Frommer's

British Columbia & the Canadian Rockies

4th Edition

by Bill McRae

with Donald Olson

Here's what the critics say about Frommer's:

"Amazingly easy to use. Very portable, very complete."

—*Booklist*

"Detailed, accurate, and easy-to-read information for all price ranges."

—*Glamour Magazine*

"Hotel information is close to encyclopedic."

—*Des Moines Sunday Register*

"Frommer's Guides have a way of giving you a real feel for a place."

—*Knight Ridder Newspapers*

WILEY

Wiley Publishing, Inc.

Published by:

Wiley Publishing, Inc.

111 River St.
Hoboken, NJ 07030-5774

ISBN-13: 978-0-471-77883-7
ISBN-10: 0-471-77883-4

Editor: Alexia Meyers
Production Editor: Katie Robinson
Cartographer: Andrew Murphy
Photo Editor: Richard Fox
Production by Wiley Indianapolis Composition Services

Front cover photo: Vancouver Island: Carmanah Walbran Provincial Park, pathway in forest
Back cover photo: Yoho National Park: Emerald Lake, canoes at a dock

For information on our other products and services or to obtain technical support, please contact our Customer Care Department within the U.S. at 800/762-2974, outside the U.S. at 317/572-3993 or fax 317/572-4002.

Wiley also publishes its books in a variety of electronic formats. Some content that appears in print may not be available in electronic formats.

Manufactured in the United States of America

5 4 3 2 1

Contents

List of Maps

Acknowledgments

The editorial staff at Frommer's would like to thank the following tourism and hotel representatives for providing assistance (and, in some cases, going above and beyond the call of duty) when it was needed: Heather McGillivray at Tourism Victoria; Kate Colley Lo at Tourism Vancouver; Janice Greenwood and Mika Ryan at Tourism British Columbia; Heather Jeliazkov at Tartan Public Relations; Joan Bloom at M Booth & Associates; Linda Chin and John Nicholson at the Pacific Palisades; Lori Holland at Fairmont Hotels & Resorts; Susana Petti at Delta Hotels; Molly Cahill at Pan Pacific Hotels & Resorts; Joanna Tsaparas at The Wedgewood; Lisa Magee at the Listel Vancouver; Angela Nielsen at the Vancouver Aquarium Marine Science Center; and David Clarke at the Butchart Gardens.

An Invitation to the Reader

In researching this book, we discovered many wonderful places—hotels, restaurants, shops, and more. We're sure you'll find others. Please tell us about them, so we can share the information with your fellow travelers in upcoming editions. If you were disappointed with a recommendation, we'd love to know that, too. Please write to:

Frommer's British Columbia & the Canadian Rockies, 4th Edition
Wiley Publishing, Inc. • 111 River St. • Hoboken, NJ 07030-5774

An Additional Note

Please be advised that travel information is subject to change at any time—and this is especially true of prices. We therefore suggest that you write or call ahead for confirmation when making your travel plans. The authors, editors, and publisher cannot be held responsible for the experiences of readers while traveling. Your safety is important to us, however, so we encourage you to stay alert and be aware of your surroundings. Keep a close eye on cameras, purses, and wallets, all favorite targets of thieves and pickpockets.

About the Authors

Bill McRae was born and raised in rural eastern Montana, though he spent the better years of his youth attending university in Great Britain, France, and Canada. He has previously written about Montana and Utah for Moon Publications and about the Pacific Northwest and Seattle for Lonely Planet. Other publications he has written for include *National Geographic* and *Microsoft Expedia.* Bill is also coauthor of *Frommer's Canada.* He makes his home in Portland, Oregon.

Donald Olson is a novelist, playwright, and travel writer. He has published several novels, most recently *The Confessions of Aubrey Beardsley* and, under the pen name of Swan Adamson, *My Three Husbands* and *Confessions of a Pregnant Princess.* His plays have been staged in the U.S. and Europe. Donald Olson's travel stories have appeared in *The New York Times, Travel & Leisure, Sunset, National Geographic* books, and many other publications. He is the author of *England For Dummies* (winner of the 2002 Lowell Thomas Travel Writing Award for Best Guidebook), *London For Dummies, Germany For Dummies,* and *Frommer's Irreverent Guide to London.*

Frommer's Star Ratings, Icons & Abbreviations

Every hotel, restaurant, and attraction listing in this guide has been ranked for quality, value, service, amenities, and special features using a **star-rating system.** In country, state, and regional guides, we also rate towns and regions to help you narrow down your choices and budget your time accordingly. Hotels and restaurants are rated on a scale of zero (recommended) to three stars (exceptional). Attractions, shopping, nightlife, towns, and regions are rated according to the following scale: zero stars (recommended), one star (highly recommended), two stars (very highly recommended), and three stars (must-see).

In addition to the star-rating system, we also use **seven feature icons** that point you to the great deals, in-the-know advice, and unique experiences that separate travelers from tourists. Throughout the book, look for:

Finds	Special finds—those places only insiders know about
Fun Fact	Fun facts—details that make travelers more informed and their trips more fun
Kids	Best bets for kids and advice for the whole family
Moments	Special moments—those experiences that memories are made of
Overrated	Places or experiences not worth your time or money
Tips	Insider tips—great ways to save time and money
Value	Great values—where to get the best deals

The following **abbreviations** are used for credit cards:

AE	American Express	DISC	Discover	V	Visa
DC	Diners Club	MC	MasterCard		

Frommers.com

Now that you have the guidebook to a great trip, visit our website at **www.frommers.com** for travel information on more than 3,000 destinations. With features updated regularly, we give you instant access to the most current trip-planning information available. At Frommers.com, you'll also find the best prices on airfares, accommodations, and car rentals—and you can even book travel online through our travel booking partners. At Frommers.com, you'll also find the following:

- Online updates to our most popular guidebooks
- Vacation sweepstakes and contest giveaways
- Newsletter highlighting the hottest travel trends
- Online travel message boards with featured travel discussions

What's New in British Columbia & the Canadian Rockies

All of western Canada is gearing up to welcome the Winter Olympic Games in 2010—even though this international sporting event is still some years away, there's lots of new construction and anticipatory prettification going on across British Columbia. While both Vancouver and Whistler, which will play host to the games, are, naturally enough, getting ready to roll out the red carpet, other areas of western Canada are anticipating lots of spillover from the games themselves and from the heightened media attention surrounding them. Following are a few of the new and noteworthy changes that visitors will encounter in western Canada.

GETTING AROUND BY TRAIN **Rocky Mountaineer Vacations** (© 800/665-7245 or 604/606-7245; www.rocky mountaineer.com), which operates high-end scenic rail tours between Vancouver and the Canadian Rockies, is opening two new rail lines in 2006. The **Whistler Mountaineer** will travel from Vancouver to Whistler along the highly scenic Sea-to-Sky corridor. The **Fraser Discovery Route** continues from Whistler along the former BC Rail *Cariboo Prospector* route, stopping overnight in Quesnel before continuing on to Prince George and east to Jasper, where the train joins to existing Rocky Mountaineer routes. These new lines allow more options for loop train journeys through the Pacific Northwest and the Rocky Mountains.

VANCOUVER The biggest news in Vancouver is that the city, along with nearby Whistler Blackcomb Resort, will host the 2010 Olympic Winter Games. Preparations are already visible, and the excitement in the city is palpable.

Vancouver's dining scene continues to flourish. In 2005, the always-fabulous **West,** 2881 Granville St. (© 604/738-8938), won *Vancouver* magazine's prestigious Best Restaurant award. Chef David Hawksworth won top honors as Best Chef.

For the scoop on Vancouver's newest and best, see chapter 4.

VICTORIA Improvements to an old logging road have resulted in the new **Pacific Marine Circle Tour.** The 52km (32-mile) loop road, which opened in 2005, makes it easier to get to Port Renfrew, Sooke, Jordan River, and Lake Cowichan on a daylong circular tour from Victoria. For details, check with the **Tourism Victoria Visitor Info Centre,** 812 Wharf St. (© 800/663-3883; www. tourismvictoria.com).

For more on British Columbia's capital city, see chapter 5.

GULF ISLANDS The recently reinvented and refurbished **Galiano Oceanfront Inn & Spa,** Galiano Island (© 877/530-3939; p. 129), will open 10 executive suites in 2006, all sharing the wondrous view and facilities at this exemplary island retreat.

For additional information on Galiano and other Gulf Islands, see chapter 6.

SOUTHERN VANCOUVER ISLAND

Calling all food lovers! The beloved Fairburn Farm B&B is under new management as the **Fairburn Farm Culinary Retreat & Guesthouse** (Duncan; ℂ 250/746-4637; p. 145). With a busy schedule of cooking lessons, mushroom hunts, farm tours, and winery visits—plus comfy rooms in a historic farmhouse—this lovely farm is the place for a Slow-Food-seeking holiday.

See chapter 6 for up-to-date recommendations on Southern Vancouver Island.

CENTRAL VANCOUVER ISLAND

Getting back and forth between Vancouver and Nanaimo is easier and faster than ever with the new **HarbourLynx** passenger ferry (ℂ 866/206-5969; p. 152). This new service departs from city-center docks on both ends of the journey, without the rigmarole of the car ferries that depart from ports on the outskirts of the city.

Downtown Nanaimo is undergoing a major construction project. Scheduled for completion in 2008, the **Vancouver Island Conference Centre** will offer 3,530 sq. m (38,000 sq. ft.) of meeting space, plus provide a new home for the Nanaimo Museum and a new Marriott hotel.

The **Old House Restaurant** (Courtenay; ℂ 250/338-5406; p. 183) is preparing to get into the lodging business. Adjacent to this very handsome heritage home smack on the Courtenay River will be a suite of 10 luxury rooms, all with views and easy access to some of the best dining in central Vancouver Island.

Chapter 7 offers full coverage of Central Vancouver Island.

NORTHERN VANCOUVER ISLAND

Sadly, the **Kwagiulth Museum and Cultural Center** on Quadra Island has closed. One of the top collections of Northwest Native carving and ritual items from potlatch ceremonies, the museum has struggled in recent years to find funding to keep its exhibits open. For the foreseeable future, the museum will remain closed.

See chapter 8 for more information and updates on Northern Vancouver Island.

THE SUNSHINE COAST & WHISTLER

In Powell River, the **Beach Gardens Resort** (ℂ 800/663-7070; p. 206) is opening a new wing of hotel rooms directly above the resort's private marina. These new rooms are a welcome addition to the otherwise downbeat lodging scene in Powell River.

Whistler continues to preen as it readies to host the ski events for the 2010 Winter Olympics. Be aware that the Sea-to-Sky Highway (Hwy. 99) between Vancouver and Whistler is undergoing a lot of construction in advance of the Olympics, and major delays and traffic snarls are almost unavoidable. The Whistler Blackcomb Resort website, **www.whistlerblackcomb.com**, provides information on scheduled delays and construction alerts.

The already stellar selection of luxury hotels in Whistler edged up another notch with the opening of two new hotels. Near the base of Blackcomb Mountain, the **Four Seasons Resort Whistler,** 4591 Blackcomb Way (ℂ 888/935-2460 or 604/935-3400), is easily the most refined and elegant of Whistler's hotels, with a feeling of monumentality that's in keeping with the grandeur of the outdoor setting. Despite the scale of the common rooms, the guest rooms and suites are very beautifully decorated in soothing colors, dark leather, and rich woods. Finally, a decor that manages to look rustic and elegant at the same time.

Near the base of Whistler Mountain, the **Pan Pacific Whistler Village Centre,** 4299 Blackcomb Way (ℂ 888/905-9995 or 604/905-2999), is an exquisite all-suite hotel designed for very discriminating guests. The rooms in this adult- and couples-oriented hotel are large and wonderfully furnished, with floor-to-ceiling windows that capture mountain vistas. This quiet enclave of refinement is just steps from the surging nightlife in Whistler Village.

For the lowdown on the ski scene and the resorts at Whistler, see chapter 9.

THE OKANAGAN VALLEY The summer of 2003's wildfire season in British Columbia witnessed the fiery destruction of trestles and rail lines on the historic Kettle Valley Railroad in the **Okanagan Valley.** After substantial private fund-raising and a pledge of money from the federal government, the process of rebuilding the trestles has begun. During the summer of 2005, three of the Myra Canyon trestles were replaced, and—if work continues as planned—by the end of 2006 half the damaged trestles will have been replaced. The rails-to-trails Kettle Valley Railroad was a favorite mountain biking destination.

The beloved **Hotel Eldorado** (Kelowna; © 250/763-7500; p. 289) has added a new wing with 30 suites and guest rooms. With its mix of old and new luxury accommodations, excellent dining, and a boat-in bar, the lakefront Eldorado is, deservedly, more popular than ever.

Chapter 12 has more detail on happenings in the Okanagan Valley.

CALGARY The formerly formulaic Holiday Inn just south of downtown was an inexpensive, no-fuss lodging. Now recreated as the **Hotel Arts,** 119 12th Ave. SW (© 800/661-9378), it's at the center of Calgary's much-hyped Arts District and is head-to-toe dripping in contemporary design and trendy installations. We're all familiar with the boutique hotel; now all welcome the gallery hotel.

Calgary's accommodations and more are described in chapter 14.

GATEWAYS TO THE CANADIAN ROCKIES: EDMONTON The sleepy art scene in Alberta's capital city is about to get a Post Modern zap. The stern **Edmonton Art Gallery,** 2 Sir Winston Churchill Sq. (© **780/422-6223**), has long served as a reliquary for the works of Prairie artists and as bunker for traveling art exhibits. However, gallery officials in 2005 announced plans for both a new name and a new look. Under its new moniker, the **Alberta Gallery of Art** will receive a C$48-million (US$38-million) upgrade that will turn an adjacent subway station entrance into a grand entryway to the gallery and add 2,787 sq. m (30,000 sq. ft.) to the building. Construction is slated to begin in 2007. The centerpiece of Los Angeles architect Randall Stout's flowing and curling design is a twisted ribbon of steel that wraps all the way around the building.

For other ideas of what Edmonton has to offer, see chapter 14.

THE CANADIAN ROCKIES The **Baker Creek Lodge** (east of Lake Louise; © 403/522-3761; p. 376) has completed an expansion of its handsome, rustic lodges. Although these log cabins are newly built, they will fulfill all your fantasies about western vacations spent in the woods.

The **Post Hotel** (Lake Louise; © 800/661-1586; p. 378)—the elegant Relais & Châteaux lodge with some of Banff National Park's top dining and lodging options—has opened **Temple Mountain Spa.** This destination spa offers 297 sq. m (3,200 sq. ft.) of superlative facilities and the latest in treatments.

Jasper isn't the kind of place that seeks the limelight, but when the Food Network came to town to film a segment of its program *Opening Soon,* the mountain town had its moment in the lights. The show captured the opening stresses and triumphs of the **Jasper Brewing Company,**

624 Connaught Dr. (© **780/852-4111**), the town's first true brewpub. With the film crews safely departed, this friendly pub with great bistro fare is a fantastic addition to Jasper's youthful nightlife scene.

For in-depth coverage of the Canadian Rockies, see chapter 15.

1

The Best of British Columbia & the Canadian Rockies

British Columbia and the Canadian Rockies, which stretch across the provincial border into Alberta, are extravagantly scenic and quietly sophisticated. The diversity of landscapes is astounding: You'll travel from cactus-studded desert to soaring mountaintops and on to wilderness ocean beaches. You can visit traditional Native Canadian villages, thread through market stalls in the largest Chinese community outside of Asia, and cheer on cowboys at an old-fashioned rodeo.

As for creature comforts, British Columbia and the Rockies are famed for their luxury hotels, rustic guest ranches, quiet inns, and B&Bs. And the food? With Alberta beef, Pacific salmon, and some of the world's most fertile farm and orchard land, these two provinces champion excellent regional cuisine.

Finally, there's no better place to get outdoors and enjoy yourself. These areas are flush with ski resorts and golf courses, hiking is a near universal passion, and you'll find no better spot on earth to try your hand at adventure sports like sea kayaking, trail riding, or scuba diving.

This guide is chock-full of recommendations and tips to help you plan and enjoy your trip to western Canada; the following are the best of the best, places and experiences you won't want to miss.

1 The Best Travel Experiences

- **Wandering Vancouver's West End:** Vancouver is one of the most cosmopolitan cities in the world, and wandering the streets, people-watching, and sipping cappuccinos at street cafes can fill an entire weekend. Stroll up Robson Street with its busy boutique-shopping scene, turn down cafe-lined Denman Street, then stride into 405-hectare (1,000-acre) Stanley Park, a gem of green space with old-growth cedars, miles of walkways, and the city's excellent aquarium. See chapter 4.

- **Taking Tea in Victoria:** Yeah, it's a little corny, but it's also fun—and delicious. Tea, scones, clotted cream—who

said the British don't know good food? The afternoon tea at the Empress is world-renowned, a little stuffy, and very expensive; if that doesn't sound like fun to you, we'll show you other places where tea is more reasonably priced and a lot less formal. See chapter 5.

- **Ferrying through the Gulf Islands:** The Gulf Islands, a huddle of clifflined, forested islands between Vancouver Island and the British Columbia mainland, can only be reached via ferry. Hop from island to island, staying at excellent country inns and B&Bs; peddle the quiet farm roads on your bike, stopping to visit artists' studios or to quaff a pint in a cozy rural pub. The romantic getaway you've been dreaming of starts and ends right here on these idyllic islands. See chapter 6.

- **Traveling the Inside Passage:** The 15-hour Inside Passage ferry cruise aboard the MV *Queen of the North* takes you from Vancouver Island's Port Hardy along an otherwise inaccessible coastline north to Prince Rupert, near the southern tip of the Alaska Panhandle. Orcas swim past the ferry, bald eagles soar overhead, and the dramatic scenery—a narrow channel of water between a series of mountain islands and the craggy mainland—is utterly spectacular. See chapter 10.

- **Wine Tasting in the Okanagan Valley:** The Okanagan Valley in central British Columbia has some of the most arid climatic conditions in Canada, but with irrigation, grape varietals like merlot, cabernet sauvignon, and pinot noir flourish here. Vineyards line the edges of huge, glacier-dug lakes and clamber up the steep desert-valley walls. Taste delicious wines, go for a swim, play some golf, eat at excellent restaurants, and do it all again tomorrow. See chapter 12.

- **Skiing the Canadian Rockies:** You can hit all three ski areas in Banff National Park with a one-price ticket, using the frequent shuttle buses to ferry you and your skis from resort to resort. The skiing is superlative, the scenery astounding, and—best of all—you can stay at Banff's luxury hotels for a fraction of their astronomical summer rates. See chapter 15.

- **Riding Herd at a Guest Ranch:** The edge of the Great Plains nudges up to the face of the Canadian Rockies in Alberta, making this some of the most fertile and beautiful ranching country anywhere. For more than a century, ranches have welcomed guests to their rustic lodges and cabins, offering trail rides, cattle drives, evening barbecues, and barn dances that'll keep you entertained whether you're a greenhorn or an old hand. See p. 252.

2 The Best Active Vacations

- **Hiking the West Coast Trail:** Hiking the entire length of the rugged 69km (43-mile) West Coast Trail, from Port Renfrew to Bamfield on Vancouver Island, takes 5 to 7 days, but it's truly the hike of a lifetime. This wilderness coastline, edged with old-growth forest and lined with cliffs, is utterly spectacular, and can be reached only on foot. If you're not up for it, consider an 11km (7-mile) day trip on the more easily accessible stretch just south of Bamfield. See p. 166.

- **Scuba Diving off Vancouver Island:** According to no less an authority than Jacques Cousteau, the waters off Vancouver Island offer some of the best diving in the world. Nanaimo and Port Hardy are popular departure points, with outfitters ready to drop you into the briny world of the wolf eel, yellow-edged cadlina, and giant Pacific octopus. See chapters 7 and 8.

- **Kayaking Clayoquot Sound:** Paddle a kayak for 4 or 5 days through the waters of Clayoquot Sound on Vancouver Island's wilderness west coast, from the funky former fishing village of Tofino to a natural hot-springs bath near an ancient Native village. Along the way, you'll see thousand-year-old trees and glaciers, whales, and bald eagles. And if the pocketbook allows, you can stop in at resorts that offer some of the best cuisine in the world. See p. 172.

- **Salmon Fishing from Campbell River:** Even though salmon fishing is not what it once was, Campbell River is still the "Salmon-Fishing Capital of the World." Join a day trip with an outfitter and fish the waters of Discovery Passage. Get ready to hook the big one! Even if your trophy salmon gets away (or you're required to release it), you'll see plenty of wildlife: bald eagles, seals, even orcas and porpoises. See p. 185.

- **Rafting the Chilcotin and Fraser Rivers:** This 3-day white-water extravaganza flushes you from the slopes of the glaciered Coast Range down through shadowy canyons to the roiling waters of the mighty Fraser River, second in North America only to the Columbia River in power and size. A number of outfitters in Williams Lake offer river options ranging from half-day thrill rides to multiday trips with catered camping. See p. 257.

- **Canoeing Bowron Lakes Provincial Park:** Every summer, canoeists and kayakers set out to navigate a perfect 120km (74-mile) circle of six alpine lakes, with minimal portages in between. There are no roads or other signs of civilization beyond the launch point, except some well-placed cabins, campsites, and shelters. The full circuit is a 7-day trip, but the memories will last a lifetime. See p. 263.

- **Heli-Skiing near Golden:** Helicopters lift adventurous skiers to the tops of the Selkirk and Purcell mountains that rise just west of Golden, accessing acres of virgin powder far from the lift lines and crowds of traditional ski resorts. **CMH Heli-Skiing** (© 800/661-0252) offers a variety of holidays, most based out of its private high-country lodges and reached only by helicopter. See p. 303.

- **Cross-Country Skiing at Canmore:** The 1988 Olympic cross-country skiing events were held at Canmore, on the edge of Banff National Park. The routes at the **Canmore Nordic Centre** (© 403/678-2400) are now open to the public and offer 70km (43 miles) of world-class skiing. See p. 352.

- **Lodge-to-Lodge Trail Riding in Banff National Park:** See the park's backcountry without getting blisters on your feet. Instead, get saddle-sore as you ride horseback on a 3-day excursion, spending the nights in remote but comfortable mountain lodges. **Warner Guiding and Outfitting** (© 800/661-8352) provides all meals and lodging, plus oats for Silver. See p. 363.

3 The Best Nature- & Wildlife-Viewing

- **Tide Pools at Botanical Beach near Port Renfrew:** Waves have eroded potholes in the thrust of sandstone that juts into the Pacific at Botanical Beach, which remain water-filled when the waves ebb. Alive with starfish, sea anemones, hermit crabs, and hundreds of other sea creatures, these potholes are some of the best places on Vancouver Island to explore the rich intertidal zone. See p. 137.

- **Bald Eagles near Victoria:** Just a few miles north of Victoria is one of the world's best bald eagle–spotting sites: Goldstream Provincial Park. Recent counts put the number of eagles wintering here at around 4,000. (Jan is the best month for viewing, though there are eagles here year-round.) See p. 140.

- **Gray Whales at Pacific Rim National Park:** Few sights in nature match observing whales in the wild. March is the prime viewing time, as the whales migrate north from their winter home off Mexico. During March, both Tofino and Ucluelet celebrate the Pacific Rim Whale Festival; outfitters offer whale-watching trips out onto the Pacific. See chapter 7.

- **Orcas at Robson Bight:** From whale-watching boats out of Telegraph Cove or Port McNeill, watch orcas (killer whales) as they glide through the Johnstone Strait in search of salmon, and rub their tummies on the pebbly beaches at Vancouver Island's Robson Bight. See p. 196.

- **Spawning Salmon at Adams River:** Every October, the Adams River fills with salmon, returning to their home water to spawn and die. While each autumn produces a large run of salmon, every fourth year (the next are 2006 and 2010), an estimated 1.5 to 2 million sockeye salmon struggle upstream to spawn in the Adams River near Squilax. Roderick Haig-Brown Provincial Park has viewing platforms and interpretive programs. See p. 269.

- **Songbirds and Waterfowl at the Columbia River Wetlands:** Between Golden and Windermere, the Columbia River flows through a valley filled with fluvial lakes, marshes, and streams—perfect habitat for hundreds of species, including moose and coyotes. Protected as a wildlife refuge, the wetlands are on the migratory flyway that links Central America to the Arctic; in spring and fall, the waterways fill with thousands of birds—over 270 different species. Outfitters in Golden operate float trips through the wetlands. See p. 305.

- **Elk in Banff National Park:** You won't need to mount an expedition to sight elk in Banff: They graze in the city parks and on people's front lawns. To see these animals in their own habitat, take the Fenlands Trail just west of Banff to Vermillion Lakes, another favorite grazing area. See chapter 15.

- **Black Bears in Waterton Lakes National Park:** There are black bears throughout the Canadian west, but chances are good you'll spot a bear or two along the entry road to Waterton Lakes National Park, where the open grasslands of the prairies directly abut the sheer faces of the Rocky Mountains (remember, bears are originally prairie animals). See p. 399.

4 The Best Family-Vacation Experiences

- **The Beaches near Parksville and Qualicum Beach:** The sandy beaches near these towns warm in the summer sun, then heat the waters of Georgia Strait when the tides return. Some of the warmest ocean waters in the Pacific Northwest are here, making for good swimming and family vacations. See chapter 7.

- **The MV *Lady Rose* (© 800/663-7192):** This packet steamer delivers mail and merchandise to isolated marine communities along the otherwise inaccessible Alberni Inlet, the longest fiord on Vancouver Island's rugged west coast. Along the way, you may spot eagles, bears, and porpoises. The MV *Lady Rose* is large enough to be stable, yet small enough to make this daylong journey from Port Alberni to Bamfield and back seem like a real adventure. See p. 165.

- **The Okanagan Lakes:** Sunny weather, sandy lake beaches, and miles of clean, clear water: If this sounds like the ideal family vacation, then head to the lake-filled Okanagan Valley. Penticton and Kelowna have dozens of family-friendly hotels, watersports rentals, and lakeside parks and beaches. Mom and Dad can enjoy the golf and wineries as well. See chapter 12.

- **Fort Steele Heritage Town** (© 250/ 426-7352): In 1864, the frontier community of Fort Steele was a mining boomtown with a population of 4,000. Twenty years later, the town was practically abandoned, soon becoming a ghost town. Now a provincial heritage site, Fort Steele again bustles with life: The town has been largely rebuilt, other historic structures have been moved in, and daily activities with living-history actors give this town a real feel of the Old West. See p. 309.

- **Fort Calgary Historic Park** (© 403/ 290-1875): This reconstruction of the Mountie fort on the banks of the Bow River—and the genesis for the city of Calgary—has always been interesting, as volunteers have been in the process of rebuilding the original fort. In the last couple years, critical mass has been reached and new/old Fort Calgary is really taking shape: It's gone from a good idea to a great attraction. But what's really cool is

that the labor has been volunteer and that all the work was done using tools and techniques from the 1880s. Take the kids and give them a lesson in history and volunteerism! See p. 323.

- **The Kicking Horse River:** One of the best white-water rafting trips in the Rockies is on the Kicking Horse River near Golden. While it's the treacherous Class IV rapids that give the river its fame, there are also stretches gentle enough for the entire family. Better yet, most outfitters run simultaneous trips on both sections of the river, so part of your brood can run the rapids while the other enjoys a leisurely float through lovely Rocky Mountain scenery. See p. 304.

- **West Edmonton Mall** (© 800/661- 8890): Okay, so it's a mall. But what a mall! Within its 483,000 sq. m (5.2 million sq. ft.) are 800 stores and a mammoth entertainment center that contains a complete amusement park, roller coaster, bungee-jumping platform, and lake-size swimming pool with real sand beaches and rolling waves. You can also ice skate, watch performing dolphins, ride a submarine, attend movies at 19 theaters—oh, and get your shopping done, too. See p. 336.

5 The Best Places to Rediscover Native Canadian Culture & History

- **Quw'utsun' Cultural Centre** (Duncan; © 877/746-8119): North of Victoria, this facility contains a theater, carving shed, ceremonial clan house, restaurant, and art gallery, all dedicated to preserving traditional Cowichan history and culture. Try to visit when the tribe is preparing a traditional salmon bake. See p. 143.

- **Alert Bay** (off Vancouver Island): One of the best-preserved and still vibrant Native villages in western

Canada, Alert Bay is a short ferry ride from northern Vancouver Island. Totem poles face the waters, and cedar-pole longhouses are painted with traditional images and symbols. The **U'Mista Cultural Centre** (© 250/974-5403) contains a collection of carved masks, baskets, and potlatch ceremonial objects. See p. 198.

- **Gwaii Haanas National Park Reserve** (Queen Charlotte Islands): A UNESCO World Heritage Site and a Canadian national park, this is the ancient homeland of the Haida people. Located on the storm-lashed Queen Charlottes, it isn't easy or cheap to get to: You'll need to kayak, sail, or fly in on a floatplane. But once here, you'll get to visit the prehistoric village of Ninstints, abandoned hundreds of years ago and still shadowed by decaying totem poles. See p. 234.

- **'Ksan Historical Village** (Hazelton; ⓒ 877/842-5518): The Gitxsan people have lived for millennia at the confluence of the Skeena and Bulkley rivers, hunting and spearing salmon from the waters. On the site of an ancient village near present-day Hazelton, the Gitxsan have built a pre-Contact replica village, complete with longhouses and totem poles. No ordinary tourist gimmick, the village houses a 4-year carving school, Native-art gift shop, traditional-dance performance space, artists' studios, restaurant, and visitor center. See p. 241.

- **Secwepemc Museum & Heritage Park** (Kamloops; ⓒ 250/828-9801): This heritage preserve contains a Native Secwepemc village archaeological site from 2,400 years ago, plus re-creations of village structures from five different eras. It's not all just history here: The Shuswap, as the Secwepemc are now called, also perform traditional songs and dances and sell art objects. See p. 265.

6 The Best Museums & Historic Sites

- **Museum of Anthropology** (Vancouver; ⓒ 604/822-3825): Built to resemble a traditional longhouse, this splendid museum on the University of British Columbia campus contains one of the finest collections of Northwest Native art in the world. Step around back to visit two traditional longhouses. See p. 83.

- **Royal British Columbia Museum** (Victoria; ⓒ 888/447-7977): The human and natural history of coastal British Columbia is the focus of this excellent museum. Visit a frontier main street, view lifelike dioramas of coastal ecosystems, and gaze at ancient artifacts of the First Nations peoples. Outside, gaze upward at the impressive collection of totem poles. See p. 107.

- **The Museum at Campbell River** (Campbell River; ⓒ 250/287-3103): The highlight of this regional museum is a multimedia presentation that retells a Native Indian myth using carved ceremonial masks. Afterwards, explore the extensive collection of contemporary aboriginal carving, then visit a fur trapper's cabin and see tools from a pioneer-era sawmill. See p. 186.

- **North Pacific Historic Fishing Village** (Port Edward; ⓒ 250/628-3538): Salmon canning was big business in northern British Columbia in the early 20th century. Located on the waters of Inverness Passage, this isolated cannery built an entire working community of 1,200 people—complete with homes, churches, and stores—on boardwalks and piers. Now a national historic site, the mothballed factory is open for tours, and you can even spend a night at the old hotel. See p. 229.

- **Fort St. James National Historic Site** (Vanderhoof; ⓒ 250/996-7191): In summer, the rebuilt log Fort St. James trading post hums with activity, as actors play the roles of explorers, traders, and craftspeople. This open-air museum of frontier life is a replica of the first non-Native structure in British Columbia, constructed in 1806. See p. 243.

- **Barkerville** (83km/51 miles east of Quesnel; © **250/994-3332**): Once the largest city west of Chicago and north of San Francisco—about 100,000 people passed through during the 1860s—the gold-rush town of Barkerville is one of the best-preserved ghost towns in Canada. Now a provincial park, it comes to life in summer, when costumed "townspeople" go about their frontier way of life amid a completely restored late-Victorian pioneer town. See p. 262.
- **Glenbow Museum** (Calgary; © **403/268-4100**): One of Canada's finest museums, the Glenbow has fascinating displays on the Native and settlement history of the Canadian Great Plains, plus changing art shows and thematic exhibitions. The gift shop is a good place to find local crafts. See p. 323.
- **Bar U Ranch National Historic Site** (Longview; © **403/395-2212**): A working ranch established in the 1880s, the Bar U preserves the artifacts and lifestyles of Alberta's cattle-ranching past. This is still a real ranch: You might catch a rodeo one day, a calf branding the next. See p. 332.

7 The Most Scenic Views

- **Vancouver from Cloud Nine** (© **604/662-8328**): Situated on the top floor of the tallest building in Vancouver, towering 42 floors above the city, the rotating restaurant/lounge Cloud Nine has 360-degree views that go on forever.
- **The Canadian Rockies from Eagle's Eye Restaurant** (© **250/344-8626**): The Kicking Horse Mountain Resort isn't just the newest skiing area in the Canadian Rockies. This exciting development also boasts the highest-elevation restaurant in all of Canada. The Eagle's Eye sits at the top of the slopes, 2,410m (7,905 ft.) above sea level. Ascend the gondola to find eye-popping views of high-flying glaciered crags—and excellent cuisine. See p. 307.
- **Calgary Tower** (© **403/266-7171**): At 191m (626 ft.), this is one landmark that you'll want to get on top of. From the windows of this revolving watchtower, you'll see the face of the Rocky Mountains to the west and the endless prairies to the east. If you like the view, stay for dinner or a drink. See p. 322.
- **Flightseeing over Banff and Jasper National Parks:** Fly over some of the most dramatic landscapes in North America. **Alpenglow Aviation** (© **888/244-7117**) offers flights along the Continental Divide in the Rockies, culminating with views of the Columbia Icefields, the world's largest nonpolar ice cap. See p. 304.
- **Sulphur Mountain in Banff National Park:** Ride the gondola up to the top of Sulphur Mountain for tremendous views of the cliff-faced mountains that frame Banff. Hike the ridge-top trails, have lunch in the coffee shop, or run through an entire roll of film. See p. 365.
- **Moraine Lake in Banff National Park:** Ten snow-clad peaks towering more than 3,000m (10,000 ft.) rear up dramatically behind this tiny, eerily green lake. Rent a canoe and paddle to the mountains' base. See p. 376.
- **Waterton Lakes from the Garden Court Restaurant at the Prince of Wales Hotel** (© **403/859-2231**): There are lots of great views of the Canadian Rockies, but perhaps the most singular is the view from the Prince of Wales Hotel, high above Waterton Lake. With blue-green water stretching back between a series of rugged snowcapped peaks, the view is at once intimate and primeval. See p. 402.

8 The Most Dramatic Drives

- **The Sea-to-Sky Highway:** Officially Highway 99, this drive is a lesson in geology. Starting in West Vancouver, the amazing route begins at sea level at Howe Sound and the Squamish Cliffs—sheer rock faces rising hundreds of feet—then up a narrowing fiord, climbing up to Whistler, at the crest of the rugged, glacier-clad Coast Mountains. Continue over the mountains and drop onto Lillooet. Here, on the dry side of the mountains, is an arid plateau trenched by the rushing Fraser River. See p. 208.
- **The Sunshine Coast:** Highway 101 follows the mainland British Columbia coast from West Vancouver, crossing fiords and inlets twice on ferries on its way to Powell River. On the east side rise the soaring peaks of the Coast Mountains, and to the west lap the waters of the Georgia Strait, with the green bulk of Vancouver Island rising in the middle distance. From Powell River, you can cross over to Vancouver Island on the BC Ferries service to Comox. See chapter 7.
- **Williams Lake to Bella Coola:** Start at the ranching town of Williams Lake, and turn your car west toward the looming Coast Mountains. Highway 20 crosses the arid Fraser River plateau, famed for its traditional cattle ranches, until reaching the high country near Anaheim Lake. After edging through 1,500m (4,920-ft.) Heckman Pass, the route descends what the locals simply call "The Hill": a 32km (20-mile) stretch of road that drops from the pass to sea level with gradients of 18%. The road terminates at Bella Coola on the Pacific, where summer-only ferries depart for Port Hardy on northern Vancouver Island. See p. 258.
- **The Icefields Parkway** (Hwy. 93 through Banff and Jasper national parks): This is one of the world's grandest mountain drives. On a road trip back to the ice ages, you'll climb past glacier-notched peaks to the Columbia Icefields, a sprawling cap of snow, ice, and glacier at the very crest of the Rockies. See p. 380.

9 The Best Walks & Rambles

- **Vancouver's Stanley Park Seawall:** Stroll, jog, run, blade, bike, skate, ride—whatever your favorite mode of transport is, use it, but by all means get out here and explore this wonderful park. See p. 64.
- **Victoria's Inner Harbour:** Watch the boats and aquatic wildlife come and go while walking along a pathway that winds past manicured gardens. The best stretch runs south from the Inner Harbour near the Parliament Buildings, past the Royal London Wax Museum. See chapter 5.
- **Strathcona Provincial Park:** Buttle Lake, which lies at the center of Strathcona Provincial Park, is the hub of several hiking trails that climb through old-growth forests to misty waterfalls and alpine meadows. Return to the trail head, doff your hiking shorts, and skinny-dip in gem-blue Buttle Lake. See p. 192.
- **Johnston Canyon in Banff National Park:** Just 24km (15 miles) west of Banff, Johnston Creek cuts a deep, very narrow canyon through limestone cliffs. The trail winds through tunnels, passes waterfalls, edges by shaded rock faces, and crosses the chasm on footbridges before reaching a series of iridescent pools, formed by springs that bubble up through highly colored rock. See p. 362.

- **Plain of Six Glaciers Trail in Banff National Park:** From Chateau Lake Louise, a trail rambles along the edge of emerald-green Lake Louise, then climbs up to the base of Victoria Glacier. At a rustic teahouse, you can order a cup of tea and scones—each served up from a wood-fired stove—and gaze up at the rumpled face of the glacier. See p. 376.

- **Maligne Canyon in Jasper National Park:** As the Maligne River cascades from its high mountain valley to its appointment with the Athabasca River, it carves a narrow, deep chasm in the underlying limestone. Spanned by six footbridges, the canyon is laced with trails and interpretive sites. See p. 382.

10 The Best Luxury Hotels & Resorts

- **Fairmont Hotel Vancouver** (Vancouver; ✆ **800/441-1414**): Built by the Canadian Pacific Railway on the site of two previous Hotel Vancouvers, this landmark opened in 1929. The château-style exterior, the lobby, and even the guest rooms—now thoroughly restored—are built in a style and on a scale reminiscent of the great European railway hotels. See p. 67.

- **The Fairmont Empress** (Victoria; ✆ **800/441-1414**): Architect Francis Rattenbury's masterpiece, the Empress has charmed princes (and their princesses), potentates, and movie moguls since 1908. If there's one hotel in Canada that represents a vision of bygone graciousness and class, this is it. See p. 99.

- **Hastings House Country Estate** (Salt Spring Island; ✆ **800/661-9255**): This farm matured into a country manor and was then converted into a luxury inn. The manor house is now an acclaimed restaurant; the barn and farmhouse have been remade into opulent suites. You might feel like you've been transported to an idealized English estate, if it weren't for those wonderful views of the Pacific. See p. 124.

- **Poets Cove Resort & Spa** (South Pender Island; ✆ **888/512-7638**): Poets Cove may be on a remote bay on a rural island, but don't let the isolation fool you. New and dazzling, the resort has beautifully furnished rooms, villas, and cottages, all overlooking a peaceful harbor. The spa, restaurant, and facilities are absolutely first class. See p. 134.

- **Wickaninnish Inn** (Tofino; ✆ **800/333-4604**): Standing stalwart in the forest above the sands of Chesterman Beach, this new log, stone, and glass structure boasts incredible views over the Pacific and extremely comfortable luxury-level guest rooms. The dining room is equally superlative. See p. 176.

- **Four Seasons Resort Whistler** (Whistler; ✆ **888/935-2460** or 604/935-3400): This grand—even monumental—hotel is the classiest place to stay in Whistler, which is saying something. This is a hotel with many moods, from the Wagnerian scale of the stone-lined lobby to the precise gentility of the guest rooms to the faint and welcome silliness of the tiled and back-lit stone fixtures of the restaurant. This is a hotel that's not afraid to make big statements. See p. 216.

- **Fairmont Palliser** (Calgary; ✆ **800/441-1414**): Calgary's landmark historic hotel, the Palliser is permeated with good breeding and high style. The magnificent lobby looks like an Edwardian gentlemen's club, and the guest rooms are large and luxurious. See p. 324.

- **Fairmont Hotel Macdonald** (Edmonton; ℂ 800/441-1414): When the Canadian Pacific bought and refurbished this landmark hotel, all of the charming period details were preserved, and the inner workings were modernized and brought up to snuff. The result is an elegant but still-friendly small hotel. From the tuxedoed bellman to the gargoyles on the walls, this is a real class act. See p. 337.
- **Rimrock Resort Hotel** (Banff; ℂ 800/661-1587): Banff is known for its scenery and its high prices; this is one of the few luxury hotels whose rates are actually justified. New and architecturally dramatic, it steps nine stories down a steep mountain slope. A fantastic marble lobby, great restaurant, and handsomely appointed bedrooms complete the package. See p. 368.

- **Fairmont Chateau Lake Louise** (Lake Louise; ℂ 800/441-1414): First of all, there's the view: Across a tiny gem-green lake rise massive cliffs, shrouded in glacial ice. And then there's the hotel: Part hunting lodge, part palace, the Chateau is its own community, with sumptuous boutiques, sports-rental facilities, nine dining areas, and beautifully furnished guest rooms. See p. 377.
- **Post Hotel** (Lake Louise; ℂ 800/661-1586): Quietly gracious hospitality in a dramatic Canadian Rockies setting is the hallmark of this luxurious lodge. The original log-built dining room and bar remain from the 1940s, now joined by a new hotel wing with extremely comfortable and beautifully furnished rooms. The "F" suites are the most desirable. See p. 378.

11 The Best B&Bs & Country Inns

- **West End Guest House** (Vancouver; ℂ 604/681-2889): This 1906 heritage home is filled with an impressive collection of Victorian antiques. Fresh-baked brownies accompany evening turndown service, and the staff is thoroughly professional. See p. 71.
- **Andersen House Bed & Breakfast** (Victoria; ℂ 250/388-4565): Your hosts outfit their venerable 1891 Queen Anne home in only the latest decor, from raku sculptures to carved-wood African masks. Their taste is impeccable—the old place looks great. See p. 99.
- **Old Farmhouse B&B** (Salt Spring Island; ℂ 250/537-4113): The Old Farmhouse is an 1894 farmstead with a newly built guesthouse. The welcome you'll get here is as engaging and genuine as you'll ever receive, and the breakfasts are works of art. See p. 125.
- **Galiano Oceanfront Inn & Spa** (Galiano Island; ℂ 877/530-3939):

Combine a magical island view, a wonderfully inventive restaurant, a full-service spa, plus luxury-level rooms, and you get this very handsome inn. Flanked by gardens and filled with major Northwest Native art, the Galiano Inn wears its high style very comfortably. See p. 129.
- **Woodstone Country Inn** (Galiano Island; ℂ 888/339-2022): The quintessential small country inn, Woodstone combines a marvelous edge-of-the-forest ambience with fine folk art and sculpture. The elegant but friendly atmosphere here is like staying with friends who are great cooks and who have great taste. See p. 129.
- **Oceanwood Country Inn** (Mayne Island; ℂ 250/539-5074): Overlooking Navy Channel, this inn offers top-notch lodgings and fine dining in one of the most extravagantly scenic locations on the west coast. Admirably, the inn maintains an array of prices that range from affordable and cozy

garden-view rooms to luxury-level suites that open onto hot-tub decks and hundred-mile views. See p. 132.

- **Fairburn Farm Culinary Retreat & Guesthouse** (© 250/746-4637): This rambling farmhouse B&B sits amid some of the most bountiful farmland in Canada—so start cooking. This unusual operation is part culinary school, part country inn, and part pilgrimage site for Slow Food–movement devotees. Come here to learn more about regional foods and wines, and stay for the *terroir.* See p. 145.

- **Melville Grant Inn** (Gabriola Island; © 866/247-5444): This inn sits in the middle of an island meadow, with views onto Georgia Strait and the Gulf Islands. The perfect spot for a romantic getaway, the rooms are opulent and indulgently comfortable, a perfect counterpoint to the wild rocky bluffs, forests, and beaches just outside your door. See p. 159.

- **Otella's, A Wine Country Inn** (Kelowna; © 888/858-8596): High in the hills above Kelowna, Otella's is a discreetly elegant small B&B that focuses on fine art, fine furniture, and restrained good taste. Food and wine lovers take note: Your hosts are very knowledgeable about the local wine and restaurant scene, and your breakfasts here, prepared by the chef-owner, will be the perfect start to a day seeking sun and fine wine in the Okanagan. See p. 290.

- **Mulvehill Creek Wilderness Inn and Bed & Breakfast** (Revelstoke;

© 877/837-8649): Equidistant to a waterfall and Arrow Lake, this remote inn in the forest has everything going for it: nicely decorated rooms with locally made pine furniture, a beautiful lounge with fireplace, decks to observe the hens and the garden (each of which does its bit for breakfast), and gracious hosts who exemplify Swiss hospitality. Swimming, boating, fishing—it's all here. See p. 297.

- **Union Bank Inn** (Edmonton; © 780/423-3600): Not quite a B&B, not quite a hotel, the absolutely charming Union Bank Inn is something in between. Right downtown, this marble-faced 1910 bank sat vacant for many years before being redeveloped as an inn and restaurant. Each bedroom was individually decorated by one of Edmonton's top interior designers. See p. 339.

- **Thea's House** (Banff; © 403/762-2499): A vision of stone, pine, and antique carpets, Thea's is a newly built bed-and-breakfast just 5 minutes from downtown Banff. "Elegant Alpine" is Thea's style, a cross between a log lodge and a vision out of *Architectural Digest.* Perfect for a romantic getaway. See p. 369.

- **Mountain Home Bed & Breakfast** (Banff; © 403/762-3889): All the comforts of home, plus commodious rooms and thoughtful hospitality. There are bigger and fancier places, but this is one of the best all-in-one B&B packages in the Rockies—and it's just steps from downtown Banff. See p. 371.

12 The Best Lodges, Wilderness Retreats & Log-Cabin Resorts

- **Tigh-Na-Mara Resort Hotel** (Parksville; © 800/663-7373): Comfortably rustic log cabins in a forest at beach's edge: Tigh-Na-Mara has been welcoming families for decades, and

the new luxury log suites are just right for romantic getaways. See p. 163.

- **Strathcona Park Lodge** (Strathcona Provincial Park; © 250/286-3122): A summer camp for the whole family is what you'll find at Strathcona Park Lodge, with rustic lakeside cabins and guided activities that range from sea kayaking and fishing to rock climbing and mountaineering. See p. 194.

- **Miles Inn on the T'Seax** (New Aiyansh, © **250/633-2636**): In the north, when you get to the end of the road and come face-to-face with the wilderness, it's a comfort and wonder to find this marvelous backcountry lodge. Miles Inn combines sophisticated lodging, First Nation artwork, and the friendly and knowledgeable welcome of hosts ready to help you explore the untamed woodlands along the Nisga'a River. See p. 240.

- **Buffalo Mountain Lodge** (Banff, © **800/661-1367**): Rustic charm meets upscale comfort on the Tunnel Mountain bluff behind Banff. Buffalo Mountain Lodge is centered on a large, handsome log lodge building with an intimate fireplace-dominated bar and elegant dining room. The woodsy, holiday-card-perfect atmosphere extends to the guest rooms, with fireplaces, slate-tiled bathrooms, and balconies overlooking the forests. Definitely worth the splurge. See p. 373.

- **Tekarra Lodge** (Jasper; © **888/962-2522**): Quaint little cabins ring a central lodge building at this well-loved getaway. The cabins are atmospherically rustic; best of all, you're a mile distant from Jasper's busy town center. See p. 390.

- **Becker's Chalets** (Jasper; © **780/852-3779**): These very attractive new cabins are set right along the Athabasca River. Some units are as large as houses. Jasper's best restaurant is here as well. See p. 389.

- **Overlander Mountain Lodge** (Jasper East; © **877/866/2330**): Forget the wildly overpriced rooms in Jasper Townsite and stay here, just .5km (¼ mile) outside the park gates. Lovely new cabins plus a handsome older lodge with a good restaurant make this an in-the-know favorite. See p. 391.

- **Emerald Lake Lodge** (Yoho National Park; © **800/663-6336**): Location, location, location: Sumptuous lakeside cabins at the base of the Continental Divide make this a longtime favorite family-vacation spot. See p. 397.

13 The Best Restaurants for Northwest Regional Cuisine

See "A Taste of British Columbia & the Canadian Rockies," in the appendix, for more information on the style of cuisine unique to this region.

- **Lumière** (Vancouver; © **604/739-8185**): From its early days, Lumière has been in the running for best restaurant in Vancouver. You won't be disappointed by the French-influenced Pacific Rim cuisine here. See p. 79.

- **Blue Crab Bar and Grill** (Victoria; © **250/480-1999**): You might think that the food would have a hard time competing with the view at this restaurant in the Coast Hotel, but you'd be wrong. The creative chef serves up the freshest seafood, the presentation is beautiful, and the dishes are outstanding. See p. 103.

- **Sooke Harbour House** (Sooke; © **250/642-3421**): This small country inn has one of the most noted restaurants in all of Canada. Fresh regional cuisine is the specialty, with an emphasis on local seafood. Views over the Strait of Juan de Fuca to Washington's mighty Olympic Mountains are spectacular. See p. 138.

- **Masthead Restaurant** (Cowichan Bay; © **250/748-3714**): Sitting above a busy marina, with islands and mountains rising in the distance, the Masthead's views are spectacular and its trappings—the century-old clapboard structure was built as a fine hotel—are charming. But the food here is absolutely up-to-date, an exploration of Vancouver Island's rich *terroir*. See p. 146.

- **Shelter** (Tofino; © **250/725-3353**): Fine dining in Tofino has always been synonymous with The Pointe, the wonderful restaurant at the Wickaninnish Inn. But the tourist boom in Tofino created an explosion of fantastic new places in this remote corner of Vancouver Island. Check out Shelter for its youthful vigor and absolutely fresh and authentic flavors—everything is right off the boat or just off the land. See p. 178.

- **Bearfoot Bistro** (Whistler; © **604/932-3433**): The food scene in Whistler is extremely dynamic, as you'd expect at North America's top ski resort and soon-to-be Olympic host. To get noticed amid Whistler's many restaurants requires something special—and Bearfoot Bistro's got it. With very inventive food served in three- or five-course meals, this is like having a cutting-edge Iron Chef in charge of your dinner. See p. 221.

- **Fresco** (Kelowna; © **250/868-8805**): Another exciting new restaurant at the epicenter of the fast-growing Okanagan wine district, Fresco brings together fresh local ingredients and sophisticated preparations in a classy but casual dining room. The chef/owner has cooked in the top restaurants in Canada: He came to Kelowna to open his first solo effort. See p. 292.

- **All Seasons Café** (Nelson; © **250/352-0101**): Innovative preparations and rich, hearty flavors are the hallmarks of the cuisine at this superlative restaurant in a downtown Nelson heritage home. Food this stylish and up-to-date would pass muster anywhere; to find it in Nelson is astonishing. See p. 315.

- **Belvedere** (Calgary; © **403/265-9595**): The moody, noirish atmosphere of this elegant fine-dining room lights up when the food arrives: Easily one of western Canada's top restaurants, Belvedere offers an inventive dining experience focused on Pan-Canadian ingredients and impeccable French-by-way-of-Tokyo technique. See p. 327.

- **River Café** (Calgary; © **403/261-7670**): You'll walk through a quiet, tree-filled park on an island in the Bow River to reach this bustling place. At the restaurant's center, an immense wood-fired oven and grill produce smoky grilled meats and vegetables, all organically grown and freshly harvested. On warm evenings, picnickers loll in the grassy shade. See p. 328.

- **Hardware Grill** (Edmonton; © **780/423-0969**): Although located in one of Edmonton's first hardware stores, there's nothing antique about the food at the Hardware Grill. A very broad selection of inventive appetizers makes it fun to snack your way through dinner. See p. 341

- **Maple Leaf Grille & Spirits** (Banff; © **403/760-7680**): In a soaring, two-story dining room that's at once rustic and classy, the Maple Leaf serves up Banff's most sophisticated mountain cuisine. The menu focuses on regional ingredients, fresh preparations, and a friendly unstuffy welcome that lets you relax into having a great time with inventive, delicious food. See p. 373.

14 The Best Festivals & Special Events

- **Vancouver's Three F Festivals:** The Folk, the Fringe, and the Film are the three F's in question. The Folk Fest brings folk and world-beat music to a waterfront stage in Jericho Park. The setting is gorgeous, the music great, and the crowd something else. Far more urban is the Fringe, a festival of new and original plays that takes place in the arty Commercial Drive area. The plays are wonderfully inventive; better yet, they're short and cheap. In October, the films of the world come to Vancouver. Serious film buffs buy a pass and see all 500 flicks (or as many as they can before their eyeballs fall out). See p. 58.

- **Celebration of Light** (Vancouver): This 3-night fireworks extravaganza takes place over English Bay in Vancouver. Three of the world's leading fireworks manufacturers are invited to represent their countries in competition against one another, setting their best displays to music. On the fourth night, all three companies launch their finales. See p. 59.

- **Market in the Park** (Salt Spring Island): The little village of Ganges fills to bursting every Saturday morning, as local farmers, craftspeople, and flea marketers gather to talk, trade, and mill aimlessly. With all ages of hippies, sturdy housewives, fashion-conscious Eurotrash, and rich celebrities all mixed together, the event has the feel of a weird and benevolent ritual. See p. 123.

- **World Championship Bathtub Race** (Nanaimo): Imagine guiding a clawfoot tub across the 58km (36-mile) Georgia Strait from Nanaimo to Vancouver: That's how this hilarious and goofily competitive boat race began. Nowadays, dozens of tubbers attempt the crossing as part of late July's weeklong Marine Festival, with a street fair, parade, and ritual boat burning and fireworks display. See p. 153.

- **Calgary Stampede:** In all of North America, there's nothing like the Calgary Stampede. Of course it's the world's largest rodeo, but it's also a series of concerts, an art show, an open-air casino, a carnival, a street dance—you name it, it's undoubtedly going on somewhere here. In July, all of Calgary is a party—and you're invited. See p. 318.

- **Klondike Days** (Edmonton): July's Klondike Days commemorate the city's key role as a departure point to the Klondike gold fields in the Yukon. The Sourdough River Raft Race pits dozens of homemade boats against the strong currents of the North Saskatchewan River. The whole city gets decked out in its turn-of-the-20th-century finery for the street fairs, music events, parades, and general high jinks. See p. 335.

2

Planning Your Trip to British Columbia & the Canadian Rockies

Here's where you'll find tips on when to visit, what documents you'll need, and where to get more information. Planning ahead can make all the difference between a smooth trip and a bumpy ride.

1 The Regions in Brief

Canada's westernmost province, British Columbia, and the Canadian Rockies region, which stretches into the province of Alberta, are incredibly diverse, with many distinct regions that vary both in geography and culture.

Vancouver is one of the most beautiful and cosmopolitan cities in the world. While there are certainly good museums and tourist sights, what we love most are the incredible mosaic of people and languages, the bustle of the streets, the mountains reaching down into the sea, and the wonderful food. Kayaking and canoeing are just off your front step in False Creek and the Georgia Strait, and skiing just up the road at **Whistler/ Blackcomb Mountain Resorts,** one of the continent's greatest ski areas.

Vancouver Island is a world apart from busy urban Vancouver. At the island's southern tip is the British Columbia capital of **Victoria,** a small, charming city that makes a lot of fuss about its Merry Olde Englishness. In summer, the crowds can be off-putting, the sham Britishness eye-rollingly silly. But in the off season, Victoria is just a beautifully preserved frontier town in a magnificently scenic seaside location.

The rest of the mountainous island ranges from rural to wild. It would be easy to spend an entire vacation just on Vancouver Island, especially if you take a few days for **sea kayaking** on the island's wilderness west coast near **Tofino,** or off the east coast in the beautiful **Gulf Islands.** Or you can learn to **scuba dive:** No less an authority than Jacques Cousteau has claimed that these waters are some of the best diving environments in the world. Vancouver Island is also home to dozens of First Nations Canadian bands. If you're shopping for **Native arts,** this is the best single destination in western Canada.

From the northern tip of Vancouver Island, you can board a BC Ferries cruiser and take the 15-hour trip through the famed **Inside Passage** to Prince Rupert, a port town just shy of the Alaska Panhandle. Getting a glimpse of the dramatically scenic Inside Passage is what fuels the Alaska-to-Vancouver cruise-ship industry; by taking this route on BC Ferries, you'll save yourself thousands of dollars and catch the same views. From Prince Rupert, you can journey out to the mystical **Queen Charlotte Islands,** the ancient homeland of the Haida people, or

British Columbia

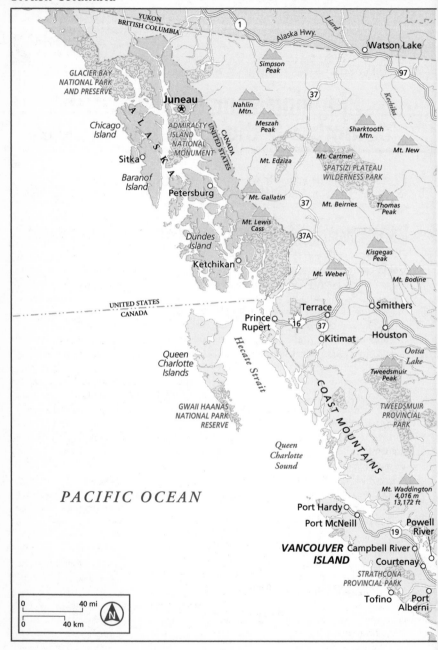

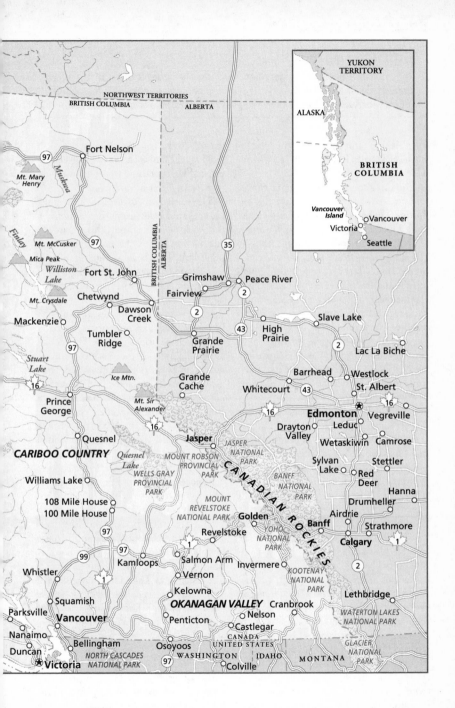

⌒Tips Planning Ahead

The road trip between Calgary and Vancouver includes a series of the most popular destinations in Canada. If you're planning to make this memorable journey, be sure to make lodging reservations as far in advance as possible.

---

turn inland and drive up the glacier-carved Skeena River valley to **Prince George,** on the Fraser River.

You can also get to the upper reaches of the Fraser River from Vancouver by following Highway 99 north past Whistler and Lillooet to the **Cariboo Country.** This route follows the historic Cariboo Trail, a gold-rush stagecoach road blazed in the 1860s. The road now leads through cattle- and horse-covered grasslands, past 19th-century ranches, and by lakes thick with trout. The gold rush started at **Barkerville,** which is now one of the best-preserved ghost towns in North America. In addition to this great family destination, the Cariboo Country offers the province's best **guest ranches** and rustic lakeside **fishing resorts.**

The Thompson River meets the Fraser River south of Lillooet. This mighty river's southern fork has its headwaters in the **Shuswap Lakes,** a series of interconnected lakes that are favorites of houseboaters. The north fork of the Thompson River rises in the mountains of **Wells Gray Provincial Park,** one of British Columbia's neglected gems. Hiking and camping are as compelling as in the nearby Canadian Rockies, but without the overwhelming crowds.

One of the best summer family destinations in western Canada is the **Okanagan Valley.** Stretching from the U.S.–Canadian border nearly 200km (124 miles) north to Vernon, this arid canyon is filled with glacier-dug lakes, which in summer become the playground for all manner of watersports. The summer heat is also good for wine grapes: This is the center for British Columbia's growing wine industry. Add to

that a dozen golf courses and excellent lodging and dining in the cities of **Penticton** and **Kelowna,** and you've got the makings for an excellent vacation.

The **Canadian Rockies** are among the most dramatically scenic destinations in the world. Unfortunately, this is hardly a secret—you'll find the entire area dripping with tourists in summer and early fall. **Banff** and **Jasper** national parks in Alberta are especially busy and expensive; however, it's hard to find fault with the sheer beauty of these places. If you don't like the crowds and high prices, we cover several other options as well. The British Columbia side of the Rockies contains mountain parks that are much less busy, including **Yoho, Glacier,** and **Kootenay** national parks, plus **Mount Robson Provincial Park.** Another spectacular mountain retreat is **Waterton Lakes National Park,** which joins the United States' Glacier National Park. You can also save money by staying outside the parks at Canmore and near Hinton, both in Alberta, or at Golden, British Columbia.

These considerations aside, spending several days in the Rockies should remain a part of any western Canadian itinerary. Despite the crowds, the town of **Banff** is charming and filled with great hotels and fine restaurants; **Lake Louise** is a magical sight; and the **Icefields Parkway,** which joins Banff and Jasper parks, is completely spellbinding. Throughout this area, chances are good you'll see lots of **wildlife,** like black bears, moose, bighorn sheep, mountain goats, and elk. The parks all offer marvelous outdoor recreation, including **hiking, mountain biking, climbing,** and **skiing.**

Calgary, the city that oil built, is a friendly town in the foothills of the Rockies. One of the most prosperous cities in all of Canada, Calgary is still a ranchers' town, and the disparity between its role as a cow town and world oil center is one of its principal charms. The dichotomies are never more apparent than during the **Calgary Stampede,** the world's largest rodeo and an excuse for turning the city into one huge party. You can also thank Calgary's prosperity for its wonderful restaurant scene.

Edmonton, the capital of Alberta, sits high above the North Saskatchewan River at the center of a vast, farm-covered plain. This welcoming city's historic Old Strathcona district is great for strolling and eating. While Edmonton lacks the high spirits and urbane attitude of Calgary, it's no slouch when it comes to fine dining and excellent hotels. And if you enjoy shopping—or swimming, carnival rides, or performing dolphins—then you must visit the **West Edmonton Mall,** one of the world's largest shopping centers. Like a cross between Disneyland, Las Vegas, and the Gap, West Ed Mall is unlike any mall you've ever seen.

2 Visitor Information

For advance information on British Columbia, contact **Tourism British Columbia,** P.O. Box 9830, Stn. Prov. Govt., 1803 Douglas St., 3rd Floor, Victoria, BC V8W 9W5 (© **800/435-5622** or 250/356-6363; www.hellobc.com).

To request information on Alberta, contact **Travel Alberta,** Box 2500, Edmonton, AB T5J 2Z4 (© **800/252-3782;** www.travelalberta.com).

For information on Canada's national parks, contact **Parks Canada National Office,** 25 Eddy St., Gatineau, Quebec K1A 0M5 (© **888/773-8888;** www.pc.gc.ca).

For Canada-wide travel information, see the official tourism site for Canada at **www.travelcanada.ca**.

The excellent travel directories **www.canadatravel.ca** and **www.canada.world web.com** have thousands of links to websites for destinations and activities across the country.

Here are some other useful provincial and city sites:

- **British Columbia:** www.discoverbc. com, www.travel.bc.ca
- **Alberta:** www.explorealberta.com, www.discoveralberta.com
- **Vancouver:** www.tourism-vancouver. org
- **Whistler:** www.whistler.com; www. whistlerblackcomb.com
- **Victoria:** www.victoriabc.com
- **Banff:** www.banfflakelouise.com, www.banff.com
- **Calgary:** www.tourismcalgary.com, www.discovercalgary.com
- **Edmonton:** www.discoveredmonton. com, www.edmonton.com.

3 Entry Requirements & Customs

ENTRY REQUIREMENTS

All visitors to Canada must be able to provide proof of citizenship. A passport is the easiest and most convenient method of proving citizenship. If you don't have a passport, you'll need to carry an official birth certificate (photocopies can be refused) and a picture ID with your home address.

However, this will soon change. The Intelligence Reform and Terrorism Prevention Act of 2004 requires that by January 1, 2008, travelers to and from Canada (and other neighboring countries) have a passport or other documentation to enter or reenter the States. If you are a U.S. citizen, you will also be required to carry a U.S. passport to enter

---

Tips Passport Savvy

When traveling, safeguard your passport in an inconspicuous, inaccessible place like a money belt and keep a copy of the critical pages with your passport number in a separate place. If you lose your passport, visit the nearest consulate of your native country as soon as possible for a replacement.

Canada and to reenter the U.S. from Canada and other countries within the Western Hemisphere. For the latest information on entry requirements between the U.S. and Canada, see http://travel.state.gov/travel.

Permanent U.S. residents who aren't U.S. citizens must have their Alien Registration Cards (green cards). If you plan to drive into Canada, be sure to bring your car's registration papers and proof of insurance.

Citizens of most European countries and of former British colonies and certain other countries (Israel, Korea, and Japan, for instance) do not need visas but must carry passports. Entry visas are required for citizens of more than 130 countries. Entry visas must be applied for and received from the Canadian embassy in your home country. For more on entry requirements to Canada, see the Citizenship and Immigration website visitors' services page at **www.cic.gc.ca/english/visit/index.html**.

An important point: Any person under 18 traveling alone requires a letter from a parent or guardian granting him or her permission to travel to Canada. The letter must state the traveler's name and the duration of the trip. It's essential that teenagers carry proof of identity; otherwise, their letter is useless at the border.

Although it is rare, immigration officials may prevent the entry of visitors who appear to pose a health risk, those they doubt will be able to support themselves and their dependents in Canada, or those whose willingness and means to return to their home country is in doubt. Also, immigration officials can prevent the entry of foreign nationals who have a criminal record. This includes any convictions for driving while intoxicated.

For information on how to get a passport, see "Fast Facts" at the end of this chapter—the websites listed provide downloadable passport applications as well as the current fees for processing passport applications. For an up-to-date country-by-country listing of passport requirements, visit the "Foreign Entry Requirements" page of the U.S. State Department website at **http://travel.state.gov/foreignentryreqs.html**.

BRINGING CHILDREN INTO CANADA If you are traveling with children, you should carry identification for each child. Divorced parents who share custody of their children should carry copies of the legal custody documents. Adults who are not parents or guardians should have written permission from the parents or guardians to supervise the children. When traveling with a group of vehicles, parents or guardians should travel in the same vehicle as the children when arriving at the border. Customs officers are looking for missing children and may ask questions about the children who are traveling with you.

CUSTOMS
WHAT YOU CAN BRING INTO CANADA

Customs regulations are very generous in most respects but get pretty complicated when it comes to firearms, plants, meats, and pets.

For details concerning Customs regulations, contact the **Customs and Revenue Agency,** 1st Floor, 2265 St. Laurent Blvd., Ottawa, ON K1G 4K3 (🕾 **800/461-9999** or 204/983-3500 within Canada, 506/636-5064 within the U.S.; www.ccra-adrc.gc.ca).

WHAT YOU CAN TAKE HOME FROM CANADA

Returning **U.S. citizens** who have been away for *at least 48 hours* are allowed to bring back, once every 30 days, $800 worth of merchandise duty-free. You'll be charged a flat rate of 3% duty on the next $1,000 worth of purchases. Be sure to have your receipts handy. On mailed gifts, the duty-free limit is $100. For specifics on what you can bring back, download the invaluable free pamphlet *Know Before You Go* online at **www.customs.gov**. (Click on TRAVELER INFORMATION, then KNOW BEFORE YOU GO.) Or contact the **U.S. Customs Service,** 1300 Pennsylvania Ave. NW, Washington, DC 20229 (🕾 **877/287-8867**), and request the pamphlet.

U.K. citizens should contact **HM Customs & Excise** at 🕾 **0845/010-9000** (020/8929-0152 from outside the U.K.), or consult their website at **www.hmce.gov.uk** for Customs information.

The duty-free allowance in **Australia** is A$900 or, for those under 18, A$450. For Customs information, call the **Australian Customs Service** at 🕾 **1300/363-263,** or log on to **www.customs.gov.au**.

The duty-free allowance for **New Zealand** is NZ$700. For Customs information, contact **New Zealand Customs,** The Customhouse, 17–21 Whitmore St., Box 2218, Wellington (🕾 **04/473-6099** or 0800/428-786; www.customs.govt.nz).

4 Money

The Canadian dollar is stronger than it has been in many years, and Canadian prices are not as low as they once were for travelers using U.S. dollars.

CURRENCY

Canadian currency is counted in dollars and cents, just like the currency system in the U.S. However, in addition to pennies, nickels, dimes, and quarters, there are 1- and 2-dollar coins. (There are no 1- or 2-dollar bills.) Dollar coins are bronze-plated coins and bear the picture of a loon—hence their nickname "loonies." There's also a two-toned 2-dollar coin sometimes referred to as a "twoonie." Paper currency begins with $5 bills.

Exchanging currency is pretty straightforward and can be done at most banks. The easiest way to procure Canadian currency, however, is simply to withdraw money from an ATM (see below).

Often, Canadian businesses will accept U.S. dollars in payment, making the conversion at the till. If you do spend American money at Canadian establishments, you should understand how the conversion is done. Often by the cash register there'll be a sign reading U.S. CURRENCY X%, offering a standard exchange rate.

⌒Tips The Canadian Dollar & the U.S. Dollar

The prices cited in this guide are given first in Canadian dollars (C$), then in U.S. dollars (US$); amounts over $10 have been rounded to the nearest dollar. Note that the Canadian dollar is worth less than the American dollar but buys nearly as much in the way of goods and services. As we go to press, US$1 is worth about C$1.25 or C$1 is worth about US80¢, and that is the exchange rate used to figure the prices in this guide.

> ### ⌐Tips Dear Visa: I'm Off to Prince Rupert!
>
> Some credit card companies recommend that you notify them of any impending trip abroad so that they don't become suspicious when the card is used numerous times in a foreign destination and block your charges. As a precaution, always carry more than one card on your trip; if one card doesn't work for any number of reasons, you'll have a backup card just in case.

This percentage, say 25%, is the "premium"—it means that for every U.S. greenback you hand over, the cashier will see it as $1.25 in Canadian dollars. Currency conversions at the till rarely provide the best rates of exchange, so it's best to shop around.

ATMs

The easiest and best way to get cash away from home is from an ATM (automated teller machine); you'll generally get the best rate of exchange as well. The **Cirrus** (© 800/424-7787; www.mastercard.com) and **PLUS** (© 800/843-7587; www.visa. com) networks both have ATMs operating in British Columbia and Alberta. If your ATM card is associated with a small community bank or credit union, it may not work at all ATMs in Canada, particularly the non-bank ATMs found in convenience stores and public facilities. In such cases, simply find a bank ATM on your card's network.

Be sure you know your personal identification number (PIN) before you leave home and be sure to find out your daily withdrawal limit before you depart. Also keep in mind that many banks impose a fee every time a card is used at a different bank's ATM, and that fee can be higher for international transactions (up to $5 or more) than for domestic ones (where they're rarely more than $1.50).

TRAVELER'S CHECKS

You can get traveler's checks at almost any bank. **American Express** offers checks in both U.S. and Canadian currency denominations. You'll pay a service charge ranging from 1% to 4%. You can also get American Express traveler's checks over the phone by calling © **800/221-7282.**

Visa offers traveler's checks for both U.S. and Canadian currency denominations at Citibank locations nationwide, as well as at several other banks. The service charge ranges between 1.5% and 2%; checks come in denominations of $20, $50, $100, $500, and $1,000. Call © **800/732-1322** for information. **MasterCard** also offers traveler's checks. Call © **800/223-9920** for a location near you.

If you choose to carry traveler's checks, be sure to keep a record of their serial numbers separate from your checks in the event that they are stolen or lost. You'll get a refund faster if you know the numbers.

CREDIT CARDS

Credit cards are a safe way to carry money, they provide a convenient record of all your expenses, and they generally offer good exchange rates. Your credit card company will likely charge a commission (1%–3%) on every foreign purchase you make, but unless you plan on buying lots of items, on most purchases in Canada you'll still get the best deal with credit cards when you factor in things such as ATM fees and higher traveler's check exchange rates.

Canadian businesses honor the same credit cards as in the U.S. Visa and MasterCard are the most common, though American Express is also normally accepted in hotels and restaurants catering to tourists. Discover and Diner's Club cards are accepted less frequently.

5 When to Go

THE WEATHER Canada west of the Rocky Mountains has generally mild winters, with snow mostly at the higher elevations. Even though spring comes early—usually in March—gray clouds can linger through June. Dry summer weather is assured only after July 1, but often continues through October. The Canadian Rockies are often socked in with cloud and rain throughout the summer; plan to spend several days here to assure that you'll catch at least some good weather. In winter, the Rockies fill with snow, but frequently the weather is not as cold as you'd expect. Chinook winds from the prairies can bring warm air systems, boosting temperatures up to early spring levels. On the prairies of Alberta, winters can be fiercely cold and windy. If you plan to travel across the prairies or through the Rockies in winter, be sure to have snow tires and chains.

As a general rule, spring runs from mid-March to mid-May, summer from mid-May to mid-September, fall from mid-September to mid-November, and winter from mid-November to mid-March. Remember that your car should be winterized through March and that snow sometimes falls as late as May.

Evenings tend to be cool everywhere, particularly on or near water. In late spring and early summer, you'll need a supply of insect repellent if you're planning bush travel or camping.

For up-to-date weather conditions, check out **http://weatheroffice.ec.gc.ca** or www.weather.ca.

HOLIDAYS Canadian national holidays include New Year's Day, Good Friday, Easter Monday, Victoria Day (in mid- to late May, the weekend before U.S. Memorial Day), Canada Day (July 1), Labour Day (first Mon in Sept), Thanksgiving (in mid-Oct), Remembrance Day (Nov 11), Christmas Day, and Boxing Day (Dec 26).

British Columbia and Alberta also celebrate a provincial holiday (called British Columbia or Alberta Day), usually on the first Monday of August.

FESTIVALS & SPECIAL EVENTS Western Canada has some wonderfully unique festivals and events, from Nanaimo's World Championship Bathtub Race to the rowdy Calgary Stampede. Each community's special events are listed in the regional chapters that follow.

6 Travel Insurance

Check your existing insurance policies and credit card coverage before you buy travel insurance. You may already be covered for lost luggage, canceled tickets, or medical expenses. The cost of travel insurance varies widely, depending on the cost and length of your trip, your age, health, and the type of trip you're taking. Canada's national health insurance system will not cover non-Canadians; Canadian doctors and hospitals can bill U.S. health insurers or European health systems, so bring appropriate documentation or insurance cards.

TRIP-CANCELLATION INSURANCE Trip-cancellation insurance helps you get your money back if you have to back out of a trip, if you have to go home early, or if your travel supplier goes bankrupt. Allowed reasons for cancellation can range from sickness to natural disasters to the State Department declaring your destination unsafe for travel. In this unstable world, trip-cancellation insurance is a good buy if you're getting tickets well in advance. Insurance policy details vary, so read the fine print—and especially make sure that your airline or cruise line is on the list of carriers covered in case of bankruptcy. For information, contact one of the following insurers: **Access America** (☎ 800/284-8300; www.accessamerica. com); **Travel Guard International** (☎ 800/ 826-1300; www.travelguard.com); **Travel Insured International** (☎ 800/243-3174; www.travelinsured.com); and **Travelex Insurance Services** (☎ 800/228-9792; www.travelex-insurance.com).

MEDICAL INSURANCE   Most health insurance policies cover you if you get sick away from home—but check, particularly if you're insured by an HMO. If you require additional medical insurance, try **MEDEX International** (☎ 800/527-0218 or 410/453-6300; www.medex assist.com) or **Travel Assistance International** (☎ 800/821-2828; www.travel assistance.com); for general information on services, call the company's Worldwide Assistance Services, Inc., at ☎ **800/ 777-8710.**

LOST-LUGGAGE INSURANCE   On international flights (including U.S. portions of international trips), baggage is limited to approximately $9.07 per pound, up to approximately $635 per checked bag. If you plan to check items more valuable than the standard liability, see if your valuables are covered by your homeowner's policy, or get baggage insurance as part of your comprehensive travel-insurance package.

If your luggage is lost, immediately file a lost-luggage claim at the airport, detailing the luggage contents. For most airlines, you must report delayed, damaged, or lost baggage within 4 hours of arrival. The airlines are required to deliver luggage, once found, directly to your house or destination free of charge.

7 Health & Safety

STAYING HEALTHY

In general, Canada poses no particular health threats to travelers. You can drink water directly from the tap anywhere in the country.

Canada's health care system is similar to that in the U.S. Hospitals have emergency rooms open 24 hours for emergency care. In addition, most cities also have walk-in clinics where nonemergency treatment is available, or you can ask about a doctor at your hotel. Most clinics take credit cards, though they may be able to bill your private insurance directly.

WHAT TO DO IF YOU GET SICK AWAY FROM HOME

If you suffer from a chronic illness, consult your doctor before your departure. For conditions like epilepsy, diabetes, or heart problems, wear a **MedicAlert Identification Tag** (☎ 800/825-3785; www. medicalert.org), which will immediately alert doctors to your condition and give them access to your records through MedicAlert's 24-hour hot line.

Pack **prescription medications** in your carry-on luggage, and carry prescription medications in their original containers, with pharmacy labels—otherwise they won't make it through airport security. Also bring along copies of your prescriptions in case you lose your pills or run out. Note that prescription drugs are substantially cheaper in Canada than in the U.S. Don't forget an extra pair of contact lenses or prescription glasses. Carry the generic name of prescription medicines, in case a local pharmacist is unfamiliar with the brand name.

The United States **Centers for Disease Control and Prevention** (☎ 800/311-3435; www.cdc.gov) provides up-to-date information on necessary vaccines and health hazards by region or country.

8 Specialized Travel Resources

TRAVELERS WITH DISABILITIES

Most disabilities shouldn't stop anyone from traveling. There are more options and resources out there than ever before. A clearinghouse of official Canadian federal government information on disability issues, including those related to travel and transportation, is available from Persons with Disabilities Online, www.pwd-online.ca. The Canadian Paraplegic Association (© 800/720-4933; www.canparaplegic.org) can offer advice for mobility-challenged travelers as well as address issues for those with spinal cord injuries or with other physical disabilities. From the national website, you can click to find provincial organizations.

A World of Options, a 658-page book of resources for travelers with disabilities, covers everything from biking trips to scuba outfitters. It costs US$18 (C$22.50) and is available from **Mobility International USA,** P.O. Box 10767, Eugene, OR 97440 (© 541/343-1284 voice and TDD; www.miusa.org).

Many travel agencies offer customized tours and itineraries for travelers with disabilities. **Flying Wheels Travel** (© 507/451-5005; www.flyingwheelstravel.com) offers escorted tours and cruises that emphasize sports and private tours in minivans with lifts. **Accessible Journeys** (© 800/846-4537 or 610/521-0339; www.disabilitytravel.com) caters specifically to slow walkers and wheelchair travelers and their families and friends.

Organizations that offer assistance to disabled travelers include the **Moss Rehab Hospital** (www.mossresourcenet.org), which provides a library of accessible-travel resources online; the **Society for Accessible Travel and Hospitality** (© 212/447-7284; www.sath.org; annual membership fees: US$45 adults, US$30 seniors and students), which offers a wealth of travel resources for all types of disabilities

and informed recommendations on destinations, access guides, travel agents, tour operators, vehicle rentals, and companion services; and the **American Foundation for the Blind** (© 800/232-5463; www.afb.org), which provides information on traveling with Seeing Eye dogs.

For more information specifically targeted to travelers with disabilities, check out the quarterly magazine *Emerging Horizons* ($14.95 per year, $19.95 outside the U.S.; www.emerginghorizons.com).

GAY & LESBIAN TRAVELERS

Canada is one of the most gay-tolerant travel destinations in the world. Witness the fact that same-sex unions are recognized in a number of provinces and that the entire nation has nondiscrimination protection for gays and lesbians. While not every rural village is ready for the circuit party set, most gay travelers will encounter little adversity.

A good clearinghouse for information on gay Canada is the website **www.gaycanada.com**, which features news and links to gay-owned or -friendly accommodations and business across Canada.

SENIOR TRAVEL

Mention the fact that you're a senior citizen while traveling in Canada and frequently you can receive discounted admission prices to cultural and tourist attractions. In most Canadian cities, people over the age of 65 qualify for reduced admission to theaters, museums, and other attractions, as well as discounted fares on public transportation. It is less common to receive discounts on lodging, though it does happen so it is worth asking when you make your lodging reservations.

Members of **AARP** (formerly known as the American Association of Retired Persons), 601 E St. NW, Washington, DC 20049 (© 800/424-3410 or 202/434-2277; www.aarp.org), can get discounts on hotels, airfares, and car rentals. AARP offers members a wide range of benefits, including a magazine and a monthly newsletter. Anyone over 50 can join. The Canadian affiliate can be reached at **www.aarpcanada.net**.

Parks Canada offers a discounted annual pass to the Canadian national park system for those 65 years of age and older. The discount amounts to about one-quarter off the regular adult rate.

Many reliable agencies and organizations target the 50-plus market. **Elderhostel** (© **877/426-8056**; www.elderhostel.org) arranges study programs for those aged 55 and over (and a spouse or companion of any age) in British Columbia and the Rockies. Most programs include airfare, accommodations in university dormitories or modest inns, meals, and tuition.

FAMILY TRAVEL

Note: See "Entry Requirements & Customs" earlier for guidelines on traveling with children in Canada.

Destinations such as the Canadian Rockies are especially attractive to families, as outfitters make it easy to arrange guided hiking, biking, white-water rafting, and horseback riding excursions tailored to your family simply by talking to your hotel's concierge.

Throughout this guide, kid-friendly activities are marked with **a kids icon**— these destinations feature activities or facilities that your children may enjoy. Most hotels in Canada offer free lodging for children under 16 to 18 traveling with parents, and also offer complimentary continental breakfast.

If your travel plans take you to Vancouver, consider buying a copy of *Frommer's Vancouver with Kids* (Wiley Publishing, Inc.).

9 Planning Your Trip Online

SURFING FOR AIRFARES

The "big three" online travel agencies, **Expedia.com, Travelocity,** and **Orbitz** sell most of the air tickets bought on the Internet (expedia.ca and travelocity.ca in Canada; expedia.co.uk and opodo.co.uk in the U.K.). Each has different business deals with the airlines and may offer different fares on the same flights, so it's wise to shop around. Expedia and Travelocity will also send you **e-mail notification** when a cheap fare becomes available to your favorite destination.

Also remember to check **airline websites,** especially those for low-fare carriers whose fares are often misreported or simply missing from travel agency websites. **WestJet** (www.westjet.com) offers flights between major and secondary Canadian airports, plus a few U.S. cities, at extremely attractive prices, but only on their own website. Even with major airlines, you can often shave a few bucks

from a fare by booking directly through the airline and avoiding a travel agency's transaction fee. But you'll get these discounts only by **booking online.** For the websites of airlines that fly to and from your destination, go to "Getting There," below.

Great **last-minute deals** are available through free weekly e-mail services provided directly by the airlines. Sign up for weekly e-mail alerts at airline websites or check megasites that compile comprehensive lists of last-minute specials, such as **Smarter Living** (smarterliving.com). For last-minute trips, **Site59.com** in the U.S. and **Lastminute.com** in Europe often have better deals than the major-label sites.

If you're willing to give up some control over your flight details, use an **opaque fare service** such as **Priceline** (www.priceline.com; www.priceline.co.uk for Europeans) or **Hotwire** (www.hotwire.com). Both offer rock-bottom prices

Frommers.com: The Complete Travel Resource

For an excellent travel-planning resource, we highly recommend **Frommers. com** (www.frommers.com). We're a little biased, of course, but we guarantee that you'll find the travel tips, reviews, monthly vacation giveaways, and online-booking capabilities thoroughly indispensable. Among the special features are our popular **Message Boards,** where Frommer's readers post queries and share advice (sometimes even our authors show up to answer questions); **Frommers.com Newsletter,** for the latest travel bargains and insider travel secrets; and **Frommer's Destinations Section,** where you'll get expert travel tips, hotel and dining recommendations, and advice on the sights to see for more than 3,000 destinations around the globe. When your research is done, the **Online Reservations System** (www.frommers.com/ book_a_trip) takes you to Frommer's preferred online partners for booking your vacation at affordable prices.

in exchange for travel on a "mystery airline" (all well-known carriers) at a mysterious time of day, often with a mysterious change of planes en route. Hotwire tells you flight prices before you buy; Priceline offers you the opportunity of buying regular sale fares or playing their "name our price" game. If you're new at this, the helpful folks at **BiddingForTravel** (www. biddingfortravel.com) do a good job of demystifying Priceline's prices.

For much more about airfares and savvy air-travel tips and advice, pick up a copy of *Frommer's Fly Safe, Fly Smart* (Wiley Publishing, Inc.).

SURFING FOR HOTELS

Hotel discount websites often turn up great deals on hotels in Canada. Last-minute rooms for popular tourist destinations, such as Banff and Jasper, are frequently sold over the Internet through discount brokers. You may not get exactly the room type you wanted, but the discounts range from 30% to 50%.

It's a gambling game, of course, as there is no guarantee that the hotel or the room you want will become available at the last minute. But if you're willing to

take a chance and don't mind monitoring websites, then you might get a chance to stay at hotels you could not otherwise afford.

Canadian hotels are well represented on U.S.-based discount hotel websites. Of the "big three" sites, **Expedia.com** may be the best choice, thanks to its long list of special deals. **Travelocity** runs a close second. Hotel specialist sites **hotels. com** and **hoteldiscounts.com** are also reliable. An excellent free program, **Travel-Axe** (www.travelaxe.net), can help you search multiple hotel sites at once, even ones you may never have heard of. It covers a number of cities in British Columbia and Alberta. If you plan on buying a hotel room online, be sure to consult it first.

The website at **www.bbcanada.com** offers an outstanding selection of Canadian B&Bs nationwide.

Priceline is an even better bet for hotels in Canada than for airfares; you can pick the neighborhood and quality level of your hotel (though its hotel rating system has some flaws) before offering up your money. Again, consult **www.biddingfor travel.com** before placing a hotel bid.

Tips Staying in Touch

Most cities and towns in British Columbia have at least one place where you can access your e-mail and the Internet. Although there's no definitive directory for cybercafes in B.C., two places to start looking are at **www. cybercaptive.com** and **www.netcafeguide.com**. Aside from formal cybercafes, most **public libraries** across the world offer Internet access free or for a small charge.

If you prefer to use a **cellphone** to stay in touch with home or the office, note that just because your phone works at home, doesn't mean it'll work in Canada, especially if you're using a **GSM (Global System for Mobiles)** phone. Renting a phone is a good option. Two good wireless rental companies are **InTouch USA** (© 800/872-7626; www.intouchglobal.com) and **Road-Post** (© 888/290-1606 or 905/272-5665; www.roadpost.com). Give them your itinerary, and they'll tell you what wireless products you need.

SURFING FOR RENTAL CARS

For booking rental cars online, the best deals are usually found at rental-car company websites, although all the major online travel agencies also offer rental-car reservations services. **Travelocity** is the best major site to consult as its rental quotes usually include the myriad of taxes all renters need to pay. **Priceline** works well for rental cars, too; the only "mystery" is which major rental company you get, and for most travelers the difference between Hertz, Avis, and Budget is negligible.

10 Getting There

BY PLANE Western Canada is linked with the United States, Europe, and Asia by frequent nonstop flights. Calgary and Vancouver are the major air hubs; regional airlines connect to smaller centers.

Air Canada (© **888/247-2262;** www.aircanada.ca), Canada's dominant airline, has by far the most flights between the United States and Canada, and also offers service to the U.K. out of Calgary and Vancouver. Air Canada also has a number of partner airlines, such as **Air Canada Jazz,** that fly to secondary cities. Flights on these airlines can be booked from the main Air Canada website.

Most major U.S. carriers also fly daily between cities in Canada and the States—these include **American Airlines** (© 800/433-7300; www.aa.com), **Continental** (© 800/525-0280; www.continental.com),

Delta (© 800/221-1212; www.delta.com), **Northwest** (© 800/447-4747; www.nwa.com), **United** (© 800/241-6522; www.ual.com), and **US Airways** (© 800/428-4322; www.usair.com).

International airlines with nonstop service to Vancouver include **British Air** (© 800/247-9297 in the U.S. and Canada, 0845/773-3377 in the U.K.; www.ba.com), **KLM** (© 800/447-7747 in the U.S. and Canada for KLM partner Northwest Airlines), **Lufthansa** (© 800/581-6400 in Canada, 800/563-5954 in the U.S., or 0803/803-803 in Germany; www.lufthansa.com), **Qantas** (© 800/227-4500 in the U.S. and Canada; www.qantas.com), and **SAS** (© 800/221-2350 in the U.S. or Canada; www.scandinavian.net). Asian airlines that fly into Vancouver include **China Airlines** (© 800/

227-5118 or 604/682-6777 in Vancouver; www.china-airlines.com), **Cathay Pacific** (© 800/233-2742; www.cathay-usa.com), **Japan Air Lines** (© 800/525-3663; www.japanair.com), and **Korean Air** (© 800/438-5000; www.koreanair.com). Additionally, **Air Canada** offers international flights from Mexico, most cities in northern Europe, and many centers in Asia. Canada's **Air Transat** (© 866/847-1112; www.airtransat.com) offers still more options from Europe and Latin America.

Another option is to fly into Seattle, Washington. Airfares are frequently less expensive to Seattle, and the difference in distance to destinations such as the Okanagan Valley, the Canadian Rockies, and Vancouver Island is negligible (driving from Seattle to Vancouver, for instance, takes about 2½ hr.). Seattle's **Sea-Tac Airport** has nonstop flights from London, Copenhagen, Frankfurt, Seoul, Tokyo, and Hong Kong, among others.

BY CAR   With the longest open border on Earth, it makes sense that many U.S. travelers will consider driving their own car to Canada. There are scores of border crossings between Canada and the U.S. (the U.S. freeway system enters at 13 different locations). However, not all border crossings keep the same hours and many are closed at night. Before you set off to cross the border at a remote location, ascertain if it will be open when you arrive there.

In addition to having the proper ID to cross into Canada (see "Entry Requirements & Customs," earlier in this chapter), drivers may also be asked to provide proof of car insurance and show the car registration. If you're driving a rental car, you may be asked to show the rental agreement. It's always a good idea to clean your car of perishable foodstuffs before crossing the border; fruit, vegetables, and meat products may be confiscated and may lead to a full search of the car. Remember if you're going hunting that firearms are allowed across the border only in special circumstances.

Once in Canada, you'll find that roads are generally in good condition. There are two major highway routes that cross Canada east to west. **Highway 1,** which is largely four lanes, travels from Victoria on the Pacific to St. John's in Newfoundland a total of 8,000km (4,960 miles)—with some ferries along the way. The **Yellowhead Highway (Hwy. 16)** links Winnipeg to Prince Rupert in B.C. along a more northerly route.

BY TRAIN   Amtrak (© 800/USA-RAIL; www.amtrak.com) can get you into Canada at a few border points, where you can connect up with Canada's **VIA Rail** (© 888/VIA-RAIL; www.viarail.ca) system. On the West Coast, the *Cascades* runs from Eugene, Oregon, to Vancouver, British Columbia, with stops in Portland and Seattle. Amtrak-operated buses may also connect segments of these routes.

Tips **Sample Distances between Major Cities**

From **Vancouver** to: Seattle, 227km (141 miles); Calgary, 975km (605 miles); Edmonton, 1,159km (719 miles)

From **Victoria** to: Toronto, 4,687km (2,906 miles)

From **Calgary** to: Edmonton, 294km (182 miles); Montréal, 3,700km (2,294 miles)

Amtrak and VIA Rail both offer a North American Railpass, which gives you 30 days of unlimited economy-class travel in the U.S. and Canada. Remember that the Railpass doesn't include meals; you can buy meals on the train or carry your own food.

BY BUS   **Greyhound Canada** (© 800/ 661-8747 in Canada; www.greyhound. ca) operates the major intercity bus system in Canada, with frequent cross-border links to cities in the U.S. northern tier (many

more than what's offered by Amtrak). In general, Greyhound offers cross-border service along routes where the U.S. freeway system enters Canada. The company offers several discount-pass options for travel in Canada (or both the U.S. and Canada). Prices and details vary; check the website or call for more information.

BY FERRY   Ocean ferries operate from Seattle, Anacortes, and Port Angeles, Washington, to Victoria, British Columbia. For details, see chapters 4 and 5.

11 Packages for the Independent Traveler

Package tours are simply a way to buy the airfare, accommodations, and other elements of your trip (such as car rentals, airport transfers, and sometimes even activities) at the same time and often at discounted prices—kind of like one-stop shopping.

One good source of package deals is the airlines themselves. Most major airlines offer air/land packages, including **Air Canada,** which offers an array of package deals specially tailored to trim the costs of your vacation. Collectively, these packages come under the title "Air Canada Vacations." This term covers a whole series of travel bargains ranging from city packages to fly/drive tours, escorted tours, motor-home travel, and ski holidays. For details, pick up the brochure from an Air Canada office, or visit www.aircanadavacations.com.

Other airlines offer Canadian package holidays, including **American Airlines Vacations** (© 800/321-2121; www.aa vacations.com), **Delta Vacations** (© 800/ 221-6666; www.deltavacations.com),

Continental Airlines Vacations (© 800/ 301-3800; www.coolvacations.com), and **United Vacations** (© 888/854-3899; www. unitedvacations.com).

Several big **online travel agencies**— Expedia.com, Travelocity, Orbitz, Site59, and Lastminute.com—also do a brisk business in packages. If you're unsure about the pedigree of a smaller packager, check with the **Better Business Bureau** in the city where the company is based, or go online to **www.bbb.org**. If a packager won't tell you where it's based, don't fly with them.

Before you invest in a package tour, get some answers. Ask about the **accommodation choices** and prices for each. You'll also want to find out what **type of room** you get. If you need a certain type of room, ask for it; don't take whatever is thrown your way.

Finally, look for **hidden expenses.** Ask whether airport departure fees and taxes, for example, are included in the total cost. And remember that, with a package tour, you'll likely have to pay most of the costs up front in one lump sum.

12 Escorted General-Interest Tours

Escorted tours are structured group tours, with a group leader. The price usually includes everything from airfare to hotels, meals, tours, admission costs, and local transportation.

These tours can take you to the maximum number of sights in the minimum amount of time with the least amount of hassle, and are particularly convenient for people with limited mobility. On the downside, an escorted tour often requires a big deposit up front, lodging and dining choices are predetermined, and you'll get little opportunity for individual sightseeing or interacting with locals.

Before you invest in an escorted tour, ask about the **cancellation policy** and think strongly about purchasing trip-cancellation insurance (see "Travel Insurance," earlier in this chapter). Also get a complete schedule of the trip, and inquire about the **size** of the group, the **demographics** (age, gender breakdown, singles or couples, and so on) of the tour, and discuss what is—and is not—included in the **price**. Ask about the **accommodation choices** and prices for each. And, finally, if you plan to travel alone, you'll need to know if a **single supplement** will be charged and if the company can match you up with a roommate.

TOUR OPERATORS

Collette Tours, 62 Middle St., Pawtucket, RI 02860 (ⓒ **800/340-5158;** www.collettevacations.com), offers a wide variety of escorted trips by bus and train, including several in the Pacific Northwest and the Rockies. Order any of Collette's tour brochures by phone or on their website.

Brewster Transportation and Tours, P.O. Box 1140, Banff, Alberta T0L 0C0 (ⓒ **800/661-1152;** www.brewster.ca), offers a wide variety of tours throughout Canada, both escorted and independent. Their offerings include motor-coach and train excursions, ski and other winter vacations, city and resort combination packages, chartered day tours by bus, and independent driving tours. Highlights include a visit to the Columbia Icefield in Jasper National Park; many packages in the Rockies include stays at guest ranches.

Travel by train lets you see the Rockies as you never would in a bus or behind the wheel of a car. The **Rocky Mountaineer Vacations,** 1150 Station St., 1st Floor, Vancouver, BC V6A 2X7 (ⓒ **877/460-3200;** www.rockymountaineer.com), bills its *Rocky Mountaineer* as "The Most Spectacular Train Trip in the World." During daylight hours between mid-April and mid-October, this sleek blue-and-white train winds past foaming waterfalls, ancient glaciers, towering snowcapped peaks, and roaring mountain streams. The *Rocky Mountaineer* gives you the options of traveling east from Vancouver; traveling west from Jasper, Calgary, or Banff; or taking round-trips. There's also a tour offering a VIA Rail connection from Toronto, or packages that include links to the Inside Passage from Prince Rupert to Victoria. Tours range from 2 to 12 days, with stays in both the mountains and cities.

John Steel Railtours (ⓒ **800/988-5778;** www.johnsteel.com) offers both escorted and independent tour packages, many through the Rockies and the west and a few in other regions, which combine train and other forms of travel. VIA Rail and BC Rail operate the train portions of John Steel tours. Packages run from 5 to 12 days, at all times of year, depending on the route, and combine stays in major cities and national parks.

13 Getting Around

BY CAR

Canada has scores of rental-car companies, including **Hertz** (ⓒ 800/263-0600 in Canada, 800/654-3131 in the U.S.; www.hertz.com), **Avis** (ⓒ 800/272-5871 in Canada, 800/230-4898 in the U.S.; www.avis.com), **Dollar** (ⓒ 800/800-4000; www.dollar.com), **Thrifty** (ⓒ 800/THRIFTY; www.thrifty.com), **Budget** (ⓒ 800/268-8900 in Canada, 800/527-0700 in the U.S.; www.budget.com), **Enterprise** (ⓒ 800/268-8900 in Canada, 800/RENTACAR in the U.S.; www.enterprise.com), and **National Car**

Rental (© 800/CAR-RENT in Canada and the U.S.; www.nationalcar.com). Nevertheless, rental vehicles tend to get tight during the tourist season, from around mid-May to summer. It's a good idea to reserve a car as soon as you decide on your vacation.

Several rental-car agencies offer roadside assistance programs in Canada. In case of an accident, a breakdown, a dead battery, a flat tire, a dry gas tank, getting stuck, or locking yourself out of your car, call your agency's 24-hour number. For **Hertz** call © 800/654-5060, for **Avis** call © 800/354-2847, for **Dollar** call © 800/800-4000, for **Budget** call © 800/858-5377, for **National** call © 800/268-9711 or 800/227-7368, and for **Enterprise** call © 800/307-6666.

Members of the **American Automobile Association (AAA)** should remember to take their membership cards since the **Canadian Automobile Association (CAA;** © **800/222-4357;** www.caa.ca) extends privileges to them in Canada.

GASOLINE Though Canada (specifically Alberta) is a major oil producer, gasoline isn't particularly cheap. Gas sells by the liter and pumps for anywhere from about C75¢ to C95¢ (US60¢–US76¢) per liter, or about C$3.15 to C$4 (about US$2.50–US$3.20) per U.S. gallon. (Note that the term "gallon" in Canada usually refers to the imperial gallon, which amounts to about 1¼ U.S. gallons.) Gasoline prices will vary from region to region.

DRIVING RULES Canadian driving rules are similar to regulations in the United States. Wearing seat belts is compulsory (and enforced) in all provinces, for all passengers. Children under 5 must be in child restraints. Motorcyclists must wear helmets. Throughout the country, pedestrians have the right-of-way and crosswalks are sacrosanct. The speed limit on the autoroutes (limited-access highways) is usually 100kmph (62 mph). In all provinces, right turns on red are permitted after a full stop, unless another rule is posted. Drivers must carry proof of insurance in Canada at all times.

BY PLANE

Deregulation has resulted in a number of excellent new airlines in Canada that offer no-frills but perfectly comfortable air travel. These airlines rely on the Internet to create savings in booking flights, so you'll need Internet access to learn about them. **WestJet** (© **888/937-8538;** www.westjet.com) offers the most flights in western Canada.

BY TRAIN

Most of Canada's passenger rail traffic is carried by the government-owned **VIA Rail** (© **888/VIA-RAIL** within Canada or 416/236-2029; www.viarail.ca). Virtually all of Canada's major cities (save Calgary) are connected by rail.

The problem with traveling on VIA Rail in western Canada is that the train only runs 3 days a week. If you want to link your visit between destinations in Alberta and British Columbia with a train journey, you may be out of luck unless your schedule is very flexible. Also, most trains in rural Canada run overnight—the leg between Vancouver and Kamloops, for instance—negating the sightseeing value of the ride.

You can buy a **Canrailpass,** C$778 (US$622) in high season and C$486 (US$389) in low season, giving you 12 days of unlimited economy-class travel in one 30-day period throughout the VIA Rail national network. Seniors 60 and over, students, and youths 17 or under receive a 10% discount on all fares. Class upgrades are available for a fee each time you ride.

BY BUS

While many Americans may not relish the option of traveling by bus while in Canada, in fact Greyhound Canada (© **800/661-8747;** www.greyhound.ca) offers far superior service and coverage to Greyhound in the U.S. Not only are the buses newer and cleaner, and the bus stations better kept up than in the U.S., Greyhound is often the only option for land transport in many parts of British Columbia due to the relatively minimal coverage by VIA Rail.

14 The Active Vacation Planner

See the individual destination chapters for specific details on how and where to enjoy the activities below.

BIKING Most of western Canada's highways are wide and well maintained, and thus well suited for long-distance bicycle touring. Most resort areas offer rentals (it's a good idea to call ahead and reserve a bike).

While most hiking trails are closed to mountain bikes, other trails are developed specifically for backcountry biking. Ask at national park and national forest information centers for a map of mountain-bike trails.

Probably the most rewarding biking anywhere is in Banff and Jasper national parks. The Icefields Parkway is an eye-popping route that leads past soaring peaks and glaciers.

CANOEING & KAYAKING Low-lying lakes and rivers form vast waterway systems across the land. Multiday canoeing trips make popular summer and early fall expeditions; you'll see lots of wildlife and keep as gentle a pace as you like. The Bowron Lakes in the Cariboo Country make an excellent weeklong paddle through wilderness.

DIVING An amazing array of marine life flourishes amid the 2,000 shipwrecks off the coast of British Columbia. Divers visit the area year-round to see the Pacific Northwest's unique underwater fauna and flora, and to swim among the ghostly remains of 19th-century whaling ships and 20th-century schooners.

The Pacific Rim National Park's Broken Group Islands is home to a multitude of sea life; the waters off the park's West Coast Trail are known as "the graveyard of the Pacific" for the hundreds of shipwrecks. Nanaimo and Campbell River, on Vancouver Island, are both centers for numerous dive outfitters.

FISHING Angling is enjoyed across western Canada. However, the famed salmon fisheries along the Pacific Coast face highly restricted catch limits in most areas, and outright bans on fishing in others. Not all salmon species are threatened, though, and rules governing fishing change quickly, so check locally with outfitters to find out if a season will open while you're visiting. Trout are found throughout the region, some reaching great size in the lakes in the British Columbia interior.

Fishing in Canada is regulated by local governments or tribes, and appropriate licenses are necessary. Angling for some fish is regulated by season; in some areas, catch-and-release fishing is enforced. Be sure to check with local authorities before casting your line.

If you're looking for a great fishing vacation with top-notch accommodations, contact **Oak Bay Marine Group,** 1327 Beach Dr., Victoria (✆ **800/663-7090** or 250/598-3366; www.obmg. com), which operates nine different resorts. Three are on Vancouver Island; the other lodges are on remote islands and fiords along the north coast.

HIKING Almost every national and provincial park in Canada is webbed with trails, ranging from easy nature hikes to long-distance backcountry trails. Late summer and early fall are good times to visit, since trails in the high country may be snowbound until July. For many people, the Canadian Rockies, with their abundance of parks and developed trail systems, provide the country's finest hiking. Before setting out, request hiking and trail information from the parks and buy a good map.

HORSEBACK RIDING   Holidays on horseback have a long history in western Canada, and most outfitters and guest ranches offer a variety of options. Easiest are half-day rides on an easygoing horse, with sufficient instruction to make you feel comfortable no matter what your previous riding ability. Multiday pack trips take riders off into the backcountry, with lodging in tents or at rustic camps. These trips are best for those who don't mind roughing it: You'll probably go a day or two without showers and end up saddle sore and sunburned. The Canadian Rockies in Alberta are filled with guest ranches offering a wide range of horseback activities.

SEA KAYAKING   One of the best places to practice sea kayaking is in the sheltered bays, islands, and inlets along the coast of British Columbia; kayaks are especially good for wildlife-viewing. Most coastal towns have rentals, instruction, and guided trips. Handling a kayak isn't as easy as it looks, and you'll want to have plenty of experience in sheltered coves before heading out into the surf. Be sure to check the tide schedule and weather forecast before setting out, as well as what the coastal rock formations are. You'll need to be comfortable on the water and ready to get wet, as well as be a strong swimmer.

SKIING   Canada, a mountainous country with heavy snowfall, is one of the world's top ski destinations. Both downhill and cross-country skiing are open to all ages, though downhill skiing carries a higher price tag: A day on the slopes, with rental gear and lift ticket, can easily top C$100 (US$80).

For downhill skiing, the Canadian Rockies and the Whistler/Blackcomb resort near Vancouver are the primary destinations. In 2010, the Alpine and Nordic skiing competitions for the Winter Olympics will be held at Whistler. The 1988 Winter Olympics were held at Nakiska, just outside Banff National Park, and the park itself is home to three other ski areas, including Lake Louise, the country's largest. If you're just learning to ski, then the easier slopes at Banff Mount Norquay are made to order. Readers of *Condé Nast Traveler* repeatedly award Whistler/Blackcomb the title of best ski resort in North America.

Almost all downhill areas also offer groomed cross-country ski trails. Canmore Nordic Centre, in Alberta, was the site of the 1988 Olympic cross-country competition, and is now open to the public.

WHITE-WATER RAFTING   Charging down a mountain river in a rubber raft is one of the most popular adventures for many people visiting Canada's western mountains. Trips range from daylong excursions, which demand little of a participant other than sitting tight, to long-distance trips through remote backcountry. Risk doesn't correspond to length of trip: Individual rapids and water conditions can make even a short trip a real adventure. You should be comfortable in water, and a good swimmer if you're floating an adventurous river.

Jasper National Park is a major center for short yet thrilling white-water trips. Another excellent destination is the Kicking Horse River near Golden, British Columbia.

FAST FACTS: British Columbia & the Canadian Rockies

American Express There are offices in Vancouver, Victoria, Calgary, and Edmonton; see the regional chapters that follow for addresses and phone numbers. To report lost or stolen traveler's checks, call © **800/221-7282.**

Business Hours Standard business hours in Canada are similar to those in the U.S., usually 10am to 6pm. It is common for stores to be closed on Sundays, particularly outside of the larger cities and major tourist areas.

Drugstores Drugstores and pharmacies are easily found throughout western Canada and almost every major city has a 24-hour drugstore. As in the U.S., there are a number of national chain pharmacies, including Shoppers Drug Mart and Rexall. In addition, most Safeway grocery stores in Canada also have in-store pharmacies. Many prescription-only drugs in the United States are available over the counter in Canada, and pharmacists are more likely to offer casual medical advice than their counterparts in the States. If you're not feeling well, a trip to see a pharmacist might save you a trip to the doctor.

Electricity Canada uses the same electrical plug configuration and current as the United States: 110 to 115 volts, 60 cycles.

Embassies & Consulates All embassies are in Ottawa, the national capital; the U.S. embassy is at 490 Sussex Dr. (© **613/238-5335;** www.usembassycanada.gov). You'll find **U.S. consulates** in Alberta at 615 Macleod Trail SE, 10th Floor, Calgary (© **403/266-8962**), and in British Columbia at Mezzanine, 1095 W. Pender St., Vancouver (© **604/685-4311;** www.amcits.com).

There's a **British consulate general** at 777 Bay St., Suite 2800, Toronto (© **416/593-1290;** www.britain-in-canada.org), and an **Australian consulate general** at Suite 316, 175 Bloor St. E., Toronto (© **416/323-1155;** www.ahc-ottawa.org).

Emergencies In life-threatening situations, call © **911.**

Liquor Laws In British Columbia, all beer, wine, and spirits are sold only in government liquor stores, which keep very restricted hours and charge extortionate prices. Alberta's liquor laws more resemble those in the United States, and the minimum drinking age there is 18 (in British Columbia, it's 19), though you still need to go to liquor stores for all forms of alcohol, including beer and wine.

Mail Standard mail in Canada is carried by **Canada Post** (© **800/267-1177** within Canada, or 416/979-8822 from the U.S.; www.canadapost.ca). At press time, it costs C50¢ (US40¢) to send a first-class letter or postcard within Canada and C85¢ (US68¢) to send a first-class letter or postcard from Canada to the United States. First-class airmail service to other countries is C$1.45 (US$1.15) for the first 20 grams. Rates go up frequently. If you put a return address on your letter, make sure it's Canadian; otherwise, leave it without. Delivery time can be unaccountably slow between Canada and the States, and all U.S. letter mail travels by air: Expect a letter from Calgary to take a week to reach Seattle.

Maps Both provincial tourist offices (see "Visitor Information," earlier in this chapter) produce excellent road maps. The Alberta map is free; the British Columbia map costs C$3.95 (US$3.15) and can be purchased from any travel information center or from **Davenport Maps,** Suite 201, 2610 Douglas St., Victoria (☎ **250/384-2621;** maps@davenportmaps.com).

Newspapers & Magazines In addition to local newspapers, the *Globe and Mail* and the *National Post,* both based out of Toronto, are distributed nationally. *Macleans* is a Canadian weekly newsmagazine along the lines of *Newsweek* or *Time.*

Passports **For Residents of the United States:** Whether you're applying in person or by mail, you can download passport applications from the U.S. State Department website at **http://travel.state.gov.** For general information, call the **National Passport Agency** (☎ **202/647-0518).** To find your regional passport office, either check the U.S. State Department website or call the **National Passport Information Center** (☎ **900/225-5674);** the fee is 55¢ per minute for automated information and $1.50 per minute for operator-assisted calls.

For Residents of the United Kingdom: To pick up an application for a passport, visit your nearest passport office, major post office, or travel agency or contact the **United Kingdom Passport Service** (☎ **0870/521-0410;** www.ukpa. gov.uk).

For Residents of Ireland: You can apply for a passport at the **Passport Office,** Setanta Centre, Molesworth Street, Dublin 2 (☎ **01/671-1633;** www.irlgov.ie/ iveagh). You can also apply at 1A South Mall, Cork (☎ **021/272-525)** or at most main post offices.

For Residents of Australia: You can pick up an application from your local post office or any branch of Passports Australia, but you must schedule an interview at the passport office to present your application materials. Call the **Australian Passport Information Service** at ☎ **131-232,** or visit the government website at **www.passports.gov.au.**

For Residents of New Zealand: You can pick up a passport application at any New Zealand Passports Office or download it from their website. Contact the **Passports Office** at ☎ **0800/225-050** in New Zealand or 04/474-8100, or log on to **www.passports.govt.nz.**

Pets To enter Canada, dogs and cats from the U.S. that are at least 3 months old need signed and dated certificates from a veterinarian verifying that they have been vaccinated against rabies within the last 3 years. The certificate must clearly identify the animal. For information on other pets, contact the **Canadian Food Inspection Agency's (CFIA)** Import Service Centre at **www.ccra.gc.ca.**

Smoking Smoking indoors is much more restricted in Canada than in the U.S. or Europe. Before you light up, check on provincial or city smoking laws, which are becoming more restrictive by the day. Restaurants are now nonsmoking, and bars will have no-smoking sections. Many inns and B&Bs don't permit smoking at all.

Taxes Throughout Canada, you will be charged a federal **goods and service tax (GST),** a 7% tax on virtually all goods and services. In all provinces except Alberta, there is an additional provincial sales tax added to purchases and financial transactions, and all provinces and some municipalities levy a hotel room tax. Other provinces instead levy a 15% **harmonized sales tax (HST),** which combines their provincial sales taxes with the GST. Some hotels and shops include the GST or HST in their prices; others add it on separately. When included, the tax accounts for the odd hotel rates, such as C$66 per day, that you might find on your final bill.

Thanks to a government provision designed to encourage tourism, you can **reclaim the GST** or **HST** portion of your hotel bills (or half of tour-package bills) and the price of goods you've purchased in Canada—in due course. In order to apply for a refund, your purchase amounts (before taxes) of eligible accommodation and goods on which you paid GST/HST or TVQ (Quebec sales tax) must total at least C$200, and, each individual receipt for your eligible goods must show a minimum purchase amount of C$50 before taxes.

The rebate doesn't apply to car rentals or restaurant meals; nor does it usually include provincial sales tax, which is normally not refundable. And the GST isn't levied on airline tickets to Canada bought in the United States. To obtain GST or HST refunds, you must submit all your original receipts (which will be returned) with an application form. You can get the forms in some of the larger hotels, in some duty-free shops, or by phone at ✆ 800/66-VISIT in Canada or 613/991-3346 outside Canada.

Receipts from several trips during the same year may be submitted together. Claims of less than C$500 (US$310) can be made at certain designated duty-free shops at international airports and border crossings. You will need to present your receipts for validation, have your purchased goods available for inspection by Customs officers, and have proof that you are leaving Canada (such as departing plane tickets) and perhaps proof of your date of entry into Canada. Otherwise, you can mail the forms to **Visitor Rebate Program,** Canada Customs and Revenue Agency, Summerside Tax Centre, 275 Pope Rd., Suite 104, Summerside, PE C1N 6C6.

Telephones The Canadian phone system is exactly the same as the system in the United States. Canadian phone numbers have 10 digits: The first three numbers are the area code, which corresponds to a province or division thereof, plus a seven-digit local number. To call a number within the same locality, usually all you have to dial is the seven-digit local number. If you're making a long-distance call (out of the area or province), you need to precede the local number with a 1 plus the area code.

- **To call Canada:** If you're calling Canada from the United States, simply dial 1 plus the 10-digit number, just as if you were dialing a domestic long-distance number in the U.S. Likewise, to call the U.S. from Canada, just dial 1 plus the number.
- **To make international calls:** To make international (non-U.S.) calls from Canada, first dial 011 and then the country code (U.K. 44, Ireland 353, Australia 61, New Zealand 64). Next you dial the area code and number. For example, if you wanted to call the Australian High Commission in London, you would dial ✆ **011-44-870-162-0822.**
- **For directory assistance:** Dial ✆ **411.** If that doesn't work, dial 1 + area code + 555-1212.
- **For operator assistance:** If you need operator assistance in making a call, dial ✆ **0** (zero).

- **Toll-free numbers:** Numbers beginning with 800, 888, 877, and 866 within Canada are toll-free.

Time Zone Most of British Columbia is in the Pacific Time zone, 3 hours earlier than Eastern Standard Time. A sliver of British Columbia, stretching from Golden down to Cranbrook, and all of Alberta is on Mountain Time, an hour later than the rest of the province. So when it's noon in New York City, it's 9am in Victoria and 10am in Calgary. From the first Sunday in April to the last Sunday in October, daylight saving time is in effect in both provinces; clocks are advanced by 1 hour.

Tipping For good service in a restaurant, tip 15% to 20%. Tip hairdressers or taxi drivers 10%. Bellhops get C$1 (US80¢) per bag; for valets who fetch your car, a C$2 (US$1.60) tip should suffice.

Useful Phone Numbers **Canadian Customs and Revenue** (© 204/983-3500); **U.S Department of Customs and Border Protection** (© 202/354-1000); **U.S. Department of State Travel Advisory** (© 202/647-5225; manned 24 hours); **U.S. Passport Agency** (© 202/647-0518); **U.S. Centers for Disease Control International Traveler's Hot Line** (© 404/332-4559).

3

Suggested Itineraries in British Columbia & the Canadian Rockies

Canada's two westernmost provinces are not only large, they are also packed with amazing must-see scenery and destinations. The following itineraries focus on the top areas covered by this book: the Canadian Rockies, and especially Banff and Jasper national parks; Vancouver, Victoria, the Pacific coast, and islands of British Columbia; and the route between these areas. Many travelers make the journey between the Canadian Rockies and Vancouver in a couple days of driving, but there are very good reasons to slow down and linger in B.C.'s highly photogenic interior, particularly if you're a golfer or wine aficionado.

1 The Canadian Rockies in 1 Week

An outdoor-oriented exploration of the gateway cities and national parks of the Rockies can begin in either Calgary or Edmonton—simply reverse this itinerary to begin in Alberta's capital.

Day ❶: Exploring Calgary

Take a day to explore Calgary, the energetic city that Albertan oil built, beginning at the Eau Claire Market and the adjacent **Prince's Island Park** (p. 322). The **Stephen Avenue** area (p. 327), about all that remains of the city's historic downtown, is now a pedestrian area and home to many restaurants, street performers, and night clubs. The **Glenbow Museum** (p. 323), one of Canada's top art and cultural institutions, is also here, and is a good destination if the weather turns.

If you have kids along, consider a visit to the **Canada Olympic Park** (p. 322), where some of the competition for the 1988 Winter Olympics took place. In addition to visiting the top of the ski jump platform, you can also take a ride down the luge slope year-round.

Days ❷ & ❸: Banff & Environs

From Calgary, follow Highway 1 west toward the Rockies. Within an hour, you'll pass beneath the soaring peaks of Canmore and enter **Banff National Park** (chapter 15). **Banff Townsite** (chapter 15) is filled with grand hotels, modern lodges, B&B inns, plus innumerable restaurants and pubs. You could easily spend most of a day just exploring the town, particularly if you like to shop. However, you'll also want to spend another day exploring the natural sites around Banff, which include boat tours on **Lake Minnewanka** (p. 366), float trips down the **Bow River** (p. 363), day-hiking **Johnston Canyon** (p. 362), and riding the gondola to the top of **Sulphur Mountain** (p. 365).

Day ❹: Lake Louise

Although just an hour to the west of Banff, **Lake Louise** (p. 376) is its own destination. Explore the lake, with its fantastic château-style hotel going eye-to-eye with a glacier. Hiking trails lead to the toe of the glacier where you can replenish yourself with tea and scones at a wilderness teahouse. In the next valley over, Moraine Lake is perhaps even more dramatic, with 10 spirelike peaks rising above a placid lake. The year-round **gondola** at Lake Louise Ski Resort transports hikers to alpine meadows (p. 351). (From Lake Louise, road trippers with a westering urge can follow Highway 1 over the Rockies' Kicking Horse Pass and head toward Vancouver; see next itinerary.)

Day ❺: Traveling the Icefield Parkway

It will take a full day to travel the phenomenal **Icefields Parkway** between Lake Louise and Jasper (p. 380), which crosses Sunwapta Pass beneath the massive Columbia Icefields. Stop to view waterfalls, hike to hidden lakes, and have tea at mountain lodges. Explore the Columbia Icefield, at the very crest of the Rockies, aboard specially built Snocoaches, which can safely venture out onto the surface of the icefield.

Day ❻: Jasper & Environs

The town of **Jasper** (p. 382) doesn't offer the alpine shopping mall experience of Banff, so after strolling through the small town center, head out on a hiking or biking trail to explore the mountains—trails start right in town. Driving to **Maligne Lake** (p. 385) for a boat tour of the Canadian Rockies' largest glacier lake is another option, as is signing up for a white-water raft trip on one of the area's many rivers. If you're a golfer, the course at Jasper Park Lodge is among the most noted in Canada.

Day ❼: Edmonton

Leave the park by heading east on the Yellowhead Highway to **Edmonton,** Alberta's capital (p. 332). Spend the afternoon exploring the city's trendy **Old Strathcona** neighborhood (p. 336), the domed legislative building, and the art gallery district around High Street. Spend your final evening in Alberta in one of Edmonton's excellent restaurants. In the morning, return to Calgary via Highway 2 to catch your flight back home.

2 The Back Roads of Interior B.C. in 1 Week

Don't just zoom between the Canadian Rockies and Vancouver—take time to explore the significantly less crowded Purcell and Selkirk mountains, the Okanagan wine country, and detour through Whistler on your way to Vancouver.

Day ❶: Exploring B.C.'s Mountain Parks

Savvy outdoor enthusiasts know that just west of crowded Banff and Jasper parks are three much less busy but equally stunning national parks, Yoho, Glacier, and Revelstoke. From Lake Louise, follow Highway 1 west over the Continental Divide, where **Yoho Park** (p. 395) offers Canada's second-highest waterfall, **Glacier Park** (p. 300) features hiking trails to the base of icefields, and Revelstoke boasts the **Meadows in the Sky Parkway** (p. 299), leading to flower-spangled alpine meadows. Spend the night in the charming mountain town of **Revelstoke** (p. 294).

Days ❷ & ❸: The Okanagan Wine Country

Head west from Revelstoke, then drop south on Highway 97A at Sicamous. The landscape quickly changes from lush forests to arid desert highlands. The

The Canadian Rockies or Interior B.C. in 1 Week

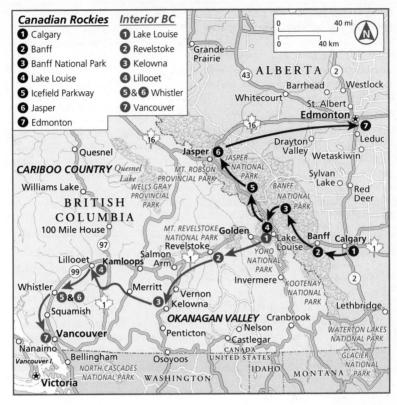

Canadian Rockies
1. Calgary
2. Banff
3. Banff National Park
4. Lake Louise
5. Icefield Parkway
6. Jasper
7. Edmonton

Interior BC
1. Lake Louise
2. Revelstoke
3. Kelowna
4. Lillooet
5 & 6. Whistler
7. Vancouver

Okanagan Valley (chapter 12), filled with 128km-long (80-mile) Okanagan Lake, is a fruit-growing paradise now famous for its burgeoning wine industry. After arriving in **Kelowna** (p. 283), relax at the city's sandy lake beachfront and check out the bustling restaurant scene. The following day, explore the valley's more than 70 **wineries** (p. 287), many of them south of Kelowna toward Penticton. The same irrigation that supports wine grapes sprinkles golf courses—some of B.C.'s top courses overlook Okanagan Lake.

Day 4: West to Whistler

This is a road-trip day, starting on the so-called Peachland Connector (Hwy. 97c) that connects the Okanagan Valley to Merritt. From Merritt, leave the freeway

and follow secondary roads to **Lillooet** (p. 251). At this historic town on the Fraser River begins one of the most dramatic mountain roads in British Columbia, climbing up the Cayoosh Valley, cresting the Coastal Mountains and dropping into Whistler, one of the continent's top mountain resorts.

Days 5 & 6: Whistler

Whistler (see chapter 9) gained its fame as a ski destination—there's a reason that the 2010 Winter Olympic ski events will be held at the exemplary **Whistler/ Blackcomb Resort** (p. 209)—but today Whistler is as busy in summer as winter. If you're a shopper, exploring the shops in **Whistler Village** (p. 208) can take most of a day, and with four championship golf courses nearby, duffers will find plenty of challenges. In summer, there's **glacier skiing** through August (p. 210), and hiking and biking trails start at the village edge. **Nightlife** in Whistler is very lively (p. 223), with a **dining** scene (p. 220) to rival Vancouver.

Day ❼: Drive to Vancouver
From Whistler, Highway 99 drops from mountain heights to sea level along the scenic **Sea-to-Sky Highway** (p. 208), before entering Vancouver from the north. With major pre-Olympic road construction along this route, allow at least 3 hours to reach **Vancouver** (see chapter 4).

3 The Wild & the Sophisticated on Vancouver Island in 1 Week

Vancouver Island is home to rugged, nearly inaccessible rainforests and wilderness coastlines; the island also offers very sophisticated dining and lodging, often in the remote backcountry itself. This is the allure of exploring coastal British Columbia: After a challenging day sea-kayaking remote archipelagoes or hiking old-growth forest, you return to three-star lodging and dining.

Day ❶: The Gulf Islands
Begin your journey in Vancouver, driving to the ferry terminal at Tsawwassen to cross to the **Gulf Islands** (see chapter 6). BC Ferries links to five of these charmingly rural islands, and which island you choose will depend on your interests and inclinations. We recommend Salt Spring Island for its broad range of facilities and multiple ferry routes.

Day ❷: Duncan & the Cowichan Valley
Catch the morning **BC Ferries** (p. 114) run to Vancouver Island (from Salt Spring Island, take the Vesuvius/Crofton ferry) and travel north to **Duncan and the Cowichan Valley** (see chapter 6). This beautiful agricultural area is home to excellent wineries and organic farms and dairies. Just outside Duncan, the **Quw'utsun' Cultural Centre** (p. 143) preserves native Cowichan traditional ways of life, and downtown Duncan is studded with totem poles.

Days ❸, ❹ & ❺: Tofino
From Duncan, drive north to Parksville and the junction with Highway 4. This road to Tofino and Vancouver Island's wild west coast is long and windy, so allow 3 hours to make the journey from Parksville. However, Tofino and the **Long Beach** portion of the Pacific Rim National Park (p. 166) are certainly worth the journey. Outfitters make it simple to get out onto calm and isolated bays on sea kayaks—a popular trip crosses a sound to visit a natural **hot springs** (p. 173). Rainforest **hikes,** deep-sea **fishing** trips, ocean **wildlife** viewing tours and lingering on the splendid sandy **beaches** are other options (p. 172).

The B&Bs and lodges in Tofino are first-rate. Many are nestled above remote beaches at the edge of the forest; others cling to rocky headlands. Some of Vancouver Island's most notable restaurants are here, and the local seafood is exquisite.

Day ❻: Courtenay
Cross back to the east side of Vancouver Island from Tofino, but turn north at Parksville and drive up Highway 19 to the twin cities of **Courtenay and Comox** (see chapter 7). If you have kids in tow, consider signing them up for a fossil dig tour with the local museum; golfers might play a round on the excellent local course, while the eco-minded will relish a sunset kayak tour on the wildlife-rich Courtenay River estuary.

Vancouver Island in 1 Week

1. Gulf Islands
2. Duncan
3. Parksville
4. Long Beach (Pacific Rim Nat'l Park)
5. Tofino
6. Courtenay
7. The Sunshine Coast

Day ⑦: Returning to Vancouver
The following day, cross from Comox via BC Ferries to the mainland and Powell River, and journey to Vancouver along the scenic **Sunshine Coast** (see chapter 9).

4 The Best of Vancouver in 1 Day

This tour is meant to show off Vancouver as a whole, giving you an overview of what makes it so uniquely appealing. There are some places where you'll be exploring on foot, others where you'll drive to reach your destination. Nature, art, culture, and coffee are all part of today's itinerary. Start: Tourism Vancouver Touristinfo Centre, Burrard and Cordova streets.

❶ Canada Place
Start your day outside, on the upper (deck) level of the city's giant **convention center** and **cruise-ship terminal** (p. 53), which juts out into Burrard Inlet across from the Touristinfo Centre. From here

you'll get a good sense of Vancouver's natural and urban topography, with the North Coast Mountains rising up before you; low-rise, historic Gastown to the east; Stanley Park to the west; and a forest of glass residential towers in between.

The Best of Vancouver in 1 Day

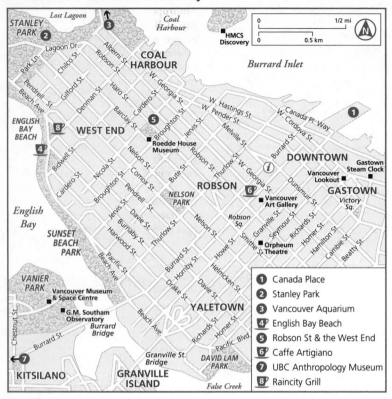

0 ——————— 1/2 mi
0 ——————— 0.5 km

Legend:
1. Canada Place
2. Stanley Park
3. Vancouver Aquarium
4. English Bay Beach
5. Robson St & the West End
6. Caffe Artigiano
7. UBC Anthropology Museum
8. Raincity Grill

Canada Place is busiest in summer, when up to four giant cruise ships may dock in one day.

2 Stanley Park ★★★

You can't really appreciate **Stanley Park** (p. 82) by driving through it in a car, so park your vehicle and head in on foot via Lagoon Drive. Surrounded by a famed pedestrian seawall, this giant peninsular park invites hours of exploration. A 1-hour carriage ride is the perfect way to see the highlights, including an amazing collection of totem poles, giant trees, and landscaped areas.

3 Vancouver Aquarium Marine Science Centre ★★

One of the best aquariums in North America is located right in Stanley Park.

Have a look especially at the Arctic Canada exhibit with its beluga whales, and the Marine Mammal Deck, where you can see Pacific white-sided dolphins, sea otters, and other denizens of Pacific Northwest waters. See p. 82.

4 ENGLISH BAY BEACH ★

If the weather is warm, take off your shoes and enjoy the grass, sand, and sunshine at **English Bay Beach** (p. 86), an all-season gathering spot on the south side of Stanley Park. You can pick up picnic eats or find take-out food on nearby Denman Street.

5 Robson Street & the West End

How you explore the West End is up to you. You can walk from English Bay

Beach down Denman Street and then turn south on **Robson Street** (p. 89), taking in as much of the throbbing shopping and cafe scene as you want. It's also fun to explore the West End as a living neighborhood—the most densely populated in North America!

---

6 CAFFÈ ARTIGIANO ☆☆
For the best latte in town, as well as grilled Italian sandwiches and snacks, stop in at this busy cafe right across from the Vancouver Art Gallery. There's a perfect people-watching patio in front (p. 78).

---

7 UBC Anthropology Museum ☆☆☆
Hop into your car for the roughly 20-minute drive to the outstanding **Anthropology Museum at the University of British Columbia** (p. 83). Here, in one of North America's preeminent collections of First Nations Art, you'll encounter powerful totem poles, spirit masks, and totemic objects, all richly carved and profoundly mysterious.

8 Dinner
In the last decade, Vancouver has become one of the top dining cities in the world, filled with superb restaurants of all kinds. For a romantic dinner that will introduce you to the best of Vancouver's "eat local" food philosophy, reserve a table at **Raincity Grill,** where the windows overlook English Bay, and the regional cuisine is a perfect excuse to linger (p. 77).

5 The Best of Victoria in 1 Day

Victoria is less than a quarter of the size of Vancouver, and you can easily hit the highlights in 1 day if you arrive on an early ferry. The scenic ferry ride—from Vancouver, Seattle, Anacortes, or Port Angeles—is part of the fun. Although it's easy to experience Victoria on foot, by bike, and using public transportation, having a car will help to maximize your sightseeing.

1 Inner Harbour
Victoria's official facade, epitomized by a pair of landmark buildings designed by Francis Rattenbury, is reminiscent of an era that promoted the idea of a British Empire. A stroll along the Inner Harbour takes you past the **Provincial Legislature** ☆, a massive stone edifice completed in 1898, and the famous Fairmont Empress Hotel, which dates from 1908 (p. 99). Along the busy waterfront you'll also find information on whale-watching excursions (p. 110), a popular Victoria pastime.

2 Royal British Columbia Museum ☆☆☆
The highlight of this excellent museum (p. 107) is the First Peoples Gallery, an absorbing and thought-provoking showplace of First Nations art and culture. The

other exhibits pale by comparison, but do have a look at the life-size woolly mastodon if he's on display.

---

3 FAIRMONT EMPRESS ☆☆
Tea at the Empress (p. 103) is a traditional affair that has remained a real treat despite its fame. Make it your main meal of the day (seatings at 12:30, 2, 2:30, and 5pm), and be sure to reserve in advance.

---

4 Butchart Gardens ☆☆☆
This century-old garden (p. 105) is one of the gardening wonders of the world, meticulously planned and impeccably maintained. Though hordes of tourists can jam the paths in the summer months, time your visit for late afternoon and

The Best of Victoria in 1 Day

1 Inner Harbour
2 Royal B.C. Museum
3 Fairmont Empress
4 Butchart Gardens
5 Il Terrazzo Ristorante

Information *(i)*

CHINATOWN

Herald St.
Fisgard St.
Pandora Ave.
Johnson St.
Yates St.
Fort St.

OLD TOWN

DOWNTOWN

Bastian Square

Victoria Harbour

Inner Harbour

Belleville St.

Burdett Ave.

Richardson St.

Government House

THUNDERBIRD PARK

Southgate St.

Fairfield Rd.

MACDONALD PARK

Toronto St.

BEACON HILL PARK

May St.

Dallas Rd.

Upper Harbour

Store St.
Government St.

Esquimalt Rd.
Johnson St. Bridge
Market Square

Wharf St.
Douglas St.
Blanshard St.
Quadra St.
Cook St.
Vancouver St.

Fort St.
Rockland Ave.
Moss St.
Linden Ave.

Montreal St.
Superior St.
Menzies St.
Simcoe St.
Oswego St.
Niagara St.
Medana St.
Government St.
Douglas St.
Cook St.

0   1/2 mi
0   0.5 km

SAANICH

VICTORIA

WEST BAY

Area of Detail

you'll have more room, plus you can stay for the fabulous summer fireworks display.

5 Dinner

If there's time, have dinner at **Il Terrazzo Ristorante** (p. 104). Victoria's best Italian restaurant serves delicious, northern-Italian dishes and has a lovely patio for outdoor, summertime dining.

4

Vancouver

If you really want to understand **Vancouver,** stand at the edge of the Inner Harbour (the Canada Place cruise ship terminal makes a good vantage point) and look around you. To the west you'll see Stanley Park jutting out into the waters of Burrard Inlet. To the north rise snow-capped mountains. To the east is the low-rise brick-faced Old Town.

Vancouver is majestic and intimate, sophisticated and completely laid back, a bustling world-class city that somehow manages to combine its contemporary, urban-centered consciousness with the free-spirited magnificence of nature on a grand scale.

Vancouver is probably one of the newest, most cosmopolitan cities you'll ever visit. There's a youthfulness, too, a certain Pacific Northwest chic (and cheek) that comes from being used in so many movies that Vancouver is sometimes called "Hollywood North." Nature figures big in that equation, but so does enlightened city planning and the diversity of cultures. Vancouver is a place that awakens dreams and desires.

The city's history is in its topography. Thousands of years ago a giant glacier carved out a deep trench and piled up a gigantic moraine of rock and sand. When the ice retreated, water from the Pacific flowed in and the moraine became a peninsula, flanked on one side by a deep natural harbor (today's Inner Harbour) and on the other by a river of glacial meltwater (the Fraser River). Vast forests of fir and cedar covered the land and wildlife flourished. The First Nations tribes that settled in the area developed rich cultures based on cedar and salmon.

Some 10,000 years later, a surveyor for the Canadian Pacific Railroad (CPR) came by, took in the peninsula, the harbor, and the river, and decided he'd found the perfect spot for the CPR's new Pacific terminus. He kept it quiet until the company had bought up most of the land around town. Then the railway moved in, and the city of Vancouver was born.

Vancouverites have seemingly all fallen in love with the outdoors and every kind of outdoor pursuit—hiking, in-line skating, mountain biking, downhill and cross-country skiing, kayaking, windsurfing, rock climbing, parasailing, snowboarding. (The international resort town of Whistler, which will take center stage during the Winter Olympics in 2010, is just 2 hr. north of downtown Vancouver.) And when not skiing or kayaking, they're drinking coffee or eating out. Bursting with an incredible variety of cuisines, Vancouver has become one of the world's top restaurant cities, making a name for itself with its unique Pacific Northwest cooking.

And the rest of the world has taken notice. The World Council of Cities ranked Vancouver second only to Geneva for quality of life. It's also one of the 10 best to visit, according to *Condé Nast Traveler.* And the International Olympic Committee chose Vancouver to host the 2010 Olympic Winter Games. Heady stuff, particularly for a spot that less than 20 years ago was routinely derided as the world's biggest mill town.

1 Essentials

GETTING THERE

BY PLANE **Vancouver International Airport** (© 604/207-7077; www.yvr.ca) is 13km (8 miles) south of downtown Vancouver on uninhabited Sea Island. Daily direct flights between major U.S. cities and Vancouver are offered by **Air Canada** (© 888/247-2262; www.aircanada.ca), **Alaska Airlines** (© 800/252-7522; www.alaskaair.com), **American Airlines** (© 800/433-7300; www.aa.com), **Continental** (© 800/231-0856; www.continental.com), **Northwest Airlines** (© 800/447-4747; www.nwa.com), and **United Airlines** (© 800/241-6522; www.united.com). Domestically, both Air Canada and the cheaper discount airline **WestJet** (© 888/WEST-JET or 800/538-5696; www.westjet.com) offer flights to most Canadian cities.

Tourist information kiosks on Level 2 of the Main and International arrival terminals (© **604/207-0953**) are open daily from 8am to 11pm. **Parking** is available at the airport for both loading passengers and long-term stays (© **604/207-7077** for all airport services inquiries). A **shuttle bus** links the terminals. There is an international departure surcharge of C$15 (US$12) per person for international air travelers outside of North America, C$10 (US$8) for passengers traveling within North America (including Hawaii and Mexico), and C$5 (US$4) for passengers on flights within British Columbia or the Yukon.

Heading into Vancouver, take the Arthur Laing Bridge, which leads directly to Granville Street, the most direct route to downtown. The **YVR Airporter** (© **604/946-8866**) provides **airport bus service** to downtown Vancouver's major hotels. It leaves from Level 2 of the Main Terminal every 15 minutes daily from 6:30am until midnight for the 30-minute ride to downtown Vancouver. The one-way fare is C$12 (US$9.60) for adults, C$8 (US$6.40) for seniors, and C$5 (US$4) for children. Bus service to the airport leaves from selected downtown hotels every half-hour between 5:35am and 10:55pm. Scheduled pickups serve the bus station, Four Seasons, Hotel Vancouver, Waterfront Centre Hotel, Georgian Court, Sutton Place, Landmark, and others. Ask the bus driver on the way in or your hotel concierge for pickup stops and times.

Getting to and from the airport via **public transit** is a pain. Public buses, operated by **Translink** (© **604/953-3333;** www.translink.bc.ca), are slow, and you have to transfer to get downtown: Catch bus no. 424 at ground level of the domestic terminal; it will take you to Airport Station. From there, bus no. 98B will take you downtown. B.C. Transit fares are C$3.25 (US$2.60) during peak hours and C$2.25 (US$1.80) on weekends and after 6:30pm. You must have the exact fare because drivers do not make change. Transfers are free in any direction within a 90-minute period.

The average **taxi** fare from the airport to downtown Vancouver is C$25 (US$20) plus tip. **LimoJet** (© **604/273-1331;** www.limojetgold.com) offers flat-rate stretch-limo service at C$39 (US$31) per trip (not per person) plus tip from downtown to the airport, and can easily accommodate six people. Drivers accept all major credit cards.

BY TRAIN **VIA Rail Canada,** 1150 Station St., Vancouver (© **888/842-7245;** www.viarail.ca), connects with Amtrak at Winnipeg, Manitoba. From there, you travel on a spectacular route that runs between Calgary and Vancouver. Lake Louise's beautiful alpine scenery is just part of this enjoyable journey. **Amtrak** (© **800/872-7245;** www.amtrak.com) has regular service from Seattle, from which you can connect to many major West Coast cities.

The main **Vancouver railway station** is at 1150 Station St., near Main Street and Terminal Avenue just south of Chinatown. You can reach downtown Vancouver from there by cab for about C$10 (US$8). One block from the station is the SkyTrain Main Street Station, providing quick access to the downtown area. A one-zone SkyTrain ticket (covering the city of Vancouver) is C$2.25 (US$1.80).

BY BUS   Greyhound Canada Bus Lines (© 604/482-8747; www.greyhound.ca) and **Pacific Coach Lines** (© 604/662-8074; www.pacificcoach.com) have their terminals at the Pacific Central Station, 1150 Station St. Pacific Coach Lines provides service between Vancouver and Victoria. The cost is C$39 (US$31) one-way per adult and includes the ferry; daily departures are between 5:45am and 7:45pm. Pacific Coach Lines will also pick up passengers from most downtown hotels; call © 604/662-8074 to reserve.

BY CAR   You'll probably be driving into Vancouver along one of two routes. **U.S. Interstate 5** from Seattle becomes **Highway 99** when you cross the border at the Peace Arch. The 210km (130-mile) drive from Seattle takes about 2½ hours. On the Canadian side of the border you'll drive through the cities of White Rock, Delta, and Richmond; pass under the Fraser River through the George Massey Tunnel; and cross the Oak Street Bridge. The highway ends there and becomes Oak Street, a busy urban thoroughfare heading into town. Turn left at the first convenient major arterial (70th Ave., 57th Ave., 49th Ave., 41st Ave., 33rd Ave., 16th Ave., or 12th Ave.) and proceed until you hit the next major street, which will be Granville Street. Turn right on Granville Street. This street heads directly into downtown Vancouver on the Granville Street Bridge.

Trans-Canada Highway 1 is a limited-access freeway running all the way to Vancouver's eastern boundary, where it crosses the Second Narrows bridge to North Vancouver. When traveling on Highway 1 from the east, exit at Cassiar Street and turn left at the first light onto Hastings Street (Hwy. 7A), which is adjacent to Exhibition Park. Follow Hastings Street 6.4km (4 miles) into downtown. When coming to Vancouver from Whistler or parts north, take Exit 13 (the sign says TAYLOR WAY, BRIDGE TO VANCOUVER) and cross the Lions Gate Bridge into Vancouver's West End.

BY SHIP & FERRY   The **Canada Place** cruise ship terminal at the base of Burrard Street (© 604/665-9085; www.portvancouver.com) is a city landmark. Topped by five eye-catching white Teflon sails, Canada Place Pier juts out into the Burrard Inlet and is at the edge of the downtown financial district. **Princess Cruises, Holland America, Royal Caribbean, Crystal Cruises, Norwegian Cruise Lines, World Explorer Majesty Cruise Line,** and **Hanseatic, Seabourn,** and **Carnival** cruise lines dock at Canada Place and the nearby Ballantyne Pier to board passengers headed for Alaska via British Columbia's Inside Passage. Public-transit buses and taxis greet new arrivals, but you can also easily walk to many major hotels, including the Pan-Pacific and Hotel Vancouver.

BC Ferries (© 888/223-3779 in B.C. only, or 250/386-3431; www.bcferries.bc.ca) has three routes operating between Vancouver and Vancouver Island. The one-way fare in peak season is C$11 (US$8.80) for adults, C$5.25 (US$4.20) for children 5 to 11, and C$36 (US$29) per car. Children under 5 ride free. In the summer it is advisable to reserve a space when traveling with a vehicle, especially on long weekends and to and from the Gulf Islands. Call BC Ferries reservations at © 888/724-5223 (in B.C. only), or 604/444-2890.

Greater Vancouver Area

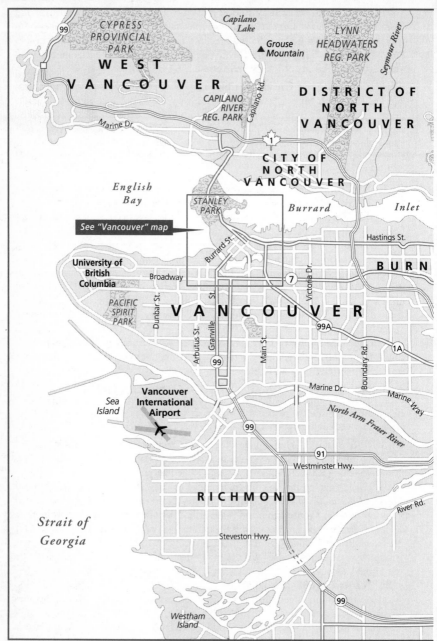

CYPRESS PROVINCIAL PARK

Capilano Lake

LYNN HEADWATERS REG. PARK

Grouse Mountain

Seymour River

W E S T
V A N C O U V E R

99

Marine Dr.

CAPILANO RIVER REG. PARK

Capilano Rd.

D I S T R I C T   O F
N O R T H
V A N C O U V E R

1

C I T Y   O F
N O R T H
V A N C O U V E R

English Bay

STANLEY PARK

See "Vancouver" map

Burrard   *Inlet*

Hastings St.

Burrard St.

Victoria Dr.

B U R N

University of British Columbia

Broadway

7

PACIFIC SPIRIT PARK

Dunbar St.

V A N C O U V E R

99A

Arbutus St.

Granville St.

Main St.

Boundary Rd.

1A

99

Marine Dr.

Marine Way

North Arm Fraser River

Sea Island

Vancouver International Airport

✈

99

91

Westminster Hwy.

R I C H M O N D

River Rd.

Strait of Georgia

Steveston Hwy.

99

Westham Island

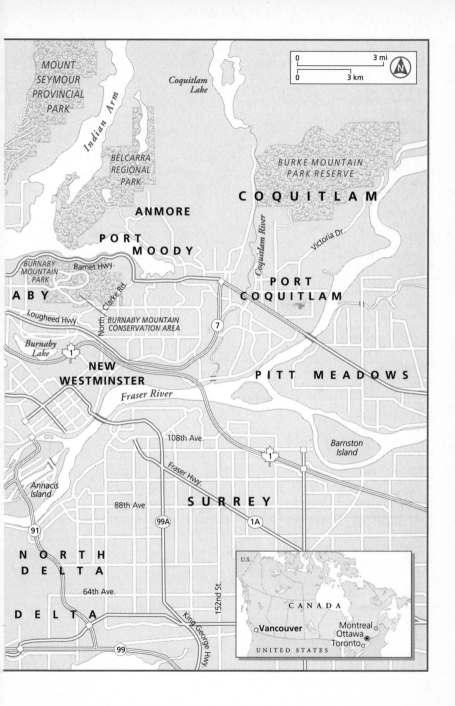

MOUNT
SEYMOUR
PROVINCIAL
PARK

Indian Arm

Coquitlam
Lake

BELCARRA
REGIONAL
PARK

BURKE MOUNTAIN
PARK RESERVE

C O Q U I T L A M

ANMORE

P O R T
M O O D Y

Victoria Dr.

Coquitlam River

BURNABY
MOUNTAIN
PARK

Barnet Hwy.

A B Y

North Clarke Rd.

P O R T
C O Q U I T L A M

Lougheed Hwy.

BURNABY MOUNTAIN
CONSERVATION AREA

7

Burnaby
Lake

1

NEW
WESTMINSTER

Fraser River

P I T T   M E A D O W S

108th Ave.

Fraser Hwy.

1

Barnston
Island

Annacis
Island

88th Ave.

S U R R E Y

91

99A

1A

N O R T H
D E L T A

152nd St.

D E L T A

64th Ave.

King George Hwy.

99

US.

C A N A D A

Vancouver

Montreal
Ottawa
Toronto

UNITED STATES

0   3 mi
0   3 km

N

Vancouver

ACCOMMODATIONS ■
The Aston Rosellen Suites at Stanley Park **16**
Barclay House in the West End **25**
Beachside City View Bed & Breakfast **10**
Buchan Hotel **17**
The Fairmont Hotel Vancouver **54**
Georgian Court Hotel **68**
Granville Island Hotel **40**
Kenya Court Ocean Front Guest House **34**
Lonsdale Quay Hotel **12**
Pacific Palisades Hotel **24**
Pan Pacific Hotel Vancouver **55**
Sheraton Vancouver Wall Centre Hotel **50**
Sunset Inn & Suites **28**
The University of British Columbia Conference Centre **33**
West End Guest House **23**
Westin Bayshore Resort & Marina **18**
YWCA Hotel/Residence **67**

DINING ◆
Banana Leaf **20**
The Beach House at Dundarave Pier **9**
Bin 941 Tapas Parlour **49**
Bishop's **36**
Blue Water Cafe and Raw Bar **47**
C **30**
Caffe Artigiano **53**
The Cannery **62**
Cin Cin **52**
Coast **45**
The Five Sails **56**
Glowbal Grill & Satay Bar **46**
Gusto **11**
Hapa Izakaya **22**
Il Giardino di Umberto Ristorante **29**
Incendio **61**
Lumière **41**
Memphis Blues Barbeque House **43**
The Naam Restaurant **35**
Olympia Oyster & Fish Co. Ltd. **51**

(Continued, right)

Beaver Lake
STANLEY PARK
Lost Lagoon
Coal
Lagoon Dr.
Chilco St.
W. Georgia St.
Alberni St.
Robson St.
Gilford St.
Denman St.
Bidwell St.
Haro St.
Pendrell St.
Beach Ave.
Barclay St.
Nelson St.
ENGLISH BAY BEACH
WEST END
Cardero St.
Nicola St.
Broughton St.
Comox St.
Jervis St.
Davie St.
Burnaby St.
Harwood St.
Pacific St.
Beach Ave.
English Bay
SUNSET BEACH PARK
Ogden Ave.
Whyte Ave.
VANIER PARK
Burrard Bridge
Vancouver Museum
KITSILANO BEACH PARK
Cornwall Ave.
Granville Bridge
Granville Island
Cartwright St.
W. 1st Ave.
KITSILANO
W. 3rd Ave.
W. 5th Ave.
W. 7th Ave.
W. Broadway

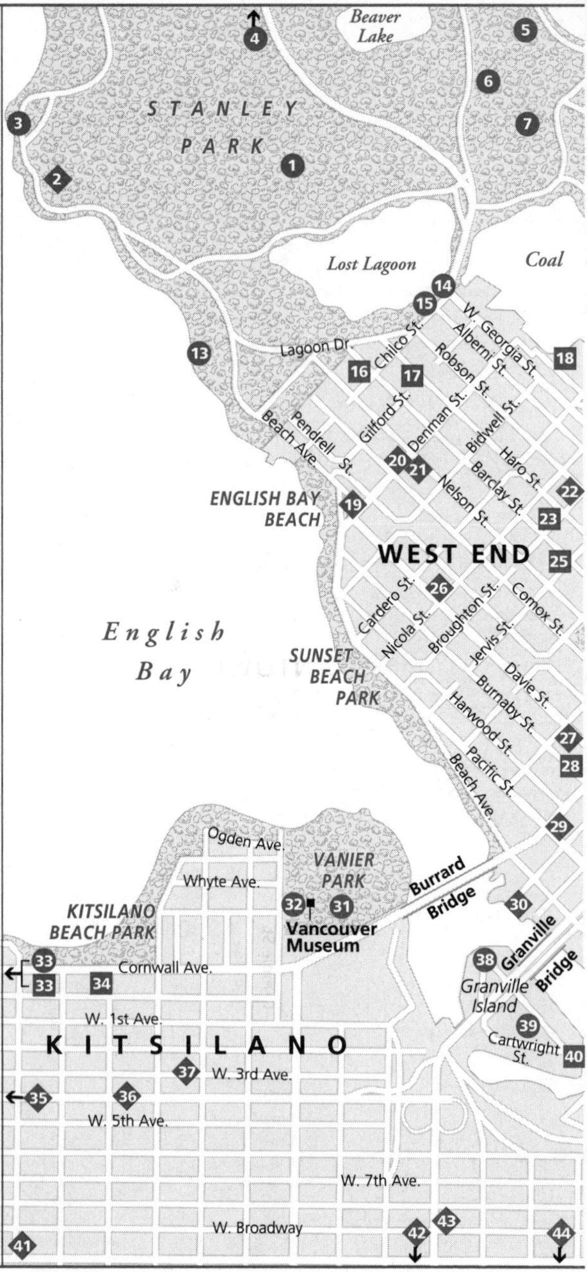

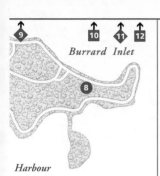

ATTRACTIONS ●

Capilano Suspension Bridge & Park **4**
Dr. Sun Yat-sen Classical Chinese Garden **64**
Granville Island Public Market **38**
Granville Island's Water Park and Adventure Playground **39**
Grouse Mountain Resort **4**
H.R. MacMillan Space Centre **31**
Harbour Centre Tower **58**
Horse-Drawn Carriage Ride **14**
Lost Lagoon Nature House **15**
Miniature Railway **6**

Museum of Anthropology **33**
Science World British Columbia **66**
Second Beach **13**
Stanley Park **1**
Stanley Park Children's Farm **7**
Steam Clock **59**
Storyeum **60**
Third Beach **3**
Totem Poles **8**
Vancouver Aquarium Marine Science Centre **5**
Vancouver Art Gallery **57**
Vancouver Museum **32**

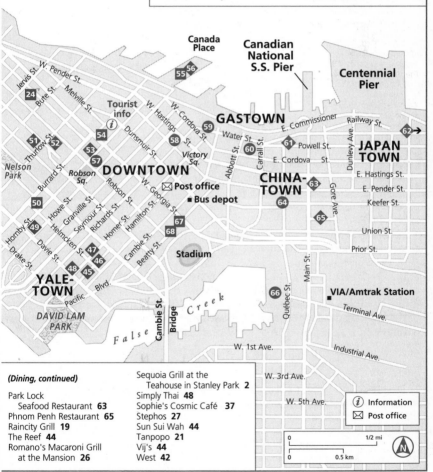

(Dining, continued)

Park Lock Seafood Restaurant **63**
Phnom Penh Restaurant **65**
Raincity Grill **19**
The Reef **44**
Romano's Macaroni Grill at the Mansion **26**

Sequoia Grill at the Teahouse in Stanley Park **2**
Simply Thai **48**
Sophie's Cosmic Café **37**
Stephos **27**
Sun Sui Wah **44**
Tanpopo **21**
Vij's **44**
West **42**

(i) Information
⊠ Post office

Special Events & Festivals

The first event of the year is the annual **New Year's Day Polar Bear Swim** at English Bay Beach; thousands of hardy citizens show up in elaborate costumes to take a dip in the icy waters of English Bay. On the second Sunday in January, the **Annual Bald Eagle Count** takes place in Brackendale, about an hour's drive north of Vancouver on the Sea to Sky Highway. The count starts at the Brackendale Art Gallery (℡ **604/898-3333**).

In late January or early February (dates change yearly), the **Chinese New Year** is celebrated with 2 weeks of firecrackers, dancing dragon parades, and other festivities.

The Vancouver Playhouse International Wine Festival (www.playhouse winefest.com) in late March or early April (dates change yearly) is a major wine-tasting event featuring the latest international vintages. Each winery sets up a booth where you may try as many varieties as you like. The April **Vancouver Sun Run** (www.sunrun.com) is Canada's biggest 10K race, featuring 40,000 runners, joggers, and walkers who race through 10 scenic kilometers. The run starts and finishes at BC Place Stadium.

The late June to early July **International Children's Festival** (℡ 640/708-5655; www.vancouverchildrensfestival.com) features plays and music; it's held in Vanier Park on False Creek. The **VanDusen Flower and Garden Show,** at the VanDusen Botanical Garden, 5251 Oak St. (℡ 604/878-9274), is Vancouver's premier flora gala. The late June **Alcan Dragon Boat Festival** (www.canadadragonboat.com) features more than 150 local and international teams racing huge dragon boats. Four stages of music, dance, and Chinese acrobatics also take place as part of the events at the Plaza of Nations (℡ 604/688-2382).

During the **Vancouver International Jazz Festival** (℡ 604/872-5200; www.jazzvancouver.com) in late June and early July, more than 800 international jazz and blues players perform at 25 venues around town. On **Canada Day** (July 1) Canada Place Pier hosts an all-day celebration including music and dance and an evening fireworks display over the harbor to top off the entertainment. The second or third weekend in July brings the **Vancouver Folk Music Festival** (℡ 604/602-9798; www.thefestival.bc.ca). International folk music is played outdoors at Jericho Beach Park.

The most direct route between Vancouver and Victoria is the **Tsawwassen–Swartz Bay ferry,** which runs every 2 hours between 7am and 9pm. The crossing takes 95 minutes. Driving distance from Tsawwassen to Vancouver is about 20km (12 miles). Take Highway 17 from Tsawwassen until it merges with Highway 99 just before the George Massey Tunnel; then follow the driving directions to Vancouver given in "By Car," above. BC Transit has regular bus service from Vancouver to Tsawwassen and from Swartz Bay to Victoria.

The **Mid-Island Express** operates between Tsawwassen and Duke Point, just south of Nanaimo. The 2-hour crossing runs eight times daily between 5:15am and 10:45pm.

Running July to September, the **Bard on the Beach Shakespeare Festival** in Vanier Park (✆ **604/739-0559**; www.bardonthebeach.org) presents Shakespeare's plays in a tent overlooking English Bay.

During the **HSBC Celebration of Light** (www.celebration-of-light.com) in late July and early August, three international fireworks companies compete for a coveted title by launching their best displays rigged to explode in time to accompanying music over English Bay Beach. Don't miss the grand finale on the fourth night. In the last week of July and first week of August, the **Vancouver International Comedy Festival** (www.comedyfest.com) features comedians from all over Canada and the United States performing at a variety of venues around town.

On BC Day (the first Sun in Aug) the **Vancouver Pride Parade** (✆ **604/687-0955**; www.vanpride.bc.ca), a colorful gay-and-lesbian parade covers a route along Denman and Davie streets, beginning at noon. In August, the **Abbottsford International Air Show** (✆ **604/852-8511**; www.abbotsfordairshow.com) features barnstorming stuntmen and precision military pilots flying everything from Sopwith Camels to VTOLs and stealth bombers.

Mid-August to Labour Day, the **Pacific National Exhibition** (✆ **604/253-2311**; www.pne.ca) offers everything from big-name entertainment to a demolition derby, livestock demonstrations, logger sports competitions, fashion shows, and North America's finest all-wooden roller coaster.

On Labour Day weekend, the **Molson Indy** (✆ **604/684-4639**; www.molsonindy.com) roars around the streets of False Creek, attracting more than 500,000 spectators. Later in September, the **Vancouver Fringe Festival** (✆ **604/257-0350**; www.vancouverfringe.com) highlights the best of Vancouver's independent theater.

Every October, the **Vancouver International Film Festival** (✆ **604/685-0260**; www.viff.org) features 250 new works, revivals, and retrospectives, representing filmmakers from 40 countries. Throughout December, the **Christmas Carol Ship Parade** (www.carolship.org) lights up Vancouver Harbour; harbor cruise ships decorated with colorful Christmas lights sail around English Bay while onboard guests sip cider and sing Christmas Carols.

The **Horseshoe Bay–Nanaimo ferry** has eight daily sailings, leaving Horseshoe Bay near West Vancouver and arriving 95 minutes later in Nanaimo. To reach Vancouver from Horseshoe Bay, take the Trans-Canada Highway (Hwy. 1) east and then take Exit 13 (Taylor Way) to the Lions Gate Bridge and downtown Vancouver's West End.

VISITOR INFORMATION
TOURIST OFFICES & PUBLICATIONS   **Tourism Vancouver Touristinfo Centre,** 200 Burrard St. (✆ **604/683-2000;** www.tourismvancouver.com), is your single-best travel information source about Vancouver and the North Shore. Tourism Vancouver can help you buy bus passes and pick up maps, brochures, and travel guides.

The staff is outgoing and can be very helpful if you need directions or recommendations. If you have trouble finding accommodations, the office has catalogs of registered hotels and B&Bs; the staff will even make reservations for you. The Info Centre is open from May to Labour Day daily from 8am to 6pm; the rest of the year, it's open Monday through Friday from 8:30am to 5pm and Saturday from 9am to 5pm.

If you plan to see more of this beautiful province, **Super Natural British Columbia** (© **800/663-6000** or 604/663-6000; www.hellobc.com) can help you.

The glossy city magazine *Vancouver* (© **604/877-7732**) is loaded with information and attitude. "VanMag," as it's also known, is available on newsstands and on the Web at **www.vanmag.com**.

CITY LAYOUT

Think of the downtown peninsula as being like an upraised thumb on the mitten-shaped Vancouver mainland. Stanley Park, the West End, Yaletown, and Vancouver's business and financial center are located on the thumb, which is bordered to the west by English Bay, to the north by Burrard Inlet, and to the south by False Creek. The mainland part of the city, the mitten, is mostly residential, with a sprinkling of businesses along main arterial streets. Both mainland and peninsula are covered by a simple rectilinear street pattern.

On the downtown peninsula, there are four key **east–west streets. Robson Street** starts at BC Place Stadium on Beatty Street, flows through the West End's more touristed shopping district, and ends at Stanley Park's Lost Lagoon on Lagoon Drive. **Georgia Street**—far more efficient for drivers than the pedestrian-oriented Robson— runs from the Georgia Viaduct on the eastern edge of downtown through Vancouver's commercial core; it then carries on through Stanley Park and over the Lions Gate Bridge to the North Shore. Three blocks north of Georgia is **Hastings Street,** which begins in the West End, runs east through downtown, and then skirts Gastown's southern border as it runs eastward to the Trans-Canada Highway. **Davie Street** starts at Pacific Boulevard near the Cambie Street Bridge, travels through Yaletown into the West End's more residential shopping district, and ends at English Bay Beach.

Tips What's West

When figuring out what's where in Vancouver, the thing to keep in mind is that this is a city where property is king, and the word "west" has such positive connotations that folks have always gone to great lengths to associate it with their particular patch of real estate. Thus, you have the **West End** and the **West Side** and **West Vancouver,** which improbably enough is located immediately beside **North Vancouver.** It can be a bit confusing for newcomers, but fortunately each west has its own distinct character. The West End is a high-rise residential neighborhood located on the downtown peninsula. The West Side is one whole half of Vancouver, from Ontario Street west to the University of British Columbia. (The more working-class **East Side** covers the mainland portion of the city, from Ontario St. east to Boundary Rd.) Very tony West Vancouver is a city to itself on the far side of Burrard Inlet. Together with its more middle-class neighbor, North Vancouver, it forms an area called the **North Shore.**

Tips **Finding an Address**

In many Vancouver addresses, the suite or room number precedes the building number. For instance, 100–1250 Robson St. is Suite 100 at 1250 Robson St. Downtown, Chinatown's **Carrall Street** is the east–west axis from which streets are numbered and designated. Westward, numbers increase progressively to Stanley Park; eastward, numbers increase approaching Commercial Drive. For example, 400 W. Pender would be 4 blocks from Carrall Street heading toward downtown; 400 E. Pender would be 4 blocks on the opposite side of Carrall Street. Off the peninsula the system works the same, but **Ontario Street** is the east–west axis. Also, all east–west roads are avenues (for example, Fourth Ave.), while streets (for example, Main St.) run exclusively north–south.

Three **north–south downtown streets** will get you everywhere you want to go in and out of downtown. Two blocks east of Stanley Park is **Denman Street,** which runs from West Georgia Street at Coal Harbour to Beach Avenue at English Bay Beach. This main West End thoroughfare is where locals dine out. It's also the shortest north–south route between the two ends of the Stanley Park Seawall.

Eight blocks east of Denman is **Burrard Street,** which starts near the Canada Place Pier and runs south through downtown, crosses the Burrard Street Bridge, and then forks. One branch, still **Burrard Street,** continues south and intersects West Fourth Avenue and Broadway Avenue before ending at West 16th Avenue on the borders of Shaughnessy. The other branch becomes **Cornwall Avenue,** which heads west through Kitsilano, changing its name to **Point Grey Road** and then **N.W. Marine Drive** before entering the University of British Columbia campus.

Granville Street starts near the Waterfront Station on Burrard Inlet and runs the entire length of downtown, crosses the Granville Bridge to Vancouver's West Side, and carries on south across the breadth of the city before crossing the Arthur Laing Bridge to Vancouver International Airport.

On the mainland portion of Vancouver, the city's east–west roads are successively numbered from First Avenue at the downtown bridges to 77th Avenue by the banks of the Fraser River. By far, the most important east–west route is **Broadway** (formerly Ninth Ave.), which starts a few blocks from the University of British Columbia (UBC) and extends across the length of the city to the border of neighboring Burnaby, where it becomes the **Lougheed Highway.** In Kitsilano, **West Fourth Avenue** is also an important east–west shopping and commercial corridor. Intersecting with Broadway at various points are a number of important north–south commercial streets, each of which defines a particular neighborhood. The most significant of these streets are (from west to east) **Macdonald Street** in Kitsilano, **Granville Street, Cambie Street, Main Street,** and **Commercial Drive.**

NEIGHBORHOODS IN BRIEF

DOWNTOWN Most of Vancouver's commercial and office space lives in the sort of square patch starting at Nelson Street and heading north to the harbor, with Homer Street and Burrard Street forming the east and west boundaries respectively. Many of the city's best hotels are also found in this area, clustering especially near the water's edge. The most interesting avenues for visitors are Georgia and Granville streets. Georgia Street—in addition to being the prime address for class A commercial property—is where you'll find the Vancouver Art Gallery, the Coliseum-shaped Vancouver Public Library, and the Pacific Centre regional shopping mall. Vancouver's recently revived great white way, Granville Street is the home of bars and clubs and theaters and pubs and restaurants.

THE WEST END The high-rise West End owes more to Manhattan than to the sprawling cities of the west. All the necessities of life are contained within the West End's border: great cafes, good nightclubs, many and varied bookshops, and some of the best restaurants in the city. That's part of what makes it such a sought-after address, but it's also the little things, like the street trees, the mix of high-rise condos and old Edwardians, and the way that, in the midst of such an urban setting, you now and again stumble on a view of the ocean or the mountains.

GASTOWN The oldest section of Vancouver, Gastown's charm shines through the souvenir shops and panhandlers. It's the only section of the city that has the feel of an old Victorian town—the buildings stand shoulder to shoulder and cobblestones line the streets. It's also the place to look for a new and experimental art gallery, or a young fashion designer setting up shop on a little back street, or even a "Legalize Marijuana" campaigner selling grow lights and cannabis seeds out of a storefront cafe. The neighborhood is named for a saloonkeeper—Gassy Jack Deighton— who talked the local mill hands into building a saloon as Vancouver's first

structure in return for all the whiskey they could drink. Nowadays, Gastown is still liberally endowed with pubs and clubs—it's one of two or three areas where Vancouverites congregate when the sun goes down.

CHINATOWN Chinatown's a kick, mostly because there's little that's overtly touristy about it. For the thousands of Cantonese-speaking Canadians who live in the surrounding neighborhoods, it's simply the place they go to shop. And for many others who have moved to more outlying neighborhoods, it's still one of the best places to come and eat. The area was settled about the same time as the rest of Vancouver, by migrant laborers brought in to build the Canadian Pacific Railway. For visitors, the fun is to simply wander, look, and taste.

YALETOWN & FALSE CREEK NORTH Vancouver's former warehouse district, Yaletown has long since been converted to an area of apartment lofts, nightclubs, restaurants, high-end furniture shops, and a fledgling multimedia biz. For visitors, it features some interesting cafes and patios, some high-end shops, and a kind of gritty urban feel that you won't find elsewhere in Vancouver. This old-time authenticity provides an essential anchor to the brand spanking new bevy of towers that has arisen in the past 10 years on Pacific Boulevard along the north edge of False Creek.

GRANVILLE ISLAND Part crafts fair, part farmers' market, part artist's workshop, part mall, and part heavy industrial site, Granville Island seems to have everything you could name: theaters, pubs, restaurants, artists' studios, bookstores, crafts shops, an art school, a hotel, a cement plant, and lots and lots of people. One of the most enjoyable ways to experience the

Granville Island atmosphere is to head down to the Granville Island Public Market, grab a latte, then wander outside to enjoy the view of the boats, the buskers, and the children chasing flocks of squawking seagulls.

KITSILANO In the '60s Kitsilano was Canada's Haight-Ashbury, a slightly seedy enclave with coffeehouses, head shops, and lots of incense and long hair. Nowadays, it's thoroughly yuppified and a fun place to wander. There are great bookstores and trendy furniture and housewares shops, lots of consignment clothing stores, snowboard shops, coffee everywhere, and lots of places to eat. Indeed, every third storefront is a restaurant. The best parts of Kitsilano are the stretch of West Fourth Avenue between Burrard and Balsam streets, and West Broadway between Macdonald and Alma streets.

COMMERCIAL DRIVE Known as "The Drive" to Vancouverites, the 12-block section from Venables Street to East Sixth Avenue has a counterculture feel. There are posters for Cuba Libre! rallies, and bits of graffiti reading "Smash Capitalism!" But The Drive also has an immigrant feel. The first wave of Italians left cafes such as **Calabria,** 1745 Commercial Dr. (© **604/253-7017**) and **Caffe Amici,** 1344 Commercial Dr. (© **604/255-2611**). More recent waves of Portuguese, Hondurans, and Guatemalans have also left their mark. And lately, lesbians and vegans and artists have moved in. Shops and restaurants reflect the mix. Think Italian cafe next to the Marxist bookstore across from the vegan deli selling yeast-free Tuscan bread.

PUNJABI MARKET India imported. Most of the businesses on this 4-block stretch of Main Street, from 48th up to 52nd avenues, are run by and cater to Indo-Canadians, primarily Punjabis. The area is best seen during business hours, when the fragrant scent of spices wafts out from food stalls, while the sound of Hindi pop songs blares from hidden speakers. Young brides hunt through sari shops or seek out suitable material in discount textile outlets. **Memsaab Boutique,** 6647 Main St. (© **604/322-0250**), and **Frontier Cloth House,** 6695 Main St. (© **604/325-4424**), specialize in richly colored silk saris, shawls, fabrics, and costume jewelry. A good place to eat is **Nirvana,** 2313 Main St. (© **604/ 872-8779**), which offers a medley of Indian favorites.

2 Getting Around

BY PUBLIC TRANSPORTATION The **Translink** (© **604/521-0400;** www. translink.bc.ca) system includes electric buses, SeaBus catamaran ferries, and the magnetic-rail SkyTrain. The eco-friendly, highly reliable, inexpensive system runs everywhere from 5am to 2am, even the beaches and ski slopes. Schedules and routes are available at the Touristinfo Centre, at major hotels, online, and on buses. For general public transportation information, call © **604/953-3333.**

Fares are the same for bus, ferry, and train. A one-way, one-zone fare (including all of central Vancouver) costs C$2.25 (US$1.80). A two-zone fare—C$3.25 (US$2.60)—is required to travel to nearby suburbs such as Richmond or North Vancouver. After 6:30pm on weekdays and all day on weekends and holidays, you can travel anywhere in all three zones for C$2.25 (US$1.80). **DayPasses,** good on all public transit, cost C$8 (US$6.40) for adults and C$6 (US$4.80) for seniors, students, and children. They can be used for unlimited daily travel, including weekends and holidays.

Drivers do not make change, so you need exact fare or a valid transit pass. You can buy passes from ticket machines at stations, Touristinfo Centres, both SeaBus terminals, convenience stores, drugstores, and outlets displaying the FARE DEALER sign.

The **SkyTrain** services 20 stations along its 35-minute trip from downtown Vancouver east to Surrey through Burnaby and New Westminster. **SeaBus** catamaran ferries take passengers, cyclists, and wheelchair riders on a scenic 12-minute commute between downtown's Waterfront Station and North Vancouver's Lonsdale Quay. The crossing is a two-zone fare on weekdays until 6:30pm.

BY TAXI   Cab fares start at C$2.30 (US$1.85) and increase at a rate of C$1.25 (US$1) per kilometer, plus C30¢ (US25¢) per minute at stoplights or in stalled traffic. In the downtown area, you can expect to travel for less than C$10 (US$8) plus tip. The typical fare for the 13km (8-mile) drive from downtown to the airport is C$25 (US$20). Taxis are easy to find in front of major hotels, but flagging one down can be tricky. Most drivers are usually on radio calls. But thanks to built-in satellite positioning systems, if you call for a taxi, it usually arrives faster than if you go out and hail one. Call for a pickup from **Black Top** (© **604/731-1111**), **Yellow Cab** (© **604/681-1111**), or **MacLure's** (© **604/731-9211**).

BY CAR   You won't need a car to see the city, but you may want one to explore the environs. If you're over 25 and have a major credit card, you can rent a vehicle from **Avis,** 757 Hornby St. (© **800/879-2847** or 604/606-2868); **Budget,** 501 W. Georgia St. (© **800/472-3325** or 604/668-7000); **Enterprise,** 585 Smithe St. (© **800/ 736-8222** or 604/688-5500); **Hertz Canada,** 1128 Seymour St. (© **800/263-0600** or 604/606-4711); **National/Tilden,** 1130 W. Georgia St. (© **800/387-4747** or 604/685-6111); or **Thrifty,** 1015 Burrard St. or 1400 Robson St. (© **800/847-4389** or 604/606-1666). These firms all have counters and shuttle service at the airport as well. To rent a recreational vehicle, contact Go West Campers, 1577 Lloyd Ave., North Vancouver (© **800/661-8813** or 604/987-5288; www.go-west.com).

All major downtown hotels have guest parking, either in-house or at nearby lots; rates vary from free to C$26 (US$21) per day. There's public parking at **Robson Square** (enter at Smithe and Howe sts.), the **Pacific Centre** (Howe and Dunsmuir sts.), and **The Bay** department store (Richards near Dunsmuir St.). You'll also find larger **parking lots** at the intersections of Thurlow and Georgia, Thurlow and Alberni, and Robson and Seymour. Metered **street parking** isn't *impossible* to come by, but rules posted on signs are strictly enforced. Cars are towed away when the 3pm no-parking rule goes into effect on many major thoroughfares, and unmetered parking on side streets is often reserved for neighborhood residents. If your car is towed away or you need a towing service and aren't a CAA or an AAA member, call **Unitow** (© **604/251-1255**) or **Busters** (© **604/685-8181**).

BY BICYCLE   Vancouver's a great place to bike. There are plenty of places to rent a bike along Robson and Denman streets near Stanley Park. A trip around the **Stanley Park Seawall** 🚲🚲 is one of Vancouver's premier sightseeing experiences. Bike routes are designated throughout the city. Paved paths crisscross through parks and along beaches, and new routes are constantly being added. Helmets are mandatory and riding on sidewalks is illegal except on designated bike paths.

You can take your bike on the SeaBus anytime at no extra charge. All the West Vancouver blue buses (including the bus to the Horseshoe Bay ferry terminal) can carry two bikes, first-come, first-served, and free of charge. In Vancouver, only a limited number of suburban routes allow bikes on the bus: bus no. 351 to White Rock, bus no. 601 to South Delta, bus no. 404 to the airport, and the 99 Express to UBC. For more information, see "Bicycling & Mountain Biking," later in this chapter.

BY MINIFERRY   Crossing False Creek to Vanier Park or Granville Island on one of the blue miniferries is cheap and fun. The **Aquabus** (© **604/689-5858;** www.aquabus.bc.ca) docks at David Lam Park, the south foot of Hornby Street, the Arts Club on Granville Island, Yaletown at Davie Street, Science World, and Stamp's Landing. Ferries operate daily from 7am to 10:30pm (8:30pm in winter), as frequently as every 15 to 30 minutes from 10am to 5pm (later in May–June). One-way fares vary from C$2.50 to C$5 (US$2–US$4) for adults and C$1.25 to C$3 (US$1–US$2.40) for seniors and children. A day pass costs C$12 (US$9.60) for adults, C$11 (US$8.80) for seniors, and C$8 (US$6.40) for children. You can take a scenic 40-minute harbor tour for C$8 (US$6.40) adults, C$6 (US$4.80) seniors, and C$5 (US$4) children.

FAST FACTS: Vancouver

American Express   The office is at 666 Burrard St. (© **604/669-2813**). It's open Monday through Friday from 8:30am to 5:30pm and Saturday from 10am to 4pm.

Area Codes   The telephone area code for the lower mainland, including greater Vancouver and Whistler, is **604.** The area code for Vancouver Island, the Gulf Islands, and the interior of the province is **250.**

Business Hours   Vancouver **banks** are open Monday through Thursday from 10am to 5pm and Friday from 10am to 6pm. Some banks, like Canadian Trust, are also open on Saturdays. **Stores** are generally open Monday through Saturday from 10am to 6pm. Last call at the city's **restaurant bars** and **cocktail lounges** is 2am.

Consulates   The **U.S. Consulate** is at 1075–1095 W. Pender St. (© **604/685-4311**). The **British Consulate** is at 800–1111 Melville St. (© **604/683-4421**). The **Australian Consulate** is at 1225–888 Dunsmuir St. (© **604/684-1177**). Check the Yellow Pages for other countries.

Currency Exchange   Banks and ATMs have a better exchange rate than most foreign exchange bureaus (the latter charge transaction and service fees).

Dentist   Most major hotels have a dentist on call. **Vancouver Centre Dental Clinic,** Vancouver Centre Mall, 11–650 W. Georgia St. (© **604/682-1601**), is another option. You must make an appointment. The clinic is open Monday through Wednesday 8:30am to 6pm, Thursday 8:30am to 7pm and Friday 9am to 6pm.

Doctor   Hotels usually have a doctor on call. **Vancouver Medical Clinics,** Bentall Centre, 1055 Dunsmuir St. (© **604/683-8138**), is a drop-in clinic open Monday through Friday from 8am to 4:45pm. Another drop-in medical center, **Carepoint Medical Centre,** 1175 Denman St. (© **604/681-5338**), is open daily from 9am to 9pm.

Emergencies   Dial © **911** for fire, police, ambulance, and poison control.

Hospitals   **St. Paul's Hospital,** 1081 Burrard St. (© **604/682-2344**), is the closest facility to downtown and the West End. West Side Vancouver hospitals include **Vancouver General Hospital Health and Sciences Centre,** 855 W. 12th Ave.

(© 604/875-4111), and **British Columbia's Children's Hospital,** 4480 Oak St. (© 604/875-2345). In North Vancouver, there's **Lions Gate Hospital,** 231 E. 15th St. (© 604/988-3131).

Internet Access Free Internet access is available at the Vancouver **public library** Central Branch, 350 W. Georgia St. (© 604/331-3600). Just across the street, **Webster's Internet Cafe,** 340 Robson St. (© 604/915-9327), charges for access but generally has a machine free. At the other end of Robson Street there's **Cyber Space Internet Café** (© 604/684-6004). Or, for some late night surfing, try **Internet Coffee,** 1104 Davie St. (© 604/682-6668).

Liquor Laws The legal drinking age in British Columbia is 19. Spirits are sold only in government liquor stores, but beer and wine can be purchased from specially licensed, privately owned stores and pubs. LCBC (Liquor Control of British Columbia) stores are open Monday through Saturday from 10am to 6pm (some are open until 11pm).

Newspapers & Magazines The two local papers are the *Vancouver Sun* (www.vancouversun.com), published Monday through Saturday, and *The Province* (www.canada.com/vancouver/theprovince), published Sunday through Friday mornings. The free weekly entertainment paper, *The Georgia Straight* (www.straight.com), comes out on Thursday. *Where Vancouver,* a shopping/tourist guide, can be found in your hotel room or at Tourism Vancouver.

Pharmacies **Shopper's Drug Mart,** 1125 Davie St. (© 604/685-6445), is open 24 hours. Several Safeway supermarket pharmacies are open late; the one on Robson and Denman is open until midnight.

Police For emergencies, dial © **911.** Otherwise, the **Vancouver City Police** can be reached at © 604/717-3535.

Post Office The **main post office** (© 800/267-1177) is at West Georgia and Homer streets (349 W. Georgia St.). It's open Monday through Friday from 8am to 5:30pm. You'll also find post office outlets in Shopper's Drug Mart and 7-11 stores with longer opening hours.

Restrooms Hotel lobbies are your best bet for downtown facilities. The shopping centers like Pacific Centre and Sinclair Centre, as well as the large department stores like the Bay, also have restrooms.

Safety Overall, Vancouver is a safe city; violent-crime rates are quite low. However, property crimes and crimes of opportunity (such as items being stolen from unlocked cars) occur disturbingly frequently, particularly downtown. Vancouver's Downtown East Side, between Gastown and Chinatown, is a troubled neighborhood and should be avoided at night.

Taxes Hotel rooms are subject to a 10% tax. The **provincial sales tax (PST)** is 7% (excluding food, restaurant meals, and children's clothing). For specific questions, call the **B.C. Consumer Taxation Branch** (© 604/660-4524).

Most goods and services are subject to a 7% **federal goods and services tax (GST).** Save your receipts. You can get a refund on short-stay accommodations and all shopping purchases. Each purchase must be greater than C$50 (US$36), and you must have a total of at least C$200 (US$144) to file a claim. (This refund doesn't apply to car rentals, parking, restaurant meals, room service, tobacco, or alcohol.) For details on the GST, call ℂ **800/668-4748** in Canada or 902/432-5608 outside Canada, or visit **www.ccra-adrc.gc.ca/visitors**.

Time Zone Vancouver is in the Pacific time zone, as are Seattle and San Francisco. Daylight saving time applies April through October.

Weather Call ℂ **604/664-9010** or 604/664-9032 for weather updates; dial ℂ **604/666-3655** for marine forecasts. Each local ski resort has its own snow report line. Cypress Ski area's is ℂ **604/419-7669**; Whistler/Blackcomb's is ℂ **604/687-7507** (in summer it also provides events listings for the village).

3 Where to Stay

There are lots of rooms and lots of choices, from world-class luxury hotels to moderately priced hotels and budget B&Bs and hostels. Most of the hotels are in the downtown area or in the West End. Central Vancouver is small and easily walkable, so in both these neighborhoods you'll be close to major sights, services, and nightlife. Reservations are recommended June through September and during holidays. If you arrive without a reservation or have trouble finding a room, call **Super Natural British Columbia** at ℂ **800/435-5622** or **Tourism Vancouver** at ℂ **604/683-2000.** If you prefer to stay in a B&B, **Born Free Bed & Breakfast of BC,** 4390 Frances St., Burnaby, BC V5C ZR3 (ℂ **800/488-1941** or 604/298-8815; www.vancouverbandb.bc.ca), specializes in matching guests with establishments.

DOWNTOWN & YALETOWN
VERY EXPENSIVE

The Fairmont Hotel Vancouver ✿✿   Thanks to a C$75-million renovation, the grande dame of Vancouver's hotels has been restored to her former glory. A landmark in the city since 1939, and located directly across from busy Robson Square and the Vancouver Art Gallery, the hotel has been completely brought up to 21st-century standards but retains its very old-fashioned, traditional elegance. The rooms are spacious, quiet, and comfortable, if not particularly dynamic in layout or finish. The bathrooms gleam with marble floors and sinks and have the kind of solid tubs that you just don't find anywhere anymore. The courtyard suites feature a large luxuriously furnished living room, separated from the bedroom by French glass doors. A state-of-the-art spa features day packages and a la carte treatments including body scrubs and wraps.

900 W. Georgia St., Vancouver, BC V6C 2W6. ℂ 800/441-1414 or 604/684-3131. Fax 604/662-1929. www.fairmont. com. 556 units. High season C$339–C$519 (US$271–US$415) double; low season C$289–C$429 (US$231–US$343) double. Children under 18 stay free in parent's room. AE, DC, DISC, MC, V. Parking C$25 (US$20). **Amenities:** 2 restaurants; bar; indoor pool; health club; excellent spa; Jacuzzi; sauna; concierge; tour desk; car rental; business center; shopping arcade; salon; 24-hr. room service; massage; babysitting; laundry service; same-day dry cleaning; non-smoking rooms; rooms for those with limited mobility; Fairmont Gold executive-level. *In room:* A/C, TV w/pay movies, dataport, minibar, coffeemaker, hair dryer, iron.

Pan Pacific Hotel Vancouver ✿✿✿   This 23-story luxury hotel atop Canada Place is a key landmark on the Vancouver waterfront. Despite its size, the hotel excels in comfort and service, and it provides the most spectacular views of any hotel in the city. Book a deluxe harbor- and mountain-view room and you can wake to see sunshine on the mountains of the North Shore, floatplanes taking off from Burrard Inlet, and cruise ships arriving and departing just below your window. Rooms are spacious and comfortable with contemporary furnishings and large luxurious Bathrooms. Guests have free use of a heated outdoor pool and Jacuzzi overlooking the harbor. In 2005, the hotel opened its new health club (daily use fee), and Spa Utopia opened in 2004. Café Pacifica has one of the best breakfast buffets in the city and is open for casual meals all day; The Five Sails restaurant (p. 74), open for dinner only, is the hotel's fine-dining option.

300–999 Canada Place, Vancouver, BC V6C 3B5. ✆ **800/937-1515** in the U.S., or 604/662-8111. Fax 604/685-8690. www.panpacific.com. 504 units. May–Oct C$490–C$640 (US$392–US$512) double, C$640–C$2,200 (US$512–US$1,760) suite; Nov–Apr C$390–C$480 (US$312–US$384) double; C$480–C$2,000 (US$384–US$1,600) suite. AE, DC, DISC, MC, V. Valet parking C$27 (US$22). **Amenities:** 2 restaurants; bar; outdoor heated pool; health club; spa; Jacuzzi; sauna; concierge; tour desk; business center; shopping arcade; 24-hr. room service; massage; babysitting; laundry service; same-day dry cleaning; nonsmoking floors; squash court. *In room:* A/C, TV w/pay movies, dataport w/high-speed Internet, minibar, coffeemaker, hair dryer, iron, safe.

Sheraton Vancouver Wall Centre Hotel ✮   The tallest—and the largest—hotel in the city, the Wall Centre is hard to miss. The hotel occupies a curved spire of black glass and a second, earlier tower, with a fountain-filled urban garden between. It may remind you of a futuristic corporate office park, a feeling that's unfortunately reinforced in the rooms, which have floor-to-ceiling polarized glass windows that look out onto great views but can't be opened, so it's like you're always wearing sunglasses. This is upscale Sheraton at its best (or worst, if you hate huge hotels), and it caters to a lot of tour groups. A vast lobby has nice touches such as a gold-leaf staircase, custom furniture, and hand-blown glass chandeliers. The guest rooms have clean, contemporary, blond-wood furnishings and nice bathrooms. Guests have the use of a 12,000-square-foot state-of-the-art health club with an indoor pool; an Ayurvedic wellness spa is attached.

1088 Burrard St., Vancouver, BC V6Z 2R9. ✆ **800/325-3535** or 604/331-1000. Fax 604/893-7200. www.sheraton wallcentre.com. 733 units. C$299 (US$239) double. AE, DC, MC, V. Valet parking C$20 (US$16). **Amenities:** 2 restaurants; 2 bars; indoor pool; health club; spa; Jacuzzi; sauna; concierge; tour desk; business center; salon; 24-hr. room service; same-day laundry and dry cleaning; nonsmoking rooms; executive level rooms. *In room:* A/C, TV w/pay movies, minibar, coffeemaker, hair dryer, iron, safe, high-speed Internet, bathrobes.

MODERATE

Georgian Court Hotel ✮ (Value)   This modern, 14-story brick hotel dating from 1984 is located just steps from BC Place Stadium, GM Place Stadium, the Queen Elizabeth Theatre, the Playhouse, and the Vancouver Public Library. You can walk to Robson Square in about 10 minutes. Guest rooms are relatively large and nicely decorated with good-size bathrooms. While big-time celebs are usually whisked off to top hotels, their entourages often stay at the Georgian Court, as it provides amenities and extras such as complimentary high-speed Internet access.

773 Beatty St., Vancouver, BC V6B 2M4. ✆ **800/663-1155** or 604/682-5555. Fax 604/682-8830. www.georgian court.com. 180 units. May 1–Oct 15 C$165–C$215 (US$132–US$172) double; Oct 16–Apr 30 C$115–C$160 (US$92–US$128) double. AE, DC, MC, V. Parking C$9 (US$7.20). **Amenities:** Restaurant; bar; health club; Jacuzzi; sauna; concierge; business center; limited room service; babysitting; laundry service; dry cleaning; nonsmoking rooms. *In room:* A/C, TV, dataport w/high-speed Internet, minibar, hair dryer, iron.

INEXPENSIVE

YWCA Hotel/Residence ✮ (Value)   Built in 1995, this attractive 12-story residence next door to the Georgian Court Hotel is an excellent choice for travelers (both male or female) as well as families with limited budgets. Bedrooms are simply furnished; some have TVs. Three communal kitchens are available for guests' use and all guest rooms have their own minifridges. Other perks include three TV lounges and free access to the best gym in town at, fittingly, the nearby co-ed YWCA Fitness Centre.

733 Beatty St., Vancouver, BC V6B 2M4. © 800/663-1424 or 604/895-5830. Fax 604/681-2550. www.ywcahotel. com. 155 units, 53 with private bathroom. C$57–C$88 (US$46–US$70) double with shared bathroom; C$76–C$134 (US$61–US$107) double with private bathroom. Additional person C$10 (US$8). AE, MC, V. Parking C$8 (US$6.40) per day. **Amenities:** Access to YWCA facility; coin-operated laundry; nonsmoking rooms. *In room:* A/C, TV in some rooms, dataport, fridge, hair dryer.

THE WEST END
EXPENSIVE
Listel Vancouver ★★ *(Finds*   What makes the Listel unique is its artwork. Hallways and suites on the top two floors are decorated with original artworks from the Buschlen Mowatt Gallery (Vancouver's preeminent international gallery), or with artifacts from the UBC Anthropology Museum. In addition, this Listel has a killer location, right at the western end of the Robson Street shopping and restaurant strip. The interior of this boutique hotel is luxurious without being flashy. Rooms feature top-quality bedding and handsome furnishings. The roomy upper-floor suites facing Robson Street, with glimpses of the harbor and mountains beyond, are the best bets here. Each is individually decorated with handsome furniture, and some have cozy window banquettes. Some bathrooms are larger than others, with separate soaker tub and shower. There's evening jazz at O'Doul's, the hotel's restaurant and bar; during the Vancouver International Jazz Festival in late June, it's the scene of late-night jam sessions with world-renowned musicians.

1300 Robson St., Vancouver, BC V6E 1C5. © 800/663-5491 or 604/684-8461. Fax 604/684-7092. www.listel-vancouver. com. 129 units. May–Sept C$260 (US$195) standard double, C$320 (US$240) gallery room double, C$600 (US$450) suite; Oct–Apr C$220 (US$165) standard double, C$260 (US$195) gallery room double, C$350 (US$263) suite. AE, DC, DISC, MC, V. Parking C$19 (US$14). **Amenities:** Restaurant; bar; exercise room; Jacuzzi; concierge; limited room service; same-day laundry/dry cleaning; nonsmoking hotel; executive-level rooms. *In room:* A/C, TV w/pay movies, dataport w/high-speed Internet, minibar, coffeemaker, hair dryer, iron.

Pacific Palisades Hotel ★★★ *(Finds*   Sherbet yellows and apple greens with pastel-colored fabrics, bright splashes of color, and whimsical touches make this hotel bright and welcoming to the young and the young at heart (though the ubiquitous rock music playing in the lobby can be annoying, depending on your mood and musical tastes). Guest rooms are spacious, airy, and equipped with kitchenettes (with minibar items priced at corner-store prices). The one-bedroom suites boast large living/dining rooms and balconies. Other perks are the complimentary afternoon wine tasting in the art gallery, the complimentary yoga program, the kid- and pet-friendly atmosphere, the large indoor pool, and fitness rooms. Plus, you're right on trendsetting Robson Street, minutes from beaches, shopping, cafes, and restaurants.

1277 Robson St., Vancouver, BC V6E 1C4. © 800/663-1815 or 604/688-0461. Fax 604/688-4374. www.pacific palisadeshotel.com. 233 units. May 1–Oct 15 C$245 (US$196) double, C$275 (US$220) suite; Oct 16–Apr 30 C$185 (US$148) double, C$275 (US$220) suite. AE, DC, DISC, MC, V. Valet parking C$26 (US$21). **Amenities:** Restaurant; bar; indoor lap pool; excellent health club; spa services; Jacuzzi; sauna; bike rentals; concierge; tour desk; business center; 24-hr. room service; massage; babysitting; coin laundry and laundry service; same-day dry cleaning; nonsmoking rooms; basketball court; yoga program. *In room:* A/C, TV, dataport w/high-speed Internet, kitchenette, minibar, fridge, coffeemaker, hair dryer, iron, bathrobes.

Westin Bayshore Resort & Marina ★★★ *(Kids*   This is the only resort hotel in Vancouver and it has its own marina in case you want to arrive by boat. The enormous lobby with its acres of marble and huge fireplace makes for an impressive entry to this venerable hotel which recently underwent a C$55-million renovation. Perched on the water's edge overlooking Stanley Park on one side and the city and Coal Harbour marina on the other, the Bayshore is just a short stroll from Canada Place Pier and downtown. The finishes throughout are top quality, and the size of the hotel (which includes a new conference center) makes it like a small city. Rooms in the original 1961 building have been completely refurbished with classic-looking decor, high-tech amenities, comfortable lighting, and floor-to-ceiling windows that open wide. In the newer tower, the rooms are spacious and bright with balconies and large windows. The circular outdoor pool is reputedly the largest in North America; there's a second indoor pool plus a full gym; all manner of spa treatments are available. This family-friendly hotel provides children with their own welcome package and organizes Super Saturdays, a behind-the-scenes tour of the hotel's operations and movie night for the young ones, giving the parents the night off.

1601 Bayshore Dr., Vancouver, BC V6G 2V4. © **800/937-8461** or 604/682-3377. Fax 604/687-3102. www.westin bayshore.com. 510 units. C$360–C$470 (US$288–US$376) double; C$550–C$695 (US$440–US$556) suite. Children under 19 stay free in parent's room. AE, DC, MC, V. Self-parking C$18 (US$14); valet parking C$20 (US$16). **Amenities:** 2 restaurants; bar; indoor and outdoor pool; health club; full-service spa; Jacuzzi; sauna; watersports rental; children's programs; concierge; tour desk; business center; shopping arcade; 24-hr. room service; massage; babysitting; laundry service; same-day dry cleaning; nonsmoking rooms. In room: A/C, TV w/pay movies, dataport w/high-speed Internet, minibar, coffeemaker, hair dryer, iron.

MODERATE

The Aston Rosellen Suites at Stanley Park ★ (Kids)　Staying at The Aston Rosellen
is like having your own apartment in the West End. Stanley Park and the seawall are just a few blocks away and busy Denman Street is just 3 blocks east. Though the hotel offers a no-frills stay, it is a favorite among travelers, with a high rate of repeat guests. The largest apartment—107 sq. m (1,150 sq. ft.)—is known as the director's suite. Other apartments are smaller, but none are really skimpy. The one-bedroom suites sleep four comfortably, and all units come with full kitchens, making them a great option for families. A 3-night minimum stay is required; rates drop for longer stays.

100–2030 Barclay St., Vancouver, BC V6G 1L5. © **888/317-6648** or 604/689-4807. Fax 604/684-3327. www.rosellen suites.com. 31 units. May–Sept C$199 (US$159) 1-bedroom apt, C$249–C$299 (US$199–US$239) 2-bedroom apt, C$399 (US$319) penthouse; Oct–Apr C$139 (US$111) 1-bedroom apt, C$169–C$229 (US$135–US$183) 2-bedroom apt, C$299 (US$239) penthouse. Minimum 3-night stay. Rates include up to 4 people in a 1-bedroom apt and 6 in a 2-bedroom apt. Cots and cribs free. AE, DC, DISC, MC, V. Limited parking C$5 (US$4); reserve when booking room. **Amenities:** Access to nearby health club and tennis courts; coin laundry; nonsmoking rooms. In room: TV, dataport, kitchen, coffeemaker, hair dryer, iron.

Barclay House in the West End ★★ (Finds)　The Barclay House bed-and-breakfast
is located on one of the West End's quiet maple-lined streets just a block from historic Barclay Square. The elegant parlors and dining rooms are perfect for lounging on a rainy afternoon or sipping a glass of complimentary sherry before venturing out for dinner in the trendy West End. On a summer day, the front porch with its wooden Adirondack chairs makes a cozy place to read. All rooms are beautifully furnished in Victorian style; a number of the pieces are family heirlooms. Modern conveniences such as CD players, TV/VCRs, and luxurious bathrooms blend in perfectly. The Penthouse offers skylights, a fireplace, and claw-foot tub; the South Room contains a queen-size brass bed and an elegant sitting room.

1351 Barclay St., Vancouver, BC V6E 1H6. © **800/971-1351** or 604/605-1351. Fax 604/605-1382. www.barclay house.com. 5 units. C$125–C$245 (US$100–US$196) double. MC, V. Free parking. **Amenities:** Access to nearby fitness center; concierge; massage; nonsmoking rooms. *In room:* TV/VCR w/pay movies, fridge, hair dryer, iron, video library, wireless Internet access.

Sunset Inn & Suites *(Value) (Kids)* Just a couple of blocks from English Bay on the edge of the residential West End, the Sunset Inn offers spacious accommodations in a great location for a very reasonable price. Units are either studios or one-bedroom apartments and come with fully equipped kitchens and dining areas. Like many other hotels in this part of town, the Sunset Inn started life as an apartment building, which means that the rooms are larger than your average hotel room, and all have balconies. The view gets better as the rooms ascend higher, but the price remains the same, so book early or just ask to be put in an upper floor. For those traveling with children, the one-bedroom suites have a separate bedroom and a pullout couch (two in the larger one-bedrooms) in the living room. The rooms on the top two floors have been redone with crisp forest-green walls and hardwood furnishings. Lower floors retain a kind of early '80s pastel look, but are slowly being upgraded. If style matters, request a refurnished unit when making your reservation.

1111 Burnaby St., Vancouver, BC V6E 1P4. © **800/786-1997** or 604/688-2474. Fax 604/669-3340. www.sunsetinn.com. 50 units. C$89–C$219 (US$71–US$175) studio; C$99–C$289 (US$79–US$231) 1-bedroom suite. Extra person C$10 (US$8). Children under 12 stay free in parent's room. Weekly rates available. AE, DC, MC, V. Free parking. **Amenities:** Exercise room; coin laundry; nonsmoking rooms. *In room:* TV, dataport w/high-speed Internet, kitchen, coffeemaker, iron, free wireless Internet access.

West End Guest House *(Finds)* A heritage home built in 1906, the West End Guest House is a handsome example of what the neighborhood looked like before concrete towers and condos replaced the original Edwardian homes in the early '50s. Decorated with early-20th-century antiques and a serious collection of vintage photographs of Vancouver taken by the original owners, this is a calm respite from the hustle and bustle of the West End. The seven guest rooms feature feather mattresses, down duvets, and your very own resident stuffed animal. The Grand Queen Suite, an attic-level bedroom with skylights, brass bed, fireplace, sitting area, and claw-foot bathtub, is the best and most spacious room; number 7 is quite small. Owner Evan Penner pampers his guests with a scrumptious breakfast and serves iced tea and sherry in the afternoon (on the back second-floor balcony in the summer). Throughout the day, guests have access to a pantry stocked with home-baked munchies and refreshments.

1362 Haro St., Vancouver, BC V6E 1G2. © **888/546-3327** or 604/681-2889. Fax 604/688-8812. www.westendguest house.com. 7 units. C$95–C$255 (US$76–US$204) double. Rates include full breakfast. AE, DISC, MC, V. Free off-street parking. **Amenities:** Complimentary bikes; business center; laundry service; nonsmoking facility. *In room:* TV/VCR, dataport, hair dryer.

INEXPENSIVE

Buchan Hotel Built in 1926, this three-story building is tucked away on a quiet tree-lined residential street in the West End, less than 2 blocks from Stanley Park and Denman Street and 15 minutes by foot from the business district. Like the Kingston (see above) downtown, this is a small European-style budget hotel that doesn't bother with frills or charming decor; unlike the Kingston, it isn't a B&B, so you won't get breakfast. The standard rooms are quite plain; be prepared for cramped quarters and tiny bathrooms, half of which are shared. The best rooms in the house are the executive rooms. These four front-corner rooms are nicely furnished and have private bathrooms. The hotel also offers in-house bike and ski storage as well as a reading lounge.

1906 Haro St., Vancouver, BC V6G 1H7. © **800/668-6654** or 604/685-5354. Fax 604/685-5367. www.buchan hotel.com. 60 units, 30 with private bathroom. C$45–C$75 (US$36–US$60) double with shared bath; C$70–C$95

(US$56–US$76) double with private bath; C$110–C$135 (US$88–US$108) executive room. Children 12 and under stay free in parent's room. Weekly rates available. AE, DC, MC, V. Limited street parking available. **Amenities:** Lounge; coin laundry; nonsmoking hotel. *In room:* TV, hair dryer, iron (on request), no phone.

THE WEST SIDE
EXPENSIVE

Granville Island Hotel 🌟 *Finds*   One of Vancouver's best-kept secrets, this hotel is tucked away on Granville Island in a waterfront setting just a short stroll from theaters, galleries, and the fabulous public market. Rooms in the original wing are fancier, but the new wing is fine, too. Rooms are fairly spacious with traditional, unsurprising decor and large bathrooms with soaker tubs; some units have balconies and views over False Creek. The best rooms and views are in the penthouse suites in the new wing. The only potential drawback to a stay here is the commute. When the False Creek ferries are running, it's a quick ride to Yaletown. After 10pm, however, you're looking at a cab ride or an hour walk. That said, there's a fair amount happening on the Island after dark, and the hotel's waterside restaurant and brewpub are wonderful hang-out spots.

1253 Johnston St., Vancouver, BC V6H 3R9. © **800/663-1840** or 604/683-7373. Fax 604/683-3061. www.granville islandhotel.com. 85 units. Oct–Apr C$170 (US$136) double, C$360 (US$288) penthouse; May–Sept C$270 (US$216) double, C$460 (US$368) penthouse. AE, DC, DISC, MC, V. Parking C$7 (US$5.60). **Amenities:** Restaurant; brewpub; access to nearby health club and tennis courts; small exercise room; Jacuzzi; bike rental; concierge; tour desk; car-rental desk; business center; limited room service; massage; babysitting; laundry; same-day dry cleaning; nonsmoking rooms. *In room:* A/C, TV w/pay movies, dataport w/high-speed Internet, minibar, coffeemaker, hair dryer, iron.

MODERATE

Kenya Court Ocean Front Guest House 🌟 *Finds*   From the street this unusual B&B simply looks like the three-story 1926 apartment house that it is. But press button no. 5, and your hosts will welcome you into their unusual and surprisingly pleasant establishment. There are, in fact, some permanent tenants in the building, but there are also five furnished apartments rented on a B&B basis. Not only is the house in a fantastic (if busy) location, directly across the street from Kits Beach, one of the most popular spots in Vancouver, but every unit has a view of English Bay, downtown Vancouver, and the Coast Mountains. On the ground floor there's a very nice little studio with a Murphy bed; other suites are much larger, with a living room, bathroom, separate bedroom (or two), and full kitchen. In the mornings, you climb up a spiral staircase and are served breakfast in a glass-walled solarium on the roof. One thing to keep in mind: In the summer, Kits Beach and Cornwall Avenue running past it are very busy; this can be either a plus or a minus, depending on your point of view.

2230 Cornwall Ave., Vancouver, BC V6K 1B5. © **604/738-7085.** h&dwilliams@telus.net. 5 units. C$155–C$175 (US$124–US$140) double. No credit cards. Garage or street parking. **Amenities:** Outdoor pool; tennis court and jogging trails nearby; nonsmoking facility. *In room:* TV, fax, kitchenette, fridge, coffeemaker, hair dryer, iron.

INEXPENSIVE

The University of British Columbia Conference Centre *Finds* *Value*   The Centre is a half-hour bus ride from downtown to pretty Point Grey—a convenient location if you plan to spend a lot of time in Kitsilano or at the university itself. Although space is usually available, don't expect luxury. The 17-story Walter Gage Residence offers new and comfortable accommodations, many on upper floors with sweeping views of the city and ocean. One- and six-bedroom suites have private bathrooms, kitchenettes, TVs, and phones. Each studio suite has a twin bed; each one-bedroom suite features a queen-size bed; the six-bedroom View Apartment suites—a particularly good deal for families—feature one double bed and five twin beds. Located next door, the year-round Gage Court suites have two twin beds in one bedroom and a queen-size Murphy bed in the sitting room.

5961 Student Union Blvd., Vancouver, BC V6T 2C9. (C) 604/822-1000. Fax 604/822-1001. www.ubcaccommodation. com. About 1,900 units. Gage Towers units available May 10–Aug 26; Pacific Spirit Hostel units available May 15–Aug 19. Gage Towers: C$42–C$71 (US$34–U$57) single with shared bathroom; C$99–C$199 (US$79–US$159) studio, 1-, or 6-bedroom suites with private bathroom. Pacific Spirit Hostel: C$25 (US$20) single; C$50 (US$40) double. Located adjacent to the Gage Residence, the 47 West Coast Suites are available year-round: C$129–C$170 (US$103–US$136) suite. AE, MC, V. Parking C$5 (US$4). Bus: 4, 10, or 99. **Amenities** (nearby on campus): Restaurant; cafeteria; pub; Olympic-size swimming pool; public golf course; tennis courts; weight room; sauna for C$5 (US$4) per person; video arcade; laundry; all rooms nonsmoking. *In room:* TV, hair dryer.

THE NORTH SHORE
EXPENSIVE
Lonsdale Quay Hotel ✦   Directly across the Burrard Inlet from the Canada Place Pier, the Lonsdale Quay Hotel is at the water's edge above the Lonsdale Quay Market at the SeaBus terminal. An escalator rises from the midst of the market's food, crafts, and souvenir stalls to the front desk on the third floor. The rooms are simply furnished and tastefully decorated, without the grandeur or luxurious touches of comparably priced downtown hotels. Nevertheless, the hotel has unique and fabulous harbor and city views, and is only 15 minutes by car or bus from Grouse Mountain Ski Resort. Smoking is not permitted.

123 Carrie Cates Court, North Vancouver, BC V6M 3K7. (C) **800/836-6111** or 604/986-6111. Fax 604/986-8782. www.lonsdalequayhotel.com. 70 units. High season C$125–C$225 (US$100–US$180) double or twin, C$350 (US$280) suite; low season C$90–C$165 (US$72–US$132) double or twin, C$250 (US$200) suite. Extra person C$25 (US$20). Senior discount available. AE, DC, DISC, MC, V. Parking C$10 (US$8); free on weekends and holidays. SeaBus: Lonsdale Quay. **Amenities:** 2 restaurants; small exercise room; spa; bike rental; children's play area; concierge; tour desk; shopping arcade; limited room service; massage; babysitting; laundry service; same-day dry cleaning; executive-level rooms. *In room:* A/C, TV, dataport, minibar, coffeemaker, hair dryer, iron.

MODERATE
Beachside City View Bed & Breakfast ✦ *Finds*   Joan Gibbs' B&B is in a new and comfortably grand house located in the upscale West Vancouver area known as "The British Properties," a 10-minute drive from downtown. There are three choices of accommodations: two bedrooms with bathroom between are rented as one unit; the enormous Honeymoon Suite has its own balcony and a luxurious bathroom with Jacuzzi and separate shower; and the family-friendly ground-floor Garden Suite has a bedroom, full-size kitchen, two bathrooms, and glass doors out to the garden. The upper-floor rooms enjoy sweeping views of Burrard Inlet, the Lion's Gate Bridge, Stanley Park, and the skyline of downtown Vancouver. The house is beautifully furnished and full of fine detailing; guests also have use of the private swimming pool. A full breakfast is served in a lovely, light-filled dining room.

1180 Renton Place, West Vancouver, BC V7S 2K7. (C) **800/563-3311** or 604/922-7773. Fax 604/926-8073. www.beach. bc.ca. 3 units. C$200–C$250 (US$160–US$200) double. Rates include breakfast tray. MC, V. Free parking. Bus: 254. **Amenities:** Outdoor heated pool; nonsmoking hotel. *In room:* TV/VCR w/free videos, fridge, coffeemaker, hair dryer, iron, wireless Internet, microwave.

4 Where to Dine

Vancouver is one of North America's top dining cities, and it shows: Its residents dine out more frequently than other Canadians. Because Vancouverites have come to expect top quality—yet they absolutely refuse to pay stratospheric prices—Vancouver is a steal for the discerning visitor.

DOWNTOWN & YALETOWN
VERY EXPENSIVE

C ✸✸✸ SEAFOOD/PACIFIC NORTHWEST   Eating at Vancouver's most creative seafood restaurant is an experience in itself. The location on False Creek is sublime; the dining room is a cool and white; and the staff can tell you the name of the fisher or farmer for each ingredient. Expect exquisite surprises and imaginative preparations: fresh Kushi oysters with a tingling mignonette fizz, or "virtual smoked" salmon atop a glass vial that releases beechwood smoke essence; a piece of hibiscus mousse atop fresh sweet Dungeness crab lightly infused with chipotle. For a really memorable dining experience, order the seven-course sampling menu. Savor the exquisite cuisine and paired wines as you watch the sun go down over the marina.

1600 Howe St. ℂ **604/681-1164.** www.crestaurant.com. Reservations advised. Main courses C$28–C$49 (US$22–US$39); taster box C$35 (US$28); sampling menu C$90 (US$72). AE, DC, MC, V. Daily 5:30–11pm; Mon–Fri 11:30am–2:30pm (from May until Labour Day). Valet parking C$7 (US$5.60). Bus: 1 or 2.

The Five Sails ✸✸✸ PACIFIC NORTHWEST/SEAFOOD   The view of Coal Harbour, Stanley Park, and the Coast Mountains is utterly magical. And, given that this restaurant serves the enormous Pan Pacific Hotel atop Canada Place Convention Centre and cruise ship terminal, the food is surprisingly good—inventive without being too clever. Try the Voyage of Discovery, a fresh seafood platter featuring Pacific prawns, Dungeness crab, clams, and sushi. Other tasty appetizers include an ahi tuna carpaccio and smoked B.C. salmon. Main courses feature pan-seared halibut, oven-roasted lobster, crispy sea bass, and a slow-roasted B.C. sockeye. The cellar offers a substantial list of wines from B.C. and around the world.

999 Canada Place Way, in the Pan Pacific Hotel. ℂ **604/891-2892.** Reservations recommended. Main courses C$26–C$45 (US$21–US$36). AE, DC, MC, V. Daily 6–9:30pm (Fri–Sat until 10pm). SkyTrain: Waterfront.

EXPENSIVE

Blue Water Cafe and Raw Bar ✸✸✸ SEAFOOD   Since opening in the fall of 2000, Blue Water Cafe in Yaletown has become one of Vancouver's hottest restaurants. If you had to describe this busy, buzzy place in one word it would be *fresh,* as in fresh, seasonal seafood; only the best from sustainable and wild fisheries makes it onto the menu. If you love sushi, the raw bar under the direction of Yoshihio Tabo offers up some of the city's best Japanese-style sushi and sashimi. Frank Pabst, the restaurant's executive chef, creates his dishes in another large open kitchen. For starters, try a medley of Kushi oysters with various toppings. Main courses depend on whatever is in season: It may be spring salmon, halibut, Dungeness crab, or, my favorite dish, smoked B.C. black cod served with ricotta gnocchi, green asparagus, potatoes, and fresh horse-radish cream. The desserts are fabulous, too, especially the frozen espresso parfait. A masterful wine list and an experienced sommelier assure fine wine pairings.

1095 Hamilton St. at Helmcken. ℂ **604/688-8078.** www.bluewatercafe.net. Reservations advised. Main courses C$23–C$35 (US$18–US$28). AE, DC, MC, V. Daily 5pm–midnight. Valet parking C$6.50 (US$5.20). Bus: 2.

Coast ✸✸✸ *Finds* SEAFOOD/INTERNATIONAL   This dashing Yaletown restaurant has quickly became a culinary and people-watching spot of note. The handsome dining room has a special community table so lucky diners can watch Chef Sean Riley at work. You may have ahi sashimi and avocado salad or a wild white sea tiger prawn cocktail. From the grill, you could order wild B.C. salmon, South Pacific John Dory, Indian Ocean tiger prawns, or hand-harvested scallops. "Off-shore" temptations include Alaskan king crab gnocchi or Louisiana blackened snapper. Land-based dishes include beef tenderloin and Moroccan-spiced Australian lamb sirloin. Accompany your meal with a recommended wine from Coast's large cellar.

1257 Hamilton St. (©) **604/685-5010**. www.coastrestaurant.ca. Reservations recommended. Main courses C$24–C$35 (US$19–US$28). AE, DC, MC, V. Daily 4:30–11pm. Bus: 1 or 22.

Glowbal Grill & Satay Bar 𝒢𝒢 FUSION   Glowbal occupies a top spot in trendy Yaletown, with good food and a bright, buzzy atmosphere. Start with one of their famous martinis and delicious satays or tempura artichokes with fresh crab meat. Then, go with whatever is fresh: It may be wild salmon with Dungeness crab gnocchi, or crusted sea bass with braised tomatoes and red pepper gratin. Service is fun and friendly, the wine list exemplary. After hours of dining, the truly in-crowd heads to Afterglow, the small lounge behind the dining room.

1079 Mainland St. (©) **604/602-0835**. www.glowbalgrill.com. Reservations recommended. Main courses C$19–C$29 (US$15–US$23). AE, DC, MC, V. Sun–Thurs 11am–midnight; Fri–Sat 11am–1am. Bus: 2.

Il Giardino di Umberto Ristorante 𝒢𝒢 ITALIAN   After more than 25 years, Il Giardino still serves up some of the best Italian fare in town. The menu leans towards Tuscany with an emphasis on pasta and game. Entrees include classics such as spaghetti carbonara and *osso buco* with saffron risotto. Daily specials—often outstanding seafood dishes—make the most of seasonal fresh ingredients. For dessert try the mandarin orange/blood orange *panna cotta* or lemon mascarpone gelato with hazelnut pound cake. The comprehensive wine list is well-chosen.

1382 Hornby St. (between Pacific and Drake). (©) **604/669-2422**. Fax 604/669-9723. www.umberto.com. Reservations required. Main courses C$14–C$33 (US$11–US$26). AE, DC, MC, V. Mon–Fri 11:30am–3pm; Mon–Sat 6–11pm. Closed holidays. Bus: 1 or 22.

MODERATE
Bin 941 Tapas Parlour 𝒢 TAPAS   Still booming 5 years on, Bin 941 remains the place for trendy tapas. True, the music's loud and the room's too small, but the food that alights on the bar or the eight tiny tables is delicious and fun to eat. Look especially for local seafood offerings like scallops and tiger prawns in bonito butter sauce. Sharing is unavoidable in this sliver of a bistro, so come prepared for socializing. So successful was the original model that Bin 942 has opened up at 1521 W. Broadway ((©) **604/734-9421**). By 8pm there's a long line of the hip and hungry.

941 Davie St. (©) **604/683-1246**. www.bin941.com. Reservations not accepted. All plates are C$10–C$14 (US$8–US$11). MC, V. Daily 5pm–2am. Bus: 4, 5, or 8.

Simply Thai 𝒢 THAI   Finally, authentic Thai in the heart of Yaletown. Watch chef and owner Siriwan in the open kitchen as he cooks up northern and southern Thai dishes. *Gai satay* features succulent pieces of grilled chicken breast marinated in coconut milk and spices and dipped in peanut sauce, while the strange but delicious *cho muang* consists of violet-colored dumplings stuffed with minced chicken. Main courses run the gamut: noodle dishes and coconut curries with beef, chicken, or pork, as well as a good number of vegetarian options. Don't miss the *tom kha gai*, a deceptively simple-looking coconut soup with chicken, mushrooms, and lemon grass.

1211 Hamilton St. (©) **604/642-0123**. Reservations recommended on weekends. Main courses C$9–C$17 (US$7.20–US$14). AE, DC, MC, V. Mon–Fri 11:30am–3pm; daily 5–10pm. Bus: 2.

INEXPENSIVE
Olympia Oyster & Fish Co. Ltd. *Finds* FISH AND CHIPS   This little hole in the wall, just off Robson, Vancouver's trendiest shopping street, serves up the city's best

fish and chips. On any given day you'll find West End residents, German tourists, and well-heeled shoppers vying for counter space. There are only a few tables and a window-seat counter, plus three sidewalk tables (weather permitting), but the fish is always fresh and flaky and can be grilled if you prefer. Choose from sole, halibut, or cod, which may be combined with oysters or prawns, too. If you want to take home smoked salmon, the staff will wrap it up or ship it if you prefer.

820 Thurlow St. ℂ 604/685-0716. Main courses C$6–C$10 (US$4.80–US$8). AE, MC, V. Mon–Sat 11am–8pm; Sun 11:30am–7pm. Bus: 5.

GASTOWN & CHINATOWN
EXPENSIVE
The Cannery ✦ SEAFOOD   With its seafaring memorabilia and fishing nets, The Cannery has charm . . . But many come here for the stunning view. You'll find good, traditional seafood too, often alder-grilled, with ever-changing specials. One classic dish is salmon Wellington—salmon, shrimp, and mushrooms baked in a puff pastry. Meat lovers can get a grilled New York steak or Alberta beef tenderloin. Chef Frederic Couton has been more inventive of late, but when a 1971 institution is still going strong, no one's *too* keen to rock the boat. The wine and desserts are stellar.

2205 Commissioner St., near Victoria Dr. ℂ 604/254-9606. www.canneryseafood.com. Reservations recommended. Main courses C$16–C$28 (US$13–US$22). AE, DC, DISC, MC, V. Mon–Fri 11:30am–2:30pm; Mon–Sat 5:30–10:30pm; Sun 5:30–9:30pm. Closed Dec 24–26. Bus: 7 to Victoria Dr. From downtown, head east on Hastings St., turn left on Victoria Dr. (2 blocks past Commercial Dr.), then right on Commissioner St.

MODERATE
Park Lock Seafood Restaurant ⒦ⁱᵈˢ CHINESE/DIM SUM   If you've never done dim sum, Park Lock in the heart of Chinatown is a good place to give it a try, despite the schlocky country-and-western music. From 8am to 3pm daily, waitresses wheel carts loaded with Chinese delicacies past the tables. When you see something you like, just point and ask for it. The final bill is based upon how many little dishes are left on your table. Dishes include spring rolls, *hargow* (shrimp dumplings) and *shumai* (steamed shrimp, beef, or pork dumplings), prawns wrapped in fresh white noodles, small steamed buns, sticky rice cooked in banana leaves, curried squid, and lots more.

544 Main St. (at E. Pender St., on the 2nd floor). ℂ 604/688-1581. Reservations recommended. Main courses C$10–C$25 (US$8–US$20); dim sum dishes C$2.50–C$6 (US$2–US$4.80). AE, MC, V. Daily 7:30am–4pm; dinner Fri–Sun 5–9:30pm. Bus: 19 or 22.

INEXPENSIVE
Incendio ✦ Ⓕⁱⁿᵈˢ PIZZA   If you're looking for something casual and local that won't be full of other tourists reading downtown maps, this little Gastown hideaway is great. The 22 pizza combinations are served on fresh, crispy crusts baked in an old wood-fired oven. Pastas are homemade, and you're encouraged to mix and match—try the mussels with spinach fettuccine, capers, and tomatoes in lime butter. The wine list is decent; the beer list is inspired. And there's a patio. Much to the delight of Kitsilano residents, a second location with a slightly larger menu has opened next to the Fifth Avenue movie theater at 2118 Burrard (ℂ 604/736-2220).

103 Columbia St. ℂ 604/688-8694. Main courses C$8–C$12 (US$6.50–US$10). AE, MC, V. Mon–Thurs 11:30am–3pm and 5–10pm; Fri 11:30am–3pm and 5–11pm; Sat 5–11pm; Sun 4:30–10pm. Closed Dec 23–Jan 3. Bus: 1 or 8.

Phnom Penh Restaurant VIETNAMESE   This family-run restaurant, serving a mixture of Vietnamese and slightly spicier Cambodian cuisine, is a perennial contender for, and occasional winner of, *Vancouver* magazine's award for the city's best Asian restaurant. The walls are adorned with artistic renderings of ancient Cambodia's capital, Angkor. Khmer dolls are suspended in glass cases, and the subdued lighting is a welcome departure from the harsh glare often found in inexpensive Chinatown restaurants. Try the outstanding hot-and-sour soup, loaded with prawns and lemon grass. The deep-fried garlic squid served with rice is also delicious. For dessert, the fruit-and-rice pudding is an exotic treat.

244 E. Georgia St., near Main St. (Ⓒ 604/682-5777. Dishes C$5.15–C$9.25 (US$4.10–US$7.40). AE, MC. Daily 10am–10pm. Bus: 8 or 19.

THE WEST END

Cin Cin 🐨🐨 MODERN ITALIAN   Celebrities, models, politicians, and hungry Vancouverites all frequent this wonderful restaurant. The rustic dining room surrounds a wood-fired oven, while the heated terrace is a pleasant people-watching spot. An exemplary menu is divided into "Old World" and "New World." Pasta includes spaghetti with boar bacon carbonara and a melt-in-the-mouth ravioli stuffed with fresh salmon and black cod. From the grill come savory dishes such as panko-crusted halibut, veal chops, free-range chicken, and buffalo strip loin. Pizza comes with toppings such as Parma prosciutto with rosemary, asparagus, roasted garlic, and fontina cheese. The wine list is extensive, the service is exemplary, and the desserts divine.

1154 Robson St. (Ⓒ 604/688-7338. www.cincin.net. Reservations recommended. Main courses C$18–C$38 (US$14–US$30); tasting menus C$69 (US$55). AE, DC, MC, V. Mon–Fri 11:30am–2:30pm; daily 5–11pm. Bus: 5 or 22.

Raincity Grill 🐨🐨🐨 PACIFIC NORTHWEST   This top-starred restaurant, which opened on English Bay in 1990, is a gem—painstaking in preparation, arty in presentation, and yet completely unfussy in atmosphere. Raincity Grill was one of the very first restaurants in Vancouver to embrace the "buy locally, eat seasonally" concept. The menu focuses on seafood, game, and poultry, and organic vegetables from British Columbia and the Pacific Northwest. The room is long and low and intimate, perfect for romantic dining. To sample a bit of everything, I recommend the seasonal tasting menu, an incredible bargain at C$50 (US$40), or C$80 (US$64) with wine pairings. Recent tasting menu highlights included wasabi leaf-wrapped beef; grilled Coho salmon with oyster mushroom, pea tip salad, and rhubarb broth; Fraser Valley duck breast; a creamily delicious selection of artisan cheeses from Vancouver Island; and a rose-and-buttermilk panna cotta. The award-winning wine list is huge and, in keeping with the restaurant's philosophy, sticks pretty close to home. From May through Labour Day Raincity opens a takeout window on Denham Street where you can get delicious gourmet dishes to go, priced at C$4.95 to C$9.95 (US$4–US$8).

1193 Denman St. (Ⓒ 604/685-7337. www.raincitygrill.com. Reservations recommended. Main courses C$21–C$32 (US$17–US$26). AE, DC, MC, V. Daily 5–10:30pm; Sat–Sun brunch 10:30am–2:30pm. Bus: 1 or 5.

Sequoia Grill at the Teahouse in Stanley Park PACIFIC NORTHWEST   One of Vancouver's most venerable seaside landmarks, the Teahouse was updated in 2004 to make it more contemporary. Come for sunset-watching and romantic relaxation as you start your meal with wok-fried squid with Thai chiles and oyster sauce. Main courses bring B.C. salmon, grilled ahi, mushroom risotto, classic coq au vin, and New York steak. The view here is perhaps more memorable than the food; after the sun sets, the lights cast a magical glow on the trees and garden.

Ferguson Point, Stanley Park. (Ⓒ 604/669-3281. www.vancouverdine.com. Reservations recommended. Small plates C$8–C$11 (US$6.40–US$8.80); main courses C$11–C$28 (US$8.80–US$22). AE, DC, MC, V. Mon–Fri 11:30am–2:30pm;

small plates daily 2:30–5:30pm; daily 5:30–9:45pm; Sat brunch 11:30am–2:30pm; Sun brunch 10:30am–2:30pm. Bus: 23, 35, or 135.

MODERATE

Hapa Izakaya ★★ JAPANESE   Dinner comes at disco decibels in this hot Japanese "eat-drink place" (the literal meaning of Izakaya). The menu features nontraditional dishes such as bacon-wrapped asparagus or fresh tuna belly chopped with spring onions served with munch-size bits of garlic bread. There are options for non-sushi eaters such as a scrumptious Korean hot pot. The martini and sake lists are both sophisticated and lengthy. The crowd is a third Japanese, a third Chinese, and a third well-informed Westerners. Service is fast, and prices are reasonable.

1479 Robson St. ℂ **604/689-4272**. No reservations accepted 6–8pm. Dinner main courses C$8–C$12 (US$6.40–US$9.60). AE, MC, V. Sun–Thurs 5:30pm–midnight; Fri–Sat 5:30pm–1am. Bus: 5.

Romano's Macaroni Grill at the Mansion *Kids* FAMILY STYLE/ITALIAN Housed in a stone mansion, Romano's is a fun chain restaurant with a Southern Italian menu. This isn't high-concept cuisine, but the food is simple and consistently good. Pastas are definite favorites. Your kids will love the children's menu, which features lasagna and meatloaf as well as tasty pizzas. It's more fun to dine outside on the patio (with heat lamps), which is among the best in town.

1523 Davie St. ℂ **604/689-4334**. Reservations advised. Main courses C$8–C$16 (US$6.40–US$13); children's courses C$4.95–C$7 (US$4–US$5.60). AE, DC, MC, V. Mon–Thurs noon–1pm; Fri–Sat noon–11pm. Bus: 5.

Tanpopo JAPANESE   A partial view of English Bay, a large patio, and a huge menu. But the line of people waiting 30 minutes or more every night for a table are here for the all-you-can-eat sushi. The unlimited fare includes the standard makis and sashimi as well as cooked items such as *tonkatsu,* tempura, chicken *kara age,* and broiled oysters. Tanpopo takes only an arbitrary percentage of reservations for dinner each day. Otherwise, you can ask to sit at the sushi bar.

1122 Denman St. ℂ **604/681-7777**. Reservations recommended for groups. Main courses C$7–C$19 (US$5.60–US$15); all-you-can-eat sushi C$22 (US$18) for dinner, C$12 (US$9.60) for lunch. AE, DC, MC, V. Daily 11:30am–10pm. Bus: 5.

INEXPENSIVE

Banana Leaf ★ MALAYSIAN   One of the city's best spots for Malaysian, Banana Leaf is just a hop and a skip from English Bay. The menu includes inventive specials such as mango-and-okra salad, delicious south-Asian mainstays such as *gado gado* (a salad with hot peanut sauce) or *mee goreng* (fried noodles with vegetables topped by a fried egg), and occasional variations such as an assam curry (seafood in hot and sour curry sauce) that comes with okra and tomato. For dessert, don't pass up *pisang goring*—fried banana with ice cream. The small room is tastefully decorated in dark tropical woods; the rather unadventurous wine list features a small selection of inexpensive reds and whites. Service is very friendly.

1096 Denman St. ℂ **604/683-3333**. (also 820 W. Broadway; ℂ **604/731-6333**). www.bananaleaf-vancouver.com. Main courses C$7–C$15 (US$5.60–US$12). AE, MC, V. Sun–Thurs 11:30am–10pm; Fri–Sat 11:30am–11pm. Bus: 5.

Caffè Artigiano ★★ *Finds* CAFE   This is latte-making elevated to an art form. Pop in for a light lunch and a pastry too. And the little outdoor patio is perfect for people-watching right across from the art Gallery. The original location at West Pender and Thurlow is less intimate.

763 Hornby St. ✆ **604/685-5333**. www.caffeartigiano.com. Sweets and sandwiches C$8 (US$6.40). Sun–Thurs 6:30am–5pm; Fri–Sat 6:30am–6pm (W. Pender location not open Sun). Bus: 22.

Stephos *Value* GREEK A fixture on the Davie Street dining scene, Stephos has been packing them in since Zorba was a boy. The cuisine is simple Greek fare at its finest and cheapest. Customers line up outside for a seat amid Greek travel posters, potted ivy, and whitewashed walls (the average wait is about 10–15 min., but it could be as long as 30 min., as once you're inside, the staff will never rush you out the door). Order some pita and dip (hummus, spicy eggplant, or garlic spread) while you peruse the menu. An interesting appetizer is the *avgolemono* soup, a delicately flavored chicken broth with egg and lemon, accompanied by a plate of piping hot pita bread. When choosing a main course, keep in mind that portions are huge. The roasted lamb, lamb chops, fried calamari, and a variety of souvlakia are served with rice, roast potatoes, and Greek salad. The beef, lamb, or chicken pita come in slightly smaller portions served with fries and *tzatziki*.

1124 Davie St. ✆ **604/683-2555**. Reservations accepted for parties of 5 or more. Main courses C$4.25–C$10 (US$3.40–US$8). AE, MC, V. Daily 11am–11:30pm. Bus: 5.

THE WEST SIDE
VERY EXPENSIVE

Bishop's ✿✿✿ PACIFIC NORTHWEST Dining here is an expensive proposition, but Bishop's is among the top five restaurants in Vancouver. All ingredients are locally grown, seasonal, and organic. Appetizers may include Dungeness crab cakes with pear-cranberry chutney or grilled Pacific squid with lemon-ginger aioli. Typical entrees include roasted wild spring salmon with rhubarb compote, grilled spot prawns and smoked salmon risotto, or rack of lamb with garlic mashed potatoes. Among the wines are a few Pacific Coast vintages.

2183 W. Fourth Ave. ✆ **604/738-2025**. www.bishopsonline.com. Reservations required. Main courses C$30–C$38 (US$24–US$30). AE, DC, MC, V. Mon–Sat 5:30–11pm; Sun 5:30–10pm. Closed Jan 1–15. Bus: 4 or 7.

Lumière ✿✿✿ FRENCH Lumière's preparation and presentation are immaculately French, while ingredients are resolutely local—making for surprises such as fresh ginger with veal, or raspberry foie gras. Rob Feenie's tasting menus are a series of 8 or 10 delightful plates that change seasonally. Choose an all-vegetarian tasting menu, a meat-and-seafood menu, or a three-course a la carte menu. Or the adjoining **Lumière Tasting Bar** allows you to sample smaller dishes. The intrepid Feenie is also the force behind the more casual **Feenie's,** right next door.

2551 W. Broadway. ✆ **604/739-8185**. www.lumiere.ca. Reservations required for restaurant, not accepted for bar. Tasting menus C$100–C$130 (US$80–US$104). AE, DC, MC, V. Restaurant Tues–Sun 5:30–9:30pm; tasting bar Tues–Sun 5:30–11pm. Bus: 9 or 10.

EXPENSIVE

West ✿✿✿ FRENCH/PACIFIC NORTHWEST I'm just going to come out and say it: I had one of the best meals of my life at West, and I wasn't surprised when it won the 2005 Best Restaurant and Best Chef award from *Vancouver* magazine. This is a restaurant where details matter, high standards reign, and cooking is a fine art. And yet it's not stuffy or stiff. You'll want to dress up, though, and you'll want to linger over your food, prepared by executive chef David Hawksworth. The credo at this award-winning restaurant is deceptively simple: "True to our region, true to the seasons." That means that fresh, organic, locally harvested seafood, game, and produce are transformed into extraordinary creations. Small plates—such as steak tartare with quail's egg—can be snacked on at the bar or ordered as an appetizer. The menu changes three to four times a week, but first courses may include house-made ravioli with spot prawns and basil or sweet pea soup with bacon and crostini; for a second course you might find roasted halibut filet with wild mushrooms, braised pork belly with warm celery and salsify salad, or cider-braised veal cheeks with roasted tongue. For the ultimate dining experience, try one of the seasonal tasting menus—a multi-course progression through the best the restaurant has to offer; there's also an early prix-fixe menu served until 6pm. A carefully chosen wine list includes a selection of affordable wines; you can purchase wines by the glass and half-bottles. If you're really into cooking, reserve one of the two "chef tables" directly adjacent to the kitchen.

2881 Granville St. ✆ **604/738-8938**. www.westrestaurant.com. Reservations recommended. Main courses C$16–C$41 (US$13–US$33); tasting menus C$71–C$94 (US$57–US$75); early prix-fixe menu until 6pm C$35 (US$28). AE, DC, MC, V. Mon–Fri 11:30am–2:30pm; daily 5:30–11pm. Bus: 8.

MODERATE

Memphis Blues Barbeque House ✦ BARBEQUE   This hole-in-the-wall has made a name for itself with *real* southern barbecue. Ribs come out tender enough to pull apart with your fingers; beef brisket is juicy and tender; and the pork butt is slow cooked until you can pull it apart with a fork. Those three meats (plus catfish and Cornish game hen) are essentially what's offered here. There's now a second location at 1342 Commercial Dr. (✆ **604/215-2565**).

1465 W. Broadway. ✆ **604/738-6806**. Reservations not accepted. Main courses C$7–C$9 (US$5.60–US$7.20); complete meals C$13–C$31 (US$10–US$25). AE, DC, MC, V. Mon–Thurs 11am–10pm; Fri 11am–midnight; Sat noon–midnight; Sun noon–10pm. Bus: 4, 7, or 10.

Vij's ✦✦✦ INDIAN   Waiting patrons huddled under Vij's violet neon sign are offered tea and *papadum* bread. The menu changes monthly, though recent choices include coconut curried chicken and saffron rice and marinated pork medallions with garlic-yogurt curry and *nan* (flatbread). Vegetarian selections include curried vegetable rice pilaf with cilantro cream sauce and Indian lentils with *nan* and *raita* (yogurt-mint sauce). Vij recently opened Rangoli next door, for lunch and take-away.

1480 W. 11th Ave. ✆ **604/736-6664**. Reservations not accepted. Main courses C$14–C$24 (US$11–US$19). AE, DC, MC, V. Daily 5:30–10pm. Closed Dec 24–Jan 8. Bus: 8 or 10.

INEXPENSIVE

The Naam Restaurant ✦ (Kids) VEGETARIAN   Vancouver's oldest vegetarian and natural-food restaurant still retains a pleasant granola feel. The decor is simple, earnest, and welcoming: well-worn wooden tables and chairs, plants, a mix of local art, and a nice garden patio. The brazenly healthy fare ranges from veggie burgers and burritos to tofu teriyaki, Thai noodles, and pita pizzas. The sesame spice fries are a local institution. The Naam caters to vegans with specialties such as the macrobiotic Dragon Bowl of brown rice, tofu, peanut sauce, sprouts, and steamed vegetables.

2724 W. Fourth Ave. ✆ **604/738-7151**. www.thenaam.com. Reservations accepted on weekdays only. Main courses C$5–C$11 (US$4–US$8.80). AE, MC, V. Daily 24-hr. Live music nightly 7–10pm. Bus: 4 or 22.

Sophie's Cosmic Café (Kids) FAMILY STYLE/AMERICAN   Sophie's is easily identifiable by the giant silver knife and fork bolted to the storefront. Inside, every available space has been crammed with toys and knickknacks from the 1950s and 1960s. So, understandably, children are inordinately fond of Sophie's. Crayons and coloring paper are always on hand. The menu is simple: pastas, burgers and fries, great milkshakes, and a few classic Mexican dishes. The slightly spicy breakfast menu is hugely popular with Kitsilano locals; waits can stretch to half an hour or more on Sunday mornings.

2095 W. Fourth Ave. © 604/732-6810. www.sophiescosmiccafe.com. Main courses C$5–C$17 (US$4–US$14). MC, V. Daily 8am–9:30pm. Bus: 4 or 7.

THE EAST SIDE
EXPENSIVE

Sun Sui Wah ★★ (Kids) CHINESE/DIM SUM/SEAFOOD   One of the most elegant and sophisticated Chinese restaurants in town, the award-winning Sun Sui Wah is known for its seafood. Fresh and varied, the catch of the day can include fresh crab, rock cod, geoduck, scallops, abalone, oyster, or prawns. Dim sum is a treat; just point and choose. There are also plenty of choices for meat lovers and vegetarians.

3888 Main St. © 604/872-8822. www.sunsuiwah.com. (Also in Richmond: 102 Alderbridge Place, 4940 No. 3 Rd.; © 604/273-8208). Main courses C$11–C$50 (US$8.80–US$40). AE, DC, MC, V. Daily dim sum 10:30am–3pm and 5–10:30pm. Bus: 3.

MODERATE

The Reef ★ (Value) CARIBBEAN   The "JERK" in the phone number refers to a spicy marinade of bay leaves, scotch bonnets, allspice, garlic, soya, green onions, vinegar, and cloves. Choose the signature jerk chicken breast, and you have a good meal at a bargain price. Other dishes are equally delightful, including a tropical salad of fresh mango, red onion, and tomato; shrimp with coconut milk and lime; grilled blue marlin; and Trenton spiced ribs. Afternoons, the tiny patio is drenched in sunlight, while in the evenings a DJ spins the sounds of the Islands.

4172 Main St. © 604/874-JERK. www.thereefrestaurant.com. Main courses C$9–C$15 (US$7.20–US$12). AE, DC, MC, V. Sun–Wed 11am–midnight; Thurs–Sat 11am–1am. Bus: 3.

THE NORTH SHORE

The Beach House at Dundarave Pier ★★ PACIFIC NORTHWEST   Diners on the heated patio get a panoramic view of English Bay and more sunshine, but they miss out on the rich interior of this restored 1912 teahouse. The food is consistently good—innovative, but not too experimental. Appetizers include soft-shell crab with salt-and-fire jelly; black tiger prawns sautéed in vermouth; and grilled portobello mushroom with Okanagan Valley goat cheese. Entrees include herb-marinated chicken breast, flat-iron steak atop a potato and leek cake, and baked striped sea bass with basil mousse and rock prawns. The wine list is award winning.

150 25th St., West Vancouver. © 604/922-1414. www.atthebeachhouse.com. Reservations recommended. Main courses C$16–C$36 (US$13–US$29); tasting menus C$30 (US$24). AE, DC, MC, V. Daily 11am–10pm. Bus: 255 to Ambleside Pier.

Gusto ★ ITALIAN   The menu at this father-and-son operation focuses on Central Italy, and the comfortable and pleasant dining room is bathed in warm earth tones and has a rustic decor. Signature main courses include pistachio-crusted sea bass; duck breast with Frangelico, toasted pine nuts, and grilled orange; and the outstanding *spaghetti quattro,* a spicy concoction of minced chicken, black beans, garlic, and chile.

1 Lonsdale Ave., North Vancouver. © 604/924-4444. www.quattrorestaurants.com. Reservations recommended. Main courses C$10–C$32 (US$8–US$26). AE, DC, MC, V. Mon–Fri 11:30am–2pm; daily 5–10pm. SeaBus to Lonsdale Quay.

5 Exploring Vancouver

Note: See the Downtown Vancouver map on p. 57 to locate most of the sights discussed in this chapter.

THE TOP ATTRACTIONS

DOWNTOWN & THE WEST END

Stanley Park 🏛🏛🏛 *Kids*   The jewel of Vancouver, Stanley Park is a 400-hectare (1,000-acre) rainforest jutting out into the ocean from the busy West End. Exploring this park in North America's second-largest urban forest is one of Vancouver's quintessential experiences. Shaded walking trails meander through towering western red cedar and Douglas fir, manicured lawns, flower gardens, and placid lagoons. The famed **seawall** runs along the waterside, allowing cyclists and pedestrians to experience the interface of forest, sea, and sky. One of the most popular attractions in the park is the **totem poles** at Brockton Point. The area around the totem poles features open-air displays on the Coast Salish First Nations and a small gift shop/visitor information center. The park is home to lots of wildlife, including beavers, coyotes, bald eagles, raccoons, trumpeter swans, brant geese, ducks, and skunks. For directions and maps, visit the **Lost Lagoon Nature House** (© 604/257-8544; 10am–7pm July 1–Labour Day, weekends only outside this period; free admission). On Sundays they offer Discovery Walks of the park. Equally nature-focused but with way more wow is the **Vancouver Aquarium** (see below). There's also the **Stanley Park's Children's Farm** (© 604/257-8530), a petting zoo with peacocks, rabbits, calves, donkeys, and Shetland ponies. Next to the petting zoo is **Stanley Park's Miniature Railway** 🏛 (© 604/257-8531), a diminutive steam locomotive that pulls passenger cars on a circuit through the woods. For swimmers, there's **Third Beach** and **Second Beach,** the latter with an outdoor pool beside English Bay. A free shuttle bus that stops at most of the park's attractions circles the park every 15 minutes. There's also a wonderful **horse-drawn carriage ride** that begins near Lost Lagoon.

Stanley Park. © 604/257-8400. www.city.vancouver.bc.ca/parks. Parking Apr–Sept 6am–9pm C$6 (US$4.80); Oct–Mar 7am–6pm C$3 (US$2.40). Park does not close. Park attractions late June to Labour Day daily 9:30am–7pm; Labour Day to late June daily 10am–5:30pm. Bus: 23, 35, or 135; free "Around the Park."

Vancouver Aquarium Marine Science Centre 🏛🏛🏛 *Kids*   One of North America's largest and best, the Vancouver Aquarium houses more than 8,000 marine species, most in meticulously re-created environments. In the icy-blue Arctic Canada exhibit, beluga whales whistle and blow water at unwary onlookers. Human-size freshwater fish inhabit the Amazon rainforest gallery, while overhead, an atrium houses three-toed sloths, brilliant blue and green poison tree frogs, and piranhas. Regal angelfish glide through a re-creation of Indonesia's Bunaken National Park coral reef, and blacktip reef sharks menacingly scour the Tropical Gallery's waters. (Call for the shark and sea otter feeding times.) The Pacific Canada exhibit is dedicated to sea life of the B.C. waters, including Pacific salmon and the giant Pacific octopus. On the Marine Mammal Deck, there are sea otters, sea lions, beluga whales, and a Pacific white-sided dolphin. During shows, aquarium staff explain the behavior of these impressive mammals. The aquarium offers several behind-the-scenes tours that allow visitors to interact with some of the marine wildlife—call or consult the website for details.

Stanley Park. © 604/659-FISH. www.vanaqua.org. Admission C$17 (US$14) adults, C$13 (US$10) seniors, students, and youths 13–18, C$9.50 (US$7.60) children 4–12, free for children under 4. Late June to Sept 1 daily 9:30am–7pm;

Sept 2 to late June daily 10am–5:30pm. Bus: 135; "Around the Park" shuttle bus June–Sept only. Parking C$5 (US$4) summer, C$3 (US$2.40) winter.

Vancouver Art Gallery ★★   The VAG demonstrates what sets Canadian and West Coast art apart from the rest of the world. There is an impressive collection of paintings by B.C. native **Emily Carr,** as well as rotating exhibits of sculpture, graphics, photography, and video art. For younger audiences, the Annex Gallery offers rotating educational exhibits.

750 Hornby St. ℂ **604/662-4719** or 604/662-4700. www.vanartgallery.bc.ca. Admission C$13 (US$9.50) adults, C$9 (US$6.75) seniors, C$8 (US$6) students, C$30 (US$23) family, free for children 12 and under, Thurs 5–9pm by donation. Mon–Wed and Fri–Sun 10am–5:30pm; Thurs 10am–9pm. Closed Mon in fall and winter. SkyTrain: Granville. Bus: 3.

THE WEST SIDE

Granville Island ★★★ *(Kids)*   Once a declining industrial site, Granville Island now houses so many galleries, artist studios, restaurants, and theaters that a day may not be enough to experience it all. Shop for crafts, grab some fresh seafood, enjoy a great dinner, attend Shakespeare in the park, rent a yacht, or stroll along the waterfront. Plan to spend some time in the **Granville Island Public Market,** one of the best all-around markets in the world. Check the website for upcoming events and festivals or stop by the information center, behind the Kids Market.

Located on the south shore of False Creek, under the Granville Street Bridge. For studio and gallery hours and other information about Granville Island, contact the information center at ℂ **604/666-5784.** www.granville-island.net. The market is open daily 9am–6pm.

Museum of Anthropology ★★★   A classic Native post-and-beam structure made out of poured concrete and glass, this museum houses one of the world's finest collections of West Coast Native art. Artifacts flank the ramp leading to the Great Hall's **collection of totem poles.** Haida artist Bill Reid's touchable cedar bear and sea wolf sculptures sit at the Cross Roads; Reid's masterpiece, *The Raven and the First Men,* is worth the price of admission all by itself. The huge carving in yellow cedar depicts a Haida creation myth, in which Raven—the trickster—coaxes humanity out into the world from its birthplace in a clamshell. The **Masterpiece Gallery** contains argillite sculptures, beaded jewelry, and hand-carved ceremonial masks. Curators have recently begun salting contemporary Native artworks in among the old masterpieces—a sign that West Coast art is alive and well. On the grounds behind the museum are two **longhouses** built in the Haida tribal style and 10 hand-carved totem poles.

Moments **360 Degrees of Vancouver**

The most popular (and most touristed) spot from which to view Vancouver's skyline is high atop the space needle observation deck at the **Lookout!, Harbour Centre Tower,** 555 W. Hastings St. (ℂ **604/689-0421**). It's a great place for first-time visitors who want a panorama of the city. The glass-encased Skylift whisks you up 166m (544 ft.) to the rooftop deck in less than a minute. The 360-degree view is remarkable. (Yes, that is Mt. Baker looming above the southeastern horizon.) Skylift admission is C$10 (US$8) for adults, C$9 (US$7.20) for seniors, C$7 (US$5.60) for students and youth, C$4 (US$3.20) children 6 and under. It's open daily in summer from 8:30am to 10:30pm and in winter from 9am to 9pm.

6393 NW Marine Dr. (at Gate 4). © **604/822-5087.** www.moa.ubc.ca. Admission C$9 (US$7.20) adults, C$7 (US$5.60) seniors, students, children 6–18, free for children under 6, free Tues 5–9pm. May 21–Aug Wed–Mon 10am–5pm, Tues 10am–9pm; Sept–May 20 Wed–Sun 11am–5pm, Tues 11am–9pm. Closed Dec 25–26. Bus: 4, 10, or 99 (10-min. walk from UBC bus loop).

Science World British Columbia 🖈 *Kids*   Science World is impossible to miss. It's in the big blinking geodesic dome on the eastern end of False Creek. Inside, it's a hands-on scientific discovery center where you and your kids can light up a plasma ball, walk through a 160-sq.-m (1,722-sq.-ft.) maze, wander through the interior of a camera, create a cyclone, watch a zucchini explode as it's charged with 80,000 volts, stand inside a beaver lodge, play in wrist-deep magnetic liquids, create music with a giant synthesizer, and watch mind-blowing three-dimensional slide and laser shows as well as other optical effects. In the OMNIMAX Theatre, you can take a stunning trip through a coral reef. Science World also hosts many spectacular traveling exhibitions.

1455 Quebec St. © **604/443-7443.** www.scienceworld.bc.ca. Admission C$13 (US$10) adults, C$8.50 (US$6.80) seniors, students, children 4–17, free for children under 4, C$43 (US$34) family pass, including 2 adults and 4 children. Combination tickets available for OMNIMAX film. Mon–Fri 10am–5pm; Sat–Sun and holidays 10am–6pm. Sky-Train: Main Street–Science World.

Vancouver Museum   The Vancouver Museum is dedicated to amassing evidence of the city's history, from its days as a Native settlement and European outpost to the city's early-20th-century maturation into a modern urban center. The exhibits allow visitors to walk through the steerage deck of a 19th-century passenger ship, peek into a Hudson's Bay Company frontier trading post, or take a seat in an 1880s Canadian Pacific Railway passenger car. Re-creations of Victorian and Edwardian rooms show how early Vancouverites decorated their homes. Rotating exhibits include a display of the museum's collection of neon signage from Vancouver's former glory days as the West Coast's glitziest neon-sign-filled metropolis during the 1940s and 1950s.

1100 Chestnut St. © **604/736-4431.** www.vanmuseum.bc.ca. Admission C$10 (US$8) adults, C$8 (US$6.40) seniors, C$6 (US$4.80) youths 4–19. Fri–Wed 10am–5pm; Thurs 10am–9pm. Bus: 22, then walk 3 blocks south on Cornwall Ave. Boat: Granville Island Ferry to Heritage Harbour.

GASTOWN & CHINATOWN
Dr. Sun Yat-sen Classical Chinese Garden 🖈   This small reproduction of a Classical Chinese Scholar's garden truly is a remarkable place, but to get the full effect it's best to take the free guided tour. Untrained eyes will only see a pretty pond surrounded by bamboo and funny shaped rocks. The engaging guides, however, can explain this unique urban garden's Taoist yin-yang design principle, in which harmony is achieved through dynamic opposition. This is one of two Classical Chinese gardens in North America (the other is in Portland, Oregon) created by master artisans from Suzhou, the garden city of China.

578 Carrall St. © **604/689-7133.** www.vancouverchinesegarden.com. Admission C$8.25 (US$6.60) adults, C$6.75 (US$5.40) seniors, C$5.75 (US$4.60) children 6–18 and students, free children under 5, C$18 (US$14) family pass. Free guided tour included. May 1–June 14 daily 10am–6pm; June 15–Aug daily 9:30am–7pm; Sept daily 10am–6pm; Oct–Apr daily 10am–4:30pm. Bus: 19 or 22.

NORTH VANCOUVER & WEST VANCOUVER
Grouse Mountain Resort 🖈   Once a small local ski hill, Grouse is now a year-round recreational park. Only a 15-minute drive from downtown, the **SkyRide gondola** transports you to the mountain's 1,110m (3,641-ft.) summit in 8 minutes. (Hikers and cardio fiends can take a near vertical trail called the Grouse Grind.) The view from the top

is one of the best around. You'll also find a restaurant, large-screen theater (Theatre in the Sky) with wildlife features, an endangered wildlife refuge, ski and snowboard area, hiking and snowshoeing trails, skating pond, children's snow park, interpretive forest trails, a fun lumberjack show, helicopter tours, mountain bike trails, sleigh rides, and a Native feast house. Many of these activities are free with your SkyRide ticket, and they should be, since there's no other way to justify the exorbitant admission fee.

6400 Nancy Greene Way, North Vancouver. © 604/984-0661. www.grousemountain.com. SkyRide C$30 (US$24) adults, C$28 (US$22) seniors, C$17 (US$14) youths 13–18, C$11 (US$8.80) children 5–12, free for children under 4. SkyRide free with advance Observatory Restaurant reservation. Daily 9am–10pm. Bus: 232, then transfer to bus no. 236. SeaBus: Lonsdale Quay, then transfer to bus no. 236. By car, take Hwy. 99 north across Lions Gate Bridge, take North Vancouver exit to Marine Dr., then up Capilano Rd. for 5km (3 miles).

VANCOUVER'S PLAZAS, PARKS & GARDENS

Unlike many cities, Vancouver's great urban gathering places stand not at the center but on the periphery, on two opposite sides of the **seawall** that runs around Stanley Park: **English Bay,** on the south side of Denman Street, and **Coal Harbour,** on the northern, Burrard Inlet, side are where Vancouverites go to stroll and be seen. On warm sunny days, these two areas are packed.

Designed by architect Arthur Erickson to be Vancouver's central plaza, **Robson Square**—downtown, between Hornby and Howe streets from Robson to Smithe streets—has never really worked. The square, which anchors the north end of the Provincial Law Courts complex designed by Erickson in 1972, suffers from a basic design flaw: It's sunk one story below street level and next to impossible to access. The Law Courts complex, which sits on a higher level, raised above the street, is beautifully executed with shrubbery, cherry trees, sculptures, and a triple-tiered waterfall, but Robson Square below is about as appealing as a drained swimming pool. Just opposite Robson square, however, the steps of the **Vancouver Art Gallery** are a great people-place, filled with loungers, political agitators, and old men playing chess. It just goes to show you that grandiose urban theory and urban design, especially back in the 1970s, didn't always take the human element into account.

Library Square—a few blocks east from Robson Square at the corner of Robson and Homer streets—is an example of a new urban space that really works. It's immensely popular with locals and has been since it opened in 1995. People sit on the steps, bask in the sunshine, read, harangue passersby with half-baked political ideas, and generally seem to enjoy themselves.

Park and garden lovers are in heaven in Vancouver. The wet, mild climate is ideal for gardening, and come spring the city blazes with blossoming cherry trees, rhododendrons, camellias, azaleas, and spring bulbs. Roses are a favorite summer bloom. You'll see gardens everywhere, and urban gardens with fountains have been incorporated into most of the city's new development. Nature is part of the scheme here. For general information about Vancouver's parks, call © **604/257-8400** or try www.parks.vancouver.bc.ca. For information on **Stanley Park,** the queen of them all, see "The Top Attractions," above.

On the West Side you'll find the magnificent **UBC Botanical Garden,** one of the largest living botany collections on the West Coast, and the sublime **Nitobe Japanese Garden.**

In Chinatown, the **Dr. Sun Yat-sen Classical Chinese Garden** (see "The Top Attractions," above) is a small, tranquil oasis in the heart of the city, built by artisans from Suzhou, China; right next to it, accessed via the Chinese Cultural Centre on

Pender Street, is the pretty (and free) **Dr. Sun Yat-sen Park,** with a pond, walkways, and plantings.

On the West Side, **Queen Elizabeth Park** *&*—at Cambie Street and West 33rd Avenue—sits atop a 150m-high (492-ft.) extinct volcano and is the highest urban vantage point south of downtown, offering panoramic views in all directions (although leafy deciduous trees now block some of the best views). Along with the rose Garden in Stanley Park, it's Vancouver's most popular location for wedding-photo sessions, with well-manicured gardens and a profusion of colorful flora. There are areas for lawn bowling, tennis, pitch-and-putt golf, and picnicking. The **Bloedel Conservatory** (*©* **604/257-8584**) stands next to the park's huge sunken garden, an amazing reclamation of an abandoned rock quarry. A 42m-high (138-ft.) domed structure, the conservatory houses a tropical rainforest with more than 100 plant species as well as free-flying tropical birds. Admission to the conservatory is C$4.25 (US$3.40) for adults, with discounts for seniors and children. Take bus no. 15 to reach the park.

VanDusen Botanical Gardens *&*, 5251 Oak St., at W. 37th Ave. (*©* **604/878-9274;** www.vandusengarden.org), is located just a few blocks from Queen Elizabeth Park and the Bloedel Conservatory. In contrast to the flower fetish displayed by Victoria's famous Butchart Gardens (see chapter 5), Vancouver's 22-hectare (54-acre) botanical garden concentrates on whole ecosystems. From trees hundreds of feet high down to the little lichens on the smallest of damp stones, the gardeners at VanDusen attempt to re-create the plant life of an enormous number of different environments. Depending on which trail you take, you may find yourself wandering through the Southern Hemisphere section, the Sino-Himalayan garden, or the northern California garden where giant sequoias reach for the sky. Should all this tree gazing finally pall, head for the farthest corner of the garden where you'll find a devilishly difficult Elizabethan garden maze. Admission April through September is C$7.75 (US$6.20) adults, C$5.50 (US$4.40) seniors, C$5.75 (US$4.60) youth 13 to 18, C$4 (US$3.20) children 6 to 12, C$18 (US$14) families, free for children under 6. Admission is about C$2 (US$1.60) less from October through March. Open daily 10am to dusk. Take bus 17.

Adjoining UBC on the city's west side at Point Grey, **Pacific Spirit Regional Park,** called the **Endowment Lands** by long-time Vancouver residents, is the largest green space in Vancouver. Comprising 754 hectares (1,862 acres) of temperate rainforest, marshes, and beaches, the park includes nearly 35km (22 miles) of trails ideal for hiking, riding, mountain biking, and beachcombing.

6 Outdoor Pursuits

BEACHES A great place for viewing sunsets, **English Bay Beach** *&&* lies at the end of Davie Street off Denman Street and Beach Avenue. On **Stanley Park**'s western rim, **Second Beach** is a quick stroll north from English Bay Beach. A playground, a snack bar, and an immense heated ocean-side **pool** *&* (*©* **604/257-8370**), open from May through September, makes this a great spot for families. Farther along the seawall lies secluded **Third Beach.** South of English Bay Beach, near the Burrard Street Bridge, is **Sunset Beach. Kitsilano Beach** *&*, along Arbutus Drive near Ogden Street, has a huge heated **pool** *&*. Below UBC's Museum of Anthropology is **Wreck Beach** *&*, Canada's largest nude beach. You get down to Wreck Beach by taking the very steep Trail 6 on the UBC campus near Gate 6 down to the water's edge.

BICYCLING & MOUNTAIN BIKING The most popular cycling path in the city runs along the **seawall** *&&&* around the perimeter of Stanley Park. Another popular route is the **seaside bicycle route,** a 15km (9¼-mile) ride that begins at English Bay and continues around False Creek to the University of British Columbia. Cycling maps are available at most bicycle retailers and rental outlets.

Serious mountain bikers love the trails on **Grouse Mountain** (see "The Top Attractions," above). The very steep **Good Samaritan Trail** on **Mount Seymour** connects to the Baden-Powell Trail and the Bridle Path near Mount Seymour Road. Locals bike the cross-country ski trails on **Hollyburn Mountain** in **Cypress Provincial Park.** Closer to downtown, **Pacific Spirit Park** and **Burnaby Mountain** offer excellent beginner and intermediate off-road trails.

Hourly rentals run around C$5 (US$4) for a one-speed "Cruiser" to C$9 (US$7.20) for a top-of-the-line mountain bike; C$15 to C$40 (US$12–US$32) for a day, helmets and locks included. Popular rental shops include **Spokes Bicycle Rentals & Espresso Bar,** 1798 W. Georgia St. (© **604/688-5141;** www.spokesbicyclerentals. com); and **Alley Cat Rentals,** 1779 Robson St., in the alley (© **604/684-5117**). Helmets are mandatory and will be included in your bike rental.

BOATING   You can rent 4.5- to 5m-long (15–16 ft.) power boats for a few hours or weeks at **Bonnie Lee Boat Rentals,** 1676 Duranleau St., Granville Island (© **866/ 933-7447** or 604/290-7441; www.bonnielee.com). A 5m (16-ft.) sport boat for four costs C$50 (US$40) per hour or C$300 (US$240) for 8 hours. **Jerry's Boat Rentals,** Granville Island (© **604/644-3256**), is steps away with similar deals. **Delta Charters,** 3500 Cessna Dr., Richmond (© **800/661-7762** or 604/273-4211; www.deltacharters. com), has weekly or monthly rates for skippered boats for four.

CANOEING & KAYAKING   Both placid, urban False Creek and the incredibly beautiful 30km (19-mile) North Vancouver fiord known as Indian Arm have launching points that can be reached by car or bus. Prices range from about C$35 (US$28) per 2-hour minimum rental to C$65 (US$52) per 5-hour day for single kayaks and about C$60 (US$48) for canoe rentals.

Ecomarine Ocean Kayak Centre, 1668 Duranleau St., Granville Island (© **888/ 425-2925** or 604/689-7575; www.ecomarine.com), has hourly, daily, and weekly kayak rentals; courses; and tours. **Deep Cove** (© **604/929-2268;** www.deepcove kayak.com) offers hourly and daily rentals of canoes and kayaks as well as lessons and customized tours. **Lotus Land Tours,** 2005–1251 Cardero St. (© **800/528-3531** or 604/684-4922; www.lotuslandtours.com), runs guided kayak tours on Indian Arm, with transportation to and from Vancouver, a barbecue salmon lunch, and incredible scenery. One-day tours cost C$149 (US$119) for adults, C$75 (US$60) for children.

ECO-TOURS   From November to January, **Lotus Land Tours** (see "Canoeing & Kayaking," above) offers float trips on the Squamish River to see bald eagles up close. **Rockwood Adventures** (© **888/236-6606** or 604/980-7749; www.rockwood adventures.com) has guided walks of the North Shore rainforest, complete with a trained naturalist, stops in Capilano Canyon and at the Lynn Suspension Bridge, and a gourmet lunch, for C$75 (US$60).

FISHING   Five species of salmon, rainbow and Dolly Varden trout, steelhead, and sturgeon abound in the local waters around Vancouver. Anglers need a nonresident saltwater or freshwater license, available from tackle shops, sporting goods stores, resorts, service stations, marinas, charter boat operators, and department stores. Saltwater (tidal waters) fishing licenses cost C$7.50 (US$6) for 1 day, C$20 (US$16) for

3 days, and C$35 (US$28) for 5 days. Fly-fishing in national and provincial parks requires special permits, which you can get at any park site.

Hanson's Fishing Outfitters, 102–580 Hornby St. (© **604/684-8988;** www. hansons-outfitters.com), **Granville Island Boat Rentals,** 1696 Duranleau St. (© **604/ 682-6287;** www.granvilleislandboatrentals.com), and **Bonnie Lee Fishing Charters Ltd.,** 1676 Duranleau St., Granville Island (© **604/290-7447;** www.bonnielee.com), are reputable outfitters.

GOLF   The **Vancouver Board of Parks and Recreation** (© **604/257-8400;** www. city.vancouver.bc.ca/parks), maintains excellent public golf courses citywide. **Langara Golf Course,** 6706 Alberta St., around 49th Avenue and Cambie Street (© **604/713-1816**), is one of the most popular courses. Greens fees range from C$25 to C$52 (US$20–US$42) for an adult, with discounts for seniors, youths, and weekday tee times. To reserve, call © **604/280-1818** up to 5 days in advance. The public **University Golf Club,** 5185 University Blvd. (© **604/224-1818**), is a great 6,560-yard, par-71 course with a clubhouse, pro shop, locker rooms, bar and grill, and sports lounge. For substantial discounts and short-notice tee times at more than 30 Vancouver-area courses, try calling **A-1 Last Minute Golf Hot Line** (© **800/684-6344** or 604/878-1833).

HIKING   Good trail maps are available from **International Travel Maps and Books,** 539 Pender St. (© **604/687-3320;** www.itmb.com), or pick up a local trail guide at any bookstore.

For a challenge without a huge time commitment, hike the **Grouse Grind** from the bottom of **Grouse Mountain** (see "The Top Attractions," above); then buy a one-way ticket down on the SkyRide gondola. If you're looking for a bit more scenery with a bit less effort, take the SkyRide up to the **Grouse chalet** and start your hike at 1,100m (3,608 ft.).

Lynn Canyon Park, Lynn Headwaters Regional Park, Capilano River Regional Park, Mount Seymour Provincial Park, Pacific Spirit Park, and **Cypress Provincial Park** have good trails that wind up through stands of Douglas fir and cedar and contain a few serious switchbacks.

ICE SKATING   Robson Square has free skating on a rink on Robson Street between Howe and Hornby streets from November to April. The **West End Community Centre,** 870 Denman St. (© **604/257-8333**), also rents skates at its enclosed rink, open October through March. The enormous **Burnaby 8 Rinks Ice Sports Centre,** 6501 Sprott, Burnaby (© **604/291-0626**), is the Vancouver Canucks' official practice facility. Call ahead to check hours for public skating.

SAILING   **Cooper Boating Centre,** 1620 Duranleau St. (© **604/687-4110;** www. cooperboating.com), offers chartered cruises, boat rentals, and sail-instruction packages. Rentals range from C$160 (US$128) daily in the off season to C$500 (US$400) in peak season.

SKIING & SNOWBOARDING   Vancouverites can ski before work and after dinner at the three ski resorts in the North Shore mountains. In 2010, these local mountains will play host to the Freestyle and Snowboard events in the Winter Olympics.

Grouse Mountain Resort, 6400 Nancy Greene Way, North Vancouver (© **604/ 984-0661,** snow report 604/986-6262; www.grousemountain.com), has four chairs, two beginner tows, two T-bars, and 24 alpine runs. The resort has night skiing, special events, instruction, and a half pipe for snowboarders. Lift tickets good for all-day skiing are C$42 (US$34) for adults, C$32 (US$26) for seniors and youths, and C$18 (US$14) for children 5 through 12; children under 4 go free.

Mount Seymour Provincial Park, 1700 Mt. Seymour Rd., North Vancouver (℡ **604/986-2261,** snow report 604/986-3999; www.mountseymour.com), with the area's highest base elevation, has four chairs and a tow. Lift tickets are C$36 (US$29) all day for adults, C$25 (US$20) for seniors, C$29 (US$23) for youths 12 to 19, C$19 (US$15) for children 6 to 11. Shuttle service is available during ski season from various locations on the North Shore, including the Lonsdale Quay SeaBus. For more information, call ℡ **604/986-2261.**

Cypress Bowl, 1610 Mt. Seymour Rd. (℡ **604/926-5612,** snow report 604/419-7669; www.cypressmountain.com), has the area's longest vertical drop. Full-day lift tickets are C$42 (US$34) for adults, with reduced rates for youths, seniors, and children.

Cypress Mountain Sports, 510 and 518 Park Royal S., West Vancouver (℡ **604/878-9229**), offers shuttle service to and from the ski area. Round-trip tickets are C$9 (US$7.20).

SWIMMING   Vancouver's midsummer salt water temperature rarely exceeds 65°F (18°C). There are **heated outdoor pools** at **Kitsilano Beach** and **Second Beach** (see "Beaches," above). The **Vancouver Aquatic Centre,** 1050 Beach Ave. (℡ **604/665-3424**), has a heated Olympic pool. The coed **YWCA Fitness Centre,** 535 Hornby St. (℡ **604/895-5777;** www.ywcavan.org), has a six-lane ozonated pool. UBC's **Aquatic Centre,** 6121 University Blvd. (℡ **604/822-4522;** www.aquatics.ubc.ca), designates hours for public use.

WHITE-WATER RAFTING   Only a 1½-hour drive from the city is **Chilliwack River Rafting** (℡ **800/410-7238;** www.dowco.com/chilliwackrafting), whose half-day trips cost C$89 (US$71) for adults. A 2½-hour drive, **Reo Rafting,** 845 Spence Way, Anmore (℡ **800/736-7238** or 604/461-7238; www.reorafting.com), offers 1-day packages for C$125 (US$100).

WILDLIFE-WATCHING   From April through October, **Vancouver Whale Watch,** 12240 Second Ave., Richmond (℡ **604/274-9565;** www.vancouverwhalewatch.com), and **Steveston Seabreeze Adventures,** 12551 No. 1 Rd., Richmond (℡ **604/272-7200;** www.seabreezeadventures.ca), offer excursions to sight whales and other wildlife.

To hook up with local Vancouver birders, try the **Vancouver Natural History Society** (℡ **604/737-3074;** www.naturalhistory.bc.ca/VNHS).

WINDSURFING   Rent a board at **Jericho** and **English Bay beaches** ✯. Equipment sales, rentals (including wet suits), and instruction can be found at **Windsure Windsurfing School,** 1300 Discovery St., at Jericho Beach (℡ **604/224-0615;** www.windsure.com).

7 Shopping

Robson Street is the spot for high-end fashions. The 10-block stretch of **Granville Street** from Sixth Avenue up to 16th Avenue is where Vancouver's old money comes to shop for classic fashions. **Water Street** in **Gastown** features knickknacks, antiques, cutting-edge furniture, First Nations art, and funky basement retro shops. **Main Street** from 19th Avenue to 27th Avenue means antiques and lots of 'em, while **Granville Island,** beneath the Granville Street Bridge, is one of the best places to pick up salmon or other seafood. It's also a great place to browse for gifts.

ANTIQUES   The **Vancouver Antique Centre,** 422 Richards St. (℡ **604/669-7444;** Bus: 20), sells china, glass, Orientalia, military objects, jewelry, and watches. **Uno**

Langmann Ltd., 2117 Granville St. (© **604/736-8825;** www.langmann.com; Bus: 4), caters to upscale shoppers.

BOOKS Since 1957, the locally owned chain **Duthie Books,** 2239 W. Fourth Ave., Kitsilano (© **604/732-5344;** www.duthiebooks.com; Bus: 4), has been synonymous with good books. On Granville Island, **Blackberry Books,** 1663 Duranleau St. (© **604/ 685-4113;** www.bbooks.ca; Bus: 50), focuses on art, architecture, and cuisine. **Chapters,** 788 Robson St. (© **604/682-4066;** www.chapters.ca; Bus: 5), is pleasant, with little nooks and comfy benches. **Little Sister's Book & Art Emporium,** 1238 Davie St. (© **604/669-1753;** www.littlesistersbookstore.com; Bus: 1), has the largest selection of lesbian, gay, bisexual, and transgender books. **International Travel Maps,** 552 Seymour St. (© **604/687-3320;** www.itmb.com; Bus: 4), fulfills all your travel needs.

DEPARTMENT STORES Since the establishment of its early trading posts, **The Bay** (Hudson's Bay Company), 674 Granville St. (© **604/681-6211;** www.hbc.com; Bus: 4), has built its reputation on quality goods. Buy a Hudson's Bay woolen "point" blanket (the colorful stripes originally represented how many beaver pelts each blanket was worth in trade), or you'll also find wares from Hilfiger, Polo, DKNY, Ellen Tracy, Anne Klein II, and Liz Claiborne.

FASHION For something uniquely West Coast, don't miss the singular First Nations designs of **Dorothy Grant,** 250–757 W. Hastings St. (© **604/681-0201;** www.dorothygrant.com; Bus: 4). **Dream,** 311 W. Cordova (© **604/683-7326;** Bus: 1), is one of the few places to find the early collections of local designers. **Zonda Nellis Design Ltd.,** 2203 Granville St. (© **604/736-5668;** www.zondanellis.com; Bus: 4), offers a line of hand-painted silks.

FIRST NATIONS ART **Images for a Canadian Heritage,** 164 Water St. (© **604/ 685-7046;** www.imagesforcanada.com; Bus: 1), is a government-licensed First Nations art gallery. **Hill's Native Art,** 165 Water St. (© **504/686-4249;** www.hills nativeart.com; Bus: 1), established in 1946, sells moccasins, ceremonial masks, Cowichan sweaters, wood sculptures, totem poles, silk-screen prints, soapstone sculptures, and jewelry. The **Lattimer Gallery,** 1590 W. Second Ave. (© **604/732-4556;** www.lattimergallery.com; Bus: 4), presents museum-quality displays of ceremonial masks, totem poles, argillite sculptures, and gold and silver jewelry.

FOOD At **Chocolate Arts,** 2037 W. Fourth Ave. (© **604/739-0475;** Bus: 4), look for the all-chocolate diorama in the window—it changes every month or so. **Murchie's Tea & Coffee,** 970 Robson St. (© **604/669-0783;** www.murchies.com; Bus: 5), is a Vancouver institution. **The Lobsterman,** 1807 Mast Tower Rd. (© **604/ 687-4531;** www.lobsterman.com; Bus: 50), is one of the city's best spots to pick up seafood, which can be packed for air travel. And the **Salmon Village,** 779 Thurlow St. (© **604/685-3378;** www.salmonvillage.com; Bus: 4), specializes in salmon of all varieties.

GIFTS For a range of basic souvenirs (lumberjack shirts, Cowichan sweaters, T-shirts, and trinkets), try **Canadian Impressions at the Station,** 601 Cordova St. (© **604/681-3507;** Bus: 1).

JEWELRY **Henry Birk & Sons Ltd.,** 698 W. Hastings St. (© **604/669-3333;** Bus: 7), has a long tradition of designing beautiful jewelry and watches. On Granville Island, **The Raven and the Bear,** 1528 Duranleau St. (© **604/669-3990;** Bus: 50), is a great spot for native jewelry.

SPORTING GOODS   Everything you'll ever need for the outdoors is at **Mountain Equipment Co-op,** 130 W. Broadway (℃ **604/872-7858;** www.mec.ca; Bus: 9).

8 Vancouver After Dark

For an overview of Vancouver's nightlife, pick up a copy of the weekly tabloid *The Georgia Straight,* the glossy *Vancouver* magazine (www.vanmag.com), or *Xtra! West,* the free gay-and-lesbian biweekly tabloid. The **Vancouver Cultural Alliance Arts Hot Line** (℃ **604/684-2787;** www.allianceforarts.com) is a great source for all performing arts, music, theater, literary events, art films, and dance, including where and how to get tickets. **Ticketmaster** (Vancouver Ticket Centre), 1304 Hornby St. (℃ **604/280-3311;** www.ticketmaster.ca; Bus: 4), has 40 outlets in the greater Vancouver area. With a credit card, you can buy tickets over the phone and pick them up at the venue.

Three major Vancouver theaters regularly host touring performances are the **Orpheum Theatre,** 801 Granville St. (Bus: 7); the **Queen Elizabeth Theatre,** 600 Hamilton St. (Bus: 5); and the **Vancouver Playhouse.** The three share a phone and website (℃ **604/665-3050;** www.city.vancouver.bc.ca). On the campus of UBC, the **Chan Centre for the Performing Arts,** 6265 Crescent Rd. (℃ **604/822-2697;** www.chancentre.com), hosts a winter concert series; its acoustics are the best in town.

THE PERFORMING ARTS

Theater isn't only an indoor pastime here. There's an annual summertime Shakespeare series called **Bard on the Beach,** in Vanier Park (℃ **604/737-0625;** www.bardonthebeach.org; Bus: 22). You can also bring a picnic dinner to Stanley Park and watch **Theatre Under the Stars** (℃ **604/687-0174;** www.tuts.bc.ca; Bus: 35), which features popular musicals and light comedies. For more original fare, don't miss **Vancouver's Fringe Festival** (℃ **604/257-0350;** www.vancouverfringe.com). The Fringe features more than 500 innovative and original shows each September, all costing under C$10 (US$7.20).

The **Arts Club Theatre Company** presents live theater in two venues: the Granville Island Stage at the Arts Club Theatre, 1585 Johnston St. (Bus: 50), and the Stanley Theatre, 2750 Granville St. (Bus: 8). For information on both theaters, call ℃ **604/687-1644** or go to www.artsclub.com. Housed in Vancouver's Firehall No. 1, the **Firehall Arts Centre,** 280 E. Cordova St. (℃ **604/689-0926;** www.firehall.org; Bus: 4), is home to three cutting-edge companies: the Firehall Theatre Company, Touchstone Theatre, and Axis Mime. Expect experimental and challenging plays.

In a converted early-1900s church, the **Vancouver East Cultural Centre** (the "Cultch" to locals), 1895 Venables St. (℃ **604/251-1363;** www.vecc.bc.ca; Bus: 20), hosts avant-garde theater productions, children's programs, and art exhibits.

Originally built as the Ford Centre in 1996, **The Centre in Vancouver for Performing Arts,** 777 Homer St. (℃ **604/602-0616;** www.centreinvancouver.com), was hailed as Vancouver's newest prime entertainment venue until its owner went bankrupt. The theater sat empty until the spring of 2002 when four brothers from Hong Kong re-opened the venue to bring big productions to town.

OPERA   The **Vancouver Opera,** 500–845 Cambie St. (℃ **604/683-0222;** www.vanopera.bc.ca; Bus: 17), alternates between obscure or new works and older, more popular favorites. English supertitles projected above the stage help audiences follow the dialogue of the lavish productions.

CLASSICAL MUSIC   The extremely active **Vancouver Symphony,** 601 Smithe St. (✆ **604/876-3434;** www.vancouversymphony.ca; Bus: 7), presents a number of series: great classical works, light classics, modern classics and ethnic works, popular and show tunes, and music geared toward school-age children. Other classical groups in town include the **Vancouver Bach Choir,** 805–235 Keith Rd., West Vancouver (✆ **604/921-8012;** www.vancouverbachchoir.com); the **Vancouver Cantata Singers,** 5115 Keith Rd., West Vancouver (✆ **604/921-8588;** www.cantata.org.); and the **Vancouver Chamber Choir,** 1254 W. Seventh Ave. (✆ **604/738-6822;** www. vancouverchamberchoir.com).

DANCE   The recently opened **Scotiabank Dance Centre,** 677 Davie St. (✆ **604/ 606-6400;** www.vkool.com/dancentre), provides a new focus point for the Vancouver dance community. For fans of modern and original dance, the time to be here is early July, when the **Dancing on the Edge Festival** (✆ **604/689-0691;** www.dancing ontheedge.org) presents 60 to 80 envelope-pushing original pieces over a 10-day period. **Ballet British Columbia,** 502–68 Water St. (✆ **604/732-5003;** www.ballet bc.com; Bus: 4), is a young company that strives to present innovative works.

COMEDY & LIVE-MUSIC CLUBS   Performers with the **Vancouver Theatre Sports League** (✆ **604/687-1644;** www.vtsl.com) rely on a basic plot supplemented by audience suggestions the actors take and improvise on, often to hilarious results. Performances are in the Arts Club Theatre, 1585 Johnston St., Granville Island (Bus: 50), with shows costing C$16 (US$13) weekends and C$10 (US$8) weeknights.

The old-style suspended hardwood dance floor makes the **Commodore Ballroom,** 868 Granville St. (✆ **604/739-7469;** www.commodoreballroom.com), the best place in Vancouver to catch a midsize band—be it R&B, jazz, blues, hip-hop, or pop. For folk, the **WISE Hall,** 1882 Adanac (✆ **604/254-5858;** Bus: 20), is the place to be, with a cover running C$5 to C$15 (US$4–US$12). And for blues, go to the smoky, sudsy old **Yale Hotel,** 1300 Granville St. (✆ **604/681-9253;** www.theyale.ca; Bus: 4), with a Thursday-to-Saturday cover of C$5 to C$12 (US$4–US$10).

BARS, PUBS & LOUNGES   **Lift,** 333 Menchions Mews (✆ **604/689-5438**), built on piers behind the Westin Bayshore Resort, is Vancouver's newest glamour hot-spot, offering the most dramatic views in town as well as such luxe features as an illu-minated onyx bar. The food has yet to impress, but the bar/lounge scene is hot on weekends. The **Atlantic Trap and Gill,** 612 Davie St. (✆ **604/806-6393;** Bus: 4), is an east-coast sea shanty of a place, where the regulars know the words to every song. On Granville Street, **The Lennox Pub,** 800 Granville St. (✆ **604/408-0881**), is a comfortable spot for a drink with an extensive beer list, including such hard-to-find favorites as Belgian Kriek, Hoegaarden, and Leffe. There is a great selection of single-malt scotches, too. In Gastown, **The Irish Heather,** 217 Carrall St. (✆ **604/688-9779**), is a bright, pleasant Irish pub with numerous nooks and crannies, some of the best beer in town, and a menu that does a lot with the traditional Emerald Isle spud. **The Shark Club Bar and Grill,** 180 W. Georgia St. (✆ **604/687-4275;** Bus: 5), is the city's premier sports bar. If you're looking for a brewpub, **Steamworks Pub & Brewery,** 375 Water St. (✆ **604/689-2739;** Bus: 7), is your best bet. Choose from a dozen in-house beers, from dark Australian-style ales to light, refreshing wheat lagers. **The Yaletown Brewing Company,** 1111 Mainland St. (✆ **604/688-0039;** Bus: 2), also offers good home-brewed fare.

View junkies will think they've died and gone to heaven at **Cloud Nine,** 1400 Rob-son St., on the 42nd floor of the Empire Landmark Hotel (✆ **604/662-8328;** Bus:

5). This sleek hotel-top lounge rotates six degrees a minute, offering an ever-changing and always-fabulous view of the city. Cover is C$5 (US$4) Friday and Saturday after 8:30pm.

DANCE CLUBS   You get two venues for the price of one at Gastown's **The Purple Onion,** 15 Water St. (© **604/602-9442;** www.purpleonion.com; Bus: 4). The Club room is a dance floor pure and simple; in the Lounge a house band squeals out funky danceable jazz for a slightly older crowd. The cover runs C$5 to C$7 (US$4–US$5.50). The dance-oriented **Richards on Richards,** 1036 Richards St. (© **604/687-6794;** www.richardsonrichards.com; Bus: 7), has been packing 'em in for close to 2 decades, and the cover is C$5 to C$40 (US$4–US$32). **Sonar,** 66 Water St. (© **604/683-6695;** www.sonar.bc.ca; Bus: 4), is Vancouver's purest hip-hop house joint; it was named one of world's top-20 nightclubs by Britain's *Ministry* magazine. The cover runs C$5 to C$10 (US$4–US$8). A converted movie theatre, **The Plaza Cabaret,** 881 Granville St. (© **604/646-0064**), makes a great nightclub with its high ceilings and spacious dance floor. Cover is C$6 to C$10 (US$5–US$8).

GAY & LESBIAN BARS   Open Monday to Saturday from noon to 6pm, the **Gay Lesbian Transgendered Bisexual Community Centre,** 2–1170 Bute St. (© **604/684-5307;** www.lgtbcentrevancouver.com; Bus: 1), has information on the current hot spots, but it's probably easier just to pick up a free copy of *Xtra West!,* available in most downtown cafes.

The **Dufferin Pub,** 900 Seymour St. (© **604/683-4251;** Bus: 7), is home to the city's glitziest drag show, Buff at the Duff. The rest of the time (and before, during, and after many of the shows) the DJs play a mix of sounds to keep you grooving. **The Odyssey,** 1251 Howe St. (© **604/689-5256;** Bus: 4), is the hippest, happeningest gay/mixed dance bar in town, with a cover of C$3 to C$5 (US$2.40–US$4). The **Heritage House Hotel,** 455 Abbott St. (© **604/685-7777;** Bus: 4), is home to two gay bars, Charlie's Lounge and the slightly seedy Chuck's Pub, and one lesbian locale, the Lotus Cabaret. Cover at the Lotus is C$4 to C$7 (US$3.20–US$5.50). The Lotus offers a big bar, little alcoves for sitting, an adequate dance floor, and an upbeat atmosphere. The crowd is normally mixed, but on Fridays it's women only. **The Fountain Head Pub,** 1025 Davie St. (© **604/687-2222**), does a good imitation of a gay version of *Cheers.* Limited cruising has been known to happen.

CASINOS   There's no alcohol and there are no floor shows, but on the other hand, you haven't really lived until you've sat down for some serious gambling with a room full of Asian big shots trying to re-create the huge night they had in Happy Valley or Macau. To try your luck, head over to the **Great Canadian Casino Downtown,** 1133 W. Hastings St. (© **604/682-8415;** Bus: 23), open daily from noon to 4am. For blackjack, roulette, pai gow poker, and mini-baccarat you can also try the **Royal Diamond Casino,** 750 Pacific Blvd., in the Plaza of Nations (© **604/899-1061;** www.rdc.com; Bus: 2). Here you can play high roller from noon to 4am daily.

5

Victoria

In an Arcadian parkland of oak and fir at the edge of a natural harbor, Victoria spent the better part of the 20th century in a reverie, looking back to its glorious past as an outpost of England at the height of the Empire. It was a busy trading post and booming colonial city in the 19th century, but Victoria's lot began to fade soon after Vancouver was established in the 1880s. When its economy finally crashed early in the 20th century, shocked Victorians realized they were looking at a future with nothing much to live on but some fabulous Tudor and Victorian architecture, a beautiful natural setting, and a carefully cultivated sense of Englishness. So they decided to market that.

So successful was the sales job that the Victorians themselves began to believe they inhabited a little patch of England. They began growing rose gardens, which flourished in the mild Pacific climate, and cultivated a taste for afternoon tea with jam and scones. For decades, the reverie continued unabated. But as it was discovered that few in the world shared a taste for English cooking, Victoria's restaurants embraced seafood and ethnic and fusion cuisines. And lately, with visitors more interested in exploring the natural world, Victoria has quietly added whale-watching and mountain-biking trips to its traditional tours on London-style double-decker buses. Victoria is now the only city in the world where you can zoom out on a zodiac in the morning to see a pod of killer whales and make it back in time for a lovely afternoon tea with all the trimmings.

1 Essentials

GETTING THERE

BY PLANE **Victoria International Airport** (© 250/953-7500; www.cyyj.ca) is near the Sidney ferry terminal, 26km (16 miles) north of Victoria off the Patricia Bay Highway (Hwy. 17). **Air Canada** (© 888/247-2262 or 800/661-3936; www.air canada.com) and **Horizon Air** (© 800/547-9308; www.horizonair.com) offer direct connections from Seattle, Vancouver, Portland, Calgary, Edmonton, Saskatoon, Winnipeg, and Toronto. Canada's low-cost airline **WestJet** (© 888/WEST-JET; www.west jet.com) offers flights to Victoria from Kelowna, Calgary, Edmonton, and other destinations. WestJet service extends to a few U.S. cities as well.

Commuter airlines include **Air B.C.** (© 888/247-2262); **Harbour Air Sea Planes** (© 604/274-1277 or 250/384-2215; www.harbour-air.com); **Pacific Spirit Air** (also known as Tofino Air; © 800/665-2359; www.tofinoair.ca), which serves Victoria in addition to the south and north Gulf Islands from Vancouver Airport and Tofino; **Pacific Coastal Airlines** (© 604/273-8666; www.pacific-coastal.com); and **West Coast Air** (© 800/347-2222; www.westcoastair.com). **Kenmore Air** (© 800/543-9595; www.kenmoreair.com) and **Helijet Airways** (© 800/665-4354; www.helijet.com) offer flights between Seattle and Victoria.

Victoria

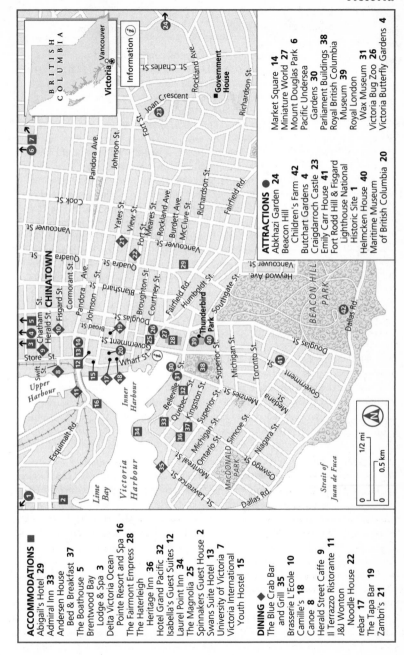

ACCOMMODATIONS ■
Abigail's Hotel 29
Admiral Inn 33
Andersen House
  Bed & Breakfast 37
The Boathouse 5
Brentwood Bay
  Lodge & Spa 3
Delta Victoria Ocean
  Pointe Resort and Spa 16
The Fairmont Empress 28
The Haterleigh
  Heritage Inn 36
Hotel Grand Pacific 32
Isabella's Guest Suites 12
Laurel Point Inn 34
The Magnolia 25
Spinnakers Guest House 2
Swans Suite Hotel 13
University of Victoria 7
Victoria International
  Youth Hostel 15

DINING ◆
The Blue Crab Bar
  and Grill 35
Brasserie L'Ecole 10
Camille's 18
Canoe 8
Herald Street Caffe 9
Il Terrazzo Ristorante 11
J&J Wonton
  Noodle House 22
rebar 17
The Tapa Bar 19
Zambri's 21

ATTRACTIONS ●
Abkhazi Garden 24
Beacon Hill
  Children's Farm 42
Butchart Gardens 4
Craigdarroch Castle 23
Emily Carr House 41
Fort Rodd Hill & Fisgard
  Lighthouse National
  Historic Site 1
Helmcken House 40
Maritime Museum
  of British Columbia 20
Market Square 14
Miniature World 27
Mount Douglas Park 6
Pacific Undersea
  Gardens 30
Parliament Buildings 38
Royal British Columbia
  Museum 39
Royal London
  Wax Museum 31
Victoria Bug Zoo 26
Victoria Butterfly Gardens 4

95

Special Events & Festivals

So many flowers bloom during the temperate month of February in Victoria that the city holds an annual **Flower Count** (© 250/383-7191). Toward the end of May, thousands of yachts sail into Victoria Harbor during the **Swiftsure Yacht Race** (© 250/953-2033; www.swiftsure.org). The last week of May brings the **Harbour Festival,** a 10-day festival that features heritage walks, entertainment, and music (© 250/953-2033). In late June, the **Jazz Fest International** (© 250/388-4423; www.vicjazz.bc.ca) brings jazz, swing, bebop, fusion, and improv from around the world. The provincial capital celebrates **Canada Day** (July 1) with music, food, and fireworks. From mid-July to late August, the **Victoria Shakespeare Festival** (© 250/360-0234) presents performances around the Inner Harbour. In August, **First Peoples Festival** (© 250/384-3211) highlights the culture and heritage of the First Nations tribes with dances, performances, carving demonstrations, and heritage displays, while the **Victoria Dragon Boat Festival** (© 250/472-2628; www.victoriadragonboat.com) features 2 days of races on the Inner Harbour. The **Royal Victoria Marathon** (© 250/658-4520; www.royalvictoria marathon.com), an annual October race, attracts runners from around the world. In November, the **Great Canadian Beer Festival** (© 250/952-0360; www.gcbf.com) features the province's best microbreweries. And Victoria rings in the New Year with **First Night** (© 250/380-1211), a family-oriented New Year's Eve celebration with free acts at many downtown venues.

The **Akal Airporter shuttle bus** (© 250/386-2525) makes it to town in about half an hour; the fare is C$15 (US$12) one-way. A limited number of hotel courtesy buses also serve the airport. A cab ride to downtown costs about C$45 (US$34) plus tip. **Empress Cabs** and **Blue Bird Cabs** (see "Getting Around," below) make airport runs.

Several **car-rental firms** have desks at the airport, including Avis, Budget, Hertz, and National. (See "Getting Around," below.)

BY TRAIN   **VIA Rail** (© 888/842-7245 in Canada; www.viarail.ca) has a Vancouver Island sightseeing train, the *Malahat,* that travels once a day (in each direction) between Courtney and Victoria, with stops in Chemainus, Nanaimo (where you can connect to the mid-island ferry terminal), Parksville, or Qualicum Beach. The *Malahat* departs Victoria's **E&N Station,** 450 Pandora Ave. (near the Johnson St. Bridge) at 8:15am, arrives in Courtney at 12:50pm, departs Courtney in the other direction at 1:30pm, and arrives back in Victoria at 6pm.

BY BUS   The **Victoria Bus Depot** is at 700 Douglas St., behind The Fairmont Empress hotel. **Greyhound Bus Lines** (© 800/231-2222 or 604/482-8747; www. greyhound.com) has daily bus service to major Canadian cities and Seattle. **Pacific Coach Lines** (© 250/385-4411; www.pacificcoach.com) offers daily service to and from Vancouver. **Island Coach Lines** (© 250/385-4411; www.victoriatours.com) has daily scheduled runs to Nanaimo, Port Alberni, Campbell River, and Port Hardy.

BY FERRY   For information on travel by **ferry,** see "Getting There" in chapter 4. Exiting the Swartz Bay ferry terminal by **car,** you'll be on Highway 17 which leads directly to downtown where it becomes Blanshard Street, 3 blocks from the harbor.

VISITOR INFORMATION

TOURIST OFFICES & MAGAZINES   On the Inner Harbour's wharf, across from The Fairmont Empress hotel, is the **Tourism Victoria Visitor Info Centre,** 812 Wharf St. (© **250/953-2033;** www.tourismvictoria.com). If you didn't reserve a room before you arrived, you can go to this office or call its **reservations hot line** (© **800/663-3883** or 250/953-2033) for last-minute bookings at hotels, inns, and B&Bs.

For details on the after-dark scene, pick up a copy of *Monday* magazine (© **250/382-6188;** www.mondaymag.com/monday), free in cafes and record shops.

CITY LAYOUT

Victoria is on the southeastern tip of Vancouver Island, across from Washington state's snow-capped Olympic Peninsula. The areas of most interest to visitors, including the **downtown** and **Old Town,** are at the eastern edge of the **Inner Harbour.**

Victoria's central landmark is **The Fairmont Empress** hotel on Government Street, right across from the Inner Harbour wharf. The provincial **Legislative Buildings** and the **Royal BC Museum** are next-door.

Government Street goes through Victoria's main downtown shopping-and-dining district. **Douglas Street,** running parallel to Government Street, is the main business thoroughfare as well as the road to Nanaimo and the rest of the island.

2 Getting Around

Victoria is a great city for walking, and most of its points of interest are accessible in less than 30 minutes on foot. However, there are a number of transportation options.

BY BUS   The **Victoria Regional Transit System (B.C. Transit),** 520 Gorge Rd. (© **250/382-6161;** www.bctransit.com), operates 40 bus routes through greater Victoria as well as to nearby towns. Schedules, routes, fares, and passes are available at the Visitor Info Centre (see "Visitor Information," above).

BY FERRY   Crossing the harbors with the blue 12-passenger **Victoria Harbour Ferries** (© **250/708-0201;** www.victoriaharbourferry.com) is cheap and fun. The cost per hop is C$3.50 (US$2.80) for adults and C$1.50 (US$1.20) for children.

BY CAR   Rental agencies include **Avis,** 1001 Douglas St. (© **800/879-2847** or 250/386-8468); **Budget,** 757 Douglas St. (© **800/268-8900** or 250/953-5300); **Hertz,** 655 Douglas St. (© **800/263-0600** or 250/360-2822); and **National,** 767 Douglas St. (© **800/227-7368** or 250/386-1312). Metered **street parking** is readily available in the downtown area, and there are parking lots at **View Street** between Douglas and Blanshard, **Johnson Street** off Blanshard Street, **Yates Street** north of Bastion Square, **the Bay** on Fisgard at Blanshard, and at major downtown hotels.

BY BIKE   Biking is the easiest way to get around the downtown and beach areas. There are bike lanes throughout the city and paved paths at parks and beaches. You can rent bikes from **Cycle B.C.,** 747 Douglas St. (© **250/380-2453;** www.cyclebc.com).

BY TAXI   Drivers don't always stop on city streets for flag-downs, so call for a pickup from **Empress Cabs** (© **250/381-2222;** www.empresstaxi.com) or **Blue Bird Cabs** (© **250/382-4235;** www.taxicab.com).

BY PEDDLE-CAB   Cabbies with legs of steel will pedal you around for C$1 to C$2 (US80¢–US$1.60) per minute. Two- and four-seater cabs wait at the Inner Harbour, or call **Kabuki Kabs** (✆ 250/385-4243; www.kabukikabs.com) for 24-hour service.

FAST FACTS: Victoria

American Express The office is at 1213 Douglas St. (✆ 250/385-8731) and is open Monday through Friday 8:30am to 4:30pm and Saturday 10am to 4pm.

Emergencies Dial ✆ 911 for fire, police, ambulance, and poison control.

Hospitals Local hospitals include the **Royal Jubilee Hospital**, 1900 Fort St. (✆ 250/370-8000; emergency 250/370-8212) and the **Victoria General Hospital**, 1 Hospital Way (✆ 250/727-4212; emergency 250/727-4181).

Internet Access **Stain Internet Café**, 609 Yates St. (✆ 250/382-3352), is open 10am to 2pm. Closer to the Legislature, try the James Bay Coffee and Books, 143 Menzies St. (✆ 250/386-4700), open 7:30am to 10pm.

Pharmacies **Shopper's Drug Mart**, 1222 Douglas St. (✆ 250/381-4321; bus: 5 to View St.), is open Monday through Friday 7am to 8pm, Saturday 9am to 7pm, and Sunday 9am to 6pm.

Police Dial ✆ 911. The **Victoria City Police** can also be reached by calling ✆ 250/995-7654.

Post Office The **main post office** is at 714 Yates St. (✆ 250/953-1352).

---

3 Where to Stay

Most accommodations are in the Old Town or around the Inner Harbour. Reservations are absolutely essential May through September. If you have trouble finding a room, **Tourism Victoria** (✆ 800/663-3883 or 250/382-1131) can make reservations for you.

INNER HARBOUR
VERY EXPENSIVE

Delta Victoria Ocean Pointe Resort and Spa 🌟🌟 (Kids)   The OPR is a big, bright, modern hotel with a grand lobby, commanding views of downtown, the Legislature, the Fairmont Empress, and the busy harbor itself. The rooms here are nice and big, and so are the bathrooms. The decor, like the hotel itself, is a blend of contemporary and traditional; comfortable beds have duvets and fine linens. A few extra dollars buys a few extra perks, such as breakfast and evening hors d'oeuvres in the third-floor lounge. All guests have use of the big indoor pool, whirlpool, and a fully equipped gym with racquetball and tennis courts. Lots of guests come for the tranquil, Zen-like spa—one of the best in Victoria.

45 Songhees Rd., Victoria, BC V9A 6T3. ✆ 800/667-4677 or 250/360-2999. Fax 250/360-1041. www.deltahotels.com. 250 units. C$129–C$399 (US$103–US$319) double; C$350–$1,299 (US$280–US$1,039) suite. Children under 17 stay free in parent's room. AE, DC, MC, V. Underground valet parking C$12 (US$10). Bus: 24 to Colville. **Amenities:** 2 restaurants; bar; indoor pool; outdoor tennis courts; health club; full-service spa; Jacuzzi; sauna; concierge; 24-hr. business center; 24-hr. room service; in-room massage; babysitting; same-day dry cleaning; nonsmoking rooms; executive level rooms; rooms for those w/limited mobility. *In room:* A/C, TV/VCR w/pay movies, dataport w/high-speed Internet, minibar, coffeemaker, hair dryer, iron, safe, robes, complimentary newspaper.

The Fairmont Empress ✒ Francis Rattenbury's harborside creation is the most famous landmark on the waterfront. Think twice, however, before throwing down the plastic. Standard rooms cost more and offer less than you can find elsewhere in the city: small rooms with smaller bathrooms and little in the way of view. For some, the hotel's fabulous location and its first-class amenities—large pool, good weight room, luxurious Willow Stream spa, lounge, restaurant, tea lobby—make up for this lack of personal space. The 80 Deluxe rooms are bigger, with high ceilings and—for 60 of them anyway—a view of the harbor. The 12 Signature rooms are corner rooms. Top of the heap are the Fairmont Gold rooms with high arched ceilings, wide windows, king beds, a big desk, CD player, and—finally—bathrooms with soaker tubs and shower. If you can't afford a Fairmont Gold or a Signature room, just come here for afternoon tea.

721 Government St., Victoria, BC V8W 1W5. ☎ **800/441-1414** or 250/384-8111. Fax 250/381-4334. www.fairmont. com/empress. 477 units. C$179–C$569 (US$143–US$455) double; C$279–C$1,300 (US$223–US$1,040) suite. AE, DC, DISC, MC, V. Underground valet parking C$19 (US$15). Bus: 5. **Amenities:** 2 restaurants; bar/lounge; tea room; indoor pool; high-quality health club; spa; Jacuzzi; sauna; concierge; business center; shopping arcade; limited room service; in-room massage; babysitting; laundry service; same-day dry cleaning service; nonsmoking rooms; executive level room; rooms for those w/limited mobility. *In room:* TV w/pay movies, dataport w/high-speed Internet, hair dryer, iron.

Hotel Grand Pacific ✒✒✒ The Grand Pacific is more luxurious than the Delta Ocean Pointe and has rooms that are generally more spacious than those at the Fairmont Empress. Like those other two hotels, the Grand Pacific has its own spa; its health club is better than the others, and features a huge ozonated indoor pool. All rooms have balconies and are attractively and comfortably furnished. Standard rooms face the Olympic Mountains and Ogden Point or, for a bit more money, the Inner Harbour. Suites provide the best views, overlooking the harbor and the Empress. And the fabulous luxury suites feature huge bathrooms, fireplaces, and several balconies.

463 Belleville St., Victoria, BC V8V 1X3. ☎ **800/663-7550** or 250/386-0450. Fax 250/380-4473. www.hotelgrand pacific.com. 304 units. C$152–C$286 (US$122–US$229) double; C$212–C$320 (US$170–US$256) suite. Extra person C$30 (US$24). AE, DC, DISC, MC, V. Free self-parking; valet parking C$10 (US$8). Bus: 30 to Superior and Oswego sts. **Amenities:** 2 restaurants; cafe; bar; indoor pool; squash courts; superior health club; full-service spa; Jacuzzi; concierge; tour desk; business center; 24-hr. room service; massage; babysitting; laundry service; dry cleaning; nonsmoking rooms. *In room:* A/C, TV w/pay movies, dataport w/high-speed Internet, minibar, coffeemaker, hair dryer, iron, safe, robes.

EXPENSIVE

Andersen House Bed & Breakfast ✒✒ The art and furnishings in the Andersen House are drawn from the old British Empire and a good bit of the modern world beyond: hand-knotted Persian rugs, raku sculptures, large cubist-inspired oils, and carved-wood African masks. The sun-drenched Casablanca room on the top floor boasts Persian rugs, a four-poster queen-size bed, and a lovely boxed window seat. All rooms have private entrances and books, CD players, and CDs; all feature soaker tubs or two-person Jacuzzis. The Andersens also run the Baybreeze Manor (☎ **250/721-3930;** www.baybreezemanor.com), a farmhouse 15 minutes from downtown.

301 Kingston St., Victoria, BC V8V 1V5. ☎ **250/388-4565.** Fax 250/721-3938. www.andersenhouse.com. 4 units. June–Sept C$195–C$275 (US$156–US$220) double; Oct–May C$115–C$195 (US$92–US$156) double. Rates include breakfast. MC, V. Some free off-street parking. Bus: 30 to Superior and Oswego sts. Children under 12 not accepted. **Amenities:** Jacuzzi; nonsmoking rooms. *In room:* TV/VCR, coffeemaker, hair dryer, iron.

The Haterleigh Heritage Inn ✒ This exceptional B&B captures the essence of Victoria's romance with a combination of antique furniture, original stained-glass windows, and attentive personal service. The rooms feature high arched ceilings, large windows, sitting areas, and large bathrooms, some with hand-painted tiles and Jacuzzi tubs. A full gourmet breakfast with organic produce is served family style at 8:30am. There's also complimentary sherry in the drawing room each evening.

243 Kingston St., Victoria, BC V8V 1V5. ℂ 866/234-2244 or 250/384-9995. Fax 250/384-1935. www.haterleigh.com. 7 units. C$135–C$355 (US$108–US$284) double. Rates include full breakfast. MC, V. Free parking. Bus: 30 to Superior and Montreal sts. **Amenities:** Jacuzzi; dataport w/high-speed Internet; nonsmoking facility. *In room:* Hair dryer, robes.

Laurel Point Inn ✫✫✫   This art-filled, resort-style hotel reflects the elegant simplicity of Japanese artistic principals and is a refreshing change from the chintz and florals. The price is greater for rooms facing the Inner Harbour, though the Outer Harbour views are actually just as good. Rooms in the older north wing are nice enough, but the south wing is where you want to be: All rooms here are suites featuring blond wood with black marble accents, shoji-style sliding doors, Asian artworks, and spacious bathrooms with deep soaker tubs and floor-to-ceiling glassed-in showers.

680 Montreal St., Victoria, BC V8V 1Z8. ℂ 800/663-7667 or 250/386-8721. Fax 250/386-9547. www.laurelpoint.com. 200 units. C$114–C$279 (US$91–US$223) double; C$169–C$329 (US$135–US$263) suite. Children under 18 stay free in parent's room. Additional person C$15 (US$12). AE, DC, DISC, MC, V. Free valet parking. Bus: 30 to Montreal and Superior sts. Small dogs accepted for C$25 (US$20). **Amenities:** Restaurant; bar; indoor pool; complimentary access to YMCA facilities; Jacuzzi; concierge; business center; 24-hr. room service; massage; babysitting; same-day dry cleaning; nonsmoking facility; rooms for those w/limited mobility. *In room:* A/C, TV, dataport w/high-speed Internet, coffeemaker, hair dryer, iron, safe.

MODERATE

Admiral Inn *(Value) (Kids)*   Comfortable, clean rooms and reasonable rates attract travelers in search of a harbor view at a price that doesn't break the bank. The rooms are pleasant and comfortably furnished, a bit motel-like, with small bathrooms and balconies or terraces. More expensive rooms come with a kitchenette with small fridge and stove. The suites come with full kitchens. Some units can sleep up to six (on two double beds and a double sofa bed). The owners provide sightseeing advice as well as extras like free bicycles, free local calls, and an Internet terminal in the lobby.

257 Belleville St., Victoria, BC V8V 1X1. ℂ 888/823-6472 or ℂ/fax 250/388-6267. www.admiral.bc.ca. 29 units. C$99–C$219 (US$79–US$175) double; C$129–C$249 (US$103–C$199) suite. Extra person C$10 (US$8). Children under 12 stay free in parent's room. Rates include continental breakfast. AE, DC, MC, V. Free parking. Bus: 5 to Belleville and Government sts. **Amenities:** Complimentary bikes; coin laundry; dry cleaning; nonsmoking rooms; complimentary Internet access. *In room:* A/C, TV, kitchenette or kitchen in some, fridge, coffeemaker, hair dryer, iron.

Spinnakers Guest House ✫ *(Value)*   Spinnakers offers good accommodations at a moderate price in two separate buildings, under the same ownership as Spinnakers Brew Pub. The 1884 heritage building on Catherine Street is more luxurious with queen beds, lovely furnishings, in-room Jacuzzis (except for no. 4, which only has a shower), fireplaces, high ceilings, and lots of light. The three units on Mary Street are really self-contained apartments, perfect for a longer stay or for families. The drawbacks are a lack of personal service and the 10- to 20-minute walk to downtown.

308 Catherine St., Victoria, BC V9A 3S3. ℂ 877/838-2739 or 250/384-2739. Fax 250/384-3246. www.spinnakers.com. 10 units. C$129–C$249 (US$103–US$199) double. Rates include full breakfast at the brewpub. AE, DC, MC, V. Free parking. Bus: 24 to Catherine St. **Amenities:** Nonsmoking rooms.

DOWNTOWN & OLD TOWN
EXPENSIVE
Abigail's Hotel ✫✫   If you like small, personalized, bed-and-breakfasts, you'll enjoy this impeccably maintained property. Not all rooms come with all the frills, but

pampering is always an objective. In the original building, some of the 16 rooms are bright and sunny and beautifully furnished, with pedestal sinks and goose-down comforters. Others feature soaker tubs and double-sided fireplaces, so you can relax in the tub by the light of the fire. The six Celebration Suites in the Coach House addition are done in a mission style, have TVs (the other rooms don't), and four-poster beds. Abigail's chef prepares a multi-course gourmet breakfast.

906 McClure St., Victoria, BC V8V 3E7. © **866/347-5054** or 250/388-5363. Fax 250/388-7787. www.abigails hotel.com. 23 units. C$149–C$475 (US$119–US$380) double. Rates include full breakfast. AE, MC, V. Free parking. Bus: 1 to Cook and McClure sts. Children under 10 not accepted. **Amenities:** Concierge; dry cleaning; nonsmoking facility; complimentary afternoon tea. *In room:* TV (in some rooms), hair dryer, iron, Jacuzzi (in some rooms), bathrobes.

The Magnolia 𝒦𝒦 If you want a small downtown boutique hotel with personalized service and a taste of luxury at a reasonable price, this is a good choice. The small lobby, with a fireplace, chandelier, and overstuffed chairs, has a clubby Edwardian look. The room decor is classic, with high-quality linen, down duvets, and quality furnishings. The spacious marble bathrooms are perhaps the best in Victoria, with walk-in showers and deep soaker tubs. The windows extend floor to ceiling, letting in lots of light. The Diamond Suites feature a sitting room with fireplace. The hotel has a good restaurant, a fine microbrewery, and a full-service Aveda day spa.

623 Courtney St., Victoria, BC V8W 1B8. © **877/624-6654** or 250/381-0999. Fax 250/381-0988. www.magnolia hotel.com. 63 units. C$169–C$329 (US$135–US$263) double; C$289–C$499 (US$231–US$399) suite. Rates include continental breakfast. AE, DC, MC, V. Valet parking C$10 (US$8). Bus: 5 to Courtney St. **Amenities:** Restaurant; bar; access to nearby health club; spa; concierge; salon; limited room service; massage; laundry service; same-day dry cleaning; executive rooms. *In room:* A/C, TV w/pay movies, dataport w/high-speed Internet, minibar, fridge, coffeemaker, hair dryer, iron, bathrobes, complimentary newspaper.

MODERATE

Isabella's Guest Suites 𝒦 *Finds* Two suites above Willie's Bakery & Cafe provide affordable, fun, and stylish accommodation in the heart of the city. Bright colors, upscale rustic furniture, high ceilings, and large windows make this a great home base for exploring Victoria. The front suite is a large, elegantly furnished studio with a bed/sitting room that opens into a dining room and full kitchen. The second unit, a one-bedroom suite, overlooks the alley and patio of Il Terrazzo Ristorante (see "Where to Dine," below). The bathroom has a lovely claw-foot tub, breakfast is included and served at the bakery, parking is free, and you have your own front door.

537 Johnson St., Victoria, BC V8W 1M2. © **250/595-3815.** Fax 250/381-8415. www.isabellasbb.com. 2 units. C$130–C$150 (US$104–US$120) double. Rates include continental breakfast. Free parking. Bus: 5. *In room:* TV, full kitchen, hair dryer, iron.

Swans Suite Hotel 𝒦𝒦 *Kids* This hotel, restaurant, brewpub, and nightclub all in one is one of Old Town's best-loved buildings. Swans is small, friendly, and charming with quirky layouts in the suites. All have fully equipped kitchens, dining areas, living rooms, and queen-size beds. The two-bedroom suites are like little town houses, accommodating up to six comfortably. The huge penthouse suite features fabulous Pacific Northwest artwork and is perfect for a special occasion. The deck offers city and harbor views, best appreciated from the rooftop hot tub.

506 Pandora St., Victoria, BC V8W 1N6. © **800/668-7926** or 250/361-3310. Fax 250/361-3491. www.swanshotel.com. 30 units. C$185–C$205 (US$148–US$164) studio; C$225–C$369 (US$180–US$295) suite. Children under 12 stay free in parent's room. AE, DC, DISC, MC, V. Parking C$12 (US$9.60). Bus: 23 or 24 to Pandora Ave. **Amenities:** Restaurant;

brewpub; limited room service; laundry service; same-day dry cleaning; nonsmoking facility. *In room:* TV, dataport w/high-speed Internet, kitchen, coffeemaker, hair dryer, iron.

INEXPENSIVE

Victoria International Youth Hostel   This hostel in the heart of Old Town has two kitchens (stocked with utensils), a dining room, TV lounge with VCR, game room, library, laundry facilities, indoor bike lockup, 24-hour security, and hot showers. The dorms are on the large side (16 to a room), and a couple of family rooms are available.

516 Yates St., Victoria, BC V8W 1K8. © 250/385-4511. Fax 250/385-3232. www.hihostels.ca. 104 beds. International Youth Hostel members C$20 (US$16); nonmembers C$21 (US$17). MC, V. Parking on street. Bus: 70 from Swartz Bay ferry terminal. **Amenities:** Game room; tour desk; laundry facilities; room for those w/limited mobility.

OUTSIDE THE CENTRAL AREA
EXPENSIVE

Brentwood Bay Lodge & Spa ★★★ *(Finds)*   Awarded membership in the prestigious Small Luxury Hotels of the World, this contemporary lodge offers the best of everything, including a fabulous spa, boat shuttle to Butchart Gardens, and eco-adventures. The rooms are gorgeous, with handcrafted furnishings, fireplaces, luxurious bathrooms with soaker tubs and body massage showers, balconies, and king beds fitted with the highest quality Italian linen. The fine dining room, offers seasonal menus focusing on foraged and organic local ingredients, plus a wine-tasting bar with a selection of fine wines from the resort's award-winning cellar. You can also dine in the casual pub. The hotel has its own marina and is a licensed PADI dive center.

849 Verdier Ave. (on Brentwood Bay), Victoria, BC V8M 1C5. © 888/544-2079 or 250/544-2079. Fax 250/544-2069. www.brentwoodbaylodge.com. 33 units. C$295–C$495 (US$236–US$396) double; C$345–C$845 (US$276–US$676) suite. Rates include breakfast. AE, DC, MC, V. Free parking. Take Pat Bay Hwy. north to Keating Crossroads, turn left (west) to Saanich Rd., turn right (south) to Verdier Ave. **Amenities:** Restaurant; pub; cafe; heated outdoor pool; full-service spa; Jacuzzi; concierge; 24-hr. room service; laundry; dry cleaning; nonsmoking facility. *In room:* A/C, TV/DVD, dataport w/high-speed Internet, minibar, coffeemaker, hair dryer, iron, bathrobes, slippers, fireplaces, hot tubs (in suites), complimentary newspaper, entertainment system.

MODERATE

The Boathouse ★ *(Finds)*   It's a short row (or a 25-min. walk) to Butchart Gardens from this secluded red cottage in Brentwood Bay. The cottage is at the end of a very long flight of stairs behind the owner's home with a stunning view all the way up Finlayson Arm. Toilet and shower facilities are in a separate bathhouse, 17 steps back uphill. All the makings for a delicious continental breakfast are provided in the evening, plus free coffee and newspaper delivery. Just below the boathouse is a floating dock, moored to which is a small dinghy reserved for guest use.

746 Sea Dr., Brentwood Bay, Victoria, BC V8M 1B1. © 866/654-9370 or 250/652-9370. http://members.shaw.ca/boathouse. 1 unit. C$215 (US$172) double with continental breakfast; C$195 (US$146) double without breakfast. 2-night minimum. AE, MC, V. Free parking. Closed Oct–Mar. Bus: 75 to Wallace Dr. and Benvenuto Ave. No children under 18. *In room:* Fridge, coffeemaker, hair dryer, iron.

INEXPENSIVE

University of Victoria Housing, Food, and Conference Services *(Value)*   One of the best deals going (when classes aren't in session), all rooms have single or twin beds and basic furnishings. There are bathrooms, pay phones, and TV lounges on every floor; and linens, towels, and soap are provided. The disadvantage is that the campus is about a half-hour drive away from the city center.

P.O. Box 1700, Sinclair at Finerty Rd., Victoria, BC V8W 2Y2. (✆ **250/721-8395**. Fax 250/721-8930. www.hfcs.uvic.ca. 898 units. May–Aug C$45 (US$36) single; C$56 (US$45) twin; C$160 (US$128) suite (sleeps 4 people). Rates include full breakfast and taxes. MC, V. Parking C$5 (US$4). Closed Sept–Apr. Bus: 4 or 14 to University of Victoria. **Amenities:** Indoor pool; access to athletic facilities for an extra C$5 (US$3.75) per day; coin laundry; nonsmoking rooms.

4 Where to Dine

Victoria's dining scene offers a mix of cuisine from around the world. Head inland from Wharf Street where the ranks of tourists thin and quality jumps tremendously.

THE INNER HARBOUR & THE OLD TOWN
EXPENSIVE

The Blue Crab Bar and Grill ✺✺ SEAFOOD   While other top-end restaurants in town have moved to sourcing all or nearly all ingredients locally, the Crab supplies itself from the world—scallops from Alaska, lamb from New Zealand, mahimahi from Hawaii, duck from the Fraser Valley, and halibut from B.C. The award-winning wine list (*Wine Spectator* award of excellence in 2003 and 2004) features mid-range and top-end vintages, drawn mostly from B.C., Washington, and California. One of the best bets for seafood, the Blue Crab also has a killer view.

146 Kingston St., in the Coast Hotel. (✆ **250/480-1999**. Reservations recommended. Main courses C$24–C$35 (US$19–US$28). AE, DC, MC, V. Daily 6:30am–10:30pm (dinner from 5pm). Bus: 30 to Erie St. or harbor miniferry to Coast Hotel.

Brasserie L'Ecole ✺✺ FRENCH   This small, pleasant room in the middle of Chinatown offers simple country French cooking at reasonable prices. L'Ecole's menu changes daily, depending on what comes in fresh from Victoria's hinterland farms. Preparation is simple, no big reductions or complicated *jus,* just shellfish, local fish, meats with red wine sauces, and fresh vegetables with vinaigrettes. L'Ecole has won a bevy of awards in its few short years on the scene.

1715 Government St. (✆ **250/475-6262**. www.lecole.ca. Reservations recommended. Main courses C$18 (US$14). AE, MC, V. Tues–Sat 5:30–11pm.

Moments Taking Afternoon Tea

Okay, so it's expensive and touristy. But if you want the experience, you may as well go for the best. **The Fairmont Empress** ✺✺, 721 Government St. ((✆ **250/384-8111**), serves tea in a busy and beautifully ornate room at the hotel. Prices run from C$26 to C$52 (US$21–US$42). For that, you'll be pampered with berries and cream; smoked salmon, cucumber, and carrot and ginger sandwiches; scones, preserves, and thick Jersey cream. There are four seatings a day: 12:30, 2, 2:30, and 5pm; reservations are essential in the summer.

Just as historic is **Point Ellice House,** 2616 Pleasant St. ((✆ **250/380-6506**). Tea costs C$17 (US$14) and includes a tour of the mansion, plus a game of croquet. Open 10am to 4pm (tea served 11am–3pm) April 1 through Labour Day.

"Afternoon Tea at the Gardens," at the **Butchart Gardens Dining Room Restaurant** ✺✺, 800 Benvenuto Ave. ((✆ **250/652-4422;** bus: 75), is a memorable experience. Savor this fine tradition for C$22 to C$29 (US$18–US$23) per person, daily noon to 5pm April 1 through Labor Day.

Camille's ✿✿ PACIFIC NORTHWEST   The most romantic of Victoria's restaurants, Camille's decor contrasts white linen with century-old exposed brick, stained-glass lamps, and antique books. The ever-changing menu uses only the freshest local ingredients and displays a love for cheeky invention: think duck confit salad with slices of mandarin orange on a bed of baby greens or citrus and coffee marinated pork tenderloin. A delicate roasted rack of lamb is also a perennial specialty. The reasonable and extensive wine list comes with liner notes that are amusing and informative.

45 Bastion Sq. ✆ 250/381-3433. www.camillesrestaurant.com. Reservations recommended. Main courses C$22–C$34 (US$18–US$27). AE, MC, V. Daily 5:30–10pm.

MODERATE

Canoe ✿ PUB/PACIFIC NORTHWEST   Casual Canoe—one of the loveliest and liveliest brewpub restaurants in Victoria, with a fabulous outdoor patio overlooking the harbor—offers intriguing variations on standard pub fare, including thin-crust pizzas with grilled lamb or chile prawns, and a Brewmaster's Plate with smoked oysters, chorizo sausage, and marinated grilled vegetables. Or dine upstairs on finer fare, such as crisp-skinned wild salmon; premium strip loin steak; penne pasta with wild mushrooms; or tagine, a North African stew.

450 Swift St. ✆ 250/361-1940. www.canoebrewpub.com. Reservations recommended for weekend dinner and Sun brunch. Main courses C$11–C$32 (US$9–US$26); pub fare and bar snacks C$4–C$15 (US$3.25–US$12). AE, MC, V. Daily 11am–midnight.

Herald Street Caffe ✿ PACIFIC NORTHWEST   The cuisine at Herald Street Caffe, a converted old warehouse, is sophisticated without going too far over the top. Appetizers may include crab cakes with cilantro-lime pesto and roasted corn and tomato salsa. Portions are generous with entrees such as free-range chicken, duck, and lamb dishes, and several pastas. For dessert, don't miss the Boca Negra, a chocolate cake with rich chocolate bourbon sauce and fresh raspberries. The Caffe offers 20 martinis, and for oenophiles, French, Canadian, and local B.C. wines.

546 Herald St. ✆ 250/381-1441. Reservations required. Main courses C$17–C$39 (US$14–US$31). AE, DC, MC, V. Daily 5–10pm; Sat–Sun brunch 11am–3pm. Bus: 5.

Il Terrazzo Ristorante ✿ ITALIAN   This charming spot in a converted heritage building is always a contender for Victoria's best Italian. The food hails from northern Italy—wood-oven-roasted meats and pizzas as well as homemade pastas. But there's also an emphasis on fresh produce and local seafood, with appetizers such as thinly sliced smoked tuna over fresh arugula with horseradish dressing and entrees such as spaghetti with clams in a spicy sauce of white wine, garlic, chiles, and tomatoes. The mood is bustling and upbeat; there's an atmospheric courtyard furnished with flowers, marble tables, wrought-iron chairs, and heaters. That, a good chianti, and a piping hot *pizzetta* are enough to keep even the fiercest chill at bay.

555 Johnson St., off Waddington Alley. ✆ 250/361-0028. www.ilterrazzo.com. Reservations recommended. Main courses C$14–C$37 (US$11–US$30). AE, MC, V. Mon–Sat 11:30am–3pm (Oct–Apr no lunch on Sat); daily 5–10pm. Bus: 5.

The Tapa Bar ✿ *Finds* TAPAS   The perfect meal for the commitment-shy, tapas are small and flavorful plates that you combine together to make a meal. Tapas to be sampled in this warm and welcoming spot include fried calamari, palm hearts, chicken chipotle, and grilled portobello mushrooms. Whatever else you order, however, don't pass up on the *gambas al ajillo*—shrimp in a rich broth of garlic. The martini list is long enough to keep the place packed till the witching hour.

620 Trounce Alley. ℭ **250/383-0013**. Tapas plates C$7–C$15 (US$5.60–US$12). AE, MC, V. Mon–Thurs 11:30am–11pm; Fri–Sat 11:30am–midnight; Sun 11am–10pm.

Zambri's ℛ *Finds* ITALIAN   This little deli-restaurant in a strip mall has earned accolades for its honest and fresh Italian cuisine served in a no-nonsense style. The lunch menu, served cafeteria style, includes five daily pasta specials and a handful of entrees such as fresh rockfish or salmon. In the evenings, the atmosphere is slightly more formal with table service and a regularly changing a la carte menu. Menu items veer from penne with sausage and tomato to pasta with chicken liver pâté or peas and Gorgonzola. Many diners come for the three-course dinner (C$38/US$30).

110–911 Yates St. ℭ **250/360-1171**. Reservations not accepted. Lunch C$6–C$15 (US$4.80–US$12); dinner C$10–C$25 (US$8–US$20). MC, V. Tues–Sat 11:30am–3pm and 5–9pm.

INEXPENSIVE
J&J Wonton Noodle House ℛ *Finds* CHINESE   You won't find better noodles anywhere in Victoria. The kitchen is glassed in, so you can watch the chefs spinning out noodles and whisking soups through woks into bowls. Lunch specials are good and cheap, so expect a line of locals at the door. If you miss the specials, soups, noodles, and other dishes are also quick, delicious, and inexpensive.

1012 Fort St. ℭ **250/383-0680**. Main courses C$11–C$16 (US$8.80–US$13); lunch specials C$6–C$13 (US$4.80–US$10). MC, V. Tues–Sat 11am–2pm and 4:30–8:30pm. Bus: 5.

rebar ℛℛ *Kids* VEGETARIAN   Rejoice: rebar is the city's premier purveyor of veggie comfort food. Not only tasty, but fun, rebar is a great spot to take the kids for brunch or breakfast. The room is bright and funky, and the service is friendly and casual. The food tends toward the simple and wholesome, including quesadillas, omelets, and crisp salads. The over 80 blends of juices are the crown jewels.

50 Bastion Sq. ℭ **250/361-9223**. www.rebarmodernfood.com. Main courses C$7.50–C$16 (US$6–US$13). AE, MC, V. Mon–Thurs 8:30am–9pm; Fri–Sat 8:30am–10pm; Sun 8:30am–3:30pm. Reduced hours in the winter. Bus: 5.

5 Exploring Victoria
THE TOP ATTRACTIONS
British Columbia Aviation Museum ℛ   This must for plane buffs is crammed with a score of original, rebuilt, and replica airplanes, from the first Canadian-designed craft ever to fly, to more modern water bombers and helicopters.

1910 Norseman Rd., Sidney (adjacent to Victoria International Airport). ℭ **250/655-3300**. www.bcam.net. Admission C$7 (US$5.60) adults, C$5 (US$4) seniors, C$3 (US$2.40) students, free for children under 12. Summer daily 10am–4pm; winter daily 11am–3pm. Closed Dec 25. Bus: Airport.

Butchart Gardens ℛℛℛ   The Butcharts transformed their lovely house and many gardens into a wonderfully resplendent attraction. Evenings in summer, the gardens are beautifully illuminated with softly colored lights, and musical entertainment is provided. You can even watch fireworks displays on Saturdays in July and August. In addition, a very good lunch, dinner, and afternoon tea are offered.

800 Benvenuto Ave., Brentwood Bay. ℭ **866/652-4422** or 250/652-4422; dining reservations 250/652-8222. www. butchartgardens.com. Admission June 15–Sept C$22 (US$18) adults, C$11 (US$9) youths 13–17, C$2.50 (US$2) children 5–12, free for children under 5; admission price reduced in spring, fall, and winter. Gates open daily 9am–sundown (call for seasonal closing time); visitors can remain in gardens for 1 hr. after gate closes. Bus: 75 or the Gray Line shuttle from the Victoria Bus Station, C$4 (US$3.20) one-way. Shuttle departure times vary seasonally; call ℭ **250/388-5248** for exact times. Take Blanshard St. (Hwy. 17) north toward the ferry terminal in Saanich, then turn

left on Keating Crossroads, which leads directly to the gardens—about 20 min. from downtown Victoria; follow the trail of billboards.

Craigdarroch Castle ✦ In the highlands above Oak Bay, Robert Dunsmuir's home is a stunner. The four-story castle is filled with opulent Victorian splendor—detailed woodwork, Persian carpets, stained-glass windows, paintings, and sculptures. The castle also hosts events, including theater performances, concerts, and dinner tours.

1050 Joan Crescent (off Fort St.). © 250/592-5323. www.craigdarrochcastle.com. Admission C$10 (US$8) adults, C$6.50 (US$5.20) students, C$3.50 (US$2.80) children 5–12, children under 5 free. June 15 to Labour Day daily 9am–7pm; Labour Day to June 14 daily 10am–4:30pm. Closed Dec 25, 26, and Jan 1. Bus: 11 to Joan Crescent. Take Fort St. out of downtown, just past Cook, and turn right onto Joan.

Fort Rodd Hill & Fisgard Lighthouse National Historic Site The light has long been automated, but exhibits recount stories of its keepers, their house, and the terrible shipwrecks that gave this coastline its ominous moniker "the graveyard of the Pacific." Adjoining the lighthouse, **Fort Rodd Hill** is a preserved 1890s coastal artillery fort that still sports camouflaged searchlights, underground magazines, and its original guns.

603 Fort Rodd Hill Rd. © 250/478-5849. Admission C$4 (US$3.20) adults, C$3 (US$2.40) seniors, C$2 (US$1.60) children 6–16, C$10 (US$8) families, free for children under 6. Mar–Oct daily 10am–5:30pm; Nov–Feb daily 9am–4:30pm. No public transit.

Maritime Museum of British Columbia Displays illustrate maritime history, from the early explorers to the fur trading and whaling era to the days of grand ocean liners and military conflict. There's an impressive collection of ship models and paraphernalia—uniforms, weapons, gear—along with photographs and journals.

28 Bastion Sq. © 250/385-4222. www.mmbc.bc.ca. Admission C$8 (US$6.40) adults, C$5 (US$4) seniors, C$3 (US$2.40) students, C$2 (US$1.60) children 6–11, C$20 (US$16) families, free for children under 6. Daily 9:30am–4:30pm. Closed Dec 25. Bus: 5 to View St.

Miniature World _Kids_ It sounds cheesy, but Miniature World is actually kinda cool, with re-creations of battle scenes, 18th-century dress balls, a CPR railway running across a miniature Canada, a circus, and scenes from Mother Goose and Charles Dickens stories. And most of these displays do something: The train moves at the punch of a button and the circus rides whirl around and light up as simulated darkness falls.

649 Humboldt St. © 250/385-9731. www.miniatureworld.com. Admission C$9 (US$7.20) adults, C$8 (US$6.40) youths, C$7 (US$5.60) children, free for children under 4. Summer daily 8:30am–9pm; winter daily 9am–5pm. Bus: 5, 27, 28, or 30.

Pacific Undersea Gardens _Kids_ Locals aren't keen on this conspicuous structure, but your kids may enjoy it. Sharks, eels, poisonous stonefish, sea anemones, starfish, sturgeon, salmon, and a remarkably photogenic huge octopus (reputedly the largest in captivity) cruise these protected waters. There's an hourly underwater show in which a diver-naturalist catches and explains a variety of the undersea fauna.

490 Belleville St. © 250/382-5717. www.pacificunderseagardens.com. Admission C$8.50 (US$6.80) adults, C$7.50 (US$6) seniors, C$6 (US$4.80) youths 12–17, C$4.50 (US$3.60) children 5–11, free for children under 5. Sept–Apr daily 9:30am–5pm; May–June daily 9:30am–6pm; June–Sept daily 9am–8:30pm; Jan–Feb closed Tue–Wed. Bus: 5, 27, 28, or 30.

Parliament Buildings (Provincial Legislature) ✦ Built for nearly C$1 million, these buildings are an architectural gem. The 40-minute tour is worth it to see the fine mosaics, marble, woodwork, and stained glass. And if you see a harried-looking man surrounded by a pack of minicam crews, it's likely just another B.C. premier getting hounded out of office by the aggressive media: Politics is a blood sport in B.C.

501 Belleville St. $\mathbb{C}$ 250/387-3046. www.protocol.gov.bc.ca. Free admission. Late May to Labour Day daily 9am–5pm; Sept to late May Mon–Fri 9am–5pm. Tours offered every 20 min. in summer (up to 23 times a day). In winter hours call ahead for the tour schedules as times vary due to school group bookings. No tours noon–1pm.

Royal British Columbia Museum $\mathcal{R}\mathcal{R}\mathcal{R}$ *Kids*   One of the world's best regional museums, the Royal B.C. has a mandate to present the land and the people of coastal British Columbia. The **Natural History Gallery** showcases the coastal flora, fauna, and geography from the Ice Age to the present. The **Modern History Gallery** presents the recent past, including historically faithful re-creations of Victoria's downtown and Chinatown, and the **First Peoples Gallery** is an incredible showpiece of First Nations art and culture. The museum also has an **IMAX theater.** Be sure to stop by **Thunderbird Park,** beside the museum, where Natives carve totem poles.

675 Belleville St. $\mathbb{C}$ 888/447-7977 or 250/387-3701. www.royalbcmuseum.bc.ca. Admission C$13 (US$10) adults, C$8.70 (US$7) seniors/students/youths, C$34 (US$27) families, children under 6 free. Combination museum and Imax C$21 (US$17) adults, C$17 (US$14) seniors/youths, C$18 (US$15) students. Daily 9am–5pm; Imax daily 9am–8pm. Closed Dec 25 and Jan 1. Bus: 5, 28, or 30.

Victoria Butterfly Gardens $\mathcal{R}$ *Kids*   Hundreds of exotic colorful butterflies flutter freely through this lush tropical greenhouse. Species range from the tiny Central American Julia (small and bright orange) to the Southeast Asian Giant Atlas Moth (brown and red, with a wingspan of about a foot). Helpful biologists are on hand, and there's a display where you can see the beautiful creatures emerge from their cocoons.

1461 Benvenuto Ave. (P.O. Box 190), Brentwood Bay. $\mathbb{C}$ 877/722-0272 or 250/652-3822. www.butterflygardens.com. Admission C$9.50 (US$7.60) adults, C$8.50 (US$6.80) students and seniors, C$5.50 (US$4.40) children 5–12, free for children under 5. Mar 1–May 13 and Oct daily 9:30am–4:30pm; May 14–Sept 30 daily 9am–5:30pm. Closed Nov–Feb. Bus: 75.

ARCHITECTURAL HIGHLIGHTS & HISTORIC HOMES

Perhaps the most intriguing downtown edifice isn't a building at all but a work of art. The walls of **Fort Victoria,** which once covered much of downtown, have been demarcated in the sidewalk with bricks bearing the names of original settlers and fur traders. Look in the sidewalk on Government Street at the corner of Fort Street.

Most of the retail establishments in Victoria's Old Town area are housed in 19th-century shipping warehouses that have been carefully restored. You can take a **self-guided tour** of these buildings, most of which were erected between the 1870s and 1890s and whose history is recounted on easy-to-read outdoor plaques.

Some of the British immigrants built magnificent estates and mansions. Don't miss architect Francis Rattenbury's crowning turn-of-the-20th-century achievements—the provincial **Parliament Buildings,** 501 Belleville St. (completed in 1898), and the opulent **Fairmont Empress Hotel,** 721 Government St. (completed in 1908).

Helmcken House, 610 Elliot St. Sq. ($\mathbb{C}$ **250/361-0021**), is the oldest house in B.C. on its original site. Originally a three-room log cabin, the house still contains its original furnishings, imported from England.

Emily Carr House $\mathcal{R}$, 207 Government St. ($\mathbb{C}$ **250/383-5843**), is the birthplace of painter/writer Emily Carr. Restored rooms have been hung with reproductions of her art or quotes from her writings.

Point Ellice House $\mathcal{R}$, 2616 Pleasant St. ($\mathbb{C}$ **250/380-6506**), the summer gathering place for Victoria's Victorian elite, is now open to the general public.

PARKS & GARDENS

The 62-hectare (154-acre) **Beacon Hill Park** stretches from Southgate Street to Dallas Road between Douglas and Cook streets. Hike up Beacon Hill to get a clear view of the Strait of Georgia, Haro Strait, and Washington's Olympic Mountains. The children's farm, aviary, tennis courts, bowling and putting greens, cricket pitch, wading pool, playground, and picnic area make this a wonderful place to spend time with the family.

Government House, the official residence of the Lieutenant Governor, is at 1401 Rockland Ave. in the Fairfield district. The house itself is closed to the public, but the formal gardens are open and well worth a wander. The rose garden is sumptuous.

Abkhazi Garden ✸, 1964 Fairfield Rd. (© **250/598-8096;** www.conservancy. bc.ca), is a jewel created by Prince and Princess Nicholas Abkhazi. The dramatic site contains quiet woodland, rocky slopes, and gorgeous vistas. Hours are 1 to 5pm Wednesday through Sunday in April to September. Admission is C$7.50 (US$6) adults, C$5 (US$4) seniors and students, and C$15 (US$12) for a family.

Just outside downtown, **Mount Douglas Park** offers great views of the area, several hiking trails, and—down at the waterline—a picnic/play area with a trail leading to a good walking beach. Forty-five minutes southwest of town, **East Sooke Park** ✸ is a 1,400-hectare (3,458-acre) microcosm of the West Coast wilderness: jagged seacoast, Native petroglyphs, and hiking trails up to a 270m (886-ft.) hilltop.

ORGANIZED TOURS

BUS TOURS   Gray Line of Victoria, 700 Douglas St. (© **250/388-5248;** www.gray linewest.com), conducts a number of tours of Victoria and the Butchart Gardens. The 1½-hour "Grand City Drive" costs C$19 (US$15) for adults and C$9.50 (US$7.60) for children ages 6 to 12.

SPECIALTY TOURS   Victoria Harbour Ferries, 922 Old Esquimalt Rd. (© **250/ 708-0201**), offers a terrific 45-minute **Inner and Outer Harbour tour** ✸ for C$14 (US$11) for adults and C$7 (US$5.60) for children under 12. A 50-minute **Gorge Tour** ✸ takes you to the gorge opposite the Johnson Street Bridge, where tidal falls reverse with each change of the tide. The Gorge Tour costs C$16 (US$13) for adults, C$14 (US$11) for seniors, and C$8 (US$6.40) for children.

Heritage Tours and Daimler Limousine Service, 713 Bexhill Rd. (© **250/474- 4332**), guides you through the city, Butchart Gardens, and Craigdarroch Castle in a six-passenger British Daimler limousine for C$65 (US$52) per hour per vehicle.

Tallyho Horse-Drawn Tours, 2044 Milton St. (© **250/383-5067;** www.tallyho tours.com), has conducted tours of Victoria in horse-drawn carriages and trolleys since 1903. Fares are C$15 (US$12) for adults, C$9 (US$7.20) for students, C$7 (US$5.60) for children 17 and under.

To get a bird's-eye view of Victoria, take a 30-minute tour with **Harbour Air Seaplanes,** 1234 Wharf St. (© **800/665-0212** or 250/384-2215; www.harbour-air.com). Rates are C$99 (US$79) per person or C$79 (US$63) if there are four or more in your party; C$54 (US$43) for children under 12.

WALKING TOURS   Victoria Bobby Walking Tours (© **250/995-0233;** www.walkvictoria.com) offers a leisurely story-filled walk around Old Town with a former English bobby as guide. Tours depart at 11am daily, May through September 15, from the Visitor Centre on the Inner Harbour; cost is C$15 (US$12) per person.

The **Old Cemetery Society of Victoria** (℗ 250/598-8870; www.oldcem.bc.ca) runs cemetery tours, such as the popular **Lantern Tours of the Old Burying Ground** ✶ in July and August. Cost is C$10 (US$7.20) per adult, C$25 (US$18) per family.

Discover the Past (℗ 250/384-6698; www.discoverthepast.com) organizes interesting year-round walks; in the summer, **Ghostly Walks** explores the haunted Old Town, Chinatown, and historic waterfront; check the website for rates and other walks.

Walkabout Historical Tours (℗ 250/592-9255; www.walkabouts.ca) covers the Fairmont Empress, Victoria's Chinatown, Antique Row, and Old Town Victoria.

Victoria Heritage Foundation (℗ 250/383-4546; vhf@pinc.com), offers the excellent *James Bay Heritage Walking Tour,* available at the Visitor Info Centre.

6 Outdoor Pursuits

Biking, eco-touring, skiing, parasailing, kayaking, canoeing, fishing, diving, and hiking are all popular in Victoria. **Sports Rent,** 611 Discovery St. (℗ 250/385-7368; www.sportsrentbc.com), meets all your equipment and watersports rental needs.

BIKING   The 13km (8-mile) **Scenic Marine Drive** bike path begins at Dallas Road and Douglas Street, at the base of Beacon Hill Park. The paved path follows the walkway along the beaches before winding up through the residential district on Beach Drive. The **Inner Harbour pedestrian path** has a bike lane for cyclists who want to take a leisurely ride around the entire city seawall. The new **Galloping Goose Trail** runs from Victoria west through Colwood and Sooke all the way up to Leechtown.

Bikes and child trailers are available at **Cycle BC Rentals,** 747 Douglas St. (year-round) or 950 Wharf St. (May–Oct). Call ℗ 250/885-2453 or go to www.cyclebc.ca.

BIRDING   The **Victoria Natural History Society** (℗ 250/479-2054 for events) runs regular weekend birding excursions.

BOATING   Kayaks, canoes, rowboats, and powerboats are available from **Great Pacific Adventures,** 811 Wharf St. (℗ 877/733-6722 or 250/386-2277; www.great pacificadventures.com).

CANOEING & KAYAKING   **Ocean River Sports,** 1437 Store St., Victoria, BC V8W 3J6 (℗ 800/909-4233 or 250/381-4233; www.oceanriver.com), can equip you with everything from kayaks to life jackets, tents, and camping gear. Costs for a single kayak range from C$14 (US$10) per hour to C$42 (US$30) per day. The company also offers numerous **guided tours** ✶ of the Gulf Islands and the B.C. west coast.

Blackfish Wilderness Expeditions (℗ 250/216-2389; www.blackfishwilderness. com) offers a kayak/boat/hike combo where you get a head start by boat to the protected waters of the Discovery Islands. After you explore the coves and inlets and eat a picnic lunch, a naturalist takes you on a hike around one of the islands. Day tours start at C$69 (US$50) per person.

FISHING   Saltwater fishing's the thing and **Adam's Fishing Charters** (℗ 250/370-2326; www.adamsfishingcharters.com) and the **Marine Adventure Centre** (℗ 250/995-2211) are good places to start. You need a nonresident fishing license, which is available at tackle shops for C$14 (US$11) for 1 day for nonresidents and C$12 (US$9.60) for B.C. residents. **Robinson's Sporting Goods Ltd.,** 1307 Broad St. (℗ 250/385-3429), is a reliable source for information, recommendations, lures, licenses, and gear. For the latest fishing hot spots and recommendations on tackle and lures, check out **www.sportfishingbc.com.**

GOLFING   The **Cedar Hill Municipal Golf Course,** 1400 Derby Rd. (✆ **250/ 595-3103**), is an 18-hole public course 3km (2 miles) from downtown Victoria; day-time greens fees are C$38 (US$30) and twilight fees (after 3pm) are C$23 (US$18). The **Cordova Bay Golf Course,** 5333 Cordova Bay Rd. (✆ **250/658-4075;** www. cordovabaygolf.com), features 66 sand traps and some tight fairways. Greens fees are C$60 to C$65 (US$48–$52); the twilight fee is C$55 (US$44). The **Olympic View Golf Club,** 643 Latoria Rd. (✆ **250/474-3673**), is one of the top 35 golf courses in Canada. Amid 12 lakes and a pair of waterfalls, this 18-hole, 6,414-yard course is open daily year-round. Fees are C$65 to C$75 (US$52–US$60) and twilight fees are C$30 to C$40 (US$24–US$32). Call **Last Minute Golf Hot Line** at ✆ **800/ 684-6344** for substantial discounts. **Island Links Hot Line** (✆ **866/266-GOLF**) acts as a booking agent for courses around Vancouver Island and will provide trans-portation from your hotel to the course.

HIKING   Island Adventure Tours (✆ **866/812-7103;** www.islandadventuretours. com) offers a half-day guided **Rainforest Walk** for C$39 (US$31) or C$95 (US$76). For the deluxe Juan de Fuca experience, sign-up for a 3-day catered backpacking **trip along this rugged West Coast trail** for C$499 (US$399).

Coastal Connections Interpretive Nature Hikes, 1027 Roslyn Rd. (✆ **250/480-9560**), offers naturalist-guided tours for groups of 10 or more. A 6-hour rainforest hike, including a gourmet picnic lunch, provides a wonderful introduction to this unique ecosystem. The hike costs C$79 (US$63) per person.

PARAGLIDING   A new company, **Vancouver Island Paragliding** (✆ **250/886-4165;** www.viparagliding.com), offers tandem paraglide flights. The pilot steers, you hang in and enjoy the adrenaline rush.

WATERSPORTS   The **Crystal Pool & Fitness Centre,** 2275 Quadra St. (✆ **250/ 361-0732**), with lap pool; children's pool; diving pool; sauna; whirlpool; and steam, weight, and aerobics rooms is Victoria's main aquatic facility. **Beaver Lake** has life-guards on duty as well as picnicking facilities along the shore. **Windsurfers** skim along outside the Inner Harbour and on Elk Lake when the breezes are right. French Beach, on the way to Sooke Harbour, is also a popular local windsurfing spot.

WHALE-WATCHING   Naturalist guides point out orcas (killer whales), gray whales, sea lions, porpoises, and harbor seals on excursions by **Seafun Safaris Whale Watching,** 950 Wharf St. (✆ **877/360-1233** or 250/360-1200; www.seafun.com). Fares are C$99 (US$79) for adults and C$69 (US$55) for children.

Oak Bay Beach Hotel and Marine Resort, Oak Bay Beach Hotel, 1175 Beach Dr. (✆ **800/668-7758** or 250/598-4556; www.oakbaybeachhotel.com), offers 3½-hour whale-watching charters daily on vessels with restroom facilities and bar service.

7 Shopping

Victoria has dozens of little specialty shops that appeal to every taste and whim, and because the city is built to such a pedestrian scale, you can wander from place to place seeking your treasure.

ANTIQUES   Many of the best stores are in **Antique Row,** a 3-block stretch on Fort Street between Blanshard and Cook streets. Though farthest from downtown, **Faith Grant's Connoisseur Shop Ltd.,** 1156 Fort St. (✆ **250/383-0121**), is the best.

ARTS & CRAFTS   Starfish Glassworks, 630 Yates St. (© **250/388-7827;** www. starfishglass.bc.ca), is both a glass-blowing artists' studio, where you can watch pieces being created, and a gallery where contemporary glass pieces are sold.

A DEPARTMENT STORE The **Hudson's Bay Company** (© **250/385-1311**), Canada's oldest department store, sells everything from housewares to fashions to cosmetics and, of course, the trendy Hudson's Bay woolen point blankets.

FASHION   Breeze, 1150 Government St. (© **250/383-8871**), is a high-energy fashion outlet that carries a number of affordable and trendy lines for women, plus accessories. **Hughes Ltd.,** 564 Yates St. (© 250/381-4405), is a local favorite for contemporary women's fashions. The Plum Clothing Co., 1298 Broad St. (© **250/381-5005**), features quality dressy casuals. For men's fashions, try **British Importers,** 1125 Government St. (© **250/386-1496**).

FOOD   Rogers' Chocolates, 913 Government St. (© **250/384-7021;** http://rogers chocolates.com), is a Victoria institution housed in an appropriately old-fashioned shop loaded with tempting treats that will satisfy even a discerning chocoholic. **Murchies,** 1110 Government St. (© **250/383-3112**), offers specialty teas, including the custom blend served at the Fairmont Empress hotel's afternoon tea.

JEWELRY Ian MacDonald of **MacDonald Jewelry,** 618 View St. (© **250/382-4113**), designs and crafts all his own jewelry. At the **Jade Tree,** 606 Humboldt St. (© **250/388-4326**), you'll find British Columbia jade crafted into necklaces, bracelets, and other wearables.

NATIVE ART All the coastal tribes are represented in the **Alcheringa Gallery,** 665 Fort St. (© **250/383-8224**), along with a significant collection of pieces from Papua New Guinea. **Cowichan Trading Ltd.,** 1328 Government St. (© **250/383-0321**), sells a mix of T-shirts and gewgaws in addition to fine Cowichan sweaters, masks, and silver jewelry. **Hill's Native Art,** 1008 Government St. © **250/385-3911**), features exquisite native art, including masks, carvings, and jewelry.

OUTDOOR CLOTHES & EQUIPMENT   Ocean River Sports, 1824 Store St. (© **250/381-4233**), is the place to go to arrange a sea-kayak tour. It's also a good spot for outdoor clothing and camping knickknacks.

8 Victoria After Dark

Victoria is never going to set the world on fire, but revelers form a mass large enough to keep a number of reactions going. You just have to know where to look.

THEATER The **Royal Theatre,** 805 Broughton St. (© **250/361-0820;** box office 250/386-6121; www.rmts.bc.ca), hosts concerts like Victoria Symphony concerts, dance recitals, and touring stage plays. The **Belfry Theatre,** 1291 Gladstone St. (© **250/385-6815;** www.belfry.bc.ca), is a nationally acclaimed theatrical group that stages four productions October to April and a summer show in August. Another source of theater and event info is the **CHEK-by-phone** line at © **250/389-6460.**

LIVE-MUSIC CLUBS   Lucky, 517 Yates St. (© **250/382-5825**), is currently the hottest spot in Victoria. This low cavernous space has a pleasantly grungy feel like Seattle's Pioneer Square. DJs spin house and trance on the weekends, with bands often showing up earlier in the week. **Legends,** 919 Douglas St. (© **250/383-7137**), below street level in the Strathcona Hotel, covers the gamut from afro-pop to blues to zydeco. **Steamers,** 570 Yates St. (© **250/381-4340**), is the city's premium blues bar.

LOUNGES, BARS & PUBS   A truly unique experience, the **Bengal Lounge** in the Empress hotel, 721 Government St. (© **250/384-8111**), is one of the last outposts of the old empire, except the martinis are ice cold and jazz plays in the background. **The Reef,** 533 Yates St. (© **250/388-5375**), is a funky reggae lounge with great martinis, good tunes, and an occasional DJ. **Canoe,** 450 Swift St. (© **250/361-1940**), is one of the most pleasant spots going to hoist a pint after a long day's sightseeing. **Big Bad John's,** 919 Douglas St., in the Strathcona Hotel (© **250/383-7137**), is Victoria's only hillbilly bar—a low, dark warren of a place, with inches of discarded peanut shells on the plank floor and a crowd of drunk and happy rowdies. **Spinnakers Brewpub,** 308 Catherine St. (© **250/386-BREW** or 250/386-2739), has one of the best views and some of the best beer in town.

GAY & LESBIAN BARS   **Hush,** 1325 Government St. (© **250/385-0566;** C$5/US$4 cover on weekends), features top-end touring DJs. **Electric Avenue,** 1601 Store St. (© **250/920-0018;** C$5/US$4 cover on weekends), is a gay cabaret and burlesque; it also has leather and fetish nights. Call ahead—or check *Monday* magazine (www.mondaymag.com/monday)—before coming.

Southern Vancouver Island & the Gulf Islands

Stretching more than 450km (279 miles) from Victoria to the northwest tip of Cape Scott, Vancouver Island is one of the most fascinating destinations in Canada, a mountainous bulwark of deep-green forests, rocky fiords, and wave-battered headlands. For an area so easily accessible by car, the range of wildlife here is surprising: Bald eagles float above the shorelines, seals and sea lions slumber on rocky islets, and porpoises and orca whales cavort in narrow passes between islands.

The British Columbia capital, Victoria, is the ideal place to begin exploring the entire island; see chapter 5 for complete coverage of the city.

Duncan, the "City of Totem Poles" in the Cowichan Valley north of Victoria, reveals another facet of Vancouver Island culture. This lush green valley is the ancestral home of the Cowichan tribe, famed for its hand-knit sweaters; it also houses some of the island's best wineries and organic farms, making it a gastronomical hub.

Nestled just off the island's east coast lie the Gulf Islands. The fact that they are only reached by a confusing network of ferries just enhances their sense of remoteness and mystery. Part arty, counterculture enclave, part trophy-home exurb, and part old-fashioned farm and orchard territory, the Gulf Islands are full of contradictions and charm. The largest, Salt Spring Island, is a haven for artists who are attracted to its mild climate and pastoral landscapes.

Running down the spine of Vancouver Island is a lofty chain of mountains that functionally divides the island into west and east. In the west, which receives the full brunt of Pacific storms, vast rainforests grow along inaccessible, steep-sided fiords. Paved roads provide access in only a few places, and boat charters, ferries, and floatplanes are the preferred means of transport.

The east side of Vancouver Island, and in particular the area from Nanaimo southward, is home to the vast majority of the island's population of 750,000. The climate here is drier and warmer than on the storm-tossed west coast, and agriculture is a major industry. Tourism is also key to the local economy: The southeast portion of Vancouver Island has the warmest median temperatures in all of Canada, and tourists and retirees flood the area in search of rain-free summer days.

While the Gulf Islands and the southern portions of Vancouver Island were long ago colonized by European settlers, the original First Nations peoples are very much a part of cultural and political life in the area. Historically, the Pacific coast of British Columbia was one of the greatest centers of art and culture in Native America, and this past is beautifully preserved in many museums and in several villages. Modern-day First Nations artists are very active, and nearly every town has galleries and workshops filled with their exquisite carvings, paintings, and sculpture.

This chapter covers the southern portion of Vancouver Island, along with the Gulf Islands. For the area from Nanaimo to Courtenay/Comox and including the West Coast Trail and Pacific Rim National Park, see chapter 7, "Central Vancouver Island." In chapter 8, "Northern Vancouver Island," we discuss the portion of the island from the town of Campbell River northward, including Strathcona Provincial Park.

1 Essentials

GETTING THERE

BY PLANE   **Victoria** is the island's major air hub, with jet, commuter-plane, and floatplane service from Vancouver and Seattle. See chapter 5 for details.

Both standard commuter aircraft and floatplanes provide regularly scheduled service to a number of other island communities from both Victoria and from Vancouver. All of the southern Gulf Islands, as well as many towns, can be reached by scheduled harbor-to-harbor floatplane service, either from Vancouver International's seaplane terminal or from downtown Vancouver's Coal Harbour terminal. In fact, it's easy to arrange a chartered floatplane for almost any destination along coastal Vancouver Island. Since floatplanes don't require airport facilities, even the most remote fishing camp can be as accessible as a major city.

Commercial airline service is provided by **Air Canada** (© **888/247-2262;** www.air canada.com), **Horizon Air** (© **800/252-7522;** www.alaskaair.com), **Pacific Coastal** (© **800/663-2872;** www.pacific-coastal.com), and **WestJet** (© **877/952-4638;** www. westjet.com).

Commuter seaplane companies that serve Vancouver Island include **Harbour Air Seaplanes** (© **800/665-0212** or 604/688-1277; www.harbour-air.com), **Tofino Air** (© **866/486-3247** for Tofino base, 888/436-7776 for Sechelt base, or 800/665-2359 for Gabriola base; www.tofinoair.ca), and **Baxter Aviation** (© **800/661-5599,** 604/ 683-6525, or 250/754-1066; www.baxterair.com).

BY FERRY   **BC Ferries** (© **888/BCFERRY,** or 250/386-3431; www.bcferries.com) operates an extensive year-round network that links Vancouver Island, the Gulf Islands, and the mainland. Major routes include the crossing from Tsawwassen to Swartz Bay and to Nanaimo, and from Horseshoe Bay (northwest of Vancouver) to Nanaimo. In summer, reserve in advance. Sample fares are included in the regional sections that follow. If you're taking a car, beware: ticket prices add up quickly. You may want to leave the car on the mainland and travel by bus, taxi, or air.

Washington State Ferries (© **888/808-7977** in Washington, 206/464-6400 in the rest of the U.S., or 250/381-1551 in Canada; www.wsdot.wa.gov/ferries) has daily service from Anacortes, in Washington, to Sidney, on Vancouver Island. One-way fares for a car and driver are around US$45 in high season.

The year-round passenger ferries run by **Victoria Clipper** (© **800/888-2535** or 206/448-5000; www.victoriaclipper.com) depart from Seattle's Pier 69; adult round-trip tickets range from US$123 to US$133.

From Port Angeles, Washington, the year-round (except for a 2-week maintenance break in Jan) Black Ball Transport's car ferry **MV Coho** (© **360/457-4491** in Port Angeles, or 250/386-2202 in Victoria; www.cohoferry.com) offers service to Victoria for US$11 per adult foot passenger, US$40 per vehicle. Also from Port Angeles, from mid-May to the end of September, foot passengers and bicyclists can pay US$21 round-trip to hop on the *Victoria Express* (© 800/633-1589 or 360/452-8088 in the U.S., or 250/361-9144 in Victoria; www.victoriaexpress.com).

In summer only, **Victoria/San Juan Cruises'** daily *Victoria Star 2* (© 800/443-4552; www.whales.com) passenger ferry travels between Bellingham and Victoria via the San Juan Islands. Round-trip adult fares range from US$79 to US$89.

BY BUS   One of the easiest ways to get to Vancouver Island destinations is by bus. Conveniently, the bus will start its journey from a city center (such as Vancouver), take you directly to the ferry dock and onto the ferry, and then deposit you in another city center (Victoria or Nanaimo). A lot of the hassle of ferry travel is minimized, and the costs are usually lower than other alternatives. (If you're traveling to Vancouver on VIA Rail, bus connections are easy—the bus and train share the same terminal.)

Pacific Coach Lines (© 800/661-1725 or 604/662-8074; www.pacificcoach.com) offers bus service via BC Ferries from Vancouver to Victoria. The one-way fare is C$35 (US$28) for adults, C$23 (US$18) for seniors, and C$18 (US$14) for children under 12. **Greyhound Canada** (© 800/661-8747 or 604/482-8747; www.greyhound. ca) provides eight daily trips between Vancouver and Nanaimo. Fares are C$28 (US$22) one-way.

VISITOR INFORMATION
For general information on Vancouver Island, contact **Tourism Vancouver Island,** Suite 203, 335 Wesley St., Nanaimo (© **250/754-3500;** fax 250/754-3599; www. islands.bc.ca). Also check out **www.vancouverisland.com**.

GETTING AROUND
While Vancouver Island has an admirable system of public transport, getting to remote sights and destinations is difficult without your own vehicle.

BY FERRY   **BC Ferries** (© 888/BCFERRY or 250/386-3431; www.bcferries.com) routes link Vancouver Island ports to many offshore islands, including the southern Gulf Islands of Denman, Gabriola, Galiano, Hornby, Kuper, Mayne, the Penders, Salt Spring, Saturna, and Thetis (see chapter 7). None of these islands has public transport, so once there, you'll need to hoof it, hitch it, hire a taxi, or arrange for bike rentals. Most innkeepers will pick you up from the ferry if you've reserved in advance.

BY TRAIN   Another charming way to get around Vancouver Island is on **VIA Rail**'s **E&N Railiner,** also known as the *Malahat* (© 888/VIA-RAIL or 250/383-4324; www.viarail.ca), which makes a daily round-trip run from Victoria to Courtenay in period passenger cars. The *Malahat* passes through some of the most beautiful landscapes on the east coast of Vancouver Island, taking about 4½ hours each way. Your ticket allows you to get on and off as many times as you'd like: You can stop at Duncan, Chemainus, Nanaimo, Parksville, or Qualicum Beach and catch the return train back, or take the next day's train north. Prices are very reasonable, especially with 7-day advance purchase. A round-trip between Victoria and Courtenay can cost as little as C$58 (US$46). *Note:* The *Malahat* has no baggage car, and checked-baggage service is not available.

BY BUS   **Vancouver Island Coach Lines** (© **250/388-5248,** or book through Greyhound © **800/661-8747;** www.greyhound.ca) runs buses between Victoria and Nanaimo with stops at smaller centers along Highway 1 (see "By Car," below).

BY CAR   The southern half of Vancouver Island is well served by paved highways. The trunk road between Victoria and Nanaimo is **Highway 1,** the Trans-Canada. This

Vancouver Island

busy route alternates between four-lane expressway and congested two-lane highway, and requires some patience and vigilance, especially during the summer months. North of Nanaimo, the major road is **Highway 19,** which is now almost all four-lane expressway, a particular improvement being the new 128km (79-mile) **Inland Highway** section between Parksville and Campbell River. The older sections of 19, all closer to the island's east coast, are now labeled 19A. North of Campbell River, a long, unimproved section of Highway 19 continues all the way to Port Hardy. The other major paved road system on the island, **Highway 4,** connects Parksville with Port Alberni and on to Ucluelet and Tofino, on the rugged west coast. This road is mostly two-lane, and portions of it are extremely winding and hilly. Access to gasoline and car services is no problem, even in more remote north Vancouver Island.

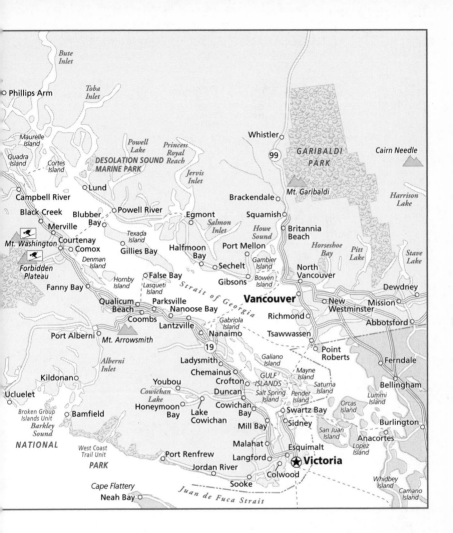

Rental cars are readily available. Agencies include **Avis** (© **800/272-5871** in Canada, 800/230-4898 in the U.S.; www.avis.com), **Budget** (© **800/268-8900** in Canada, 800/527-0700 in the U.S.; www.budget.com), and **National** (© **800/CAR-RENT** in Canada and the U.S.; www.nationalcar.com).

2 The Gulf Islands ✶✶✶

The Gulf Islands are a collection of several dozen mountainous islands that sprawl across the Strait of Georgia between the British Columbia mainland and Vancouver Island. While only a handful of the islands are served by regularly scheduled ferries, this entire area is popular with boaters, cyclists, kayakers, and sailboat enthusiasts. Lying in the rain shadow of Washington State's Olympic Mountains, the Gulf Islands

The Gulf Islands

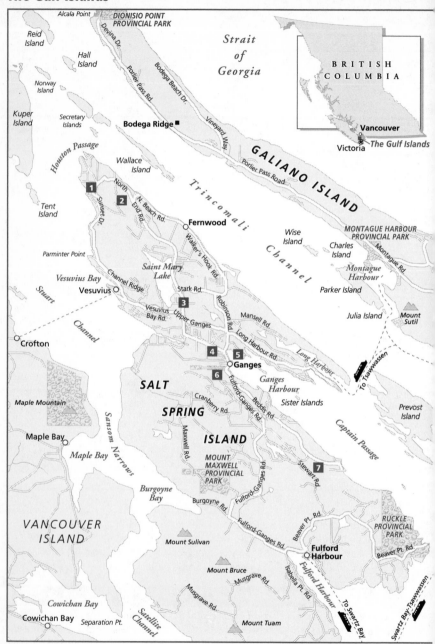

My, what an inefficient way to fish.

Ring toss, good. Horseshoes, bad.

Faster! Faster! Faster!

We take care of the fiddly bits, from providing over 43,000 customer reviews of hotels, to helping you find our best fares, to giving you 24/7 customer service. So you can focus on the only thing that matters. Goofing off.

✱* travelocity®
You'll never roam alone.™

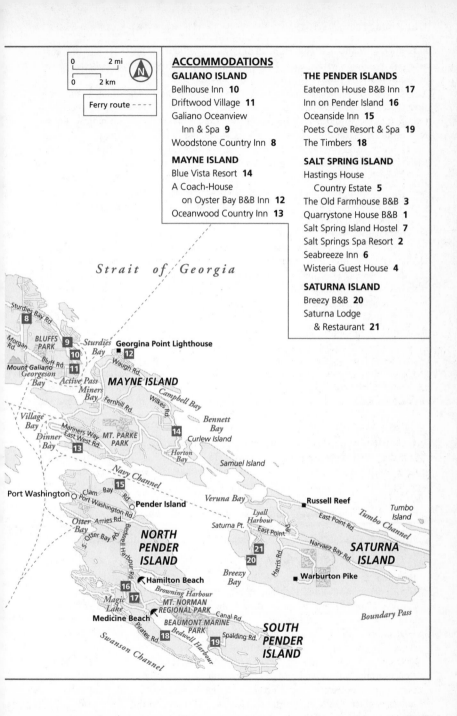

ACCOMMODATIONS

GALIANO ISLAND
Bellhouse Inn **10**
Driftwood Village **11**
Galiano Oceanview
    Inn & Spa **9**
Woodstone Country Inn **8**

MAYNE ISLAND
Blue Vista Resort **14**
A Coach-House
    on Oyster Bay B&B Inn **12**
Oceanwood Country Inn **13**

THE PENDER ISLANDS
Eatenton House B&B Inn **17**
Inn on Pender Island **16**
Oceanside Inn **15**
Poets Cove Resort & Spa **19**
The Timbers **18**

SALT SPRING ISLAND
Hastings House
    Country Estate **5**
The Old Farmhouse B&B **3**
Quarrystone House B&B **1**
Salt Spring Island Hostel **7**
Salt Springs Spa Resort **2**
Seabreeze Inn **6**
Wisteria Guest House **4**

SATURNA ISLAND
Breezy B&B **20**
Saturna Lodge
    & Restaurant **21**

Strait of Georgia

Sturdies Bay Rd.
8
Morgan Rd.
BLUFFS PARK
9 Sturdies
Bluff Rd. Bay
10
11
Mount Galiano
Georgeson
Bay
Active Pass
Miners
Bay
Village Bay
Mariners Way
East West Rd.
Dinner
Bay
13

Sturdies Bay
12 Georgina Point Lighthouse
Waugh Rd.
MAYNE ISLAND
Campbell Bay
Fernhill Rd.
Wilkes Rd.
MT. PARKE PARK
14
Bennett Bay
Curlew Island
Horton Bay

Navy Channel
15
Port Washington
Clam Bay
Port Washington Rd.
Pender Island
Otter Bay
Amies Rd.
Otter Bay Rd.
Bedwell Harbour Rd.
NORTH PENDER ISLAND
16
Hamilton Beach
17
Magic Lake
Browning Harbour
MT. NORMAN REGIONAL PARK
Medicine Beach
BEAUMONT MARINE PARK
Pirates Rd.
18 Bedwell Harbour
Canal Rd.
19 Spalding Rd.
SOUTH PENDER ISLAND
Swanson Channel

Samuel Island
Veruna Bay
Russell Reef
Lyall Harbour
Saturna Pt.
East Point
Breezy Bay
21
20
Harris Rd.
East Point Rd.
Narvaez Bay Rd.
SATURNA ISLAND
Warburton Pike
Tumbo Island
Tumbo Channel
Boundary Pass

0   2 mi
0   2 km
N

Ferry route - - - -

have the most temperate climate in all of Canada, without the heavy rainfall that characterizes much of coastal British Columbia. In fact, the climate here is officially listed as semi-Mediterranean!

The Gulf Islands are the northern extension of Washington's San Juan Islands, and they share those islands' farming and seafaring past. Agriculture, especially sheep raising, is still a major industry. The past few decades, however, have seen radical changes in traditional island life: The sheer beauty of the land- and seascapes, the balmy climate, and relaxed lifestyle have brought in a major influx of new residents. These islands were a major destination for Vietnam War–era draft evaders, many of whom set up homes, farms, and businesses here. The islands quickly developed a reputation as a countercultural hippie enclave, a reputation they still maintain. Even as one generation's radicals gray and become the islands' business class, younger generations of free spirits have come to grow organic vegetables, explore an artistic urge, and hang out in the coffee shops.

The 1990s witnessed a parallel but different land rush. High-tech moguls, Hollywood stars, and other wealthy refugees from urban centers have been moving to the islands in droves. The quality of facilities has shot up: The islands now boast fine restaurants, elegant inns, and a multitude of galleries. In fact, the Gulf Islands are noted across Canada as a major center for crafts and arts.

The population influx is having some unexpected consequences. Groundwater is a precious commodity on these arid islands, and some inns will ask guests to monitor their water use. Adding to the problem is that saltwater aquifers underlie parts of the islands: A well of corrosive salt water doesn't do anyone much good.

Despite the one-direction migration, the Gulf Islands remain a charming destination. The islands are still underdeveloped, and some of the best restaurants and lodgings are tucked away in forests down long roads. There's little in the way of organized activities: no water slides, theme parks, and few major resorts; just incredible scenery, great biking and kayaking, lovely inns, and fine dining.

Gulf Islands National Park Reserve, 2220 Harbour Rd., Sidney, BC V8L 2P6 (© **250/654-4000;** www.pc.gc.ca), protects 34 sq. km (13 sq. miles) of the islands' unique marine ecosystem on 15 islands and more than 50 islets, plus 26 sq. km (10 sq. miles) of marine areas. A large portion of the reserve is on smaller Gulf Islands, such as Prevost, Portland, D'Arcy, and Tumbo, which have no BC Ferries service and can only be reached by kayak, canoe, water taxi, or private boat. Land on Mayne, and

---

Tips A Note for Families

If you're traveling with kids, the Gulf Islands are a fairly inhospitable place to secure accommodations. Nearly all B&Bs have listed minimum ages for guests (usually 12 or 16), and there are only a few standard motels or cottage resorts where families are welcome. Note that for all accommodations, it's mandatory to make reservations well in advance, as the ferry system doesn't exactly make it easy to just drive on to the next town to find a place to stay.

One option for families is to rent a cottage or private home. **Gulf Island Vacation Rentals,** 5402 Wilson Rd., Pender Island, BC V0N 2M1 (© **877/662-3414;** www.gulfislandvacationrentals.com), is a clearinghouse of private homes, bed-and-breakfast rooms, and cottages available for rental on the Gulf Islands.

North and South Pender islands are included in the park, though it is Saturna—the most remote and undeveloped of the islands served by BC Ferries—that has the most parkland acreage. Visitor facilities are minimal.

ESSENTIALS
GETTING THERE
BY FERRY **BC Ferries** (© **888/BCFERRY** in B.C., or 250/386-3431; www.bc ferries.bc.ca) operates four different runs to the southern Gulf Islands (five if you count Horseshoe Bay to Bowen Island), from Tsawwassen on the British Columbia mainland, and from Swartz Bay, Crofton, and Nanaimo on Vancouver Island. The system was designed primarily to get commuters to their jobs on the mainland or in Victoria. Getting exactly where you want to be, exactly when you want to be there, is anything but straightforward (and, in fact, not always possible). Be aware that the ferries are not particularly large; to ensure that you make the one you want, arrive at least 15 minutes early (30 min. on summer weekends). You can make reservations on the routes from Tsawwassen, but not on the other runs.

Ticket pricing is confusing. There are separate fares for drivers, passengers, and vehicles, plus fees for bikes, kayaks, and canoes on most runs. Tickets from Vancouver Island (Chemainus, Crofton, Nanaimo, or Swartz Bay) are calculated as return fares; that is, when you buy a ticket and depart from one of these ports, you don't have to buy an additional ticket if you are returning to the same port. However, all fares via Tsawwassen are one-way: You pay going and coming. To make it more puzzling, outward-bound fares from Tsawwassen are more expensive than the same journey back to the mainland. Sample peak-season fares: a car and two passengers from Swartz Bay to Salt Spring Island, C$37 (US$30); a single foot passenger, C$7 (US$5.60).

The ferry schedule is also confusing so give yourself plenty of time to study it. You can get to any of the major southern Gulf Islands (that is, Gabriola, Galiano, Mayne, the Penders, Salt Spring, and Saturna) from Swartz Bay or Tsawwassen.

If you are planning to visit several islands, consider purchasing a 4- or 7-day **Sail-Pass** (www.bcferries.com/sailpass) from BC Ferries, which can reduce both fares and confusion. The SailPass is a one-price ticket that allows you to travel along 20 ferry routes in southern B.C., including those routes servicing the Gulf Islands (except for travel along the Inside Passage routes or to the Queen Charlottes). The ticket includes passage for a vehicle plus two adults (more adults can be added to the ticket by paying more). A 4-day ticket is C$149 (US$119), and a 7-day ticket is C$179 (US$143), which, given normal use, will represent a savings of about one-third over regular fares. The only hitch is that you need to pre-purchase the SailPass—you can't buy one at the ferry terminal. They can be ordered from the BC Ferry website above (allow a week for delivery) or purchased the same day from the **Tourism Vancouver Info Centre,** 200 Burrard St. (© **604/683-2000**), open Monday to Saturday 8:30am to 6:30pm; **Peace Arch Provincial Visitor Info Centre,** 356 Hwy. 99, Surrey (© **604/531-7352**), daily 9am to 5pm; and **Vancouver International Airport Visitor Info Centre** (© **604/207 0953**), daily 8am to midnight.

BY PLANE   A number of commuter airlines offer regular floatplane service from either Vancouver Harbour or Vancouver International Airport. One-way tickets to the islands usually cost C$75 to C$85 (US$60–US$68) per person, not a bad fare when you consider the time and hassle involved in taking a ferry. However, floatplanes are small and seats sell out quickly, so reserve ahead of time. Call **Harbour Air Seaplanes**

Tips Make Saturna Your First Stop

If you're planning to make a circuit of the five southern Gulf Islands, consider starting with Saturna Island. Saturna is far easier to reach by ferry from Swartz Bay on Vancouver Island than it is from its sister Gulf Islands (to get to Saturna from Tsawwassen on the mainland requires a change of ferries). In fact, there's not even scheduled service between Saturna and Salt Spring Island. However, for reasons unknown, once on Saturna it's not difficult to continue on to other islands.

(© **800/665-0212** or 604/688-1277; www.harbour-air.com), **Seair Seaplanes** (© **800/447-3247** or 604/273-8900; www.seairseaplanes.com), or **Tofino Air** (© **800/ 665-2359** for Gabriola base; www.tofinoair.ca).

VISITOR INFORMATION

For general information on the Gulf Islands, contact **Tourism Vancouver Island,** Suite 203, 335 Wesley St., Nanaimo (© **250/754-3500;** www.islands.bc.ca). Another good comprehensive resource is **www.gulfislands.com**.

GETTING AROUND

Most innkeepers will pick up guests at the ferry or floatplane terminals, if given sufficient notice. There's also taxi service on most islands. Though these taxis are unregulated, most will quote you a fixed price for a journey when you phone to reserve the trip. Be sure to confirm the price when you're picked up. Note, however, that there aren't many options if you don't like the price!

BY BICYCLE   Winding country roads and bucolic landscapes make the Gulf Islands a favorite destination for cyclists. Although the islands' road networks aren't exactly large—and roads are quite steep and narrow—it can be great fun to bike the back roads, jump a ferry, and peddle to an outlying pub for lunch. Bikes can be taken onboard BC Ferries for a small surcharge. Note, though, that the narrow roads really fill up in summer, making them more idyllic for cycling other times of the year. Several parks have designated mountain-bike trails. Rentals are available on most islands.

BY KAYAK   The Gulf Islands' lengthy and rugged coastline, plus their proximity to other more remote island groups, make them a good base for kayaking trips. Most of the islands have kayak outfitters; however, not all of them will offer rentals separate from guided tours. If you're an experienced kayaker and just want to rent a kayak, call ahead to inquire. Kayaks and canoes can be taken on the ferries for a small fee.

SALT SPRING ISLAND

The largest of the Gulf Islands, Salt Spring is—to the outside world—a bucolic getaway filled with artists, sheep pastures, and cozy B&Bs. While this image is mostly true, Salt Spring is also a busy cultural crossroads: Movie stars, retirees, high-tech telecommuters, and hippie farmers all rub shoulders here. The hilly terrain and deep forests afford equal privacy for all lifestyles, and that's the way the residents like it.

Salt Spring is divided geographically into three distinct lobes. In fact, the island looks as if it were once three separate islands that somehow got pushed together. Most of the population lives in the area around Ganges and Vesuvius; the rugged lower third of the island is the least developed. Although Salt Spring's configuration makes for a lot of coastline, there are very few beaches; instead, the island's underlying granite forms headlands that drop straight into the sea.

GETTING THERE   Salt Spring Island is served by three different routes on **BC Ferries** (© **888/BC-FERRY** or 250/381-5452; www.bcferries.com). From Tsawwassen on the mainland, ferries depart two to four times a day for Long Harbour, on the island's northeast coast. If you're on Vancouver Island, you can choose the Crofton–Vesuvius Bay run or the Swartz Bay (Victoria) to Fulford Harbour crossing.

Regular floatplane service operates from Vancouver International Airport and Vancouver's Inner Harbour seaplane terminal to Ganges Harbour. See "Essentials" (p. 114) for contact information.

VISITOR INFORMATION   The **Salt Spring Chamber of Commerce** operates a visitor center at 121 Lower Ganges Rd. (© **250/537-5252;** www.saltspringisland.bc.ca).

GETTING AROUND   If you don't have a car, you will need to rely on a bike or call **Silver Shadow Taxi** (© **250/537-3030**). **Gulf Islands Water Taxi** (© **250/537-2510;** www.saltspring.com/watertaxi) offers speedboat service between Salt Spring, Mayne, and Galiano islands on Wednesdays and Saturdays in summer (June 9–Sept 1), plus Pender and Saturna islands on all school days during the rest of the year. There are morning and late afternoon scheduled services for commuters and students; charters are also available. The taxi leaves from Government Dock in Ganges Harbour. Fares are C$15 (US$12) from any one point to another, or C$25 (US$20) for a round-trip. Reservations are recommended; bikes are transported free of charge.

EXPLORING THE ISLAND

With a year-round population of 10,000 residents, Salt Spring is served by three ferries, making it by far the easiest of the Gulf Islands to visit. Not coincidentally, Salt Spring also has the most facilities for visitors. The center of island life is **Ganges,** a little village with gas stations, grocery stores, and banks, all overlooking a busy pleasure-boat harbor. You can easily spend from an hour to most of a day poking around the art galleries, boutiques, and coffee shops here.

In fact, the island is famed across Canada as an artists' colony and many people visit expressly to see the studios of local artists and craftspeople. Stop by the visitor center for the **Studio Tour Map,** which pinpoints 42 island artists—glass blowers, painters, ceramists, weavers, carvers, sculptors, many of whom are available to visit.

Pegasus Gallery, Mouat's Mall, 1–104 Fulford-Ganges Rd. (© **800/668-6131** or 250/537-2421; www.pegasusgalleryca.com), displays a mix of contemporary Canadian painting and sculpture as well as Native carving and basketry. On Fridays from 5 to 9pm, a dozen Ganges galleries remain open late for the **Gallery Walk.** From mid-May to mid-September, **ArtCraft** (© **250/537-0899;** www.artcraftgallery.ca) features

---

Moments The Mother of All Saturday Markets

Not to be missed is **Market in the Park** ✿ (www.saltspringmarket.com), held April through October, Saturdays from 8am to 4pm, on the waterfront's Centennial Park. The market brings together a lively mix of craftspeople, farmers, musicians, and bakers. It's great fun, and a good chance to shop for local products. As you might guess, the people-watching is matchless.

the work of more than 250 local artists at Mahon Hall, just north of Ganges at Park Drive and Lower Ganges Road.

BIKING Although Salt Spring has the best network of paved roads, it's not the best island for cycling. With ferries unleashing cars throughout the day, there's a lot more traffic here than you'd expect. However, these same ferries—plus the **Gulf Islands Water Taxi** (see "Getting Around," above)—make Salt Spring a convenient base for cyclists. For rentals (starting at C$15/US$12 for 2 hr.), contact **Salt Spring Kayaking,** 2923 Fulford-Ganges Rd., on the Fulford Harbour wharf (© **250/537-4664;** www.saltspring.com/sskayak).

HIKING **Ruckle Provincial Park** (http://wlapwww.gov.bc.ca/bcparks), on the southeast corner of the island, is the largest provincial park in the Gulf Islands; its entrance is 10km (6¼ miles) from the Fulford Harbour ferry terminal on Beaver Point Road. Eight kilometers (5 miles) of trails wind through forests to rocky headlands where the tide-pool exploring is excellent; some trails are designated for mountain bikes. Ruckle Park is also the only public campground on Salt Spring.

KAYAKING **Island Escapades,** 118 Natalie Lane (© **888/529-2567** or 250/537-2537; www.islandescapades.com), offers a 2-hour introduction to kayaking on the placid waters of Cusheon Lake, for C$40 (US$32), with guided 3-hour ocean tours for C$55 (US$44). **Sea Otter Kayaking,** 149 Lower Ganges Rd. (© **877/537-5678;** www.saltspring.com/kayaking), rents kayaks and canoes, starting at C$20 (US$16) an hour. Guided tours are C$40 (US$32) for 2 hours. **Saltspring Kayaking,** 2923 Fulford-Ganges Rd. (© **250/537-4664;** www.saltspring.com/sskayak), offers rentals and 2-hour guided tours from C$38 (US$25). They also offer 2-day guided tours of the new Gulf Islands National Park for C$275 (US$220).

WHERE TO STAY

Ruckle Provincial Park, off Beaver Point Road (© **250/391-2300;** http://wlap www.gov.bc.ca/bcparks), has 70 walk-in sites and eight reservable sites for C$14 (US$11). **Salt Spring Island Hostel,** 640 Cusheon Lake Rd. (© **250/537-4149;** www.beacom.com/ssihostel), which offers 23 dorm beds, plus a tepee and treehouse, closed its doors in 2005 but promises to reopen in May 2006. Call ahead.

Hastings House Country Estate ✿✿ In the 1930s, an English couple built a replica of a 16th-century Sussex estate, now known as the Manor House, on the site of an old trading post. Almost all of the original structures have been converted into beautifully furnished accommodations. The Manor House now serves as the restaurant and library, with two guest suites on the second floor. The farmhouse contains two two-story suites, and the old trading post is now a cottage suite. Architecturally most ingenious are the five suites in the old barn, which offer all of the luxuries you'd expect from a modern five-star hotel plus spa. The owners have recently added the three-bedroom Churchill cottage, with excellent views of the grounds and harbor, plus the newly-constructed Hillside suites, which offer very graciously furnished rooms. All units are outfitted with antiques and fireplaces; most have deep soaker tubs.

While the rooms are full of character, what really sets Hastings House apart is its incredible 10-hectare (25-acre) setting. This charming inn is just east of Ganges, in a forested valley that drops directly onto Ganges Harbour. Cheviot ewes trim the meadow grass, the gardens provide vegetables for the excellent restaurant (see "Where to Dine," below), and the old orchard bears sour cherries, apples, and pears. Idyllic only begins to describe this idealized English manor.

160 Upper Ganges Rd., Salt Spring Island, BC V8K 2S2. ℭ 800/661-9255 or 250/537-2362. Fax 250/537-5333. www.hastingshouse.com. 18 units. From C$475 (US$380) double. Extra person C$85 (US$68) per night. Rates include full breakfast and tea. Weekly cottage rental available. Off season 1-, 2-, 3-, and 5-night packages available. AE, MC, V. Closed mid-Nov to mid-Mar. Children must be 16 or older. **Amenities:** Restaurant; golf course and tennis courts nearby; spa including massage; free bikes and scooters; laundry service; dry cleaning. *In room:* Dataport, minibar, hair dryer, iron, CD player.

Old Farmhouse B&B 🅐🅐

One of the best-loved accommodations in the Gulf Islands, the Old Farmhouse combines top-quality lodgings and great multi-course breakfasts. This Victorian-era homestead was built in 1894 amid 1.2 hectares (3 acres) of meadows and orchards—in fact, the enormous 500-year-old arbutus (or madroño) tree in the front yard may be the world's largest. The bedrooms are in a stylistically harmonious guesthouse adjoining the original farmhouse. Each room has a balcony or patio; the decor incorporates just the right country touches—floral wallpaper, wainscoted walls—without lapsing into Laura Ashley excess. The farm's old chicken house has been transformed into the charming Chateau de Poulet, a cozy one-bedroom suite with a king bed. The extensive meadows are perfect for lolling with a book or playing a game of croquet.

1077 N. End Rd., Salt Spring Island, BC V8K 1L9. ℭ 250/537-4113. Fax 250/537-4969. www.oldfarmhouse.ca. 5 units. C$185 (US$148) double. Rates include full breakfast. MC, V. Call to inquire about children and pets. **Amenities:** Common room; Internet access; nonsmoking facility. *In room:* Hair dryer, no phone.

Quarrystone House B&B 🅐

If you're looking to add a rural touch to your Salt Spring Island vacation, this is your lodging. At the northern end of Salt Spring Island, on a farm surrounded by orchards and sheep pastures is Quarrystone House, a tranquil getaway with great views and very comfortable rooms. Accommodations are in a newly built structure—separate from the main house to ensure privacy—and are spacious and nicely furnished; one is a two-bedroom unit. You can stroll through gardens and meadows and meet sheep, goats, and ponies. Yet, the only thing countrified about Quarrystone House is the location; each room has a fireplace, balcony or patio, Jacuzzi tub, and luxury amenities. Best of all are the sunset views over Stewart Channel and Vancouver Island.

1340 Sunset Dr., Salt Spring Island, BC V8K 1E2. ℭ 250/537-5980. Fax 250/537-5937. www.quarrystone.com. 4 units. C$135–C$185 (US$108–US$148) double. Low season rates available. Rates include breakfast. MC, V. *In room:* TV/VCR, fridge, coffeemaker, hair dryer, Jacuzzi, fireplace, microwave, snacks, robes.

Salt Springs Spa Resort

Salt Spring's notorious saltwater aquifers are put to good use at this ocean-side day spa and chalet on the north end of the island. The center offers a variety of facials, massage, aromatherapy, and mineral baths utilizing the spa's salt spring water. Even if you're not into the spa scene, Salt Springs Spa Resort is worth considering for its new knotty-pine chalets, which face the busy waters of Trincomali Channel and overlook Wallace Island. Each rustic-looking unit has a fireplace, porch, and two tubs: a therapeutic tub with jetted mineral water and a soaker tub.

1460 N. Beach Rd., Salt Spring Island, BC V8K 1J4. ℭ 800/665-0039 or 250/537-4111. Fax 250/537-2939. www.saltspringresort.com. 13 chalets. Late June through Aug C$199–C$299 (US$156–US$239) double; Sept–Oct, Mar to late June, and Dec 21–31 C$129–C$219 (US$103–US$175) double; Nov–Feb except winter holidays C$109–C$199 (US$87–US$159) double. 2- and 3-bedroom suites available. Extra person C$20 (US$16) per night. 2-night minimum stay in summer. Packages available. AE, MC, V. Free parking. Children must be 16 or older. **Amenities:** Golf course nearby; spa; free rowboats and bikes; game room; massage; coin-op laundry; nonsmoking facility. *In room:* Kitchen, fridge, coffeemaker, hair dryer, no phone.

Seabreeze Inne *(Value) (Kids)*   An alternative to Salt Spring's expensive B&Bs, the Seabreeze is a well-maintained motel just south of Ganges. All rooms are clean and nicely furnished; some have electric fireplaces. Kitchen units are available. Guests can use a large deck with grapevine-covered arbors, picnic tables, and a barbecue.

101 Bittancourt Rd., Salt Spring Island, BC V8K 2K2. © **800/434-4112** or 250/537-4145. Fax 250/537-4323. www.seabreeze inne.com. 29 units. Mar–May 14 C$79–C$109 (US$63–US$87) double; May 15–June and Sept 18–Oct C$75–C$169 (US$60–US$135) double; July–Sept 17 C$95–C$189 (US$76–US$151) double; Nov–Feb C$59–C$85 (US$47–US$68) double. Extra person C$25 (US$20). 2-night minimum stay on weekends, 3-night minimum stay on holidays. AE, DC, DISC, MC, V. Senior discounts and weekly rates available. Package tours by moped available. Dogs accepted by approval; add C$20 (US$16) per day. **Amenities:** Golf course nearby; Jacuzzi; scooter rental; concierge; tour/activities desk; coin-op laundry. *In room:* TV, dataport, kitchen (in some), coffeemaker.

Wisteria Guest House *(★★) (Finds)*   This rambling inn, tucked off a side street in Ganges, was once a small nursing home. There's little evidence of its institutional past, however, as the new owners have done a sensational job of updating the rooms, adding new features, and injecting lots of color and energy into the operation. In the main guesthouse, there are two sets of rooms that share adjacent bathrooms. These inexpensive rooms are perfect for friends or families traveling together, functioning like a small apartment. The two additional guest rooms, two studios with private entrances, and stand-alone cottage all have private baths. All rooms are spacious, beautifully decorated, and absolutely ship-shape; and, as you might expect—one of the owners was formerly the pastry chef at the New York Westin Hotel—there's a comfortable central lounge and dining area where you'll enjoy a fantastic breakfast. Expect this small inn to just get better and better.

268 Park Dr., Salt Spring Island, BC V8K 2S1. © **250/537-5899.** Fax 250/537-5644. www.wisteriaguesthouse.com. 9 units. From C$89 (US$71) guest room double with shared bathroom; from C$129 (US$103) guest room double en suite bathroom; from C$139 (US$111) studio double; from C$99 (US$79) cottage (does not include breakfast). AE, MC, V. Children must be 10 or older. **Amenities:** Common room w/TV and fireplace; nonsmoking facility. *In room:* No phone.

WHERE TO DINE

Artist's Bistro *(★)* INTERNATIONAL   Alfresco waterfront dining is just one of the delights of Artist's Bistro. This classy restaurant combines Continental flair with Northwest fish and produce, resulting in an outstanding menu rich in temptation. Start with smoked salmon and avocado salad with horseradish dressing, or try Gambas "Pil Pil"—sizzling shrimp in garlic, hot peppers, and fresh herbs. Pork tenderloin "Normandy" is a fall favorite, served with apples in cider, brandy, and cream sauce. Local halibut filet is wrapped in chard leaves, steamed, and served with saffron and leek coulis. The bright dining room is festive in any season, and service is exceptional.

Grace Point Sq., Ganges. © **250/537-1701.** www.artistsbistro.com. Reservations recommended. Main courses C$28–C$39 (US$22–US$31). MC, V. Wed–Mon 6–9pm. Above Ganges harbor near the intersection of Fulford Ganges Rd. and Purvis Rd.

Calvin's *(★)* CANADIAN   If you ask a local where to eat in Ganges, chances are she'll recommend Calvin's, a friendly, bustling restaurant with good prices and flavorful food. Ingredients are fresh and local, like the island lamb available in multiple preparations. Wild fish is often available on the broad menu that ranges from traditional schnitzel to Northwest bouillabaisse, a tangy tomato broth rich with salmon, mussels, clams, and halibut. Surprisingly, Calvin's is also a great spot for Thai food as the Thai-born chef frequently offers Bangkok specialties. In good weather, deck seating overlooks the marina. The charmingly energetic Swiss owners will make you feel very welcome—if you want stuffy, formal service, this isn't your restaurant.

133 Lower Ganges Rd. ℭ 250/538-5551. Reservations suggested. Dinner main courses C$16–C$27 (US$13–US$22). MC, V. Tues–Sat 11:30am–2pm and 5pm to closing.

Hastings House ✿✿ PACIFIC NORTHWEST   Easily the most elegant culinary experience on the island, the rose-covered Relais & Châteaux dining room at Hastings House combines old-world sophistication with the freshest of ingredients. Menus incorporate local produce and fish; many of the herbs and vegetables are grown on the grounds. The evening begins with cocktails served by the fireplace. The five-course meal includes an appetizer (perhaps ahi sashimi and prosciutto salad with onion marmalade), an excellent soup, a small seafood course (such as gingered scallops with citrus cream), and a choice of four main dishes: Salt Spring lamb is nearly always featured, as is local salmon or other seasonal fish. A three-course meal is also available for smaller appetites.

160 Upper Ganges Rd. ℭ 250/537-2362. www.hastingshouse.com. Reservations required. Prix-fixe 5-course dinner C$95 (US$76). AE, MC, V. Summer (mid-June to mid-Oct) seating at 7:30pm; spring and fall (mid-Mar to mid-June and mid-Oct to mid-Nov) seating at 7pm. Closed mid-Nov to mid-Mar.

House Piccolo CONTINENTAL   Located in a heritage home in Ganges, House Piccolo offers excellent food and a good wine list in moderately formal surroundings. The Finnish origins of the chef are reflected in the northern European accents on the unusual menu, particularly the fish specials that feature the best of the local catch. You might see salmon chowder Finlandia; local black cod drizzled with red wine, honey, and balsamic vinegar reduction; or roasted venison with rowan- and juniper-berry-scented demi glace.

108 Hereford Ave., Ganges. ℭ 250/537-1844. www.housepiccolo.com. Reservations recommended. Main courses C$18–C$29 (US$14–US$23). AE, DC, MC, V. Daily 5–9pm.

Oystercatcher Seafood Bar & Grill   If you're looking for a relaxing spot for a drink and some tempting eats, consider the Oystercatcher. Above Shipstone's Pub (with outdoor seating on the waterfront) this smartly atmospheric bar and grill features a menu that spans the gulf between pub fare and fine dining: You can get a burger or a plate of fresh shucked oysters, fish and chips or fire-grilled local lamb rack with three-mustard sauce. The same menu is available on both levels. Service is youthful and friendly, and the barman pours a number of local brews and wines.

104 Manson Rd. ℭ 250/537-5041. Reservations accepted. Main courses C$12–C$34 (US$9.60–US$27). MC, V. Daily 11:30am–11pm.

GALIANO ISLAND

Galiano is an elongated string bean of an island stretched along the Gulf Islands' eastern flank. Though Galiano looks, on the map, like just a long, skinny sand spit, it is in fact quite mountainous, with rocky, cliff-faced shorelines and dense forests.

Galiano is the closest Gulf Island to Vancouver, and many of the properties here are second homes of the city's elite. The rural yet genteel feel of the island is perfect for a romantic getaway or a relaxing break from the hassles of urban life. However, don't come to Galiano looking for high-octane nightlife or boutique shopping. There isn't much of a town on the island, just a few shops and galleries at Sturdies Bay. However, there are a number of notable and unique eateries and excellent inns and B&Bs.

GETTING THERE   BC Ferries serves Sturdies Bay from both Tsawwassen and Swartz Bay. Floatplanes serve Galiano Island from the docks at Montague Harbour.

Harbour Air Seaplanes and **Seair Seaplanes** are your best options here. For contact information, see "Essentials," earlier in this chapter.

VISITOR INFORMATION Contact **Galiano Island Chamber of Commerce** (© **866/539-2233;** www.galianoisland.com). A seasonal information booth sits at the top of the ferry dock ramp.

GETTING AROUND For taxi or bus service, call **Galiano Island Shuttle** (© **250/ 539-0202;** www.gogaliano.com).

EXPLORING THE ISLAND

Galiano is perhaps the most physically striking of the Gulf Islands, particularly the mountainous southern shores. Mount Sutil, Mount Galiano, and the exposed cliffs above Georgeson Bay (simply called the Bluffs) rise above sheep-filled meadows, shadowy forests, and fern-lined ravines. **Active Pass,** the narrow strait that separates Galiano from Mayne Island, is another scenic high spot: All the ferry and much of the pleasure craft traffic between Vancouver and Victoria negotiates this turbulent, cliff-lined passage. Watch the bustle of the boats and ferries from **Bellhouse Provincial Park,** a picnicking area at the end of Jack Road, or head to **Montague Harbour Provincial Park,** a beautiful preserve of beach and forest.

Like Salt Spring Island, Galiano is also a center for artists and craftspeople. **Galiano Art Gallery,** in Sturdies Bay on Madrona Street (© **250/539-3539**), displays the work of many Gulf Island painters and sculptors. Just up the road on Sturdies Bay Road, also check out **Art and Soul Craft Gallery** (© **250/539-2944**).

BIKING The farther north you go on Galiano, the more remote, making this area a favorite among cyclists. While you won't have to worry too much about traffic on the 30km-long (19-mile) paved road that runs up the island's west side, there are enough steep ascents to keep your attention focused. Mountain bikers can follow unmaintained logging roads that skirt the eastern shores. Contact **Galiano Bicycle Rental,** 36 Burrill Rd. (© **250/539-9906;** www.galianoisland.com/galianobicycle), for rentals. A full day's rental is C$28 (US$22).

HIKING Several short hikes lead to Active Pass overlooks, including the trail to the top of 330m (1,082-ft.) Mount Galiano and the cliff-edge path in Bluffs Park. Bodega Ridge is a park about two-thirds of the way up the island, with old-growth forest, wildflowers, and views of the distant Olympic and Cascade mountain ranges.

KAYAKING & BOATING Home to otters, seals, and bald eagles, the gentle waters of Montague Harbour are a perfect kayaking destination. **Gulf Island Kayaking** (© **250/539-2442;** www.seakayak.ca) offers a variety of guided part- and whole-day trips, including a 3-hour sunset paddle for C$45 (US$36). If you want to really get away, consider a custom multiday kayaking/camping trip. Gulf Island Kayaking also offer kayak rentals from its base at the Montague Harbour marina.

WHERE TO STAY

The only campground is at **Montague Harbour Provincial Marine Park** (© **250/ 539-2115** for reservations, or 250/391-2300 for information; http://wlapwww. gov.bc.ca/bcparks) with 40 sites (15 walk-in and 25 drive-in; a portion of each take reservations) for C$17 (US$14). The camp offers beach access, but no showers or flush toilets.

Bellhouse Inn ⚜ If you're looking for historic charm and a scenic location, the Bellhouse Inn is hard to beat. The 1890 farmhouse sits in a grassy meadow above a private beach. The views of Mayne Island across Active Pass are stunning, and orcas sometimes frolic right in front of you. The 2.4 hectares (6 acres) of grounds retain the feel of the old farm, with fruit trees lining the property and sheep grazing in the fields. Each bedroom has a private balcony, and one has a Jacuzzi. The lounge, filled with vintage furniture and period art, is a great spot to curl up with a book. The proprietor also sails a 13m (43-ft.) boat during the summer months; for a fee you can take a trip out into the pass.

29 Farmhouse Rd., Galiano Island, BC V0N 1P0. (©) **800/970-7464** or 250/539-5667. Fax 250/539-5316. www. bellhouseinn.com. 3 units. Mid-July to Labour Day C$135–C$195 (US$108–US$156) double; check website for lower shoulder and off-season rates. Rates include breakfast. 2-night minimum stay on weekends and holidays. MC, V. Children must be 16 or older. **Amenities:** Lounge; golf course nearby; in-room massage. *In room:* Hair dryer, iron, no phone.

Driftwood Village (Kids) (Finds)   This venerable choice is perfect as a comfortable retreat for couples or in summer as a laid-back vacation with the kids and pets in tow. The cottages, of differing vintages and styles, are scattered around a .8-hectare (2-acre) garden complete with ponds, flowers, and fruit trees. Most have fireplaces and decks with views onto Sturdies Bay, and all are decorated with a sense of eclectic artfulness that will instantly bring back youthful memories of idealized lakeside holidays.

205 Bluff Rd. E., Galiano Island, BC V0N 1P0. (©) **888/240-1466** or 250/539-5457. Fax 250/539-5058. www.driftwood cottages.com. 10 units. C$105 (US$84) studio double; C$125 (US$100) 1-bedroom heritage double; C$145 (US$116) 1- or 2-bedroom luxury double; C$159 (US$127) Jacuzzi suite. Off-season and shoulder-season rates available. Extra person C$10–C$20 (US$8–US$116). Rates include ferry pickup. MC, V. Pets accepted for C$10 (US$8) per night. **Amenities:** Jacuzzi; badminton court. *In room:* TV or TV/VCR, kitchen, fridge, coffeemaker, no phone.

Galiano Oceanfront Inn & Spa (reverse-A)(reverse-A)   Formerly the Galiano Lodge and one of the original accommodations on Galiano Island, the inn—with an unrestricted vista onto the harbor, the busy boat traffic on Active Passage, and the lighthouse on Mayne Island—is now a top destination in the Gulf Islands. Unique in the islands, the Galiano Inn is just a 5-minute stroll from the ferry dock, so guests can leave the car on the mainland. Galiano Inn also offers some of the largest and most comfortable rooms on the island. Each of the very plush rooms has a fireplace, a patio or balcony with stunning water views, and extras such as bathrobes and CD players. Rooms with king beds have Jacuzzi tubs, while others have soaker tubs; all bathrooms have glass-walled shower stalls. One room is wheelchair accessible. Another 10 executive suites are planned for 2006. The Atrevida restaurant, with notable regional cuisine (p. 130), is in a separate, even more stunning building filled with Northwest Native art; Madrona del Mar Spa, a complete beauty and wellness center, shares the waterfront building. A large garden courtyard with a fountain greets guests, while a new garden addition includes a koi pond, herb and vegetable beds for the restaurant, and outdoor treatment areas for the spa; a path leads to a small sandy beach.

134 Madrona Dr., Galiano Island, BC V0N 1P0. (©) **877/530-3939** or 250/539-3388. Fax 250/539-3333. www.galiano inn.com. 10 units. C$170–C$350 (US$122–US$252). Off-season rates available. Rates include full breakfast. MC, V. Free parking. **Amenities:** Restaurant (Atrevida, p. 130); lounge; golf course nearby; spa; outdoor hot tub; kayaking/ boat rentals nearby; tour/activities desk; courtesy limo; business center; British Columbia wine and gourmet shop; room service; laundry service; gardens; 1 room for those w/limited mobility. *In room:* Minibar, fridge, coffeemaker, hair dryer, wireless Internet, Jacuzzi, CD player, robes, fireplace.

Woodstone Country Inn (reverse-A)(reverse-A)   A quintessential small country inn, Woodstone is one of the most refined lodgings on Galiano. It sits among fir trees overlooking a series of meadows, which serve as a de facto bird sanctuary. The entire inn is decorated with restrained but exquisite taste: You'll find not only the owner's collection of art from

world travels but canvases from renowned local painters. Woodstone's architecture is such that all rooms are large and unique; many second floor rooms also have dramatic dormered ceilings. Our favorite is the Dogwood room, with beautiful oak paneling, fine furnishings, and a vast window with views of the valley. All units have fireplaces, some have soaker tubs, and one is wheelchair accessible. Rooms on the main floor have small private patios. The restaurant (see "Where to Dine," below) serves fine cuisine.

743 Georgeson Bay Rd., RR 1, Galiano Island, BC V0N 1P0. ℂ 888/339-2022 or 250/539-2022. Fax 250/539-5198. www.woodstoneinn.com. 12 units. C$129–C$195 (US$103–US$156) double. Rates include full breakfast and afternoon tea. Packages available. AE, MC, V. Closed Dec–Jan. Children must be 15 or older. **Amenities:** Restaurant; lounge; golf course nearby; concierge; tour/activities desk; business center; in-room massage; nonsmoking facility; 1 room for those w/limited mobility. *In room:* Hair dryer, no phone.

WHERE TO DINE

The convivial **Daystar Market Café** (ℂ **250/539-2800**) is just north of Sturdies Bay at the intersection of Georgeson Bay and Porlier Pass roads. Part of an organic- and health-food store, it serves mostly vegetarian meals for lunch and dinner daily. **Montague Café,** at the Montague Harbour Marina (ℂ **250/539-5733**), offers light dining right on the water. **Hummingbird Pub,** 47 Sturdies Bay Rd. (ℂ **250/539-5472**), is a friendly, woodsy spot for beer and a burger.

Atrevida Dining Room ⋇⋇ PACIFIC NORTHWEST This gorgeous dining room in the Galiano Oceanfront Inn has one of the best views in the Gulf Islands, literally overlooking the harbor and ferry traffic on Active Pass: a nine-sided post-and-beam room with glass walls lets you take it all in. The small, focused menu, featuring wild salmon, local chicken, and island lamb, is enhanced with seasonal fish and shellfish specials from the local catch. In fact, much of the produce and fish is bought directly from farmers and fishers, who deliver their goods to the pier outside the dining room; hope that the local diver has brought in a catch of the small native scallops. Much thought goes into the wine list, which is full of unusual choices from local micro-wineries (there are over 25 on the islands). The goal—amply reached—is to wed island wines and regional ingredients into a unique expression of Gulf Islands cuisine. In summer months, lunch and dinner is served on the patio, while in winter the focus is the dining room's huge stone fireplace.

134 Madrona Dr. (ℂ **250/539-3388.** Reservations suggested. Main courses from C$18–C$30 (US$15–US$24). MC, V. Dinner daily from 5:30; lunch served July–Labour Day only. Call for hours.

Woodstone Country Inn ⋇⋇ INTERNATIONAL The Wisteria Dining Room at the Woodstone is one of the top restaurants in the Gulf Islands. The menu is a compelling blend of classic French cuisine enlivened with vivid international flavors. You might find grape-leaf-wrapped baked Cornish hen on walnut risotto, or sockeye salmon glazed with orange and ginger atop sautéed pea shoots. The daily menu includes a choice of three entrees—meat, fish, or vegetarian—accompanied by homemade bread, soup, and a delightful salad. Desserts, which aren't included in the prix fixe, usually include the outstanding bread pudding with rum sauce. The wine list is a mix of Okanagan, California, and French vintages. The professionalism of the staff combined with a convivial atmosphere make dining here an enchanting experience.

743 Georgeson Bay Rd., RR 1. ℂ **888/339-2022** or 250/539-2022. Reservations required. 3-course dinner C$28–C$33 (US$22–US$26). AE, MC, V. Daily seating from 6–8:30pm.

MAYNE ISLAND

Bucolic Mayne Island is a medley of rock-lined bays, forested hills, and pastureland. Mayne was once a center of Gulf Island agriculture, noted for its apple and tomato production. Many of the island's early farmhouses remain, and a rural, lived-in quality is one of Mayne's most endearing features.

GETTING THERE   **BC Ferries** serves Mayne Island with regularly scheduled runs from both Tsawwassen and Swartz Bay. **Harbour Air, Tofino Air,** and **Seair Seaplanes** all offer floatplane service between Mayne and Vancouver. For contact information, see "Essentials," earlier in this chapter.

VISITOR INFORMATION   Contact the **Mayne Island Community Chamber of Commerce,** Box 2, Mayne Island, BC V0N 2J0 (no phone; www.mayneisland chamber.ca).

GETTING AROUND   Call **M.I.D.A.S. Taxi** at *©* **250/539-3132** or 250/539-0181 for a ride.

EXPLORING THE ISLAND

Miner's Bay is by default the commercial center of the island, though in most locales this somewhat aimless collection of homes and businesses wouldn't really qualify as a village. It's this understated approach to life that provides Mayne Island with its substantial charm. Don't let the rural patina fool you: Some of the lodgings and restaurants are world-class, and even though organized activities are few, it's hard to be bored on such a lovely island.

Mayne doesn't boast the provincial parks and public lands that the other Gulf Islands do, though there are several beach access sites that provide opportunities for swimming in warm weather, and beachcombing during other times of the year. **Bennett Bay,** on the northeast coast, is the best swimming beach. **Campbell Bay,** just northwest, is another favorite pebble beach. **Dinner Bay Park** is lovely for a picnic.

On a sunny day, the grounds of the **Georgina Point Lighthouse** offer dramatic views. Located on the island's northern tip, this lighthouse juts into Active Pass and overlooks the southern shores of Galiano Island, less than a mile away.

Mayne Island is home to a number of artists; the widely available map of the island lists more than 20 studios that are open to visitors. The pottery of **John Charowsky,** 490 Fernhill Rd. (*©* **250/539-3488**), is especially attractive.

BIKING   Mayne is one of the best islands for cyclists. The rolling hills provide plenty of challenges, yet the terrain is considerably less mountainous than that of the other islands. For rentals, contact **Mayne Island Kayaks & Canoe Rentals,** below.

HIKING   The roads on Mayne are usually quiet enough that they can also serve as paths for hikers. Those looking for more solitude should consider **Mount Parke Regional Park,** off Fernhill Road in the center of the island. The park's best views reward those who take the 1-hour hike to Halliday Viewpoint.

KAYAKING & BOATING   Mayne Island Kayak & Canoe Rentals (*©* **250/539-5599;** www.maynekayak.com), at Seal Beach in Miner's Bay, rents kayaks and canoes for C$22 (US$16) for 2 hours, or C$42 (US$30) for a full day. The company will drop off kayaks at any of six launching points on the island, and, if you get stranded, will even pick up kayaks (and too-weary kayakers) from other destinations. If you'd rather let the wind do the work, call **Island Charters** (*©* **250/539-5040**). A half-day sailboat excursion (C$140/US$112 for two) lets you explore the coasts of Mayne, Saturna, and the Pender islands; or you can arrange for the sailboat to deliver you to other island destinations.

WHERE TO STAY

Blue Vista Resort *Kids*   This venerable resort is that rare Gulf Island lodging: a place where kids and pets are welcome. On the warm eastern side of Mayne Island—close to beaches, kayaking, and hiking—the comfortable, unfussy cabins are a great value and come with full kitchen, deck, and barbecue; some have a fireplace. You have a choice of studio, one-, and two-bedroom cabins; one-bedroom units have ramps for wheelchair access. Blue Vista is also a great location for an active holiday, with sea kayak rentals and tours into the new Gulf Islands National Park Reserve, plus bike rentals.

563 Arbutus Dr., Mayne Island, BC V0N 2J0. © **877/535-2424** or 250/539-2463. www.bluevistaresort.com. 8 units. C$65–C$83 (US$52–US$66) studio; C$75–C$105 (US$60–US$84) 1-bedroom cottage; C$90–C$120 (US$72–US$96) 2-bedroom cottage. Extra person C$10 (US$8). Off-season and weekly rates available. MC, V. Pets accepted in 2 cottages for C$6 (US$4.80) per night. **Amenities:** Kayak and canoe rentals; bike rentals; laundry service; nonsmoking facility; rooms for those w/limited mobility. *In room:* TV, kitchen, fridge, coffeemaker, no phone.

A Coach-House on Oyster Bay B&B Inn *←*   This modern home on a private bay (3km/2 miles from the ferry terminal) was designed to look like one of Mayne Island's old heritage farm homes, but with up-to-date comforts. Each unit has a gas fireplace, patio or balcony, and private entrance, plus nice touches such as robes and complimentary sherry. Two of the rooms have their own private hot tubs. A path from the inn leads to an outdoor hot tub and gazebo, perched just 3m (10 ft.) from the tide line on a rock ledge. From here, the views across the Strait of Georgia are magnificent. Otters frequently come into the bay, and orcas gather just offshore. Deer feel so at home that they sometimes sleep right in the garden. Coach-House is convenient to the Georgina Point Lighthouse. In summer, the water along the small private beach is warm enough for swimming.

511 Bayview Dr., Mayne Island, BC V0N 2J0. © **888/629-6322** or 250/539-3368. Fax 250/539-3355. www.acoach house.com. 3 units. C$170–C$210 (US$136–US$168) double. Off-season rates available. Rates include breakfast. 2-night minimum stay in summer and on holidays. AE, MC, V. **Amenities:** Common area; Jacuzzi; kayak and canoe rentals; free bikes and tennis rackets; nonsmoking facility. *In room:* Hair dryer, wireless Internet, fireplace, no phone.

Oceanwood Country Inn *←←←*   This luxury property is one of the best places to stay in the Gulf Islands. A gem of understated elegance, it has an excellent restaurant, attentive staff, spacious rooms with sumptuous furnishings, and just the right blend of comfortable formality and relaxed hospitality. All but one of the rooms have magnificent views of Navy Channel and Saturna Island. The original inn's rooms are smaller and less expensive, yet still comfortable and beautifully outfitted; two have balconies. The rooms in the new wing are truly large, with private decks, two-person tubs, and fireplaces. The Wisteria Suite is a three-tiered unit with two baths, multiple decks, and an outdoor soaker tub.

The inn's public rooms are equally impressive. Facing the gardens are a comfortable living room and library, separated by a double-sided fireplace. The dining room is one of the most sophisticated places to eat on the Gulf Islands (see "Where to Dine," below).

630 Dinner Bay Rd., Mayne Island, BC V0N 2J0. © **250/539-5074.** Fax 250/539-3002. www.oceanwood.com. 12 units. Mid-June to mid-Sept C$179–C$349 (US$143–US$279); mid-Sept to Oct 31 and Mar 2 to mid-June C$139–C$299 (US$111–US$239). Extra person C$25 (US$20). Rates include full breakfast and afternoon tea. MC, V. Closed Nov 1–late Mar. **Amenities:** Restaurant; bar; golf course nearby; Jacuzzi; sauna; free bikes; in-room massage; nonsmoking facility. *In room:* Hair dryer, no phone.

WHERE TO DINE

Manna Bakery Café, on Fernhill Road in Miner's Bay's tiny strip mall (© **250/539-2323**), is the place to go for a cappuccino and fresh-baked cinnamon roll. Just above the marina in Miner's Bay, the **Springwater Lodge** (© **250/539-5521**) is a comfortably ramshackle pub/restaurant with great views; try the fish and chips.

Oceanwood Country Inn ☆☆ PACIFIC NORTHWEST   Refined yet robust, the cuisine at Oceanwood is one of the Gulf Islands' best expressions of up-to-date, full-flavored cooking. The chef unites the rich bounty of Northwest fish, meat, game, and produce in a daily-changing tableau of impressive tastes and textures. Try the local paupiettes of sole with herb gnocchi and blackberry vinaigrette, or the grilled duck breast with cranberry demi glace served on foie gras–stuffed ravioli. The dining room overlooks a lily pond and garden; the decor is handsome but unfussy.

630 Dinner Bay Rd. © **250/539-5074**. www.oceanwood.com. Reservations required. 4-course prix-fixe menu C$48 (US$38). MC, V. Daily, most sittings 6–8pm. Closed Nov to late Mar.

THE PENDER ISLANDS

The Penders consist of North and South Pender islands, separated by a very narrow channel that's spanned by a one-lane bridge. North Pender is much more developed, though that's all relative out in the Gulf Islands. It has a rather startling housing development on its southwest side, a 1970s suburb plopped down on an otherwise rural island. Neither of the Penders seems to share the long-standing farming background of the other Gulf Islands, so forests are thick and all-encompassing. The Penders do have some lovely beaches and public parks with good hiking trails. Toss in a handful of local artists, and you have the recipe for a tranquil island retreat.

GETTING THERE   **BC Ferries** serves Pender Island with regularly scheduled runs from both Tsawwassen and Swartz Bay. The commuter airlines mentioned in previous sections also offer floatplane service to and from Vancouver. For more information, see "Essentials," earlier in this chapter.

VISITOR INFORMATION   The **Pender Island Visitor Info Centre,** 2332 Otter Bay Rd. (©/fax **250/629-6541**), is open from May 15 to September 2. Or check out the chamber of commerce website at www.penderislandchamber.com.

EXPLORING THE ISLANDS

Mount Norman Regional Park, which encompasses the northwest corner of South Pender Island, features hiking trails through old-growth forest to wilderness beaches and ridge-top vistas. Access to trails is just across the Pender Island bridge.

The extensive network of roads makes these islands good destinations for cyclists. Rentals are available at **Otter Bay Marina,** 2311 McKinnon Rd. (© **250/629-3579**), where you'll also find **Mouat Point Kayaks,** 1615 Storm Crescent (© **250/629-6767**). If beachcombing or sunning are more your style, try **Hamilton Beach** on the east side of North Pender, or **Medicine Beach** and the beaches along **Beaumont Marine Park,** both of which flank Bedwell Harbour.

WHERE TO STAY

If you want to rent a house on one of the Gulf Islands, one of the best options is **The Timbers** ☆☆ (© **877/662-3414** or 250/629-6040; www.thetimbers.net), a 22-hectare (55-acre) waterfront property on the western shores of Bedwell Harbour that offers five beautifully decorated, fully furnished cottages, each with private beach, hot tub, covered deck or patio, and use of an ozonated swimming pool and a children's play area. Cottages range from one-bedroom units with loft beds that sleep two to six, to three-bedroom, two-bathroom units that are, at 139 sq. m (1,500 sq. ft.), essentially houses, and can sleep eight. Each cottage has a full kitchen, fireplace or gas stove, TV/VCR, plus luxe features like slate floors and locally milled alder floors. In summer, week-long rentals are required, starting at C$1,699 (US$1,359) for up to six people. In off seasons, rates can drop to C$171 (US$137) per night for up to four people, with a 3-night minimum. For more information, contact **Gulf Island Vacation Rentals,** 5402 Wilson Rd., Pender Island, BC V0N 2M1 (© **866/472-7982** or 250/629-6040).

Eatenton House B&B Inn

This contemporary B&B offers wonderful gardens and views of both the forest and the sparkling waters of Browning Harbour. The spacious rooms are great for groups; the largest is essentially a suite with two bedrooms. Nice touches include silk robes and large towels. A fireplace commands the dining area and antiques-filled sitting room. On nice afternoons, the deck is where you'll be spending most of your time.

4705 Scarff Rd., Pender Island, BC V0N 2M1. © **888/780-9994** or 250/629-8355. Fax 250/629-8375. www.penderislands.com. 3 units. C$95–C$135 (US$76–US$108) double. Extra person C$20 (US$16). Rates include full breakfast. Honeymoon, off-season, and anniversary packages available. MC, V. Children must be 15 or older. **Amenities:** Golf course nearby; Jacuzzi; nonsmoking facility. *In room:* TV w/VCR, hair dryer, teakettle, no phone.

Inn on Pender Island *(Kids* *(Value*

The Inn on Pender Island is the name given to an enterprising complex at the center of North Pender. Nine large, unfussy units are housed in a modern motel building. Pets and kids are welcome. These basic rooms are a real deal in the otherwise expensive Gulf Islands. Also part of the complex are three log cabins. Each has a kitchenette and deck; two have hot tubs. These, too, are a great value when you consider the sky's-the-limit prices of comparable lodgings. Likewise, the restaurant is a just-fine place to eat, with good Northwest cuisine.

4709 Canal Rd., N. Pender Island, BC V0N 2M0. © **800/550-0172** or 250/629-3353. Fax 250/629-3167. 12 units. C$79–C$89 (US$63–US$71) lodge double; C$149 (US$119) cabin. Extra person C$10 (US$8). Lodge rates include breakfast. V. Small pets allowed for C$2 (US$1.60). **Amenities:** Restaurant; Jacuzzi; business center. *In room:* TV/VCR, kitchenette (in cabins only), fridge, coffeemaker.

Oceanside Inn

Cantilevered above a rocky cliff overlooking Navy Channel and Mayne Island, the Oceanside Inn ranks among the most private getaways on the Penders. The arbutus trees that line the shore are home to bald eagles and turkey buzzards. The dramatic setting alone strongly recommends the place. Two rooms have fireplaces. All units have private entrances, private decks with outdoor hot tubs, and bathrobes.

4230 Armadale Rd., N. Pender Island, BC V0N 2M3. © **800/601-3284** or 250/629-6691. www.penderisland.com. 3 units. C$139–C$239 (US$–US$191) double. Rates include full breakfast. Off-season rates and multiday escape and honeymoon packages available. V. Children must be 18 or older. Closed mid-Oct to early Apr. **Amenities:** Golf course nearby; private hot tubs; tour/activities information; in-room massage; beach access on property; Internet access in common area; nonsmoking facility. *In room:* Fridge, hair dryer, iron, no phone.

Poets Cove Resort and Spa *(★★★*

This very impressive new resort shows what a difference an investment of C$48 million can make. Poets Cove opened in 2004 on the former Bedwell Harbour Resort site, which served for many years as a rustic boating lodge and the Canadian Customs office for U.S. and Canadian pleasure-boat traffic. Like a butterfly losing its cocoon, the newly built resort has emerged as a classy and sprawling complex that includes a 22-room Arts and Crafts–style lodge complete with upscale spa, fitness center, ballroom, casual restaurant/pub, and fine-dining restaurant, plus 15 cottages and nine luxury-apartment-like villas. Furnishings are top-quality, and the attention to detail is exquisite. Lodge rooms have soaker tubs, tiled showers, fireplaces, and balconies with views over Bedwell Harbour, while the cottages and villas are spacious units (several boast three bedrooms) with full kitchens, fireplaces, balconies or decks, two bathrooms, and—in addition to indoor soaker tubs—outdoor hot tubs in many. The refined solitude makes it easy to forget that incredible recreation waits just outside the door, but the kayak and charter boat rental at the activity center can help you remember. Or simply enjoy one of the two swimming pools (one for adults only). Poets Cove sets the gold standard for marina resorts in southwest British Columbia; you can't go wrong here.

9801 Spalding Rd., S. Pender Island, BC V0N 2M3. ✆ **888/512-7638** or 250/629-2100. Fax 250/629-2110. www.poets cove.com. 46 units. C$159–$289 (US$127–US$231) double lodge rooms; C$319–C$449 (US$255–US$359) 2-bedroom villas; C$419–C$549 (US$335–US$439) 3-bedroom villa; C$349–C$479 (US$279–US$383) 2-bedroom cottage; C$419–C$649 (US$335–US$519) 3-bedroom cottage. Extra person C$50 (US$40). AE, MC, V. **Amenities:** Restaurant (see Aurora, below); bar; 2 swimming pools; tennis courts; fitness center; spa; sports equipment rental; concierge; market; deli; coin-op laundry; activity center; marina. *In room:* TV/DVD, fridge, coffeemaker, hair dryer, iron, kettle, fireplace, balcony or patio, robes, soaker tubs.

WHERE TO DINE

Aurora ⟳⟳ PACIFIC NORTHWEST   The swank dining room at Poets Cove Resort combines excellent food, a romantic setting, and terrific views—this is easily the most sophisticated place to eat on the Penders. Unsurprisingly, the menu features local fish and shellfish, including oysters on the half shell, wild salmon and halibut, and other seasonal fish specials. Local lamb is also a standout; and lavender-dusted sirloin is served over warm goat cheese and vegetable terrine with carrot couscous. One wall of the warmly formal dining room is dominated by a huge stone fireplace, and another by a bank of wine bottles, but you'll spend more time taking in the lovely view of the harbor and islands. Casual dining is also available in Syrens Lounge, which opens onto a voluminous patio.

In Poets Cove Resort and Spa, 9801 Spalding Rd. ✆ **250/629-2100.** Reservations recommended. Main courses C$27–C$30 (US$22–US$24). AE, MC, V. Daily 5–10pm.

Hope Bay Café ⟳⟳ NEW CANADIAN   Northeast of North Pender Island is Hope Bay, a tiny community perched above a rocky harbor. When the old general store at Hope Bay, open since 1903, burned down a few years ago, a group of island artists and merchants pooled resources to rebuild a new commercial center in this lovely waterfront spot. In the corner with the best views is the Hope Bay Café, a very pleasant, light-filled dining room whose informality veils some very serious and delicious cooking. It's a classic story: big-city-trained chef comes to small community and cooks fantastic food. Get here before the crowds do. While the printed menu is small, and includes dishes such as Dungeness crab with three dipping sauces or pan-seared salmon with Thai curry sauce, the real attractions are the specials that vary seasonally as local ingredients become available. Baked guinea hen with a gravy of wild mushrooms, fennel, and port is superb.

4301 Bedwell Harbour Rd. ✆ **250/629-6668.** Main courses C$14–C$26 (US$11–US$21). MC, V. Mon–Fri 10am–3:30pm and 5–8:30pm; Sat 9am–3:30pm and 5–8:30pm; Sun 9am–3pm. Call to confirm off-season hours.

SATURNA ISLAND

The most remote of the southern Gulf Islands, Saturna is both pristine and, compared with its neighbors, mostly vacant—it has only about 350 residents. Whereas other islands are best described as rural, Saturna is truly wild. It's not surprising that the new Gulf Islands National Park Reserve has its largest presence on Saturna: About half the island is now protected as reserve land.

Served by direct ferries from Swartz Bay and a few indirect sailings from Tsawwassen, Saturna is hard to get to. It's easiest to ferry to Vancouver Island and then back out, or over to Pender Island, which has direct sailings to Saturna. If you are planning to visit all the Gulf Islands, start your journey on Saturna; for reasons that defy logic, it's easier to get away from Saturna by ferry than it is to get to it.

Any visit to Saturna should include a stop at **Saturna Island Family Estate Winery** (© 877/918-3388 or 250/539-3521), a small, well-established winery in an extremely dramatic setting. Perched between massive cliffs and the sea, the setting is reminiscent of Corsica. The tasting room, open daily 11am to 4:30pm from May to October, is reached by a precipitous single track road with a 20 percent grade. The tasting room also offers soups and salads for lunch.

Its remoteness makes Saturna a favorite destination of outdoorsy types. The island boasts nice beaches, including Russell Reef, Veruna Bay, and Shell Beach at **East Point Park.** This park, with its still-active lighthouse, is a good spot to watch for orcas. Hikers can drive to **Mount Warburton Pike** and follow the **Brown Ridge Nature Trail.** Views from this craggy cliff-faced peak are astonishing, taking in southern Vancouver Island, the San Juan Islands, and the Olympic Peninsula. Kayakers can explore the rocky islets surrounding **Tumbo Island,** just offshore Saturna's eastern peninsula. Facilities are few and far between, though in several cases, exemplary. For more information, check out **www.saturnatourism.com**.

WHERE TO STAY & DINE

In addition to the excellent dining room at the Saturna Lodge (below), there is also a deli and cafe at the **Saturna General Store,** 101 Narvaez Bay Rd. (© **250/539-2936**).

Breezy Bay B&B   Twenty hectares (49 acres) of farmland surround this 1890s farmhouse, which overlooks sheep and llama pastures and cliff-lined Breezy Bay. The interior of the house is lined with wainscot and period moldings, and a stone fireplace dominates the lounge and library. The cozy bedrooms share two bathrooms. Paths lead to the beach, with access for swimming and kayaking. Children are welcome.

131 Payne Rd., Saturna Island, BC V0N 2Y0. © 250/539-5957. Fax 250/539-3339. http://saturnacan.net/~breezy. 4 units. C$85 (US$68) double. Extra person C$25 (US$20). Rates include full breakfast. No credit cards. Closed Oct–Mar. *In room:* No phone.

Saturna Lodge & Restaurant   This well-established resort, which began its life as a 1940s boarding house, has been revamped into a very comfortable, upscale country inn. If your idea of an island getaway is seclusion and genteel comfort, this is your lodging. Set amid gardens, with views onto Boot Cove, the lodge has taken on a winery theme—each of the charming guest rooms is named for a wine or grape varietal. The top of the line is the Sauterne Room, a large suite with soaker tub, private deck, and king bed. Families will like the suite of ground floor rooms with private entrances, where a twin-bed room and a queen room share a large bathroom. The attractive main-floor lounge overlooks the gardens and has a fireplace, small library, and television.

For most guests, the highlight of a stay here is a meal at the restaurant. The menu features Saturna Island lamb, local seafood, and organic produce. In good weather, the menu offers barbecued meats and fish from the outdoor grill. Three-course meals are

C$39 (US$31); a la carte selections are also available. There's a well-chosen wine list, featuring wines from Saturna and the other islands, as well as some from around British Columbia.

130 Payne Rd., Saturna Island, BC V0N 2Y0. ℂ **888/539-8800** or 250/539-2254. Fax 250/539-3091. www.saturna.ca. 7 units. C$120–C$195 (US$96–US$156) double. Rates include 3-course breakfast. Special packages available. MC, V. Closed Dec–Jan. Pets allowed in 3 garden rooms for C$20 (US$16) per night. **Amenities:** Restaurant; bar; Jacuzzi; free bikes; tour/activities desk; business center; nonsmoking facility. *In room:* TV/DVDs available, hair dryer, no phone.

3 West of Victoria: Sooke & Beyond

Sooke: 30km (19 miles) W of Victoria

Following Highway 14 west from Victoria, the suburbs eventually thin; by the time you reach Sooke, the vistas open up to the south, where Washington's Olympic Mountains prop up the horizon. There are a number of reasons to explore this part of the island.

Highway 14 gives access to beaches and parks with good swimming and recreation, finally leading to Port Renfrew, the southern trail head for the famous West Coast Trail (see chapter 7). Port Renfrew is a rough-and-ready seaside village whose main claim to fame is its deep-sea fishing; but it is also known as one of the termini of the West Coast Trail. Day-trippers from Vancouver also come out to visit **Botanical Beach Provincial Park** ✿, an area with spectacular tide-pool formations, unique geology, and one of the richest intertidal zones on the entire North American west coast. About 4km (2½ miles) south of Port Renfrew, Botanical Beach is a ledge of sandstone that juts out into the churning waters of the Strait of Juan de Fuca. Over the millennia, tidal action has carved out pits and pools, in which you'll find sea urchins, clams, periwinkles, giant anemones, chitons, and sea stars. In spring and fall, watch for gray whales. Check local tide tables to maximize opportunities for wildlife-viewing and tide pool exploration: a low tide of 1.2m (4 ft.) or less is best. Picnic facilities and toilets are available.

Ambitious backcountry drivers can make a loop journey from Highway 14. From Port Renfrew, a good logging road leads up the San Juan River valley, connecting to the southern shores of Cowichan Lake just west of Duncan. You can make this drive in 1 day, or divide the trip up by planning to spend the night camping at Cowichan Lake or at one of Duncan's moderately priced hotels.

The civilized reason to make the journey west from Victoria is the superlative Sooke Harbour House, one of the most renowned small inns in all of Canada.

IN & AROUND SOOKE

The little town of Sooke doesn't offer a lot to divert the visitor, but there are a number of recreation areas nearby that warrant a stop. **Sooke Potholes Provincial Park** preserves a curious geologic formation. The Sooke River flows down a series of rock ledges, pooling in waist-deep swimming holes before dropping in waterfalls to another series of pools and waterfalls. In July and August, the normally chilly river water warms up. The trails that link the pools are nice for a casual hike. There are more trails in adjacent **Sooke Mount Provincial Park.** To reach these parks, drive west on Route 14 almost to the town of Sooke; turn right on Sooke River Road. Fifteen kilometers (9¼ miles) west of Sooke is **French Beach Park,** a sand-and-gravel beach that's one of the best places to watch for gray whales. The park has 69 campsites.

WHERE TO STAY

Markham House B&B and Honeysuckle Cottage ☆☆   On the outskirts of Sooke, nestled in the woods, sits this admirably well-executed Tudor-style home on 4 hectares (10 acres) of landscaped grounds. The rooms are outfitted with antiques, featherbeds, and duvets. The cottage has its own kitchenette, woodstove, and hot tub. The main house features an elegant parlor with fireplace, plus a hot tub. Breakfasts are sumptuous and healthy. Outside, you can sit by the trout pond, play bocce, or practice your golf swing on the minifairway and green. Of course, you may also want to head out to the water or explore the region's parks, and your gracious hosts will help you make plans.

1775 Connie Rd., Victoria, BC V9C 4C2. © 888/256-6888 or 250/642-7542. Fax 250/642-7538. www.markham house.com. 4 units. July–Sept and mid-Dec to Jan 3 C$105–C$215 (US$84–US$172) double; Oct to mid-Dec and Jan 4–Jun C$95–C$175 (US$76–US$140) double. Rates include full breakfast and afternoon tea. AE, DC, DISC, MC, V. Take Sooke Rd. (Hwy. 14) west from Victoria 25km (16 miles); turn left on Connie Rd. Pets allowed in cottage. Not suitable for children. **Amenities:** Swimming pool, golf course, tennis nearby; room service; laundry service; croquet; badminton; hot tub; gazebo; nonsmoking facility. *In room:* TV/VCR, fireplace, wireless Internet access, robes.

Point-No-Point Resort ☆   Get away from it all in your own little cabin on the ocean, with 16 hectares (40 acres) of wilderness around you, a wide, rugged beach in front of you, and nothing to do but laze the day away in your hot tub. This resort has been welcoming guests since 1950. All cabins have fireplaces and kitchens; newer ones have hot tubs and decks, and two are wheelchair accessible. Lunch and dinner can be had in the sunny dining room; its tables are conveniently equipped with binoculars, so you won't miss a bald eagle as you eat. In summer, the resort runs a fishing boat charter.

1505 West Coast Hwy. (Hwy. 14), Sooke, BC V0S 1N0. © 250/646-2020. Fax 250/646-2294. www.pointnopoint resort.com. 25 units. C$165–C$280 (US$132–US$224) cabin double. 2- or 3-night minimum stay on weekends and holidays. Off-season rates available. Summer fishing packages available. AE, MC, V. Free parking. Pets allowed for C$10 (US$8) per night and C$100 (US$80) refundable dog deposit. No children in cabins with hot tubs. **Amenities:** Restaurant/teahouse; in-room massage; laundry service; rooms for those w/limited mobility. *In room:* Kitchen, fridge, coffeemaker, no phone.

Sooke Harbour House ☆☆☆   This inn at the foot of a beautiful pebble-and-sand spit, 30km (19 miles) west of Victoria, has earned an international reputation for the warmth of its welcome, quality of its food and lodging, and the drama of its vistas. One of the great things about Sooke Harbour House is that the whole operation seems effortless and graceful while in fact an extraordinary amount of work and attention is geared toward the comfort of the guests. Each individually decorated suite boasts a fireplace, bathrobes, antiques, fresh flowers, and views of the water—most have unusual nooks and corners that make them unique. One unit is wheelchair accessible. The three top-floor rooms, very spacious suites with 6m (20-ft.) cathedral ceilings and beautiful furnishings, are perfect for romantic getaways. All but one of the rooms have decks overlooking the inn's splendid gardens and onto Sooke Harbour, where otters swim and dive, and many have Jacuzzis with a waterfront view. Massages and spa treatments can be arranged by appointment. The entire inn is absolutely filled with art—in fact, the quantity of art in Sooke Harbour House's common spaces makes it one of the largest public art collections on Vancouver Island. The extensive gardens, which grow many of the herbs and flowers that appear on your dinner table, are also fascinating; the gardener leads tours each morning. A nice perk is the easy access to the spit, a public park that juts out into the mouth of Sooke Harbour, breaking the rougher waters of the Strait of San Juan de Fuca. It's a nice stroll out and back—perfect for watching the sunset, as well

(Moments Hiking the Juan de Fuca Marine Trail

This long-distance hiking trail links China Beach Park, just past the town of Jordan River, to Botanical Beach Provincial Park, near Port Renfrew, along a stretch of near-wilderness coastline. Similar to the famed West Coast Trail but less extreme, the rugged 47km (29-mile) trail offers scenic beauty, spectacular hiking, wildlife-viewing, and roaring surf in its course along the Pacific coastline of the Strait of Juan de Fuca. Most of the trail is designed for strenuous day or multiday hiking. Unlike the West Coast Trail, it can be easily broken down into daylong segments between trail heads accessed along Highway 14: China Beach, Sombrio Beach, Parkinson Creek, and Botanical Beach. Plan on 3 days to hike the entire length; campsites are regularly spaced along the trail.

Conditions are always changing, so obtain up-to-date information before proceeding by checking the trail head information shelters. If you're camping, keep a tide chart handy and refer to trail head postings about points that will be impassable at high tide. Wear proper footwear—the trail gets very muddy—and appropriate clothing, plus rain gear if you're going to camp. And leave a plan of your trip (including which trail you're hiking), with arrival and departure times, with a friend or relative. Also, don't leave a car full of valuables in the trail-head parking lots—break-ins are common.

For information on Juan de Fuca Marine Park, contact **BC Parks,** South Vancouver Island District, 2930 Trans-Canada Hwy., Victoria (© **250/391-2300;** http://wlapwww.gov.bc.ca/bcparks).

---

as seals, otters, and birds. Sooke Harbour House has one of the best restaurants in Canada (see "Where to Dine," below).

1528 Whiffen Spit Rd., Sooke, BC V0S 1N0. © **800/889-9688** or 250/642-3421. Fax 250/642-6988. www.sooke harbourhouse.com. 28 units. May to mid-Oct and winter holidays C$335–C$575 (US$268–US$460); mid-Oct to Apr other than holidays C$250–C$355 (US$200–US$284). Rates include in-room breakfast and brown-bag lunch. Children 6 and under stay free in parent's room. Dinner C$69 (US$55) extra. Off-season discounts available. AE, MC, V. Free parking. Take the Island Hwy. (Hwy. 1) to the Sooke/Colwood turnoff (Junction Hwy. 14). Follow Hwy. 14 to Sooke. About 1.6km (1 mile) past the town's 3rd traffic light, turn left onto Whiffen Spit Rd. Pets allowed for C$30 (US$24) per night. **Amenities:** Restaurant; spa services; bike rentals; concierge; tour/activities desk; room service; babysitting; laundry service; art gallery; garden tours; 1 room for those w/limited mobility. *In room:* Fridge, coffeemaker, hair dryer, iron, steam shower, Jacuzzi.

WHERE TO DINE

17 Mile House PUB For inexpensive but reliable fare, the 17-mile House has the most character in the area. Built in the late 1800s, this establishment became a regional hub in the 1920s when it installed the only phone around. Today, you can sup on a nice salad, burger, or one of many pasta, meat, or seafood entrees while admiring the old wood, brick, and tile interior. You might tap out a tune on the pub's 150-year-old piano or settle for a game of billiards; Saturdays feature live music.

5126 Sooke Rd. © **250/642-5942.** www.17milehouse.com. Main courses C$8–C$24 (US$6.40–US$19). Sun–Thurs 11am–11pm; Fri–Sat 11am–midnight. MC, V. On Sooke Rd. (Hwy. 14) between Connie Rd. and Gillespie Rd. Victoria bus no. 61.

Sooke Harbour House ✦✦✦ NORTHWEST COAST Acclaimed as one of the best restaurants in Canada, Sooke Harbour House treats you to a sensual culinary experience using almost all local ingredients, with an emphasis on the tastes of the Pacific Northwest and the produce of the inn's own gardens. The restaurant is situated at the rear of the inn, a rambling white house on a bluff, and offers a quiet atmosphere with spectacular views. A fall menu might feature hot and sour cabbage broth with Dungeness crab and a sweet corn pirogi, smoked salmon with nasturtium-leaf puree, and rack of lamb marinated with coriander and juniper berry and served with quince sage syrup. A la carte selections are available on weekends only. With advance notice, the kitchen will prepare a seven- to nine-course gastronomical adventure for C$99 (US$71). If you're ready for a splurge, the sommelier will pick a pairing for each dish from a wine list that's one of *Wine Spectator's* "best in the world."

1528 Whiffen Spit Rd., Sooke. ⓒ 250/642-3421. www.sookeharbourhouse.com. Reservations required. Main courses C$29–C$38 (US$23–US$30); Sun–Thurs prix-fixe 4-course menu C$69 (US$55). AE, MC, V. Daily 5–9pm. Take the Island Hwy. to the Sooke/Colwood turnoff (Junction Hwy. 14). Continue on Hwy. 14 to Sooke. About 1.5km (1 mile) past the town's 3rd traffic light, turn left onto Whiffen Spit Rd.

4 North of Victoria: Goldstream Provincial Park ⊛

North of Victoria, the Island Highway climbs up over the high mountain ridge called the Malahat, shedding the suburbs as it climbs. Goldstream Provincial Park is a tranquil arboreal setting that overflowed with prospectors during the 1860s gold-rush days, hence its name. Today, its natural beauty attracts hikers, campers, and birders who stop to spend a few hours or days in the beautiful temperate rainforest.

Hiking trails take you past abandoned mine shafts and tunnels as well as stands of Douglas fir, lodgepole pine, red cedar, indigenous yew, and arbutus trees. The **Gold Mine Trail** leads to Niagara Creek and the abandoned mine. The **Goldstream Trail** goes to the salmon-spawning areas (you might also catch sight of mink and river otters racing along this path).

Three species of salmon make **annual salmon runs** up the Goldstream River during the months of October, November, December, and February. Visitors can easily observe this natural wonder along the riverbanks. Goldstream is also a major attraction for bird-watchers, as numerous bald eagles winter here each year. January is the best month for spotting these majestic creatures.

For information on all provincial parks on the South Island, contact **BC Parks** (ⓒ 250/391-2300; www.env.gov.bc.ca/bcparks). Goldstream Park's **Freeman King Visitor Centre** (ⓒ 250/478-9414) offers guided walks and talks, plus programs geared towards kids throughout the year. It's open daily from 9:30am to 6pm; there is a C$3 (US$2.40) per day vehicle fee. Take Highway 1 about 20 minutes north of Victoria.

WHERE TO STAY

The Aerie Resort ⊛⊛ It's safe to say, there's nothing else on Vancouver Island like this Relais & Châteaux member designed to accommodate the most discriminating— even extravagant—tastes. The Aerie is a sprawling Mediterranean-style villa resort with opulent rooms and suites, dining rooms, and spa facilities scattered amid 14 hectares (35 acres) of gardens and fir forest. Austrian-born owner Maria Schuster dreamed of transporting the style and grandeur of private estates along the French and Italian Riviera to the Pacific Northwest. The result is a series of neo-Palladian villas boasting sumptuous furnishings and top-of-the-line—some would say, over the top— decor. Dior duvets sit atop gargantuan four-poster beds; expect amenities to include CD players, bathrobes, fresh-cut flowers, and chocolate truffles. King-bed suites have balconies, fireplaces, and Jacuzzi or soaker tubs; others are two-story. Suites in the unparalleled Villa Cielo development are in a newer building even higher up the mountain, making it more private and attractive to celebrities. As its name implies, Villa Cielo offers jaw-dropping views from its perch in the sky over Finlayson Arm and Victoria, projecting a sense of place and occasion more suited to a European palace than a rugged Canadian mountain peak. Facilities include a helipad, a spa offering a variety of treatments, and an outdoor wedding chapel. Most guests also sample the excellent cuisine in the dining room (see below).

600 Ebedora Lane, P.O. Box 108, Malahat, BC V0R 2L0. ℂ 800/518-1933 or 250/743-7115. Fax 250/743-4766. www. aerie.bc.ca. 29 units. Late May to mid-Oct C$295–C$345 (US$236–US$276) double, C$395–C$775 (US$316– US$620) suite; Mar 28 to late May C$255–C$335 (US$204–US$268) double, C$365–C$695 (US$292–US$556) suite; mid-Oct to Mar 27 C$195–$275 (US$156–US$220) double, C$325–$650 (US$260–US$520) suite. Rates include a full breakfast. Packages available. AE, DC, MC, V. Free parking. Take Hwy. 1 north to the Spectacle Lake turnoff; take the 1st right and follow the winding driveway up. **Amenities:** Restaurant; lounge; indoor pool; golf courses nearby; tennis court; full service spa; concierge; limited room service; in-room massage; laundry service; complimentary wireless Internet access; nonsmoking facility. *In room:* A/C, TV (VCRs available), dataport, minibar, fridge, coffeemaker, hair dryer, iron.

WHERE TO DINE

The Aerie 𝕲𝕲 FRENCH/NORTHWEST   Ornate. Overwhelming. Over the top? Depends on your tastes. The dining room of this villa boasts panoramic views, a gold-leaf ceiling, chandeliers, and faux-marble columns. When it comes to the cooking, over-the-top might be a good thing. If you like formal service but innovative cuisine, there are few better restaurants in western Canada. Consider, for example, lime-scented papaya and Dungeness crab terrine with white gazpacho, or poached halibut with quince and grapefruit bouillon and rhubarb foam. If you like this kind of cutting-edge cuisine, consider the six-course Discovery Tasting Menu (C$100/US$80), where the chef's imagination really takes flight. An excellent selection of brandies and coffee will take you over the peak and down the far side.

600 Ebedora Lane, Malahat. ℂ 250/743-7115. www.aerie.bc.ca. Reservations required. Main courses C$35–C$42 (US$28–US$33). AE, DC, MC, V. Daily noon–2pm and 5:30–10pm. Free parking. Take Hwy. 1 to the Spectacle Lake turnoff; take the 1st right and follow the winding driveway.

Six Mile Pub PUB   The Six Mile was popular with sailors when the Esquimalt Naval Base opened nearby in 1864, then became the hub for provincial bootleggers during Prohibition. With a lively bar and intimate dining rooms, it still has broad appeal. You can enjoy the ambience of the fireside room, which has an oak bar with stained glass, or the beautiful scenery from the patio. The food is seasoned with fresh herbs from the garden. Start with one of the house brews, then move on to a juicy prime rib or tasty veggie burger.

494 Island Hwy., View Royal. ℂ 250/474-3663. www.sixmilepub.com. Main courses C$7–C$16 (US$5.60–US$13). AE, DC, MC, V. Mon–Thurs 11am–11pm; Fri–Sat 11am–1am; Sun 10am–10pm. At the View Royal/Colwood exit off Island Hwy., approximately 10km (6¼ miles) north of Victoria.

5 Duncan & the Cowichan Valley

Duncan: 57km (35 miles) N of Victoria

The Cowichan Valley is one of the richest agricultural areas on Vancouver Island. The Cowichan Indians have lived in the valley for millennia, and today the band's reservation spreads immediately to the south of the town of Duncan. European settlers, drawn by the valley's deep soil and warm temperatures, established farms here in the

1870s. Although the orchards and sheep pastures of yore remain, the valley's providential location also makes it one of the few sites in western British Columbia for vineyards, a new and booming crop.

For visitors, the town of Duncan, at the center of the valley, may seem a pretty low-key place, but its centrality to excellent recreation and cultural sights makes it a comfortable hub for exploring this part of Vancouver Island. Cowichan Lake is a popular summertime getaway, with swimming beaches and boating. Maple Bay and Cowichan Bay are marina-dominated harbor towns with good pubs and restaurants, plus enchanting views. And don't forget those wineries: Cowichan Valley is home to several good ones, most with tasting rooms open to the public.

ESSENTIALS

GETTING THERE   Duncan is 57km (35 miles) north of Victoria on Highway 1. It's also a stop on the **E&N Railiner.** For information, contact **VIA Rail** (© **888/VIA-RAIL** or 250/383-4324; www.viarail.ca). **Vancouver Island Coach Lines** (© **250/388-5248,** or book through Greyhound © **800/661-8747;** www.greyhound.ca) offers bus transport from Victoria to Duncan. A one-way fare from Victoria to Duncan is C$10 (US$8).

VISITOR INFORMATION   The **Duncan Visitor Information Centre,** 381A Trans-Canada Hwy. (© **250/746-4636**), is open from April 15 to October 15. Online, go to **www.city.duncan.bc.ca.** For year-round information on the entire valley, contact the **Cowichan Tourism Association,** 25 Canada Ave., Duncan (© **888/303-3337;** http://warmland.ca).

EXPLORING THE AREA
DUNCAN: THE CITY OF TOTEM POLES

Duncan is a welcoming city of 5,330, with a mix of First Nations peoples and descendants of European settlers. Congested Highway 1 runs to the east of the old town center, and you'll miss Duncan's old-fashioned charm if you don't get off the main drag (follow signs for Old Town Duncan).

Downtown Duncan still bustles with stationers, dress shops, bakeries, haberdasheries, cafes, candy shops—it's the quintessential small and friendly Canadian town. The main reason to make a detour downtown is to see the city's impressive collection of modern **totem poles.** The First Nations peoples of this region are famed for their carving skills. However, most historic totem poles are now in museums or are rotting in front of abandoned villages, and for a long time few Native Canadians had any reason to keep the old skills and traditions alive. In the 1980s, the mayor of Duncan began an ambitious project of commissioning local First Nations artists to carve new totem poles, which were then erected around the city. Today, with more than 80 totem poles rising above the downtown area, Duncan's public art is one of the world's largest collections of modern totem carving, a wonderful assemblage that represents the continuation of an ancient art form unique to the Northwest coast.

The totem poles are scattered around the city, mostly in the pedestrian-friendly downtown area: Simply follow the yellow shoe-prints on the pavement. You can also take a free guided tour, which starts from in front of the Cowichan Valley Museum, at the E&N Railway station, Station Street, and Canada Avenue. The tours are given from May to mid-September, Tuesday through Saturday, from 10am to 4pm. Reserve for groups of five or more by calling the **Duncan Business Improvement Area Society** (© **250/715-1700**).

The B.C. Forest Discovery Centre *Kids* This 41-hectare (100-acre) site explores the history of the logging industry. Over the years, the focus of the exhibits has shifted from an unreflective paean to tree cutting to a more thoughtful examination of sustainable forestry practices, woodland ecosystems, and the role (sometimes surprising) of wood products in our lives. No matter what you may think of logging as a practice, the history of forestry in British Columbia is fascinating, and this museum does a good job of presenting both the high and low points. Kids will love the vintage steam train, which circles the grounds on narrow-gauge rails.

2892 Drinkwater Rd., 2km (1¼ miles) north of Duncan on Hwy. 1 (near Somenos Lake). © 250/715-1113. www.bc forestmuseum.com. Admission C$9 (US$7.20) adults, C$8 (US$6.40) seniors and students 13–18, C$5 (US$4) children 5–12. May 12–Labour Day daily 10am–6pm; Apr 13–May 11 and Sept 4–Oct 8 daily 10am–4pm. Closed Oct 9–Apr 12.

Quw'utsun' Cultural Centre *ⓕ* The Cowichan (Quw'utsun') people were the original inhabitants of this valley, and the tribe's cultural history and traditional way of life are the focus of Quw'utsun' Centre, on the southern edge of downtown Duncan ("Quw'utsun'" means "warming your back in the sun"). The parklike enclosure along the Cowichan River contains several modern longhouse structures flanked by totem poles. Join a guided tour of the village, or take a seat in the theater to watch the excellent presentation *The Great Deeds,* a retelling of Cowichan myth and history. At the building devoted to traditional carving, you can talk to carvers as they work, and even take up a chisel yourself. In fall, the center hosts interpretive cultural/ecological tours of the Cowichan River and the life cycle of its salmon.

The Cowichan tribes are famous for their bulky sweaters, knit with bold motifs from hand-spun raw wool. The gallery at Quw'utsun' is the best place in the valley to buy these sweaters (expect to pay around C$250/US$200), as well as carvings, prints, jewelry, and books. In summer, the cafe serves traditional foods. Thursday through Saturday in July and August, there's a midday alder-planked salmon barbecue feast with drumming and storytelling. Call ahead for details.

200 Cowichan Way. © 877/746-8119 or 250/746-8119. www.quwutsun.ca. Admission C$13 (US$10) adults, C$11 (US$8.80) seniors and students 13–17, C$2 (US$1.60) children 12 and under and First Nations individuals, C$25 (US$20) families. May–Sept daily 9am–5pm; Oct–Apr daily 10am–5pm.

COWICHAN BAY

This small but busy port town edges along the mouth of the Cowichan River. Many visitors come to walk the boardwalks and admire the boats amid the sounds, smells, and sights of a working harborside village, just 7km (4¼ miles) southeast of Duncan. The **Cowichan Bay Maritime Centre,** 1761 Cowichan Bay Rd. (© **250/746-4955;** www.classicboats.org), tells the story of the clash of Native and European cultures in the Cowichan Valley. It also serves as a workshop for the building of wooden boats. Hours are daily from 9am to dusk between April and October with admission by donation. Be sure to stop at **Hilary's Cheese Company** and **True Grain Bread,** sharing space at 1725 Cowichan Bay (© **250/746-7664**). This outlet for local farm cheeses and artisanal and organic bread makes a perfect stop for outfitting a picnic.

MAPLE BAY & GENOA BAY

Maple Bay is a lovely harbor town 7km (4¼ miles) northeast of Duncan. Take Tzouhalem Road east to Maple Bay Road, then head northeast. Although not a major destination, it's worth the short drive just to take in the view—a placid bay of water beneath steep-sloped mountains. Ponder the vista at the **Brigantine Inn** *ⓕ*, on Beaumont Avenue (© **250/746-5422**), a friendly pub with local brews and a bayside deck, or the **Grapevine on the Bay Café,** 6701 Beaumont Ave. (© **250/746-0797**), where the specialty is local mussels; open Wednesday through Sunday 11:30am to 8:30pm. If you're into **diving,** Maple Bay is worth exploring—it's said to have been one of Jacques Cousteau's favorite dive spots in the world!

Genoa Bay is directly south of Maple Bay. This tiny harbor is actually on Cowichan Bay, though the mountainous terrain mandates that overland transport make a circuitous route around Mount Tzouhalem. Again, the point of the journey is the charm of the location. Enjoy a drink or a meal at **The Genoa Bay Cafe** (see "Where to Dine," below), a floating restaurant in the midst of extraordinary visual wonder.

COWICHAN VALLEY VINEYARDS

The warm summers and mild winters of the Cowichan Valley make this one of the few areas in western British Columbia where wine grapes flourish. Pinot noir, pinot gris, Marechal Foch, and Gewürztraminer are popular varietals. The following wineries welcome guests, and most will arrange tours with sufficient notice. For more information, see **www.islandwineries.ca**.

Blue Grouse Vineyards and Winery, 4365 Blue Grouse Rd., south of Duncan, off Lakeside Road near Koksilah Road (© **250/743-3834;** www.bluegrousevineyards.com), is open for tastings from 11am to 5pm Wednesday through Sunday year-round.

Cherry Point Vineyards, 840 Cherry Point Rd., near Telegraph Road southeast of Cowichan Bay in eastern Cobble Hill (© **250/743-1272;** www.cherrypointvineyards. com), is one of the most prominent Cowichan Valley wineries, with national awards to prove it. The tasting room is open daily from 10am to 6pm.

Zanatta Winery and Vineyards, 5039 Marshall Rd., south of Duncan near Glenora (© **250/748-2338;** www.zanatta.ca), is open March through December, Wednesday through Sunday from noon to 5pm. Its restaurant, Vinoteca, is one of the best places to eat in the area (see "Where to Dine," below).

A newer vineyard in the region is **Godfrey-Brownell,** west of Duncan at 4911 Marshall Rd. (© **250/748-4889**). The winery is generally open for tastings daily from 10am till 5pm.

A twist on the local scene is **Merridale Cider,** 1230 Merridale Rd., Cobble Hill, west of Highway 1 (© **800/998-9908** or 250/743-4293; www.merridalecider.com), which produces both apple and pear cider. Tastings are available daily 10am to 6pm. In addition, meals are available on-site at **La Pommeraie Bistro** Monday through Sunday from 11:30am to 4pm for lunch, and Friday and Saturday evenings from 5pm for dinner.

WHERE TO STAY
IN & AROUND DUNCAN

Best Western Cowichan Valley Inn   Duncan's most comfortable full-service lodging is conveniently located for visiting the B.C. Forest Discovery Centre. Its handsomely furnished guest rooms offer numerous amenities. A wheelchair-accessible room is available. Choices is one of the best family restaurants in Duncan, and the hotel's beer-and-wine shop is one of the best places in town to purchase local wines.

6474 Trans-Canada Hwy., Duncan, BC V9L 6C6. © **800/927-6199** or 250/748-2722. Fax 250/748-2207. www.bc travel.com/bestwestern. 42 units. C$105–C$149 (US$84–US$119) double. Extra person C$6 (US$4.30). Children 16 and under stay free in parent's room. Senior and AAA discounts available. AE, DC, DISC, MC, V. Free parking. Located 2km (1¼ miles) north of Duncan. Pets allowed with approval. **Amenities:** Restaurant; pub; small heated outdoor pool; golf course nearby; exercise room; tour/activities desk; volleyball court; beer-and-wine store; 1 room for those w/limited mobility. *In room:* A/C, TV, dataport, fridge, coffeemaker, hair dryer, iron.

Fairburn Farm Culinary Retreat & Guesthouse ★★ *Finds*   If you dream of an idealized back-to-the-land farm vacation with a focus on exploring regional cuisine and wines, then this is your destination. Picturesque Fairburn Farm, in existence since the frontier days of the Cowichan Valley, consists of 53 working hectares (131 acres) plus forested areas with trails. It has long been an excellent working-farm B&B with a resident herd of Italian water buffalo used to produce fresh mozzarella cheese. Under the new management of Mara Jernigan, Fairburn Farm has stepped up to the future: a rural culinary getaway complete with cooking lessons with guest chefs in the exhibition kitchen; farm, vineyard, and farmers' market tours; seasonal food-related events; and comfy lodging in the rambling old farmhouse. In addition to cooking classes and special events, Fairburn Farm also offers dinner service to overnight guests on Thursday, Friday, and Saturday evenings (and other evenings with advance notice). A cottage with two bedrooms and kitchen—perfect for family vacations—is available in summer.

Its beautifully preserved farmhouse boasts high ceilings, antique moldings, tiled fireplaces, and a broad porch. Some of the individually decorated rooms offer fireplaces, Jacuzzi tubs, and mountain views. But the center of energy is the kitchen. Jernigan is one of Canada's leaders in the Slow Food movement, and Fairburn Farm is a forum for her warm, country-style hospitality and a showcase for the wealth of wonderful food and wine produced in the Cowichan Valley. The focus of a stay at Fairburn Farm may be mushroom-hunting expeditions, bread-making forums, tours of local farms, vineyards, cideries, cheese-making operations, and trips to the Duncan farmers' market—one of the best in B.C.—to buy the freshest and most flavorful ingredients for Saturday's dinner, a multi-course exploration of the valley's bounty. Visitors can be as hands-on as they wish, or you can simply stay here as a B&B guest. Fairburn Farm has become an epicenter for thoughtful exploration of fine regional food on Vancouver Island, and, if you're serious about cooking and wine, you should definitely put the farm on your itinerary. Call ahead to find out what's on the calendar during your stay, as events are timed to the cycles of the season and harvest.

3310 Jackson Rd., Duncan, BC V9L 6N7. ℂ **250/746-4637.** Fax 250/746-4317. www.fairburnfarm.bc.ca. 5 units. May–Oct C$130–C$175 (US$104–US$140) guesthouse double; Nov–Apr C$100–C$155 (US$80–US$124) guesthouse double; Apr–Oct C$175 (US$140) cottage per night, 3-night minimum; C$900 (US$720) cottage per week (does not include breakfast). Breakfast included in room rates. Extra person C$20 (US$16). MC, V. Free parking. **Amenities:** Common room; nonsmoking facility. *In room:* No phone.

Travelodge Silver Bridge Inn   Its reasonably priced, well-maintained rooms make the Silver Bridge a good choice. King-bed units have fridges; honeymoon suites boast gas fireplaces and double Jacuzzis. Located next to the Cowichan River, the motel is within walking distance of the Quw'utsun' Cultural Centre. The pub, with an attractive shaded deck, is in a converted century-old house.

140 Trans-Canada Hwy., Duncan, BC V9L 3P7. ℂ **888/858-2200** or 250/748-4311. Fax 250/748-1774. www. travelodgeduncan.com. 34 units. C$99–C$179 (US$79–US$143) double. Extra person C$10 (US$8). AAA, senior, weekly, group, corporate, and sports-team rates available. AE, DC, MC, V. Free parking. Pets allowed for C$10 (US$8) per night. **Amenities:** Restaurant; pub; golf course nearby; limited room service; laundry service; same-day dry cleaning. *In room:* A/C, TV, dataport, fridge (in king-bed rooms), coffeemaker, hair dryer.

IN COWICHAN BAY

Dream Weaver B&B ★   This handsome Victorianesque structure with wraparound porch is newly constructed as a B&B, offering stylish and large units with expansive views across the bay. The location—right above the harbor—couldn't be better. The top-of-the-line room is also top-of-the-house: The very spacious Magnolia Suite encompasses the entire attic floor, complete with dormers and quirky ceiling angles, fireplace, soaker tub, and picture window. Each suite has its own character, and is decorated with rich colors and fabrics—plus a dash of knowing restraint. All rooms have private bathrooms.

1682 Botwood Lane, Cowichan Bay, BC V0R 1N0 ☎ **888/748-7689** or 250/748-7688. www.dreamweaverbedand breakfast.com. C$100–C$150 (US$80–US$120). Extra person C$25 (US$20). MC, V. Free parking. **Amenities:** TV/DVD, fridge, coffeemaker, CD player, fireplace.

Oceanfront Grand Resort and Marina   This newly renovated hotel sits immediately above the marina in Cowichan Bay, with incredible views of the harbor and the peaks of Salt Spring Island. The upgraded rooms all have oceanfront views, full kitchens, and separate living rooms. Best of all, you're just steps from the marina, where you can rent a kayak, charter a sailboat, or have a drink and watch the tides.

1681 Botwood Lane, Cowichan Bay, BC V0R 1N0. ☎ **800/663-7898** or 250/701-0166. Fax 250/701-0126. www.the grandresort.com. 57 units. C$139–C$195 (US$111–US$156) double. Extra person C$10 (US$8). Children 12 and under stay free in parent's room. AE, DISC, MC, V. Free parking. **Amenities:** Restaurant; bar; heated indoor pool; gym; hot tub; boat rental; beer and wine sales. *In room:* TV, coffeemaker, hair dryer, iron.

WHERE TO DINE
IN & AROUND DUNCAN

Just Jakes   BURGERS/LIGHT DINING   This laid-back, funky restaurant is a cross between a fern bar and a soda fountain, and the staff is young and engaging. The menu offers a wide selection of burgers, salads, steaks, and pasta: pleasantly passé food that perfectly mirrors Duncan's attractively slow-paced downtown.

45 Craig St. ☎ **250/746-5622.** www.justjakes.ca. Reservations recommended. Main courses C$6–C$22 (US$4.80–US$18). AE, MC, V. Mon–Thurs 11am–9pm; Fri–Sat 11am–10pm.

Vinoteca ☆ *Finds*   FRESH LOCAL/COUNTRY ITALIAN   A combination wine-tasting room and country-style restaurant, Vinoteca is located in a historic farmhouse at the Vigneti Zanatta vineyards (see "Cowichan Valley Vineyards," above). The menu plays counterpoint to the wines produced here. The dishes are based on hearty country fare; you might choose oven-roasted Cornish hen stuffed with figs and apples, with rosemary mustard and citrus *jus*. As much as possible, the ingredients used at Vinoteca are grown on the farm or nearby.

At Vigneti Zanatta Winery, 5039 Marshall Rd., near Glenora south of Duncan (call for directions). ☎ **250/709-2279.** www.zanatta.ca/vinoteca.htm. Reservations recommended. Main courses C$12–C$28 (US$9.60–US$22). MC, V. Mar–Dec Wed–Sun seatings noon–3:30pm and from 6pm; other nights possible by reservation. Closed Jan–Feb.

IN COWICHAN BAY

Masthead Restaurant ☆☆ WEST COAST   The building that now houses the Masthead was the town's original hotel. Its dining room now serves the area's finest Northwest cuisine. Under the guidance of chef Andrew Stevens, nothing is ordinary here. Appetizers include succulent Dungeness crab cakes served with avocado and tomato tartare. Local duck breast is seared and served with sweet corn, ginger, and blackberry port reduction. A real showstopper is the halibut, pan-fried with a hazelnut crust and served with an orange-ginger-butter sauce. The leg of lamb with a cardamom-scented tomato syrup is another standout. The airy dining room manages to seem nicely traditional without being cloying. In good weather, sit out on the deck.

1705 Cowichan Bay Rd., Cowichan Bay. ☎ **250/748-3714.** www.themastheadrestaurant.com. Reservations recommended. Main courses C$19–C$29 (US$15–US$23). MC, V. Daily from 5pm.

Rock Cod Café SEAFOOD   Rock Cod Café has the best fish and chips in the area. From the deck, you can watch the fish coming in off the boats. The chalkboard menu is crammed with whatever else is fresh. Since the cafe has a liquor license—something most British fish and chip shops can't boast—you can turn a humble meal of halibut and fries into an afternoon's worth of pleasure.

4–1759 Cowichan Bay Rd., Cowichan Bay. ☎ 250/746-1550. Reservations recommended in summer. Main courses C$6–C$14 (US$5–US$11). MC, V. Daily 11am–9pm.

IN GENOA BAY

The Genoa Bay Cafe ☞ PACIFIC NORTHWEST   One of the most delightful dining experiences in the Duncan area is found at the relaxed yet stylish Genoa Bay Cafe. From the dining room or the deck, you can follow the to-ing and fro-ing of pleasure boats and see towering forested bluffs reflected in the waters of the bay. Appetizer favorites include calamari with roasted red pepper pesto. Local roast leg of lamb served with mango chutney glaze is the house specialty, but it's given a close run by the slow-roasted ribs with apple-cranberry barbecue sauce and wild coho salmon with blue cheese and pecan glaze. Summer weekends bring live jazz, plus specials such as plank-roasted salmon grilled on a spit. What makes a meal here so satisfying—besides the dramatic scenery and peaceful atmosphere—is the food's perfect blend of restaurant sophistication and hearty home cooking.

5100 Genoa Bay Rd., Genoa Bay Marina, Genoa Bay. ☎ 250/746-7621. Reservations recommended. Main courses C$16–C$38 (US$13–US$30); 3-course tasting menu C$40 (US$32). MC, V. Nov–Mar Thurs 5:30–9pm, Fri–Sun 11:30am–2:30pm and 5:30–8:30pm; Apr and Oct Wed–Sun 11:30am–2:30pm and 5:30–8:30pm; June–Sept daily 11:30am–2:30pm and 5:30–9pm. Call to confirm off-season hours.

6 En Route to Nanaimo

CHEMAINUS: THE CITY OF MURALS

Settled in the 1850s by European farmers, Chemainus quickly became a major timber-milling and -shipment point, due to the town's Horseshoe Bay, the oldest deepwater port on the Canadian west coast. Prosperity saw the building of handsome homes and a solid commercial district. By the mid–20th century, the sawmills here were among the largest in the world, fed by the seemingly unending supply of wood from Vancouver Island's vast old-growth forests.

When the mills closed in 1983, the town slid into decline. Economic prospects for Chemainus seemed dim until someone had the bright idea of hiring an artist to paint a mural depicting the town's history. Tourists took notice, and soon mural painting became the raison d'être of this town of only slightly more than 3,500 residents. Chemainus claims to be Canada's largest permanent outdoor art gallery. Much of downtown is now covered with murals, most dealing with area history and local events.

Stop by the **Chemainus Visitor Info Centre,** 9758 Chemainus Rd. (☎ **250/ 246-3944**), open from May to early September, for a walking-tour map of the murals, or go to **www.muraltown.com** for an online map. Across the street from the visitor center in Heritage Park is an informational kiosk where you can join a horse-drawn wagon tour of the murals for C$5 (US$4) for adults, C$2.50 (US$2) for kids. Or simply follow the yellow shoe-prints painted on the sidewalks.

Much of the town is quiet and pedestrian-oriented, making it a pleasant place for a stroll and a good spot for lunch. **Old Town Chemainus,** along Willow and Maple streets, is filled with Victorian cottages converted into shops and cafes. The **Chemainus**

Theatre, 9737 Chemainus Rd. (© **800/565-7738** or 250/246-9820; chemainustheatre festival.ca), is a late-19th-century opera house that now serves as a popular dinner theater. The season runs February through December; call ahead to reserve.

WHERE TO STAY & DINE

There aren't lots of choices for fine dining in Chemainus. **Willow Street Café,** 9749 Willow St. (© **250/246-2434**), is a hip eatery serving up sandwiches, wraps, and salads; the deck is the best people-watching perch in town; open daily from 9am to 5pm. **Kudo's Japanese Restaurant,** 9875 Maple St. (© **250/246-1046**), serves sushi and other Japanese cuisine and is open for lunch and dinner daily.

Bird Song Cottage Bed & Breakfast ⚐ Filled with Victorian bric-a-brac and unusual objets d'art, Bird Song is an enchanting, English-style garden cottage. The owners, both professional musicians, admit to being "a bit theatrical." Rather an understatement: Whimsy pervades the place, from the extensive collection of Victorian hats (which guests are encouraged to try on) to the grand piano and Celtic harp. The exterior continues the theme, with a wraparound porch and turreted veranda, burbling fountains, and loads of architectural gingerbread. Everything here is over the top, but lovingly so. The guest rooms are beautifully outfitted, with quality linens and fresh flowers. Two units have TV/VCRs. Breakfasts are elaborate affairs. The proprietors of Bird Song also operate **Castlebury Cottage,** designed as a "folly"—a small, whimsical, European-style castle that offers private, luxurious, and fully modern accommodations with TV/VCR, kitchen, fridge, coffeemaker, and other amenities. The upstairs Camelot suite has a fireplace, canopy bed, and two-person marble soaker tub. The style is thoroughly baroque, with lots of ornate flourishes and rough frescoed walls. The downstairs Sonnet suite is smaller but similarly appointed.

9909 Maple St., Chemainus, BC V0R 1K1. © 250/246-9910. Fax 250/246-2909. www.birdsongcottage.com. Birdsong Cottage: 3 units. C$115–C$125 (US$92–C$100) double. Extra person C$25 (US$20). Rates include breakfast and evening tea. Extended-stay, group, and wedding packages available. Castlebury Cottage: 2 units. May–Sept Camelot suite C$285–C$325 (US$228–US$260), Sonnet suite C$140 (US$112); Oct–Apr Camelot suite C$230–C$285 (US$184–US$228), Sonnet suite C$125 (US$120). Rates include breakfast basket. 2-night minimum on holiday weekends. Weekly rates available. AE, MC, V. **Amenities:** Golf course nearby; courtesy limo. *In room:* Hair dryer, iron, no phone.

CEDAR & YELLOW POINT

South of Nanaimo, a forested peninsula juts out into the waters of the Georgia Strait. The land is rural and mostly undeveloped. The little community of Cedar is as close as the area comes to a town; this wouldn't qualify as much of a destination if it weren't for the fact that one of Vancouver Island's most popular lodges and one of its best restaurants are located here. It's a short drive from Nanaimo, and a detour through the forests and farmland makes for a pleasant break from Highway 1.

WHERE TO STAY

Yellow Point Lodge ⚐⚐ *(Value* Beloved Yellow Point Lodge is located on 73 hectares (180 acres) of forested waterfront, with over 2.5km (1½ miles) of rocky beach and secluded coves. This family-operated resort was established in the 1930s. The three-story log-and-stone building has an enormous lobby, a huge fireplace, and a dining room with communal tables, all with wondrous views of Vancouver Island and the southern Gulf Islands. Inside the lodge are a number of comfortable hotel-like rooms, all with ocean views; scattered around the woods are cabins and cottages in a wide range of styles. Most basic are the beach cabins and the rustic Beach Barracks with communal wash houses. Some of the more luxurious one-, two-, and three-bedroom cottages have fireplaces. One room is appointed for those with disabilities.

Hiking trails are on the property and in nearby provincial parks. Good, home-style meals are served in the dining room, where a real sense of camaraderie develops among the guests. If this unique blend of summer camp and luxury resort appeals to you, be sure to reserve well ahead—the lodge is a summer tradition for people of all incomes. Part of the charm of Yellow Point is that there are affordable lodging options here for almost everyone, and everyone gets the same friendly service.

3700 Yellow Point Rd., Ladysmith, BC V9G 1E8. ℂ 250/245-7422. Fax 250/245-7411. www.yellowpointlodge.com. 53 units, 27 with private bathroom, most with shower only. C$123–C$198 (US$98–US$158) double. Rates include all meals. AE, MC, V. Ferry, bus, train, or airport shuttle available for small fee. Children must be 14 or older. **Amenities:** Outdoor saltwater pool; golf course nearby; tennis courts; Jacuzzi; sauna; free bikes; free kayaks and canoes; massage; volleyball and badminton courts; nonsmoking facility. *In room:* Fridge (in some cabins), coffeemaker (in some cabins), no phone.

WHERE TO DINE

The Crow & Gate ✿ *Finds* PUB   This Tudor-style pub on a 4-hectare (10-acre) farm is a friendly haven of English style. It looks straight out of the Cotswolds, with low ceilings, handcrafted beams, and gleaming brass accents complemented by a brick fireplace and leaded-glass windows. The menu offers roast beef and Yorkshire pudding, shepherd's pie, and roasted Cornish game hen. In summer, sit out on the flower-decked patio.

2313 Yellow Point Rd. ℂ 250/722-3731. www.crowandgate.com. Reservations recommended. Main courses C$8–C$18 (US$6.40–US$14). MC, V. Daily 11am–midnight; closes early when not busy and on some holidays (call ahead). Take the old Island Hwy. (Hwy. 19) north past Cassidy, or exit Island Hwy. 1 at Hwy. 19 to Cedar and Harmac. Cross the Nanaimo River, then turn right on Cedar Rd., which leads onto Yellow Point Rd. Continue for 1.6km (1 mile).

The Mahle House ✿✿ PACIFIC NORTHWEST   The Mahle (pronounced "Molly") House is located in a tiny country town, in a salmon-pink heritage home overlooking a park. From this unlikely address, it has developed a huge reputation for excellent regional cuisine emphasizing locally grown, mostly organic produce and meats. On the weekly changing menu you might choose venison with a chanterelle sauce or Chinook salmon, scallops, and porcupine prawns with saffron aioli and lemon oil. The award-wining wine list is extensive. The restaurant also offers bargain nights: a Wednesday five-course dinner for C$32 (US$26), a Thursday tapaslike "grazing platter" for C$44 (US$35) for two, and a three-course Sunday "country dinner" for C$29 (US$23).

At Cedar Rd. and Hemer Rd., Cedar. ℂ 250/722-3621. www.mahlehouse.ca. Reservations recommended. Main courses C$14–C$36 (US$11–US$29). AE, MC, V. Wed–Sun from 5pm. Closed Dec 21–29 and Jan 1–15.

7

Central Vancouver Island

Central Vancouver Island's major population center is Nanaimo, the arrival point for visitors taking ferries from the mainland and the site of a major 19th-century coal-mining operation. The city has moved away from its dependence upon resource extraction and is now sparkling with redevelopment, taking advantage of its scenic location—overlooking a bay full of islands, the choppy waters of Georgia Strait, and the glaciated peaks of the mainland.

In sharp contrast to the serenity of the island's east coast, the wild, raging beauty of the Pacific Ocean on Vancouver Island's west coast entices photographers, hikers, kayakers, and divers to explore Pacific Rim National Park, Long Beach, and the neighboring towns of Ucluelet, Tofino, and Bamfield. Thousands of visitors arrive between March and May to see

Pacific gray whales pass close to shore as they migrate north to their summer feeding grounds. More than 200 shipwrecks have occurred off the shores in the past 2 centuries, luring even more travelers to this eerily beautiful underwater world. And the park's world-famous West Coast Trail beckons intrepid backpackers to brave the 5- to 7-day hike over the rugged rescue trail—established after the survivors of a shipwreck in the early 1900s died from exposure because there was no land-access route for the rescuers.

On east-central Vancouver Island, the towns of Parksville, Qualicum Beach, Courtenay, and Comox are famous for their warm, sandy beaches and numerous golf courses.

Note: See the "Vancouver Island" map (p. 116) to locate areas covered in this chapter.

1 Essentials

GETTING THERE
BY PLANE   See chapter 5 for details on flights to **Victoria,** the main air hub for all of Vancouver Island.

Nanaimo and Comox/Courtenay have regular air service. **Air Canada Jazz** (© 888/247-2262; www.aircanada.com) offers service to Vancouver from Nanaimo. **Pacific Coastal Airlines** (© 800/663-2872; www.pacific-coastal.com) and Air Canada connector Central Mountain Air fly to/from Comox and Vancouver, while **WestJet** (© 877/952-4638; www.westjet.com) provides Comox with nonstop service to/from Edmonton and Calgary.

Smaller towns in central Vancouver Island can be reached via floatplane, either from Vancouver International's seaplane terminal or from downtown Vancouver's Coal Harbour terminal.

Commuter seaplane companies include **Harbour Air Seaplanes** (© 800/665-0212 or 604/688-1277; www.harbour-air.com), **Tofino Air** (© 866/486-3247 for

Tofino base, 888/436-7776 for Sechelt base, or 800/665-2359 for Gabriola base; www.tofinoair.ca), and **Baxter Aviation** (© **800/661-5599,** 604/683-6525, or 250/ 754-1066; www.baxterair.com).

BY FERRY   BC Ferries (© **888/223-3779** or 250/386-3431; www.bcferries.com) links Vancouver Island, the Gulf Islands, and the mainland. Major routes include the crossing from Tsawwassen to Swartz Bay and to Nanaimo, and from Horseshoe Bay (northwest of Vancouver) to Nanaimo. In summer, reserve in advance. Sample fares are included in the regional sections that follow.

BY BUS   One of the easiest ways to get to and from Vancouver Island destinations is by bus. **Greyhound Canada** (© **800/661-8747** or 604/482-8747; www.greyhound. ca) provides six daily trips between Vancouver and Nanaimo. Fare is C$18 (US$14) one-way.

VISITOR INFORMATION

For information on central Vancouver Island, contact **Tourism Vancouver Island,** Suite 203, 335 Wesley St., Nanaimo (© **250/754-3500;** www.islands.bc.ca). Also check out **www.vancouverisland.com**.

GETTING AROUND

While Vancouver Island has an admirable system of public transport, getting to remote sights and destinations is difficult without your own vehicle.

BY FERRY   BC Ferries (© **888/223-3779** or 250/386-3431; www.bcferries.com) routes link Vancouver Island ports to many offshore islands.

BY TRAIN   A scenic way to travel is on **VIA Rail**'s **E&N Railiner,** the *Malahat* (© **888/VIA-RAIL** or 250/383-4324; www.viarail.ca), which runs from Victoria to Courtenay. See p. 179 for details.

BY BUS   Island Coach Lines (© **250/724-1266**) operates regular daily service between Victoria and Tofino/Ucluelet via Nanaimo. The 6-hour trip arrives in Tofino at 12:45pm and costs C$55 (US$44). The bus stops in Nanaimo and can pick up visitors arriving from Vancouver by ferry. The **Tofino Bus** (© **866/986-3466;** www.tofino bus.com) also offers daily bus service from Victoria and Vancouver to Tofino/Ucluelet via Nanaimo. A one-way ticket from Victoria is C$50 (US$40).

BY CAR   The southern half of Vancouver Island is well served by paved highways. The trunk road between Victoria and Nanaimo is **Highway 1,** the Trans-Canada, which requires some patience, especially during the busy summer months. North of Nanaimo, the major road is **Highway 19,** which is a four-lane expressway for almost all of its duration, a particular improvement being the 128km (79-mile) **Inland Highway** between Parksville and Campbell River. The older sections of 19, all closer to the island's east coast, are now labeled 19A. The other major paved road system on the island, **Highway 4,** connects Parksville with Port Alberni and on to Ucluelet and Tofino, on the rugged west coast. This road is mostly two-lane, and portions of it are extremely winding and hilly.

Rental-car agencies include **Avis** (© **800/272-5871** in Canada, 800/230-4898 in the U.S.; www.avis.com), **Budget** (© **800/268-8900** in Canada, 800/527-0700 in the U.S.; www.budget.com), and **National** (© **800/CAR-RENT** in Canada and the U.S.; www.nationalcar.com).

2 Nanaimo & Gabriola Island

Nanaimo: 113km (70 miles) N of Victoria

For over a century, Vancouver Island's second-largest city (pop. 79,000) was the center of vast coal-mining operations, without much in the way of cultural niceties. In the last 30 years, however, Nanaimo has undergone quite a change. With its redeveloped waterfront, scenic surroundings, good restaurants and lodging, and a location central to many other Vancouver Island destinations, downtown Nanaimo makes a pleasant stop for a few days. Note, however, that Nanaimo is a fairly sprawling city, complete with lots of suburban strip malls and plenty of traffic, so it may not hold the same charm as the island's less populous destinations.

Just a 20-minute ferry ride from Nanaimo Harbour is Gabriola Island, though it feels a world away. Gabriola makes a marvelous day trip, providing a little of everything—sandy beaches, galleries, petroglyph sites, tide pools, and a sense of wooded serenity.

ESSENTIALS
GETTING THERE

BY PLANE   Regular service between Vancouver and Nanaimo Airport, 24km (15 miles) south of the city, is offered by **Air Canada Jazz** (© **888/247-2262;** www.air canada.com).

Harbour Air Seaplanes (© **800/665-0212** or 604/688-1277; www.harbour-air. com) and **Baxter Aviation** (© **800/661-5599,** 604/683-6525, or 250/754-1066; www.baxterair.com) offer floatplane flights from Vancouver to Nanaimo Harbour.

BY CAR   Nanaimo is 113km (70 miles) from Victoria via Highway 1, the Trans-Canada Highway. At Nanaimo, Highway 1 crosses Georgia Strait via the Horseshoe Bay ferry. North of Nanaimo, the main trunk road becomes Highway 19. It's 161km (100 miles) from Nanaimo to Campbell River, 206km (128 miles) to Tofino.

BY FERRY   BC Ferries (© **888/223-3779** or 250/386-3431; www.bcferries.com) operates two major runs to Nanaimo. The crossing from Horseshoe Bay in West Vancouver to Nanaimo's Departure Bay terminal is one of the busiest in the system; expect delays especially at rush hour and summer weekends. New PacifiCat Ferries cut the normal 1½-hour crossing down to just over an hour. The Tsawwassen ferry arrives and departs at Nanaimo's Duke Point terminal, just south of town off Highway 1. Tickets for both ferries are C$11 (US$8.80) per passenger and C$38 (US$30) per car, with slightly lower midweek and low season prices. In addition to the BC Ferries service, **HarbourLynx** (© **866/206-5969;** www.harbourlynx.com) offers ferry service between downtown Nanaimo and downtown Vancouver. Fare is C$25 (US$20) one-way.

BY TRAIN   The **E&N Railiner** operates daily service between Victoria and Courtenay. For information, contact **VIA Rail** (© **888/VIA-RAIL** or 250/383-4324; www. viarail.ca).

BY BUS   Greyhound Canada (© **800/661-8747** or 604/482-8747; www.greyhound. ca) provides eight daily trips between Vancouver and Nanaimo. Non-Greyhound buses continue both north and south from Nanaimo, though you can use Greyhound to book seats.

VISITOR INFORMATION

Contact **Tourism Nanaimo,** Beban House, 2290 Bowen Rd. (© **800/663-7337** or 250/756-0106; www.tourismnanaimo.com). In summer, an **info center** operates out of the Bastion, at Pioneer Waterfront Plaza.

GETTING AROUND

Nanaimo Regional Transit System (© **250/390-4531;** www.rdn.bc.ca) provides public transport in the Nanaimo area. Fares are C$2 (US$1.60) for adults and C$1.75 (US$1.40) for seniors and youths. For a cab, call **AC Taxi** (© **800/753-1231** or 250/753-1231) or **Swiftsure Taxi** (© **250/753-8911**).

The **BC Ferries** route to Gabriola Island leaves from behind the Harbour Park Shopping Centre on Front Street (note that this is not the same dock as either the Tsawwassen- or Horseshoe Bay–bound ferries), roughly every hour between 7am and 11pm. In summer, the round-trip fare is C$6.30 (US$5) per person, plus C$16 (US$13) for a car. You can bring your bike free of charge.

EXPLORING NANAIMO

Nanaimo's steep-faced waterfront has been restructured with tiers of walkways, banks of flowers, marina boardwalks, and floating restaurants. Called **Pioneer Waterfront Plaza,** the area fills on Fridays with the local farmers' market. The **Bastion,** a white fortified tower, rises above the harbor as a relic of the 1850s when this area was the site of a Hudson's Bay Company trading post (it now holds a summer tourist information center).

Nanaimo's busy natural port has ferry links to Vancouver, Horseshoe Bay, and to Tsawwassen to the south, as well as to lovely **Gabriola Island** and to **Newcastle Island,** a car-free provincial park on the harbor's northern flank. Throughout the day, floatplanes buzz in and out of the boat basin, shuttling commuters back and forth to Vancouver. If you're up for a run, the **Harbourside Walkway** stretches 4km (2½ miles) from the heart of the city all the way to Departure Bay.

The old downtown, just behind the Bastion and centered on Commercial, Front, and Bastion streets, is a series of pleasant winding streets behind the harbor. **Artisan's Studio,** 70 Bastion St. (© **250/753-6151**), is a co-op gallery that displays the work of local artists and craftspeople.

⌜Moments Only in Nanaimo: The World Championship Bathtub Race

From its beginnings in 1967, Nanaimo's signature summer draw has grown into a weeklong series of events that shows off the city's good-natured spirit. In the early days, fewer than half of the original racing vessels—old claw-foot tubs fitted with engines—completed the crossing of 58km (36-mile) Georgia Strait from Nanaimo Harbour to Vancouver's Fisherman's Cove. These days, most contestants race in specially designed tubs that look like single-person speedboats. The race is the climax of July's **Marine Festival,** which includes a street fair, parade, and traditional "Sacrifice to the Bathtub Gods." For information, go to http://bathtub.island.net.

Nanaimo

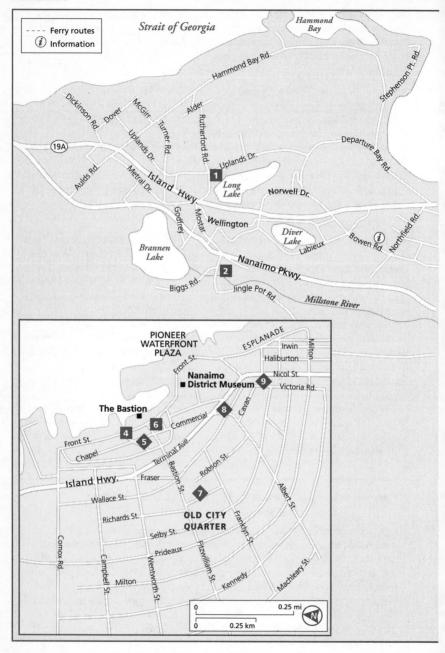

Ferry routes

ⓘ Information

Strait of Georgia

Hammond Bay

Hammond Bay Rd.

Dickinson Rd.

Dover

McGirr

Turner Rd.

Alder

Rutherford Rd.

Stephenson Pt. Rd.

Uplands Dr.

Departure Bay Rd.

19A

Aulds Rd.

Metral Dr.

Island Hwy.

Uplands Dr.

1

Long Lake

Norwell Dr.

Bowen Rd.

ⓘ

Northfield Rd.

Godfrey

Mostar

Wellington

Diver Lake

Labieux

Brannen Lake

Nanaimo Pkwy.

2

Biggs Rd.

Jingle Pot Rd.

Millstone River

PIONEER WATERFRONT PLAZA

ESPLANADE

Irwin

Milton

Front St.

Haliburton

Nicol St.

Nanaimo District Museum

9

Victoria Rd.

The Bastion

6

Commercial

8

Cavan

4

5

Front St.

Chapel

Terminal Ave.

Bastion St.

Robson St.

Island Hwy.

Fraser

7

Albert St.

Wallace St.

Franklyn St.

OLD CITY QUARTER

Comox Rd.

Richards St.

Selby St.

Prideaux

Fitzwilliam St.

Kennedy

Machleary St.

Campbell St.

Wentworth St.

Milton

0   0.25 mi

0   0.25 km

N

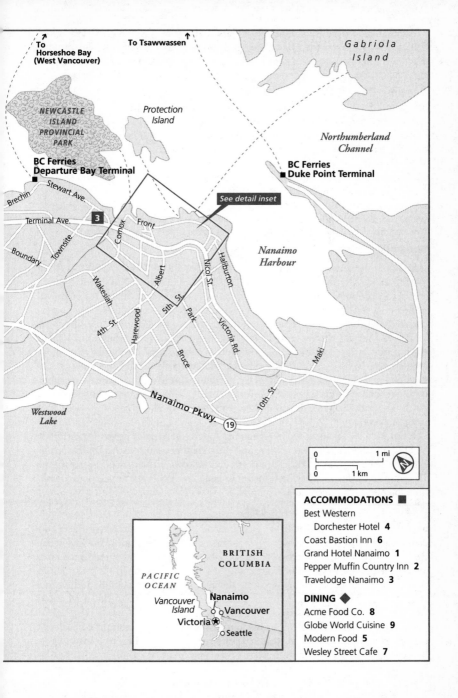

To Horseshoe Bay (West Vancouver)

To Tsawwassen

Gabriola Island

NEWCASTLE ISLAND PROVINCIAL PARK

Protection Island

Northumberland Channel

BC Ferries
Departure Bay Terminal

BC Ferries
Duke Point Terminal

Stewart Ave.

Brechin

Terminal Ave. **3**

Front

Comox

Boundary

Townsite

Wakesiah

Albert

4th. St.

Harewood

5th St.

Park

Bruce

Nicol St.

Haliburton

Victoria Rd.

Maki

See detail inset

Nanaimo Harbour

10th St.

Westwood Lake

Nanaimo Pkwy. **(19)**

0   1 mi
0   1 km

BRITISH COLUMBIA

PACIFIC OCEAN

Vancouver Island

Nanaimo
Vancouver
Victoria ✪
Seattle

ACCOMMODATIONS ■
Best Western
  Dorchester Hotel **4**
Coast Bastion Inn **6**
Grand Hotel Nanaimo **1**
Pepper Muffin Country Inn **2**
Travelodge Nanaimo **3**

DINING ◆
Acme Food Co. **8**
Globe World Cuisine **9**
Modern Food **5**
Wesley Street Cafe **7**

Another good stroll is the **Old City Quarter,** an uptown section of the city center that was severed from the harborfront area when the Island Highway cut through downtown. Now reached from the harbor by walking up the Bastion Street overpass, the 3-block area has been redeveloped into housing, boutiques, and fine restaurants.

Nanaimo District Museum Nanaimo's regional museum is a worthwhile introduction to the area's past, first as a home for the Snunéymuxw (the name from which Nanaimo derives) people and then as an industrial boomtown. An intriguing exhibit links painted dioramas of traditional Snunéymuxw life with a simulation of an archaeological dig near Discovery Bay in 1992. In drawers beneath the dioramas are the actual artifacts found at the site and pictured in the paintings. A gift shop sells wooden carvings from the local Snunéymuxw. The museum will relocate to the new and adjacent Nanaimo Convention Center in 2008.

100 Cameron Rd. ℂ 250/753-1821. www.nanaimomuseum.ca. Admission C$2 (US$1.60) adults, C$1.75 (US$1.40) seniors, C75¢ (US60¢) children 6–12. May 24–Labour Day daily 10am–5pm; day after Labour Day to May 23 Tues–Sat 10am–5pm. From Front St., head up Museum Way, then left on Gordon St. and left again on Cameron Rd.

FERRYING TO NEWCASTLE ISLAND

Just outside Nanaimo harbor, **Newcastle Island Provincial Park** (ℂ 250/391-2300 for BC Parks, South Vancouver Island District) is an ideal destination for hikers, cyclists, and campers. The island was home to two Salish Indian villages before British settlers discovered coal here in 1849. The Canadian-Pacific Steamship Company purchased the island in 1931, creating a resort with a dance pavilion, teahouse, and floating hotel. The 300-hectare (750-acre) island has now largely returned to its natural state. It now attracts outdoorsy types with its many trails; selected walks range from 2km to 4km (1¼–2½ miles). The popular **Mallard Lake Trail** leads through the wooded interior toward a freshwater lake; the **Shoreline Trail** runs across steep cliffs, onto sand and gravel beaches suitable for swimming, and up to a great eagle-spotting perch. The park maintains 18 **campsites,** with toilets, wood, fire pits, and water. Rate is C$14 (US$11).

From April to Canadian Thanksgiving (mid-Oct), the **Scenic Ferries** (ℂ 250/753-5141) run leaves daily between 10am and early evening from the wharf at the peninsula tip of **Maffeo-Sutton Park** (just north of downtown). The round-trip fare for the 10-minute crossing is C$5 (US$4) for adults and C$4 (US$3.20) for seniors and children; bikes are C$2 (US$1.60).

EXPLORING GABRIOLA ISLAND

Much of Gabriola (pop. 4,000) is reached along North Road and South Road, two country lanes that provide a loop route around the island. A third road, Taylor Bay Road, departs from the ferry dock to access Gabriola's rocky northern reaches. It takes about half an hour to drive from one end of the island to the other.

The main commercial center is just up the hill from the ferry terminal and is often referred to as **Folklife Village.** Stop by **Gabriola Artworks,** 575 North Rd. (ℂ 250/247-7412), an excellent gallery of local arts and crafts.

Sandwell Provincial Park is one of Gabriola's nicest beaches and picnic areas, with paths leading through old-growth forests and to views of the Entrance Island lighthouse. Turn off North Road onto Barrett Road and follow the signs.

At the southern end of Gabriola is Silva Bay, a marina resort featuring an excellent restaurant and pub. Nearby is **FOGO Folk Art Studio** ✿, 3065 Commodore Way (ℂ 250/247-8082; www.fogoart.com). The artists' intricately carved characters perfectly capture the quirks of human nature. Wandering around the studio grounds is a true delight. Just south of Silva Bay is **Drumbeg Provincial Park,** which has a good swimming beach.

Gabriola Island and the area around Nanaimo are rich in prehistoric **petroglyph rock carvings.** On the South Road, near the United Church (about 10km/6¼ miles from the ferry terminal), a short path leads to a mix of fantastical creatures and abstract shapes scratched in sandstone. Park in the church lot and follow the signs. Note that the Snunéymuxw regard these petroglyphs as sacred and frown on people taking pictures or rubbings of them.

Taylor Bay Road leads to more parks and beaches on the north end of the island. **Gabriola Sands Provincial Park** protects two of the island's best beaches, at Taylor Bay and Pilot Bay. Toward the end of the road (now called Berry Point Rd.) is the **Surf Lodge,** 885 Berry Point Rd. (© **250/247-9231**), with a pub and restaurant overlooking the Georgia Strait.

OUTDOOR PURSUITS

BUNGEE JUMPING   The **Bungy Zone** (© **888/668-7771,** 800/668-7874, or 250/753-5867; www.bungyzone.com), off the Island Highway 15 minutes south of Nanaimo, is North America's first legal bridge jump, sending you over the Nanaimo River for C$100 (US$80). For another adrenaline rush at this recreation hot spot (which also includes sky-diving, paintball, and a high-elevation swing), consider a ride on the new zip-line (C$60/US$48), which launches daredevils, attached to a steel cable by a climbing harness, across a wooded canyon at speeds near 100kmph (60 mph).

DIVING 𝕽𝕽   While all of the waters off Vancouver Island are known for their superior diving opportunities, those around Nanaimo benefit from the efforts of the Nanaimo Dive Association, which is working to make Nanaimo a world-class diving destination. Rather unique are three artificial reefs formed by the sinking of decommissioned cargo ships just off the Nanaimo coastline. The HMCS *Saskatchewan* and the HMCS *Cape Breton* together form a reef 228m (760 ft.) in length. A third boat, the rescue tug RivTow Lion, lies in shallow water just off Newport Island and is used for training. One of the single best dives in the Northwest is at **Dodds Narrows,** between Vancouver Island and Mudge Island. It boasts outstanding visibility, a high concentration of wildlife, and dramatic rock formations. Other area dives include **Snake Island Wall,** with a drop-off that seems to extend into the abyss.

Ocean Explorers Diving, 1956 Zorkin Rd., near Departure Bay (© **800/233-4145** or 250/753-2055; www.oceanexplorersdiving.com), offers charter dives and packages that include 1 night's accommodation and two boat dives, with prices starting at C$159 (US$127). Day rate for a single dive is C$55 (US$44; minimum of two divers). Another local dive outfitter, **Mamro Adventures,** 1–5765 Turner Rd., Suite 203 (© **250/756-8872;** www.mamro.com), can accommodate six passengers on trips of 1 to 10 days. Popular excursions include Port Hardy, famed for its dense marine-mammal population, and the Gulf Islands, Sunshine Coast, and Georgia Strait.

WHERE TO STAY

IN NANAIMO

Best Western Dorchester Hotel 𝕽   The Dorchester stands on the most venerable spot in Nanaimo: the site of the Hudson's Bay Company trading post in the 1850s, and then of the city's old opera house. Reminders of the opera-house days remain: The handsome chandeliers are all original, as are the ornate columns flanking the dining room. Guest rooms are comfortably furnished, though not exactly spacious. For the price, quality, and excellent downtown location, the Dorchester is hard to top. Pay a bit extra for a bayside room—the view is fantastic. Check the hotel website for seasonal Internet rates not available elsewhere. Rooms for those with disabilities are available.

70 Church St., Nanaimo, BC V9R 5H4. ✆ 800/661-2449 or 250/754-6835. Fax 250/754-2638. www.dorchester nanaimo.com. 65 units. C$100–C$160 (US$80–US$128) double. Extra person C$10 (US$8) per night. Senior, AAA, and Internet discounts, and corporate and off-season rates available. AE, DC, DISC, MC, V. Free parking. Pets accommodated for C$20 (US$16) per night. **Amenities:** Restaurant; lounge; golf course nearby; laundry service; same-day dry cleaning; rooms for those w/limited mobility. *In room:* TV, dataport, coffeemaker, hair dryer, iron.

Coast Bastion Inn ⭐

At this modern high-rise hotel at the heart of downtown, every room boasts a waterfront view, and the Harbourside Walkway scene is just seconds away. It's worth the splurge for a superior room, with upgraded amenities and views from two sides. Two wheelchair-accessible rooms are available. The hotel connects to the Port Theatre complex.

11 Bastion St., Nanaimo, BC V9R 6E4. ✆ 800/663-1144 or 250/753-6601. Fax 250/753-4155. www.coasthotels.com. 177 units. High season C$165–C$289 (US$132–US$231) double; C$235–C$270 (US$188–US$216) suite. Extra person C$10 (US$8). Senior and AAA discounts, theater packages, and off-season rates available. AE, DC, DISC, MC, V. Pets allowed for C$10 (US$8) per day. Valet parking C$9 (US$7.20); self-parking C$4.50 (US$3.60). **Amenities:** Restaurant; lounge; exercise room; Jacuzzi; sauna; concierge; 24-hr. room service; in-room massage; babysitting; laundry service; same-day dry cleaning; rooms for those w/limited mobility. *In room:* A/C, TV w/pay movies, dataport, coffeemaker, hair dryer, iron.

Grand Hotel Nanaimo ⭐

The Grand Hotel is the area's most luxurious lodging. Rooms range from 56-sq.-m (600-sq.-ft.) suites with two TVs, fireplace, kitchenette, and a king bed to simpler but still very comfortable standard rooms. Deluxe rooms have jetted tubs and fireplaces; many rooms have balconies. There are two wheelchair-accessible units. The public areas are handsome, particularly the lobby with its soaring ceilings and chandelier. The Grand Hotel is about a 10-minute drive northwest of city center.

4898 Rutherford Rd., Nanaimo, BC V9T 4Z4. ✆ 877/414-7263 or 250/758-3000. Fax 250/729-2808. www.thegrand hotelnanaimo.ca. 72 units. C$139–C$269 (US$111–US$215) double. Extra person C$10 (US$8) per day. Senior and AAA discounts available. AE, DC, DISC, MC, V. **Amenities:** Restaurant; lounge; indoor pool; golf course nearby; exercise room; limited room service; laundry service; same-day dry cleaning; rooms for those w/limited mobility. *In room:* A/C, TV, dataport, coffeemaker, hair dryer, iron, voice mail.

Pepper Muffin Country Inn ⭐ *Kids*

This country B&B on 2.4 hectares (6 acres) offers a rural getaway just minutes from downtown. A stream plays host to beaver, otter, and trout; and local crags are home to pileated woodpeckers and turkey buzzards. Although newly constructed as an inn, the building was designed with quirky angles and rooflines, and is tastefully furnished with antiques. Each bedroom has a balcony and a private en suite bathroom. At breakfast, you'll learn what Pepper Muffin refers to: savory corn muffins flecked with jalapeño pepper. Bike trails and lakes are accessible nearby.

3718 Jingle Pot Rd., Nanaimo, BC V9R 6X4. ✆ 250/756-0473. Fax 250/756-0421. www.peppermuffin.com. 3 units. C$95–C$125 (US$76–US$100) double. Rates include breakfast. AE, MC, V. **Amenities:** Outdoor Jacuzzi; golf courses nearby; nonsmoking facility. *In room:* TV/VCR, hair dryer, wireless Internet access, bathrobes.

Travelodge Nanaimo

A midprice motel with a great location, this Travelodge is just a few blocks from the Vancouver ferry, and a short walk to downtown. All of the clean, comfortable rooms have balconies or patios. The front desk can help you arrange activities around Nanaimo.

96 Terminal Ave. N., Nanaimo, BC V9S 4J2. ⓒ **800/667-0598** or 250/754-6355. Fax 250/754-1301. www.travelodge nanaimo.com. 78 units. July–Aug C$100–C$124 (US$80–US$99) double; June and Sept C$85–C$13 (US$68–US$90) double; Oct–May C$89–C$117 (US$71–US$94) double. Extra person C$6 (US$4.80). Rates include continental break-fast. Senior and AAA discounts available. AE, DISC, MC, V. Free parking. Pets allowed for C$10 (US$8) per night. **Amenities:** Golf course nearby; exercise room; sauna; coin-op laundry; dry cleaning. *In room:* TV, dataport, cof-feemaker, hair dryer.

ON GABRIOLA ISLAND

Melville Grant Inn ⓡ *Finds*   This classy B&B sits on over 2 hectares (5 acres) of woods and meadows, and is a tranquil refuge. The rooms are large and beautifully fur-nished with quality linens and amenities; each has a spa tub and fireplace. The com-mon areas are rather opulently furnished. The staff is happy to help organize any activity you'd like—perhaps a day visiting local artisans, or an afternoon exploring the island on a kayak. An especially fun outing is a picnic boat trip, where the staff pro-vides a picnic basket and a boat ride to a secluded beach; the boat returns to pick you up at a prearranged time. Meals feature island-grown eggs and produce.

2310 Windecker Dr., Gabriola Island, BC V0R 1X7. ⓒ **866/247-5444** or 250/247-9687. Fax 250/247-9689. 4 units. C$209 (US$167) double. Rates include candlelit breakfast. MC, V. Not suitable for children. *In room:* A/C, TV, hair dryer, whirlpool tub.

WHERE TO DINE

In central Nanaimo there are two casual spots worth knowing about. **Tina's Diner,** 187 Commercial St. (ⓒ **205/753-5333**), is a classic '50s diner for big eggy breakfasts and sandwiches for lunch. **McClean's Specialty Foods,** 426 Fitzwilliam St. (ⓒ **250/ 754-0100**), offers over 150 varieties of cheese, including many from Vancouver Island, plus other picnic comestibles. This is also an excellent spot to savor a cup of tea and a Nanaimo Bar, the famed bar cookie invented here as a snack for local coal miners.

Acme Food Co. ⓡⓡ *Finds* ECLECTIC   In an arrowhead-shaped building on down-town Nanaimo's busiest corner, the Acme offers five page's worth of menu choices, everything from sushi to pizza, curry to steaks. Everything at this chic cocktail bar and '90s-retro dining room was delicious. The sashimi and sushi rolls are particularly good while both pizza, pasta, and burger "kits" encourage DIY creativity. Cocktail tapas are also excellent, and even the steaks and seafood, like grilled five-spice salmon and raw oysters with ponzu sauce, are memorable. This is a great place to bring a group of peo-ple with differing food tastes, which is exactly how it's done in Nanaimo. The Acme is one of the top hang-outs for the city's young urban hip.

14 Commercial St. ⓒ **250/753-0042**. Reservations recommended. Main courses C$8–C$23 (US$6.40–US$18). MC, V. Daily 11am–midnight.

Glow World Cuisine ⓡ TAPAS   Glow offers excellent cocktails and tapas in addi-tion to debonair good looks in the city's century-old fire hall. The dining room is dra-matic—7.5m (25-ft.) ceilings, towering windows, modern art, colorful draperies and curious wood-slat coved ceilings—and a large menu provides the gastronomic drama. Seared foie gras is served with grilled peaches, and grilled lamb loin comes with licorice *jus*. Local oysters on the half shell are winners, but 2 days later we were still talking about the grilled pork ribs in thyme tamarind sauce. Tapas here are large—two'll do ya, though you'll be tempted, as we were, to skip dessert and have more ribs.

7 Victoria Rd. ⓒ **250/741-8858**. Reservations recommended. Tapas $C6–C$16 (US$4.80–US$13). MC, V. Daily 5–11pm; Sun 10:30am–2pm.

Tips **Two Popular Pubs**

In summer, for a pint of ale and a burger in a marvelous location, take the 10-minute Protection Connection ferry ride to the **Dinghy Dock Floating Marine Pub,** on Protection Island (© 250/753-2373). It's exactly what its name says—a floating pub—and boasts spectacular sunset views of Nanaimo and the Vancouver Island mountains. The ferry leaves on the hour from the Commercial Inlet boat basin, below Pioneer Waterfront Plaza.

You'll get a wonderful view of the harbor from the **Lighthouse Bistro and Pub,** off Harbourside Walkway at 50 Anchor Way (© 250/754-3212; http://nanaimo.ark.com/~litehse). Open daily from 11am to midnight and until 1am in summer (the restaurant closes earlier), this floating pub is adjacent to the city's floatplane base—watch these boats take off just beside your table.

Modern Food ✻ NEW CANADIAN This chic, arty cafe is a good spot to have a quiet meal, or meet friends for late-night dessert and coffee. One menu is devoted to tapas, like almond-crusted baked brie with cranberry apple compote and West Coast fish cakes in creamy chipotle sauce, while another features "hand helds" or sandwiches. Main dishes feature local meats and vegetables—the Veggie Stack, a tower of portobello mushrooms, mashed yams, tomatoes, and won tons, is a nice break from rich meat dishes. With contemporary art on the red brick walls, Modern Food's setting exudes a level of casual sophistication unusual for Nanaimo.

221 Commercial St. © 250/754-5022. Main courses C$12–C$19 (US$9.60–US$15). MC, V. Sun–Mon 11am–11pm; Thurs–Sat 11am–midnight.

Wesley Street Café ✻✻ WEST COAST CONTEMPORARY Nanaimo's premier fine-dining restaurant serves the city's most up-to-date food in a comfortably formal Old Town Quarter dining room. Chef Daniel Caron pairs European preparations with regional Northwest flavors, as in local clams and mussels in a peach cider broth, and stuffs double cut pork chops with figs and apples. Monday through Thursday, the cafe offers three-course dinners for an unbelievable C$25 (US$20). The huge wine list features many B.C. selections. Live jazz is hosted every Saturday night.

321 Wesley St. © 250/753-6057. www.wesleycafe.com. Reservations required. Main courses C$14–C$26 (US$11–US$21). AE, MC, V. Mon–Fri 11:30am–2:30pm and 5:30–10pm; Sat–Sun noon–2:30pm.

3 Parksville & Qualicum Beach

37km (23 miles) N of Nanaimo

These twin resort towns near the most popular beaches on Vancouver Island now market themselves as the tourist region of Oceanside. Spending a week here is a family tradition for many residents of British Columbia. With miles of sand and six golf courses, it's the perfect base for a relaxing vacation. Parksville (pop. 10,500) and Qualicum Beach (pop. 7,500) are also good stopping-off points for travelers making the trip to or from Victoria and Tofino.

ESSENTIALS

GETTING THERE **Vancouver Island Coach Lines** (© 250/388-5248 or book through Greyhound © 800/661-8747; www.greyhound.ca) offers bus transport from

Nanaimo to the Parksville and Qualicum area along the Highway 1/Highway 19 corridor; one-way fare from Victoria to Parksville is C$28 (US$22). **VIA Rail's E&N Railiner,** or the *Malahat* (© **888/VIA-RAIL** or 250/383-4324; www.viarail.ca), stops in both towns on its daily trip from Victoria to Courtenay. **KD Air** (© **800/ 665-4244,** 604/688-9957, or 250/752-5884; www.kdair.com) flies daily from Vancouver to the Qualicum Beach Airport for C$225 (US$180) round-trip. Otherwise, the closest available air service is at Nanaimo or Comox.

VISITOR INFORMATION   For information on Qualicum Beach, contact the **Qualicum Beach Visitor Information Centre,** 2711 W. Island Hwy., Qualicum Beach, BC V9K 2C4 (© **250/752-9532;** www.qualicum.bc.ca). For information on Parksville and to get a free visitor's guide, contact the **Parksville Visitor Info Centre,** 1275 E. Island Hwy., P.O. Box 99, Parksville, BC V9P 2G3 (© **250/248-3613;** www. chamber.parksville.bc.ca).

EXPLORING THE AREA

While Qualicum Beach and Parksville share similar beaches and are all but connected by country-club developments and marinas, there are differences. Parksville has several large resorts and beachfront hotels, and is more of a developed strip without much of a town center. In contrast, Qualicum Beach has more of a town center with shopping and cafes—but this part of town is a few miles inland, away from the beach.

In Qualicum Beach, you can access the beach from many points along Highway 19A, the old Island Highway. Likewise, in Parksville, the beach is accessible downtown from the old Island Highway, near the junction of Highway 4A, and at the adjacent Parksville Community Beach and Playground. However, the best beaches are preserved in **Rathtrevor Beach Provincial Park,** just east of Parksville's town center. The 348-hectare (860-acre) park offers trails, bird-watching sites, and a campground.

Note: If you're looking for miles of broad, white-sand strands lapped by azure water, you might be surprised. The sea is quite shallow here, with a very gentle slope. When the tide goes out, it exposes hundreds of acres of gray-sand flats. When the tide is in, the beach disappears beneath the shallow waters. There are benefits to this: The summer sun bakes the sand while the tide is out, so when the tide comes back in, the shallow water is warmed by the sand, thus making the water agreeable for swimming.

When you're not on the beach, one particularly good place to stop in Qualicum Beach is the **Old School House,** 122 Fern Rd. W. (© **250/752-6133;** www.theold schoolhouse.org), which now houses galleries, studios, and a gift shop.

There's no better place for a garden stroll than the Milner Gardens and Woodland, 2179 W. Highland Hwy. (© **250/752-6153;** www.milnergardens.org), a heritage garden recently opened to the public. Comprising 24 hectares (60 acres) of old-growth, Douglas-fir forest and 4 hectares (10 acres) of planted gardens, the Milner Gardens are part of a 1930s estate, which also includes a historic home where Queen Elizabeth II once stayed. Given to the local university in 1996, the estate was gradually turned into a destination garden by a small army of horticulture students and local volunteers. Plantings include an artist's garden and many unusual rhododendrons, at their most colorful in late spring. Paths thread through the forests, and garden tours are available. Afternoon tea is served in the Milner house. Open 10am to 5pm daily from early May through Labour Day, and Thursday through Sunday from March 1 to early May, and Labour Day through the second weekend of Oct; C$10 (US$8) adults, C$6 (US$4.80) students 12 and older.

HORNE LAKE CAVES PROVINCIAL PARK

West of Qualicum Beach, **Horne Lake Caves Provincial Park** (© 250/954-4600 for Strathcona Park District) offers access to a lakeside park area, with camping and canoeing, and a system of caves on the slopes of the Beaufort Range (bring at least two sources of light, and, in summer, rent a helmet from the park office). From mid-June to Labour Day, the park offers guided tours, like the family-oriented Riverbend Cave Interpretive Program. The park is located 26km (16 miles) west of Qualicum Beach, off Exit 75 from Highway 19 or 19A. For more adventure, contact **Island Pacific Adventures/Horne Lake Adventures** (© 250/757-8687; www.hornelake.com) to reserve space on its 3-hour Wet and Wild Expedition (C$49/US$39), which features climbing and splashing through part of the cave system.

HITTING THE LINKS

There are six golf courses in the Parksville–Qualicum Beach area, and over a dozen within an hour's drive. **Eagle Crest Golf Club,** 2035 Island Hwy., Qualicum Beach (© 800/567-1320 or 250/752-9744; www.eaglecrest.bc.ca), is an 18-hole, par-71 course with an emphasis on shot making and accuracy. **Pheasant Glen Golf Resort,** 1025 Qualicum Rd., Qualicum Beach (© 877/407-4653 or 250/752-8786; www. pheasantglen.com), now has 18 holes, half of them links-style. **Qualicum Beach Memorial,** 115 Crescent Rd. W., Qualicum Beach (© 250/752-6312), has 9 holes, stunning ocean views, and a restaurant. **Arrowsmith Golf and Country Club,** north of Qualicum Beach at 2250 Fowler Rd. (© 250/752-9727; www.golfarrowsmith.com), is a family-oriented course with 18 holes and a par-61 rating.

    Fairwinds, east of Parksville at 3730 Fairwinds Dr., Nanoose Bay (© 250/468-7666; www.fairwinds.bc.ca), is a challenging 18-hole, par-71 course with ocean views and lots of trees. **Morningstar Golf Club** ✸, 525 Lowry's Rd., Parksville (© 250/248-2244; www.morningstar.bc.ca), is an 18-hole, par-72 championship course with a 74 rating. Designed by Les Furber, it has seaside links and fairways that run in and out of the woods. Each of the above has a driving range, clubhouse, pro shop, and green from C$45 to C$66 (US$36–US$53) for 18 holes.

WHERE TO STAY

Campsites at **Rathtrevor Beach Provincial Park** (© 800/689-9025 for reservations, or 250/248-9449 in the off season) go for C$14 to C$22 (US$11–US$18); it's open in July and August.

Maclure House B&B Inn   This ivy-covered, half-timbered 1921 mansion—with leaded glass, high ceilings, and ornate moldings—was modeled after a Scottish hunting lodge. Bedrooms are tastefully decorated according to British Empire themes (Rudyard Kipling once stayed in the Blue Room). Two units face the ocean and share a balcony. The Ocean Suite boasts a fireplace and an incredible bathroom with original fixtures.

1015 E. Island Hwy., Parksville, BC V9P 2E4. © 250/248-3470. Fax 250/248-5162. www.maclurehouse.com. 4 units. Mid-June to mid-Sept C$130–C$200 (US$110–US$150) double; mid-Sept to mid-June C$110–C$150 (US$88–US$120) double. Extra person C$12–C$21 (US$9.60–US$17). Rates include 3-course breakfast and afternoon treats. Special packages available. AE, MC, V. **Amenities:** Restaurant (see "Where to Dine," below); lounge; golf courses nearby; tennis court; concierge; coin-op laundry; laundry service; dry cleaning. *In room:* Hair dryer, no phone.

Pacific Shores Resort and Spa ✸   Pacific Shores is a large time-share development perched above a half-mile of waterfront in a grove of arbutus and fir trees. Trails lead across the property, which includes its own fish hatchery. Most impressive are the extensive gardens—if you see a plant you like, you may be able to purchase a cutting from the nursery. The Aquaterre Spa offers a full selection of spa treatments. The Landing West Coast Grill offers regional fine dining plus two saltwater aquariums as walls—reportedly, the largest private aquarium in B.C. Accommodations include basic hotel-style units or large suites with up to two bedrooms, a kitchen, fireplaces, a balcony, and two bathrooms, one with a jetted tub; it's a good idea to call and discuss the various unit configurations with the reservations staff. Families are welcome and minimum stays of a week are preferred in summer. But you usually will also have the option to rent a hotel-style room for shorter stays. Several rooms offer wheelchair access. Resort staff can help you book activities with local outfitters.

1–1600 Stroulger Rd., Nanoose Bay, BC V9P 9B7. (C) **866/986-2222** or 250/468-7121. Fax 250/468-2001. www.pacific-shores.com. 132 units. C$110–C$315 (US$88–US$252) 1- or 2-bedroom condo. AE, DISC, MC, V. Free parking. **Amenities:** Restaurant; large indoor pool with "ozonated" water; health club with full weight room; Jacuzzis; sauna; free kayaks, canoe, and rowboat; massage; laundry service; use of 2 computers with Internet access; convenience store and deli; outdoor children's play area; rooms for those w/limited mobility. *In room:* TV/VCR, dataport, kitchen, fridge, coffeemaker, iron.

Quality Resort Bayside (Value)

Perched right above the sands in central Parksville, this resort offers bounteous amenities at moderate prices. Half of the rooms face the beach, and the other half look onto the mountains of Vancouver Island. Heron's offers West Coast cuisine, with summer seating on the deck. The bar features darts, pool, and satellite sports broadcasts.

240 Dogwood St., Parksville, BC V9P 2H5. (C) **877/424-6423** or 250/248-8333. Fax 250/248-4689. www.quality resortparksville.com. 59 units. Oct–Mar C$89–C$109 (US$71–US$87) double; Apr–June C$99–C$129 (US$79–US$103) double; July–Sept C$109–C$139 (US$87–US$1,111) double. Extra person C$10 (US$8). AE, DC, DISC, MC, V. Free parking. Pets allowed for C$15 (US$12). **Amenities:** Restaurant; bar; indoor pool; golf course nearby; full-service health club and spa; Jacuzzi; sauna; bike rentals; tour/activities desk; business center; limited room service; in-room massage; babysitting; laundry service; same-day dry cleaning. *In room:* TV, dataport, coffeemaker, hair dryer, iron.

Tigh-Na-Mara Resort Hotel (R)(R) (Kids)

This time-honored log-cabin resort just keeps getting better. Established in the 1940s on a forested waterfront beach (near Rathtrevor Beach Provincial Park), Tigh-Na-Mara has expanded over the years: more cottages, lodge-style rooms, and beautifully furnished condo-style suites with stunning ocean views. Accommodations include studio and one-bedroom lodge rooms, plus one- and two-bedroom cottages. The duplex cottages can be converted to sleep eight. The new ocean-side condo units all have views as well as balconies or patios. All rooms and cottages have fireplaces and full bathrooms, and almost all have a kitchen. The cottages are comfortably lived-in and homey, while the condos are new and lavish. The new Grotto Spa is B.C.'s largest and offers a mineral pool, body and massage treatments, plus facials, waxing, manicures, and skin and hair care. Families will appreciate the lengthy list of supervised child-friendly activities (many of them free), such as swimming lessons, and small amenities such as video rentals and babysitting (for a fee). In season, try your hand at shell fishing on the resort's beach. The restaurant in the log-and-stone lodge serves an eclectic version of Northwest cuisine and has a children's menu, lounge, and Friday barbecues and dances in summer.

1155 Resort Dr., Parksville, BC V9P 2E5. (C) **800/663-7373** or 250/248-2072. Fax 250/248-4140. www.tigh-na-mara.com. 210 units. July–Aug C$209–C$289 (US$167–US$231) double. Rates vary throughout the year. Extra person C$8–C$15 (US$6.40–US$12). Weekly rates available. Varying minimum stays apply in mid-summer, on holidays, and weekends. AE, DC, DISC, MC, V. Free parking. 1 pet allowed per cottage Sept–June, add C$2 (US$1.60) per day. **Amenities:** Restaurant; bar; indoor pool; golf courses nearby; unlit tennis court; full spa facilities; sauna; paddle boats; bike rental; children's programs; concierge; tour/activities desk (summer); car-rental desk; business center; in-room massage; babysitting; coin-op laundry; laundry service; dry cleaning; nonsmoking rooms. *In room:* TV, data-port, fridge, coffeemaker.

WHERE TO DINE

Beach House Café INTERNATIONAL   The flavors of Asia and Austria mingle at this popular beachside restaurant. An outstanding choice is the Madras shrimp and fruit coconut-milk curry, also available as a vegetarian dish by request. On the European side of the menu, the Jagerschnitzel (veal medallions with wild-mushroom sauce) is a standout. The dining room is comfortable, filled with sun and views.

2775 W. Island Hwy., Qualicum Beach. (©) **250/752-9626.** Reservations suggested. Main courses C$10–C$19 (US$8–US$15). MC, V. Daily 11am–2:30pm and 5–10pm.

Kalvas Restaurant SEAFOOD   Kalvas is the locals' special-occasion restaurant, a rustic-looking lodge with a bustling dining room. The specialties are steaks and seafood prepared in traditional supper-club style: sole amandine, New York steak, steamed Dungeness crab served with drawn butter, and nine preparations of Fanny Bay oysters.

180 Molliet St., Parksville. (©) **250/248-6933.** Reservations recommended. Main courses C$12–C$60 (US$9.60–US$48). MC, V. Sun–Fri 5–10pm; Sat 5–11pm.

Lefty's Fresh Foods HEALTHY/INTERNATIONAL   Originally a vegetarian eatery, Lefty's has added healthy chicken and meat dishes. The emphasis is on modern comfort food: salads, sandwiches, burgers, pasta, stir-fries, and focaccia pizzas. In addition to the original Qualicum Beach location, there's now also a Lefty's in Parksville.

710 Memorial St., Qualicum Beach, and 101–280 E. Island Hwy., Parksville. (©) **250/752-7530** (Qualicum) and **250/954-3886** (Parksville). www.leftys.tv. Main courses C$8–C$20 (US$6.40–US$16). AE, DC, MC, V. Thurs–Sat 8am–10pm (to 9pm off season); Sun–Wed 8am–8pm.

Maclure House Restaurant INTERNATIONAL   This Tudor-style mansion is perfect for a romantic meal. Guests are seated in the wood-paneled dining room, library, or music room, each with a fireplace and garden views. In summer, tables spill out onto the flagstone veranda. The menu has a good selection of salads and pastas, plus Indian curries. The specialty is rack of lamb, crusted with Dijon mustard and pecans. The snug lounge is a wonderful spot for a drink.

1015 E. Island Hwy., Parksville. (©) **250/248-3470.** www.maclurehouse.com. Reservations advised. Main courses C$14–C$35 (US$11–US$28). AE, MC, V. Daily 8:30am–2:30pm and 5–8pm.

Saigon Garden VIETNAMESE   Vietnamese food isn't as common in Canada as in the United States, making this excellent outpost even more of a treat. Order favorites like *pho* (noodle soup) and specialties such as *com tay cam do bien,* a seafood hot pot with prawns, scallops, squid, royal mushrooms, and lily flowers in a delicate fish broth.

118 Craig St., Parksville. (©) **250/248-5667.** Reservations not needed. Main courses C$6–C$12 (US$4.80–US$9.60). V. Mon–Sat 11am–9pm. Free delivery after 3pm in the Parksville area.

Shady Rest Waterfront Pub & Restaurant CANADIAN   Both the restaurant and the pub here have outdoor seating, and both serve the same Qualicum Beach–style comfort food. The appetizer menu is extensive, and entrees range from stir-fries to burgers, plus the freshest local seafood.

3109 W. Island Hwy., Qualicum Beach. © **250/752-9111.** Reservations recommended for the restaurant. Main courses C$10–C$18 (US$8–US$14). MC, V. Restaurant daily 8am–9pm; pub-food service Sun–Thurs 11am–9pm, Fri–Sat 11am–10pm. Pub open until 1am Fri–Sat.

4 En Route to Vancouver Island's Wild West Coast

From Parksville, Highway 4 cuts due west, climbing up over the mountainous spine of Vancouver Island before dropping into Port Alberni, at the head of the Pacific's Alberni Inlet. From here, you can join the mail boats **MV *Lady Rose* &** and **MV *Frances Barkley* &** as they ply the inlet's narrow waters, delivering mail, supplies, and passengers to isolated communities. Bamfield, the southern terminus of the mail-boat run, is one of the two departure points for the West Coast Trail. Mail boats from Port Alberni also negotiate the waters of Barkley Sound and the Broken Group Islands before arriving at Ucluelet, a gentrifying fishing port.

THE DRIVE TO PORT ALBERNI

West of Parksville is the **North Island Wildlife Recovery Centre,** 1240 Leffler Rd., Errington (© **250/248-8534;** www.northislandwildliferecoverycenter.org), which takes in injured and orphaned wildlife. Its eagle flight cage is the largest in Canada. It's open mid-March through October, daily from 10am to 4pm. Take a left from Highway 4 onto Bellevue Road; turn right onto Ruffels Road and then left onto Leffler Road.

Just 3km (1¾ miles) west of the junction with Highway 19, turn south to **Englishman's Falls Provincial Park.** Easy trails lead to both the upper and lower falls. Picnic tables and a basic campground are available.

Below the cliffs of 1,818m (5,963-ft.) Mount Arrowsmith, Highway 4 passes along the shores of **Cameron Lake.** The western end of the lake is preserved as **MacMillan Provincial Park,** with a magnificent stand of old-growth forest called Cathedral Grove.

Finally, you'll reach **Port Alberni,** a hard-working town of nearly 20,000. The busy port is home to a number of fishing charters and boat-tour companies, as well as the mail boats that offer day trips to Bamfield and Ucluelet. If you need a hotel, consider the **Coast Hospitality Inn,** 3835 Redford St. (© **800/663-1144** or 250/723-8111; www.coasthotels.com), with doubles from C$129 (US$103); or the **Best Western Barclay Hotel,** 4277 Stamp Ave. (© **800/563-6590** or 250/724-7171; www.bestwesternbarclay.com), with rooms from C$129 (US$103) in high season.

MV *LADY ROSE* & & MV *FRANCES BARKLEY* &

Lady Rose Marine Services (© **800/663-7192** Apr–Sept, or 250/723-8313; www.ladyrosemarine.com) operates two packet freighters that deliver mail and supplies to communities along the Alberni Inlet and Barkley Sound. The boats take sightseers to the wild outback of Vancouver Island, for a fascinating glimpse into the daily life of remote fishing and logging communities. You'll likely spot bald eagles, bears, orcas, and porpoises. Year-round, the freighters depart from north Harbour Quay at 8am on Tuesday, Thursday, and Saturday. They head to Bamfield via Kildonan, with an hour-long layover before returning to Port Alberni at 5:30pm. From the first Friday in July to the first Friday in September, there's an additional 8am Friday sailing from Port Alberni to Bamfield. The company also operates from Sechart (see the box on p. 171).

June through September, freighters depart on Monday, Wednesday, and Friday at 8am for Ucluelet via Sechart near the Broken Group Islands, arriving back in Port Alberni at 7pm. The freighters also convey kayakers bound for the Broken Group

Islands. Lady Rose Marine Services drops off kayakers at Sechart, on a spur of Vancouver Island across from the islands themselves; kayakers then make the crossing on their own (Oct–May the freighters will drop kayakers at the islands with advance notice). From the first Sunday in July to the first Sunday in September, there's an extra 8am Sunday sailing to Bamfield via Sechart.

One-way fare to Bamfield is C$25 (US$20); round-trip fare is C$50 (US$40). One-way fare to Ucluelet is C$28 (US$22); the round-trip fare is C$55 (US$44). You can go to Kildonan for C$18 (US$14) each way, or to Sechart for C$25(US$20). Children 8 to 15 pay half the adult fare. Bring windproof jackets and hats, as the weather can change dramatically during the course of the trip. Reservations are required.

5 The West Coast Trail (★ & Pacific Rim National Park (★

The west coast of Vancouver Island is a magnificent area of old-growth forests, stunning fiords (or "sounds" in local parlance), rocky coasts, and sandy beaches. And although **Pacific Rim National Park** (**www.pc.gc.ca**) was established in 1971, it wasn't until 1993 that the area really exploded into the greater consciousness. That was when thousands of environmentalists from around the world gathered to protest the clear-cutting of old-growth forests in Clayoquot Sound. When footage of the protests ran on the evening news, people who saw the landscape for the first time were moved to come experience it firsthand. Tourism in the area has never looked back.

Three units make up the park. Along the southwest coast is a strip of land that contains the 75km (47-mile) **West Coast Trail,** which runs between Port Renfrew (covered in chapter 6) and Bamfield (see above). Though considered one of the world's great hikes, the grueling 5- to 7-day journey—with frequent dangerous river crossings and rocky scrambles—is not for the inexperienced. **Broken Group Islands** is a wilderness archipelago in the mouth of Barkley Sound, and a popular diving and kayaking spot (p. 171). **Long Beach** fronts onto the Pacific between Ucluelet and Tofino. Long Beach is more than 30km (19 miles) long, broken here and there by rocky headlands and bordered by tremendous groves of cedar and Sitka spruce. Park entry is C$10 (US$8) per vehicle, per day.

The town of **Ucluelet** (pronounced "you-*clue*-let," meaning "safe harbor") sits on the southern end of the Long Beach peninsula, on the edge of Barkley Sound. Though it has a winter population of only 1,900, thousands of visitors arrive between March and May to see the Pacific gray whales.

At the far northern tip of the peninsula, **Tofino** (pop. 1,600) borders beautiful Clayoquot Sound. Hikers and beachcombers come to Tofino simply for the scenery. Others use it as a base from which to explore the sound—It's the center of the local

---

Tips Special Events

About 20,000 Pacific gray whales migrate to this area annually. During the second week of March, the **Pacific Rim Whale Festival** ★ (② 250/726-7742 or 250/725-3414; www.island.net/~whalef) is held in Tofino and Ucluelet. The annual whale migration is celebrated with whale-watching hikes; First Nations storytelling, music, dancing, and art; children's activities; and contests.

Pacific Rim National Park

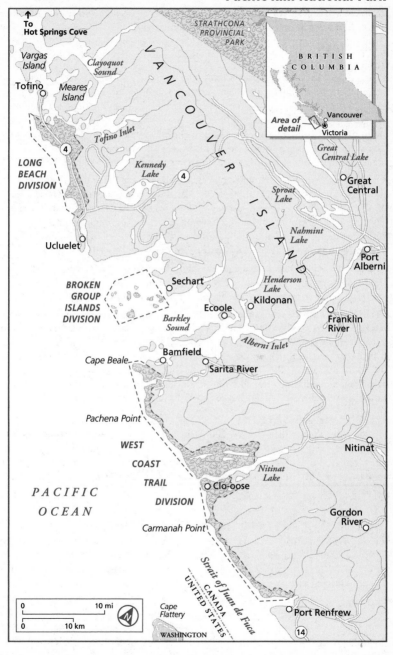

To
Hot Springs Cove

STRATHCONA
PROVINCIAL
PARK

Vargas
Island

Clayoquot
Sound

Tofino

Meares
Island

VANCOUVER ISLAND

BRITISH
COLUMBIA

Area of
detail

Vancouver

Victoria

Great
Central Lake

Tofino Inlet

LONG
BEACH
DIVISION

Kennedy
Lake

4

4

Sproat
Lake

Great
Central

Ucluelet

Nahmint
Lake

Port
Alberni

BROKEN
GROUP
ISLANDS
DIVISION

Sechart

Henderson
Lake

Kildonan

Franklin
River

Barkley
Sound

Ecoole

Alberni Inlet

Cape Beale

Bamfield

Sarita River

Pachena Point

WEST

COAST

TRAIL

DIVISION

Nitinat

Nitinat
Lake

Clo-oose

PACIFIC

OCEAN

Gordon
River

Carmanah Point

0   10 mi

0   10 km

Cape
Flattery

Strait of Juan de Fuca

CANADA
UNITED STATES

Port Renfrew

14

WASHINGTON

eco-tourism business. No small number of travelers arrive here with eating in mind: This remote town is noted for its excellent restaurants.

ESSENTIALS
GETTING THERE

BY PLANE   **Sonic Blue Airways** (℃ **800/228-6608** or 604/278-1608; www.sonic blueair.com) offers flights between Vancouver International Airport and Tofino. Return fare to/from Vancouver starts at C$280 (US$224); flying time is 45 minutes. **Craig Air** (℃ **877/886-3466** or 250/266-0267; www.craigair.com) provides air service from Victoria and Vancouver to Tofino; one-way fare is C$145 (US$116). **Sound Flight** offers air service between the Seattle area and Tofino (℃ **866/921-3474** or 425/254-8064; www.soundflight.net). One-way transport is US$250 (C$313).

BY CAR   Tofino, Ucluelet, and Long Beach all lay near the end of Highway 4 on the west coast of Vancouver Island. From Nanaimo, take the Island Highway (Hwy. 19) north for 52km (32 miles). Just before the town of Parksville is a turnoff for Highway 4, which leads to the mid-island town of Port Alberni (38km/24 miles) and then to the coastal towns of Tofino (135km/84 miles west of Port Alberni) and Ucluelet (103km/64 miles west). The road is well paved but windy after Port Alberni.

BY FERRY   A 4½-hour ride aboard the **Lady Rose Marine Services** (℃ **800/663-7192** Apr–Sept, or 250/723-8313; www.ladyrosemarine.com) MV *Lady Rose* takes you from Port Alberni to Ucluelet. See p. 165 for more information.

BY BUS   **Island Coach Lines** (℃ **250/724-1266**) operates regular daily service between Victoria and Tofino/Ucluelet. The 6-hour trip, departing Victoria at 5:30am and arriving in Tofino at 12:45pm, costs C$55 (US$44) to Tofino. The bus also stops in Nanaimo and can pick up passengers arriving from Vancouver on the ferry. The **Tofino Bus** (℃ **866/986-3466;** www.tofinobus.com) also offers daily bus service from Victoria and Vancouver to Tofino/Ucluelet. A one-way ticket from Victoria to Tofino is C$50 (US$40).

VISITOR INFORMATION

The **Ucluelet Visitor Info Centre,** 100 Main St., by Government Wharf on Ucluelet Harbour (℃ **250/726-4641;** www.uclueletinfo.com), is open July through September, Monday through Friday from 11am to 5pm. You should also check out **www.ucluelet.com**. The **Tofino Visitor Info Centre,** 1426 Pacific Rim Hwy. (℃ **250/725-3414;** www.tofinobc.org), is open March through September, Monday through Friday from 11am to 5pm.

THE HIKE OF A LIFETIME: THE WEST COAST TRAIL

The rugged West Coast Trail has gained a reputation as one of the world's greatest extreme hiking adventures. Each year, about 9,000 people tackle the entire challenging 75km (47-mile) route, and thousands more hike the very accessible 11km (6¾-mile) **oceanfront stretch** at the northern trail head near Bamfield. Imperative for the full hike are a topographic map and tidal table, stamina for rock climbing as well as hiking, and advanced wilderness-survival and minimum-impact camping knowledge. Go with at least two companions, pack weatherproof gear, and bring 15m (50 ft.) of climbing rope per person. Only 52 people per day are allowed to enter the main trail (26 from Port Renfrew, 26 from Bamfield), and registration with the park office is mandatory. Most people make the hike in 5 to 7 days.

Moments **Diving the Graveyard of the Pacific**

The waters off the park's West Coast Trail are known throughout the world as "the graveyard of the Pacific." Hundreds of 19th- and 20th-century shipwrecks silently attest to the hazards of sailing without an experienced guide in these unforgiving waters. Underwater interpretive trails narrate the history of the area—rated among the world's best by The Cousteau Society. Check out **www. 3routes.com/na/can/bc/09/index.html** for an index of diving outfitters.

The West Coast Trail land is temperate coastal rainforest dominated by old-growth spruce, hemlock, and cedar. The topography ranges from sandy beaches to rocky headlands and wide sandstone ledges. Caves, arches, tidal pools, and waterfalls add variety to the shoreline.

Call **Super Natural BC** (*✆* **800/435-5622** or 250/387-1642) after March 1 to schedule your entry reservation for the coming May-through-September season. In summer, you can also contact the **parks service** (*✆* **250/728-3234** or 250/647-5434; www.pc.gc.ca) for information. Make your reservations as early as possible. There's a C$25 (US$20) booking fee and C$110 (US$88) trail-use fee. If you want to try your luck, there are six daily first-come, first-served wait-list openings at each trail head information center—Gordon River at the south end and Pachena Bay at the north end. The park service says you'll probably wait 1 to 3 days for an opening.

UCLUELET

When fishing was the premier industry on the coast, a constant flow of ships frequented Ucluelet's processing and packing plants. With the boom in eco-tourism, however, the town is scrambling to reinvent itself. It now offers a few fine B&Bs and cabin resorts but has yet to catch up to Tofino. Ucluelet is cheaper though, just as close to Long Beach, and more likely to have vacancies in the high season.

Fishing, kayaking, and whale-watching are the main attractions. For custom fishing charters, contact **Roanne Sea Adventures,** in the boat basin (*✆* **250/726-4494;** www.roanne.ca). To combine lodging with your fishing expedition, check out **Island West Resort,** 1990 Bay St. (*✆* **250/726-7515;** www.islandwestresort.com), or, for more luxury, Oak Bay Marine Group's **Canadian Princess Resort** (see below).

Subtidal Adventures, 1950 Peninsula Rd., in the West Ucluelet Mall (*✆* **877/444-1134** or 250/726-7336; www.subtidaladventures.com), offers whale-watching trips, kayaking expeditions, and even an archaeological tour. **Aquamarine Adventures,** Small Craft Harbour Floathouse 200, near the base of Hemlock Street (*✆* **866/726-7727** or 250/726-7727; www.westcoastwhales.com), operates whale-watching tours that let passengers listen to whales through the boat's hydrophone system, plus historical tours of the Broken Group Islands. **Majestic Ocean Kayaking,** 1167 Helen Rd. (*✆* **800/889-7644** or 250/726-2868; www.oceankayaking.com), also runs various kayak trips.

The 3km (1¾-mile) **Wild Pacific Trail** takes you out to the Amphitrite Lighthouse, a prime whale-watching spot. See also "Outdoor Pursuits" under "Tofino," below, for guided walks offered by **Long Beach Nature Tour Company** *✖*.

WHERE TO STAY

Canadian Princess Resort If you're coming to Ucluelet to fish—or even if you're not—the Canadian Princess Resort is an enjoyable and high spirited place to stay. You can lodge either on land in standard hotel-style rooms or in traditional bunk-roomed cabins onboard the Canadian Princess, a former survey ship permanently moored adjacent to the hotel in Ucluelet's central Boat Basin. Hotel accommodations are very comfortable, while the ship cabins are authentically snug, with the toilet and shower down the hall. Also aboard the ship are a fine dining restaurant and two lounges all with charming maritime decor. The resort focuses on fishing trips out into the Pacific—each day, cabin cruisers set out on guided fishing trips; gear is provided.

1943 Peninsula Rd., Ucluelet, BC V0R 3A0. © **800/663-7090** or 250/726-7771. Fax 250/726-7121. www.canadian princess.com. 76 units. C$89–C$195 (US$71–US$157) double. Guided fishing packages with 2 fishing trips and 2 nights' stay begin at C$415 (US$332) in high season. AE, MC, V. Closed late Sept to late Apr. **Amenities:** Restaurant; 2 lounges; tour desk. *In room (hotel):* A/C, TV, coffeemaker, hair dryer.

Ocean's Edge B&B This remarkable little B&B sits on its own tiny peninsula jutting out into the Pacific, with only a thicket of interwoven hemlocks sheltering it from the wind and the surf of the ocean, which roars up surge channels on either side. Rooms have a single queen-size bed and are pleasant and spotless. The real attractions are the scenery and the wildlife, which abound. Owners Bill and Susan McIntyre installed a skylight in the kitchen so breakfasting guests could keep an eye on the pair of bald eagles and their chicks nesting in a 200-year-old Sitka spruce in the driveway. The former chief naturalist of Pacific Rim National Parks, Bill is a font of information and also does nature tours. See the website for information on guided hikes.

855 Barkley Crescent, Box 557, Ucluelet, BC V0R 3A0. © **250/726-7099.** Fax 250/726-7090. www.oceansedge. bc.ca. 3 units. C$130 (US$104) double. Rates include full breakfast. 2-night minimum; discounts for extended stays. MC, V. Not suitable for children. **Amenities:** Nonsmoking facility. *In room:* Binoculars, no phone.

A Snug Harbour Inn ⭐ A beautiful cliff-top B&B, A Snug Harbour Inn even overlooks its own little bay. Guests can make use of several large decks (one with a hot tub) and a monstrous telescope to watch the sea lions on the reef just offshore. The inn is luxurious—the rooms are spacious, with queen- or king-size beds, opulent bathrooms, and jetted tubs. The heart-shaped tub with a waterfall may be a bit over the top, but who's complaining? Owner Skip Rowland had the inn built by a shipwright, and the craftsmanship is evident, with wonderful woodwork and fine nautical joinery. The cottage features two luxury rooms, each with a king-size bed, jetted tub, fireplace, heated floors, and balcony. One room is wheelchair accessible, the other is pet friendly.

460 Marine Dr., Box 367, Ucluelet, BC V0R 3A0. © **888/936-5222** or 250/726-2686. www.awesomeview.com. 6 units. June–Sept C$245–C$325 (US$196–US$260) double; Nov–Feb C$175–C$205 (US$140–US$164) double; Oct and Mar–May C$205–C$255 (US$164–US$204) double. Breakfast included. DC, MC, V. Children not accepted. **Amenities:** Jacuzzi; nonsmoking rooms; access to kitchen and TV; 1 room for those w/limited mobility. *In room:* Coffeemaker, hair dryer, no phone.

WHERE TO DINE

Fine dining is only just beginning to have a presence here, as urban refugees with a flair for cooking try to make a go of coastal living. The **Matterson Teahouse and Garden,** 1682 Peninsula Rd. (© **250/726-2200**), is a great spot for lunch. Sandwiches, salads, and a great chowder are served in the cute dining room; evening hours are unusual, so be sure to call ahead. Overlooking the harbor is **Eagle's Nest Marine Pub,** 140 Bay St. (© **250/726-7515**), open Monday to Saturday 10am to midnight and

Sunday 10am to 10pm, with traditional pub grub. The **Stewart Room Restaurant** on the Canadian Princess, 1943 Peninsula (© **250/726-7771**) offers seafood and fine dining aboard a 71m (235-ft.) moored ship.

TOFINO

Once the center of massive environmental protests that drew the world's attention, Tofino is now a rather schizophrenic town—part eco-tourism outfitters, activists, and serious granolas; part former loggers and fishermen; and part Tla-o-qui-aht and Ahousaht peoples, who live mostly outside the town. Conflict was common in the early years, but recently all parties seem to have learned to get along.

The reason for Tofino's popularity is not hard to fathom. Tofino offers incredible marine vistas at the end of a thin finger of land, battered by the Pacific to the west and lapped by Tofino Sound on the east. The town is notched with tiny bays and inlets, with a multitude of islands, many of them very mountainous, just off the coast. Further east, the jagged, snow-capped peaks of Strathcona Park fill the horizon.

Tofino is becoming more crowded and subject to a particular brand of gentrification. On the beaches south of town, luxury inns serve the rarified demands of upscale travelers attracted to the area's scenery. There are more fine dining restaurants and boutiques here than can possibly be justified by the town's size. Dining is as big a draw as sea kayaking for many Tofino visitors.

Broken Group Islands

Lying off the coast of Ucluelet in Barkley Sound are the Broken Group Islands, an archipelago of about 300 islands and islets that are part of Pacific Rim National Park. Due to the relatively calm waters, abundant wildlife, and dramatic seascapes, these islands are popular destinations for experienced sea kayakers and ocean canoeists. Divers can explore historic shipwrecks as well as reefs teeming with marine life (dive outfitters operate out of Bamfield, described earlier). The underwater drop-offs shelter large populations of feather stars, rockfish, and wolf eels that grow as long as 2m (6½ ft.) and occasionally poke their heads out of their caves.

Access to the Broken Group Islands is limited. In both Bamfield and Ucluelet, you'll find a number of operators who can arrange a trip, or you can take a packet freighter from Port Alberni (see "MV *Lady Rose* & MV *Frances Barkley*" on p. 165).

Sechart is also the site of the **Sechart Whaling Station Lodge,** an operation of **Lady Rose Marine Services** (© 800/663-7192 Apr–Sept, or 250/723-8313; www.ladyrosemarine.com). It primarily serves the needs of kayakers, though it's open to anyone who wants a unique wilderness experience. Rates are C$100 (US$80) per person or C$155 (US$1,124) for two people sharing the same room, including three family-style meals a day. The only ways to get to the lodge are via the packet freighters, a **Toquart Connector Water Taxi** (© 250/720-7358) from Bamfield, or your own vessel. Kayak rentals are available. For reservations, contact Lady Rose Marine Services (above).

With all the bustle, it can be difficult at times to find solitude in what's actually still an amazingly beautiful and wild place. Accordingly, more people decide to avoid the crowds and visit Tofino in winter, to watch dramatic storms roll in from the Pacific.

OUTDOOR PURSUITS

FISHING   Sportfishing is excellent off the west coast. Long Beach is also great for bottom fishing. A nonresident saltwater or freshwater license is available at tackle shops, which also carry *BC Tidal Waters Sport Fishing Guide, BC Sport Fishing Regulations Synopsis for Non-Tidal Waters,* and the *BC Fishing Directory and Atlas.*

Sportfishing for salmon, steelhead, rainbow trout, Dolly Varden char, halibut, cod, and snapper is excellent off the west coast of Vancouver Island. **Jay's Clayoquot Ventures** (© **888/534-7422** or 250/725-2700; www.tofinofishing.com) organizes fishing charters throughout the Clayoquot Sound area. Deep sea, and both saltwater and freshwater flying-fishing excursions, are offered. The company supplies all the gear, a guide, and a boat. Prices start at a minimum of C$85 (US$68) per hour, with a minimum of 4 hours. A 10-hour fishing trip for four people on an 8m (25-ft.) boat costs C$750 (US$600).

GUIDED NATURE HIKES   Owned and operated by Bill McIntyre, former chief naturalist of the Pacific Rim National Park, the **Long Beach Nature Tour Co.** ❄ (© **250/726-7099;** www.oceansedge.bc.ca) offers guided beach walks, storm watching, land-based whale-watching tours, and rainforest tours customized to suit your group's needs.

HIKING   In and around **Long Beach,** numerous marked trails 1km to 3.5km (⅔ mile–2 miles) long take you through the thick temperate rainforest edging the shore. The **Gold Mine Trail** (about 3.5km/2 miles long) near Florencia Bay still has a few artifacts from the days when a gold-mining operation flourished here. The partially boardwalked **South Beach Trail** (less than 1.5km/1 mile long) leads through the moss-draped rainforest onto small quiet coves like Lismer Beach and South Beach, where you can see abundant life in the rocky tidal pools. The 1km (⅔ mile) **Schooner Beach Trail,** just south of Tofino, passes through mature rainforest before dropping onto scenic Schooner Beach, at the northern end of the park's Long Beach. The **Big Cedar Trail,** on Meares Island, is a 3km (2-mile) boardwalked path that was built to showcase the old-growth forest. Maintained by the Tla-o-qui-aht band, the trail has a long staircase leading up to the Hanging Garden Tree, which is said to be between 1,000 and 1,500 years old. Many Tofino outfitters offer tours and boat transportation to the trail.

In town, the paths in the 5-hectare (12-acre) **Tofino Botanical Gardens,** 1084 Pacific Rim Hwy. (© **250/725-1220;** www.tofinobotanicalgardens.com), meander past theme gardens and old-growth forest and wind down to Tofino Inlet. Admission is C$10 (US$8) for adults, C$6 (US$4.80) for students, and C$2 (US$1.60) for children under 12. Open daily from 9am to dusk.

KAYAKING   Perhaps the quintessential Clayoquot experience, and certainly one of the most fun, is to slip into a kayak and paddle out into the Sound. For beginners, half-day tours to Meares Island (usually with the chance to do a little hiking) are an especially good bet. For rentals, lessons, and tours, try **Pacific Kayak,** 606 Campbell St., at Jamie's Whaling Station (© **250/725-3232;** www.tofino-bc.com/pacifickayak). The **Tofino Sea-Kayaking Company,** 320 Main St., Tofino (© **800/863-4664** or

---

⌢Tips Hot Springs Cove

Hot Springs Cove is a natural hot spring located about 67km (42 miles) north of Tofino; it's accessible only by water. Take a water taxi, canoe, or kayak up to Clayoquot Sound to enjoy a swim in the steaming pools and bracing waterfalls. A number of kayak outfitters and boat charters offer trips here (see "Whale-Watching, Nature Tours & Birding," below). On the way, guides generally try to take some time for whale-watching as well.

250/725-4222; www.tofino-kayaking.com), offers kayaking packages ranging from 4-hour paddles around Meares Island (from C$68/US$54 per person) to weeklong paddling and camping expeditions. Instruction by experienced guides makes even your first kayaking experience a comfortable, safe, and enjoyable one.

WHALE-WATCHING, NATURE TOURS & BIRDING   Nearly a dozen outfitters conduct tours out onto the waters of Clayoquot Sound to view gray whales, bald eagles, porpoises, orcas, seals, and sea lions. March to October, **Jamie's Whaling Station,** 606 Campbell St., Tofino, BC V0R 2Z0 (② **800/667-9913** or 250/725-3919; www.jamies.com), uses a glass-bottomed 20m (65-ft.) power cruiser as well as a fleet of Zodiacs for tours to watch the gray whales. A combined Hot Springs Cove and whale-watching trip aboard a 10m (32-ft.) cruiser can be booked year-round. In addition to whale-watching and hot springs expeditions, **Seaside Adventures** (② **888/ 332-4252** or 250/725-2292; www.seaside-adventures.com) offers bear watching trips from May 1 through Sept. Fares for both companies' expeditions generally start at C$75 (US$60) per person for a 2- or 3-hour tour; customized trips can run as high as C$250 (US$200) per person for a full day.

March to November, **Remote Passages,** Meares Landing, 71 Wharf St., Tofino, BC V0R 2Z0 (② **800/666-9833** or 250/725-3330; www.remotepassages.com), runs daily 2½-hour whale-watching tours in Clayoquot Sound on Zodiac boats, costing C$69 (US$55) for adults and C$55 (US$44) for children under 12. The company also conducts a 7-hour whale-watching/hot springs trip at C$110 (US$88) for adults and C$79 (US$63) for children under 12. Reservations are recommended.

For bird enthusiasts, the protected waters of Clayoquot Sound and the beaches of Pacific Rim National Park offer fantastic viewing opportunities. **Just Birding** (② **250/725-8018;** www.justbirding.com) offers a range of bird-watching adventures, including walking tours of the beaches, paddle trips to bald eagle habitats, and boat tours for off-shore pelagic birding. Guided trips begin at C$79 (US$63) per person.

RAINY-DAY ACTIVITIES: SHOPPING, STORM-WATCHING & MORE

When you'd rather be indoors, snuggle up with a book at the **Wildside Booksellers and Espresso Bar,** Main Street (② **250/745-4222**), or get a massage or salt glow at the **Ancient Cedars Spa** at the Wickaninnish Inn (② **250/725-3100**).

Or, check out the galleries. The **Eagle Aerie Gallery,** 350 Campbell St. (② **250/ 725-3235**), constructed in the style of a Native Indian Longhouse, features the innovative work of Tsimshian artist Roy Henry Vickers. The **House of Himwitsa,** 300 Main St. (② **250/725-2017**), is also owned/operated by Native Indians. The quality and craftsmanship of the shop's artwork, masks, baskets, totems, gold and silver jewelry, and apparel are excellent. The **Reflecting Spirit Gallery,** 441 Campbell St. (© **250/725-4229**), offers medicine wheels, rocks, and crystals, as well as a great selection of Native art, carvings, wood crafts, and pottery.

Watching the winter storms from big windows has become very popular in Tofino. For a slight twist on this, try the outdoor storm-watching tours offered by the **Long Beach Nature Tour Co.** ⊀ (© **250/726-7099;** www.oceansedge.bc.ca). Owner Bill McIntyre, former chief naturalist of Pacific Rim National Park, can explain how storms work and the best locations to get close to them without getting swept away.

WHERE TO STAY

There are easily 100 or more places to stay in Tofino; the **Tofino Visitor Info Centre,** 380 Campbell St. (© **250/725-3414;** www.tofinobc.org), open March through September, Monday through Friday from 11am to 5pm, keeps a helpful list of vacancies.

Best Western Tin-Wis Resort (*Kids*)   The Tla-o-qui-aht First Nations band run this large, hotel-like lodge on MacKenzie Beach. All rooms are spacious, with oceanfront views, although more basic than you'll find at most other beachfront lodges. Options include queen loft units and deluxe king rooms with fireplaces, kitchenettes, and Jacuzzi tubs. Most units have sofa beds, making them a good choice for families.

1119 Pacific Rim Hwy., Box 380, Tofino, BC V0R 2Z0. © 800/661-9995 or 250/725-4445. Fax 250/725-4447. www.tinwis.com. 86 units. June 20–Oct 15 C$199–C$235 (US$179–US$188) double; C$345 (US$276) executive suite. Substantially lower off-season rates. Senior, AAA, and group discounts available. AE, DC, DISC, MC, V. **Amenities:** Restaurant; lounge; well-equipped exercise room; large Jacuzzi. *In room:* TV, fridge, coffeemaker, hair dryer.

The Clayoquot Wilderness Resort ⋆⋆ (*Finds*)   This upscale resort company offers an interesting twist on luxury accommodations. The Bedwell River Outpost package features safari-style luxury tent accommodations located a short boat or plane ride from Tofino on the Bedwell River. Twenty canvas platform tents, beautifully furnished with Adirondack-style furniture, Oriental rugs, antiques, and other comforts, serve as guest rooms and suites, while dining tents, a lounge tent, games tent, and even a library tent offer visitors a taste of upscale camping. The heart of the outpost is the ranch-style log cookhouse, with a towering double-sided fieldstone fireplace in the open-kitchen attended by chef Timothy May. A range of activities such as horseback riding, sailing, kayaking, and fishing are included in the package. After a full day's adventure, retreat to the three spa treatment tents for a massage or a revitalizing soak in a wood-fired hot tub. Most packages also include return airfare from Vancouver. *Note:* Clayoquot Wilderness Resort's floating resort on Quoit Bay is temporarily closed for refitting.

P.O. Box 130, Tofino, BC V0R 2Z0. © 888/333-5405 in North America or 250/725-2688. Fax 250/726-8558. www.wildretreat.com. 20 tents. March 15–Nov 30 3-day packages from C$4,750 (US$3,800) per person double occupancy. Includes all activities, meals, and transport. AE, MC, V. **Amenities:** Restaurant; bar; spa; Jacuzzi; sauna; watersports equipment; massage. *In room:* TV/VCR, hair dryer, iron.

The Inn at Tough City ⊀   This is possibly Tofino's nicest small inn and certainly the quirkiest (by the way, Tough City was an early nickname for Tofino). Built in 1996 from salvaged and recycled material, it's filled with antiques, stained glass, and bric-a-brac. The rooms are all unique, with cheerful jewel-toned walls and a dollop of thrift-store chic; several feature soaker tubs, fireplaces, or both. Some rooms have balconies. The on-site restaurant, Tough City Sushi, features seafood and sushi and is open for dinner year-round, lunch in summer season only.

350 Main St., P.O. Box 8, Tofino, BC V0R 2Z0. ℭ **877/725-2021** or 250/725-2021. Fax 250/725-2088. www.tough city.com. 8 units. Mid-May to mid-Oct C$140–C$175 (US$112–US$140) double. Shoulder and off-season discounts. AE, MC, V. Pets are allowed, C$10 (US$8). **Amenities:** Restaurant; in-room massage; laundry service; nonsmoking rooms. *In room:* TV, dataport, coffeemaker, hair dryer.

Long Beach Lodge Resort ★★

A contender for the title of Tofino's most upscale lodge is this extremely handsome log-and-stone resort perched above the waves on Cox Bay. The care and style that went into the building of the lodge and cottages is extraordinary—in fact, the Long Beach Lodge Resort was featured in *Architectural Digest* magazine. The architects and designers did a great job updating the usual back-country lodge look, making the entire resort feel both timeless and comfortably modern. The Great Room, filled with fine furniture and flanked by a huge granite fireplace and massive windows overlooking Cox Bay, is the heart of the lodge, serving as breakfast and lunch room, cocktail lounge, and a comfortable living room for snoozing, reading, and watching surfers. The dining room here has quickly gained attention for its regional fine dining. Accommodations include lodge rooms (with less expensive rooms facing the forest, not the Pacific) and free-standing duplex cottages. All feature marvelous fir furniture, slate-floored bathrooms with soaker tubs and separate showers, bathrobes, and loads of rich decor (including original artwork); some rooms have fireplaces and balconies/patios. The cottages are 93-sq.-m (1,000-sq.-ft.) dwellings with all the above, plus private hot tubs, a large sitting area with overstuffed couches and chairs, washer and dryer, and a full kitchen. The rate formula is rather complex, so check the website or call for exact rates for the date of your visit. Resort staff will help you put together outdoor activities and recreation.

1441 Pacific Rim Hwy., Box 897, Tofino, BC V0R 2Z0. ℭ **877/844-7873** or 250/725-2442. Fax 250/725-2402. www. longbeachlodgeresort.com. 61 units. Late June to Oct 1 C$269–C$429 (US$215–US$343) double; C$429 (US$343) cottage. 3-night minimum cottage stay in high season. Lower shoulder and off-season rates; packages available. Extra person C$30 (US$24). Some discounts available with 3-day minimum stays during shoulder and off season. AE, DC, MC, V. Pets allowed in some cottages. **Amenities:** Restaurant; beautifully furnished lodge "great room" with fireplace. *In room:* TV, fridge, coffeemaker, hair dryer, iron, DVD/CD player.

Middle Beach Lodge ★★

This beautiful lodge/resort complex is on a headland overlooking the ocean just south of Tofino. The rustic look was accomplished by using largely recycled beams and salvaged lumber, and as a result the lodge exudes a sense of venerability and history, despite its recent construction. Accommodations are in a variety of structures: a "beach house" with standard hotel rooms, two lodges (one family oriented, one adults only) with a mix of suites and guest rooms, and oceanfront cabins, some of which can sleep seven. Although most of the suites and cabins have decks, soaker or Jacuzzi tubs, gas fireplaces, CD players, and kitchenettes, it's a good idea to phone the lodge to discuss specific room features, as there are many subtle variations. All guests have access to two lofty common rooms overlooking the ocean. These are good spots to pour a coffee or something stronger and look out over the waves crashing in.

400 Mackenzie Beach Rd. (P.O. Box 100), Tofino, BC V0R 2Z0. ℭ **866/725-2900** or 250/725-2900. Fax 250/725-2901. www.middlebeach.com. 45 units, 19 cabins. C$135–C$225 (US$108–US$180) double; C$175–C$350 (US$140–US$280) suite; C$230–C$400 (US$184–US$320) cabin. 2-night minimum stay required Mar–Oct. Shoulder and off-season rates available. AE, MC, V. Children 12 and under not accepted at beach and some headlands accommodations. **Amenities:** Exercise room; tour desk; laundry service; nonsmoking facility. *In room:* TV/VCR (suites and cabins only), kitchenette, fridge, coffeemaker, no phone.

Red Crow Guest House ★

While the Wickaninnish and other coastal lodges show you the wild, stormy west-facing side of Tofino, the Red Crow displays the kinder, subtler beauty on the peninsula's east side. By the sheltered waters of Jensen Bay, this pleasant Cape Cod–style home sits in 2.8 secluded hectares (7 acres) of old-growth forest. Two rooms are in the lower level of the house (with private entrances), opening out onto a fabulous view of the bay—perhaps best seen from the inn's outdoor hot tub. Rooms here are large and pleasant, with queen- or king-size beds and 1920s-style furnishings. In addition, there's a charming two-bedroom garden cottage with full kitchen. Come here for the wildlife viewing (eagles, seals, and shorebirds), and stay for the breakfasts—the innkeeper is a professional chef. Guests have free use of canoes to explore offshore islands.

Box 37, 1084 Pacific Rim Hwy., Tofino, BC V0R 2Z0. ℂ/fax **250/725-2275**. www.tofinoredcrow.com. 3 units. C$165–C$180 (US$132–US$144) double. Shoulder and off-season rates available. Extra person C$20 (US$16). V. *In room:* Fridge, coffeemaker, hair dryer, CD player, no phone.

The Tides Inn on Duffin Cove
This comfy B&B offers a friendly welcome and spectacular views of Duffin Cove, an easy stroll from the village center. All rooms have en suite bathrooms, private entrances and decks or balconies, and one has a fireplace. For families or friends traveling together there's also a two-bedroom, two-bathroom suite with a wet bar, pool table, and large shared living room. At the bottom of the yard, past the hot tub, a wooden stairway leads down to a semiprivate beach.

160 Arnet Rd. (Box 325), Tofino, BC V0R 2Z0. ℂ **250/725-3765**. Fax 250/725-3325. www.tidesinntofino.com. 3 units. June 15–Sept 15 C$120–C$145 (US$96–US$116) double; Sept 16–June 14 C$95–C$125 (US$76–US$100) double. Rates include full breakfast. 2-night minimum stay. MC, V. Children under 12 not permitted. **Amenities:** Jacuzzi; nonsmoking facility. *In room:* TV/VCR, fridge, coffeemaker, hair dryer, iron, no phone.

Whalers on the Point Guesthouse
This modern hostel is one way to save money in an increasingly expensive town. Located downtown, with views of Clayoquot Sound, it offers both shared and private rooms; wheelchair-accessible rooms are available. The hostel offers discounted activities, arranged through local outfitters.

81 West St., Box 296, Tofino, BC V0R 2Z0. ℂ **250/725-3443**. Fax 250/725-3463. www.tofinohostel.com. 55 beds. May–Sept double C$75 (US$60); Oct–Apr double from C$45 (US$36); shared C$24–C$26 (US$19–US$21) per person. Hostelling International member, off-season, multiday, and family discounts available. MC, V. **Amenities:** Sauna; game room; coin-op laundry; Internet kiosk; kitchen; TV room; rooms for those w/limited mobility. *In room:* No phone.

The Wickaninnish Inn ☆☆☆
No matter which room you book at this beautiful inn of cedar, stone, and glass, you'll wake to a magnificent view of the untamed Pacific. The Wick, as it's affectionately known, is on a rocky promontory, surrounded by an old-growth spruce and cedar rainforest and the sprawling sands of Chesterman Beach. Perennially ranked as one of the top inns in North America, the Wick succeeds by blurring the distinction between outdoors and indoors through art, furnishings, architecture, and building materials. Rustic driftwood furniture, richly printed textiles, and local artwork highlight the rooms, each of which features a private balcony, oceanfront view, fireplace, down duvet, soaker tub and stone-lined shower, luxurious bath amenities, thick bathrobes, a CD player, a large-screen TV, and complimentary high-speed Internet access. Special occasion suites, particularly the Canopy Suite with custom-made furniture, "seashore" bathroom, and fiber-optic sky-scape of the summer solstice above the bed, are truly fantastic. The new Wickaninnish On the Beach is a major expansion of the inn that adds a health-club facility and library to the resort, in addition to 30 more luxury-level guest rooms. Winter storm-watching packages have become so popular that the inn is nearly as busy in winter as it is in summer. The Pointe Restaurant (see "Where to Dine," below) is one of the top dining rooms in

western Canada. The staff can arrange whale-watching, golfing, fishing, and diving packages. Affiliated with Aveda, the inn's Ancient Cedars Spa offers a host of packages and beauty and relaxation treatments.

Osprey Lane at Chesterman Beach, P.O. Box 250, Tofino, BC V0R 2Z0. © **800/333-4604** in North America or 250/725-3100. Fax 250/725-3110. www.wickinn.com. 75 units. From C$440 (US$352) double. Special packages available year-round. Reduced shoulder and off-season rates. AE, DC, MC, V. Drive 5km (3 miles) south of Tofino toward Chesterman Beach to Osprey Lane. **Amenities:** Restaurant; bar; spa; concierge; in-room massage; babysitting; non-smoking facility; rooms for those w/limited mobility. *In room:* TV, dataport, minibar, coffeemaker, hair dryer, iron.

CAMPING

The 94 campsites on the bluff at **Green Point** are maintained by Pacific Rim National Park (© **250/726-7721**). The grounds are full every day in July and August, and the average wait for a site is 1 to 2 days. Leave your name at the ranger station when you arrive to be placed on the list. You're rewarded for your patience with a magnificent ocean view, pit toilets, fire pits, pumped well water, and free firewood (no showers or hookups). Sites in July and August are C$16 to C$21 (US$13–US$17) and in the shoulder season C$12 to C$18 (US$9.60–US$14). The campground is closed October to March.

The **Bella Pacifica Resort & Campground,** 3.5km (2 miles) south of Tofino on the Pacific Rim Highway (P.O. Box 413), Tofino, BC V0R 2Z0 (© **250/725-3400;** www.bellapacifica.com), is privately owned and has 165 campsites from which you can walk to Mackenzie Beach or take the resort's private nature trails to Templar Beach. Flush toilets, hot showers, water, laundry, ice, fire pits, firewood, and full and partial hookups are available. Rates are C$20 to C$42 (US$16–US$34) per two-person campsite. Reserve at least a month in advance for a summer weekend.

WHERE TO DINE

For a cup of java and a snack, it's hard to beat the **Caffé Vincenté,** 441 Campbell St. (© **250/725-2599**), a touch of urban hip near the entrance to town. The cafe also does an excellent breakfast and lunch and serves afternoon dessert. Tofino's dining darling of the moment is **SOBO** (© **250/725-2341**) a catering wagon at the Tofino Botanical Gardens (1084 Pacific Rim Hwy.) that serves inexpensive, well-prepared lunches featuring Asian noodles as well as wraps, salads, and soups that are also available to go (C$6–C$18/US$4.80–US$14). At night, the operation moves indoors to the botanical garden visitor center. SOBO's food is certainly tasty and an inexpensive meal in Tofino is welcome, but you decide if the quality matches the hype generated by rave-up articles in *Gourmet* magazine and the *New York Times*. See The Inn at Tough City under "Where to Stay," above, for a description of **Tough City Sushi** ᕫ.

The Common Loaf Bake Shop BAKERY/CAFE   Locally famous as the gathering place for granolas and lefty rabble-rousers back when they amassed in Tofino to take their stand, the Loaf has since expanded, which just goes to show you can make money selling idealism along with your muffins. Located at the "far" end of town, the Common Loaf does baked goods really well: muffins, cookies, whole-grain breads, and sticky cinnamon buns. It also serves soups, curry, and pizza for lunch.

180 First St. © **250/725-3915.** Reservations not accepted. Main courses C$4–C$12 (US$3.20–US$9.60). No credit cards. Summer daily 8am–9pm; winter daily 8am–6pm.

The Pointe Restaurant ᕫᕫᕫ PACIFIC NORTHWEST   The famed restaurant at the Wickaninnish Inn is perched on the water's edge at Chesterman Beach, where a 280-degree view of the roaring Pacific is the backdrop to a dining experience that can only be described as pure Pacific Northwest. Top chef Andrew Springett applies his talents to an array of local ingredients, including Dungeness crab, spotted prawns, halibut, salmon, quail, lamb, and rabbit. Service is top-notch and the wine list wins awards from *Wine Spectator*. The inn's signature dishes include a salmon tasting medley; Wickaninnish Potlatch, a chunky, fragrant stew of fish, shellfish, and vegetables simmered in a thick seafood broth; and whole Dungeness crab for two with crab and chorizo risotto. Other offerings include delectable appetizers like foie gras with rhubarb compote, goat-cheese tarts, and shaved fennel salad. In addition to the seasonal a la carte menu is a specialty seafood menu.

The Wickaninnish Inn, Osprey Lane at Chesterman Beach. ℭ **250/725-3100**. Reservations required. Main courses C$29–C$42 (US$23–US$34); 4-course gastronomic menu C$75 (US$60). AE, MC, V. Daily 8am–2:30pm, 2–5pm (snacks), and 5–9:30pm.

The RainCoast Cafe WEST COAST   This cozy restaurant, just off the main street, has developed a deserved reputation for some of the best—and best value—seafood and vegetarian dishes in town. There are a number of small plates, which you can assemble into a meal, many featuring local shrimp, oysters, and clams in innovative preparations. Main courses reflect an Asian influence. Local sablefish is served with maple mirin sauce, while tandoori halibut comes with cardamom and pistachio pilaf. Start your meal off with the popular RainCoast salad—smoked salmon, sautéed mushrooms, and chèvre on a bed of greens, with maple-balsamic vinaigrette.

120 Fourth St. ℭ **250/725-2215**. Main courses C$17–C$30 (US$14–US$24). AE, MC, V. Daily 5–9:30pm.

The Schooner on Second ⚓ PACIFIC NORTHWEST   This big red barn of a building looks like the sort of place that serves up family style crab suppers—and so it did until a few years ago. However, after a major menu and decor make-over, the Schooner is now one of Tofino's top fine dining choices. As you'd expect, local fish and shellfish in hearty yet sophisticated preparations dominate the menu. The signature dish is Halibut Bowden Bay, in which local halibut is stuffed with crab, shrimp, and brie and served with an apple brandy peppercorn sauce. Wild mushrooms in port cream grace grilled lamb tenderloin. Breakfasts here are legendary—smoked salmon eggs Benedict will kick-start your vacation. In good weather, dine on the deck with views across Tofino Inlet to myriad offshore islands.

331 Campbell St. ℭ **250/725-3444**. Reservations suggested. Main courses C$14–C$36 (US$11–US$29). MC, V. Daily 9–11:30am, noon–3, and 5–9:30pm.

Shelter ⚓⚓ PACIFIC NORTHWEST   You don't come to this land-locked restaurant for the view, but, rather, for the cooking, which is remarkable in its bright flavors and textures. Shelter, which buys most of its fish and fresh ingredients directly from producers—right off the boat and right off the land—is one of the best of Tofino's new crop of restaurants. Their signature bouillabaisse is stuffed with local fish and shellfish and simmered in a fire-roasted tomato broth; a delicate halibut filet surmounts a bed of spot-prawn risotto. Local white wines dominate the wine list, chosen to highlight the delicate flavors of fish and seafood. Just as there's no ocean view in the narrow, fireplace-warmed dining room, there's also no kitschy totem poles or wooden seagulls in fishing nets. Instead, a single, heraldic surfboard, emblematic of the youthful energy of Shelter's cooking style, dominates the dining room.

601 Campbell St. ℭ **250/725-3353**. www.shelterrestaurant.com. Reservations suggested. Main courses C$16–C$27 (US$13–US$22). MC, V. Daily 5–10pm.

6 Courtenay & Comox

62km (38 miles) N of Qualicum Beach

Facing each other across the Courtenay Estuary, Comox (pop. 12,500) and Courtenay (pop. 20,000) are twin towns that provide a bit of urban polish to a region rich in outdoor recreation. Because they're north of the Victoria-to-Tofino circuit that defines much of the tourism on Vancouver Island, these towns are refreshingly untouristy. Comox has a working harbor with a fishing fleet; Courtenay, a lumber-milling center, has an old downtown core where the shops have largely transformed into boutiques, but which still seems homey. Which isn't to say that these towns lack sophistication: You'll find excellent lodging and restaurants, as well as the new and opulent Crown Isle Golf Resort. Depend on the pace of change to quicken even further: The Comox Valley is the one of the fastest-growing regions of Vancouver Island.

Courtenay and Comox are also stepping-off points for adventures in the Beaufort Mountains, just to the west. From Mount Washington Alpine Resort, trails lead into the southeast corner of Strathcona Provincial Park. There are also adventures to be had at sea level: The shallow Courtenay Estuary is home to abundant wildlife, particularly birds and sea mammals, and is a popular destination for sea kayakers.

ESSENTIALS
GETTING THERE
BY PLANE   Comox Valley Regional Airport, north of Comox, welcomes daily flights from Vancouver, Calgary, and Edmonton. The airport is served by **Pacific Coastal Airlines** (© **800/663-2872;** www.pacific-coastal.com) and **WestJet** (© **877/952-4638;** www.westjet.com).

BY FERRY   BC Ferries (© **888/BC-FERRY** in B.C., or 250/386-3431; www.bcferries.com) crosses from Powell River on the mainland to Little River, just north of Comox. Nanaimo's Duke Point and Departure Bay are the closest terminals with connections to the Vancouver area. If you'd like to see the Sunshine Coast on your way to Comox/Courtenay—and stay overnight to make it possible and worthwhile—cross from Horseshoe Bay to Langdale in Gibsons, then drive along Highway 101 to Earl's Cove in Sechelt, crossing again to Saltery Bay, finally ferrying from Westview in Powell River to Comox.

BY TRAIN & BUS   Courtenay, which is 90 minutes north of Nanaimo on Highway 19, is also the terminus for **VIA Rail's E&N Railiner,** or *Malahat* (© **888/VIA-RAIL** or 250/383-4324; www.viarail.ca), which offers daily service from Victoria.

Tips Special Events

The **Filberg Festival** attracts over 140 artists and craftspeople from across the province. It takes place at Filberg Park, with some events in the lodge and others in tents and booths. The festival includes musical entertainment and theater. It's held the first weekend of August; admission is C$10 (US$8), 13 and under free. Tickets can be purchased at **www.sidwilliamstheatre.com** or by calling © **866/898-8499** or 250/338-2420, ext. 3. For information, contact the park (see below) or the festival coordinator (© **250/334-9242;** www.filbergfestival.com).

Vancouver Island Coach Lines (© **250 388-5248,** or book through Greyhound © **800/661-8747;** www.greyhound.ca) offers bus transport from Nanaimo to the Comox and Courtenay area along the Highway 19 corridor. One-way fare from Victoria to Courtenay is C$39 (US$31).

VISITOR INFORMATION

Contact the **Comox Valley Visitor Info Centre,** 2040 Cliffe Ave., Courtenay (© **888/357-4471** or 250/334-3234; www.tourism-comox-valley.bc.ca).

EXPLORING THE AREA

Highway 19A becomes Cliffe Avenue as it enters Courtenay. It then crosses the Courtenay River and continues north toward Campbell River, bypassing the old town centers of both Courtenay and Comox. This is a comparative blessing, as it allows these commercial districts to quietly gentrify without four lanes of traffic shooting past. The new Inland Highway 19 bypasses the towns altogether; the Comox Valley Parkway exit will take you from the highway over to Cliffe Avenue.

COURTENAY

Courtenay's town center revolves around Fourth, Fifth, and Sixth streets just west of the Courtenay River. It's a pleasant place for a stroll, with a number of boutiques, art galleries, and housewares shops to browse. It's also the heart of Courtenay's dining and coffee shop culture.

Stop by the **Comox Valley Art Gallery,** Duncan Avenue at Sixth Street (© **250/334-2983**), a public contemporary exhibition space for local and regional artists. The gallery shop carries the work of more than 100 artists. The **Artisans Courtyard,** 180B Fifth St. (© **250/338-6564;** www.artinglass.org), is a co-op with more than 60 members. Next door is the **Potter's Place,** 180A Fifth St. (© **250/334-4613**), which offers the works of 29 potters, ranging from porcelain to raku.

The **Courtenay District Museum & Paleontology Centre,** 207 Fourth St. (© **250/334-0686;** www.courtenaymuseum.ca), tells the story of the region's First Nations peoples with a good collection of masks, basketry, and carvings. The museum's highlight is a 12m (39-ft.) cast skeleton of an elasmosaur, a Cretaceous-era marine reptile. (The Comox Valley was once covered by a tropical sea, and the area now yields a wealth of marine fossils.) July and August (and on a more limited basis Apr–June, and in Sept) the museum leads 3-hour **fossil tours** of its paleontology lab and to a local fossil dig; C$20 (US$16) adults, C$18 (US$14) seniors and students, C$13 (US$10) children, or C$55 (US$44) per family. Call ahead for reservations. Admission to the museum alone is C$3 (US$2.40) adults and C$2.50 (US$2) seniors and children 12 and over. Summer hours are Monday to Saturday 10am to 5pm and Sunday 12 to 4pm. Winter hours are Tuesday to Saturday 10am to 5pm.

COMOX

The old center of Comox is small, with just a few shops and cafes to tempt travelers. What's definitely worth exploring, however, is the **marina area** in Comox Harbour. Walkways offer views of the boats and the bay; rising above it all are the jagged peaks of Strathcona Park. Another excellent place for a stroll is **Filberg Lodge and Park,** 61 Filberg Rd. (© **250/334-9242;** www.filbergfestival.com/lodge.html). A full 3.6 hectares (9 acres) of lawn and forest, plus a petting zoo, surround a handsome Arts and Crafts–style home. Once a private residence, the lodge is now open for tours from 11am to 5pm on Easter weekend plus weekends in May and September, and daily from July to Labour Day.

PARKS & BEACHES

Continue past the marina on Comox Road to **Gooseneck Park,** a local favorite. **Saratoga Beach** and **Miracle Beach Provincial Park** are about a half-hour drive north of Courtenay on Highway 19. **Seal Bay Regional Nature Park and Forest,** 24km (15 miles) north of Courtenay off Highway 19, is a 714-hectare (1,764-acre) preserve laced with hiking and mountain-biking trails. Hours are from 6:30am to 11pm.

OUTDOOR PURSUITS

GOLF   One of the finest courses on Vancouver Island is **Crown Isle Resort & Golf Community** ⚑, 399 Clubhouse Dr., Courtenay (© **888/338-8439** or 250/703-5050; www.crownisle.com). This 18-hole links-style championship course has already hosted the Canadian Tour. Facilities are lavish, including an eye-popping clubhouse, steam rooms, and a hotel and villas (see "Where to Stay," below).

KAYAKING   With the Courtenay Estuary and Hornby, Tree, and Denman islands an easy paddle away, sea kayaking is very popular. **Comox Valley Kayaks,** 2020 Cliffe Ave., Courtenay (© **888/545-5595** or 250/334-2628; www.comoxvalleykayaks.com), offers rentals, lessons, and tours. Rentals start at C$20 (US$16) for 2 hours.

SKIING   **Mount Washington Alpine Resort** ⚑ (© **888/231-1499** or 250/338-1386, or 250/338-1515 for snow report; www.mtwashington.bc.ca) is a 5-hour drive from Victoria and open year-round (for hiking or skiing, depending on the season). The summit reaches 1,588m (5,209 ft.), and the mountain averages 8.6m (28 ft.) of snow per year. A 488m (1,601-ft.) vertical drop and 50 groomed runs are served by six lifts and a beginners' tow. Fifty-five kilometers (34 miles) of Nordic track–set and skating trails connect to Strathcona Provincial Park. The **Raven Lodge** has restaurants, equipment rentals, and locker rooms, while the Bear and Deer lodges offer accommodation. Lift rates are C$51 (US$41) for adults, C$42 (US$34) for seniors and students, and C$28 (US$22) for kids 7 to 12. Take the Strathcona Parkway 37km (23 miles) to Mount Washington, or use turnoff 130 from Inland Highway 19.

WHERE TO STAY

The **Travelodge Courtenay,** 2605 Island Hwy. (© **800/795-9486** or 250/334-4491; www.travelodgecourtenay.com), offers extras at a relatively modest cost. The motel's clean, unfussy rooms start at C$79 (US$63).

Coast Westerly Hotel   The Coast Westerly presents a rather off-putting visage: The three-story slant-fronted wall of glass that encases the lobby probably seemed like a stylish idea when the hotel was first built . . . But once you get past the exterior, you'll discover that the guest rooms are spacious and nicely furnished, with a full complement of extras like an indoor pool and health club. The back wing offers rooms with balconies, some overlooking the river. The Coast Westerly is just south of Courtenay's vibrant downtown area, near the shopping centers along Cliffe Avenue.

1590 Cliffe Ave., Courtenay, BC V9N 2K4. © **800/668-7797** or 250/338-7741. Fax 250/338-5442. www.coastwesterly hotel.com. 108 units. C$119–C$159 (US$95–US$127) double. Extra person C$10 (US$8). Off-season and senior rates available. Ski and golf packages available. AE, MC, V. Pets accepted. **Amenities:** Restaurant; pub; lounge; indoor pool; golf course nearby; exercise room; Jacuzzi; sauna; limited room service; liquor store. *In room:* A/C, TV w/pay movies, dataport, coffeemaker.

Greystone Manor B&B ⚑ *(Finds)*   For many guests, the high point of a stay here is a chance to wander the lush .6-hectare (1½-acre) gardens. The charming innkeepers claim that gardening wasn't even a particular passion in their lives until they bought this property. But a passion it has now become: Every year, they put in more than 3,500 bedding plants. The house itself is a handsome 1918 Tudor-style Craftsman. Guests share a magnificent wood-paneled sitting room with loads of unpainted moldings, a grand piano, and comfy couches.

4014 Haas Rd., Courtenay, BC V9N 9T4. ℂ 250/338-1422. www.bbcanada.com/1334.html or http://greystone manorbb.com. 3 units. C$95 (US$76) double. Rates include full breakfast. MC, V. Children must be 13 or older. **Amenities:** Nonsmoking facility. *In room:* Hair dryer, no phone.

Kingfisher Oceanside Resort and Spa ★★

Located 7km (4½ miles) south of Courtenay, this long-established resort has modernized with an added bank of beachfront suites and a classy spa. The older motel units are large, nicely furnished rooms with balconies or patios, most with views of the pool and the Strait of Georgia. The newer one-bedroom suites are splendid, each with a full kitchen, two TVs, fireplace, and balcony that juts out over the beach; most suites have a two-person whirlpool tub in addition to a full bathroom with heated tile floors. Our favorite is no. 401, on the end of the building, with banks of windows on two sides. Two rooms are available for people with disabilities.

The **Kingfisher restaurant** is one of the best places to eat in Courtenay. The spa offers a wide selection of treatments and body work. Trained technicians offer thalassotherapy baths and wraps, massage, reiki, and facials. Guests also have access to a steam cave. *Note:* Smoking is not permitted on the premises.

4330 Island Hwy. S., Courtenay, BC V9N 9R9. ℂ 800/663-7929 or 250/338-1323. Fax 250/338-0058. www.kingfisher spa.com. 64 units. From C$165 (US$132) double; C$200 (US$160) suite. Extra person C$15 (US$12). Golf, ski, fishing, spa, and women's wellness packages available. Senior discounts available. AE, DC, DISC, MC, V. Free parking. Pets allowed in 3 rooms, add C$10 (US$8). **Amenities:** Restaurant; outdoor pool; golf course nearby; unlit tennis court; exercise room; spa; Jacuzzi; sauna; canoe and kayak rentals; activities desk; courtesy limo; business center; 24-hr. room service; massage; babysitting; coin-op laundry; laundry service; dry cleaning; nonsmoking rooms; executive-level rooms; rooms for those w/limited mobility. *In room:* TV (suites w/VCR), dataport, fridge, coffeemaker, hair dryer.

The Villas at Crown Isle Resort ★★ *Value*

For the money, these villas are an incredible deal. Located at Crown Isle Golf Resort, they overlook the first fairway and are just yards from the spectacular clubhouse. The suites are truly large and filled with luxury touches: Many have gourmet kitchens, Jacuzzis, fireplaces, VCRs, and balconies. A newer building has well-appointed hotel-style rooms. Villa guests have access to the fitness equipment in the resort clubhouse, a full spa, and, of course, there's that golf course.

399 Clubhouse Dr., Courtenay, BC V9N 9G3. ℂ 888/338-8439 or 250/703-5000. Fax 250/703-5035. www.crown isle.com. 54 units. Nov–Apr from C$109 (US$87) fairway room, from C$149 (US$119) villa; Oct from C$119 (US$95) fairway room, from C$189 (US$9,151) villa; May–Sept from C$129 (US$103) fairway room, from C$249 (US$199) villa. Extra person C$15 (US$12). Golf and ski packages available. AE, MC, V. Free parking. **Amenities:** 2 restaurants; golf course; health club; spa; business center; limited room service; laundry service; same-day dry cleaning. *In room:* TV, coffeemaker, hair dryer.

WHERE TO DINE

Atlas Café *Value* INTERNATIONAL This cafe serves up affordable, flavorful variations on world cuisine. The globe-trotting menu hops from Asia and the Mediterranean to Mexico and the Pacific Northwest. Happily, many of the dishes are vegetarian. Portions are large, so this is a good destination for a hungry group with different tastes. Although some of the specials reach toward the C$20 (US$16) range, the majority of dishes are between C$11 to C$15 (US$8.80–US$12). The decor is quite sophisticated—the bar is an aquamarine jewel box and the dining room boudoir red. The only downside: The wine list is extremely limited, especially considering B.C.'s burgeoning wine culture.

250 Sixth St., Courtenay. ✆ **250/338-9838.** www.comoxvalleyrestaurants.ca/atlas.htm. Reservations accepted for parties of 6 or more only. Main courses C$7–C$19 (US$5.60–US$15). MC, V. Mon 8:30am–3:30pm; Tues–Sat 8:30am–10pm; Sun 8:30am–9pm.

The Black Fin Pub PUB/CANADIAN   On the short walk from downtown Comox to the marina, you'll pass this hospitable pub overlooking the harbor. The menu is large and, for a pub, quite interesting; some of the appetizers feature Thai and Chinese flavors. Entrees range from schnitzel to curry chicken. The usual burgers and sandwiches are also in abundance. Sunday brunch is served until 2pm, and there's an afternoon tea on Monday and Thursday. The entire pub is smoke-free.

132 Port Augusta St., Comox. ✆ **250/339-5030.** Reservations accepted for parties of 4 or more in early evening. Main courses C$8–C$15 (US$6.40–US$12). AE, MC, V. Food service Sun–Thurs 11am–10pm; Fri–Sat 11am–10:30pm. Hours may be extended in summer.

Kingfisher Oceanside Restaurant ✿ SEAFOOD/CONTINENTAL   The dining room at this resort brings together waterfront views with high-quality cuisine. If you're staying at the Kingfisher to partake of the new spa services, you'll be pleased with the spa menu, which features low-fat, low-calorie entrees such as poached halibut jardiniere. On the regular menu, one popular entree is cedar plank–baked salmon with a chutney of sage and blackberries. Also listed are steaks, schnitzels, and lamb dishes.

4330 Island Hwy. S., 7km (4½ miles) south of Courtenay. ✆ **250/338-1323.** www.kingfisherspa.com. Reservations advised. Main courses C$12–C$28 (US$9.60–US$22). AE, DC, DISC, MC, V. Daily 7–10:30am, 11:30am–2pm, and 5–10pm.

Old House Restaurant ✿ WEST COAST   In the midst of splendid gardens, and on the banks of the Courtenay River, the very charming and atmospheric Old House is located in a rambling 1930s heritage home that looks like it belongs in England's Cotswolds. With four fireplaces and rough-hewn timbers, it feels like a country lodge. The menu at this well-loved restaurant has recently been updated, and now features local and regional ingredients in a spectrum of international and West Coast dishes. Local seafood and lamb are always featured. The patio is a wonderful place for a drink.

1760 Riverside Lane, Courtenay. ✆ **250/338-5406.** www.theoldhouse.ca. Reservations recommended. Main courses C$12–C$28 (US$9.60–US$22). AE, MC, V. Sun–Thurs 11am–9pm; Fri–Sat 11am–9:30pm.

Otters Bistro SEAFOOD/PUB   Otters Bistro has the area's top view—just above the marina in Comox, with a spectacular vista across Courtenay Bay. Request a table on the deck if the weather's nice. Seafood dominates the entrees—try the medley of shellfish with onions and tomatoes, in a hearty broth of white wine, garlic, saffron, and herbs. For meat lovers, there's hunter-style schnitzel and beef tenderloin. There's an entire page worth of burgers and wraps; the same menu is available in the pub and restaurant.

1805 Beaufort Ave., Comox. ✆ **250/339-6150.** ✆ 250/339-6151 (Edgewater Pub). Reservations recommended in summer. Main courses C$8–C$18 (US$6.40–US$14). MC, V. Free parking in marina parking lot. Daily 11:30am–2:30pm and 5–9:30pm.

Toscanos ITALIAN   Toscanos is a cheerful restaurant located between downtown Comox and Comox Harbor, with a million-dollar view of the bay and distant Beaufort Mountains. The dining room is rather minimalist, lacking the rustic clutter that passes for decor in many Italian restaurants. The menu is divided between pasta dishes and chicken, veal, and seafood entrees. Desserts include classics such as tiramisu and profiteroles.

140 Port Augusta, Comox. ✆ **250/890-7575.** www.comoxvalleyrestaurants.ca/Toscanos.htm. Reservations recommended. Main courses C$11–C$24 (US$8.80–US$19). MC, V. Mon–Sat 11am–2pm and 5–9pm. Closed on major holidays.

8

Northern Vancouver Island

In this chapter, we cover the portion of Vancouver Island from the town of Campbell River—the "Salmon-Fishing Capital of the World"—northward. West of Campbell River lies Strathcona Provincial Park, the oldest provincial park in British Columbia and the largest on Vancouver Island.

The waters along the island's northeast coast near Port McNeill are home to both resident and transient orca whales; the latter move annually from Johnstone Strait to the open Pacific. In this vicinity are also two tiny unique communities: the First Nations town of Alert Bay on Cormorant Island, and Telegraph Cove, a boardwalk community on pilings above the rocky shore.

The Island Highway's final port of call, Port Hardy is the starting point for the Inside Passage ferry cruise up the northern coast. It carries passengers bound for Prince Rupert, where it meets the ferries to the Queen Charlotte Islands and to Alaska, and links to the Yellowhead Highway and Via Rail's *Skeena* run (see chapter 10 for complete coverage of these destinations).

Note: See the "Vancouver Island" map (p. 116) to locate areas covered in this chapter.

1 Essentials

GETTING THERE

BY PLANE See chapter 5 for information on Vancouver Island's major air hub, **Victoria.**

The **Campbell River and District Regional Airport,** located south of Campbell River off Jubilee Parkway, has regularly scheduled flights on commuter planes to and from Vancouver on **Pacific Coastal Airlines** (② 800/663-2872; www.pacific-coastal. com). Pacific Coastal Airlines is the only scheduled air carrier with flights to/from Port Hardy and Vancouver.

Commuter seaplane company **Kenmore Air** (② 800/543-9595; www.kenmore air.com), departs from Seattle's Lake Union or Lake Washington and flies to Campbell River/Quadra Island and Port McNeill in summer only.

BY FERRY BC Ferries (② 888/BC-FERRY or 250/386-3431; www.bcferries.com) operates a route linking Powell River to Comox, not too far south of Campbell River, but reaching Powell River from other points on the mainland requires taking two other ferries—a daunting and costly prospect for a single day's travel (p. 204 for details). Nanaimo's Duke Point and Departure Bay are the closest terminals with connections to the Vancouver area. Port Hardy also connects with Prince Rupert via a 15-hour journey that winds through the Inland Passage. Sample fares are included in the regional sections that follow.

If you're traveling with a car, you'll find that ferry ticket prices add up quickly. You may want to consider leaving the car on the mainland and traveling by bus, taxi, or air.

BY BUS   Greyhound Canada (© **800/661-8747** or 604/482-8747; www.greyhound. ca) provides eight daily trips between Vancouver and Nanaimo. Fare is C$28 (US$15) one-way. **Vancouver Island Coach Lines** (© **250/388-5248,** or book through Greyhound © **800/661-8747;** www.greyhound.ca) offers bus transport from Nanaimo to the Campbell River and Port Hardy along the Highway 19 corridor.

VISITOR INFORMATION

For information on Vancouver Island, contact **Tourism Vancouver Island,** Suite 203, 335 Wesley St., Nanaimo (© **250/754-3500;** www.islands.bc.ca). You can also check out **www.vancouverisland.com**.

GETTING AROUND

While Vancouver Island has an admirable system of public transport, getting to remote sights and destinations is difficult without your own vehicle.

BY FERRY   BC Ferries (© **888/BC-FERRY** in B.C., or 250/386-3431; www.bcferries.com) links Vancouver Island ports to many offshore islands, including Quadra, Alert Bay, and Sointula. None of these islands has public transport, so once there you'll need to hoof it, hitch it, hire a taxi, or arrange for bike rentals. Most innkeepers will pick you up if you've reserved in advance.

BY BUS   See "Getting There," above, for information on **Vancouver Island Coach Lines.**

BY CAR   North of Nanaimo, the major road on Vancouver Island is **Highway 19,** which is now almost all four-lane expressway; a particular improvement being the new 128km (80-mile) **Inland Highway** between Parksville and Campbell River. The older sections of 19, all closer to the island's east coast, are now labeled 19A. North of Campbell River, a long, unimproved section of Highway 19 continues all the way to Port Hardy. Access to gasoline is no problem, even in more remote northern areas, but don't head out on a long stretch of unpaved road without filling up.

Rental-car agencies include **Avis** (© **800/272-5871** in Canada, 800/230-4898 in the U.S.; www.avis.com), **Budget** (© **800/268-8900** in Canada, 800/527-0700 in the U.S.; www.budget.com), and **National** (© **800/CAR-RENT** in Canada and the U.S.; www.nationalcar.com).

2 Campbell River & Quadra Island

Campbell River: 45km (28 miles) N of Courtenay; 266km (165 miles) N of Victoria

Busy and utilitarian, Campbell River (pop. 33,000) gives the impression of a town that works for a living. For years, it has been known as the "Salmon-Fishing Capital of the World," but it is also home to a large pulp and paper mill. Between Quadra Island and Campbell River, the broad Strait of Georgia squeezes down to a narrow 1.6km-wide (1-mile) channel called Discovery Passage. All of the salmon that enter the Strait of Juan de Fuca near Victoria to spawn in northerly rivers funnel down into this tight churning waterway with 4m (13-ft.) tides. Historically, vast hauls of incredibly large fish have been pulled from these waters; fishing lodges have lined these shores for decades. However, salmon numbers at Campbell River have fallen drastically in recent years, and the days of pulling 60-pound chinooks from the turbulent waters are largely over. Today, you're as likely to take a wildlife-viewing trip on the sound as go fishing for salmon—and if you do fish, there are plenty of restrictions.

Salmon or no salmon, there are plenty of other attractions in and around Campbell River. An excellent museum with a world-class collection of Native artifacts heads the list, and hiking on Quadra Island and in Strathcona Provincial Park appeals to outdoorsy types. To reach Quadra Island, take the 10-minute ferry from downtown Campbell River to Quathiaski Cove, on Quadra Island. Trips depart on the hour from about 6am to 10pm (no Sun 7am sailing). Round-trip fares are C$6 (US$4.80) per adult passenger, C$15 (US$12) per vehicle; you can bring a bike for free.

ESSENTIALS

GETTING THERE   By Plane   The **Campbell River and District Regional Airport,** south of Campbell River off Jubilee Parkway, has regular flights on commuter planes from Vancouver on **Pacific Coastal Airlines** (✆ **800/663-2872;** www.pacific-coastal.com).

Commuter seaplane company **Kenmore Air** (✆ **800/543-9595;** www.kenmore air.com), departs from Seattle's Lake Union or Lake Washington and flies to Campbell River/Quadra Island in summer.

By Car   On the four-lane Inland Highway (Hwy. 19), Campbell River is 45km (28 miles) north of Courtenay and 266km (165 miles) north of Victoria. Campbell River is the end of this newly improved stretch of roadway. The old Island Highway, 19A, also runs into the center of Campbell River, right along the water as you approach town.

By Bus   **Vancouver Island Coach Lines** (✆ **250/388-5248,** or book through Greyhound ✆ **800/661-8747;** www.greyhound.ca) offers bus transport from Victoria and Nanaimo to Campbell River. One-way fare from Nanaimo to Campbell River is C$24 (US$19). (Nanaimo is the closest ferry service to the Vancouver area.)

VISITOR INFORMATION   The **Campbell River Visitor Info Centre,** 1235 Shoppers Row (✆ **250/287-4636;** http://visitorinfo.incampbellriver.com), is open from 9am to 5pm (later in summer), daily from late July to Labour Day, Monday through Saturday in shoulder seasons, and Monday through Friday from October to early May. Another good resource is **Campbell River Tourism** (✆ **800/463-4386** or 250/286-1616; www.campbellrivertourism.com).

EXPLORING CAMPBELL RIVER

Downtown Campbell River won't win any awards for quaintness. Busy Island Highway whizzes through town, and the commercial district is dominated by strip malls. One worthy stop is **Wei Wai Kum House of Treasures,** Discovery Harbour Shopping Centre, 1370 Island Hwy. (✆ **250/286-1440;** www.houseoftreasures.com), which sells carvings, totem poles, and clothing from the local Laichwiltach (aka Ligwitdaxw or Lekwiltok) tribes of the Kwakwaka'wakw First Nations people. Wei Wai Kum is home to **Gildas Box of Treasures Theatre,** a facsimile of a Laichwiltach Big House which hosts performances of traditional dances, songs, and stories.

The Museum at Campbell River 🎐 *Kids*   Campbell River's captivating museum is worth seeking out for the carvings and artifacts from local First Nations tribes; the contemporary carved masks are especially fine. Also compelling is the sound-and-light presentation *The Treasures of Siwidi,* which retells an ancient Native myth. You can see a replica of a pioneer-era cabin, tools from the early days of logging, and, in the theater, a 1914 documentary called *War of the Land Canoes.* The gift shop is a great place to buy Native art and jewelry.

Campbell River

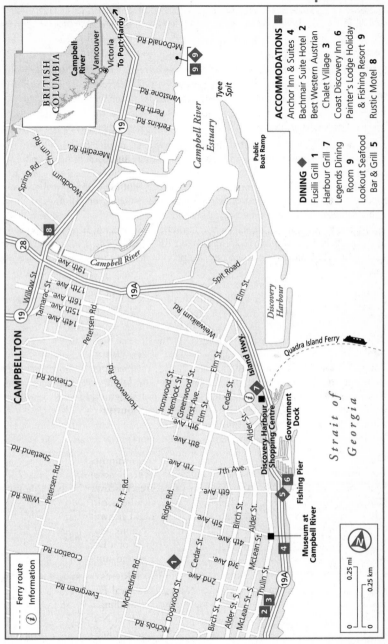

ACCOMMODATIONS
Anchor Inn & Suites **4**
Bachmair Suite Hotel **2**
Best Western Austrian
Chalet Village **3**
Coast Discovery Inn **6**
Painter's Lodge Holiday
& Fishing Resort **9**
Rustic Motel **8**

DINING
Fusilli Grill **1**
Harbour Grill **7**
Legends Dining
Room **9**
Lookout Seafood
Bar & Grill **5**

BRITISH
COLUMBIA

Campbell
River

Vancouver

Victoria

Campbell River
Estuary

Tyee
Spit

Public
Boat Ramp

To Port Hardy

McDonald Rd.

Vanstone Rd.

Perth Rd.

Perkins Rd.

Meredith Rd.

Woodburn Chum Rd.

Spring Rd.

Campbell River

19th Ave.

17th Ave.

16th Ave.

15th Ave.

14th Ave.

Tamarac St.

Willow St.

Spit Road

Elm St.

Discovery
Harbour

CAMPBELLTON

Cheviot Rd.

Homewood Rd.

Petersen Rd.

Weiwaikum Rd.

Ironwood St.

Hemlock St.

Greenwood St.

First Ave.

Elm St.

Elm St.

Cedar St.

Alder St.

9th Ave

8th Ave

7th Ave.

7th Ave.

6th Ave

5th Ave

4th Ave

3rd Ave

2nd Ave

Cedar St.

Birch St.

Alder St.

McLean St.

Thulin St.

Island Hwy.

19A

19

19

28

8

Discovery Harbour
Shopping Centre

Government
Dock

Quadra Island Ferry

Fishing Pier

Museum at
Campbell River

*Strait of
Georgia*

Shetland Rd.

Petersen Rd.

Willis Rd.

E.R.T. Rd.

Ridge Rd.

Croation Rd.

McPhedran Rd.

Evergreen Rd.

Nichols Rd.

Dogwood St.

Birch St. S.

Alder St. S.

McLean St. S.

19A

Ferry route
Information

0   0.25 mi
0   0.25 km

N

9 9

1

2 3

4

5 6

7

470 Island Hwy. (© 250/287-3103. www.crmuseum.ca. Admission C$6 (US$4.80) adults, C$4 (US$3.20) seniors and students, C$15 (US$12) families, free for children under 6. Mid-May to Sept daily 10am–5pm; Oct to mid-May Tues–Sun noon–5pm.

OUTDOOR PURSUITS

DIVING   The decommissioned **HMCS *Columbia*** was sunk in 1996 near the sea-life-rich waters of Seymour Narrows off the Quadra Island's west coast. For information on diving to this artificial reef and on other diving sites (with enticing names like Row and Be Damned, Whisky Point, Copper Cliffs, and Steep Island) in the Campbell River area, contact **Beaver Aquatics** (© **250/287-7652;** www.connected.bc.ca/~baquatics).

FISHING ℱ   The coho salmon in these waters weigh up to 9kg (20 lb.), and even these are dwarfed by the tyee—13.5kg-plus (30-lb.-plus) chinook (king) salmon. But fishing isn't what it once was in Campbell River. Some salmon runs are now catch-and-release only, and others are open for limited catches; many fishing trips are now billed more as wildlife adventures than hunting-and-gathering expeditions.

To fish here, you need nonresident saltwater and freshwater licenses, available at outdoor-recreation stores throughout Campbell River, including **Painter's Lodge Holiday & Fishing Resort,** 1625 McDonald Rd. (© **250/286-1102;** www.painters lodge.com). The staff at the lodge can also provide information on guided boats and fishing rules.

If you'd like to get out onto the waters and fish, be sure to call ahead and talk to an outfitter or the tourist center to find out what fish are running during your visit and if the seasons have opened. Because of plummeting numbers of salmon and of recent treaties with the United States, the next few years will see more restricted fishing seasons in the waters off Vancouver Island. Don't be disappointed if there's no salmon fishing when you visit or if the salmon you hook is catch-and-release only. For one thing, there are other fish in the sea: Not all types of salmon are as threatened as the coho and tyee; or, you can also consider fishing for halibut and other bottom fish. And if you really just want to get out on the water and have an adventure, consider a wildlife-viewing boat tour, offered by many fishing outfitters.

There are dozens of fishing guides in the Campbell River area, with a range of services that extend from basic to pure extravagance. Expect to pay around C$85 (US$68) per hour for 4 to 5 hours of fishing with a no-frills outfitter. A flashier trip on a luxury cruiser can cost more than C$120 (US$96) per hour. The most famous guides are associated with the Painter's Lodge and its sister property, April Point Lodge on Quadra Island. A few smaller fishing-guide operations include **Destiny Sportfishing,** 2653 Vargo Rd. (© **866/286-9610** or 250/830-7435; www.destinysportfishing.com); **CR Fishing Village,** 260 Island Hwy. (© **250/287-3630;** www.fishingvillage.bc.ca); and **Coastal Island Fishing Adventures,** 663 Glenalan Rd. (© **888/225-9776** or 250/923-5831; www.coastalislandfishing.com).

You can also check out the Info Centre's directory to fishing guides by following the links at www.visitorinfo.incampbellriver.com. Most hotels in Campbell River also offer fishing/lodging packages; ask when you reserve.

GOLF   Because it was carved out of a dense forest, you may see wildlife grazing on the fairway at **Storey Creek Golf Club,** Campbell River (© **250/923-3673;** www. storeycreek.bc.ca). Greens fees run C$40 to C$56 (US$32–US$45) for 18 holes.

HIKING   For day hikes, drive to Strathcona Provincial Park (see below) or explore Quadra Island's Mount Seymour or Morte Lake parks. For a pleasant hike closer to

Campbell River, drive west 6km (3¾ miles) on Highway 28 to **Elk Falls Provincial Park.** Easy 1- to 2-hour hikes lead to a fish hatchery and let you explore a stream with beaver ponds. From the park, you can also join the **Canyon View Trail,** a loop hike that follows the banks of the Campbell River.

WILDLIFE TOURS   Eagle Eye Adventures (✆ **250/286-0809** or 250/890-0464; www.eagleeyeadventures.com) offers a range of excursions via Zodiac and floatplane. A popular 3½-hour trip takes you up a series of sea rapids, with the chance to see bears, eagles, orcas, and sea lions. Excursions cost C$99 (US$79) for adults, C$79 (US$63) for children under 13. Check the company's website for other options. **Painter's Lodge** (see "Fishing," above) also offers wildlife-watching trips.

Check out **http://visitorinfo.incampbellriver.com/pdf/sea_to_sky.pdf** for a full listing of adventure- and wildlife-tour operators in the area.

CAMPING
The 122 campsites at **Elk Falls Provincial Park** (✆ **250/954-4600**) go for C$14 (US$11) in summer (see also "Hiking," above).

WHERE TO STAY
CAMPBELL RIVER
Anchor Inn & Suites 🏕   Each spacious room here has a balcony and ocean view. Best of all, because the Anchor Inn is on the ocean side of busy Island Highway, you won't have to look over the traffic to see the water. In addition to the standard rooms and suites, the Anchor Inn offers five styles of theme suites—Arabian, African, Arctic, English, and Western—that feature extras such as Jacuzzi tubs. (Western suites are the best choice if you have kids, as they have bunk beds hidden in a "jail cell.") And even if you're not up to an exotic hotel room, you'll like the fact that all the rooms are newly renovated and have balconies.

261 Island Hwy., Campbell River, BC V9W 2B3. ✆ **800/663-7227** or 250/286-1131. Fax 250/287-4055. www.anchor inn.ca. 76 units. C$129 (US$103) double; C$249–C$289 (US$199–C$231) theme room double. Extra person C$10 (US$8). Theme, honeymoon, golf, and fishing packages available. AE, MC, V. Free parking. **Amenities:** 2 restaurants; lounge; indoor pool; golf course nearby; exercise room; Jacuzzi; business center; coin-op laundry; laundry service; dry cleaning. *In room:* TV w/pay movies, fridge, coffeemaker, hair dryer, iron, wireless Internet access.

Bachmair Suite Hotel 🄥🄰🄻🅄🄴   This hotel on the southern edge of town offers very large and beautifully furnished rooms at moderate prices. Accommodations range from standard hotel rooms to two-bedroom suites. The suites all come with large bedrooms, kitchens, sitting rooms, and dining areas. Furnishings are exquisite: leather couches, fine carpeting, feather duvets, and hand-painted armoires. Kitchens are fully equipped with china, utensils, and appliances. Most units have balconies and views of Discovery Passage. The hotel itself—wrapped in carved-wooden-rail balconies lined by flower boxes—is handsome in the Bavarian style so favored in Canada.

492 S. Island Hwy., Campbell River, BC V9W 1A5. ✆ **888/923-2849** or 250/923-2848. Fax 250/923-2849. www.hotel bachmair.com. 23 units. C$89–C$120 (US$71–US$96) double. Extra person C$20 (US$16). Off-season rates available. Fishing charters arranged. AE, DC, MC, V. Free parking. Dogs allowed, add C$6 (US$4.80) per night. **Amenities:** Restaurant; bar next door; golf course nearby; in-room massage; babysitting; coin-op laundry; laundry service; non-smoking rooms. *In room:* TV, dataport, kitchen, fridge, coffeemaker, hair dryer, wireless Internet.

Best Western Austrian Chalet Village   Overlooking Discovery Passage, this recently renovated oceanfront hotel offers a choice of regular or housekeeping units (with kitchenettes); some rooms are in loft chalets. Most units have a fridge, and some have VCRs. The staff can arrange whale-watching, fishing, or golfing trips.

462 S. Island Hwy., Campbell River, BC V9W 1A5. © 800/667-7207 or 250/923-4231. Fax 250/923-2840. www.bw campbellriver.com. 59 units. May–Sept C$136 (US$109) double, C$189 (US$151) kitchenette unit, loft chalet, or mini-suite; Oct–Apr C$109–C$169 (US$87–US$135) all units. Extra person C$10 (US$8). Senior and AAA discounts available. AE, DC, DISC, MC, V. Pets allowed in smoking rooms only for C$5 (US$4) per night. **Amenities:** Restaurant and pub adjacent; indoor pool; golf course nearby; miniature putting green; Jacuzzi; sauna; babysitting; coin-op laundry; same-day dry cleaning; table tennis. *In room:* TV, dataport, fridge, coffeemaker, hair dryer, iron, wireless high-speed Internet.

Coast Discovery Inn   Part of the sprawling Discovery Harbour Marina and Shopping Centre, the Coast is right in the thick of downtown and offers dramatic views from its upper stories. The accommodations are spacious and nicely furnished. Superior rooms offer ocean views, bathrobes, and upgraded toiletries. One wheelchair-accessible unit is available.

975 Shoppers Row, Campbell River, BC V9W 2C4. © 800/663-1144 or 250/287-7155. Fax 250/287-2213. www.coast hotels.com. 88 units. From C$160 (US$128) double. Extra person C$10 (US$8). Family plan, senior, and AAA discounts, and corporate rates available. AE, DC, DISC, MC, V. Pets allowed for C$10 (US$8) per night. **Amenities:** Restaurant; pub; golf course nearby; exercise room; Jacuzzi; 24-hr. room service; same-day dry cleaning; 1 room for those w/limited mobility. *In room:* TV w/pay movies and Nintendo, dataport, coffeemaker, hair dryer, iron.

Painter's Lodge Holiday & Fishing Resort ♛♛   This resort has been a favorite fishing hideaway for film stars such as John Wayne, Bob Hope, and Goldie Hawn. Built in 1924 on an awe-inspiring wooded point overlooking the Discovery Passage, the lodge retains a rustic grandeur, with spacious rooms and suites decorated in natural wood and pastels. Four secluded, self-contained cottages are also available for rent. Guests can enjoy all three meals and cocktails in **Legends Dining Room** (see "Where to Dine," below), Tyee Pub, and Fireside Lounge. Amenities include guided fishing trips, and jogging and hiking trails around the grounds. Painter's Lodge is also well-equipped for business conferences. Wheelchair-accessible rooms are available.

1625 McDonald Rd., Box 460, Campbell River, BC V9W 5C1. © 800/663-7090 or 250/286-1102. Fax 250/286-0158. www.painterslodge.com. 94 units. C$189–C$299 (US$151–US$239) double; C$239–C$289 (US$191–US$231) cottage. Extra person C$12 (US$9.60). Off-season discounts available. AE, DC, MC, V. Closed mid-Oct to early Apr. **Amenities:** Restaurant; pub; lounge; heated outdoor pool; golf course nearby; 2 unlit tennis courts; exercise room; Jacuzzi; bicycle, scooter, and kayak rentals; children's center; game room; tour and activities desk; car-rental desk; babysitting; laundry service; same-day dry cleaning; nonsmoking facility; executive-level rooms; rooms for those w/limited mobility. *In room:* A/C, TV, coffeemaker, hair dryer.

Rustic Motel *Value*   Located on .8 hectare (2 acres) of parkland beside the river, the Rustic offers moderately priced rooms with everything you'll need for a comfortable stay. There are also three two-bedroom suites and a three-bedroom cabin. In summer, the Rustic is decked out with baskets of flowers.

2140 N. Island Hwy., Campbell River, BC V9W 2G7. © 800/567-2007 or 250/286-6295. Fax 250/286-9692. www. rusticmotel.com. 41 units. C$90–C$100 (US$72–US$80) double. Extra person C$10 (US$8). Kitchen C$10 (US$8) extra. Rates include continental breakfast. AE, DC, MC, V. Free parking. Pets allowed for C$5 (US$4) per night. **Amenities:** Jacuzzi; sauna; business center; coin-op laundry; barbecue. *In room:* A/C, TV, dataport, fridge, coffeemaker, hair dryer, microwave, high-speed Internet access.

QUADRA ISLAND
April Point Lodge & Fishing Resort ♛   Secluded April Point Lodge, world famous for its saltwater fishing charters, has magnificent views of the Discovery Passage. This luxury fishing resort and Painter's Lodge, just across the channel, are under the same ownership; there's free boat-taxi service between the two properties for registered guests, which makes it easy to come from Campbell River for drinks or dinner. (See the amenities listed below for other Painter's Lodge extras available to April Point

guests.) Guesthouses are tastefully furnished, with hot tubs, fireplaces, and kitchens. The lodge suites are also nicely appointed. The new Aveda Concept Spa offers luxury pampering in a Japanese-style structure overlooking the water. Facilities include helicopter access and seaplane service to Vancouver and Seattle, as well as a marina.

April Point Rd., Quadra Island, c/o Box 1, Campbell River, BC V9W 4Z9. © **800/663-7090** or 250/285-2222. www. aprilpoint.com. 36 units. C$155–C$259 (US$124–US$207) lodge; C$175–C$355 (US$140–US$284) guesthouse. Extra person C$20 (US$16) in lodge, C$30 (US$24) in guesthouse. Closed mid-Oct to early Apr. AE, DC, MC, V. **Amenities:** Restaurant (see "Where to Dine," below); sushi bar; lounge; heated outdoor pool; tennis courts; exercise room; spa, Jacuzzi; bike, scooter, and kayak rentals; children's center; tour/activities desk; car-rental desk; in-room massage; babysitting; laundry service; same-day dry cleaning; nonsmoking facility. *In room:* TV, coffeemaker, hair dryer.

Tsa-Kwa-Luten Lodge ☞ Owned by the Laichwiltach Cape Mudge Band, this modern luxury resort is designed to resemble a Native Big House. Overlooking the Discovery Passage, it offers both lodge suites and waterfront cabins. The cabins contain full kitchens; some have fireplaces and hot tubs. Some suites have lofts, Jacuzzis, or fireplaces. All units are beautifully decorated with contemporary Native art. Accommodations for travelers with disabilities are available. The staff can arrange fishing trips and heli-fishing charters.

Lighthouse Rd., Box 460, Quathiaski Cove, Quadra Island, BC V0P 1N0. © **800/665-7745** or 250/598-3366. Fax 250/ 285-2532. www.capemudgeresort.com. 34 units. C$84–C$259 (US$67–US$207) double; C$179–C$259 (US$143–US$207) suite; C$140–C$180 (US$112–US$144) cottage. Meal plans available. Children under 12 stay free in parent's room. AE, DC, MC, V. Free parking. Small pets allowed in cabins for C$10 (US$8) per day. **Amenities:** Restaurant (see "Where to Dine," below); lounge; lit tennis courts nearby; exercise room; Jacuzzi; sauna; bike rentals; massage; laundry service. *In room:* Coffeemaker, hair dryer, iron.

WHERE TO DINE
CAMPBELL RIVER

In addition to the restaurants listed below, try **Koto's,** 80 10th Ave. (© **250/286-1422**), an excellent sushi bar, open Tuesday through Friday from 11am to 2pm and Tuesday through Saturday from 5:30 to 9pm.

Fusilli Grill ITALIAN A good, casual Italian restaurant located in the suburbs southwest of downtown, Fusilli Grill makes almost all of its own pasta and utilizes local produce, meats, and seafood as much as possible. Lunch features a variety of sandwiches on fresh-baked focaccia. At dinner, there's a choice of pasta, steak, fish, and chicken dishes, plus a few Mexican and Asian options for variety.

4–220 Dogwood St. © 250/830-0090. www.fusilligrill.bc.ca. Reservations recommended. Main courses C$8–C$23 (US$6.40–US$18); evening take-out specials C$8 (US$6.40). AE, DC, MC, V. Mon 4:30–9:30pm; Tues–Fri 11am–9:30pm; Sat–Sun 4:30–9:30pm.

Harbour Grill ☞ CONTINENTAL/SEAFOOD Owned by the proprietors of the respected but now defunct Le Chateaubriand, Harbour Grill still features much of that restaurant's same quality menu in an attractive location, complete with views of Discovery Passage. The dinner menu features many worthy relics of mid-20th-century fine dining. Yes, you can actually order a real chateaubriand here, an arm-size roast of beef tenderloin drizzled with béarnaise and topped with asparagus. Other classics of Kennedy-era cuisine include duck with orange sauce and veal Oscar. In summer, fresh seafood receives more contemporary preparations. The Harbour Grill isn't exactly a food museum—for one thing, the new location is too bright and modern—it's more like time-travel cuisine, and great fun at that.

112–1334 Island Hwy., in the Discovery Harbour Mall. © 250/287-4143. www.harbourgrill.com. Reservations recommended. Main courses C$20–C$32 (US$16–US$27) and up. AE, DC, MC, V. Mon–Sat from 5:30pm.

Legends Dining Room ✸ INTERNATIONAL The dining room at Painter's Lodge is flanked entirely by windows, affording every table a view of busy Discovery Passage and the free speedboat taxi that runs between the hotel and April Point Lodge on Quadra Island. If you're having dinner here, consider hopping that water taxi for a predinner cocktail at April Point. Return with salt spray in your hair, ready for a great meal at Legends. Start with the excellent smoked salmon–stuffed mushroom caps. The entrees have regional flair—try the Cuban-style pork chops, marinated in rum and tandoori spices and served with apple and sun-dried cranberry chutney. As you'd expect at a fishing resort, fish and seafood are menu favorites.

At Painter's Lodge, 1625 McDonald Rd. ⓒ **250/286-1102.** Reservations recommended. Main courses C$12–C$31 (US$9.60–US$25). AE, DC, MC, V. Daily 7am–10pm. Closed mid-Oct to early Apr.

The Lookout Seafood Bar & Grill CANADIAN A pleasant dining room that overlooks Discovery Pass and Quadra Island, the Lookout offers a range of burgers, fish and chips, and sandwiches during the day. The dinner offerings expand to include steak, pasta, and seafood dishes—unsurprisingly, salmon is the specialty. If you're just looking for a light meal, try the tapas menu. A new patio overlooks the water.

921 Island Hwy. ⓒ **250/286-6812.** Reservations recommended in summer. Dinner main courses C$8–C$30 (US$6.40–US$24). AE, MC, V. Daily 11am–10pm.

QUADRA ISLAND
April Point Lodge & Fishing Resort NORTHWEST/SUSHI The hotel's restaurant features Northwest cuisine and floor-to-ceiling windows offering lovely views. To start, try pan-seared Fanny Bay oysters with chile-and-lime crème fraîche, or choose from the menu of the adjoining sushi bar. For an entree, opt for a daily seafood special or, if you're not in the mood for fish, filet mignon with crisp latkes and caramelized red-onion glaze is an excellent choice.

April Point Rd. ⓒ **800/663-7090** or 250/285-2222. www.aprilpoint.com. Reservations recommended. Main courses C$14–C$32 (US$11–US$26). AE, DC, MC, V. Daily 7am–10pm. Closed early Oct to mid-Apr.

Tsa-Kwa-Luten Lodge SEAFOOD The restaurant features fresh seafood and steaks prepared with Continental finesse and an eye toward Native traditions. Standouts include the venison bourguignon, with wild mushrooms and traditional bannock bread, and cedar plank–baked salmon accompanied by fresh local blackberry butter. Native dancing and entertainment are offered.

Lighthouse Rd. ⓒ **800/665-7745** or 250/598-3366. www.capemudgeresort.com. Reservations recommended. Main courses C$12–C$28 (US$10–US$22). AE, DC, MC, V. Daily 7am–9pm. Closed mid-Oct to early May.

3 Strathcona Provincial Park ⍟
38km (24 miles) W of Campbell River

British Columbia's oldest provincial park, and the largest on Vancouver Island at 250,000 hectares (617,500 acres), **Strathcona Park** is located west of Campbell River and Courtenay. Mountain peaks, many glaciated or mantled with snow, dominate the park, and lakes and alpine meadows dot the landscape. Roosevelt elk, Vancouver Island marmot and wolf, and black-tailed deer have evolved into distinct species, due to Vancouver Island's separation from the mainland. **Buttle Lake** provides good fishing for cutthroat and rainbow trout and Dolly Varden.

Summers in Strathcona are usually pleasantly warm; evenings can be cool. Winters are fairly mild except at higher elevations, where heavy snowfall is common. Snow remains year-round on the mountain peaks and may linger into July at higher eleva-tions. Rain can be expected at any time of year.

ESSENTIALS

GETTING THERE   Campbell River and Courtenay are the primary access points for the park. Highway 28 passes through the northern section of the park and provides access to Buttle Lake, 48km (30 miles) west of Campbell River. There are two access routes to the Forbidden Plateau area from Courtenay. To reach Paradise Meadows from Courtenay and Highway 19, follow signs to Mount Washington Resort via the Strath-cona Parkway. Twenty-five kilometers (16 miles) up the parkway, you'll come to the resort's Nordic Lodge road on the left. Turn onto this road and go another 1.6km (1 mile) to the Paradise Meadows parking lot. To reach Forbidden Plateau, follow the signs on the Forbidden Plateau road from Highway 19 and Courtenay. It's 19km (12 miles) to the former Forbidden Plateau ski area (now closed) and the trail head.

VISITOR INFORMATION   Contact the **BC Parks District Manager,** Box 1479, Parksville (© **250/954-4600;** http://wlapwww.gov.bc.ca/bcparks).

SEEING THE HIGHLIGHTS

The Buttle Lake area (off Hwy. 28) and the Forbidden Plateau area (accessed through Courtenay) both have something to offer visitors. Just outside the park boundaries, **Strathcona Park Lodge** (see "Where to Stay," below) offers lodging, dining, and a variety of activities. The rest of the park is largely undeveloped and requires hiking or backpacking into the alpine wilderness to see and enjoy much of its scenic splendor.

A paved road joins **Highway 28** (the Gold River Hwy.) near the outlet of **Buttle Lake** and winds its way southward, hugging the shoreline. Along this scenic road are numerous cataracts and creeks that rush and tumble into the lake.

Some of the more prominent peaks include Mount McBride, Marble Peak, Mount Phillips, and Mount Myra. **Elkhorn Mountain,** at 2,192m (7,190 ft.), is the second-highest mountain in the park. Elkhorn, along with Mount Flannigan and Kings Peak, can be seen from Highway 28. The highest point on Vancouver Island at 2,200m (7,216 ft.), the **Golden Hinde** stands almost in the center of the park to the west of Buttle Lake.

A second area of the park, **Forbidden Plateau,** is accessed by gravel road from Courtenay. Those who hike into the plateau are rewarded with an area of subalpine beauty and views that extend from the surrounding glaciers and mountains to farm-lands and forest.

The 440m (1,443-ft.) **Della Falls,** one of the 10 highest waterfalls in the world, is located in the southern section of the park, and is reached by a rugged multiday hike (see "Hiking," below).

HIKING

FROM THE BUTTLE LAKE AREA   The 3km (2-mile) **Upper Myra Falls Trail** starts just past the Westmin mine operation. This 2-hour hike leads through old-growth forests and past waterfalls. The 6.6km (4-mile) **Marble Meadows Trail** starts at Phillips Creek Marine Campsite on Buttle Lake. It features alpine meadows and limestone formations; allow 6 hours round-trip. The 900m (2,952-ft.) **Lady Falls Trail,** which begins at the Highway 28 viewing platform, takes about 20 minutes and leads to a picturesque waterfall.

FROM THE PARADISE MEADOWS TRAIL HEAD (MOUNT WASHINGTON)
The 2.2km (1⅓-mile) **Paradise Meadows Loop Trail** is an easy walk through sub-alpine meadows, taking about 45 minutes. The 14km (8⅔-mile) **Helen McKenzie–Kwai Lake–Croteau Lake Loop Trail** takes 6 hours and offers access to beautiful lakes and mountain vistas. There's designated camping at Kwai Lake. From Lake Helen McKenzie, the trail follows forested slopes over rougher terrain before rising to a rolling subalpine area to Circlet Lake, which offers designated camping. Allow 4 hours.

FROM FORBIDDEN PLATEAU The 5km (3-mile), 2-hour **Mount Becher Summit Trail** starts at the former ski lodge and goes up one of the runs to the trail head near the T-bar. It provides excellent views of the valley and Strait of Georgia.

OTHER TRAILS IN STRATHCONA PARK The **Della Falls Trail** is 32km (20 miles) round-trip. It starts at the west end of Great Central Lake (between Port Alberni and Tofino on Hwy. 4) and follows the old railway grade up the Drinkwater Valley. You must take a boat across the lake to get to the trail head. At **Ark Resort,** 11000 Great Central Lake Rd. ((C) **250/723-2657;** www.arkresort.com), you can take a high-speed water taxi or rent a motorboat or canoe. The whole trip will take 3 to 6 days. The trail passes historic railroad logging sites and accesses Love Lake and Della Lake. Some unbridged river crossings can be hazardous.

CAMPING
Buttle Lake, with 85 sites, and **Ralph River,** with 76 sites, are both located on Buttle Lake, accessible via Highway 28 (the Gold River Hwy.) west of Campbell River. Sites go for C$14 (US$10). The campgrounds have water, toilets, and firewood.

WHERE TO STAY
Strathcona Park Lodge 🦅🦅 This rustic lodge, north of Strathcona Park along upper Campbell Lake, has something to offer everyone—from families to Golden Agers—who loves the outdoors. Lodge activities include climbing and rappelling, canoeing, fishing, and swimming. The package options offered by the lodge are numerous, so call to discuss your interests. The popular Adventure Sampler package includes lodging, meals, and activities (climbing, kayaking, orienteering, hiking, and more) for 4 (C$675/US$540) or 7 days (C$1,295/US$1,036) per person, based on double occupancy. The lodge is also a lovely place to just hang out and is a good base for exploring the park. All accommodations are sparely yet comfortably furnished. Some chalet units have shared bathrooms; all other rooms have private bathrooms. The lakefront cabins with kitchens are the most charming, though you must reserve well in advance. In summer, the Whale Room serves three buffet-style meals daily. Guests sit at long communal tables.

40km (25 miles) west of Campbell River on Hwy. 28. Mailing address: Box 2160, Campbell River, BC V9W 5C5. (C) 250/286-3122. Fax 250/286-6010. www.strathcona.bc.ca. 39 units. C$50–C$88 (US$40–US$70) chalet double with shared bathroom; C$88–C$149 (US$70–US$119) double with private bathroom; C$149–C$295 (US$119–US$236) cabin. 2- or 3-night minimum stays in cabins. Off-season discounts available. MC, V. **Amenities:** Exercise room; sauna; canoe and kayak rentals; children's programs; massage; babysitting; coin-op laundry; nonsmoking facility. *In room:* No phone.

4 Telegraph Cove, Port McNeill, Alert Bay & Port Hardy
Port McNeill: 198km (123 miles) N of Campbell River

It's a winding 198km (123-mile) drive through forested mountains along the Island Highway (Hwy. 19) from Campbell River to **Port McNeill,** on northern Vancouver

Island. But the majestic scenery, crystal-clear lakes, and unique wilderness along the way make it worthwhile.

The highway rejoins the coast along **Johnstone Strait,** home to a number of orca (killer whale) pods, which migrate annually from the Queen Charlotte Strait south to these salmon-rich waters. Whale-watching trips out of Port McNeill and Telegraph Cove are the principal recreational activities; this is one of the most noted whale-watching areas in British Columbia.

Also worth a visit is the island community of **Alert Bay,** a traditional First Nations town site festooned with totem poles and carvings. The museum houses a famous collection of ceremonial masks and other artifacts.

The Island Highway's terminus, **Port Hardy,** is 52km (32 miles) north of Port McNeill. Although it's a remote community of only 5,470, Port Hardy is the starting point for three unique experiences: the Inside Passage ferry cruise (see chapter 10) to Prince Rupert; the Discovery Coast ferry cruise (see chapter 10); and the untamed rainforest and coastline of Cape Scott Provincial Park.

ESSENTIALS

GETTING THERE   There are three principal ways to get to Vancouver Island's northernmost towns and islands: by car, bus, and plane. You can also reach Port Hardy from the north via the Inside Passage ferry from Prince Rupert (see chapter 10).

By Plane   Pacific Coastal Airlines (© **800/663-2872;** www.pacific-coastal.com) flies daily from Vancouver to Port Hardy Airport. From late May to late September, **Kenmore Air** (© **800/543-9595;** www.kenmoreair.com) flies seaplanes from Seattle's Lake Union or Lake Washington to Port McNeill.

By Car   Telegraph Cove is 198km (123 miles) north of Campbell River along the Island Highway (Hwy. 19). Port McNeill is another 9km (5½ miles) north. Port Hardy is 238km (148 miles) north of Campbell River.

By Bus   Vancouver Island Coach Lines (© **250/388-5248,** or book through Greyhound © **800/661-8747;** www.greyhound.ca) offers bus transport from Victoria and Nanaimo to Port Hardy and other towns in northern Vancouver Island. One way fare from Nanaimo to Port Hardy is C$70 (US$56).

VISITOR INFORMATION   The **Port McNeill Visitor Info Centre,** 351 Shelley Crescent (© **250/956-3131;** www.portmcneill.net), is open year-round on weekdays and daily in summer from 10am to 6pm. The **Alert Bay Visitor Info Centre,** 116 Fir St. (© **250/974-5213;** www.village.alertbay.bc.ca), is open in summer daily from 9am to 6pm, and the rest of the year Monday through Friday from 9am to 5pm. The **Port Hardy Visitor Info Centre,** 7250 Market St. (© **250/949-7622;** www. ph-chamber.bc.ca), is open June through September daily from 8:30am to 7pm, and October through May Monday through Friday from 8:30am to 5pm. For additional information on northern island destinations, contact the **Vancouver Island North Visitors' Association** (© **800/903-6606** or 250/949-9094; www.vinva.bc.ca).

TELEGRAPH COVE

Telegraph Cove, 22km (14 driving miles) southeast of Port McNeill—by way of the Island Highway and then a stretch of paved and gravel road—has an unusual story. The town's handful of permanent residents lives in one of the few remaining elevated-board-walk villages on Vancouver Island, overlooking Johnstone Strait. This postcard-perfect fishing village's buildings are perched on stilts over the water, making it an entertaining destination for a stroll.

First a sawmill and fishing port, then an army camp, now a resort, Telegraph Cove bustles in summer. The town is largely dominated by comfortably rustic **Telegraph Cove Resort,** which offers many historic boardwalk homes as rental units. With a good restaurant, busy boat basin, and wonderful bay and island views, the resort village is a longtime family favorite.

WHALE-WATCHING & OTHER OUTDOOR PURSUITS

Telegraph Cove is right on the Johnstone Strait, a narrow passage that serves as the summer home to hundreds of orcas as well as dolphins, porpoises, and seals. Bald eagles also patrol the waterway, and more unusual birds pass through the area, an important stop on the Pacific Flyway.

Seventeen kilometers (11 miles) south of Telegraph Cove, the **Robson Bight Ecological Reserve** *&&* provides fascinating whale-watching. Orcas regularly beach themselves in the shallow waters of the pebbly "rubbing beaches" to remove the barnacles from their tummies. Boat tours are not allowed to enter the reserve itself, but you can watch from nearby areas. **Stubbs Island Whale-Watching,** at the end of the Telegraph Cove boardwalk (© **800/665-3066** or 250/928-3185; www.stubbs-island. com), offers tours from late May through late October in boats equipped with hydrophones, so you can hear the whales' underwater communication. These 3½-hour cruises cost from C$69 to C$79 (US$55–US$63) for adults.

From May to mid-October, **Tide Rip Tours,** 28 Boardwalk (© **888/643-9319** or 250/339-5320; www.tiderip.com), offers excursions in covered water taxis to watch grizzly bears for C$233 (US$186). Other wildlife-viewing trips are available.

For kayaking tours, contact **Telegraph Cove Sea Kayaking** (© **888/756-0099** or 250/756-0094; www.tckayaks.com), which offers guided day-long trips out onto Telegraph Cove (C$150–C$175/US$120–US$140), plus multiday expeditions out onto Johnstone Strait. Rentals are available; full-day rates start at C$50 (US$40).

WHERE TO STAY & DINE

Although both of the following establishments have mailing addresses in Port McNeill, they are located in or near Telegraph Cove.

Hidden Cove Lodge   Built years before a road reached this isolated harbor, Hidden Cove was meant to be approached by boat, and it still saves its best face for those who arrive this way. The handsome lodge, with a cathedral-ceilinged great room, is nestled beside a secluded cove. The guest rooms are clean and simply decorated. Three cabins have efficiency kitchens and decks. There's also a floating guesthouse with five rooms that share bathrooms. Hidden Cove's easy-going, unaffected atmosphere belies the fact that it attracts the rich and famous. The restaurant, open to nonguests by reservation only, serves quality international dishes. Whale-watching, birding, heli-fishing, kayaking, and hiking tours can be arranged.

Lewis Point, 1 Hidden Cove Rd., Box 258, Port McNeill, BC V0N 2R0. ©/fax **250/956-3916.** www.bcbbonly.com/ 1263.php. 15 units, 8 with private bathroom. C$145 (US$116) lodge double; C$99 (US$79) guesthouse double; C$299 (US$239) cottage. Extra person C$25 (US$20). Lodge rates include full breakfast. 2-night minimum stay in lodge and cottage. Off-season rates available. MC, V. Free parking. Take the Island Hwy. (Hwy. 19) to turnoff for Telegraph Cove/Beaver Cove; turn right and follow signs. The lodge is 6.5km (4 miles) from Telegraph Cove. **Amenities:** Restaurant; golf course nearby; Jacuzzi; in-room massage available; babysitting available; coin-op laundry; nonsmoking facility. *In room:* No phone.

Telegraph Cove Resorts   Most of the accommodations offered by Telegraph Cove Resorts are refurbished homes from the early 20th century, scattered along the boardwalk. They range from small rooms in a former fishermen's boardinghouse to three-bedroom homes that sleep up to nine. All have bathrooms and kitchens, but no phones or TVs. There are also hotel-style rooms (no kitchens) at the Wastell Manor, a large home built in 1912. Although none of the historic properties are exactly fancy, they are clean and make for a unique experience—it really is like staying in a historic logging camp. On Sunday, the resort encourages guests to join the afternoon potluck. Amenities include moorage and fishing charters. In addition, 121 campsites are a short walk from the boardwalk. Open May through October, the campground provides hot showers, laundry, toilets, fire pits, and water. Sites are C$21 to C$26 (US$17–US$21).

Box 1, Telegraph Cove, BC V0N 3J0. © 800/200-HOOK or 250/928-3131. Fax 250/928-3105. www.telegraphcove resort.com. 24 units. Mid-June to Sept C$99–C$275 (US$79–US$220) cabin, C$145–C$175 (US$116–US$140) suite; Oct 1 to mid-Oct and May 1 to June 14 C$69–C$160 (US$55–US$128) cabin, C$80–C$130 (US$64–US$104) suite. Extra person C$10 (US$8). Packages available. MC, V. Closed mid-Oct to Apr. Located 26km (16 miles) south of Port McNeill. Pets allowed in some cabins for C$5 (US$4) per night. **Amenities:** Restaurant; pub; kayak rentals; coin-op laundry. *In room:* Coffeemaker, no phone.

PORT MCNEILL & ALERT BAY

Port McNeill (pop. 3,000) is a logging and mill town—not particularly quaint—that serves as an access point for whale-watching and other wildlife tours, numerous outdoor-recreation opportunities, and the ferry to Alert Bay. Alert Bay (pop. 1,000) is a fascinating destination for anyone interested in First Nations culture. It has a world-renowned collection of totem carvings and wall murals, as well as historic buildings.

During the second week of June, the Nimpkish Reserve hosts **June Sports & Indian Celebrations** (© **250/974-5556,** the 'Namgis First Nation office) on the soccer field in Alert Bay. Traditional tests of strength and agility are demonstrated by the island's tribal members.

BC Ferries (© **888/BC-FERRY** or 250/386-3431; www.bcferries.com) runs daily service between Port McNeill and Alert Bay. The crossing takes about 45 minutes; peak fares are C$7 (US$5.60) per passenger, C$18 (US$14) per vehicle.

EXPLORING ALERT BAY

Alert Bay has a rich First Nations heritage that can be seen in its proudly preserved architecture and artifacts. It has been a Kwakwaka'wakw (Kwagiulth) village for thousands of years. The integration of Scottish immigrants into the area during the 19th and 20th centuries is clearly depicted in the design of the **Anglican Church** on Front Street (© **250/974-5401**). The cedar building was erected in 1881; its stained-glass window designs reflect a fusion of Kwakwaka'wakw and Scottish motifs. It's open in summer Monday through Saturday from 8am to 5pm.

Walk a mile from the ferry terminal along Front Street to the island's two most interesting attractions: a 53m (174-ft.) **totem pole**—the world's highest—stands next to the **Big House,** the tribal community center. The cedar totem pole features 22 figures of bears, orcas, and ravens. The Big House is usually closed to the public, but visitors are welcome to enter the grounds to get a closer look at the building, which is covered with traditional painted figures. In July and August, the **T'sasala Cultural Group** (© **250/974-5475**) presents dance performances in the Big House, usually Wednesday through Saturday. The cost is C$12 (US$9.60) for adults and C$5 (US$4) for children under 12.

A few yards down the road from the Big House is the **U'Mista Cultural Centre** ✷✷, Front Street (𝄪 **250/974-5403;** www.umista.org), which displays carved masks, cedar baskets, copper jewelry, and other potlatch artifacts. The potlatch was traditionally a highly important ceremony for the Kwagiulth: While dancers and singers clad in elaborate masks and robes performed and sang, villagers would engage in ritual gift-giving, exchanging ceremonial objects, totems, shields, and other hand-carved artifacts created especially for the ritual. However, in the 1880s, the Canadian government outlawed the ceremony as part of an effort to "civilize" the Kwagiulth, and, in 1921, its officers confiscated the entirety of the band's potlatch treasures and regalia, which was sent to museums in eastern Canada and sold to private collectors.

By the 1970s and 1980s, pressures from native groups and changes in government perspectives resulted in the partial repatriation of potlatch ceremonial artifacts to the Kwagiulth, who established the U'Mista Cultural Centre to exhibit this wondrous collection. Admission is C$5 (US$4) for adults, C$4 (US$3.20) for seniors and students, and C$1 (US80¢) for children 12 and under. The museum is open in summer, daily from 9am to 5pm, and in winter Monday through Friday from 9am to 5pm.

WHALE-WATCHING & OTHER OUTDOOR PURSUITS

Orcas, dolphins, and eagles all gather along Johnstone Strait to snack on fish that converge at this narrows between Vancouver Island and a series of tightly clustered islands.

From Port McNeill, **Mackay Whale Watching Ltd.,** 1514 Broughton Blvd. (𝄪 **877/663-6722** or 250/956-9865; www.whaletime.com), offers daily tours to Johnstone Strait on a 17m (55-ft.) passenger cruiser with hydrophone. A 4-hour trip costs C$80 (US$64).

Seasmoke Tours/Sea Orca Expeditions (𝄪 **800/668-6722** in B.C., or 250/974-5225; www.seaorca.com) offers whale-watching sailing trips from Alert Bay from June to September. Excursions aboard a 13m (44-ft.), hydrophone-equipped sailboat include baked goods and Devonshire tea. Five-hour tours cost C$79 to C$89 (US$63–US$71). Seasmoke also offers tour/lodging packages at two bungalows on Alert Bay. For more information on tour providers, as well as other businesses and attractions in Alert Bay, contact **Alert Bay Adventures,** 62c Fir St. (𝄪 **877/974-9911** or 250/974-9911; www.alertbay.com).

WHERE TO STAY & DINE

If you can't get into the recommended Telegraph Cove–area resorts and don't want to continue on to Port Hardy or Campbell River, try Port McNeill's **Dalewood Inn,** 1703 Broughton Blvd. (𝄪 **877/956-3304** or 250/956-3304; www.dalewoodinn.com), a motor inn with decent rooms starting at C$75 (US$60) in high season. Also in Port McNeill, try the 62-unit **Haida-Way Motor Inn,** 1817 Campbell Way (𝄪 **800/956-3373** or 250/956-3373; www.pmhotels.com), which rents rooms for C$99 (US$79) in summer. Both motor inns also have on-premises restaurants and pubs.

Oceanview Camping & Trailer Park, Alder Road, Alert Bay (𝄪 **250/974-5213;** fax 250/974-5470), has a great view of the Johnstone Strait and nature trails that fan out from the 23 sites. Rates are C$12 to C$16 (US$9.60–US$13). Full hookups, flush toilets, hot showers, a free boat launch, and boat tours make this a great deal. The 'Namgis Nation runs the **Gwakawe Campground,** Alert Bay (𝄪 **250/974-5274**), where C$13 (US$10) gets you a beachfront site and access to showers, laundry, water, and firewood.

In Alert Bay, the **Old Customs House Restaurant,** 19 Fir St. (© **250/974-2282**), has a menu of burgers, pasta, and fish and chips; open for three meals daily. There are also three bed-and-breakfast rooms upstairs; C$50 to C$60 (US$40–US$48) double.

Oceanview Cabins   Overlooking Mitchell Bay and only 1.6km (1 mile) from the ferry terminal, this quiet waterfront resort is Alert Bay's best value. Simply furnished, comfortable cabins contain queen beds and kitchens; two have shower-only bathrooms. Reserve a few months in advance for summer.

390 Poplar St., Alert Bay, BC V0N 1A0. © 250/974-5457. Fax 250/974-2275. www.alertbay.com/oceanview. 12 units. C$50–C$65 (US$40–US$52) double. Extra person C$5 (US$4). MC, V. *In room:* TV, no phone.

PORT HARDY

Port Hardy is the final stop on the Island Highway. This sizable community is slowly moving away from a resource-based economy: Fishing, forestry, and mining have waned—though not disappeared—and the town is gradually developing an economy based on tourism.

A principal reason to venture here is the ferry to **Prince Rupert**—in fact, the ferry is a mainstay of the local tourism industry. The night before the 15-hour Inside Passage ferry runs, the town is booked up and reservations are needed at most restaurants. Port Hardy is also the point of departure for the Discovery Coast ferry cruise (see chapter 10).

People also visit for the diving, hiking, and excellent halibut and salmon fishing. Sportfishing is very good here, as the runs of salmon in local rivers continue to be strong and are therefore open to more fishing than at threatened runs elsewhere. Port Hardy is also the launching point for a land-based journey to **Cape Scott,** a wilderness park at the northern tip of Vancouver Island. Planning has begun on a 130km (81-mile) hiking and multiuse trail along the island's northeastern coast from Shushartie Bay, just west of Port Hardy, to Cape Scott.

The **Port Hardy Museum,** 7110 Market St. (© **250/949-8143**), holds relics from early Danish settlers, plus a collection of stone tools from about 8000 B.C. found just east of town. Admission is by donation. The gift shop is one of the few places in town where you can find local carving and artwork. Hours are from mid-May to mid-October Tuesday through Saturday from 11:30am to 5:30pm, and from mid-October to mid-May Wednesday through Saturday from noon to 5pm.

OUTDOOR PURSUITS

DIVING ⚓   Diving is excellent in the Port Hardy area. **North Island Diving and Water Sports,** at Market and Hastings (© **250/949-2664**), is a full-service dive store; rentals and instruction are available. For more information on diving in the region, go to **www.3routes.com/scuba/na/can/bc/08/index.html**.

FISHING   From Port Hardy, you can arrange day charter trips with local outfitters. **Catala Charters and Lodge** (© **800/515-5511** or 250/949-7560; www.catala charters.net) offers guided fishing trips and operates the C-View B&B. **Codfather Charters** (© **250/949-6696;** www.codfathercharters.com) offers year-round fishing and accommodations in a waterfront lodge.

To simply rent a boat, contact **Hardy Bay Boat Rental,** Quarterdeck Marina at 6555 Hardy Bay Rd. (© **250/949-7048** or 250/949-0155; www.hardybayfishing.com). Rates start at C$22 (US$18) per hour or C$190 (US$152) per day.

Port Hardy is the stepping-off point for trips to remote **fishing camps,** many with long pedigrees and well-to-do clientele. One of the only camps directly accessed from

Port Hardy is **Duval Point Lodge** (① 250/949-6667; www.duvalpointlodge.com), which offers multiday packages from its base camp about 8km (5 miles) north of town (accessed by boat). Guests receive a short training session; groups are then given their own boat and pointed to the channel. From here on, you keep your own schedule and run expeditions as you see fit. Guests stay in two two-story floating lodges, each with four bedrooms, a mix of private and shared bathrooms, and a full kitchen. The outfitter provides rod and reel, bait, boat, cleaning area, and freezers. Guests do their own cooking. Guides are available, though part of the fun here is the satisfaction of running your own boat and interacting with other guests. The lodge also has two land-based log cabins, each with three bedrooms. Anyone who comes in their own boat can stay in these cabins; rates start at C$400 (US$320) for 4 midweek nights. Boat/lodging packages start at C$750 (US$600) for 3 nights/4 days of fishing and accommodation. The lodge is closed October through May. Duval Point is not for those looking for five-star comforts and pampering. But if you want access to excellent fishing and adventure with congenial hospitality, it's a great value.

If you are looking for creature comforts, one of the area's most famous and upscale fishing lodges is **Nimmo Bay Resort** (① 800/837-HELI or 250/956-4000; www.nimmo bay.com), a full-service floating resort where 3 days/3 nights at the lodge and fishing with transportation by helicopter will run you around C$5995 (US$4,796). Access is by floatplane or boat.

HIKING   For serious hikers, the best destination is **Cape Scott Provincial Park,** at the island's northwest point (see above).

KAYAKING   The dozens of uninhabited islands in the Goletas Channel directly off-shore from the **Duval Point Lodge** (see "Fishing," above) are excellent for exploration by kayak, as is the coastline west of Duval Point. **Pacific Rim Kayaking** (① 250/384-6103; www.pacificrimpaddling.com/inside_passage.htm) offers 4-day, 3-night trips based at Duval Point Lodge for C$1,355 (US$1,084).

North Island Kayak (① 877/949-7707 or 250/949-7707; www.kayakbc.ca) offers rentals, instruction, and tours. It has locations both in Port Hardy and on the Johnstone Strait, and offers a number of tours to view orcas. A daylong instruction course on calm waters is C$118 (US$94). Half-day rentals start at C$30 (US$24) for a single.

WHERE TO STAY

Port Hardy has several well-worn hotel complexes. Reserve well in advance, especially on days when the ferries run. The **Wildwoods Campsite,** Forestry Road (① 250/949-6753; ranger@island.net), is off the road to the ferry terminal. The 60 sites are a great value, offering fire pits, hot showers, toilets, beach access, and moorage for C$15 to C$20 (US$12–US$16). Tenters will like the wooded sites at **Quatse River Campground,** 5050 Hardy Rd (① 250/949-2395, www.quatsecampground.com), with 62 sites at C$16 to C$20 (US$13–US$16).

Kay's Bed & Breakfast   This conveniently located and nicely decorated B&B has a lovely ocean view and offers free pickup service from the ferry terminal. The continental breakfast features fresh baked goods. For travelers with disabilities, a ground-floor room is available with in-room breakfast. If you have kids, you'll be happily accommodated—provided you rent both main rooms.

7605 Carnarvon Rd., Box 257, Port Hardy, BC V0N 2P0. ① 800/829-0963 or 250/949-6776. www.bbcanada.com/4737. html. 2 units. C$75 (US$60) double. Extra person C$15 (US$12). Rates include continental breakfast. Off-season rates available. No credit cards. **Amenities:** Lounge; shared kitchen for guest's use; nonsmoking facility. *In room:* TV, kitchen, coffeemaker, hair dryer, no phone.

Oceanview B&B   Perched on a bluff overlooking Port Hardy Bay, Oceanview is a comfortably furnished, spotless modern home. A large room with two queen beds and a bathroom overlooks the cul-de-sac and gardens, the other spacious units offers views of the bay. Free coffee, tea, and hot cocoa are served in the evening. The hostess offers a friendly welcome and advice on local travel.

7735 Cedar Place, Box 1837, Port Hardy, BC V0N 2P0. Ⓒ/fax **250/949-8302**. www.island.net/~oceanvue. 3 units, 2 with shared bathroom. C$85–C$100 (US$68–US$80) double. Rates include continental breakfast. No credit cards. Children must be 12 or older. *In room:* TV, hair dryer, no phone.

Pioneer Inn (Port Hardy)   Pioneer Inn is located in a parklike setting on the banks of the Quatse River, 8km (5 miles) south of Port Hardy. There are often vacancies here on the nights before the ferry departs, when the downtown motels fill up. The rooms are basic but well maintained. Some units contain kitchens; there's one wheelchair-accessible room. Amenities include a campground, picnic area, and ferry shuttle service (for a fee).

4965 Byng Rd., Box 699, Port Hardy, BC V0N 2P0. Ⓒ **800/663-8744** or 250/949-7271. Fax 250/949-7334. 36 units. Mid-May to mid-Oct C$89–C$119 (US$71–US$95) double; mid-Oct to mid-May C$59–C$80 (US$47–US$64) double. Extra person C$10 (US$8). 25 RV sites C$17 (US$14) per vehicle; electricity, sewer, and water included; cable TV and telephone hookup extra. Off-season and senior discounts available. AE, MC, V. Pets allowed for C$10 (US$8). **Amenities:** Restaurant; coffee shop; golf course nearby; room service available; coin-op laundry; playground; 1 room for those w/limited mobility. *In room:* TV, coffeemaker.

Quarterdeck Inn 🏊   Opened in 1999, the Quarterdeck has more going for it than just its comparative youth. Perched directly above a busy marina, all units have great views onto a fishing and pleasure-boat port. The spacious rooms are outfitted with quality furniture; some contain kitchenettes and DVD players The staff can arrange all sorts of outdoor and cultural activities, including whale-watching and fishing charters. The Quarterdeck also has an RV park (C$20/US$16 full hookup).

6555 Hardy Bay Rd., P.O. Box 910, Port Hardy, BC V0N 2P0. Ⓒ **877/902-0459** or 250/902-0454. Fax 250/902-0454. www.quarterdeckresort.net. 40 units. C$85–$135 (US$68–US$108) double. Rates include continental breakfast. AE, DC, DISC, MC, V. Free parking. Small pets allowed for C$10 (US$8) per day. **Amenities:** Restaurant (see review below); golf course nearby; Jacuzzi; tour/activities desk; massage; coin-op laundry. *In room:* TV, coffeemaker, hair dryer.

WHERE TO DINE

IV's Quarterdeck Pub PUB/CANADIAN   This friendly pub and dining room, right above the marina, offers a large menu of appetizers, salads, sandwiches, burgers, and standards like steaks, ribs, and chicken. Locals will be quick to tell you that this is the best casual dining in Port Hardy; the clientele is a friendly mix of fishermen, tradesmen, and travelers.

6555 Hardy Bay Rd. Ⓒ **250/949-6922**. www.quarterdeckresort.net. Reservations not accepted. Main courses C$7–C$19 (US$5.60–US$15). AE, MC, V. Daily 11am–midnight.

9

The Sunshine Coast & Whistler

One of British Columbia's most scenic drives and the province's most celebrated year-round recreation center are both just north of Vancouver, making great destinations for a weekend away or a short road trip. The Sunshine Coast Highway is the name given to Highway 101 as it skirts the islands, fiords, and peninsulas of the mainland's Strait of Georgia coast. The scenery is spectacular, and the fishing and logging communities along the route offer friendly hospitality. No small part of the charm of this drive are the ferry rides: To reach road's end at Lund, you'll need to take two ferries, both offering jaw-dropping vistas of glaciered peaks floating above deep-blue waters. To make this route into a full loop trip, catch a third ferry from Powell River across the Strait of Georgia to Comox, and begin your exploration of Vancouver Island (see chapters 6, 7, and 8).

The road to Whistler is equally spectacular, as it follows fiordlike Howe Sound, flanked by cliffs and towering peaks. But there's more to do here than gawk at the landscape: Whistler is Canada's premier skiing destination in winter (and will host the ski events for the 2010 Winter Olympics) and a golf, hiking, and white-water rafting mecca in summer. Accommodations, dining, and recreational facilities are first-class, and the well-planned lodging developments have yet to overwhelm the natural beauty of the valley.

1 The Sunshine Coast

Powell River: 142km (88 miles) N of Vancouver

It's a travel writer's truism that the "getting there" part of a trip is half the fun. In the case of the Sunshine Coast—that strip of wildly scenic waterfront real estate north of Vancouver, along the mainland Strait of Georgia coast—the "getting there" is practically the entire reason for making the journey. But what a journey!

Backed up against the high peaks of the glaciated Coastal Mountain range, overlooking the tempestuous waters of the Strait of Georgia and onto the rolling mountains of Vancouver Island, this maritime-intensive trip involves two ferry rides and a lovely meandering drive between slumbering fishing villages. It eventually terminates at Lund, the end of the road for the Pacific Coast's Highway 101.

Powell River is the only town of any size along this route. Long a major lumber-milling center, Powell River is beginning to focus on tourism as a supplement to its resource-based economy. Diving in the sea-life-rich waters of the Georgia Strait is a particularly popular activity along the Sunshine Coast.

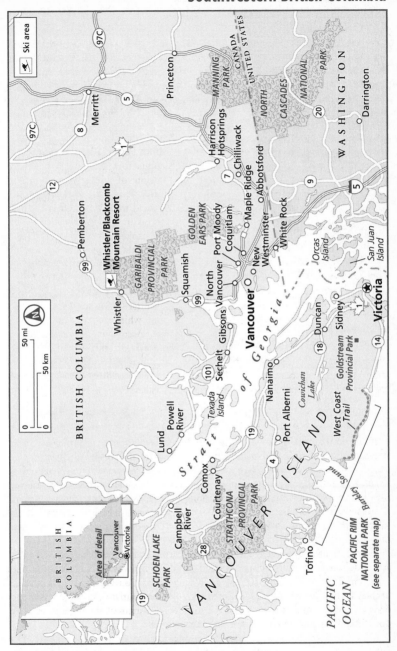

ESSENTIALS
GETTING THERE
BY CAR & FERRY   Getting to Powell River and the Sunshine Coast requires taking a couple of ferries. From West Vancouver's Horseshoe Bay **BC Ferries** (© **888/BC-FERRY** or 250/386-3431; www.bcferries.bc.ca) terminal, ferries embark for Langdale, a 40-minute crossing. Driving north along Highway 101, the road hugs the coast along the Sechelt Peninsula, terminating 81km (50 miles) later at Earls Cove, where another ferry departs for a 50-minute crossing to Saltery Bay. The fare for each ferry is C$9.15 (US$7.30) per passenger, C$33 (US$26) per car in peak season. From Saltery Bay, Powell River is another 31km (19 miles). Lund, the terminus of Highway 101, is another 28km (17 miles).

You can also cross to Comox/Courtenay, on central Vancouver Island, from Powell River. This popular 75-minute crossing makes for a scenic loop tour of British Columbia's rugged coast and islands. The fare is C$8.65 (US$6.90) per passenger, C$30 (US$24) per vehicle in peak season. (See chapter 7 for coverage of Comox and Courtenay.)

BY BUS   **Malaspina Coach Lines** (© **877/227-8287**) offers service from Vancouver to Powell River via Highway 101 and the Sechelt Peninsula.

BY PLANE   **Pacific Coastal Airlines** (© **800/663-2872** or 604/273-8666) flies from Vancouver to Powell River.

VISITOR INFORMATION   Contact the **Powell River Visitors Bureau,** 4690 Marine Ave. (© **877/817-8669;** www.discoverpowellriver.com).

EXPLORING THE AREA
Although Powell River is only 142km (88 miles) north of Vancouver, it feels light-years removed from the urban sprawl. It's probably because of the ferries: Commuting from the Sunshine Coast—the name given to the rocky, mountain-edged coastline that lies in the rain shadow of Vancouver Island—wouldn't make sense if you worked in Vancouver's financial district.

Highway 101 is a very scenic route, with soaring 3,048m (9,997-ft.) peaks to the east and the swelling blue waters of the Strait of Georgia to the west. The first town north of the Horseshoe Bay–Langdale Ferry is **Gibsons** (pop. 3,732), a bucolic seaside community that served as the setting for the 1980s TV series *The Beachcombers.* Much of the action took place in **Molly's Reach Restaurant,** 647 School Rd. (© **604/886-9710**), which has evolved from a film set of a restaurant into a real eatery with fine home-style cooking. Wander along the Gibsons Seawalk, which leads from the Government Wharf to Gibsons Marina, and watch fishing boats unload their catch. **Roberts Creek Provincial Park,** 9km (5½ miles) north of town, has a great tide-pool area that's perfect for picnicking.

Twenty-eight kilometers (17 miles) north of Gibsons is **Sechelt** (pop. 7,545), an arty little town on a sandy finger of land—all that connects the Sechelt Peninsula to mainland British Columbia. The town is a delightful clutter of galleries and cafes. The **Sechelt Indian Nation** is headquartered here; the imposing House of Hewhiwus contains a cultural center, museum, and gift shop. A couple miles north of Sechelt is **Porpoise Bay Provincial Park,** with a nice beach and riverside trail.

Continue north along Highway 101, admiring views of Vancouver Island. Drive past the Earls Cove ferry terminal to **Skookumchuck Narrows Provincial Park.** All of the seawater that lies behind 40km-long (25-mile) Sechelt Peninsula—which includes three major ocean inlets—churns back and forth through this passage in an amazing display of tidal fury. It's about an hour's walk to the park's viewing area. Tides are so fierce, they actually roar, causing boiling whirlpools and eddies.

Powell River (pop. 13,300) is dominated by one of the world's largest pulp and paper mills. That said, the town sits on a lovely location, and if you're feeling adventurous, it's a major center for diving and kayaking.

The old portion of town is called the **Homesite,** a company town that grew up alongside the original lumber mill near the harbor. The only designated National Historic Region in British Columbia, the Homesite contains more than 30 commercial buildings and about 400 residential buildings, all in late Victorian style. Ask at the visitor center for the heritage walking-tour brochure. The **Powell River Historic Museum,** 4800 Marine Dr. (© **604/485-2222**), has one of the largest archives of historic photos in the province, along with artifacts from the Native Sechelt. It's open Monday through Friday from 10am to 5pm, plus weekends from mid-May to Labour Day. Admission is C$3 (US$2.40).

From Powell River, many travelers take the ferry over to Comox/Courtenay on Vancouver Island and continue the loop back south. However, Powell River isn't the end of the road. That honor goes to tiny **Lund,** 28km (17 miles) north on Highway 101. The main reason to make the trip is to say you did it, and to pop into the century-old Lund Hotel for a drink or a meal.

OUTDOOR PURSUITS

CANOEING & KAYAKING   The Sunshine Coast, with its fiord-notched coastline, myriad islands, and protected waters, makes for excellent kayaking. The **Desolation Sound** area, north of Lund, is especially popular. The **Powell Forest Canoe Route,** a 4- to 8-day backcountry paddle, links four lakes in an 81km (50-mile) circuit. **Powell River Sea Kayaks,** 6812E Alberni St. (© **866/617-4444** or 604/483-2160; www.bcseakayak.com), offers rentals and tours.

DIVING   The center for diving along the Sunshine Coast, Powell River boasts visibility of over 30m (98 ft.) in winter, lots of sea life, and varied terrain. Area dive spots include five shipwrecks and several boats sunk as artificial reefs. **Alpha Dive Services,** 7013 Thunder Bay St. (© **604/485-6939;** www.divepowellriver.com), is one of the area's leading outfitters, with a shop in Powell River and diving operations in Okeover Inlet and Desolation Sound.

WHERE TO STAY & DINE
IN SECHELT
Four Winds B&B ✿   It's hard to imagine a more compelling site: a thrust of bare rock stretching out into the Strait of Georgia, backed up against a grove of fir and spruce. This modern home is lined with picture windows, all the better to capture the astonishing view of islands and sea, frequently visited by whales, herons, and seals. Guest rooms are beautifully decorated and have a hot tub or Jacuzzi; the suite has a balcony. Most notably, one of the owners is a licensed massage therapist, and will schedule sessions utilizing craniosacral therapy, neuromuscular, and hot stone techniques.

5482 Hill Rd., Sechelt, BC V0N 3A8. © **800/543-2989,** 604/885-3144, or 604/740-1905. Fax 604/885-3182. www.fourwindsbeachhouse.com. 3 units. C$139–C$179 (US$111–US$143) double. Rates include full breakfast. AE, MC, V. **Amenities:** Golf course nearby; spa treatments; Jacuzzi; hot tub; massage; limited laundry service; nonsmoking facility. *In room:* A/C, TV, fridge, hair dryer, DVD/VCR, wireless Internet, coffeemaker, tea.

IN POWELL RIVER

Beach Gardens Resort 🀆 Long popular with divers and kayakers, the Beach Gardens—just south of Powell River—has 48 brand-new rooms, all with incredible views overlooking Malaspina Strait. Several banks of perfectly comfortable older view rooms rent at a discount; some of these have full kitchens. Amenities include a marina, pub, and beer-and-wine store.

7074 Westminster Ave., Powell River, BC V8A 1C5. ℂ **800/663-7070** or 604/485-6267. Fax 604/485-2343. www. beachgardens.com. 66 units. C$79–C$135 (US$63–US$108) double; C$79 (US$63) cottage. Off-season rates available. AE, MC, V. Free parking. Pets allowed in ground-floor rooms. **Amenities:** Golf course nearby; watersports equipment rentals; coin-op laundry; beer-and-wine store. In room: TV, coffeemaker.

Desolation Sound Resort 🀆🀆 Twenty minutes north of Powell River on Okeover Inlet near Lund is Desolation Sound Resort, which offers luxury and a wilderness experience rolled into one. Accommodations are in extremely attractive chalets perched on high pilings above a steeply sloping shoreline. These log structures built by local craftspeople come in various configurations and sleep up to eight. Spaces are fully modern, and beautifully maintained, with cedar interiors, full kitchens, hardwood floors, and tasteful decor—some units have private hot tubs; all have decks (with gas grills) overlooking the water. Chartered boating, kayaking, or diving trips can be arranged; guests are free to use resort canoes and kayaks.

2694 Dawson Rd., Okeover Inlet, Powell River, BC V8A 4Z3. ℂ **604/483-3592.** Fax 604/483-7942. www.desolation resort.com. 9 units. July–Sept and winter holidays C$149–C$289 (US$119–US$231) double, C$229–C$424 (US$183–US$339) chalet; May–June C$129–C$259 (US$103–US$207) double, C$259–C$399 (US$167–US$319) chalet; Oct–Apr C$109–C$199 (US$87–US$159) double, C$199–C$314 (US$159–US$251) chalet. Extra person C$25 (US$20) per night. Discounts for stays over 3 nights. Packages available. AE, MC, V. Pets allowed in off season for additional charge. **Amenities:** Watersports equipment; powerboat rentals; charter cruises; free use of kayaks and canoes. In room: Kitchen, no phone.

Powell River Town Centre Hotel Right downtown, Powell River's newest hotel offers well-appointed guest rooms and a full health club. All-inclusive fishing and golf packages are available.

4660 Joyce Ave., Powell River, BC V8A 3B6. ℂ **800/663-1144** or 604/485-3000. Fax 604/485-3031. 71 units. C$99–C$169 (US$79–US$135) double. AE, DISC, MC, V. Free parking. Pets allowed for C$10 (US$8) per day. **Amenities:** Restaurant; pub; golf course nearby; exercise room; Jacuzzi; car-rental desk; business center; 24-hr. room service; babysitting; laundry service; same-day dry cleaning. In room: AC, TV w/pay movies, dataport, coffeemaker, hair dryer, high-speed wireless Internet access.

2 Whistler: North America's Premier Ski Resort 🀆

120km (74 miles) N of Vancouver

The premier ski resort in North America, according to *Ski, Snow Country,* and *Condé Nast Traveler* magazines, the **Whistler/Blackcomb** complex boasts more vertical feet, more lifts, and more ski terrain than any other ski resort in North America. And it isn't all just downhill skiing: There's also backcountry, cross-country, snowboarding, snowmobiling, heli-skiing, and sleigh riding. In summer, there's mountain biking, rafting, hiking, golfing, and horseback riding. The area got the ultimate seal of approval from the International Olympic Committee in 2003 when it landed the opportunity to stage many of the alpine events for the 2010 Winter Games. So come now to test yourself on the same slopes that tomorrow's champions will ski on.

And then there's **Whistler** itself, a full-service resort town with a year-round population of 10,000 plus 115 hotels and lodgings.

Whistler Village

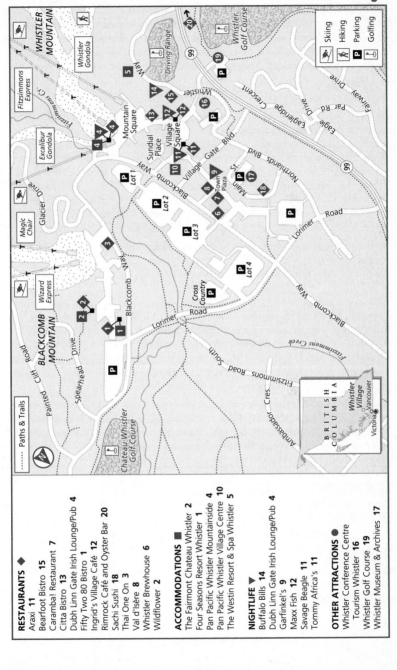

RESTAURANTS ◆
Araxi **11**
Bearfoot Bistro **15**
Carambal Restaurant **7**
Citta Bistro **13**
Dubh Linn Gate Irish Lounge/Pub **4**
Fifty Two 80 Bistro **1**
Ingrid's Village Café **12**
Rimrock Café and Oyster Bar **20**
Sachi Sushi **18**
Thai One On **3**
Val d'Isere **8**
Whistler Brewhouse **6**
Wildflower **2**

ACCOMMODATIONS ■
The Fairmont Chateau Whistler **2**
Four Seasons Resort Whistler **1**
Pan Pacific Whistler Mountainside **4**
Pan Pacific Whistler Village Centre **10**
The Westin Resort & Spa Whistler **5**

NIGHTLIFE ▼
Buffalo Bills **14**
Dubh Linn Gate Irish Lounge/Pub **4**
Garfinkel's **9**
Maxx Fish **12**
Savage Beagle **11**
Tommy Africa's **11**

OTHER ATTRACTIONS ●
Whistler Conference Centre
Tourism Whistler **16**
Whistler Golf Course **19**
Whistler Museum & Archives **17**

The towns north of Whistler, **Pemberton** and **Mount Currie,** are refreshment stops for cyclists and hikers and gateways to the icy alpine waters of **Birkenhead Lake Provincial Park** (see "Fishing," below) and the majestic **Cayoosh Valley,** which winds through the glacier-topped mountains to the Cariboo town of Lillooet (see chapter 11 for more on this town).

ESSENTIALS
GETTING THERE
By Car   Whistler is about a 2-hour drive from Vancouver along Highway 99, also called the **Sea-to-Sky Highway.** The drive is spectacular, winding along the edge of Howe Sound before climbing up through the mountains. You'll need to allow extra time for road construction over the next few years while driving this extravagantly scenic route, as road crews are widening the road in advance of the 2010 Olympics. Before you depart, check **www.tourismwhistler.com** for updates on lane and road closures so you know what you're facing. Parking at the mountain is free for day skiers; there are large parking lots along Fitzsimmons Creek between Whistler Village and Upper Village. However, most hotels will charge a fee for overnight parking.

By Bus   **Whistler Express,** 8695 Barnard St., Vancouver (© **604/266-5386** in Vancouver, or 604/905-0041 in Whistler; www.perimeterbus.com), operates door-to-door bus service from Vancouver International Airport via 16 downtown Vancouver hotels (for registered guests) to over 25 lodgings in Whistler. Buses depart seven times daily in the summer and 11 times in winter. The trip takes about 3 hours; one-way fares are C$67 (US$53) for adults and C$45 (US$36) for children. Kids under 5 ride free. Reservations are required year-round. **Greyhound,** Pacific Central Station, 1150 Station St., Vancouver (© **604/662-8051** in Vancouver, or 604/482-8747 in Whistler; www.greyhound.ca), operates service from the Vancouver Bus Depot to the Whistler Greyhound depot at 2029 London Lane. The trip takes about 2½ hours; one-way fares are C$32 (US$27) for adults and C$16 (US$13) for children ages 5 to 12.

By Train   The **Whistler Mountaineer,** a new route from Rocky Mountaineer Vacations (© **877/460-3200** or 604/606-7245), debuts in 2006. The 3-hour route links Vancouver and Whistler along the highly scenic Sea-to-Sky corridor. For schedule and fare information see **www.rockymountaineer.com**.

VISITOR INFORMATION   The **Whistler Visitor Info Centre,** 4230 Gateway Dr., Whistler, BC V0N 1B4 (© **604/932-5522;** www.whistlerchamber.com), is open daily 9am to 5pm. **Tourism Whistler** is at the Whistler Conference Centre at 4010 Whistler Way, Whistler, BC V0N 1B0, open daily 9am to 5pm (© **877/991-9988** or 604/938-2769; www.tourismwhistler.com). This office can assist you with event tickets and last-minute accommodations bookings, and can also provide general information.

GETTING AROUND
Be sure to pick up a map when you get to Whistler and study it—the curving streets are made for pedestrians but defy easy negotiation by drivers, particularly in the winter darkness. **Whistler Village** is at the base of the ski runs at Whistler Peak. **Upper Village,** at the base of Blackcomb ski runs, is just across Fiztsimmons Creek from Whistler Village. As development continues, the distinction between these two "villages" is disappearing, though Whistler Village is the center for most independent restaurants, shopping, and the youthful nightlife scene. Upper Village, centered on the Four Seasons and Fairmont Chateau Whistler hotels, is quieter and more upscale.

However, both villages are compact, and signed trails and paths link together shops, lodgings, and restaurants in the central resort area. The walk between the two village resort areas takes about 10 minutes.

Many smaller inns, B&Bs, restaurants, and services are located outside the nucleus of Whistler Village and Upper Village. **Creekside** is a large development east (down-hill) from Whistler Village (there are lifts onto Whistler Mountain from Creekside—in fact, this was the original lift base for the resort), while the shores of **Alta Lake** are ringed with residential areas and golf courses.

By Bus   The year-round Whistler and Valley Express (WAVE) **public bus system** (© 604/932-4020) offers 14 routes in the Whistler area. Buses have both bike and ski racks. Most routes cross paths at the Gondola Transit Exchange off Blackcomb Way, near the base of the Whistler Mountain lifts. One-way fares are C$1.50 (US$1.20) for adults and C$1.25 (US$1) for seniors and students. For a route map, go to www.busonline.ca.

By Taxi   The villages' taxis operate around the clock and are easy to find near the entrances to hotels. Taxi tours, golf-course transfers, and airport transport are also offered by **Airport Limousine Service** (© 800/278-8742 or 604/273-1331), **Whistler Taxi** (© 604/938-3333), and **Sea-to-Sky Taxi** (© 604/932-3333).

By Car   Rental cars are available from **Avis** in the Cascade Lodge, 4315 Northlands Blvd. (© 800/TRY-AVIS or 604/932-1236), or **Budget** at the Whistler Coast Hotel, 4005 Whistler Way (© 800/299-3199 or 604/935-4122).

SPECIAL EVENTS
Downhill ski competitions are held December to May, including the FIS Snowboard World Cup (Dec), the TELUS Winter Classic (Jan), and the TELUS World Ski & Snowboard Festival (Apr). In August, mountain bikers compete in Crankworx, Canada's premier free-ride mountain bike festival.

During the third week in July, the villages host **Whistler's Roots Weekend** (© 604/932-2394). Down in the villages and up on the mountains, you'll hear the sounds of Celtic, zydeco, bluegrass, folk, and world-beat music at free and ticketed events. The **Whistler Summit Concert Series** (© 604/932-3434) is held during August weekends.

The second weekend in September ushers in the **Whistler Jazz & Blues Festival** (© 604/932-2394), featuring live performances in the village squares and the sur-rounding clubs. **Cornucopia** (© 604/932-3434) is Whistler's premier wine-and-food festival. Held in November, the opening gala showcases top wineries from the Pacific region plus lots of food events and tastings from local chefs.

HITTING THE SLOPES
Whistler/Blackcomb Resort   **Whistler and Blackcomb Mountains,** 4545 Black-comb Way, Whistler, BC V0N 1B4 (© 866/218-9690 or 604/932-3434; snow report 604/687-1032; www.whistlerblackcomb.com), are jointly operated by Intrawest, so your pass affords access to both ski areas. You can book nearly all accommodations and activities in Whistler from their website.

From its base in Whistler Village, **Whistler Mountain** has 1,530m (5,018 ft.) of vertical and over 100 marked runs that are serviced by a total of 16 lifts. From its base in Upper Village, **Blackcomb Mountain** has 1,610m (5,280 ft.) of vertical and over 100 marked runs that are served by a total of 17 lifts. Both mountains also have bowls and glade skiing, with Blackcomb offering glacier skiing well into August. Together, the two mountains comprise the largest ski resort in North America, offering over 8,100 skiable acres—3,000 more than the largest U.S. resort.

During winter, lift tickets for 3 days of skiing on both mountains cost C$166 to C$222 (US$132–US$178) for adults, C$142 to C$189 (US$113–US$151) for youths and seniors, and C$84 to $113 (US$67–US$90) for children. Lifts are open 8:30am to 3:30pm (to 4:30pm mid-Mar to closing, depending on weather and conditions).

Whistler/Blackcomb offers **ski lessons and guides** for all levels and interests. (For skiers looking to try snowboarding, a half-day lesson plus rentals is a particularly attractive package.) Phone **Guest Relations** at © 604/932-3434 for details. Ski, snowboard, and boot **rentals** are available from the resort, and can be booked online. In addition, dozens of independent shops provide equipment rentals. **Affinity Sports** www.affinityrentals.com) has seven locations in the Whistler area, with online reservations available. **Summit Ski** (© **604/938-6225** or 604/932-6225; www.summit sport.com), has three locations in Whistler and rents high-performance and regular skis, snowboards, cross-country skis, and snowshoes.

BACKCOUNTRY SKIING   The **Spearhead Traverse,** which starts at Whistler and finishes at Blackcomb, is a well-marked backcountry route that has become extremely popular. **Garibaldi Provincial Park** (© **604/898-3678**) maintains marked backcountry trails at **Diamond Head, Singing Pass,** and **Cheakamus Lake.** These are ungroomed and unpatrolled trails, and you have to be self-reliant—you should be at least an intermediate skier, bring appropriate clothing and avalanche gear, and know how to use it. There are several access points along Highway 99 between Squamish and Whistler.

CROSS-COUNTRY SKIING   The 32km (20 miles) of easy to very-difficult marked trails at **Lost Lake** start at the Lorimer Road bridge over Fitzsimmons Creek, just west of Upper Village. Passes are C$10 (US$8); a 1-hour cross-country lesson runs about C$35 (US$28) and can be booked at the same station where you purchase your trail pass. The **Valley Trail System** in the village becomes a well-marked cross-country ski trail during winter. For more information on cross-country skiing at Whistler, go to **www.crosscountryconnection.bc.ca**.

HELI-SKIING   Whistler Heli-Skiing (© **888/HELI-SKI** or 604/932-4105; www. whistlerheliskiing.com), is one of the more established operators. A three-run day, with 1,400 to 2,300m (4,500–7,500 ft.) of vertical helicopter lift, costs C$670 (US$536) per person. A four-run day, for expert skiers and riders only, with 1,800 to 3,000m (6,000–10,000 ft.) of vertical helicopter lift, costs C$750 (US$600) per person. Both trips include a guide and lunch.

SNOWCAT SKIING AND BOARDING   Lifts and choppers aren't the only way up a mountain. **Powder Mountain Catskiing** (© **877/PWDR-FIX** or 604/932-0169; www.powdermountaincatskiing.com), uses snowcats to climb up into a private skiing area south of Whistler where skiers and boarders will find 4,000 skiable acres on two mountains. The price, C$449 (US$359) per person, includes a full day of skiing, usually six to eight runs down 2,100 to 3,000m (7,000–10,000 ft.) of vertical untracked powder, plus transport to/from Whistler, breakfast, lunch, and guides.

OTHER WINTER PURSUITS
SLEIGHING & DOG SLEDDING   Explore the old-growth forests of the Soo Valley Wildlife Preserve while mushing a team of eager Huskies. **Cougar Mountain**

(© **888/297-2222** or 604/932-4086; www.cougarmountain.ca), offers a choice of dog-sledding trips, and if the weather and terrain permit, you may even get to drive the dogs yourself. A 4-hour trip Woof Pack tour costs C$280 (US$224) for two people sharing a sled. For a sleigh ride with horses, contact **Blackcomb Horsedrawn Sleigh Rides,** 103–4338 Main St. (© **604/932-7631**). In winter, tours go out every evening and cost C$45 (US$36) for adults, C$35 (US$28) for youths 13 to 18, and C$25 (US$23) for children 12 and under.

SNOWMOBILING   The year-round ATV/snowmobile tours offered by **Canadian Snowmobile Adventures Ltd.,** Carleton Lodge (© **604/938-1616;** www.canadian snowmobile.com), are a unique way to take to the Whistler Mountain trails. Exploring the Fitzsimmons Creek watershed, a 2-hour tour costs C$119 (US$95) for a driver and C$89 (US$71) for a passenger. A nighttime snowmobile tour heads to a remote mountain cabin, where a fondue dinner awaits, for C$219 (US$175), or, for real adrenaline, consider heli-snowmobiling—catch a chopper to 1,500m (5,000 ft.) and snowmobile virgin snow above timberline (C$489/US$391).

SNOWSHOEING   **Outdoor Adventures@Whistler,** P.O. Box 1054, Whistler, BC V0N 1B0 (© **604/932-0647;** www.adventureswhistler.com), has guided tours for novices at C$69 (US$55) for 1½ hours. If you want to just rent the snowshoes and find your own way around, rentals are C$15 (US$12) per day.

WARM-WEATHER PURSUITS

BIKING   Some of the best mountain-bike trails in the village are in Whistler and Blackcomb mountains' **bike park,** which offers over 200km (124 miles) of lift-serviced trails and mountain pathways with over 1,440m (4,800 ft.) of vertical drop. The park has three access lifts and two jump areas; the trail system is labeled from beginner to gonzo. Lift tickets and park admission are C$41 (US$33) adult, C$36 (US$29) youths 13 to 18, and C$21 (US$17) kids 7 to 12. If you're not ready for daredevil riding on the mountain, the 30km (19-mile) paved Valley Trail is a pedestrian/bicycle route linking parks, neighborhoods, and playgrounds around Whistler Village. For other biking trails, check out the comprehensive Whistler Mountain Bike Guide at www.whistlermountainbike.com.

You can rent a mountain bike from a multitude of summer rental outfits including **Trax & Trails,** Chateau Whistler Hotel, 4599 Chateau Blvd., Upper Village (© **604/ 938-2017**); and from the **Whistler Bike Company,** Hilton Whistler Resort, 4050 Whistler Way, Whistler Village (© **604/938-9511**). Prices range from C$30 (US$24) per half-day for a commuting-style bike to C$60 to C$85 (US$48–US$68) per half-day for a high-end mountain bike.

CANOEING & KAYAKING   The 2-hour River of Golden Dreams Kayak & Canoe Tour offered by **Whistler Outdoor Experience,** P.O. Box 151, Whistler, BC V0N 1B0 (© **604/932-3389;** www.whistleroutdoor.com), is a great way to get acquainted with an exhilarating stretch of slow-moving glacial water that runs between Green Lake and Alta Lake behind the village of Whistler. Packages range from C$49 (US$39) per person unguided to C$79 (US$63) per person with a guide.

FISHING   Spring runs of steelhead, rainbow trout, and Dolly Varden char; summer runs of cutthroat and salmon; and fall runs of coho salmon attract anglers from around the world to the many glacier-fed lakes and rivers in the area and to **Birkenhead Lake Provincial Park,** 67km (42 miles) north of Pemberton. Bring your favorite fly rod and don't forget to buy a fishing license when you arrive. **Whistler**

Tips A Worthwhile Museum

To learn more about Whistler's unique heritage, flora, and fauna, visit the **Whistler Museum & Archives Society,** 4329 Main St., off Northlands Boulevard (© **604/932-2019**). Interesting exhibits reveal the life and culture of the Native Indian tribes that have lived in the lush Whistler and Pemberton valleys for thousands of years. There are also re-creations of the village's early settlement by British immigrants during the late 1800s and early 1900s. Admission is C$5 (US$4) for adults, C$4 (US$3.20) seniors and students, and C$3 (US$2.40) youths 7 to 18. Open mid-May to Labour Day, daily from 10am to 4pm; call for off-season hours.

Backcountry Adventures, Box 202, Whistler, BC V0N 1B0 (© **604/932-3532;** www.whistlerriver.com), offers half-day and full-day catch-and-release fishing trips in the surrounding glacier rivers. Half-day rates are C$150 (US$120) per person, based on two people, which includes all fishing gear, round-trip transport to/from the Whistler Village Bus Loop, and a snack or lunch.

GOLF   Robert Trent Jones, Jr.'s **Chateau Whistler Golf Club,** at the base of Blackcomb Mountain (© **604/938-2092,** or pro shop 604/938-2095), is an 18-hole, par-72 course. The 6,635-yard, par-72 signature course was selected in 1993 as "Canada's Best New Golf Course" by *Golf Digest* magazine. Greens fees are C$125 to C$225 (US$100–US$180), which includes power-cart rental. A multiple-award-winning golf course, **Nicklaus North at Whistler** (© **604/938-9898**) is a 5-minute drive north of the village on the shores of Green Lake. The 6,908-yard, par-71 course's mountain views are spectacular. Greens fees are C$115 to C$210 (US$92–US$183) in high season. The 6,676-yard **Whistler Golf Club** (© **800/376-1777** or 604/932-4544), designed by Arnold Palmer, features nine lakes, two creeks, and magnificent vistas. In addition to the 18-hole, par-72 course, the club offers a driving range, putting green, sand bunker, and pitching area. Greens fees are C$129 to C$193 (US$103–US$154). The Robert Cupp–designed, 7,001-yard, **Big Sky Golf and Country Club** is half an hour north at Pemberton (© **800/668-7900** or 604/894-6106). In addition to awe-striking vistas onto Mount Currie, Big Sky offers one of Canada's top teaching facilities with 2- and 3-day programs ideal for all ability levels, as well as custom schools.

HIKING   There are numerous easy hiking trails in and around Whistler. (Just remember—never hike alone, and bring plenty of water with you.) You can take lifts up to Whistler and Blackcomb mountains' trails during summer, but you have a number of other choices as well. The **Lost Lake Trail** starts at the northern end of the Day Skier Parking Lot at Blackcomb. The 30km (19 miles) of marked trails that wind around creeks, beaver dams, blueberry patches, and lush cedar groves are ideal for biking, cross-country skiing, or just strolling and picnicking.

The **Valley Trail System** is a well-marked paved trail connecting parts of Whistler. The trail starts on the west side of Highway 99 adjacent to the Whistler Golf Course and winds through quiet residential areas, as well as golf courses and parks. Garibaldi Provincial Park's **Singing Pass Trail** is a 4-hour hike of moderate difficulty. The fun way to experience this trail is to take the Whistler Mountain gondola to the top and walk down the well-marked path that ends in the village.

Beginning in 2006, Whistler Mountain's premier chairlift—the Peak Chair—will remain open in summer for transport to the mountain's 2,182m (7,160-ft.) summit for alpine sightseeing and hiking. Called the **Peak Adventure** (© **866/218-9690** or 604/932-3434; www.whistlerblackcomb.com), tickets are C$35 (US$28) adult, C$27 (US$22) seniors and youths 13 to 18, and C$15 (US$12) children 7 to 12. After the exhilarating open-air chairlift ride, take your pick from over 48km (30 miles) of alpine hiking trails including the Peak Interpretive Walk; guided hikes are available.

Nairn Falls Provincial Park is about 33km (20 miles) north of Whistler on Highway 99. It features a 1.5km (1-mile) long trail leading you to a stupendous view of the icy-cold Green River as it plunges 60m (196 ft.) over a rocky cliff into a narrow gorge on its way downstream. On Highway 99 north of Mount Currie, **Joffre Lakes Provincial Park** is an intermediate-level hike leading past several brilliant-blue glacial lakes up to the very foot of a glacier. The **Ancient Cedars** area of Cougar Mountain is an awe-inspiring grove of towering cedars and Douglas firs. Some of the trees are over 1,000 years old and measure 2.5m (9 ft.) in diameter.

RAFTING   Whistler River Adventures, Whistler Mountain Village Gondola Base (© **888/932-3532** or 604/932-3532; www.whistlerriver.com), offers five different day trips on local rivers, ranging from a placid all-generation paddle to a roaring white-water adventure. Four-hour paddle trips on the Cheakamus River are gentle enough for families (C$89/US$71 adults, C$69/US$55 youths 13–16, and C$44/US$35 children 5–12), while the 6-hour Squamish River white-water trip is for thrill seekers (C$109/US$87 adults, C$99/US$79 youths 13–16). All trips include equipment and ground transport. The 6-hour trip includes a salmon barbecue lunch.

TENNIS   The Whistler Racquet & Golf Resort, 4500 Northland Blvd. (© **604/932-1991;** www.whistlertennis.com), features three covered courts, seven outdoor courts, and a practice cage, all open to drop-in visitors. Indoor courts are C$32 (US$26) per hour and outdoor courts are C$16 (US$13) per hour. Adult and junior tennis camps are offered during summer. Camp prices range from C$295 to C$350 (US$236–US$280) for a 3-day camp; kids camps cost C$46 (US$39) per day drop-in or C$186 (US$149) for a 5-day camp. The **Mountain Spa & Tennis Club,** Hilton Whistler Resort, Whistler Village (© **604/938-2044**), and the **Chateau Whistler Resort,** Chateau Whistler Hotel, Upper Village (© **604/938-8000**), also offer courts

---

Kids   Activities for Kids

At the base of Blackcomb mountain, **Adventure Zone** offers kid-centric activities in a circuslike atmosphere. Activities and facilities include horseback riding, minigolf, trampolines, trapezes, wall climbing, gondola rides, gyroscopes, and zip-line and luge rides. Tickets are C$7 to C$15 (US$5.60–US$12); combo tickets are available; see www.whistlerblackcomb.com for more information. Based at Blackcomb Mountain, the **Dave Murray Summer Ski Camp,** P.O. Box 98, Whistler, BC V0N 1B0 (© **604/932-5765;** www.skiandsnowboard.com), is North America's longest-running summer ski camp. Junior programs cost about C$1,995 (US$1,596) per week mid-June to mid-July. The packages include food, lodging, and lift passes, as well as tennis, trapeze, and mountain-biking options.

to drop-in players. Prices run C$12 (US$9.60) per hour per court, with racquet rentals at C$5 (US$4) per hour.

There are **free public courts** at Myrtle Public School, Alpha Lake Park, Meadow Park, Millar's Pond, Brio, Blackcomb Benchlands, White Gold, and Emerald Park. Call ✆ **604/938-PARK** for details.

ZIP-LINING   One of Whistler's newest thrills is the year-round steel zip-line rides offered by **Ziptrek Ecotours** (✆ **866/935-0001** or 604/935-0001; www.ziptrek.com). Zip-lining involves gliding along a suspended steel cable using a pulley and climbing harness at speeds up to 88kmph (55 mph). Guided tours include five zip-line rides that range in height and length from 24 to 335m (80–1,100 ft.), spanning 11 hectares (33 acres) in the valley between Whistler and Blackcomb Mountains, an area of untouched coastal temperate rainforest.

Beginning in 2006, Ziptrek will add two additional zip lines down the valley between Blackcomb and Whistler mountains, taking zippers from the current course in the rainforest all the way back to Whistler Village. The first of the two new lines is 609m (2,000 ft.) long and about 61m (200 ft.) above Fitzsimmons Creek. The last line is 305m (1,000 ft.) long, joined between two five-story wooden towers.

Tickets for the five-line tour are C$98 (US$78) adult, C$78 (US$62) senior and youth 14 and under. For those not up to zip-lining, Ziptrek also offers **TreeTrek,** a network of boardwalks, aerial stairways, and bridges at heights of over 24m (80 ft.) in the tree canopy. Tickets are C$39 (US$31) adult and C$29 (US$23) senior and youth 14 and under. Check the website for prices on extended tours.

SHOPPING

You'll have absolutely no problem finding interesting places to shop in Whistler—both quality and prices are high. **Whistler Village,** and the area surrounding the **Blackcomb Mountain lift,** brim with clothing, jewelry, craft, specialty, gift, and equipment shops open daily 10am to 6pm. The **Path Gallery,** in the Tyndall Stone Lodge, 4338 Main St. (✆ **604/932-7570**), is devoted to Northwest Coast Native art, including totem poles, carved masks, and prints. **Gallery Row** in the Hilton Whistler Resort consists of the **Whistler Village Art Gallery** (✆ **604/938-3001**), the **Black Tusk Gallery** (✆ **604/905-5540**), and the **Adele Campbell Gallery** (✆ **604/938-0887**). Their collections include fine art, sculpture, and glass.

WHERE TO STAY

Lodgings in Whistler are very high quality, and the price of rooms is equally high. The hotels listed below offer superlative rooms with lots of extras. However, the smaller inns offer great value and excellent accommodations, often with services and options that can, for many travelers, make them a more attractive option than the larger hotels. At these smaller, owner-operated inns, rates usually include features that are usually available for an extra fee at hotels. These inns are located outside of the central villages and usually offer a quieter lodging experience than the hotels in Whistler Village.

In addition, Whistler is absolutely loaded with condos. To reserve a unit, which can range from studios, one- to five-bedroom furnished condos, town houses, and chalets with prices from C$125 to C$1,500 (US$100–US$1,200) a night, for many travelers the easiest thing to do is simply decide on your price point and call one of the central booking agencies, such as **Resort Quest Whistler** (✆ **800/892-2431** or 604/932-6699; www.resortquest.com/whistler) and **Rainbow Retreats Accommodations Ltd.**

Tips A Day at the Spa

Spas are definitely a growth industry in Whistler. Nearly all the large hotels now feature spas and a number of independent spas line the streets of Whistler Village. The **Spa at Chateau Whistler Resort** (*©* **604/938-2086**) is considered one of the best. Open daily 8am to 9pm, it offers massage therapy, aromatherapy, skin care, body wraps, and steam baths. Another noteworthy hotel spa is the Westin Resort's **Avello Spa,** 400–4090 Whistler Way (*©* **877/935-7111** or 604/935-3444; www.whistlerspa.com), which offers a host of spa services as well as holistic and hydrotherapy treatments. The newest and swankiest is **The Spa at Four Seasons Resort** (*©* **604/966-2620**), with 15 treatment rooms, a Vichy shower, yoga and fitness classes, and a vast assortment of luxury treatments from mineral scrubs to wildflower baths. **Sacha Spa,** 4308 Main St. (*©* **866/368-0888** or 604/966-0888; www.sachaspa.com), is a highly atmospheric day spa with exotic-themed treatment rooms and a wide selection of beauty and relaxation treatments. The therapists at **Whistler Physiotherapy** (*©* **604/932-4001** or 604/938-9001; www.whistlerphysio.com) have a lot of experience with the typical ski, board, and hiking injuries. There are three locations: 339–4370 Lorimer Rd., at Marketplace; 202–2011 Innsbruck Dr., next to Boston Pizza in Creekside; and 4433 Sundial Place in Whistler Village.

(*©* **604/932-2343;** www.rainbowretreats.com). **Whistler Accommodation** (*©* **866/905-4607** or 604/905-4607; www.whistleraccommodation.com) focuses on condos and hotels in the Upper Village.

One other excellent booking service is **Allura Direct** (*©* **866/4-ALLURA** or 604/707-6700; www.alluradirect.com), through which owners of rental properties in Whistler rent directly to the public (and you escape the 10% local hotel tax). The website offers information and photos of numerous properties located throughout Whistler. Though owners are screened—we encountered no problems and got a fabulous deal on a one-bedroom condo—quality can vary, so we recommend you do your homework and book only with those owners who accept credit cards.

One of the easiest ways to book rooms, buy ski passes, and plan activities is to visit the official Whistler Blackcomb Resort website at **www.whistlerblackcomb.com**. Most hotels and condo developments are represented at this one-stop shopping and information site.

Reservations for peak winter periods should be made by September at the latest.

IN THE VILLAGE & UPPER VILLAGE

Developed by the owners of Opus, **Adara Hotel,** 4122 Whistler Green (*©* **866/502-3272;** www.adarahotel.com), is sure to become a top choice for Whistler's trendy, urban-chic set. Rustic naturalism meets contemporary color and modern Scandinavian style at this new boutique hotel, which raises the bar on area accommodations. Rooms and suites feature spalike bathrooms with large showers and rain shower heads, luxurious beds, "floating" fireplaces, artful design details, and views of Whistler, Whistler Village, or the mountains. Ski and snowboard waxing plus equipment rentals are offered. Pets are welcome and will also be well attended to, with services such as pet sitting and dog walking available. The hotel is slated to open in 2006; check the website for details and updates.

The Fairmont Chateau Whistler ★★★   Rated the top ski resort in North America by *Condé Nast Traveler* in 2003, the Fairmont re-creates the look of a feudal castle at the foot of Blackcomb Mountain, but with every modern comfort added. Massive wooden beams support an airy peaked roof in the lobby, while in the hillside Mallard Bar, double-sided stone fireplaces cast a cozy glow on the couches and leather armchairs. Rooms and suites are very comfortable and beautifully furnished, and feature duvets, bathrobes, and soaker tubs (some offer stunning views of the slopes). Fairmont Gold Service guests can have breakfast or relax après-ski in a private lounge with the feel of a Victorian library. All guests can use the heated outdoor pool and Jacuzzis, which look out over the base of the ski hill. The hotel's spa (see above) is generally cited as the best in town. The Fairmont pays attention to the needs of skiers, with a recreation concierge, ski storage next to the slopes, and ski valets to help make pre- and après-ski as expeditious and pleasant as possible.

4599 Chateau Blvd., Whistler, BC V0N 1B4. ℂ **800/441-1414** in the U.S., 800/606-8244 in Canada, or 604/938-8000. Fax 604/938-2058. www.fairmont.com. 550 units. Winter C$399–C$435 (US$319–US$348) double, C$570–C$1,399 (US$456–US$1,119) suite; summer C$299–C$335 (US$239–US$268) double, C$425–C$1,000 (US$340–US$800) suite. AE, MC, V. Underground valet parking C$25 (US$20). Pets are welcome. **Amenities:** 2 restaurants; bar; heated indoor/outdoor pool; 18-hole golf course; 2 tennis courts; health club; outstanding spa facility; Jacuzzi; children's programs; concierge; business center; shopping arcade; 24-hr. room service; in-room massage; babysitting; coin laundry; laundry service; same-day dry cleaning; nonsmoking rooms; concierge-level rooms; secure ski and bike storage; rooms for those w/limited mobility. *In room:* A/C, TV w/movie channels, dataport, minibar, coffeemaker, hair dryer, iron, safe.

Four Seasons Resort Whistler ★★★   Whistler has its share of grand hotels, but, even in this exalted company, the Four Seasons Resort stands alone. Easily the most refined and elegant of Whistler's hotels, the Four Seasons is monumental in scale while maintaining the atmosphere of a very intimate and sophisticated boutique hotel—a rare achievement. The expansive stone, glass, and timber lobby is like a modern-day hunting lodge—but with the addition of extraordinary contemporary art—while the fine-dining Fifty Two 80 Bistro & Bar (see below) has a pleasing, slightly playful decor of stone, candy-colored tile, and back-lit onyx. The Four Seasons' urbane good taste extends to the large guest rooms, decorated in wood and cool earth tones and beautifully furnished with rich fabrics and leather furniture. All rooms have a balcony, fireplace, and very large, amenity-filled bathrooms with soaker tubs. The standard room is a very spacious 46 sq. m (500 sq. ft.), and superior and deluxe level rooms are truly large. A separate wing of the hotel contains private residences: 139- to 344-sq.-m (1,500- to 3,700-sq.-ft.) apartments with two to four bedrooms. With 15 treatment rooms, the exquisite spa at the Four Seasons Resort is Whistler's largest, and a heated outdoor pool and three whirlpool baths fill half of the hotel courtyard. The Four Seasons Resort Whistler is a très chic, très elegant monument to refinement.

4591 Blackcomb Way, Whistler, BC V0N 1B4. ℂ **888/935-2460** or 604/935-3400. Fax 604/935-3455. 273 units. July–Sept 12 and Nov 24–Dec 22 C$345–C$740 (US$276–US$592) double; Sept 13–Nov 23 and May–June C$245–C$590 (US$196–US$472) double; Dec 23–Jan 1 C$845–C$1,350 (US$676–US$1,080) double; Jan 2–Apr C$495–C$970 (US$396–US$776) double. Underground valet parking C$28 (US$22), self park C$23 (US$18). **Amenities:** Restaurant; lounge; heated outdoor pool; fitness studio; superlative spa; hot tubs; concierge; business center; 24-hr. room service; laundry service; dry cleaning; ski and bike storage; rooms for those w/limited mobility. *In room:* A/C, TV/DVD, dataport, minibar, coffeemaker, hair dryer, iron, safe, high-speed Internet access, CD player, voice mail.

Pan Pacific Whistler Mountainside ★★   The Pan Pacific's slightly older and more family-oriented, all-suite property has a lot going for it, with top-notch furnishings, kitchenettes, and loads of amenities. Comfortable as the rooms are, however, the true advantage to the Pan Pacific Mountainside is its location at the foot of the

Whistler Mountain gondola. Not only can you ski right up to your hotel, but, thanks to a large heated outdoor pool and Jacuzzi deck, you can sit at the end of the day—sipping a glass of wine, gazing up at the snowy slopes—and marvel at the ameliorative effects of warm water on aching muscles.

4320 Sundial Crescent, Whistler, BC V0N 1B4. (C) **888/905-9995** or 604/905-2999. Fax 604/905-2995. www.pan pacific.com. 121 units. Jan–Apr 16 C$309–C$749 (US$247–US$599) studio, C$459–C$909 (US$367–US$727) 1 bedroom, C$709–C$1,309 (US$567–US$1,045) 2 bedroom; Apr 17–Nov 22 C$129–C$299 (US$103–US$239) studio, C$169–C$399 (US$135–US$319) 1 bedroom, C$229–C$529 (US$183–US$423) 2 bedroom; Nov 23–Dec 31 C$309–C$749 (US$247–US$599) studio, C$459–C$909 (US$367–US$727) 1 bedroom, C$709–C$1,309 (US$567–US$1,047) 2 bedroom. AE, DC, MC, V. Underground valet parking C$20 (US$16). **Amenities:** Restaurant; pub; heated outdoor pool; fitness center; whirlpool; steam room; concierge; room service; self-serve laundry; ski, bike, and golf bag storage; nonsmoking facility; rooms for those w/limited mobility. *In room:* A/C, TV w/pay movie channels and pay Nintendo, dataport w/high-speed Internet, fridge, coffeemaker, hair dryer, iron, wireless connectivity.

The Pan Pacific Whistler Village Centre ✿✿✿

The Pan Pacific chain now has two handsome properties in Whistler, both just steps off Blackcomb Way in Whistler Village. The newest is the Pan Pacific Village Centre, opened in 2005. An all-suite boutique property, the Village Center is an imposing structure with curious gables and a dormered roofline, underscoring the fact that this is anything but an anonymous corporate hotel. All in all, suites in the Village Centre are more like apartments than hotel rooms—it's also more couples-oriented than its family-friendly sister property. All one-, two-, and three-bedroom suites have a balcony, fireplace, flat-screen TV, full kitchen with granite counters, soaker tub, bathrobes, handsome furniture, built-in cabinetry, and floor-to-ceiling windows to showcase the amazing mountain vistas. The rooms come in two equally elegant color schemes, either "dawn"—in shades of tan and light fir—or "dusk"—with darker wood tones and rich upholstery. The enormous penthouse suites are truly magnificent, with cathedral ceilings, massive stone fireplaces, multiple balconies, European appliances, and dining rooms. The Village Centre has a fitness center with sauna, massage therapy, and spa treatment rooms, plus a lap pool and two hot tubs. Rates include a full breakfast buffet and afternoon/evening hors d'oeuvres in the Pacific Lounge, a guest-only facility with an outdoor patio.

4299 Blackcomb Way, Whistler, BC V0N 1B4. (C) **888/905-9995** or 604/905-2999. Fax 604/905-2995. www.panpacific whistler.com. 82 units. Jan–Apr 16 C$459–C$909 (US$367–US$727) 1 bedroom, C$709–C$1,309 (US$567–US$1,047) 2 bedroom, C$499–C$2,499 (US$399–US$1,999) 3 bedroom penthouse; Apr 17–Nov 22 C$169–C$399 (US$135–US$319) 1 bedroom, C$229–C$529 (US$183–US$423) 2 bedroom, C$499–C$2,499 (US$399–US$1,999) 3 bedroom penthouse; Nov 23–Dec 31 C$459–C$909 (US$367–US$727) 1 bedroom, C$709–C$1,309 (US$567–US$1,047) 2 bedroom, C$499–C$2,499 (US$399–US$1,999) 3 bedroom penthouse. AE, DC, DISC, MC, V. Underground valet parking C$20 (US$16). **Amenities:** Restaurant; pub; heated outdoor pool; fitness center; whirlpool; steam room; concierge; room service; self-serve laundry; ski, bike, and golf bag storage; rooms for those w/limited mobility. *In room:* A/C, TV (w/pay movie channels, pay Nintendo, and Web TV), dataport w/high-speed Internet, fridge, coffeemaker, hair dryer, iron, wireless connectivity.

The Westin Resort and Spa Whistler ✿✿✿

A relative latecomer to the Whistler lodging scene, the all-suite Westin Resort snapped up the best piece of property in town and squeezed itself onto the mountainside at the bottom of the main ski run into the village. Both the Whistler and Blackcomb gondolas are within a few hundred yards of your doorstep. The hotel is built in the style of an enormous mountain chalet with cedar timbers and lots of local granite and basalt finishings. All 419 suites offer full kitchens, soaker tubs, slate-lined showers, and an elegant and restful decor. The beds, Westin's signature Heavenly Beds, are indeed divine. To get you going in the morning, little luxuries include a ski valet service and (no more cold toes!) a boot-warming service. That is certainly one of the reasons why, in the short period it's been open, the Westin has already grabbed several top awards. The hotel's Avello Spa is extremely well appointed for après-slope pampering, and the indoor/outdoor pool, hot tubs, steam baths, and sauna will warm up ski-weary limbs.

4090 Whistler Way, Whistler, BC V0N 1B4. ✆ **888/634-5577** or 604/905-5000. Fax 604/905-5589. www.westin whistler.com. 419 units. Apr 16–Nov 23 C$159–C$469 (US$127–US$375) junior suite, C$249–C$589 (US$199–US$471) 1-bedroom suite, C$409–C$1,049 (US$327–US$839); 2-bedroom suite; Nov 24–Apr 15 C$199–C$569 (US$159–US$455) junior suite, C$319–C$689 (US$255–US$551) 1-bedroom suite, C$519–C$1,499 (US$415–US$1,199) 2-bedroom suite. Children 17 and under stay free in parent's room. AE, DC, DISC, MC, V. Parking C$23 (US$18). **Amenities:** Restaurant; bar; indoor and outdoor pool; nearby golf course; nearby tennis courts; outstanding health club; top-notch spa; indoor and outdoor Jacuzzi; sauna; bike rental; children's program; concierge; business center; shopping arcade; salon; 24-hr. room service; massage; babysitting; laundry; dry cleaning; wireless connectivity; nonsmoking facility. *In room:* TV w/pay movies, dataport, quality appointed appliances in kitchen, coffeemaker, hair dryer, iron, safe.

OUTSIDE THE VILLAGE

Alpine Chalet Whistler 🏔🏔
This cozy alpine-style lodge sits in a quiet location near Alta Lake and the Whistler Golf Club. The entire inn, built in 2001, is designed to provide luxurious lodgings, privacy, and a welcoming sense of camaraderie in the comfortable, fireplace-dominated guest lounge. There are three room types: Alpine rooms, comfortable lodge rooms that will suit the needs of most skiers and travelers; Chalets, which are larger and feature fireplaces and other extras; and the Master Suite, the largest and most opulent room, with a fireplace, cathedral ceiling, Jacuzzi, and large private balcony. All rooms have balconies or terraces, fine linens, bathrobes, and other upscale amenities you'd expect at a classy hotel. Evening meals available by reservation.

3012 Alpine Crescent, Whistler, BC V0N 1B3. ✆ **800/736-9967** or 604/935-3003. Fax 604/935-3008. www.alpine chaletwhistler.com. 8 units. Early Jan to Apr 15 C$189–C$259 (US$151–US$207); mid-Dec to early Jan C$259–C$429 (US$207–US$343); Apr 16 to mid-Dec C$129–C$219 (US$103–US$175). Rates include full breakfast. MC, V. Free parking. **Amenities:** Guest lounge; 8-person hot tub; steam room; heated ski lockers; nonsmoking facility. *In room:* A/C, TV/VCR, dataport, hair dryer, high-speed Internet.

Cedar Springs Bed & Breakfast Lodge 🏔 *Kids*
The no-children policy at many Whistler inns can be a real challenge for families, but the Cedar Springs provides an excellent solution. Guests at this large and charming modern lodge a mile north of Whistler Village have a choice of king-, queen-, or twin-size beds in comfortably modern yet understated surroundings—two-family suites, with two queen and two twin beds, are just the ticket for families. What's more, the lodge is just next door to a park, biking paths, and a sports center with swimming pool. Cedar Springs also offers excellent accommodations for couples and solo travelers. The large honeymoon suite boasts a fireplace and balcony. Most rooms feature handmade pine furniture; all have bathrooms with heated tile floors. The guest sitting room has a TV, VCR, fireplace, and video library. A sauna and hot tub on the sun deck overlooking the gardens add to the pampering after a day of play. A gourmet breakfast is served by the fireplace in the dining room, and guests are welcome to enjoy afternoon tea. Lodge owners Jackie and Joern offer lots of extras such as complimentary shuttle service to ski lifts, heated ski gear storage, bike rentals, and free wireless Internet access.

8106 Cedar Springs Rd., Whistler, BC V0N 1B8. ✆ **800/727-7547** or 604/938-8007. Fax 604/938-8023. www.whistler inns.com/cedarsprings. 8 units, 6 with bathroom. High winter season C$175–C$229 (US$140–US$183) double; spring, summer, fall C$89–C$119 (US$71–US$95) double. Rates include full breakfast. MC, V. Take Hwy. 99 north toward Pemberton 4km (2½ miles) past Whistler Village. Turn left onto Alpine Way, go a block to Rainbow Dr., and turn left; go a block to Camino St. and turn left. The lodge is a block down at the corner of Camino and Cedar Springs

Rd. Free parking. **Amenities:** Jacuzzi; sauna; game room; courtesy car to ski slopes; nonsmoking rooms; heated ski and gear storage. *In room:* Hair dryer, free wireless Internet, no phone.

Chalet Luise B&B Inn ★★

This homey inn is just outside of Whistler Village, so park the car and walk to dining, shopping, and recreation. Chalet Luise is a very charming small inn with an equally charming hostess. The inn has just the right Bavarian touch to create a festive, holiday-card atmosphere. The guest rooms are bright and cheerful, and come with pine furniture and high-quality linens; some have fireplaces and balconies. At the back is a gazebo with hot tub; the large guest lounge has a TV, fireplace, and a self-service coffee bar with a microwave for guest use. There are a number of decks, all lovingly festooned with flower pots in summer. All rooms have private baths. Breakfast is a buffet of fresh baked goods plus a hot main course. Room rates are complex; check the website for current rates and minimum-stay requirements.

7461 Ambassador Crescent, Whistler BC V0N 1B7 © **800/665-1998** or 604/932-4187. Fax 604/938-1531. www. chaletluise.com. 8 units. Summer rates from C$129–C$169 (US$103–US$135) double. Rates include full breakfast. Low season and winter rates available on request. MC, V. Free parking. **Amenities:** Hot tub; sauna; guest laundry; bike storage; nonsmoking facility. *In room:* Hair dryer.

Durlacher Hof Pension Inn ★★ *Finds*

This lovely inn boasts both an authentic Austrian feel and a sociable atmosphere. Both are the result of the exceptional care and service shown by owners Peter and Erika Durlacher. Guests are greeted by name at the entranceway, provided with slippers, and then given a tour of the three-story chalet-style property. The rooms vary in size from comfortable to quite spacious and come with goose-down duvets and fine linens, private bathrooms (some with jetted tubs) with deluxe toiletries, and incredible mountain views from private balconies. The downstairs lounge is a treat, with a fireplace and complimentary après-ski appetizers baked by Erika. Peter and Erika are a font of knowledge about local restaurants and recreation; they will happily arrange tours and outings.

7055 Nesters Rd., Whistler, BC V0N 1B7. © **877/932-1924** or 604/932-1924. Fax 604/938-1980. www.durlacher hof.com. 8 units. Dec 18–Mar C$129–C$499 (US$103–US$399) double; June 19–Sept C$99–C$359 (US$79–US$287) double. Discounted rates for spring and fall. Extra person C$35 (US$28). Rates include full breakfast and afternoon tea. MC, V. Free parking. Take Hwy. 99 about a half-mile north of Whistler Village to Nester's Rd. Turn left and the inn is immediately on the right. **Amenities:** Jacuzzi; sauna; laundry service; dry cleaning; nonsmoking rooms; 1 room for those w/limited mobility. *In room:* TV, hair dryer, no phone.

Edgewater Lodge *Finds*

This lodge has probably the most unique location of any lodging in Whistler. It sits on a jut of land that thrusts into Green Lake, a quiet 3km (1¾ miles) north of Whistler Village. From each room, there are gum-swallowing vistas across the lake to Wedge Mountain and the ski slopes on Whistler and Blackcomb. The intimate lodge offers personal and professional service. Half the rooms are standard hotel-style bedrooms, the other half are one-bedroom suites with a sofa bed in the sitting room. All share a large lobby guest area with couches and a huge fireplace. The Edgewater is also noteworthy for its fine Northwest cuisine dining room.

The lodge is very convenient to all-season recreation—in summer, you can fish and boat in Green Lake, or test your drive on the adjacent Nicklaus North Golf Course. Come winter, in addition to downhill skiing, ice skating and cross-country skiing are right out the front door—the valley's major Nordic ski trail runs right by the property.

8841 Hwy. 99, Box 369, Whistler, BC V0N 1B0. © **888/870-9065** or 604/932-0688. Fax 604/932-0686. www. edgewater-lodge.com. 12 units. High season C$175–C$320 (US$140–US$256) double; summer C$125–C$215 (US$100–US$172). 2-night minimum stay required on weekends. Rates include breakfast. AE, MC, V. Free parking. **Amenities:** Restaurant; lounge; Jacuzzi. *In room:* TV, hair dryer, wireless Internet access.

Hostelling International Whistler _Value_   On the south edge of Alta Lake, with a dining room, deck, and lawn looking over the lake to Whistler Mountain, this hostel is extremely pleasant. There's a lounge with a wood-burning stove, a common kitchen, a piano, Ping-Pong tables, and a sauna, as well as a drying room for ski gear and storage for bikes, boards, and skis. In the summer, guests have use of a barbecue, canoe, and rowboat. As with all hostels, most rooms and facilities are shared. Beds at the hostel book up very early. Book by September at the latest for the winter ski season.

5678 Alta Lake Rd., Whistler, BC V0N 1B5. ☎ 604/932-5492. Fax 604/932-4687. www.hihostels.ca. 33 beds in 4- to 8-bed dorms. C$20–C$24 (US$16–US$19) IYHA members; C$24–C$28 (US$19–US$22) nonmembers. Family and group memberships available. MC, V. Free parking. **Amenities:** Sauna; watersports equipment; bike rental; nonsmoking facility.

Inn at Clifftop Lane 🖈🖈   This large home, built as a B&B, sits above the Whistler Valley on a quiet side street just south of Whistler Creekside. The inn strikes that perfect balance between the homeyness of a B&B and the formality of a small boutique hotel. Each of the guest rooms is spacious, with an easy chair and living area, plus a bathroom with a jetted tub and bathrobes. The home is filled with books and decorated with antiques and folk art collected during the owners' travels, lending a cheerful élan to the breakfast rooms and guest lounge. Outdoors, steps lead through the forest to a hot tub and a private deck. This a great choice for travelers seeking understated comfort and elegance with friendly, professional service.

2828 Clifftop Lane, Whistler, BC V0N 1B2. ☎ 888/281-2929 or 604/938-1229. Fax 604/938-9880. www.innat clifftop.com. 5 units. Summer low season from C$109–C$130 (US$87–US$104); winter high season from C$145–C$275 (US$116–US$220). Ski packages available. Rates include full breakfast. MC, V. Free parking. **Amenities:** Lounge; hot tub; nonsmoking facility. _In room:_ TV, hair dryer.

CAMPING

South of Whistler on the Sea-to-Sky corridor is the very popular **Alice Lake Provincial Park.** About 27km (17 miles) north of Whistler, the well-maintained campground at **Nairn Falls,** Highway 99 (☎ **604/898-3678**), is more adult-oriented, with pit toilets, pumped well water, fire pits, and firewood, but no showers. The 85 campsites at **Birkenhead Lake Provincial Park,** off Portage Road, Birken (☎ **604/898-3678**), fill up very quickly during summer. To reserve at any of these provincial parks, call **Discover Camping** at ☎ **800/689-9025.** Campsites are C$14 (US$11).

WHERE TO DINE

Whistler literally overflows with dining choices: Whistler Village alone has over 90 restaurants. You'll have no trouble finding high quality, reasonably priced food. Gourmets on the go can grab a quick, fresh, and delicious bite at **Ciao Thyme Bistro & BBKs Pub,** 4573 Chateau Blvd. (☎ **604/932-7051;** www.chefbernards.ca/restaurant), open daily from 7am to 9pm. **Ingrid's Village Café,** just off the Village Square at 4305 Skiers Approach (☎ **604/932-7000**), is another locals' favorite, for both quality and price. A large bowl of Ingrid's clam chowder costs just C$4.50 (US$3.60), while a veggie burger comes in at C$5 (US$4). It's open daily 8am to 6pm. **Thai One On,** 4557 Blackcomb Way, in the Le Chamois Hotel (☎ **604/932-4822**), is Whistler's top Thai restaurant, with house specialties like _Naim Prik Pla Talay_ from C$11 to C$18 (US$8.80–US$6.40); open daily from 5pm to 10pm. The **Whistler Brewhouse,** 4355 Blackcomb Way (☎ **604/905-2739**), is a great spot for a microbrewed ale, a plate of wood-fired pizza, or rotisserie chicken (C$15–C$23/US$12–US$18), and a seat on the patio. Open daily 11:30am to midnight, till 1am on weekends. **Sachi**

Sushi, 4359 Main St. (© **604/935-5649**), is the best of Whistler's many sushi restaurants—the udon noodles and hot pots are excellent as well; sushi rolls from C$8 to C$17 (US$6.40–US$14). Open Tuesday to Friday noon to 2:30pm and nightly 5:30 to 10pm. And for a hearty Italian meal, try **Trattoria di Umberto,** 4417 Sundial Place (© **604/932-5858;** www.umberto.com).

Araxi Restaurant & Bar 🐸🐸 ITALIAN/WEST COAST   Frequently awarded for its wine list, and voted best restaurant in Whistler, this is one of the top places to dine. And, thanks to a major renovation, Araxi now has storage enough for its famous 12,000-bottle inventory of fine B.C. and foreign wines. Outside, the heated patio seats 80 people amid barrels of flowers, while inside, the artwork, antiques, and terra-cotta tiles give it a subtle Italian ambience. The menu, however, is less Italian and more West Coast. The locally caught trout is smoked in the Araxi kitchen. Various soups and salads are made from scratch with fresh ingredients like Pemberton sheep cheese and Okanagan tomatoes. Main courses include seafood such as ahi tuna, salmon filet, and scallops. For meat lovers, the menu offers rack of lamb, tenderloin, and alder-smoked pork loin. And don't hesitate to ask for a suggestion when contemplating the nearly encyclopedic wine list.

4222 Village Sq. © **604/932-4540.** www.araxi.com. Main courses C$25–C$39 (US$20–US$31). AE, MC, V. Mid-May to Oct daily 11am–10:30pm; during ski season daily 5pm–10pm.

Bearfoot Bistro 🐸🐸🐸 NORTHWEST   One of the very best in Whistler, Bearfoot Bistro has created an enormous following for its regional, seasonal Northwest cuisine. The emphasis is on innovation, new flavors, and unusual preparations—in short, this a cutting edge restaurant for serious gastronomes. In the dining room, choose either three or five courses from the admirably broad menu, with selections such as confit Quebec foie gras and Atlantic lobster salad, pan-seared weather-vane scallops served with pork belly and wild chanterelle mushroom and sweet corn ragout, or wild turbot with Dungeness crab and leek ravioli with sea urchin cream. There's nothing ordinary about the food, or the wine list, which has earned awards from *Wine Spectator* magazine. A number of specialty tasting menus are also available. Appetizers and more casual meals are offered in the fireside room and the cozy Champagne Bar.

4121 Village Green. © **604/932-3433.** www.bearfootbistro.com. 3-course dinner C$90 (US$72); 5-course dinner C$125 (US$100). AE, MC, V. Daily 5–10pm.

Caramba! Restaurant MEDITERRANEAN   The room is bright and filled with the pleasant buzz of nattering diners. The kitchen is open, and the smells wafting out hint tantalizingly of fennel, artichoke, and pasta. Caramba! is casual dining, but its Mediterranean-influenced menu offers fresh ingredients, prepared with a great deal of pizzazz. Try the pasta, free-range chicken, or roasted pork loin. Better still, if you're feeling especially good about your dining companions, order a pizza or two; a plate of grilled calamari; some hot spinach, cheese, and artichoke-and-shallot dips; and a plate of sliced prosciutto and bullfighters toast (savory toasted Spanish bread with herbs).

12–4314 Main St., Town Plaza. © **604/938-1879.** Main courses C$11–C$18 (US$8.80–US$14). AE, MC, V. Daily 11:30am–10:30pm.

Citta Bistro INTERNATIONAL   Citta's is a favorite restaurant and nightspot, serving thin-crust pizzas, gourmet burgers, and delicious finger foods like bruschetta, spring rolls, and nachos. Its terrace is the best people-watching corner in town.

In Whistler Village Sq. © **604/932-4177.** Reservations suggested. Main courses C$7–C$15 (US$5.60–US$12). AE, MC, V. Daily 11am–1am.

Dubh Linn Gate Irish Lounge PUB   The Gate is a convincing re-creation of a Dublin pub—in fact, the structure was shipped over board by board from Ireland—with good-quality pub food, excellent beer, and, more often than not, a balladeer singing a song or two about the *auld sod*.

In the Pan Pacific Lodge Whistler, 4320 Sundial Crescent. (✆ 604/905-2999. Reservations not accepted. Main courses C$11–C$21 (US$8.80–US$17). AE, MC, V. Mon–Sat 7am–1am; Sun 7am–midnight.

Fifty Two 80 Bistro & Bar ⚓   The suave dining room at the upscale Four Seasons Resort Whistler celebrates "fire and ice"—fire from the stone fireplace and dramatic backlit onyx panels, and ice from the display of fresh fish and shellfish that greets dinners. The design may be high-concept but the food is more easygoing and hearty. For appetizers, fresh shucked oysters or seared scallops with cauliflower puree are outstanding, and old-fashioned chicken supreme is made new again with local corn and wild mushrooms. Fresh lobster, prime Canadian steaks, spit roast meats, and fresh fish entrees round out the menu. Combine the a la carte selections into three- (C$39/US$31) or four- (C$45/US$36) course dinners—a great value for sublimely prepared food.

In the Four Seasons Whistler Resort, 4591 Blackcomb Way. (✆ 604/935-3400. Main courses C$18–C$38 (US$15–US$30). AE, DC, DISC, MC, V. Daily 7am–10pm.

Rimrock Cafe and Oyster Bar ⚓ SEAFOOD   Upstairs in a long narrow room with a high ceiling and a great stone fireplace at one end, Rimrock is very much like a Viking mead hall of old. It's not the atmosphere, however, that causes people to hop in a cab and make the C$5 (US$4) journey out from Whistler Village. What draws folks in is the food. The first order of business should be a plate of oysters. Chef Rolf Gunther serves them up half a dozen ways, from raw with champagne to "cooked in hell" (broiled with fresh chiles). For my money, though, the signature Rimrock oyster is still the best: broiled with béchamel sauce and smoked salmon. Other appetizers are lightly seared ahi tuna or Québec foie gras with portobello mushrooms. Main dishes focus on seafood and game. Look for lobster and scallops in light tarragon sauce on a bed of capellini pasta, or swordfish broiled with pecans, almonds, pistachios, and a mild red Thai curry. The accompanying wine list has a number of fine vintages from B.C., California, New Zealand, and Australia.

2117 Whistler Rd. (✆ 604/932-5565. www.rimrockwhistler.com. Main courses C$24–C$40 (US$19–US$32). AE, MC, V. Daily 11:30am–11:30pm.

Val d'Isère FRENCH   The fact that the Val d'Isère is a notable French restaurant is somewhat obscured by the multi-tasking menu's many feints. Look behind the pasta and pizza to find Alsatian classics from a hearty regional cuisine that will warm you even on the coldest of days. Start with the goat-cheese soufflé, followed by braised duck on a bed of figs, red cabbage, and polenta with port-wine reduction. A classic *choucroute* (sauerkraut with sausages and pork) will be welcome after a long day on the slopes. For lighter fare—perhaps on a summer day on the patio—consider seared scallops with candied lemon-ginger sauce, accompanied by a glass of Riesling. The desserts are luscious.

4314 Main St., Whistler Town Plaza. (✆ 604/932-4666. www.valdisere-restaurant.com. Main courses C$15–C$34 (US$12–US$27). AE, MC, V. June–Oct daily 11:30am–11pm; Nov–May daily 5–10pm.

The Wildflower ⚓⚓ PACIFIC NORTHWEST   In the Fairmont Chateau Whistler, the Wildflower serves innovative cuisine in a highly sophisticated dining room—this

---

(*Moments* **Après-Ski**

"Après-ski" refers to that delicious hour after a hard day on the slopes, when you sit back with a cold drink, nurse the sore spots, and savor the glow that comes from a day well skied. On the Blackcomb side, **Merlin's Bar,** at the base ((**604/938-7735**), is the most obvious spot, but hidden away inside the Chateau Whistler Resort is something better: the **Mallard Bar** ((**604/938-8000**), one of the most civilized après-ski bars on the planet.

---

is Whistler's only four-star restaurant. The seasonal menu features fresh Pacific seafood—the pine-roasted salmon is a specialty—as well as delicious local meats from the British Columbia interior. In addition to superlative regional cuisine, the Wild-flower also offers a Canadian Wine Discovery menu, which matches special main courses with Canadian wines for C$100 (US$80).

In the Fairmont Chateau Whistler Resort, 4599 Chateau Blvd. ((**604/938-8000.** Reservations required. Main courses C$18–C$45 (US$14–US$36). AE, MC, V. Daily 6–10pm.

WHISTLER AFTER DARK

For a town of just 10,000, Whistler has a more-than-respectable nightlife scene. You'll find concert listings in the *Pique,* a free local paper available at cafes and food stores. **Tommy Africa's,** underneath the Pharmasave at the entrance to the Main Village ((**604/932-6090**), and the dark and cavernous **Maxx Fish,** in the Village Square below the Amsterdam Cafe ((**604/932-1904**), cater to the 18- to 22-year-old crowd; you'll find lots of beat and not much light. The crowd at **Garfinkel's,** at the entrance to Village North ((**604/932-2323**), is similar, though the cutoff age can reach as high as 26 or 27. The **Boot Pub,** Nancy Green Drive, just off Highway 99 ((**604/932-3338**), is crammed with young Australian ski-lift operators. **Buffalo Bills,** across from the Whistler Gondola ((**604/932-6613**), and the **Savage Beagle,** opposite Starbucks in the Village ((**604/938-3337**), cater to the 30-something crowd. Bills is bigger, with a pool table, a video ski machine, and a smallish dance floor. The Beagle has a fabulous selection of beer and bar drinks, with a pleasant little pub upstairs and a house-oriented dance floor below.

Northern British Columbia

When you're talking about the "north" in Canada, you have to be careful. Although the following destinations are certainly northerly—at least a day's very long drive from Vancouver, or by a 15-hour ferry trip from Vancouver Island—most of this chapter's towns and sights are geographically in British Columbia's mid-section. By the time you reach Prince George or Prince Rupert, however, you'll feel the palpable sense of being in the north: The days are long in summer and short in winter, and the spruce forest-lands have a primordial character. First Nations peoples make up a greater per-centage of the population here than in more southerly areas, and Native com-munities and heritage sites are common.

One of the most dramatic ways to reach northern British Columbia is by ferry. The BC Ferries Inside Passage route operates between Port Hardy, on Vancouver Island, and Prince Rupert, on the mainland; this full-day ferry run passes through mystical land- and seascapes, with excellent wildlife-viewing opportu-nities. From Prince Rupert—a fishing town with an excellent Native arts museum—you can catch another ferry to the Queen Charlotte Islands, which lie truly on the backside of beyond. Part of these islands is preserved as Gwaii Haanas' National Park Reserve, a refuge of rare flora and fauna, and the ancient home-land of the Haida people.

Inland from Prince Rupert, the Yellow-head Highway (Hwy. 16) follows the mighty Skeena and Bulkley rivers past First Nations villages and isolated ranches, finally reaching Prince George, the largest city in northern British Columbia. Prince George is also a transportation gateway. Whether you're coming west from Edmonton, east from Prince Rupert, north from Vancouver, or south from Alaska, you'll pass through this city at the junction of the Fraser and Nechako rivers.

From Highway 16, there are two options for travelers who wish to explore realms even farther north. The famed 2,280km (1,414-mile) Alaska High-way—the only overland route to the 49th state—begins at Dawson Creek. More than 960km (595 miles) of the route wind across northern British Columbia, through black-spruce forest and over the Continental Divide. The Alaska Highway exercises an irresistible attraction to die-hard road-trippers, many of them retirees with RVs. Another route north, the Stew-art-Cassiar Highway, also labeled High-way 37, leaves the Yellowhead Highway west of the Hazeltons, cutting behind the towering Coast Mountains to eventually join the Alaska Highway in the Yukon.

Frigid weather and short days make winter travel difficult in northern British Columbia; rather, explore this beautiful wilderness landscape under the glow of the summer's midnight sun.

1 The Inside Passage ⊛ & Discovery Coast

The ferry cruise along British Columbia's Inside Passage combines the best scenic elements of Norway's rocky fiords, Chile's Patagonian range, and Nova Scotia's wild coastline. Less than half a century ago, there was only one way to explore this rugged coastline: by booking the 4-day passage on an Alaska-bound cruise ship or freighter.

Since 1966, **BC Ferries** (© **888/BC-FERRY** or 250/386-3431; www.bcferries.com) has operated the **Inside Passage ferry** between Port Hardy (see chapter 8) and Prince Rupert (on the mainland, see below), with stops at the small Discovery Coast communities of Bella Coola, Ocean Falls, Shearwater, McLoughlin Bay (Bella Bella), and Klemtu. These stopovers became so popular that in 1994, the company added the **Discovery Coast ferry** to its schedule, which is dedicated to serving these remote villages. The ferry system also connects Prince Rupert to the remote **Queen Charlotte Islands,** the ancestral home of the Haida tribe (see later in this chapter).

For information on the region, contact the **Northern BC Tourism Association,** 850 River Rd., Prince George (© **800/663-8843** or 250/561-0432; www.nbctourism.com).

THE INSIDE PASSAGE ⊛

Fifteen hours may seem like a long time to be on a ferry. But you'll never get bored as the *Queen of the North* ⊛ noses its way through an incredibly scenic series of channels and calm inlets, flanked by green forested islands. Whales, porpoises, salmon, bald eagles, and sea lions line the route past the mostly uninhabited coastline. This 491km (304-mile) BC Ferries run between Port Hardy and Prince Rupert follows the same route as expensive Alaska-bound cruise ships, but at a fraction of the cost. And in midsummer, with the north's long days, the trip is made almost entirely in daylight.

The ferry from Port Hardy initially crosses a couple hours' worth of open sea—where waters can be rough—before ducking behind Calvert Island. Except for a brief patch of open sea in the Milbanke Sound north of Bella Bella, the rest of the trip follows a narrow, protected channel between the mainland and a series of islands.

The actual Inside Passage begins north of Bella Bella, as the ferry ducks behind mountainous Princess Royal and Pitt islands. The passage between these islands and the mainland is very narrow—often less than a mile wide. The scenery is extraordinarily dramatic: Black cliffs drop thousands of feet directly into the channel, notched with hanging glacial valleys and fringed with forests. Powerful waterfalls shoot from dizzying heights into the sea. Eagles float along thermal drafts, and porpoises cavort in the ferry's wake. Even in poor conditions (the weather is very unpredictable here), this is an amazing trip.

The 410-foot *Queen of the North* carries up to 750 passengers and 157 vehicles. On board, you'll find a cafeteria, snack bar, buffet-style dining, playroom, business center, and gift shop. From mid-May to early October, the ferry makes the journey north one day, returning south the next. The rest of the year, service gradually drops to about one ferry per week each way. Mid-summer one-way fares between Prince Rupert and Port Hardy are C$110 (US$88) per adult car passenger or walk-on, C$263 (US$210) for a normal-size vehicle. A car with two passengers adds up to C$483 (US$386). Reservations are mandatory. The ship's cabins rent for between C$55 and C$65 (US$44–US$52) for day use. Ferry service to/from Prince Rupert and Port Hardy continues at least once weekly the rest of the year, with somewhat lower fares. See the BC Ferries website for dates and prices.

In summer, the ferry leaves both Prince Rupert and Port Hardy at 7:30am, so under normal circumstances, you'll arrive at your destination at 10:30pm—thus you probably won't need a cabin to sleep in. You should, however, make lodging reservations at your destination in advance; by the time the ship docks and you wait to drive your car off, it can be close to midnight.

At Prince Rupert, you can also catch an **Alaska Marine Highway ferry** (© 800/ **642-0066;** www.dot.state.ak.us/amhs), which stops here on its run between Bellingham, Washington, and Skagway, Alaska. Passenger fare from Prince Rupert to Skagway is C$183 (US$146) per adult; a car and two adult passengers costs C$771 (US$617). The trip can range anywhere from 30 to 50 hours, depending on the number of stops.

THE DISCOVERY COAST PASSAGE

Also departing from Port Hardy, the Discovery Coast's *Queen of Chilliwack* connects small, mostly First Nations communities along the fiords and islands of the northern coast, including Namu, Bella Bella, Shearwater, Ocean Falls, and Klemtu. The most popular part of this run is the summer-only service to Bella Coola, which links to Highway 20, a paved and gravel road that's a day's drive from Williams Lake, in central British Columbia's Fraser Valley (see "Williams Lake" in chapter 11).

In summer, a direct ferry runs on Thursday to Bella Coola, a Tuesday circular run goes north to McLoughlin Bay and Shearwater before returning to Port Hardy via Bella Coola, and a Saturday circular run goes to the above ports as well as Klemtu and Ocean Falls before returning via Bella Coola (there's a map on the BC Ferries website to help you make sense of the different routings). The Tuesday and Saturday departures require a night on the boat. In high season, fares between Port Hardy and Bella Coola are C$115 (US$92) per adult passenger and C$231 (US$184) for a car. Note that there is no reason to take a car to any of these destinations except for Bella Coola, as there is otherwise no road system to drive on.

For sleeping, you might snag one of 110 extra-wide reclining seats. Otherwise, BC Ferries recommends bringing a tent or cot, which you can set up on the leeward side of the boat. You can rent pillows and blankets for C$5 (US$4); lockers and showers are available. Pets are allowed on board, but must remain in vehicles on the car deck; owners can descend to those decks to tend to their pets' needs.

2 Prince Rupert

491km (304 miles) N of Port Hardy; 756km (469 miles) W of Prince George

British Columbia's most northerly coastal city, Prince Rupert (pop. 17,000) is a city in transition. For years a major fishing and timber port, it is now turning to tourism to bolster its economy. Although scarcely a fancy place, Prince Rupert has much to offer travelers. Eco-tourism has taken off, sportfishing is excellent in local rivers and in the protected waters of Chatham Sound, and the town is a convenient hub for exploring the sights of the Pacific Northwest. From here, ferries go north to Alaska, west to the Queen Charlotte Islands, and south to Vancouver Island and Bellingham, Washington.

Prince Rupert exudes a hard-working, good-natured vigor, and the population is a well-integrated mix of First Nations and European-heritage Canadians. You'll experience the palpable sense of being on the northern edge of the world, which gives the

Prince Rupert

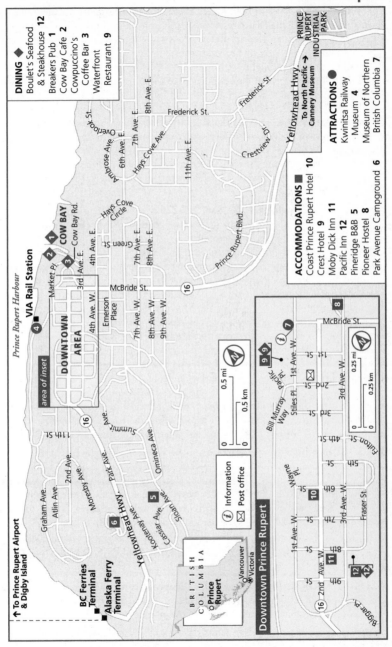

DINING ◆
Boulet's Seafood
& Steakhouse **12**
Breakers Pub **1**
Cow Bay Cafe **2**
Cowpuccino's
Coffee Bar **3**
Waterfront
Restaurant **9**

ATTRACTIONS ●
Kwinitsa Railway
Museum **4**
Museum of Northern
British Columbia **7**

ACCOMMODATIONS ■
Coast Prince Rupert Hotel **10**
Crest Hotel **9**
Moby Dick Inn **11**
Pacific Inn **12**
Pineridge B&B **5**
Pioneer Hostel **8**
Park Avenue Campground **6**

ℹ Information
✉ Post office

Downtown Prince Rupert

city—situated on a series of rock ledges above the broad expanse of the Pacific—a sense of purpose and vitality.

ESSENTIALS

GETTING THERE   By Ferry   For information on BC Ferries service from Port Hardy and Alaska Marine Highway service between southeast Alaska and Washington, see "The Inside Passage," above. For information on BC Ferries service to the Queen Charlotte Islands, see later in this chapter.

By Train   A **VIA Rail** (© **888/VIA-RAIL;** www.viarail.ca) train, the *Skeena,* operates between Prince Rupert and Prince George 4 days weekly (3 in winter). One-way fares start at C$64 (US$51) in summer season. The train follows the same route as the Yellowhead Highway along the scenic Skeena River valley. At Prince George, travelers can continue on to Jasper, with connections to the mainline Via Rail line between Vancouver and Toronto

By Plane   Air Canada Jazz (© **888/247-2262;** www.flyjazz.ca) provides service between Vancouver and Prince Rupert. **Hawkair** (© **800/487-1216;** www.hawkair.ca) also offers daily service from Vancouver.

Both these airlines fly into Prince Rupert's Digby Island airport, which is indeed on an island. Upon collecting their luggage, arriving passengers board a bus that meets every scheduled flight and transports all passengers to the ferry terminal. Once there, the entire bus boards the ferry and crosses to Prince Rupert. The bus deposits the passengers at either the Atlin Terminal (at Cow Bay) for Air Canada Jazz passengers, or at the Howard Johnson Highliner Plaza Hotel for Hawkair passengers. Taxis are available at both termini. The bus/ferry fare from the airport to Prince Rupert is included in your airline ticket so there's no fee assessed for the service while you're traveling. The entire voyage takes roughly 35 minutes. While this process may sound complex, in fact it's as simple as collecting your luggage and getting on the bus. The driver takes care of the rest.

To catch a flight from Digby Island, the process works in reverse. Air Canada Jazz passengers catch the bus at Atlin Terminal, while Hawkair passengers catch the bus at the Highliner Plaza Hotel. Both then proceed across the ferry to the airport. Call the airport bus at © **250/622-2222** to find out what time the bus leaves for your flight.

By Car   Prince Rupert is the terminus of the Yellowhead Highway, Canada's most northerly transcontinental roadway. Between Prince Rupert and Prince George, the route is 756km (469 miles) of extraordinary scenery. For car rentals, call **National** (© **800/CAR-RENT** or 250/624-5318; www.nationalcar.com). If you are planning on renting a car while in Prince Rupert, reserve well in advance, as the cars get snapped up fast, especially on days when trains or ferries arrive.

By Bus   Greyhound Canada (© **800/661-8747** or 604/482-8747; www.greyhound. ca) serves Prince Rupert and Prince George with two buses daily each way. The fare is about C$104 (US$83).

VISITOR INFORMATION   The **Prince Rupert Visitor Info Centre,** Suite 215, Cow Bay Road (© **800/667-1994** in Canada, or 250/624-5637; www.tourismprince rupert.com), is on the waterfront in the new Atlin Terminal building, about 2km (1¼ miles) from Highway 16. It's also the pickup and drop-off point for the Air Canada Jazz bus to/from Digby Island airport. The center is open year-round, Monday through Saturday from 8am to 4pm, Monday through Friday from 5:30 to 9pm, and Sunday from 8 to 11am and 5:30 to 9pm (all day in summer).

Tips **Special Events**

During the second week in June, Prince Rupert hosts **Seafest** (© 250/624-9118), which features a fishing derby, parades, games, food booths, bathtub races, and the annual blessing of the fleet.

EXPLORING THE AREA

Prince Rupert gets more than 18 hours of sunlight a day in summer. And despite its far-north location, this coastal city enjoys a mild climate most of the year. Mountain biking, cross-country skiing, fishing, kayaking, hiking, and camping are just a few of the region's popular activities.

Northern British Columbia's rich Native Indian heritage has been preserved in Prince Rupert's museums and archaeological sites. But you don't need to visit a museum to get a sense of the community's history. Relics of the city's early days are apparent in its old storefronts, miners' shacks, and churches. Built on a series of rocky escarpments, the city rises ledge by ledge, starting at the harbor with a well-established train station and the **Kwinitsa Railway Museum** (© 250/627-1915 or 250/627-3207). This area is overlooked by the old commercial center, with several blocks of turn-of-the-20th-century storefronts still busy with commerce. **Studio 9 Gallery,** 515 Third Ave. W. (© 250/624-2366), offers a selection of local, regional, and First Nation art. **Java dot Cup,** 516 Third St. (© 250/622-2822), is a lively and youthful coffeehouse and Internet cafe. The downtown area is overlooked by the historic residential area, which is dominated by massive stone churches.

The bustling **Cow Bay** district on the north waterfront, with galleries, restaurants, and the visitor center in the new Atlin Terminal building, is Prince Rupert's major center for tourist activity. Just south of Atlin Terminal is Prince Rupert's new cruise-ship dock, which serves a number of cruise lines.

Museum of Northern British Columbia   This museum displays artifacts of the Tsimshian, Nisga'a, and Haida First Nations, who have inhabited this area for more than 10,000 years. There are also artifacts and photographs from Prince Rupert's 19th-century European settlement. In summer, the museum sponsors a number of special programs, including walking tours of Prince Rupert. The gift shop is one of the best places in town to buy Native art. Also sponsored by the museum is the **Carving Shed,** a working studio located a block away on Market Place. There's no sign for the Carving Shed, but you'll recognize it as the long wooden building with a totem pole at the front door. If the door is open, that means that visitors are welcome. Be discreet while the carvers concentrate. There is no admission, but tips are welcome.

100 First Ave. © **250/624-3207.** Fax 250/627-8009. www.museumofnorthernbc.com. Admission C$5 (US$4) adults, C$2 (US$1.60) students, C$1 (US80¢) children 6–11, C$10 (US$8) families. MC, V. Summer Mon–Sat 9am–8pm, Sun 9am–5pm; winter Mon–Sat 10am–5pm.

North Pacific Historic Fishing Village ⊛   Salmon canning was one of the region's original industries, back when the salmon run up the Skeena River was one of the greatest in North America. The province's oldest working salmon-cannery village, built on the waterfront of Inverness Passage in 1889, was home to hundreds of First Nations, Japanese, Chinese, and European workers and their families. Every summer, fishing fleets dropped off their catches at the cannery, where the salmon was packed and shipped out to world markets. This company-owned community reached its apex from 1910 to 1950, when the workforce numbered 400 and the community grew to about 1,200; the cannery has been closed since 1968.

Now a National Historic Site, the North Pacific Cannery Village Museum complex includes the cannery building, various administration buildings and residences, the company store, a hotel, and a dining hall—a total of over 25 structures linked by a long boardwalk (the land is so steep here that most of the houses were built on wharves). Workers were segregated by race: the Chinese, Japanese, and Native Canadian workers had their own micro-neighborhoods along the boardwalk, all overseen by the European bosses. Guided tours of the cannery complex, offered on the hour, provide a very interesting glimpse into a forgotten way of life.

The **boardinghouse** now operates as the historically authentic B&B, the **Waterfront Inn,** which is rustic but clean and cheerful with small rooms and squeaky floors—a very unique experience. Doubles cost C$55 (US$44). The **Cannery Café** and **Forge Broiler Bar** are open during museum hours, and the **Salmon House Restaurant** (© 250/628-3273) is open 11am to 7pm year-round.

20km (12 miles) south of Prince Rupert in Port Edward. Mailing address: Box 1104, Prince Edward, BC V0V 1G0. © 250/628-3538. Admission C$12 (US$9.60) adults, C$9.95 (US$8) seniors and students, free for children 6 and under. May 15–Sept 30 daily 9am–6pm. Call for off-season hours. Take the Port Edward turnoff on Hwy. 16 and drive 5km (3 miles) past Port Edward on Skeena Dr.

ARCHAEOLOGICAL, WILDLIFE & ADVENTURE TOURS

Prince Rupert is at the center of an amazingly scenic area, but unless you have your own boat, you'll find it hard to get around. A good option is to sign on with a local tour operator. One of the most unusual excursions is the **Pike Island Archaeological Tour,** operated by the Metlakatla band of the Tsimshian First Nation. Tiny Pike Island (Laxspa'aws) is 9km (5½ miles) from Prince Rupert in Venn Passage, and is at the center of a rich archaeological area that was once one of the most densely populated regions in pre-Contact Native America. The island has three village sites which were abandoned 18 to 20 centuries ago. Although none have been excavated, guides point out the house depressions in the forest floor and discuss the midden deposits, the shellfish and bone piles that were essentially the garbage pits of these prehistoric people. Tours are offered daily from May to Labour Day, starting at 11:30am and returning to Prince Rupert at 4pm. The trails on the island are not difficult, but are not wheelchair accessible. The Pike Island tours are offered by **Seashore Charters** (© 800/667-4393 or 250/624-5645), which has an office at Atlin Terminal. Harbor tours by boat and city tours by bus cost C$20 (US$16), and whale-watching tours are C$75 (US$60).

One of Prince Rupert's most unique adventures takes you to Canada's only wildlife preserve dedicated to the grizzly bear. Access to the **Khutzeymateen Grizzly Bear Preserve,** northwest of Prince Rupert, is highly restricted, and a very limited number of outfitters can offer trips to this pristine wilderness, home to abundant numbers of *Ursus horribilis.* There's no other access to the preserve, and humans are forbidden to actually land. The most affordable option is **Palmerville Adventures** (© 888/580-2234 or 250/624-8243; www.palmerville.bc.ca), which offers trips to the preserve on jet boats. Their half-day trip combines an air flight (either by seaplane or helicopter, depending on the size of the group) plus a journey into the preserve on a covered jet boat, with rates starting at C$375 (US$300) per person. Although **Prince Rupert Adventure Tours** (© 800/201-8377 or 250/627-9166; www.westcoastlaunch.com)

is not one of the two outfitters that are allowed into the Khutzeymateen preserve itself, this outfitter does offer affordable day trips to the area near the wilderness area. Of course the grizzlies don't recognize boundaries, so the chances of viewing bears, as well as other wildlife such as eagles, seals, and mountain goats, is good. A 6-hour trip, including a sack lunch, is C$145 (US$116) for adults. This outfitter also offers a variety of whale- and wildlife-watching tours, kayak drop-off and pickup, plus the popular, 1½- to 2-hour Kaien Island Circle Tours trip, which circumnavigates Prince Rupert's Kaien Island. The trip visits the city's busy docks, the seaplane terminal, and circles the island to view wildlife and such phenomenon as reversing tidal rapids. The cost is C$45 (US$36). Tours leave from Atlin Terminal at Cow Bay.

For a historical 2-hour walking tour of the city, contact **Heritage Walking Tour** (© **250/624-3207** or 250/624-5637). It leaves daily May through August from the Museum of Northern British Columbia (see above) and is free with museum admission. A self-guided walking-tour booklet is also available for C$2 (US$1.60).

OTHER OUTDOOR PURSUITS

FISHING   Prince Rupert is famed for its excellent sportfishing. There are dozens of charter operators based in town. The **Visitor Info Centre,** in Cow Bay (© **800/667-1994** in Canada, or 250/624-5637; www.tourismprincerupert.com), or **Seashore Charters** (© **800/667-4393** or 250/624-5645) can steer you to the one that best serves your needs.

Fishing charters can range in length from a half-day to weeklong trip, and range in facilities from rough-and-ready boats to luxury cruisers. Expect a guided trip to cost from C$450 (US$360) per day. Long-established companies include **Frohlich's Fish Guiding** (© **250/627-8443;** www.fishing-charter.net) and **Predator Fishing Charters** (© **250/627-1993;** www.citytel.net/~predator), which also provides charters for diving. **Pacific Northwest BC Sea Tours and Charters' New Pacifica Charters** (© **250/624-3272** or 250/624-1964) offers outings for fishing, diving, wildlife-viewing, and photography.

HIKING   **Far West Sports,** 212 Third Ave. W. (© **250/624-2568**), is one of the best sources of information about hiking and mountain-biking trails. The area experiences annual as well as seasonal changes in trail conditions, and some hiking and backcountry ski areas are too challenging for beginners.

There are a number of good hiking options right in Prince Rupert. One trail follows Hays Creek from McBride Street down to the harbor. Just 6.4km (4 miles) east on Highway 16 is a trail head for three more wilderness hikes. The 4km (2½-mile) loop **Butze Rapids Trail** winds through wetlands to Grassy Bay and to Butze Rapids, a series of tidal cataracts. The sometimes-steep trail to the **Tall Trees** grove of old-growth cedars and to the viewpoint on **Mount Oldfield** requires more stamina. Check with the visitor center or the **North Coast Forest District Office,** 125 Market Place (© **250/624-7460;** www.for.gov.bc.ca/dnc/rec/recreation.htm), for more information.

KAYAKING & CANOEING   The waters surrounding Prince Rupert are tricky, and rough tidal swells and strong currents are common. **Skeena Kayaking** (© **250/624-5246;** www.skeenakayaking.ca) offers kayak trips along the Skeena River and to the Kutzmateen Grizzly Bear Sanctuary. A 4-hour kayak rental is C$40 (US$32).

WHERE TO STAY

The **Pioneer Hostel,** 167 Third St. E. (© **888/794-9998** or 250/624-2334; www.citytel.net/pioneer), is in a historic rooming house within easy walking distance to both downtown and Cow Bay. Under new ownership, Pioneer Hostel is well-run and clean, with accommodations from C$16 to C$35 (US$13–US$28) a person.

A mile from the ferry terminal, **Park Avenue Campground,** 1750 Park Ave. (© **800/667-1994** or 250/624-5861; fax 250/627-8009), has 77 full-hookup and 10 unserviced sites, plus open areas for tent camping. Facilities include laundry, showers, toilets, playground, and phones. Reserve in advance in summer. Rates are C$15 (US$12) for tenters to C$29 (US$23) for RVs.

Coast Prince Rupert Hotel   Right downtown, the six-story Coast offers views of the harbor and mountains from just about every spacious room. Rooms are well maintained and feature standard business travel furnishings. The hotel's one suite is a good deal at C$165 (US$132), with a king bed and a separate corner sitting room with a kitchen. Three meals daily are offered at Charlie's, just off the lobby, while drinks are available at the Rupert Pub. There's dancing 3 nights a week at Bogart's.

118 Sixth St., Prince Rupert, BC V8J 3L7. © **800/663-1144** or 250/624-6711. Fax 250/624-3288. www.coasthotels. com. 92 units. C$130 (US$104) double. Extra person C$10 (US$8). Family plan, corporate, and off-season rates, and senior and AAA discounts available. AE, DC, DISC, MC, V. **Amenities:** Restaurant; lounge; club; golf course nearby; guest passes to full-service health club; limited room service; laundry service; same-day dry cleaning; beer-and-wine store. *In room:* A/C, TV, dataport, fridge (on request), coffeemaker, hair dryer, iron, free high-speed Internet.

Crest Hotel ⊛   The Crest offers the best views in town, good dining, and beautifully furnished, though not expansive, rooms. Situated on the bluff's edge overlooking Tuck Inlet, Metlakatla Pass, and the harbor, this is one of the finest hotels in northern British Columbia. The rooms feature quality furniture, feather duvets, and a relaxed stylishness. Standard rooms come with either two doubles or one queen bed; suites feature king beds. The wood-paneled lobby and common rooms are opulent, and it's hard to imagine more impressive views anywhere than from the jutting outdoor hot tub and the well-equipped fitness room. The staff will happily set you up with fishing charters and wildlife-viewing trips. The Waterfront Restaurant is the best in town (see "Where to Dine," below), and Charley's Lounge, with a heated deck, has the city's best year-round view from a bar stool.

222 First Ave. W., Prince Rupert, BC V8J 3P6. © **800/663-8150** or 250/624-6711. Fax 250/627-7666. www.cresthotel. bc.ca. 102 units. C$147–C$167 (US$104–US$119) double; C$209–C$279 (US$167–US$223) suite. AE, MC, V. Free parking. Small pets allowed for C$10 (US$8). **Amenities:** Restaurant; coffee shop; bar; golf course nearby; health club; Jacuzzi; sauna; limited room service; dry cleaning. *In room:* TV w/pay movies, dataport, coffeemaker, hair dryer, iron, wireless high-speed Internet.

Moby Dick Inn   Well established and comfortable, the Moby Dick is a clean, unfussy choice—it's all the hotel most travelers will need while in Prince Rupert. It has a central location between downtown and the ferry docks. Rooms are nicely outfitted and some of them have harbor views. Wheelchair-accessible units are available.

935 Second Ave. W., Prince Rupert, BC V8J 1H8. © **800/663-0822** or 250/624-6961. Fax 250/624-3760. www.moby dickinn.com. C$84–C$94 (US$67–US$75) double. Children under 12 stay free in parent's room. AE, DC, DISC, MC, V. Small pets allowed. **Amenities:** Restaurant; bar; golf course nearby; Jacuzzi; sauna; limited room service; coin-op laundry; rooms for those w/limited mobility. *In room:* TV, dataport, fridge, coffeemaker, hair dryer.

Pacific Inn *(Value)*   Recently renovated, this motor lodge is a good value for its large, clean, and attractive rooms in a convenient location, midway between downtown and the ferry docks. The owners take pride in the place, and it shows. The front desk will arrange local tours and activities; Boulet's Seafood and Steakhouse (see below) is one of the best places in town to eat local seafood.

909 Third Ave. W., Prince Rupert, BC V8J 1M9. C **888/663-1999** or 250/627-1711. Fax 250/627-4212. www.pacific inn.bc.ca. 77 units. C$95–C$110 (US$76–US$88) double. Rates include continental breakfast. Off-season rates and senior discounts available. AE, MC, V. Pets allowed for C$10 (US$8). **Amenities:** Restaurant; golf course nearby; coin-op laundry across street. *In room:* TV, dataport, fridge (on request), coffeemaker, hair dryer.

Pineridge B&B 🐟🐟 This very attractive B&B sits above the town, between down-town and the ferry terminals, and offers the largest and most sophisticated rooms in Prince Rupert. The uncluttered bedrooms are furnished with quality art (the owners are also gallery owners) and feature soothing colors, handsome pine furniture, and nice touches such as bathrobes and down duvets. Guests share a large sitting room with a TV, fridge, couches, a library, phone, and games. The traditional European breakfast is a highlight of the stay. The entire house is tastefully decorated with clean-lined, modern furnishings and local art and crafts. The friendly hosts will help you plan activities and arrange charters.

1714 Sloan Ave., Prince Rupert, BC V8J 3Z9. C **888/733-6733** or 250/627-4419. Fax 250/624-2366. www.pineridge. bc.ca. 3 units. Summer C$90 (US$72) double; off season C$70 (US$56) double. Rates include full breakfast. MC, V. Follow signs to ferry terminal, turn left (or from ferry turn right) onto Smithers St., go 2 blocks, and turn right onto Sloan Ave. Not suitable for children. **Amenities:** Washer/dryer available for use (extra fee); nonsmoking facility. *In room:* Hair dryer, iron (on request), robes, no phone.

WHERE TO DINE

Cowpuccino's Coffee Bar, 25 Cow Bay Rd. (C **250/627-1395**), is a friendly, slightly funky coffee shop with good homemade muffins at breakfast and desserts in the evening.

Boulet's Seafood and Steakhouse SEAFOOD Ask the locals for the best seafood restaurant in Prince Rupert, and chances are they will recommend Boulet's. All the seafood is locally caught, and then prepared simply—many fish are simply steamed and served with light sauces to emphasize the exquisite freshness of the catch. The menu usually includes fresh Skeena salmon, halibut, rock fish, crab, prawns, shrimp, and oysters; steaks and poultry are also available. The dining room, in the Pacific Inn Hotel, is comfortably casual.

In the Pacific Inn Hotel, 909 Third Ave. W. C **250/627-1711.** Reservations suggested. Main courses C$18–C$33 (US$14–US$26). AE, MC, V. Daily 4–10pm.

Breakers Pub 🐟 PUB Breakers is a popular pub with a harbor view and well-pre-pared international food. The offerings range from salads and wraps to pasta, pizza, and grilled local fish. This is a hopping social spot, with a new game room and dance floor; the young and prosperous of Prince Rupert gather here to get happy with a microbrew or two.

117 George Hills Way (on the Cow Bay Wharf). C **250/624-5990.** Reservations not needed. Main courses C$6–C$21 (US$4.80–US$17). AE, DC, MC, V. Mon–Thurs 11:30am–midnight; Fri–Sat 11:30am–1am; Sun noon–midnight.

Cow Bay Café 🐟 PACIFIC NORTHWEST This homey place is like a little Van-couver street cafe plunked down on the edge of a dock. The casual, slightly hippie atmosphere feels refreshing so far north, and is nicely matched by the menu, which features lots of vegetarian options. Choices include salads, pastas, soups, and sand-wiches; at night, fresh fish is prepared with zest. Order dessert when you order the rest of your meal, because popular items often sell out by the end of the evening.

205 Cow Bay Rd. ⓒ 250/627-1212. Reservations recommended. Main courses C$11–C$20 (US$8.80–US$16). AE, MC, V. Tues noon–2:30pm; Wed–Sat noon–2:30pm and 6–8:30pm.

Waterfront Restaurant ⭐⭐ PACIFIC NORTHWEST   Easily Prince Rupert's most sophisticated restaurant, the Waterfront is flanked by banks of windows that overlook the busy harbor. The white-linen-and-crystal elegance of the dining room is matched by the inventiveness of the cuisine. Understandably, much of the menu is devoted to local seafood; Skeena River salmon and sea scallops are served in pesto cream, and Pacific Northwest hot pot combines local halibut, mussels, sea scallops, prawns, and salmon with tomato broth and basil oil. "Casual plates" feature smaller portions, salads, and tempting appetizers such as alder-smoked steelhead with red onions and caper berries. The wine list features a number of impressive B.C. vintages.

In the Crest Hotel, 222 First Ave. W. ⓒ 250/624-6771. www.cresthotel.bc.ca. Reservations suggested. Main courses C$17–C$36 (US$14–US$29). AE, DC, MC, V. Daily 6:30am–10pm.

3 The Queen Charlotte Islands

The misty and mysterious Queen Charlotte Islands were the muse for 19th-century painter Emily Carr, who documented her impressions of the towering totem poles and longhouses at the abandoned village of Ninstints, on Anthony Island. The islands still lure artists, writers, and photographers wishing to experience their haunting beauty.

The Queen Charlottes—also called by their Native name, Haida Gwaii—are the homeland of the Haida people. Sometimes referred to as the Vikings of the Pacific, the Haida were mighty seafarers, and during raiding forays, ranged as far south along the Pacific Coast as Oregon. The Haida were also excellent artists, carvers of both totems and argillite, a slatelike rock that they transformed into tiny totemic sculptures and pendants. The Haida today make up about half of the islands' population of 6,000.

The Queen Charlottes have a reputation as the "Canadian Galapagos," as these islands—ranging between 51km and 136km (32–84 miles) from the mainland—have evolved their own endemic species and subspecies of flora and fauna. The Canadian government preserved the southern portion of Moresby Island as **Gwaii Haanas National Park Reserve and Haida Heritage Site** ⭐. UNESCO followed suit by naming the islands a World Heritage Site.

The islands are primordial and beautiful, but visiting them requires some planning. In fact, if you're reading this in Prince Rupert and thinking about a spur-of-the-moment trip to the Charlottes, you may want to reconsider. Lodging on the islands is limited, and reservations are necessary year-round. The most interesting areas—the abandoned Haida villages—are accessible only by boat, and the Gwaii Haanas National Park limits the number of people who can daily access the archaeological sites. There are only 125km (78 miles) of paved roads, and none of them even come close to the park or the islands' wild western coastline. In short, simply showing up on the Queen Charlottes is not a good idea. The best way to visit is by arranging, in advance, to join a guide or outfitter on a kayaking, flightseeing, sailing, or boating excursion.

ESSENTIALS

GETTING THERE   By Ferry   BC Ferries (ⓒ **888/BC-FERRY** in B.C., or 250/386-3431; www.bcferries.bc.ca) crosses between Prince Rupert and Skidegate, on northerly Graham Island. The 6½- to 7-hour crossing can be quite rough; take precautions if you're prone to seasickness. Ferries run daily in summer; call ahead to reserve.

The one-way high-season tickets are C$25 (US$20) for a passenger and C$97 (US$77) for most passenger vehicles.

By Plane   **Air Canada Jazz** (© **888/247-2262;** www.flyjazz.ca) provides daily flights from Vancouver to Sandspit Airport on northern Moresby Island. **Pacific Coastal Airlines** (© **800/663-2872** or 604/273-8666; www.pacific-coastal.com) provides daily service from Vancouver's South Terminal to Masset during the summer and service three times a week during the shoulder and winter season. **North Pacific Seaplanes** (© **800/689-4234** or 250/627-1341; www.northpacificseaplanes.com) has daily float plane service between Prince Rupert and Masset (C$153/US$122 one-way) and service three times a week between Prince Rupert and Sandspit/Queen Charlotte City.

VISITOR INFORMATION   The **Queen Charlotte Islands Visitor Info Centre,** 3220 Wharf St., Queen Charlotte (© **250/559-8316;** www.qcinfo.com), is open May through September daily from 8am to 8pm. On Graham Island, the **Masset Visitor Info Centre,** 1455 Old Beach Rd., Masset (© **888/352-9292** or 250/626-3982; www.island.net/~masset), is open in July and August daily from 11am to 5pm. You can also check out **www.qcislands.net/tourism**.

GETTING AROUND   In the Queen Charlotte Islands, the island-to-island **Skidegate–Alliford Bay ferry** operates 12 daily sailings between the main islands. The fare is C$6 (US$4.80) each way or C$14 (US$11) per vehicle. With so few roads on the islands, it's fair to ask if it even makes sense to take a car on a short trip. **Budget** (© **250/559-4675**), **Rustic Car Rentals** (© **250/559-4641**), **Tilden** (© **250/626-3318**), and **Thrifty** (© **250/559-8050**) have car-rental offices on the islands.

EXPLORING THE ISLANDS

Most visitors come to the Charlottes to view its abundant and unusual wildlife, and to visit the ancient Haida villages. In both cases, you'll need to either have your own boat or arrange for a guide to get you from the islands' small settlements to the even more remote areas. The islands provide superlative wilderness adventures—camping, hiking, diving, sailing, kayaking, and fishing—although due to their isolation and sometimes extreme weather, you'll need to plan ahead before setting out.

   Graham Island is the more populous of the two major islands. **Queen Charlotte City** is a fishing and logging town with a population of about 1,200, sitting above the scenic waters of Beaverskin Bay. QCC, as the village is sometimes dubbed, has the majority of lodgings and facilities for travelers, as well as the administrative headquarters for **Gwaii Haanas National Park Reserve** (see below).

   Skidegate Village (pronounced "*skid*-a-gut"), just east of the Skidegate ferry terminal, is home to the **Haida Gwaii Museum at Quay 'Ilnagaay** (© **250/559-4643**), which houses the world's largest collection of argillite carvings, made from the slate-like stone found only in the Queen Charlottes. Admission is C$3 (US$2.40) for adults; the museum is open Monday through Friday from 10am to 5pm and Saturday and Sunday from 1 to 5pm (closed Sun Sept–May and Tues Dec–May). Next to the museum is the longhouse-style office of the **Haida Gwaii Watchmen,** the Native guardians of the islands' Haida villages and heritage sites. Ask here for information on visiting these sites.

   Heading north from Skidegate on Highway 16, **Tlell** is an old agricultural community and now somewhat of an artists' colony; watch for signs pointing to studios. Past the logging town of Port Clements, the highway ends at **Masset,** the island's largest town with a population pushing 1,500. **Old Massett,** just north of Masset, is one of the largest Haida settlements on the island, and a good place to shop for carvings and jewelry. Just north of the Masset town center, trails lead through the **Delkatla Wildlife Sanctuary,** one of the first southerly landfalls on the Pacific Flyway.

From Masset, continue north and then east on Tow Hill Road to **Naikoon Provincial Park,** where whales can be spotted from the beaches and peregrine falcons fly overhead. The **Agate Beach Campground** (© 250/847-7320) is a popular place to camp (C$14/US$11).

On **Moresby Island,** the principal center of population is **Sandspit** (pop. 460). In summer, Parks Canada operates an information center for visitors headed to the wilderness **Gwaii Haanas National Park Reserve and Haida Heritage Site** ☞. There are no roads or shore facilities in the park, and access is by boat or floatplane only. Although there are many amazing sights in this part of the Queen Charlottes, you'll need to be committed to the journey to get here: The distances are great and the costs high. If you're a dedicated wildlife watcher, it may be worth it to see the rare fauna and flora. Perhaps the most famous site in the park is **SGang Gwaay 'Ilnagaay,** or **Ninstints,** on Anthony Island, an ancient Native village revered as sacred ground by the modern-day Haida. Centuries-old totem poles and longhouses proudly stand in testimony to the culture's 10,000-year heritage.

You must attend a mandatory orientation session before entering Gwaii Haanas National Park, and reservations are required. Call **Super Natural British Columbia** at © 800/435-5622 to reserve a spot; reservations are C$15 (US$12). Only a limited number of people are allowed to enter Gwaii Haanas per day, and these are apportioned between those on organized tours and those traveling independently. Entry to the park is C$10/US$8 per day. (Six standby places are also available daily on a first-come, first-served basis.) The **Haida Gwaii Watchmen** (© 250/559-8225) manage access to SGang Gwaay 'Ilnagaay and other ancient villages in the park, and watchmen members there will explain the history and cultural significance of the sites you may visit. For more information, contact **Gwaii Haanas National Park Reserve,** Box 37, Queen Charlotte City, BC V0T 1S0 (© 250/559-8818; www.pc.gc.ca/pn-np/bc/gwaiihaanas), or the **Queen Charlotte Islands Visitor Info Centre** (© 250/559-8316; www.qcinfo.com).

TOURS & EXCURSIONS TO GWAII HAANAS NATIONAL PARK RESERVE

Outfitters must be registered with park officials; the list of authorized tour operators is the best place to start shopping for expeditions into the park. Note that the park entry fee of C$10 (US$8) per day may or may not be included in the cost of tour packages, so ask when booking.

Many outfitters, such as **Butterfly Tours Great Expeditions** (© 604/740-7018; www.butterflytours.bc.ca)—alternately booked through **Great Expeditions** (© 800/663-3364 or 604/257-2040; www.greatexpeditions.com)—offer kayaking packages that suit every age and experience level; Butterfly's 8-day tours start at C$1,950 (US$1,560). Longtime sea-kayak outfitter **Ecosummer Expeditions** (© 800/465-8884 or 250/674-0102; www.ecosummer.com) offers 7-day trips to Gwaii Haanas, with prices starting at C$1,995 (US$1,596). **Pacific Rim Paddling Company** (© 250/384-6103; www.pacificrimpaddling.com) has both 7- and 8-day kayak trips to the park, with prices from C$1,595 (US$1,276).

Sailing into Gwaii Haanas is another popular option, and most sailboat operators also have kayaks aboard for guests' use. **Bluewater Adventures** (© 888/877-1770 or

604/980-3800; www.bluewateradventures.ca) offers 8-day tours starting at C$3,145 (US$2,516). **Ocean Light II Adventures** (℃ **604/328-5339;** www.oceanlight2.bc.ca) offers 8-day Haida Gwaii sailings on a 22m (72-ft.) boat for C$3,366 (US$2,692).

South Moresby Air Charters (℃ **888/551-4222** or 250/559-4222; www.qc islands.net/smoresby) offers sightseeing seaplane flights to Hot Springs Island and SGang Gwaay 'Ilnagaay. The latter trip includes a landing at Rose Bay and a 40-minute boat ride to the ancient village, plus a guided tour. It costs C$1,795 (US$1,436) for one to four people; check the website, as weight restrictions may apply.

Diving charters around the islands, but not in Gwaii Haanas, can be arranged through **Emerald Sea Sail and Scuba** (℃ **250/635-5818;** www3.telus.net/emeraldsea).

FISHING

Langara Fishing Adventures (℃ **800/668-7544** or 604/232-5532; www.langara. com) offers fishing packages with accommodations at one of the most beautiful lodges in western Canada. Geared toward those who want to be pampered, the outfitter picks up guests at Vancouver Airport and delivers them to Langara Island, just north of Graham Island. The rooms at the Langara Island Lodge are luxurious, and the dining room serves expertly prepared Pacific Northwest dishes. Packages include air transport from Vancouver, lodging, meals, boats, tackle, weather gear, and freezing or canning of your catch. Guided fishing trips cost extra, as do whale-watching and heli-touring. Also available are fishing trips to even more remote fishing lodges in the Queen Charlottes. Rates start at C$3,495 (US$2,796) for a 4-day trip; packages are offered April to October.

For something more low-key, **Naden Lodge,** 1496 Kelkatla St., Masset (℃ **800/ 771-8933** or 250/626-3322; www.nadenlodge.bc.ca), offers B&B accommodations and guided fishing trips from a lovely location right above Masset's boat basin. Numerous charter operators can be found in Masset, Queen Charlotte, and Skidegate. Contact the **Queen Charlotte Islands Visitor Info Centre** (℃ **250/559-8316;** www. qcinfo.com) for suggestions.

WHERE TO STAY & DINE

Food on these remote islands is pretty perfunctory. Stop in at the **Mile Zero Pub,** Collison Avenue at Main Street, Masset (℃ **250/626-3210**), for a pint and a fish tale or two. The **Sandpiper Restaurant,** Collison Avenue at Orr Street in Masset (℃ **250/ 626-3672**), serves hearty portions of seafood, steaks, pasta dishes, sandwiches, and salads. **Oceana,** at 3119 Third Ave. in Queen Charlotte City (℃ **250/559-8683**), offers both Chinese and Continental cuisine, and is open for lunch and dinner.

Dorothy & Mike's Guest House   The atmosphere here is serene: A large deck overlooks the Skidegate Inlet, while gardens surround the house. The warm, cozy guest rooms are filled with local art and antiques; one suite comes with a full kitchen and all three have private entrances. All guests have access to a common area with an entertainment center and reading library. The inn is within walking distance of the ocean, restaurants, and shopping.

3127 Second Ave. (Box 595), Queen Charlotte City, BC V0T 1S0. ℃ 250/559-8439. Fax 250/559-8439. www.qc islands.net/doromike. 9 units, 3 with shared bathroom. May–Sept C$65 (US$52) double with shared bathroom; C$80–C$90 (US$64–US$72) double with private bathroom. Rates include breakfast. Off-season rates available. No credit cards. Drive 3.5km (2 miles) away from the Skidegate ferry terminal on Second Ave. *In room:* TV.

Premier Creek Lodging   Great for the budget-conscious, this heritage lodge dates back to 1910. Many rooms have great views over gardens to Bearskin Bay. There's a range of accommodations, from small, single units with shared bathrooms to suites with kitchens. There's also a full-fledged hostel in a separate building (C$19/US$14).

3101 Third Ave. (Box 268), Queen Charlotte City, BC V0T 1S0. ✆ 888/322-3388 or 250/559-8415. Fax 250/559-8198. 14 units. C$60–C$75 (US$48–US$60) double. AE, MC, V. **Amenities:** Restaurant; bike rentals. *In room:* TV, kitchen (some units only), no phone (except in larger rooms).

Sea Raven Motel   The largest lodging in the Queen Charlottes, the Sea Raven is a comfortable motel with many room types, ranging from simple single units to deluxe accommodations with decks; many have ocean views. A few units sport kitchenettes. The rooms are simply furnished, but very clean.

3301 Third Ave. (Box 519), Queen Charlotte City, BC V0T 1S0. ✆ 800/665-9606 or 250/559-4423. Fax 250/559-8617. www.searaven.com. 29 units. C$75–C$95 (US$60–US$76) double. AE, DC, MC, V. Limited street parking available. Pets allowed for C$10 (US$8). **Amenities:** Restaurant; golf course nearby; kayak and bike rentals; tour/activities desk; car-rental desk; laundry service. *In room:* TV, kitchenette (5 rooms only), coffeemaker.

Spruce Point Lodging   This rustic inn, overlooking the Hecate Strait, features rooms with private entrances as well as excellent views. Each unit has a fridge and a choice of either private shower or tub. Some rooms have full kitchen facilities, and all have complimentary tea and coffee service. The shared balcony is used as a guest lounge. Your friendly hosts can arrange kayaking packages to the surrounding islands. *Note:* Guests may smoke only on outside decks.

609 Sixth Ave., Queen Charlotte City (on Graham Island), BC V0T 1S0. ✆ 250/559-8234. www.qcislands.net/spr point. 7 units. C$80 (US$64) double. MC, V. Drive about 15 min. west on the main road away from the Skidegate ferry terminal, then turn left at Sam & Shirley's Grocery (the corner store). *In room:* TV, fridge, coffeemaker.

4 The Yellowhead Highway: From Prince Rupert to Prince George

It's a long 756km (469 miles) from Prince Rupert to Prince George. Even though it's possible to make the journey in 1 long day, it's far more pleasant to take it slowly, enjoy the scenery, and stop at some of the cultural sights along the way.

The route initially follows the glacier-carved Skeena River valley inland, through the industrial city of **Terrace** and to the **Hazeltons,** twin towns with a lovely river setting and an excellent First Nations cultural center. **Smithers,** cradled in a rich agricultural valley, is another scenic spot, and the most pleasant place along the route to spend a night. Between Burns Lake and Fort Fraser is a series of long, thin lakes, famed for trout angling and rustic fishing resorts.

ESSENTIALS
GETTING THERE   By Car   Terrace is 152km (94 miles) east of Prince Rupert on the Yellowhead Highway (Hwy. 16). From Terrace to Prince George, it's another 571km (354 miles).

By Train   VIA Rail (✆ 888/VIA-RAIL; www.viarail.ca) operates four-times-weekly service between Prince George and Prince Rupert, with stops including Smithers, New Hazelton, and Terrace. The train follows the same route as the Yellowhead Highway.

By Bus   Greyhound Canada (✆ 800/661-8747 or 604/482-8747; www.greyhound.ca) travels twice daily between Prince Rupert and Prince George. One-way fare from Prince Rupert to Terrace is about C$30 (US$24).

VISITOR INFORMATION   The **Northern BC Tourism Association,** 850 River Rd., Prince George (✆ 800/663-8843 or 250/561-0432; www.nbctourism.com), provides extensive information on the area.

TERRACE & NISGA'A MEMORIAL LAVA BEDS PROVINCIAL PARK

The Yellowhead Highway (Hwy. 16) follows the lush Skeena River valley from Prince Rupert, on the coast of the Inside Passage, to the province's interior. It's the gateway to the land-based return route from the Inside Passage ferry cruise. The long, winding valley is home to a diverse community of fishers, loggers, and aluminum and paper-mill workers in Terrace, and is the ancestral home of the Gitxsan, Haisla, Tsimshian, and Nisga'a First Nations.

If you want to understand glacial geology, this drive will provide instant illumination. It's easy to picture the steep-sided valley choked with a bulldozer of ice, grinding the walls into sheer cliffs. Streams drop thousands of feet in a series of waterfalls. There are many small picnic areas along this route; plan on stopping beside the Skeena to admire the astonishing view.

Terrace is an industrial town of about 14,000, and has only just begun to develop itself for tourism. Stop by the store at the **House of Sim-oi-Ghets,** off Highway 16 (© **250/638-1629;** www.kitsumkalum.bc.ca/house.html), a cedar longhouse owned by the Kitsumkalum tribal band of the Tsimshian Nation. It offers jewelry, carvings, bead and leather work, and moccasins.

For area information, stop by the **Terrace Visitor Info Centre,** 4511 Keith Ave. (© **800/499-1637** or 250/635-2063; www.terracetourism.bc.ca), open from June 1 to September 1 daily from 8:30am to 6pm, and September 2 to May 31 Monday through Friday from 8:30am to 4:30pm.

NORTH OF TERRACE

Forty kilometers (25 miles) northwest of town, the **Khutzeymateen Grizzly Bear Preserve** is the province's first official sanctuary of its kind. You must be part of an authorized group or accompanied by a ranger to observe these amazing creatures (see "Archaeological, Wildlife & Adventure Tours," earlier in this chapter).

North America's rarest subspecies of black bear, the **kermodei,** also makes its home in the valley. The kermodei is unique, a nonalbino black bear born with white fur. Its teddy-bear face and round ears are endearing, but the kermodei is even larger than the impressive Queen Charlotte Islands black bear.

Also north of Terrace, at the **Nisga'a Memorial Lava Beds Provincial Park,** vegetation has only recently begun to reappear on the lava plain created by a volcanic eruption and subsequent lava flow in 1750, which consumed this area and nearly all of its inhabitants.

The route to the park's near-lunar landscape begins in Terrace at the intersection of the Yellowhead Highway (Hwy. 16) and Kalum Lake Drive (Nisga'a Hwy.). Follow the paved highway north along the Kalum River past Kalum Lake. Just past Rosswood is **Lava Lake** (where the park boundary begins). While there are a number of short interpretive trails to volcanic curiosities along the parkway, the primary hiking trail is the 3km (2-mile) **Volcanic Cone Trail,** which leads through old-growth forest to a volcanic crater. To protect the site, it is required that you hire a local guide; reservations are mandatory. There are scheduled 4-hour guided hikes at noon on Saturdays and Sundays from the last weekend in June through Labour Day; cost is C$25 (US$20) adult. Call to reserve a space at the park office or © **250/638-8490.** Hikes depart from the **Nisga'a Visitor Centre** (© **250/638-9589;** www.env.gov.bc.ca/bcparks).

Continuing on Nisga'a Highway, the road picks its way across the lava flow. As you approach the Nass River, the road forks: To the left is the visitor center and to the right is the town of **New Aiyansh,** the valley's largest Nisga'a village, with basic facilities for travelers. The entire trip is 120km (74 miles); allow at least 2 hours each way.

The Nass River valley is the homeland of the Nisga'a indigenous peoples. In 1998, the Nisga'a and the Canadian federal government concluded an agreement that gives the Nisga'a tribe full title to about 2,000 sq. km (780 sq. miles) of land, a cash settlement, and powers of self-government. The tribe is opening the land reserve up for ecotourism; for information on fishing and outdoor adventure on the Nass River, contact **True North Adventures** (© 877/362-3382 or 250/362-3382).

Maps also show an unpaved road linking New Aiyansh with Highway 37 to the east. Called the Cranberry Connector by locals, it's a heavily rutted and pot-holed logging road that is perfectly passable but very slow going. If your destination is Stewart or Dease Lake, then it's worth inching your way across this shortcut (it will take about 2 hr. to make the 77km/48-mile journey to Cranberry Junction on Hwy. 37). If you are heading back toward the Hazeltons, however, you're better off returning to Terrace and driving at highway speed up Highway 16.

In winter, **Shames Mountain,** 35km (22 miles) west of town (© 877/898-4754 or 250/635-3773; www.shamesmountain.com), is known for its small crowds and huge quantities of snow. Open mid-December to mid-April, it has one double chair and one T-bar lift, along with 20 groomed trails. Lift tickets are C$39 (US$31) for adults, C$27 (US$22) for seniors and youths 13 to 18, and C$19 (US$15) for children 7 to 12. Facilities include a rental and repair shop, store, cafeteria, and pub.

WHERE TO STAY & DINE

Best Western Terrace Inn   Overlooking the surrounding mountains, this hotel's well-appointed rooms feature little touches not normally found in the backcountry. A few deluxe accommodations sport Jacuzzi tubs. Facilities include a piano bar and lounge, plus a pub with live entertainment. Lava-bed tours are available upon request.

4553 Greig Ave., Terrace, BC V8G 1M7. © 800/488-1898 or 250/635-0083. Fax 250/635-0092. www.bestwestern. com/ca/terraceinn. 62 units. C$71–C$185 (US$57–US$148) double. Group, corporate, senior, and weekend discounts available. AE, DC, DISC, MC, V. Free parking. Small pets accepted for C$10 (US$8). **Amenities:** Restaurant; bar; lounge; well-equipped exercise room; Jacuzzi; room service; laundry service; dry cleaning. *In room:* A/C, TV, dataport, coffeemaker, hair dryer.

Coast Inn of the West   This comfortable hotel in downtown Terrace offers pleasant rooms in the heart of the town. Facilities include a lounge that provides evening entertainment, a gift shop, and a restaurant open for three meals daily.

4620 Lakelse Ave., Terrace, BC V8G 1R1. © 800/663-1144 or 250/638-8141. Fax 250/638-8999. www.coasthotels. com. 58 units. C$65–C$129 (US$52–US$103) double. Senior and AAA rates available. AE, DC, DISC, MC, V. **Amenities:** Restaurant; bar; lounge; golf course nearby; limited room service; laundry service; same-day dry cleaning. *In room:* A/C, TV, dataport, coffeemaker, hair dryer.

Miles Inn on the T'seax ★★ (*Finds*)   Overlooking the Nisga'a Memorial Lava Beds Provincial Park, this beautiful hand-crafted log lodge sits above the Nass River valley. A real showcase of sophisticated hospitality in the midst of wilderness, Miles Inn offers very attractive rooms furnished with handsome furniture. The ground-floor rooms share a large bathroom; this area, with one queen room and a room with two twin beds and a large sitting area, is perfect for a family or friends traveling together. The upstairs rooms each have private bathrooms. A hot tub is available for relaxing tired muscles after a day of hiking, climbing, kayaking the Nass River, or fishing the T'seax River. Home-cooked dinners are available for an extra charge.

Nass Valley (Box 230), New Aiyansh, BC V0J 1A0. ©/fax **250/633-2636.** www.kermode.net/milesinn. 5 units, 3 with private bathroom. C$90 (US$72) double. Rates include breakfast. MC, V. **Amenities:** Jacuzzi; nonsmoking facility. *In room:* No phone.

THE HAZELTONS

The Skeena and Bulkley rivers join at the Hazeltons (pop. 2,000). Straddling two river canyons and set below the rugged Rocher de Boule mountains, the Hazeltons are actu-ally three separate towns: **Hazelton** itself, **South Hazelton,** and **New Hazelton,** all located along a 8km (5-mile) stretch. The junction of these two mighty rivers was home to the Gitxsan and Wet'suwet'en peoples, for whom the rivers provided both transport and a wealth of salmon. In the 1860s, it became the upriver terminus for riverboat traffic on the Skeena, and Hazelton became a commercial hub for miners, ranchers, and other frontier settlers farther inland.

The old town center of Hazelton, though small, still has the feel of a pioneer set-tlement. And you can get a sense of the Gitxsan culture by visiting **'Ksan Historical Village** 👍👍, off Highway 62 (© **877/842-5518** or 250/842-5544; www.ksan.org), a re-creation of a traditional village. Some of the vividly painted longhouses serve as stu-dios, where you can watch artists carve masks and hammer silver jewelry. If possible, plan your visit to coincide with a performance by the **'Ksan Performing Arts Group,** a troupe of singers and dancers who entertain visitors with music, masks, costumes, and pageantry. The shop here is a great source for Native art and gifts, and the Wilp Tokx, or the House of Eating, is a good place to try Native cooking. There's a C$2 (US$1.60) admission for entrance to a small museum and the grounds themselves. To see the interior of the longhouses, you'll need to join a guided tour, which costs C$10 (US$8) for adults, C$8.50 (US$6.80) for seniors and youths. If you take the tour, you don't have to pay the grounds fee. 'Ksan is open from April 15 to October 15 daily from 9am to 6pm. The rest of the year, only the museum and shop are open, Mon-day through Friday from 9:30am to 4:30pm.

There aren't many lodging choices, but the **28 Inn,** 4545 Yellowhead Hwy. 16, New Hazelton (© **877/842-2828** or 250/842-6006; www.28inn.com), with a dining room and pub, is clearly the best, with rooms going for C$65 (US$52). The area's best dining room is the **Hummingbird Restaurant,** 2720 Hwy. 62 (© **250/842-5628**), which serves German specialties. It's open nightly for dinner, weekdays for lunch, and Sunday brunch.

The **'Ksan Historical Village** (see above) and **Seeley Lake Provincial Park,** 9.5km (6 miles) west of New Hazelton (© **250/847-7320**), have campgrounds. For advance information on the area, call the **Hazeltons Travel Info Centre** (© **250/842-6071** in summer, 250/842-6571 Oct–May). The summer-only **visitor center** is at the junc-tion of highways 16 and 62 (Main St.).

SMITHERS & THE BULKLEY VALLEY

Smithers (pop. 6,200) is located in a stunningly beautiful valley that truly resembles the northern Alps. Flanked on three sides by vast ranges of glaciated peaks, it is cut through by the fast-flowing Bulkley River. The heart of Smithers occupies the old commercial strip on **Main Street,** which is perpendicular to the current fast food and motel haven that is Highway 16. This attractive area is lined with Bavarian-theme storefronts that offer outdoor gear, gifts, and local crafts. But what Smithers really has to offer is founds in its gorgeous mountain backdrop. With 2,621m (8,597-ft.) **Hudson Bay Mountain** rising directly behind the town, snowcapped ranges ringing the valley, and the area's fast-flowing rivers and streams, you'll feel the urge to get outdoors.

Driftwood Canyon Provincial Park, 11km (7 miles) northeast of Smithers, preserves fossil-bearing formations laid down 50 million years ago. Considered one of the world's richest fossil beds, the park has interpretive trails leading through a section of exposed creek bed, which was carved by an ice-age glacier. To get here, drive 3km (2 miles) east of Smithers and turn east on Babine Lake Road.

Regional information can be obtained from the **Smithers Visitor Info Centre,** 1411 Court St. (© **800/542-6673** or 250/847-3337; www.tourismsmithers.com). Hours are 9am to 8pm Monday to Saturday mid-May to October 1

OUTDOOR PURSUITS

HIKING The 9km (5½-mile) **Perimeter Trail** is a good place to jog; especially along the Bulkley River in Riverside Park. Two excellent hikes are on **Hudson Bay Mountain.** Three kilometers (2 miles) west of Smithers, take Kathlyn Lake Road 10km (6½ miles) to the trail head. It's an easy .8km (½-mile) stroll to view the impressive **Twin Falls.** From the same trail head, climb up to Glacier Gulch to get close to the toe of **Kathlyn Glacier.** This strenuous hike is just under 6.4km (4 miles) one-way, but allow at least 3 hours to make the climb.

Follow Hudson Bay Mountain Road west out of Smithers for 10km (6½ miles) to **Smithers Community Forest,** with an extensive trail system. The easy 4km (2½-mile) Interpretive Nature Trail makes a loop through the forest. For more rugged hiking, **Babine Mountains Recreation Area** protects 32,400 hectares (80,028 acres) of sub-alpine meadows, lakes, and craggy peaks. This roadless area is accessible only on foot, but many sights are within the range of day hikers. The **Silver King Basin Trail** passes through subalpine forest before reaching an alpine meadow that explodes with wild-flowers in July. To reach the Babine Mountains, go 3km (2 miles) east of Smithers and take Babine Lake Road.

FISHING The Bulkley River has excellent fishing for steelhead, chinook, and coho salmon, though restrictions apply. The best fishing areas on the Bulkley are from the confluence of the Morice River south of Smithers to the town of Telkwa.

WHERE TO STAY

The well-maintained **Aspen Motor Inn,** 4268 Hwy. 16 (© **800/663-7676** or 250/ 847-4551; www.hiway16.com/aspen), offers an on-site restaurant and large rooms from C$80 (US$64). **Riverside Park Municipal Campsite,** 1600 Main St. N. (© **250/ 847-1600**), has 40 sites starting at C$14 (US$11) with dry toilets, fire pits, and water.

Hudson Bay Lodge The largest and most comfortable hotel in Smithers is a popular stop for the tour-bus crowds making their way to and from the Prince Rupert ferries. Crowds notwithstanding, rooms are nicely equipped and the suite has a Jacuzzi, fireplace, and two-person shower.

3251 Hwy. 16 E. (Box 3636), Smithers, BC V0J 2N0. © 800/663-5040 or 250/847-4581. Fax 250/847-4878. www. hblodge.com. 99 units. C$113 (US$90) double. AE, DC, MC, V. Pets allowed for C$5 (US$4). **Amenities:** Restaurant (see Pepper Jack's Grill in "Where to Dine," below); coffee shop; lounge; Jacuzzi; courtesy limo. In room: A/C, TV w/pay movies, coffeemaker, hair dryer.

Stork Nest Inn *Value* The Stork Nest does more than most Smithers lodgings to look Bavarian, with gables, flowers, and a corbeled roofline. Though the rooms aren't the largest in the province, they are clean, pleasant, and nicely furnished. The honeymoon suite features a Jacuzzi; and wheelchair-accessible rooms are available.

1485 Main St. (Box 2049), Smithers, BC V0J 2N0. **©** **250/847-3831.** Fax 250/847-3852. www.storknestinn.com. 23 units. C$75–C$80 (US$60–US$64) double. Rates include full breakfast. AE, MC, V. Free parking. **Amenities:** Golf course nearby; lit tennis courts; sauna; free airport shuttle; rooms for those w/limited mobility. *In room:* A/C, TV, fridge, hair dryer (on request), iron (on request), high-speed Internet access.

WHERE TO DINE

Pepper Jack's Grill, in the Hudson Bay Lodge (see above), serves pasta, gourmet pizza, and other international cuisine. Fresh seafood is a highlight, but the stock in trade is beef. It's open daily from 5 to 10pm. The **Alpenhorn Pub and Bistro,** 1261 Main St. (**©** **250/847-5366**), is a pleasant, sports-bar type of pub with gourmet burgers, pastas, sandwiches, and ribs. It's open daily from 11am to midnight.

THE LAKES DISTRICT

Between Smithers and Prince George lies a vast basin filled with glacier-gouged lakes, dense forests, and rolling mountains. There are over 300 lakes, whose combined shorelines add up to more than 4,800km (2,976 miles). Not surprisingly, sportfishing is the main draw here, and rustic fishing lodges are scattered along the lakeshores.

But this isn't an easy place to plan a casual visit. Many of the lodges are fly-in or boat-in, and offer only weeklong fishing packages. Most are very rustic indeed. If this is what you're looking for, contact the Burns Lake Chamber of Commerce (see below), which can connect you with the lodge or outfitter that suits your needs.

If you have a day to spare and want to explore the region, there's a paved loop starting in Burns Lake that explores the shores of four of the lakes. Take Highway 35 south from Burns Lake, past Tchesinkut Lake to Northbank on François Lake. From here, take the free half-hour ferry across François Lake and continue south to Ootsa Lake. Here, the road turns west, eventually returning to François Lake, Highway 16 at Houston, and then back east to Burns Lake.

Burns Lake is nominally the center of the Lakes District, and if you end up here needing a place to stay, try the **Burns Lake Motor Inn,** on Highway 16 West (**©** **800/663-2968** or 250/692-7545). For information on the region, contact the **Burns Lake Chamber of Commerce,** 540 Yellowhead Hwy. (**©** **250/692-3773**), open in July and August daily and year-round at varying times; call for hours. You can also head online to **www.hiway16.com**.

At Vanderhoof, 133km (82 miles) east of Burns Lake, take Highway 27 north 59km (37 miles) to **Fort St. James National Historic Site** ✻ (**©** **250/996-7191;** www.pc.gc.ca/lhn-nhs/bc/stjames), one of the most interesting historic sites in northern British Columbia. Fort St. James was the earliest non-Native settlement in the province, a fur-trading fort established in 1806. In summer, costumed docents act out the roles of traders, craftsmen, and explorers. The park is open mid-May through September, daily from 9am to 5pm. Summer admission is C$6.50 (US$5.20) for adults, C$5.50 (US$4.40) seniors, C$3.25 (US$2.60) for youths 12 to 16, and C$16 (US$13) for families. Free audio-guided tours of the grounds are available in winter; call ahead to request one.

5 Prince George

396km (246 miles) W of Jasper, Alberta; 756km (469 miles) E of Prince Rupert

The largest city in northern British Columbia, Prince George (pop. 82,000) makes a natural base for exploring the sights and recreational opportunities of the province's north-central region, which is filled with forested mountains, lakes, and mighty rivers.

There has been settlement at the junction of the Fraser and Nechako rivers for millennia; the two river systems were as much a transportation corridor for the early First Nations people as for the European settlers who came later. A trading post was established in the early 1800s; the Grand Trunk Railroad, which passed through here in 1914, put Prince George on the map.

What makes the city's economic heart beat is lumber—and lots of it. Prince George is at the center of vast softwood forests, and three major mills here turn trees into pulp, and pulp into paper. The economic boom that these mills introduced has brought a relative degree of sophistication to the lumber town—there's a civic art gallery, good restaurants, and the University of Northern British Columbia.

ESSENTIALS

GETTING THERE **By Plane** **Air Canada Jazz** (© 888/247-2262; www.flyjazz.ca) provides daily service to Prince George to/from Vancouver. **WestJet** (© 888/937-8538;** www.westjet.com) also serves Prince George, offering economical flights to the rest of Canada.

By Train The *Skeena* run on **VIA Rail** (© 800/561-8630; www.viarail.ca), which operates between Prince Rupert and Jasper, stops overnight in Prince George. Connections to the main Vancouver-Toronto line are available at Jasper. The passenger service once offered by BC Rail, which connected Prince George to Vancouver via Whistler, no longer operates. But in 2006, **Rocky Mountaineer Vacations** (© 877/460-3200 or 604/606-7245; www.rockymountaineer.com) begins service along this route with its **Fraser Discovery Route** excursion trains.

By Bus **Greyhound Canada** (© 800/661-8747 or 604/482-8747; www.greyhound.ca) serves Prince George with daily buses from Vancouver. Fares begin at C$80 (US$64). Greyhound also offers daily buses between Prince Rupert and Jasper along the Yellowhead Highway.

By Car Prince George is about a third of the way across the province on the east-west Yellowhead Highway (Hwy. 16). South from Prince George, Highway 97 drops through the Cariboo District on its way to Kelowna (712km/441 miles) and Vancouver (via Hwy. 1, 808km/501 miles). From Prince George, you can also follow Highway 97 north to join the Alaska Highway at Dawson Creek (421km/261 miles).

VISITOR INFORMATION Contact the **Prince George Visitor Info Centre,** 1198 Victoria St. (© 800/668-7646 or 250/562-3700; www.nbctourism.com). It's open daily from 9am to 6pm.

GETTING AROUND The local bus system is operated by **Prince George Transit** (© 250/563-0011). For a cab, call **Emerald Taxi** (© 250/563-3333) or **Prince George Taxi Holdings** (© 250/564-4444).

⌒Kids Family Fun

The **Ol' Sawmill Bluegrass Jamboree** (© 250/564-8573), held 26km (16 miles) up North Nechako Road in mid-August, is a musical event for the whole family, with weekend camping, music workshops, arts and crafts, play areas for the kids, and many talented bluegrass performers.

Car-rental agencies include **Avis** (© 800/272-5871 in Canada, 800/230-4898 in the U.S.; www.avis.com), **Budget** (© 800/268-8900 in Canada, 800/527-0700 in the U.S.; www.budget.com), **Hertz** (© 800/263-0600 or 250/963-7454; www.hertz.com), **National** (© 800/CAR-RENT in Canada and the U.S.; www.nationalcar.com), and **Thrifty** (© 800/THRIFTY or 250/963-8711; www.thrifty.com).

EXPLORING THE AREA

Downtown Prince George is located on a spur of land at the confluence of the Fraser and Nechako rivers. The old commercial district at first seems a bit forlorn, but a stroll around the city center—concentrated along Third Avenue and George Street—reveals a down-and-dirty charm that's reminiscent of towns in the Yukon or Northwest Territories. And the prevalence of tattoo parlors, pawnshops, and old-fashioned coffee shops enhances the impression of a rough-and-ready frontier community.

The **Two Rivers Gallery** (© **888/221-1155** or 250/614-7800; www.tworiversart gallery.com) occupies a stylish space in the Civic Centre Plaza, at Patricia Boulevard and Dominion Street. This architecturally innovative, C$5-million (US$4-million) structure showcases the work of local and regional artists. There's also a sculpture garden, gift shop, and cafe. Hours are Tuesday through Saturday from 10am to 5pm, Sunday from noon to 5pm. Between May and September, it's also open Monday from 10am to 5pm. Admission is C$5 (US$4) for adults, C$4 (US$3.60) for seniors and students, and C$2 (US$1.60) for children 5 to 12. After viewing the gallery, cross Patricia Street and wander the trails in **Connaught Hill Park.** From the top of the hill are good views of the Fraser River and downtown.

At the **Prince George Native Art Gallery,** 1600 Third Ave. (© **250/614-7726;** www.pgnfc.com), you can see birch-bark art, cedar-wood carvings, beadwork, and limited-edition prints by regional Native artists. It's open Tuesday through Friday from 9am to 5pm and Saturday from 10am to 4pm, with extended summer hours possible.

There are more than 120 parks within the city limits, many of them linked by the Heritage River Trails system. The best is 36-hectare (89-acre) **Fort George Park,** on the site of the original fur-trading post. On the grounds are a First Nations burial ground, a miniature railway, a one-room schoolhouse, and the Exploration Place (© **250/562-1612;** www.theexplorationplace.com), a kid-focused science and nature museum. Adults will enjoy the history gallery, which details the customs of the region's Native Carrier people, and moves on to tell the story of the fur-trading and logging past. There are also numerous interactive science exhibits; an Internet cafe; and a SimEx theater, in which viewers' seats move in tandem with motions in films. Admission is C$8.95 (US$7.15) for adults, C$6.95 (US$5.55) for seniors and students, C$5.95 (US$4.75) for children 2 to 12, or C$21 (US$17) per family; there are also combo tickets that included admission to SimEx films. It's open daily 10am to 5pm from mid-May through mid-October, the same hours Wednesday through Sunday the rest of the year. The park is on the Fraser River end of 20th Avenue; from downtown, take Queensway Street south, then turn east on 20th Avenue.

The **Heritage River Trails** take you on an 11km (6¾-mile) circuit covering the historic sights of town. The loop starts at Fort George Park, goes along the Fraser River, passes through Cottonwood Island Park and along the Nechako River to the Cameron Street bridge, and leads through town and back to Fort George Park.

WHERE TO STAY

If you're looking for a bed-and-breakfast, try the **Prince George B&B Hot Line** (℗ **877/562-2626** or 250/562-2222; www.pgonline.com/bnb/hotline.html).

Coast Inn of the North   One of the best of British Columbia's Coast hotel chain is right in the thick of things in downtown Prince George. The guest rooms are nicely furnished; the corner suites are truly large, with king beds, a balcony, and lots of light and space (some suites have Jacuzzis). Among the numerous facilities is an indoor pool. Small pets are allowed in the guest rooms.

770 Brunswick St., Prince George, BC V2L 2C2. ℗ **800/663-1144** or 250/563-0121. Fax 250/563-1948. www.coast hotels.com. 155 units. C$135–C$170 (US$108–US$136) double. Extra person C$10 (US$8). Family plan, corporate, and off-season rates, and senior and AAA discounts available. AE, MC, V. Free parking with engine heater plug-ins. **Amenities:** 3 restaurants; pub; dance club; indoor pool; fitness center; Jacuzzis; saunas; salon; 24-hr. room service. *In room:* A/C, TV, dataport, minibar, coffeemaker, hair dryer.

Goldcap Travelodge *Value*   If you're looking for value, it's hard to beat the large, clean, unfussy rooms at the Travelodge, right downtown. Kitchen units with microwaves and fridges are available for a small extra fee. An on-site family restaurant is open for three meals daily.

1458 Seventh Ave., Prince George, BC V2L 3P3. ℗ **800/663-8239** or 250/563-0666. Fax 250/563-5775. www. travelodgeprincegeorge.com. 77 units. C$65–C$95 (US$52–US$76) double. Kitchens available for C$10 (US$8). Off-season rates and senior discounts available. AE, MC, V. Free parking. Pets accepted. **Amenities:** Sauna; guest laundry. *In room:* A/C, TV, dataport, coffeemaker.

Ramada Hotel (Downtown Prince George)   Right in the center of the city, the grandest of hotels in Prince George offers a variety of top-notch rooms—from standard to presidential—with handsome neo-Scandinavian furniture. The Tower Suites offer a selection of large business and specialty suites that include breakfast and Aveda products. Some units have Jacuzzis; all have heated bathroom floors and irons. The Ramada has the only casino in Prince George, so this is a very busy place indeed.

444 George St., Prince George, BC V2L 1R6. ℗ **800/830-8833** or 250/563-0055. Fax 250/563-6042. www.ramada princegeorge.com. 200 units. C$109–C$180 (US$87–US$144) double. Extra person C$20 (US$16). Senior discounts available. AE, DC, DISC, MC, V. Free covered parking. **Amenities:** Restaurant; bar; large indoor pool; golf course nearby; access to nearby health club; Jacuzzi; sauna; business center; limited room service; same-day dry cleaning; rooms for those w/limited mobility. *In room:* A/C, TV w/pay movies, dataport, coffeemaker.

Sandman Inn   Along Highway 97 west of downtown, the inn offers large, comfortable guest rooms including one- and two-bedroom suites. Kitchenettes and wheelchair-accessible units are available. A 24-hour Denny's restaurant is on-site. For a comfortable room that avoids downtown, this is a good choice.

1650 Central St., Prince George, BC V2M 3C2. ℗ **800/SANDMAN** or 250/563-8131. Fax 250/563-8613. www.sandman hotels.com. 144 units. C$110–C$175 (US$88–US$140) double. Senior and AAA discounts available. AE, DC, DISC, MC, V. Small pets allowed for C$5 (US$4) per day. **Amenities:** Restaurant; indoor pool; golf course nearby; sauna; limited room service; laundry service; coin-op laundry; same-day dry cleaning; rooms for those w/limited mobility. *In room:* A/C, TV, dataport, coffeemaker, hair dryer, iron (available on request).

A Tangled Garden B&B   This comfortable, centrally located home offers two guest rooms and such extras as bathrobes. One unit has a kitchenette, private entrance, queen bed, and phone; the other offers a wonderful view of the mountains. A resident cat and dog may keep you company. The hosts will pick up guests by request.

2957 Sullivan Crescent, Prince George, BC V2N 5H6. ℗ **250/964-3265.** Fax 250/964-3248. www.tangledgarden. bcbnb.ca. 2 units. C$70–C$80 (US$56–US$64) double. Extra person C$10 (US$8). Rates include full breakfast. No credit cards. Free parking with engine heater plug-ins. **Amenities:** Jacuzzi; courtesy limo; nonsmoking facility. *In room:* TV/VCR.

WHERE TO DINE

For a light meal, head to **Java Mugga Mocha**, 304 George St. (🕐 **250/562-3338**), a fun hangout for espresso drinks, sandwiches, and baked goods.

Ric's Grill STEAKHOUSE   This chic dining room serves an expanded steak and chop menu that mixes old-fashioned meat and potatoes with imaginative New Canadian cuisine. Ric's also features an impressive selection of fish and shellfish dishes, plus pasta, chicken, and salads. It's a stylish and friendly spot for dinner.

547 George St. 🕐 250/614-9096. Reservations suggested. Main courses C$14–C$32 (US$11–US$27). AE, MC, V. Mon–Thurs 11:30am–10pm; Fri 11:30am–11pm; Sat 4:30–11pm; Sun 4:30–10pm.

Waddling Duck Restaurant 🎯 PUB   The Waddling Duck looks like an olde English pub, complete with exposed beams, stone walls and a huge fireplace, but the food is up-to-date and sure to please. The pub offers over 20 choices for tapas ranging from seafood tartare or stuffed baby squid to tiny lamb chops with a pear-and-apple compote. Entrees include burgers, pizza, steaks, fresh fish, and imaginative dishes like pork loin stuffed with prosciutto, apple, and Stilton cheese. The Waddling Duck also offers a number of vegetarian options. Service is very friendly and professional.

1157 Fifth Ave. 🕐 250/561-5550. Reservations not needed. Tapas C$5–C$12 (US$4–US$9.60); main courses C$9–C$29 (US$7.20–US$23). MC, V. Daily 11am–10pm.

6 The Alaska Highway

Constructed as a military freight road during World War II to link Alaska to the Lower 48, the Alaska Highway—also known as the Alcan Highway, and Highway 97 in British Columbia—has become something of a pilgrimage route for recent retirees.

Strictly speaking, the Alaska Highway starts at Mile 1 marker in **Dawson Creek,** on the eastern edge of British Columbia, and travels north and west for 2,242km (1,390 miles) to **Delta Junction,** in Alaska, passing through the Yukon along the way. The **Richardson Highway** (Alaska Rte. 4) covers the additional 158km (98 miles) from Delta Junction to **Fairbanks.**

Popular wisdom states that if you drive straight out, it takes 3 days between Dawson Creek and Fairbanks. However, this is a very *long* winding road, and RV traffic is heavy. If you try to keep yourself to a 3-day schedule, you'll have a miserable time.

WHAT TO EXPECT

Summer is the only opportunity to repair the road, so construction crews really go to it; you can count on lengthy delays and some very rugged detours. Visitor centers along the way get faxes of daily construction schedules and conditions, so stop for updates, or follow the links to "Road Conditions" from the website **www.themilepost. com.** You can also call 🕐 **867/456-7623** for 24-hour highway information.

Although there's gas at most of the communities that appear on the road map, most close up early in the evening, and gas prices can be substantially higher than in, say, Edmonton or Calgary. You'll find 24-hour gas stations and plenty of motel rooms in the towns of Dawson City, Fort St. John, Fort Nelson, Watson Lake, and Whitehorse.

Try to be patient when driving the Alaska Highway. In high season, the entire route, from Edmonton to Fairbanks, is one long caravan of RVs. Many people have their car in tow, a boat on the roof, and several bicycles chained to the spare tire. Thus encumbered, they lumber up the highway; loath (or unable) to pass one another. These convoys of RVs stretch on forever, the slowest of the party setting the pace for all.

DRIVING THE ALASKA HIGHWAY

This overview of the Alaska Highway is not meant to serve as a detailed guide for drivers. For that, you should purchase the annual *Alaska Milepost* (www.themilepost.com), which offers exhaustive, mile-by-mile coverage of the trip (and of other road trips into the Arctic of Alaska and Canada).

The route begins (or ends) at Dawson Creek, in British Columbia. Depending on where you start, Dawson Creek is a long 590km (365-mile) drive from Edmonton or a comparatively short 406km (252 miles) from Prince George on Highway 97. Dawson Creek is a natural place to break up the journey, with ample tourist facilities. If you want to call ahead to ensure a room, try the Ramada Limited Dawson Creek, 1748 Alaska Ave. (© **800/663-2749** or 250/782-8595).

From Dawson Creek, the Alaska Highway soon crosses the Peace River and passes through **Fort St. John,** in the heart of British Columbia's far-north ranch country. The highway continues north, parallel to the Rockies. First the ranches thin, and then the forests thin. Moose are often seen from the road.

From Fort St. John to **Fort Nelson,** you'll find gas stations and cafes every 65 to 81km (40–50 miles), though lodging options are pretty dubious. Fort Nelson is thick with motels and gas stations; because it's hours from any other major service center, this is a good place to spend the night. Try the **Travelodge Fort Nelson,** 4711 50th Ave. S. (© **888/515-6375** or 250/774-3911; www.travelodgefortnelson.com).

At Fort Nelson, the Alaska Highway turns west and heads into the Rockies; from here, too, graveled **Liard Highway** (B.C. Hwy. 77; Northern Territories Hwy. 7) continues north to Fort Liard and Fort Simpson, the gateway to **Nahanni National Park,** a very worthy side trip.

From Fort Nelson, the Alaska Highway through the Rockies is mostly narrow and winding—and likely to be under construction. Once over the Continental Divide, the Alaska Highway follows tributaries of the Liard River through **Stone Mountain** and **Muncho Lake** provincial parks. Rustic lodges are scattered along the road. The lovely log **Northern Rockies Lodge** ⚜, at Muncho Lake (© **800/663-5269** or 250/776-3481; www.northern-rockies-lodge.com), offers lodge rooms and log cabins for C$99 to C$109 (US$79–US$87) and campsites for C$35 (US$28).

At the town of **Liard River,** stop and stretch your legs or go for a soak in the two nice deep-forest soaking pools at **Liard Hot Springs.** The boardwalk out into the mineral-water marsh is pleasant even if you don't have time for a dip.

As you get closer to **Watson Lake** in the Yukon, you'll notice that mom-and-pop gas stations along the road will advertise that they have cheaper gas than at Watson Lake. Believe them, and fill up: Watson Lake is an unappealing town whose extortionately priced gas is probably its only memorable feature. The **Belvedere Motor Hotel,** 609 Frank Trail (© **867/536-7714**), is the best spot to spend the night, with a restaurant and coffee shop on-site and rooms starting at C$89 (US$71).

The long road between Watson Lake and **Whitehorse** travels through rolling hills and forest to Teslin and Atlin lakes, where the landscape becomes more mountainous and the gray clouds of the Gulf of Alaska's weather systems hang menacingly on the horizon. Whitehorse is the largest town along the route of the Alaska Highway, and unless you're in a great hurry, plan to spend at least a day here.

Hope for good weather as you leave Whitehorse; the trip past **Kluane National Park** is one of the most beautiful parts of the entire route. Tucked into the southwestern corner of the Yukon, a 2-hour drive from Whitehorse, these 22,015 sq. km (8,500 sq. miles) of glaciers, marshes, mountains, and sand dunes are unsettled and virtually untouched—and designated as a **UNESCO World Heritage Site.** Bordering on Alaska in the west, Kluane contains **Mount Logan** and **Mount St. Elias,** respectively the second- and third-highest peaks in North America (Denali is the highest).

Because Kluane is largely undeveloped, casual exploration is limited to a few day-hiking trails and aerial sightseeing trips. The vast expanse of ice and rock in the heart of the wilderness is well beyond striking range of the average outdoor enthusiast. The area's white-water rapids are world-class but, likewise, not for the uninitiated.

Purists may object, but the only way most visitors are going to have a chance to see the backcountry of Kluane Park is by airplane or helicopter. **Trans North Helicopters** (© 867/668-2177 or 600/700-1034; www.tntaheli.com), at the Haines Junction airport, offers a 1-hour flight into Kluane Park and over Lowell Glacier and Lowell Lake. The per person fare is C$308 (US$246), based on a minimum group of four.

For more information on recreation in Kluane, see the website at **www.pc.gc.ca/ pn-np/yt/kluane**.

After Kluane, the Alaska Highway edges by Kluane Lake before passing Beaver Creek and crossing over into Alaska. From the border to Fairbanks is another 481km (298 miles).

11

The Cariboo Country & the Thompson River Valley

South of Prince George along Highway 97 and beyond into British Columbia's interior, the Canadian Wild West hasn't changed much in the past century. This is Cariboo Country, a vast landscape that changes from alpine meadows and thick forests to rolling prairies and arid canyons before it encounters the gigantic glacial peaks of the Coast Mountains. The Cariboo's history is synonymous with the word *gold.*

From Vancouver, the Sea-to-Sky Highway (Hwy. 99) passes through Whistler and the Cayoosh Valley, eventually descending into the town of Lillooet, which was Mile 0 of the Old Cariboo Highway during the gold-rush days of the 1860s. Prospectors and settlers made their way north up what's now called the Cariboo Gold Rush Trail (Hwy. 99 and Hwy. 97).

Highway 97 follows the gold-rush trail through the towns of 70 Mile House, 100 Mile House, 108 Mile House, and 150 Mile House. The towns were named after the mile-marking roadhouses patronized by prospectors and settlers headed north to the gold fields.

The gold-rich town of Barkerville sprang up in the 1860s after a British prospector named Billy Barker struck it rich on Williams Creek. Completely restored, the town brings the rough gold-rush days to life. The streets are only 5.5m (18 ft.) wide, thanks to a drunken surveyor. Nowadays, you can try your hand at panning for the shiny gold flakes and nuggets that still lie deep within Williams Creek.

Gold isn't the only thing that attracts thousands of visitors to this area. Cross-country skiers and snowmobilers take to the creek-side paths in winter; canoeists head a few miles north of Barkerville to a 120km (74-mile) circular route called Bowron Lakes.

From Williams Lake, back-roads enthusiasts can also drive Highway 20 west to the Pacific coastal community of Bella Coola, which in the early days of European exploration was one of the most important First Nations communities on the coast. From Bella Coola, you can catch the Discovery Coast ferry to Port Hardy on the northern tip of Vancouver Island (see chapter 10).

Due east, on the opposite side of Cariboo Country, the Thompson River valley's arid lowlands attract fishers and boaters to the shores of the lower Thompson River and the Shuswap Lakes. Heading north from this dry terrain, you'll reach a majestic 1.3-million-hectare (3.2-million-acre) forested mountain wilderness formed by glaciers and volcanoes—Wells Gray Provincial Park.

1 Cariboo Country Essentials

GETTING THERE

Whether you travel by train or by car, the trip from Whistler to Cariboo Country is a visually exhilarating experience.

BY CAR   The shortest and most scenic route from Vancouver is along Highway 99 (the Sea-to-Sky Highway) past Whistler to Lillooet, continuing to Highway 97 and turning north to 100 Mile House and points north. From Vancouver to Quesnel, it's 600km (373 miles). If you want to bypass the dramatic but slow Highway 99 and head straight up to the central Cariboo district, you can take the Highway 1 expressway east from Vancouver, then jump onto Highway 97 at Merritt.

BY TRAIN   For decades, **BC Rail** operated the *Cariboo Prospector,* which linked Vancouver to Prince George with stops in other towns in the Cariboo Country. In 2002, however, BC Rail discontinued passenger service along this route. **Rocky Mountaineer Vacations** (© 877/460-3200 or 604/606-7245), which operates the very successful excursion train service between Vancouver and Banff and Jasper in the Canadian Rockies, in 2006 begins service along this route with its **Fraser Discovery Route** excursion trains. For information, go to **www.rockymountaineer.com**. The train departs from Whistler, with an overnight stop in Quesnel before continuing on to Jasper, where the train will link with other Rocky Mountaineer Vacations trains.

BY BUS   **Greyhound Canada** (© 800/661-8747; www.greyhound.ca) travels from Vancouver through the Cariboo to Prince George via highways 1 and 97, passing through Kamloops, 100 Mile House, Williams Lake, and Quesnel. Note that these routes do not pass through Lillooet, which has no bus service.

BY PLANE   **Air Canada Jazz** (© 888/247-2262; www.flyjazz.ca) offers daily service between Quesnel and Vancouver. It also offers daily flights between Williams Lake and Vancouver. **Pacific Coastal Air** (© 800/663-2872 or 604/273-8666; www.pacific-coastal.com) links Vancouver to Anahim Lake, Bella Coola, and Williams Lake.

VISITOR INFORMATION

Contact the **Cariboo Chilcotin Coast Tourist Association,** 118A N. First Ave., Williams Lake, BC V2G 1Y8 (© 800/663-5885 or 250/392-2226; www.landwithout limits.com).

2 En Route to 100 Mile House

There's nothing subtle about the physical setting of **Lillooet** (pop. 2,058). To the west, the soaring glaciated peaks of the Coast Mountains dominate the sky. To the east rise the steep desert walls of the Fountain Range, stained with rusty red and ochre. Cleaving the two mountain ranges is the massive and roaring Fraser River. From the peaks of the Coast Range to the riverbed is a drop of nearly 2,700m (9,000 ft.)—all of this making for an incredibly dramatic backdrop to the town.

In 1858, a trail was cut from the Fraser Valley goldfields in the south to the town of Lillooet, later established as Mile 0 of the 1860s **Cariboo Gold Rush Trail.** At the big bend on Main Street, a cairn marks MILE 0 of the original Cariboo Wagon Road.

From Lillooet, Highway 99 heads north along the Fraser River Canyon, affording many dramatic vistas before turning east to its junction with Highway 97. Thirty kilometers (19 miles) north on Highway 97 is **Clinton,** the self-avowed "guest-ranch capital of British Columbia." This is certainly handsome ranch country, with broad cattle- and horse-filled valleys rolling between dry mountain walls.

Hat Creek Ranch   Now a provincial heritage site, Hat Creek House was built in 1861 and served as a stagecoach inn for miners. This open-air museum of frontier life has more than 20 period buildings, including a blacksmith shop, barn, and stable. There's also a good exhibit on the culture of the region's First Nations Shuswap tribe. In summer, concessionaires operate horse-drawn wagon and horseback rides, plus a ranch-house restaurant. You can stroll the grounds year-round; however, regular visitor services and guided tours are offered only from mid-May to the end of September.

At junction of Hwy. 99 and Hwy. 97. (C) **800/782-0922** or 250/457-9722. www.hatcreekranch.com. Admission C$8 (US$6.40) adults, C$7 (US$5.60) seniors, C$5 (US$3.20) children 6–12, C$20 (US$16) families. May–Sept 30 daily 9am–5pm (July–Aug till 6pm).

WHERE TO STAY
Big Bar Guest Ranch (Kids)   A longtime favorite for horse-focused family vacations, the Big Bar is a comfortable destination with lots of recreational and lodging options. Summer activities include riding and pack trips, or you can canoe, fish, pan for gold, bike, and go for hayrides. In winter, the ranch remains open for cross-country skiing, snowshoeing, snowmobiling, and ice fishing. The centerpiece of the property is the hand-hewn log Harrison House, built in the early 1900s, which now serves as guest lounge, with a huge stone fireplace, and game area with pool and foosball tables. The Big Bar is the quintessential old-fashioned guest ranch—not a New Age lifestyle resort—where lots of attention is spent on the quality of the horses and the wranglers. Guests will enjoy the family-style meals after a hearty day of horseback riding or hiking. In addition to 10 comfortable, no-fuss lodge rooms in the main lodge, there are four quite comfortable one-bedroom log cabins, each with a sleeping loft and fold-out couch that sleep up to eight, with full kitchens and fireplaces. In addition, other lodging options include tepees, a six-bedroom lodge, and campsites. If you're looking for an Old West adventure, not just an opportunity to dress up in a Stetson and denim, then this might be the guest ranch for you.

54km (33 miles) northwest of Clinton off Hwy. 97. Mailing address: P.O. Box 27, Jesmond, BC V0K 1K0. (C) **250/459-2333.** Fax 250/459-2400. www.bigbarranch.com. 17 units. C$230 (US$184) double occupancy in lodge rooms, including 3 meals daily; C$189 (US$151) double occupancy in cabin; C$75 (US$60) per person tepee, including meals. Extra person in lodge C$105 (US$84) adult, C$59 (US$47) child. MC, V. **Amenities:** Dining room; lounge; Jacuzzi; game room; playground. *In room:* No phone.

Cariboo Lodge Resort   There's been a log lodge on this site for well over a century—the original was built to serve frontier trappers and miners. Times have changed, and so has the Cariboo Lodge. This modern log lodge and motel offers stylish, fully modern guest rooms plus an Old West pub (complete with stuffed heads) and restaurant; the resort makes a perfect base for exploring central British Columbia. The proprietors will organize horseback rides, rafting and mountain-biking tours, and cross-country ski trips. Rooms are large and nicely furnished—without the Old West clutter you'd normally expect in such a place.

The Cariboo Country & the Thompson River Valley

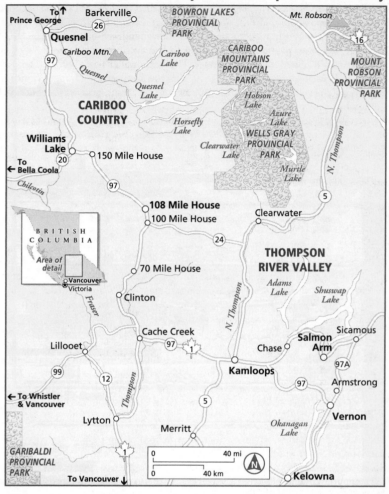

Box 459, Clinton, BC V0K 1K0. ☎ 877/459-7992 or 250/459-7992. www.cariboolodgebc.com. 23 units. C$90 (US$72) double. MC, V. **Amenities:** Restaurant; pub. *In room:* A/C, TV, fridge, coffeemaker.

Echo Valley Ranch and Spa *(Finds)* East meets West at this remarkable resort, which is both amazingly sumptuous and rather artificial. Occupying a scenic plateau with views over the Fraser River valley, Echo Valley Ranch combines features of a traditional guest ranch—horseback riding and hiking—with Thai and European spa facilities. Guest rooms are in two central lodges—three-story log buildings straight out of *House Beautiful*—or in individual cabins. Even more astonishing is the Baan Thai building, a massive four-story log structure that's half American West, half Thai palace, which contains VIP lodging, conference rooms, and Thai spa treatment space.

Guest rooms are very comfortable, and meals are served family style in the main lodge. Recreation opportunities include horseback riding, hiking, rafting, mountain biking, pack trips, and gold panning. Spa facilities include an indoor pool and Jacuzzi, plus a full selection of therapeutic, aesthetic, and hydrotherapy treatments featuring standard therapies plus Thai stretching and massage. The ranch raises its own beef, chicken, and turkey, and has an organic garden that supplies the excellent dining room. This isn't your typical guest ranch, but if you're looking for upscale spa facilities plus horseback riding, this is the place for you.

50km (31 miles) northeast of Clinton. Mailing address: P.O. Box 16, Jesmond, BC V0K 1K0. ✆ 800/253-8831 or 250/459-2386. www.evranch.com. 20 units. From C$288 (US$230) per person based on double occupancy, 3-day minimum stay; packages from C$1,914 (US$1,531) per person per week. Rates include all meals and access to all spa facilities plus horseback riding and guided activities. Packages available. MC, V. Children must be 13 or older. **Amenities:** Restaurant; lounge; indoor pool; exercise room; spa; Jacuzzi; sauna; game room; laundry service. *In room:* Fridge, coffeemaker, hair dryer, robes.

3 100 Mile House & the South Cariboo District

100 Mile House: 174km (108 miles) N of Lillooet; 320km (198 miles) S of Prince George

Named for the roadhouse inn that marked the 100th mile north of Lillooet in the days of the Cariboo gold rush, 100 Mile House (pop. 1,978) is an attractive ranching community at the heart of a vast recreational paradise. There are thousands of lakes in the valleys that ring the town, making canoeing, fishing, and boating popular activities. In winter, the gently rolling landscape, combined with heavy snowfalls, make 100 Mile House a major cross-country ski destination.

Thirteen kilometers (8 miles) north is 108 Mile House, another frontier-era community now famed for its golf course and **108 Mile House Heritage Site (✆ 250/791-5288)**. This collection of ranch buildings includes an enormous log barn built to stable 200 Clydesdales, the horsepower that drove the stagecoaches.

For information on this region, contact the **South Cariboo Visitor Info Centre,** 422 Hwy. 97 S., 100 Mile House (✆ **250/395-5353;** www.southcariboo.com).

FISHING & WATERSPORTS

100 Mile House is a pleasant enough little town, but it's the outdoor recreation in the surrounding South Cariboo Lakes District that brings most people here. There are dozens of lakes, nearly all with rustic fishing resorts as well as provincial parks offering campgrounds and public boat launches. Be sure to pick up the *Cariboo-Chilcotin Fishing Guide* at the visitor center. For tackle, licenses, and advice, head to **Donex Pharmacy,** 145 Birch St. (✆ **250/395-4004**).

One lake-filled area lies southeast of 100 Mile House along Highway 24, which connects Highway 97 with Highway 5 at Little Fort, on the Thompson River. This scenic drive climbs up along a high plateau between the watersheds of the Fraser and Thompson rivers. The road leads to so many excellent fishing lakes that it's often referred to as the "Fishing Highway."

On Sheridan Lake, the **Loon Bay Resort,** 40km (25 miles) southeast of 100 Mile House (✆ **250/593-4431;** www.loonbayresort.com), rents tackle, canoes, and motorboats; sells licenses; and maintains cabins (from C$55/US$44) and campsites.

Perhaps the most beautiful of all these lakes is **Lac des Roches,** 88km (55 miles) east of 100 Mile House. The handsome **Lac Des Roches Resort (✆ 250/593-4141;**

www.lacdesroches.com) offers boat rentals, campsites (C$15/US$12), and lakeside cabins (from C$79/US$63).

Northeast of 100 Mile House is another lake-filled valley. **Canim Lake** is the most developed, with good swimming beaches. The venerable **Ponderosa Resort** (© **250/ 397-2243;** www.ponderosaresort.com) offers boat rentals, guided fishing, and horseback riding. Motel-style rooms are C$95 (US$76), cabins are C$105 to C$120 (US$84–US$96); campsites are around C$22 (US$18). At **Canim Beach Provincial Park,** 45km (28 miles) from 100 Mile House, campsites are C$14 (US$11).

If you're looking for a wilderness canoeing experience, **Moose Valley Provincial Park** preserves a series of small glacial lakes that are linked by short portage trails. The most popular route begins at Marks Lake and links with 11 other lakes, making for a leisurely 2-day loop paddle. For more information, contact **BC Parks,** Cariboo District (© **250/398-4414;** www.env.gov.bc.ca/bcparks).

OTHER OUTDOOR PURSUITS

CROSS-COUNTRY SKIING   In February, the town hosts the **Cariboo Marathon,** a 50km (31-mile) race that draws more than 1,000 contestants. There's an extensive public trail system with 200km (124 miles) of groomed trails in the area, with some parts lit at night. Many resorts and guest ranches also have groomed trails.

GOLF   The region's finest course is undoubtedly at **108 Ranch Resort,** in 108 Mile House (© **800/667-5233** or 250/791-5211). The 18-hole championship course has undulating fairways and fast putting greens. The resort offers a driving range, a pro shop, and lessons. Midweek greens fees for 18 holes are C$40 (US$32).

WHERE TO STAY & DINE

The shipshape **Red Coach Inn,** 170 Hwy. 97 N., 100 Mile House (© **800/663-8422** or 250/395-2266), offers rooms from C$85 (US$68), just a short walk from downtown.

Hills Health & Guest Ranch   This spa and guest ranch offers a full complement of beauty and health treatments as well as activities such as horseback riding, mountain biking, hayrides, downhill skiing on the ranch's own ski area, and cross-country skiing on more than 167km (104 miles) of private trails. Popular activities include breakfast horseback rides, line-dancing lessons, and lake canoeing. The spa has a variety of offerings, including massage, facials, and reflexology. Also popular are weight-loss and physical therapy programs guided by professional nutritionists and therapists. Within the vast spa building are hydrotherapy pools, an aerobics gym, dry saunas, and 16 treatment rooms. The guest rooms feature ranch-style natural pine decor; also available are three-bedroom chalets with kitchens, plus 10 campsites (C$20/US$16). The lodge restaurant serves a unique blend of cowboy favorites and spa cuisine, specializing in fondue and hot-rock cooking. All programs, therapies, and activities can be customized to form your own personalized package vacation—this is an ambitious resort, with over 100 employees.

Hwy. 97, 108 Mile Ranch, P.O. Box 26, BC V0K 2Z0. © 250/791-5225. Fax 250/791-6384. www.spabc.com. 46 units. From C$168 (US$134) double, 2-night minimum. All-inclusive packages available. AE, DISC, MC, V. **Amenities:** 2 restaurants; lounge; indoor pool; nearby golf course; exercise room; full-service spa; bike and ski rentals; game room; salon; massage. *In room:* A/C, TV, dataport.

108 Resort and Conference Centre ⚐   This upscale hotel and resort centers on its fantastic golf course, although even if you're not a duffer, there's a lot to like here.

Other activities here include horseback riding, mountain biking, and canoeing. In winter the golf course is transformed into a vast undulating cross-country center. Guest rooms are large and beautifully furnished, all with balconies that overlook either the golf course or a small lake. Golf, cross-country-skiing, and horseback-riding packages are available. The on-site clubhouse restaurant offers good Northwest cuisine.

13km (8 miles) north of 100 Mile House. 4618 Telqua Dr., Box 2, 108 Mile Ranch, BC V0K 2Z0. ℂ **800/667-5233** or 250/791-5211. Fax 250/791-6537. www.108resort.com. 62 units and 11 campsites. C$110–C$130 (US$88–US$104) double. Extra person C$10 (US$8). Campsites C$20 (US$16) per vehicle with a C$5 (US$4) charge for electricity. Off-season rates and packages available. AE, MC, V. **Amenities:** Restaurant; bar; indoor pool; Jacuzzi; sauna; bike and canoe rentals; stables. *In room:* A/C, TV, dataport, kitchenettes (some rooms), coffeemaker, hair dryer.

Ramada Limited *(Value)* The area's newest hotel, the Ramada has large, well-furnished rooms in a variety of configurations and styles. In addition to standard hotel rooms there are king-bed suites with Jacuzzi tubs, a fireplace, and balcony; and family suites with full kitchens and an extra sofa bed. Small pets are allowed in some of the guest rooms. All in all, it's a very good value.

917 Alder Rd. (Hwy. 97), 100 Mile House, BC V0K 2E0. ℂ **877/395-2777** or 250/395-2777. Fax 250/395-2037. www.ramada.com. 36 units. From C$79 (US$63) double. Kitchens C$5 (US$4) extra. AE, MC, V. **Amenities:** Jacuzzi; sauna; coin-op laundry. *In room:* A/C, TV, dataport, coffeemaker, hair dryer.

4 Williams Lake

90km (56 miles) N of 100 Mile House; 539km (334 miles) N of Vancouver

Unabashedly a ranch town, Williams Lake (pop. 12,000) is known across the West for its large, hell's-a-poppin' rodeo, the **Williams Lake Stampede,** held the first weekend of July. It's also the gateway to the Chilcotin, the coastal mountainous area to the west. As the trade center for a large agricultural area, the little lakeside town bustles with activity.

The downtown area is west of the Highway 97 strip, centered on Oliver Street. The **Cariboo Friendship Society Native Arts and Crafts Shop,** 99 S. Third Ave. (ℂ **250/398-6831**), sells the work of local Native artists. The building that houses the shop was constructed to resemble a Shuswap pit-house dwelling. The old train depot has been in part converted into **Station House Gallery,** 1 MacKenzie Ave. N. (ℂ **250/392-6113**), with local arts and crafts.

The **Museum of the Cariboo Chilcotin,** 113 N. Fourth Ave. (ℂ **250/392-7404;** www.cowboy-museum.com), is the only museum in B.C. to focus on ranching and rodeo, honoring both the cowboys of the past and the present. The museum is home to the BC Cowboy Hall of Fame and also features an exhibit on ranching women, native arrowheads, and a replica blacksmith shop. It's open Monday through Saturday from 10am to 4pm from June through August, and 11am to 4pm Tuesday through Saturday the rest of the year. Admission is C$2 (US$1.60) adult.

For information, contact the **Williams Lake Visitor Centre,** 1148 Broadway S. (ℂ **250/392-5025;** www.williamslakechamber.com).

OUTDOOR PURSUITS

Red Shreds Bike and Board Shop, 95 S. First Ave. (ℂ **250/398-7873;** www.red shreds.com), offers a bounty of information on local hiking, mountain biking, and kayaking; bike and kayak rentals; and a number of specialty trail maps.

Moments   The Williams Lake Stampede

The **Williams Lake Stampede** is one of Canada's top rodeos, and is the only British Columbia rodeo on the Canadian Professional Rodeo Association circuit. Begun in the 1920s, the Stampede has grown into a 4-day festival held over the first weekend in July. Rodeo cowboys from across Canada and the western United States gather here to compete for prizes in excess of C$80,000 (US$64,000).

What makes the Stampede so popular is that in addition to the usual rodeo events—barrel racing, bareback and saddle bronc riding, calf roping, bull riding—there are a number of unusual competitions that provide lots of laughs and action. The Ranch Challenge pits real working cowboys from area ranches in a pouch-passing pony express race, a hilarious wild cow-milking contest, and a cattle-penning contest. There are also chariot races with two-horse teams and a chuck-wagon race with four-horse teams. In a variation on British sheepdog trials, the Top Dog Competition pits a cowboy and his ranch dog against three unruly cows. The dog puts the cows through a course of barrels, then into a pen; the fastest dog wins.

Other Old West events, such as barn dances, a parade, midway rides, and grandstand entertainment, add to the fun. Because the Stampede is very popular, accommodations go fast—make plans well ahead.

For more information, contact the Williams Lake Stampede, P.O. Box 4076, Williams Lake, BC V2G 2V2 (✆ **250/392-6585;** williamslakestampede.com). For tickets, call ✆ **800/717-6336.** Reserved seats cost C$17 (US$14) adults and C$10 (US$8) seniors/children under 12.

FISHING   There are more than 8,000 lakes in the area, and as many streams and rivers. Stop by **Harry's Sporting Supply,** 615 Oliver St. (✆ **250/398-5959**), to find out where the fish are biting.

WHITE-WATER RAFTING   The Chilko-Chilcotin-Fraser river system that runs from the Coast Mountains east is a major rafting destination, though not for the faint of heart or the unguided novice. Inquire at **Red Shreds** (see above) for information and rentals. **Chilko River Expeditions,** P.O. Box 4723, Williams Lake, BC V2G 2V7 (✆ **250/398-6711;** www.chilkoriver.com), leads a variety of trips on the three rivers, including a 1-day trip on the Chilcotin for C$110 (US$88) adults.

WHERE TO STAY

Caesar Inn   If you want a clean, no-fuss place, the Caesar Inn is a good choice. It's right downtown, service is friendly, and the restaurant Georgio's (see "Where to Dine," below) is one of the best in town.

55 Sixth Ave. S., Williams Lake, BC V2J 1K8. (✆ **800/663-6893** or 250/392-7747. Fax 250/392-4852. 100 units. C$65 (US$52) double. Kitchen C$10 (US$8) extra. Extra person C$5 (US$4). Monthly rates available. AE, MC, V. Small pets accepted. **Amenities:** Restaurant; pub; sauna; coin-op laundry. *In room:* A/C, TV, fridge.

Fraser Inn   The Fraser Inn overlooks Williams Lake from its hillside perch north of town along Highway 97. Large and modern, it offers a level of facilities not usually found in small ranch towns. Most rooms have great views.

285 Donald Rd., Williams Lake, BC V2G 4K4. ℂ **888/452-6789**, 888/331-8863 in the U.S., or 250/398-7055. Fax 250/398-8269. www.fraserinn.com. 75 units. C$70–C$110 (US$56–US$88) double. Kitchen C$10 (US$8) extra. Extra person C$7–C$10 (US$5.60–US$8). AE, MC, V. Pets accepted. **Amenities:** Restaurant; bar; exercise room; Jacuzzi; sauna; beer-and-wine store. *In room:* A/C, TV, minibar, coffeemaker.

Sandman Inn and Suites Just 2 blocks from downtown Williams Lake, the Sand-man has a newer wing of large one-bedroom suites, plus an older wing with regular motel units. You'll find the place clean, friendly, and close to everything you'll want to do in Williams Lake. A 24-hour Denny's restaurant shares the premises.

664 Oliver St., Williams Lake, BC V2G 1M6. ℂ **800/726-3626** or 250/392-6557. Fax 250/392-6242. www.sandman.ca. 59 units. C$100–C$150 (US$80–US$120) double. Senior discounts offered. AE, MC, V. Small pets allowed for C$5 (US$4) per day. **Amenities:** Restaurant; indoor pool; sauna; room service from Denny's; coin-op laundry. *In room:* A/C, TV, dataport, coffeemaker.

WHERE TO DINE

Georgio's 𝄐 GREEK/STEAKHOUSE This Greek/Canadian restaurant is far bet-ter than the dingy cafes usually found in motels. As much as possible, meats and pro-duce are sourced locally from area ranchers and farmers. The main focus is on steaks, such as the house-specialty garlic tenderloin. Other choices include Bella Coola salmon with honey-lime glaze, plus a complete selection of well-prepared Greek dishes.

In the Caesar Inn, 55 Sixth Ave. S. ℂ **250/392-7747**. Reservations recommended. Main courses C$8–C$22 (US$6.40–US$18). AE, MC, V. Daily 7am–10pm.

Laughing Loon Neighborhood Pub PUB Located just southeast of Williams Lake on Hwy. 97, this pleasant Victorian-style pub serves high-quality food in a hand-some dining room or in a lush garden setting. The menu offers pub standards such as burgers and sandwiches, plus Greek specialties and local Cariboo-area beef steaks and fresh salmon from Bella Coola.

1730 S. Broadway (Hwy 97). ℂ **250/398-5666**. Reservations not accepted. Main courses C$9–C$19 (US$7.20–US$15). AE, MC, V. Sun–Fri 11:30am–10pm; Sat 11:30am–11pm.

5 West on Highway 20 to Bella Coola

456km (283 miles) W of Williams Lake

Highway 20 cuts through a rugged land of lakes and mountains on its way to Bella Coola, a Native village on a Pacific inlet. This journey takes the adventurous driver from Williams Lake and the desert canyons of the Fraser River to glaciated peaks and finally to the shores of a narrow fiord. It's an amazingly scenic trip, but be ready for lots of gravel roads and steep grades. There aren't a lot of facilities along the way, so start out with a full tank of gas. You can easily make this trip in a day, especially in summer, but leave plenty of time to stop and explore.

After climbing up out of the Fraser Canyon, Highway 20 winds along the **Chilcotin Plateau,** miles of spacious grasslands that are home to some of the largest ranches in North America. At Hanceville, the route drops onto the **Chilcotin River,** famed for its white-water rafting and kayaking. The **Chilcotin Hotel,** in Alexis Creek (ℂ **250/394-4214**), is a popular place to stop for a home-style meal. You can camp right on the river at **Bull Canyon Provincial Parks,** with 20 sites at C$14 (US$11) a piece. The park is 10km (6¼ miles) west of Alexis Creek, 126km (78 miles) west of Williams Lake.

Just past Redstone, Highway 20 leaves the Chilcotin River and climbs up the valley. **Puntzi Lake** is home to a number of old-time fishing resorts. The **Poplar Grove Resort** (✆ **800/578-6804** or 250/481-1186) has boat and tackle rentals, and rents campsites starting at C$17 (US$14) and cabins from C$50 (US$40).

As Highway 20 presses closer to the Coast Mountains, the landscape is increasingly dotted with lakes and marshes. At the wee community of **Tatla Lake,** the pavement ends and the gravel begins. **Anahim Lake,** 328km (203 miles) west of Williams Lake and the largest settlement on the Chilcotin Plateau (pop. 522), is noted for its fishing and outdoor recreation. The **Escott Bay Resort** (✆ **888/380-8802** or 250/742-3233; www.escottbay.com) offers cabins starting at C$60 (US$48). The general store in Anahim Lake is over a century old, and its coffeepot is always on. The enormous glaciated peak that dominates the southern skyline is **Mount Waddington,** which at 4,016m (13,172 ft.) is the highest point in the Coast Mountains.

As you begin the final ascent up to 1,494m (4,900-ft.) **Heckman Pass,** note the **Rainbow Range,** 2,400m-plus (7,874-ft.) peaks that are brilliantly colored by purple, red, and yellow mineralization.

Thirty kilometers (19 miles) from Anahim Lake, Highway 20 crests Heckman Pass, and then begins **"The Hill."** Bella Coola residents had long dreamed of a road connection to the rest of the province, and a succession of provincial governments promised to build one from the Chilcotin Plateau down to the Pacific. When years went by and nothing happened—civil engineers doubted that a safe road could be made down the steep western face of the Coast Mountains—the locals took matters in their own hands. In 1953, two men in bulldozers set out, one from Heckman Pass, the other from the end of the road at the base of the Coast Mountains. In just 3 months, the two bulldozers kissed blades at the middle of the mountain, and Highway 20 was born. You'll feel your heart in your mouth on a number of occasions as you corkscrew your way down the road. The most notorious portion is 10km (6¼ miles) of gravel switchbacks, with gradients up to 18%, which drop 1,405m (4,600 ft.).

This part of Highway 20 passes through **Tweedsmuir Provincial Park,** British Columbia's second-largest park at 1 million hectares (2.5 million acres). This vast wilderness park of soaring mountains, interlocking lakes, and abundant wildlife is accessible by long-distance hiking trails, floatplane, and canoe. In fact, the Eutsuk Lake–Whitesail Lake circuit provides more than 320km (198 miles) of canoeing waters with just one portage. For information, contact **BC Parks,** 281 First Ave. N., Williams Lake (✆ **250/398-4414**).

The town at the end of the road, **Bella Coola** (pop. 992), is a disorganized little burg in a green glacier-carved valley. Ancestral home to the Bella Coola tribe, Bella Coola once held a Hudson's Bay Company trading fort, then became a fishing center for Norwegian settlers. The waterfront is a busy place in summer, with fishing and pleasure boats coming and going.

Besides the lure of the end of the road, the main reason to drive to Bella Coola is to catch the **BC Ferries Discovery Coast** service (see chapter 10). This summer-only ferry connects Bella Coola with other even more isolated coastal communities. The ferry terminates at Port Hardy, on Vancouver Island, making this an increasingly popular loop trip. The journey lasts 12 to 13½ hours. In high season, fares between Port Hardy and Bella Coola are C$115 (US$92) per adult passenger and C$231 (US$184) for a car.

WHERE TO STAY & DINE

There are basic campsites (pump your own water, pit toilets) at **Bailey Bridge Campsite** (© **250/982-2342**). See also the Bella Coola Motel, below.

Bella Coola Motel   Located right in the middle of downtown, this motel occupies the site of the old Hudson's Bay Company trading post on the waterfront. Guest rooms are spacious. RV and tent sites go for C$10 to C$20 (US$8–US$16).

1224 Clayton St., Box 188, Bella Coola, BC V0T 1C0. © **250/799-5323.** Fax 250/799-5323. www.bellacoola valley.com. 10 units. C$65–C$85 (US$52–US$98) double. Extra person C$10 (US$8). Senior and AAA discounts available. AE, DC, MC, V. Free parking. Pets conditionally accepted with deposit. **Amenities:** Canoe, bike, and scooter rentals; tour/activities desk; shuttle service; laundry service. *In room:* TV, kitchen, fridge, coffeemaker.

Bella Coola Valley Inn   This is the closest lodging to the ferry terminal, and the inn offers standard motel-style units. Extras include a BC Ferries ticket agency and the popular Smuggler's Cove Restaurant.

MacKenzie St., Box 183, Bella Coola, BC V0T 1C0. © **888/799-5316** or 250/799-5316. Fax 250/799-5610. www. bellacoolavalleyinn.com. 20 units. C$76–C$95 (US$61–US$76) double. Extra person C$10 (US$8). AE, MC, V. **Amenities:** Restaurant; pub; airport and ferry shuttle service. *In room:* TV, fridge, coffeemaker.

6 Quesnel

120km (74 miles) N of Williams Lake; 654km (405 miles) N of Vancouver; 101km (63 miles) S of Prince George

Like most other towns in the Cariboo District, Quesnel (pop. 8,500) was founded during the gold-rush years. Now mostly a logging center, Quesnel serves as gateway to the ghost town of Barkerville and to the canoe paddler's paradise, the Bowron Lakes. It also serves as the overnight stop on Rocky Mountaineer Vacations new-in-2006 train tour line, the Frazer Discovery Route. Watch for an uptick in lodging options.

Quesnel is located on a jut of land at the confluence of the Fraser and Quesnel rivers. The small downtown is almost completely surrounded by these rivers. **Ceal Tingley Park,** on the Fraser side, is a pleasant place for a stroll, and it's one of the few spots where you can get right down to the huge and powerful Fraser. Directly across the street is a Hudson's Bay Company trading post built in 1882; it currently houses a restaurant.

The main commercial strip is **Reid Street,** a block east of Highway 97. A walk along Reid Street reveals the kinds of old-fashioned shops and services that have been gobbled up by behemoths like Wal-Mart in the United States.

Over on the Quesnel River side of downtown is **Le Bourdais Park,** which contains the visitor center and the **Quesnel and District Museum and Archives,** 405 Barlow Ave. (© **250/992-9580**), which tells the story of the gold rush and has good exhibits on the Chinese who worked in the camps. It's open daily May to October; the rest of the year, Monday through Friday afternoons only.

A rodeo, river-raft races, and more than 100 other events attract thousands to Quesnel during the second week of July for **Bill Barker Days** (© **800/992-4922** in Canada, or 250/992-8716). For general information, contact the **Quesnel Visitor Info Centre,** in Le Bourdais Park, 703 Carson Ave. (© **800/992-4922** or 250/992-8716; www.northcariboo.com), open March through October.

WHERE TO STAY

Ten Mile Lake Provincial Park, 11km (6¾ miles) north of Quesnel off Highway 97 (© **250/398-4414**), has 141 campsites from C$14 (US$11). Open May through October, the park has flush toilets and showers.

Best Western Tower Inn   Right in the middle of downtown, though off the busy main thoroughfare, the Tower Inn offers clean, crisp new guest rooms. Begbie's Bar and Bistro is a popular eatery and hangout.

500 Reid St., Quesnel, BC V2J 2M9. © **800/663-2009** or 250/992-2201. Fax 250/992-5201. www.bwtowerinn.ca. 63 units. C$80–C$115 (US$64–US$92) double. Extra person C$5 (US$4). AE, MC, V. **Amenities:** Restaurant; bar. *In room:* A/C, TV/VCR w/pay movies, hair dryer.

Ramada Limited *Kids*   This well-equipped hotel is in the center of Quesnel, and while that's not promising a lot, it's more interesting than staying at a freeway exit. Next door is the city government and civic center, with a fitness center and skating rink. For the price, the rooms are nicely furnished, and there's a pool area for the kids.

383 St. Laurent Ave., Quesnel, BC V2J 2E1. © **800/992-1581** or 250/992-5575. Fax 250/995-2254. www.ramada.ca. 46 units. C$76–C$82 (US$61–US$66) double. Rates include continental breakfast. AE, MC, V. **Amenities:** Indoor pool; Jacuzzi; laundry service. *In room:* A/C, TV, dataport, coffeemaker, hair dryer.

Talisman Inn   A well-maintained older motel close to downtown, the Talisman has large, light-filled rooms that overlook a grassy courtyard. Kitchen units and executive suites are available. Some rooms have Jacuzzis, and several are equipped for those with disabilities.

753 Front St., Quesnel, BC V2J 2L2. © **800/663-8090** or 250/992-7247. Fax 250/992-3126. www.talismaninn.bc.ca. 87 units. C$68–C$86 (US$54–US$69) double; C$85–C$98 (US$68–US$78) suite; C$110 (US$81) executive suite. Extra person C$5 (US$4). Rates include continental breakfast. Corporate and senior rates available. AE, DC, DISC, MC, V. Free parking. Pets allowed in some units. **Amenities:** Golf course nearby; exercise room; spa; coin-op laundry; laundry service; same-day dry cleaning; rooms for those w/limited mobility. *In room:* A/C, TV w/pay movies, kitchenette, fridge, coffeemaker, iron.

WHERE TO DINE

Mr. Mike's West Coast Grill CANADIAN   Mr. Mike's is probably the hippest place in Quesnel, with a cocktail menu that would make a Yaletown club in Vancouver proud. The dining room serves up eclectic fare that focuses on steaks, but includes grilled salmon and boutique burgers. A few Mexican- and Thai-influenced dishes also make their way onto the menu.

450 Reid St. © **250/992-8181.** Reservations recommended. Main courses C$8–C$22 (US$6.40–US$18). AE, MC, V. Daily 10am–midnight.

River Rock Pub and Steakhouse PUB   This pub overlooks the Moffat Bridge and the Fraser River, with an outdoor deck to frame the view. The menu is broad, ranging from burgers to steaks and to East Indian specialties. Families are welcome, and you're sure to find something that will appeal to everyone.

290 Hoy St. © **250/991-0110.** Reservations not needed. Main courses C$7–C$19 (US$5.60–US$15). MC, V. Daily 11:30am–10pm.

7 East to Barkerville (★ & Bowron Lakes (★

Barkerville: 83km (51 miles) E of Quesnel

Barkerville is one of the premier tourist destinations in interior British Columbia, as well as one of the most intact ghost towns in Canada. However, what lures paddlers and campers to the Cariboo Mountains today isn't a flash of gold, but the splash of water at the Bowron Lakes. These are a chain of six major and a number of smaller interconnecting lakes that attract canoeists and kayakers who paddle and portage around the entire 115km (71-mile) circuit.

Follow the signs in Quesnel to Highway 26 east. The 87km (54-mile) drive to Barkerville takes you deep into the forests of the Cariboo Mountains, where moose and deer are often spotted from the road. The paved highway ends at Barkerville. Bowron Lakes is another 30km (19 miles) northeast on a gravel road.

EXPLORING BARKERVILLE: AN OLD WEST GHOST TOWN

The 1860 Cariboo gold rush was the reason thousands of miners made their way north from the played-out Fraser River gold deposits to Williams Creek, east of Quesnel. **Barkerville** (★ was founded on its shore after Billy Barker discovered one of the region's richest gold deposits in 1862. The town sprang up practically overnight; that year, it was reputedly the largest city west of Chicago and north of San Francisco. Many of the claims continued to produce well into the 1930s, but Barkerville's population moved on, leaving behind an intact ghost town that was designated a historic park in the 1950s.

The original 1869 **Anglican church** and 125 other buildings have been lovingly reconstructed or restored. The **Richland courthouse** stages trials from the town's past. From May to Labour Day, "townspeople" dress in period costumes. Visitors can pan for gold, dine in the Chinatown section, or take a stagecoach ride. In winter, the town becomes a haven for **cross-country skiers.** During the holidays, Barkerville hosts a special **Victorian Christmas** celebration.

Admission to the town is C$13 (US$10) adults, C$11 (US$9) seniors, C$7.25 (US$5.80) youths 13 to 17, and C$3.50 (US$2.80) children, C$29 (US$23) family. Barkerville is open year-round, daily from dawn to dusk, with interpretive activities from late May through September. For information, contact **Barkerville Historic Town,** Box 19, Barkerville, BC V0K 1B0 (© **250/994-3332;** www.barkerville.ca).

WHERE TO STAY & DINE

There are three campgrounds in **Barkerville Provincial Park,** Highway 26 (© **250/ 398-1414**), open year-round. Sites go for C$14 to C$18 (US$11–US$15). **Lowhee Campground** is the best and closest to the park entrance, with both tent and RV sites, plus showers, flush toilets, pumped well water, and a sani-station.

The Wells Hotel   Established in 1933, the 15 historic rooms at this restored hotel near Barkerville are filled with lovely antique furnishings. The hotel offers amenities that you'll truly appreciate after a day of hiking, canoeing, skiing, or gold panning: fine dining, a frothy cappuccino, and a soothing hot tub. Guest rooms are tastefully refurbished and decorated with antiques and local artwork. Some units have private bathrooms and/or fireplaces. Continental breakfast included in all rates.

Pooley St. (Box 39), Wells, BC V0K 2R0. $\textcircled{C}$ **800/860-2299** in Canada, or 250/994-3427. Fax 250/994-3494. www. wellshotel.com. 15 units. C$70–C$130 (US$56–US$104) double. Rates include breakfast. AE, MC, V. **Amenities:** 3 restaurants, including the Pooley Street Café with fine dining; pub; Jacuzzi; bike rental; massage.

PADDLING BOWRON LAKES: A CANOEIST'S PARADISE

Thirty kilometers (19 miles) northeast of Barkerville over an unpaved road, there's access to a circle of lakes that attracts canoeists and kayakers from around the world. The 123,120-hectare (304,106-acre) **Bowron Lakes Provincial Park** is a majestic paddler's paradise set against a backdrop of glacial peaks.

The 7-day circular route is 120km (74 miles) of unbroken wilderness. It begins at Kibbee Creek and Kibbee Lake, flows into Indianpoint Lake, Isaac Lake, and the Isaac River, and continues to McCleary, Lanezi, Sandy, and Una lakes before entering the final stretch: Babcock Lake, Skoi Lake, the Spectacle Lakes, Swan Lake, and finally Bowron Lake. The long, narrow lakes afford visitors a close look at both shores. You'll catch sight of moose, mountain goats, beavers, black bears, and grizzly bears. Be prepared to portage for a total of 8.5km (5¼ miles) between some of the creeks that connect the lakes. The longest single portage is 3km (1¾ miles). You must pack everything in and out of the wilderness camps.

The number of canoes and people allowed to enter the park per day is restricted in summer. Permit bookings are handled by **Super Natural British Columbia** ($\textcircled{C}$ **800/ 435-5622** or 250/387-1642). Fees for a full circuit are C$60 (US$48) per person per one-person canoe/kayak, or C$120 (US$96) per two-person canoe/kayak. There's a reservation fee of C$18 (US$14). After September 25, permits can be purchased at the **Bowron Lakes Park office,** at the start of the circuit ($\textcircled{C}$ **250/398-4414**). The park does not close in winter, but there are no rangers in the park after mid-October, so extreme caution must be used. For information on the park, contact the **District Manager,** Suite 301, 640 Borland St., Williams Lake ($\textcircled{C}$ **250/398-4414;** www.env. gov.bc.ca/bcparks).

You don't have to make the entire journey to enjoy this incredible setting. Open May through October, the **campground** at the park's entrance is a relaxing spot to camp, fish, boat, or simply observe the abundant flora and fauna.

WHERE TO STAY

Bowron Lake Lodge & Resorts   This rustic resort provides all the creature comforts you could ask for in a wilderness setting. Guests can choose from comfortable lodge rooms, cabins, or campsites. There are 5km (3 miles) of trails, 610m (2,000 ft.) of private beach, and an airstrip. Views across the lake and onto the forested craggy peaks are extremely dramatic.

Bowron Lake, 672 Walkem St., Quesnel, BC V2J 2J7. $\textcircled{C}$ **250/992-2733**. 16 units, 50 campsites. C$65–C$150 (US$52–US$120) double; C$20 (US$16) campsite. MC, V. Closed Nov–Apr. **Amenities:** Restaurant; lounge; bike, canoe, and motorboat rentals. *In room:* No phone.

8 The Thompson River Valley

Kamloops: 345km (214 miles) NE of Vancouver; 218km (135 miles) W of Revelstoke

From its juncture with the Fraser River at Lytton, the Thompson River cuts north, then east through an arid countryside grazed by cattle. **Kamloops,** a major trade center for this agricultural region, is increasingly a retirement center for refugees from the mists of the Pacific coast. In the South Thompson River valley, the **Shuswap Lakes** are popular with houseboaters. It's easy to rent a houseboat in **Salmon Arm** and navigate the 1,000km (620 miles) of waterways, landing at campsites and beaches along the way.

Rising up from the dry terrain of Kamloops, heading north along Highway 5, the road enters the cool forests of the High Country. High above the town of **Clearwater** is the pristine wilderness of **Wells Gray Provincial Park.**

KAMLOOPS

At the confluence of the north and south forks of the Thompson River, Kamloops (pop. 81,000) is the province's fifth-largest city. The forest-products industry is the city's primary economic force, although Kamloops is also a major service center for ranchers and farmers.

ESSENTIALS

GETTING THERE   You can fly into Kamloops on **Air Canada Jazz** (© 888/247-2262; www.flyjazz.ca), which operates daily 50-minute flights from Vancouver, and rent a car at the airport from **Budget** (© **800/268-8900** in Canada, 800/527-0700 in the U.S.; www.budget.com), **Discount** (© **250/372-7170;** www.discountcar. com), or **Hertz** (© **250/376-3022;** www.hertz.com).

Kamloops is a junction point for many provincial roads, including the Trans-Canada Highway and the Coquihalla toll road (Hwy. 5), the fastest route to/from Vancouver.

There are seven daily **Greyhound Canada** (© **800/661-8747;** www.greyhound.ca) buses from Vancouver; the fare is C$53 (US$42). **VIA Rail** (© **888/VIA-RAIL;** www.viarail.ca) passes through on the main transnational route. Kamloops is also the overnight stop for the Grand Canadian Railtour Company's luxury *Rocky Mountaineer* (© 800/665-7245). For more information on this train, see p. 317.

VISITOR INFORMATION   Contact the **Kamloops Visitor Info Centre,** 1290 W. Trans-Canada Hwy., at exit 368 (© **800/662-1994** or 250/347-3377; www.adventure kamloops.com).

EXPLORING THE AREA

Kamloops is a sprawling city in a wide river valley flanked by high desert mountains. A major service center for agricultural industries, Kamloops isn't exactly a tourist town. The downtown core centered around **Victoria Street,** however, is a pleasant, tree-lined area. North of downtown along the Thompson is **Riverfront Park,** a lovely expanse of green in an otherwise arid landscape. The stern-wheeler *Wanda-Sue* (© 250/374-7447) plies the river waters, providing narrated sightseeing tours.

BC Wildlife Park Kamloops *Kids*   This zoological park is home to more than 65 endangered species. Most popular is the grizzly exhibit, but you'll also see Siberian tigers, cougars, pygmy owls, and wolves. On the grounds are a miniature railroad, cafe, and playground.

17km (11 miles) east of Kamloops on Hwy. 1 at 9007 Dallas Dr. © 250/573-3242. www.bczoo.org. Admission C$9 (US$7.20) adults, C$8 (US$6.40) seniors and youths 13–16, C$6 (US$4.80) children 3–12. Reduced rates in fall, winter, and spring. Daily 8am–4:30pm; check for extended hours in summer and during holidays.

Kamloops Art Gallery This is the only public art museum in the Thompson region and the largest in the province's interior, with a collection of more than 1,200 works by Canadian artists. The gallery also mounts changing exhibits of international works.

101–465 Victoria St. © 250/828-3543. www.kag.bc.ca. Admission C$3 (US$2.40) adult and senior couples, C$2 (US$1.60) seniors and students, C$5 (US$4) families; "pay what you can" Thurs 5–9pm. Tues–Wed and Fri–Sat 10am–5pm; Thurs 10am–9pm; Sun noon–4pm.

Kamloops Museum & Archives This museum tells the story of human history in the valley, from the arrival of the Shuswap people through the frontier era and up to World War II, when Kamloops served as a principal ammunition depot for Canada. It preserves a fur trader's cabin, livery stable, and blacksmith shop.

207 Seymour St. © 250/828-3576. www.city.kamloops.bc.ca/museum. Admission by donation. Late May to mid-Sept Tues–Sat 9:30am–4:30pm.

Secwepemc Museum & Heritage Park ⊛ The Secwepemc (pronounced "*she-whep-m*," anglicized as Shuswap) people have lived along the Thompson River for thousands of years. This heritage park contains an actual archaeological site inhabited 2,400 to 1,200 years ago, plus reconstructions of traditional villages from five different eras. Also featured are song-and-dance performances; displays of native plants and their traditional uses; and a replica of a salmon-netting station.

355 Yellowhead Hwy. © 250/828-9801. www.secwepemc.org/museum.html. Admission C$6 (US$4.80) adults, C$4 (US$3.20) children 7–17 and seniors. June–Labour Day Mon–Fri 8:30am–8pm, Sat–Sun 10am–8pm; Labour Day–May Mon–Fri 8:30am–4:30pm. Summer admission includes performances.

OUTDOOR PURSUITS

FISHING There are more than 200 lakes within a 2-hour drive of Kamloops. For licenses, equipment, and advice, try **Wilderness Outfitters,** 1304 Battle St. (© 250/372-3311), an authorized Orvis shop.

FOSSIL & GEOLOGY TOURS The hills around Kamloops are filled with Eocene-era fossils, including the remains of ancient fish, insects, leaves, and flowers; they are also rich in interesting rocks, minerals, and crystals, including quartz, selenite, opals, agates, and petrified wood. Kamloops Geology and Fossil Tours provide daylong outings to fossil and mineral digs where interested amateur bone-diggers and rock hounds can excavate for treasures. The service provides gloves, safety glasses, and packing materials, plus a trained geologist to guide and instruct. For two to six adults, rates are C$70 (US$56) each, and C$25 (US$18) per accompanied child under 12.

⌠*Tips* **Special Events**

Departing from a different ranch each year, the **Kamloops Cattle Drive** ⊛ (© 800/288-5850 or 250/372-7075) has grown immensely popular over the past decade, attracting over 1,000 participants. Cattle, cowboys, and visitors from around the world ride through the High Country's rolling prairies for 6 days in mid-July, finishing with a grand arrival and party in Kamloops. Horses, gear, and even seats on the chuck wagons are available for rent.

For more information, contact **Kamloops Geology and Fossil** (✆ **250/554-2401;** www3.telus.net/bc_eocene_tours).

GOLF **Aberdeen Hills Golf Links,** 1185 Links Way (✆ **250/828-1149** or 250/ 828-1143), is an 18-hole course with panoramic views. **The Dunes,** 652 Dunes Dr. (✆ **888/881-4653** or 250/579-3300), is a Graham Cooke–designed 18-hole championship course. **Kamloops Golf & Country Club,** 3125 Tranquille Rd. (✆ **250/ 376-8020**), is an 18-hole semi-private championship course. **Pineridge Golf Course,** 4725 E. Trans-Canada Hwy. (✆ **250/573-4333**), is an 18-hole course designed to be "the best short course ever built."

Rivershore Estates and Golf Links ⚡ (✆ **250/573-4622**) is an award-winning Robert Trent Jones design and has been host to the Canadian National Championships. **Sun Peaks Resort and Golf Course,** 280 Alpine Rd. (✆ **877/828-9989** or 250/578-7222), is a Graham Cooke course adjacent to the ski-resort village at Sun Peaks. Horseback riding, shopping, and six resort hotels are close to the first tee. For family-friendly golf, **McArthur Island Golf Centre** (✆ **250/553-4211**) offers a 9-hole course, driving range, miniature golf, pro shop, and restaurant.

SKIING **Sun Peaks Resort** ⚡ on Tod Mountain Road, Heffley Creek (✆ **250/ 578-7232,** or 250/578-7232 for snow report; www.sunpeaksresort.com), is a great powder-skiing and open-run area with a vertical rise of 870m (2,854 ft.). The 85 runs are serviced by a high-speed quad, fixed-grip quad, triple chair, double chair, T-bar, and beginner platter. Snowboarders have a choice of two half pipes, one with a super-large boarder-cross. At the bottom of this 914m (3,000-ft.) run are handrails, cars, a fun box, hips, quarter pipes, transfers, and fat gaps that were designed by Ecosign Mountain Planners and some of Canada's top amateur riders. Lift tickets are C$57 (US$46) for adults, C$40 (US$32) seniors, C$49 (US$39) for youths 13 to 18, and C$30 (US$24) for children 6 to 12. The resort also offers dog sledding, snowshoeing, and cross-country and snowmobile trails.

WHERE TO STAY

In addition to the following lodgings, most of which are downtown, you'll find a phalanx of easy-in, easy-out motels at Highway 1, exit 368, south and west of the city center.

Coast Canadian Inn ⚡ Ideally located in downtown, the Coast Canadian is one of the top hotels in Kamloops, with spacious guest rooms and lots of extras, such as WebTV Internet access; superior rooms offer bathrobes and upgraded toiletries. The protected outdoor pool and hot tub area is heated for all-season use. The Pronto Restaurant is one of the best in the city (see "Where to Dine," below).

339 St. Paul St., Kamloops, BC V2C 2J5. ✆ **800/663-1144** or 250/372-5201. Fax 250/372-9363. www.coasthotels. com. 94 units. C$108–C$159 (US$86–US$127) double. Extra person C$10 (US$8). Family plan, corporate, and off-season rates, and senior discounts available. AE, DC, MC, V. **Amenities:** Restaurant; pub; outdoor pool; exercise room; Jacuzzi; sauna; 24-hr. room service; laundry service; beer-and-wine store. *In room:* A/C, TV w/pay movies and Nintendo, dataport, coffeemaker, hair dryer, iron, WebTV.

Hostelling International–Kamloops This is one of the grandest hostels in all of Canada, located in the old 1909 district courthouse. The stone-and-brick structure has been modernized, but still retains its stained-glass windows and Gothic arches. The old courtroom is now a sitting room, and the old jail cells now serve as bathrooms.

7 W. Seymour St., Kamloops, BC V2C 1E4. © **250/828-7991**. Fax 250/828-2442. www.hihostels.ca. 70 beds. C$19 (US$15) members; C$23 (US$18) nonmembers. Private rooms available. Group and off-season rates available. MC, V. **Amenities:** Game room; laundry; Internet access; bike and ski storage. *In room:* No phone.

Plaza Heritage Hotel ⋆

The Plaza began its life as *the* downtown hotel in Kamloops. A masterful renovation of this 1920s luxury lodging allows it to once again reclaim that title. The restoration preserves the vintage feel of the decor while adding luxury touches such as fine furniture and spacious bathrooms. Each room is individually decorated—some in full Victoriana, others in equally stylish understatement. There are a number of room types and bed configurations—ask the reservation clerk to specify a room that will best serve your needs. The lobby restaurant offers fine dining, while the lounge is a comfortable spot for a friendly brew.

405 Victoria St., Kamloops, BC V2C 2A9. © **877/977-5292** or 250/377-8075. Fax 250/377-8076. www.plaza heritagehotel.com. 66 units. From C$119 (US$86) double. AE, MC V. **Amenities:** Restaurant; coffee shop; lounge; beer-and-wine store. *In room:* A/C, TV, dataport, coffeemaker, hair dryer.

Scott's Inn–Downtown *(Value*

A standard motel with clean, comfortable rooms and many extra features, Scott's is located in a quiet residential neighborhood within easy walking distance of downtown. Some units have kitchenettes. Save some money here without taking a cut in quality.

551 11th Ave., Kamloops, BC V2C 3Y1. © **800/665-3343** or 250/372-8221. Fax 250/372-9444. www.scottsinn. kamloops.com. 51 units. C$66–C$80 (US$53–US$64) double. Kitchen C$10 (US$8) extra. Extra person C$6–C$10 (US$4.80–US$8). Rates include continental breakfast. Group, senior, corporate, and off-season discounts available. AE, DC, MC, V. **Amenities:** Restaurant; indoor pool; Jacuzzi; coin-op laundry. *In room:* A/C, TV, coffeemaker, hair dryer.

Travelodge Kamloops *(Value*

This downtown hotel underwent a complete remodel in 2003 and offers good value, nicely furnished rooms, and a central location. With a pool, restaurant, and sauna, the Travelodge has the features you're looking for but at an accommodating price. It's extra clean and comfortable.

430 Columbia St., Kamloops, BC. V2C 2T5. © **877/372-8202** or 250/372-8202. Fax 250/372-1459. www.travelodge. com. From C$89 (US$71) double. AE, DC, MC V. **Amenities:** Restaurant; pool; hot tub; sauna. *In room:* A/C, TV, dataport, fridge, coffeemaker.

WHERE TO DINE

Chapters Viewpoint Restaurant INTERNATIONAL/MEXICAN

Perched on a hill above Kamloops, Chapters offers a great view over the city; the terrace is the place to be for summer drinks. The menu, which features steaks, prime rib, and classic Continental specialties, also has a marked New Mexican flavor. A local favorite is the Steak Ranchero, a red pepper–marinated New York strip that's grilled and served with a topping of cheese.

In the Howard Johnson Inn & Suites, 610 Columbia St. © **250/374-3224**. Reservations recommended. Main courses C$11–C$29 (US$8.80–US$23). AE, DC, MC, V. Daily 11:30am–2:30pm and 5–10pm.

Forsters Restaurant CANADIAN

If you don't want to negotiate downtown Kamloops, try this bright and lively restaurant for good food. The house specialty is prime rib in a variety of sizes. There's also a selection of pasta, chicken, and seafood dishes.

In the Best Western Kamloops, 1250 Rogers Way. © **250/372-5312**. Reservations recommended. Main courses C$14–C$24 (US$11–US$19). AE, DC, MC, V. Daily 7–10:30am, 11:30am–2:30pm, and 5–10pm.

Pronto Restaurant ⍟ CONTINENTAL/SEAFOOD One of Kamloops's finest restaurants, Pronto is a favorite for special occasions. About half of the menu is devoted to seafood; grilled steelhead trout is dusted with lemon pepper and served with tomato-sherry sauce. The meat dishes have a European flavor, ranging from pork schnitzel to rack of lamb with mint and merlot.

In the Coast Canadian Inn, 339 St. Paul St. ℂ 250/372-5201. Reservations suggested. Main courses C$14–C$33 (US$11–US$26). AE, MC, V. Daily 5–10pm.

Ric's Mediterranean Grill ⍟⍟ GRILL Ric's has done more to revitalize the downtown dining scene than any other restaurant. Out in Kamloops, nobody cares if you mix cuisines, so you'll find a wide-ranging menu—among the lighter fare, selections such as a Thai sirloin steak salad; and from the dinner menu, chutney prawns and scallops, Tequila lime barbecued ribs, or citrus-chile-glazed swordfish. The decor matches the food; Ric's is a handsome place with warm wood furnishings and dramatic black and gold accents.

227 Victoria St. ℂ 250/372-7771. Main courses C$10–C$30 (US$8–US$24). AE, MC, V. Mon–Fri 11am–10pm; Sat–Sun 4:30–10pm.

THE SHUSWAP LAKES

From Kamloops, the South Thompson River valley extends east to the Shuswap Lakes, a series of waterways that is an extremely popular summer destination for family houseboating parties. With more than 1,000km (620 miles) of shoreline, these long, interconnected lakes provide good fishing, water-skiing, and other boating fun.

The main commercial center for the Shuswap Lakes is **Salmon Arm** (pop. 15,000), 108km (67 miles) east of Kamloops on Highway 1. While the town has plenty of facilities for the traveler, there's not much in the way of sights. The **Salmon Arm Visitor Info Centre,** 751 Marine Park Dr. NE (ℂ 250/832-2230; www.sachamber.bc.ca), is open Monday through Friday from 9am to 5pm, plus weekends June through August.

The other sizable commercial center on the lakes is **Sicamous** (pop. 3,000), which has the largest number of houseboat-rental agencies.

OUTDOOR PURSUITS

With a shoreline filled with sandy beaches, coves, and narrow channels, fishing and houseboating are the area's biggest lures.

BOAT RENTALS Sicamous Creek Marina (ℂ 250/836-4611) rents ski boats, fishing boats, and other power watercraft, as well as kayaks and canoes.

FISHING To fish here, you need a nonresident freshwater license. Pick up copies of *BC Tidal Waters Sport Fishing Guide* and *BC Sport Fishing Regulations Synopsis for Non-Tidal Waters.* Independent anglers should also get a copy of the *BC Fishing Directory and Atlas.*

GOLF There are 15 golf courses in the area, making this heaven for golfers. One of the best is the **Salmon Arm Golf Club,** 3641 Hwy. 97B SE (ℂ 250/832-4727; www.salmonarmgolf.com), an 18-hole, par-72 course that's rated among the province's top 20. Rentals and lessons are offered. Greens fees start at C$70 (US$56). Also tops is the **Shuswap Lakes Estate Golf & Country Club,** 2404 Centennial Rd., Sorrento (ℂ 888/675-2523 or 250/675-2523), offering an 18-hole, par-71 course with four lakes. Greens fees start at C$59 (US$47). Facilities include a driving range, practice greens, and a pro shop with rentals and lessons.

Tips **The Salmon Run & Other Special Events**

In January, the **Reino Keski-Salmi Loppet** (© 250/832-7740) attracts cross-country skiers from across North America to the Larch Hills Cross-Country Ski Hill in Salmon Arm.

The annual **Salmon Arm Bluegrass Festival** (© 250/832-3258), held in Salmon Arm's R. J. Haney Heritage Park on the first weekend in July, features performers from Canada, the United States, and Europe.

One of nature's most amazing phenomena, the **Adams River Salmon Run** *, takes place in late October. Every 4 years, 1.5 to 2 million sockeye salmon struggle upstream to spawn in the Adams River. Trails provide riverside-viewing, with trained staff ready to interpret the spectacle. Take the Trans-Canada Highway (Hwy. 1) to Squilax, about 10km (6¼ miles) east of Chase. Follow the signs north to Roderick Haig-Brown Provincial Park.

HIKING   On the northern shore of Shuswap Lake near Squilax, **Shuswap Lake Provincial Park** (© 250/851-3000) offers wonderful strolling, with abundant old-growth ponderosa pines. About a mile offshore, the park's **Copper Island** has a pleasant trail that leads to a high point, where boaters looking for a dry-land hike can survey the lake and surrounding countryside.

WHERE TO STAY & DINE

Many visitors hire a houseboat and cruise the lakes in a leisurely fashion (see "Houseboating on the Shuswap Lakes," below). You'll also find good land-based accommodations, though some of the lower-priced motels see pretty hard use in summer—and it shows. Because most people use the kitchens on their boats, notable restaurants haven't really taken hold here.

The 280 campsites at **Shuswap Lake Provincial Park** (© 250/851-3000), 32km (20 miles) northeast of Highway 1 at Squilax, cost C$22 (US$18) each. Facilities include hot showers and flush toilets. The 35 sites at **Silver Beach Provincial Park** (© 250/851-3000), with pit toilets and fire pits, are accessible by unpaved road from Anglemount, by ferry from Sicamous, or by boating to the north end of Seymour Arm. Rates are C$14 (US$11). There are 51 sites at **Herald Provincial Park** (© 250/851-3000), 15km (9⅓ miles) northeast of Highway 1 at Tappen, plus hot showers, pit toilets, a sani-station, and a boat launch. Sites are C$22 (US$18).

Prestige Harbourfront Resort & Convention Centre **   This new hotel is the showcase of the Shuswap Lakes. A towering castellated structure, the Harbourfront Resort is directly on the downtown lakefront and half the rooms overlook the wharf and marina, while others offer mountain views. Rooms are very stylish and comfortable, and public areas are suitably grand. Jacuzzi suites are decorated according to various themes. With loads of extras and facilities—such as a shopping arcade, beauty salon, and athletic club—this is definitely one of the best addresses in central B.C.

251 Harbourfront Dr., Salmon Arm, BC V1E 2W7. © 877/737-8443 or 250/833-5800. www.prestigeinn.com. 121 units. From C$199–C$269 double (US$159–C$215). Extra person C$20 (US$16). Golf and ski packages available. AE, DC, MC, V. **Amenities:** 2 restaurants; coffee shop; bar; indoor and outdoor pools; day spa; hot tub. *In room:* A/C, TV, dataport, fridge, coffeemaker, hair dryer, iron.

Quaaout Lodge *(Kids)*   This handsome resort draws heavily on Native tradition in its decor. Set on the shores of Little Shuswap Lake, it's owned by the Shuswap band of the Secwepemc tribe. In addition to standard rooms, there are six units containing fireplaces and Jacuzzis. The excellent restaurant offers many traditional dishes, including alder-smoked salmon, venison, and fried bannock bread. There's easy access to hiking and biking trails; other activities include fishing, cross-country skiing, and canoeing. Adventurous kids can spend a night in a tepee.

Little Shuswap Lake Rd. (Box 1215), Chase, BC V0E 1M0. ✆ **800/663-4303** or 250/679-3090. Fax 250/679-3039. http://quaaout.bcresorts.com. 72 units. C$120–C$180 (US$96–US$150) double. AE, MC, V. Free parking. Take the Trans-Canada Hwy. (Hwy. 1) through the town of Chase. About 16km (10 miles) east, turn left at the Squilax Bridge underpass. Take the overpass; the lodge is on the 1st road on the left. **Amenities:** Restaurant; indoor pool; exercise room, Jacuzzi; sauna; limited room service; playground. *In room:* A/C, TV, dataport, coffeemaker, hair dryer.

Villager West Motor Inn *(Value)*   This motel offers good value and is a 10-minute walk from central Salmon Arm and the wharf. The Villager West is adjacent to two restaurants, a water-slide complex, and the bus station. Lake tours can be arranged.

61 10th St. SW, Salmon Arm, BC V1E 1E4. ✆ **888/832-9793** or 250/832-9793. Fax 250/832-5595. 78 units. C$85–C$114 (US$68–US$91) double. Kitchen C$7 (US$5.60) extra. Extra person C$7 (US$5.60). Commercial and off-season discounts available. AE, DC, DISC, MC, V. **Amenities:** Indoor pool; Jacuzzi. *In room:* A/C, TV, dataport, kitchenette, coffeemaker, hair dryer, iron.

THE UPPER THOMPSON RIVER VALLEY

From Kamloops, the North Thompson River flows north into increasingly rugged terrain. The little town of **Clearwater** is the gateway to **Wells Gray Provincial Park,** the

---

Moments Houseboating on the Shuswap Lakes

The best way to see the lakes is to rent a houseboat; after all, Shuswap is the "Houseboating Capital of Canada." Houseboats come equipped with staterooms, bathrooms, and kitchens. All you need to bring is your bedding and food. Reserve well in advance; by late spring, all boats are usually rented for the high season, from mid-June to Labour Day. Low-season rates are up to half off the prices below. Of the numerous rental operations along the Shuswap Lakes, the following are two of the largest.

Admiral House Boats, Sicamous Creek Marina (RR 1, Site 6, Comp 30), Sicamous (✆ **250/836-4611;** www.admiralhouseboats.com), rents houseboats from April to October. Super Admiral boats, which sleep up to 10, have three private staterooms and one and a half bathrooms. Rentals are available in 3-, 4-, and 7-day increments. In high season, a week on a Super Admiral houseboat goes for C$3,295 (US$2,636).

Twin Anchors Houseboat Vacations (www.twinanchors.com) has two locations, one in Salmon Arm at 750 Marine Park Dr. (✆ **800/665-7782** or 250/832-2745), and the other in Sicamous at 101 Martin St. (✆ 800/663-4026 or 250/836-2450). It offers four types of boats, ranging from two- to four-stateroom models. A week on a two-stateroom Cruisecraft II that sleeps 15 and comes with hot tub costs C$5,460 (US$4,368) per week. Rentals are available in 3-, 4-, 5-, and 7-day increments.

---

mountain wilderness park of choice for purist hikers and outdoor adventurers as the nearby Canadian Rockies become increasingly crowded and commercialized.

Although **Greyhound** offers bus service daily between Vancouver and Clearwater, you'll need a car to explore the best areas of the High Country. Clearwater is 103km (64 miles) north of Kamloops on Highway 5.

The **Clearwater–Wells Gray Info Centre,** 425 E. Yellowhead Hwy. 5 (*©* **250/ 674-2646;** www.ntvalley.com/clearwaterchamber), is at Highway 5 and Wells Gray Park Road. From October 16 to April 14, it's open Monday through Saturday from 9am to 5pm; April 15 to June 30 and September 1 to October 15, daily from 9am to 6pm; July 1 to August 31, daily from 8am to 8pm.

EXPLORING WELLS GRAY PROVINCIAL PARK

Wells Gray Provincial Park (*©* **604/371-6400;** www.wellsgraypark.ca) is British Columbia's third-largest park, encompassing more than 526,500 hectares (1.3 million acres) of mountains, rivers, lakes, volcanic formations, glaciers, forests, and alpine meadows. Wildlife abounds, including mule deer, moose, bears, beaver, timber wolves, mink, and golden eagles.

Wells Gray has something to offer everyone: birding and wildlife-viewing, hiking, boating, canoeing, and kayaking. Guide operations offer horseback riding, canoeing, rafting, fishing, and hiking. The history enthusiast can learn about the early home-steaders, trappers, and prospectors, or about the natural forces that produced Wells Gray's many volcanoes, mineral springs, and glaciers.

Most of Wells Gray is remote wilderness that can only be viewed after a vigorous hike or canoe excursion. In the southern quarter of the park, however, a road runs 34km (21 miles) from the park entrance to Clearwater Lake. Called simply the **Corridor,** it provides access to many of the park's features as well as its campgrounds and many of its trail heads.

Twice as tall as Niagara Falls, the park's **Helmcken Falls** is Canada's fourth-highest waterfall, and is an awesome sight easily reached by paved road. Boating, canoeing, kayaking, and fishing are popular pastimes on **Clearwater, Azure, Mahood,** and **Murtle lakes.** The wilderness campgrounds along these lakes make perfect destinations for overnight canoe or fishing trips.

Multiday hiking destinations include the area around Ray Farm Homestead, Rays Mineral Spring, and the thickly forested **Murtle River Trail** that leads to **Majerus Falls, Horseshoe Falls,** and **Pyramid Mountain,** a volcanic upgrowth that was shaped when it erupted beneath miles of glacial ice that covered the park millions of years ago.

GUIDED TOURS & EXCURSIONS

Area accommodations make it easy to get out and explore the wilderness. Both **Trophy Mountain Buffalo Ranch** and **Helmcken Falls Lodge** (see "Where to Stay," below) and the **Wells Gray Guest Ranch,** Wells Gray Road (*©* **250/674-2792** or 250/674-2774; www.wellsgrayranch.com), offer a wide variety of recreational options, including horseback riding, canoeing, rafting, and hiking trips in summer, and dog sledding, cross-country snowshoeing, snowmobiling, and ice fishing in winter.

Interior Whitewater Expeditions (*©* **800/661-7238** in Canada, or 250/674-3727; www.interiorwhitewater.bc.ca) offers half- to 5-day rafting and kayaking trips.

Consider a 3-hour white-water screamer on the Clearwater River for C$85 (US$68), or a more leisurely 3-hour float down the North Thompson for C$63 (US$50).

Wells Gray Chalets & Wilderness Adventures (© **888/SKI-TREK** or 250/587-6444; www.skihike.com) offers backcountry hut-to-hut hiking and cross-country ski trips. Ian Eakins and Tay Briggs run this family-owned company that maintains three chalets nestled deep in the park. Each sleeps up to 12 and is equipped with a kitchen, bedding, sauna, and propane lighting and heat. It's the best of both worlds: You can experience untrammeled wilderness and great rural hospitality. Two of the nicest people you could hope to have as guides, Ian and Tay are extremely knowledgeable about the wildlife and history of the park. They offer guided or self-catered hiking and cross-country ski packages as well as guided 3- and 6-day canoe trips that are custom-designed for families. Guided summer hikes are roughly C$113 to C$130 (US$90–US$104) per person per day; guided winter cross-country ski trips are C$150 (US$120) per person per day.

WHERE TO STAY

Most campers head to Wells Gray Provincial Park's **Spahats, Clearwater,** and **Dawson Falls campgrounds** ℱ (© **250/851-3000**), which offer fire pits, firewood, pumped well water, pit toilets, and boat launches. Each of the 88 sites go for C$14 (US$11) per night; check the sign outside the Clearwater visitor center to make sure the grounds aren't full before driving all the way up to the park.

Dutch Lake Motel and Campground   The nicest lodging in the town of Clearwater itself, the Dutch Lake Motel overlooks its namesake lake in a quiet setting away from the highway. All guest rooms have balconies; some have kitchenettes. Canoe rentals can be arranged.

333 Roy Rd. (RR 2, Box 5116), Clearwater, BC V0E 1N0. © **877/674-3325** or 250/674-3325. Fax 250/674-2916. www.dutchlakemotel.com. 27 units. C$90–C$160 (US$72–US$125) double; campsites C$23 (US$18). Lower off-season rates. AE, MC, V. **Amenities:** Restaurant; bar; tennis courts. *In room:* A/C, TV, dataport, fridge, coffeemaker, hair dryer, iron.

Helmcken Falls Lodge ℱ   Established in the 1920s as a humble trapper's camp, this venerable property has grown into a handsome complex of buildings that includes a 1940s hand-hewn log lodge, which is now home to Wells Gray's best dining room. Accommodations are in a variety of structures, including two log buildings each with four hotel-style rooms, plus a two-story chalet building, and the original trapper's log cabin with two rustic guest rooms. Helmcken Falls Lodge is noted for its recreational activities. The lodge maintains its own horse herd and offers a variety of guided rides in the park, from 1 hour to overnight. Naturalist-led half- and full-day hikes and canoeing trips through the park are another specialty. Cross-country ski rentals are available in winter. The friendly staff can arrange a wide range of other recreational opportunities with area outfitters; families are welcome. The lodge also overlooks a 9-hole golf course. Call ahead for dinner reservations in the atmospheric log dining room, with delicious home-cooked meals. The lodge is closed October 15 to December 20 and all of April.

Wells Gray Park Rd., Box 239, Clearwater, BC V0E 1N0. © **250/674-3657.** Fax 250/674-2971. www.helmcken falls.com. 21 units. C$120–C$148 (US$96–US$118) double. Rafting and kayaking packages available. AE, MC, V. Located 35km (22 miles) north of Clearwater. **Amenities:** Restaurant. *In room:* No phone.

Nakiska Ranch 🏚🏚   Gorgeous log cabins, grazing cattle on acres of mowed meadows, and Wells Gray's majestic forests and mountains surround the main lodge of this working ranch. The six log one-bedroom cabins are the original log ranch buildings from the turn of the 20th century, but beautifully renovated and updated with full kitchens, spacious bathrooms and lovely furnishings straight out of the pages of *House Beautiful.* Each of the cabins has a private patio with gas barbecue; three have fireplaces. In addition, there are two rooms each with two twin beds and private bathrooms in the main lodge. The lodge features a TV lounge with video library; phones and fax machine are also available. Families are welcome. A full Swiss-style breakfast is available for C$12 (US$9.60) a person. Your hosts will arrange horseback rides and other recreation. Open in winter by reservation only.

Trout Creek Rd. (off Wells Gray Park Rd.), Clearwater, BC V0E 1N0. ✆ 250/674-3655. Fax 250/674-3387. www. nakiskaranch.bc.ca. 8 units. Summer C$105 (US$84) double, C$120–C$145 (US$96–US$116) cabin; winter C$89 (US$71) double, C$105–C$125 (US$84–US$100) cabin. MC, V. Drive up Wells Gray Park Rd. for 42km (26 miles); it will take about 40 min. Turn right at the ranch sign onto Trout Creek Rd. The ranch is a 10-min. drive from the park entrance. Small pets accepted. **Amenities:** Lounge. *In room:* Kitchen (cabins only), fridge, coffeemaker, hair dryer, no phone.

Trophy Mountain Buffalo Ranch Bed & Breakfast and Campground   You can't miss the small buffalo herd grazing in a pasture as you drive up the Wells Gray Park Road. Beyond this pastoral setting stand a log lodge, campsites, and camping cabins. The lodge came into existence nearly a century ago out on the North Thompson River. The abandoned structure was taken apart log by hand-hewn log and reassembled in its present location. The lodge rooms are cozy and clean; all but two have private bathrooms. The rustic camping cabins, tent sites, and RV sites are extremely well kept. Dishwashing sinks are set up on the deck of the shower house, where hot water flows liberally. Hiking and horseback-riding trails surround the ranch, and guided rides run to the cliffs overlooking the Clearwater River valley and to the base of a secluded waterfall (C$45/US$36 for a 2½-hr. trip). This friendly, unfussy guest ranch is just the spot if you're looking for clean and simple accommodations with lots of Old West atmosphere. It's open May through October only.

RR 1 (P.O. Box 1768), Clearwater, BC V0E 1N0. ✆ 250/674-3095. Fax 250/674-3131. www.buffaloranch.ca. 6 units, 15 campsites, 2 camping cabins. C$65 (US$52) double; C$16–C$19 (US$13–US$15) campsite; C$11 (US$8.80) cabin. Lodge room rates include full breakfast. MC, V. Drive up Wells Gray Park Rd. for 20km (12 miles); it will take about 20 min. Turn left at the ranch sign. *In room:* No phone.

WHERE TO DINE

The **Clearwater Country Inn,** 449 Yellowhead Hwy. E. (✆ 250/674-3121), has good home-style cooking; it's open daily from 4am to 9pm. **Helmcken Falls Lodge** (✆ 250/674-3657), described above, and the Black Horse Saloon at the **Wells Gray Guest Ranch,** Wells Gray Road (✆ 250/674-2774), offer lunch and buffet-style dinners; reservations are required. The friendly **River Café,** 73 Old N. Thompson Hwy. (✆ 250/674-0088), in Clearwater, offers salads, espresso drinks, and fresh-baked snacks.

The Okanagan Valley

Just south of the High Country on Highway 97, the arid Okanagan Valley, with its long chain of crystal-blue lakes, is the ideal destination for freshwater-sports enthusiasts, golfers, skiers, and wine lovers. Ranches and small towns have flourished here for more than a century; the region's fruit orchards and vineyards will make you feel as if you've been transported to the Spanish countryside. Summer visitors get the pick of the crop—at insider prices—from the many fruit stands that line Highway 97. Be sure to stop for a pint of cherries, homemade jams, and other goodies.

An Okanagan-region chardonnay won gold medals in 1994 at international competitions held in London and Paris. In 2000, several other Okanagan vintages picked up quite a number of medals at international competitions. And more than 70 other wineries produce vintages that are following right on their heels. Despite these coveted honors, the valley has received little international publicity. Most visitors are Canadian, and the valley isn't yet a major tour-bus destination (it's far less crowded and expensive than the more publicized California wine country, but no less extraordinary). Get here before they do.

Many retirees have chosen the Okanagan Valley as their home for its relatively mild winters and dry, desertlike summers. It's also a favorite destination for younger visitors, drawn by boating, water-skiing, sportfishing, and windsurfing on 128km-long (79-mile) Okanagan Lake. The town of Kelowna in the central valley is the hub of the province's winemaking industry and the area's largest city.

1 Essentials

GETTING THERE

BY CAR The 387km (240-mile) drive from Vancouver via the Trans-Canada Highway (Hwy. 1) and Highway 3 rambles through rich delta farmlands and the forested mountains of Manning Provincial Park and the Similkameen River region before descending into the Okanagan Valley's antelope-brush and sagebrush desert. For a more direct route to Kelowna, take the Trans-Canada Highway to the Coquihalla Toll Highway, which eliminates more than an hour's driving time. The 203km (126-mile) route runs from Hope through Merritt over the Coquihalla Pass into Kamloops.

BY BUS **Greyhound Canada** (© 800/661-8747; www.greyhound.ca) runs daily buses from Vancouver to Penticton and Kelowna, with service continuing on to Banff and Calgary. The one-way fare to Penticton is C$61 (US$50).

BY PLANE   **Air Canada Jazz** (© **888/247-2262;** www.aircanada.ca) and **WestJet** (© **888/937-8538;** www.westjet.com) offer frequent daily commuter flights from Calgary and Vancouver to Penticton and Kelowna. **Horizon Air** (© **800/252-7522;** http://horizonair.alaskaair.com) provides service to and from Seattle and Kelowna.

VISITOR INFORMATION

Contact the **Thompson Okanagan Tourism Association,** 1332 Water St., Kelowna (© **800/860-5999** or 250/860-5999; www.totabc.com), which is open daily from 9am to 6pm.

2 Touring the Wineries

British Columbia has a long history of producing wines, ranging from fantastic to truly bad. In 1859, missionary Father Pandosy planted apple trees and vineyards and produced sacramental wines for the valley's mission. Other monastery wineries cropped up, but none worried about the quality of their bottlings. After all, the Canadian government had a reputation for subsidizing domestic industries, such as book publishing and cleric wineries, to promote entrepreneurial growth.

In the 1980s, the government threatened to pull its support of the industry unless it could produce an internationally competitive product. The vintners listened. Rootstock was imported from France and Germany, and European-trained master vintners were hired to oversee the development of the vines and the winemaking process. The climate and soil conditions turned out to be some of the best in the world for winemaking, and today, British Columbia wines are winning international gold medals. Competitively priced, in the range of C$7 to C$50 (US$5.60–US$40), they represent some great bargains in well-balanced chardonnays, pinot blancs, and Gewürztraminers; full-bodied merlots, pinot noirs, and cabernets; and dessert ice wines that surpass the best muscat d'or.

The valley's more than 70 vineyards and wineries conduct free tours and tastings throughout the year. The **Okanagan Wine Festival** (© **250/861-6654;** www.owfs. com), an annual celebration of wine and food, is held at area vineyards and restaurants. Contact local visitor centers for information, as new wineries continue to open and established ones reinvent themselves with new and ever more sophisticated facilities. Vineyard restaurants are particularly in the vanguard, and many tasting rooms now offer food in addition to wine.

3 Oliver

52km (32 miles) S of Penticton

The absolute center of the Okanagan fruit-growing orchards is Oliver (pop. 4,300). What makes the area interesting to travelers, however, is its many wineries. Scarcely a tourist town, Oliver exists to serve the needs of local farmers, orchardists, and winemakers. It makes a reasonable stop if you're not obsessed with the resort and watersports lifestyle prevalent in the rest of the Okanagan Valley.

Many of the long-established wineries that put the region's name on the wine-producing map are within a short drive of Oliver. Especially proud of their location are the wineries along the "Golden Mile," situated on the slopes of the mountains west of

Oliver along Road 8. **Festival of the Grape** (© 250/498-6321; www.oliverchamber. bc.ca) occurs on the first weekend of October, and is part of the larger Okanagan Wine Festival.

Notable wineries that welcome visitors include **Domaine Combret Estate Winery,** on Road 13 (© 866/837-7647; www.combretwine.com), which has won medals at the annual Chardonnay du Monde competition in Burgundy. Call ahead for tasting room appointments.

Gehringer Brothers Estate Winery, Road 8 (© 250/498-3537), offers German-style wines, including Riesling, pinot gris, pinot noir, and pinot blanc. Try the crisp Ehrenfelser white wine, which carries intense flavors of apricot and almond. The tasting room is open June through mid-October daily.

Hester Creek Estate Winery, Road 8 (© 250/498-4435; www.hestercreek.com), has a boutique that's open daily, plus tours by appointment. Especially nice is the patio, an inviting spot for picnickers. Superior growing conditions found at Hester Creek produce intense fruit flavors.

Inniskillin Okanagan, Road 11 (© 250/498-6663; www.inniskillin.com), offers daily tours and tastings. This winery—the western operations of the famed Niagara-area winery—produces a distinct selection of red wines such as cabernet sauvignon, merlot, and pinot noir.

Tinhorn Creek Vineyards, Road 7 (© 888/846-4676; www.tinhorn.com), is one of the top Okanagan wineries. Self-guided tours allow you to linger; guided tours can be arranged by appointment. Specialties include Gewürztraminer, pinot gris, chardonnay, pinot noir, cabernet franc, merlot, and ice wine.

Adjacent to a wilderness area and bird sanctuary overlooking Vaseaux Lake, **Blue Mountain Vineyards & Cellars,** Allendale Road (© 250/497-8244; www.blue mountainwinery.com), has tours and tastings by appointment only. Due to its small output, Blue Mountain wines are available only from the winery and at fine restaurants.

International accolades are pouring in to the wines of **Burrowing Owl Estate Winery,** south of Oliver off Black Sage Road at 100 Burrowing Owl Place (© 877/ 498-0620; www.bovwine.com). In addition to a delicious and highly decorated merlot, the winery offers **The Sonora Room,** a winery restaurant that serves very up-to-date cuisine designed to match the Borrowing Owl wines (closed in winter). The winery is open for tastings from Easter through October from 10am to 5pm; in winter call ahead for an appointment.

The nicest place to stay in Oliver is the **Southwind Inn,** 34017 Hwy. 97 S. (© 800/ 661-9922 or 250/498-3442; www.winecountry.net), with high-season doubles for C$109 to C$139 (US$87–US$111). Amenities include a fine restaurant with patio, pub, and outdoor pool.

For more information on the region, contact the **Oliver Visitor Info Centre,** 36205 93rd St. (© 250/498-6321; www.oliverchamber.bc.ca).

4 Penticton

80km (50 miles) N of Oliver; 60km (37 miles) S of Kelowna; 396km (246 miles) W of Vancouver via the Coquihalla Hwy.

One of the belles of the Okanagan, Penticton (pop. 41,500) is a lovely midsize city with two entirely different lakefronts. Above the town is the toe-end of vast Okanagan Lake, to the south are the upper beaches of Lake Skaha. It's a lovely setting, and a peach of a place for a recreation-dominated holiday. "Peach" has additional significance here, as Penticton is also the center for apple, peach, cherry, and grape production. But there's a lot more to Penticton than agriculture: Facilities range from hostels to world-class resorts, and the restaurants are among the best in this part of British Columbia.

The **Penticton Visitor Info Centre** is at 888 Westminster Ave. W. (© **800/663-5052** or 250/493-4055; www.penticton.org). It also houses the British Columbia Wine Information Centre and a good wine shop with all sorts of local vintages. It's open daily 9am to 6 pm.

EXPLORING THE TOWN

It's hard to beat Penticton's location. With Okanagan Lake lapping at the northern edge of town, Lake Skaha's beaches forming the town's southern boundary, and the Okanagan River cutting between the two, Penticton has the feel of a real oasis. Hemmed in by lakes and desert valley walls, Penticton is pleasantly compact and in summer fairly hums with activity. As elsewhere in the Okanagan Valley, watersports are the main preoccupation, but Penticton also has an air of gentility that suggests there's a little more going on than just jet-skiing.

The old commercial center is along **Main Street** toward the north end of town; there's also a lot of activity along **Lakeshore Drive,** the boulevard that parallels the beachfront of Okanagan Lake. Lined with hotels and restaurants on one side, clogged with sun worshippers on the other, Lakeshore Drive is a very busy place in summer.

Right on the lakefront is the **SS *Sicamous,*** a stern-wheeler that plied the waters of Okanagan Lake from 1914 to 1935. Now preserved as a museum, it's beached in the sand, and currently houses a scale model of the historic Kettle Valley Railway. It's open in summer daily from 9am to 9pm, the rest of the year Monday through Friday from 9am to 4pm.

Even if you're not into sunbathing, a saunter along the **beachfront promenade** is called for. Beach volleyball, sand castles, and a drinks kiosk in the shape of a giant peach are just the beginning of what you'll encounter along this long, broad strand: It's prime people-watching territory.

At the eastern end of the beachfront is the **Art Gallery of the South Okanagan,** 199 Front St. (© **250/493-2928**), a showcase for local artists. The gift shop is a good spot to pick up a souvenir. Just beyond the gallery is the **Marina on Lake Okanagan** (© **250/770-2000**), where you can rent all manner of watercraft.

Tips **Special Events**

The town's big summer celebration is the **Penticton Peach Festival,** held the first week of August. It includes parades, watersports competitions, live entertainment, street dances, midway rides, and a general and pervasive air of fun.

Be the first to taste the valley's best chardonnay, pinot noir, merlot, and ice wines at the **Okanagan Wine Festival** (© **250/861-6654;** www.owfs.com), during late September and early October at wineries and restaurants throughout Penticton.

The beach along Skaha Lake is usually more laid-back than the Okanagan Lake front. The relatively more secluded nature of this beach, plus a large water park for the kids, makes it a good destination for families. **Skaha Lake Marina** (© **250/492-7368**) is at the east edge of the beach.

TOURING THE WINERIES

The two main wine-producing areas near Penticton are north along the east slopes of Okanagan Lake near the community of Naramata, and north along the west lake slopes near Summerland. From Penticton, follow Upper Bench Road, which turns into Naramata Road and leads to **Naramata,** 14km (8¾ miles) north and one of the first wine-growing regions in British Columbia.

Lang Vineyard, 2493 Gammon Rd. (© **250/496-5987;** www.langvineyards.com), was one of the first of the new generation of wineries in the province. It's open for tastings and sales daily from May to October.

Hillside Estate, 1350 Naramata Rd. (© **250/493-6274;** www.hillsideestate.com), is open daily (call ahead in midwinter). From Easter weekend until the Okanagan Wine Festival, it operates the **Barrel Room Bistro,** a patio restaurant at the winery, open for lunch daily, and dinner from late May on Friday, Saturday, and Sunday evenings only.

Lake Breeze Vineyards, 930 Sammet Rd. (© **250/496-5659;** www.lakebreeze winery.ca), opens its tasting room from May 1 to October 15 daily from 10am to 5pm. Its patio restaurant **Mahdina's** is open for lunch from May 1 to September 30.

North of Penticton along Highway 97 is another wine-producing area. **Sumac Ridge Estate Winery,** 17403 Hwy. 97 (© **250/494-0451;** www.sumacridge.com), offers tours daily from May to mid-October. Besides operating a shop and tasting room open daily year-round, the winery runs the fine **Cellar Door Bistro** (see "Where to Dine," below).

Located 43km (27 miles) north of Penticton, the **Hainle Vineyards Estate Winery,** 5355 Trepanier Bench Rd. (© **250/767-2525;** www.hainle.com), was the first Okanagan winery to produce ice wine. The wine shop is open daily for tasting **Amphora,** the winery's bistro, is open daily for lunch and dinner.

THE KETTLE VALLEY STEAM RAILWAY

The Kettle Valley Railway, which was completed in 1914 to link coastal communities to the burgeoning mining camps in Kettle River valley, became one of the Okanagan Valley's top draws after it was converted into rails-to-trails pathways for hikers and mountain bikers. Unfortunately, the massive forest fires of 2003 burned a number of the historic wooden trestles that bridged the route through steep Myra Canyon, closing it at least for now for most hiking and biking access (there are lengthy detours around the burned trestles, though they aren't for novice bikers). Public and private funding initiatives are in place to rebuild all destroyed spans and reopen the entire route.

One section of the Kettle Valley Railway, however, remains intact, and is in use by original steam trains. The **Kettle Valley Railway Society,** 18404 Bathville Rd., Summerland (© **877/494-8424** in B.C., or 250/494-8422; www.kettlevalleyrail.org), offers a 2-hour journey on a 10km (6¼-mile) section of the original track west of Summerland, 16km (10 miles) north of Penticton. From the last Thursday in June to

Labour Day, the train runs Thursday through Monday at 10:30am and 1:30pm, departing from the Prairie Valley Station off Bathville Road; from late May to late June and from Labour Day to mid-October, the train runs at the same times Saturday through Monday only. In addition, on most Saturdays there's an afternoon train that involves a "train robbery" and barbecue. Check the website for other additional runs throughout the year. Fares are C$18 (US$14) for adults, C$17 (US$13) for seniors, C$15 (US$12) for students, C$11 (US$8.80) for children 3 to 12, and C$62 (US$50) for families.

OUTDOOR PURSUITS

BIKING   Bike rentals and friendly riding advice are available at **Sun Country Cycle,** 533 Main St. (© **250/493-0686**).

BOATING & WATERSPORTS   The Okanagan Valley's numerous local marinas offer full-service boat rentals. **Okanagan Houseboat Vacations,** 291 Front St., Penticton (© **800/524-2212** or 250/492-5099; www.obc.bc.ca), rents houseboats with fully equipped kitchens that can accommodate up to 10 people. Prices for a weeklong rental begin at C$2,600 (US$2,080) in the high summer season, with substantial discounts for off-peak rentals. The **Marina on Okanagan Lake,** 291 Front St., Penticton (© **250/492-2628**), rents ski-boats, Tigersharks (similar to Jet-Skis or Sea-Doos), fishing boats, and tackle.

A popular activity is renting a rubber raft from **Coyote Cruises,** in the blue building along the river at Riverside Drive (© **205/492-2115**), then floating from Okanagan Lake down to Skaha Lake, which takes about 2 hours. On a hot day, you'll be joined by hundreds of other people in rafts, inner tubes, and rubber dinghies; the water fight of your life is almost guaranteed.

GOLF   **Penticton Golf & Country Club** (© **250/492-8727**) is an 18-hole, par-70 course just west of downtown on the Okanagan River, with rentals, a driving range, and a clubhouse. Greens fees are C$40 to C$49 (US$32–US$39). **Twin Lakes Golf Resort,** 18km (11 miles) south of Penticton off Highway 97 (© **250/497-5359**), is an 18-hole course located in a steep-walled canyon; greens fees start at C$42 (US$34).

SKIING   Cross-country and powder skiing are the Okanagan Valley's main winter attractions. Intermediate and expert downhill skiers frequent the **Apex Resort,** Green Mountain Road, Penticton (© **800/387-2739,** 250/492-2880, 250/292-8111, or 250/492-2929, ext. 2000, for snow report; www.apexresort.com), where 56 runs are serviced by one quad chair, one triple chair, one T-bar, and one beginner tow/platter. Day passes are C$53 (US$42) adult, C$43 (US$34) senior and teens, and C$32 (US$26) 12 and under. The 52km (32 miles) of cross-country ski trails are well marked and well groomed, offering both flat stretches and hilly ascents. Facilities include an ice rink, snow golf, sleigh rides, casino nights, and racing competitions.

WHERE TO STAY

There are three major lodging areas: the northern lakefront on Okanagan Lake, the southern lakefront on Lake Skaha, and the Main Street strip that connects the two. Penticton has a lot of older motels, many of which have seen years of hard use.

Bel Air Motel   This older motor-court motel is just the ticket if you don't want to spend a fortune. Guest rooms are large and stylish, and the balconies decked with flowers. You'll need to drive to get to the beaches, but otherwise it's a good, inexpensive choice, near both restaurants and shopping.

2670 Skaha Lake Rd., Penticton, BC V2A 6G1. © **800/766-5770** or 250/492-6111. Fax 250/492-8035. www.belair motel.bc.ca. 42 units. High season C$89–C$165 (US$71–US$132) double. Kitchen C$16 (US$13) extra. AE, MC, V. **Amenities:** Outdoor heated pool; Jacuzzi; sauna; coin-op laundry; playground. *In room:* A/C, TV, dataport, coffeemaker.

Best Western Inn at Penticton   Roughly midway between the two lake beaches, this Best Western is a short drive from the beach scene, but it's a handsome hotel with well-furnished rooms and especially nice facilities, such as the beautifully landscaped courtyard and banks of flowers everywhere.

3180 Skaha Lake Rd., Penticton, BC V2A 6G4. © **800/668-6746** or 250/493-0311. Fax 250/493-5556. www.best westernpenticton.com. 67 units. High season C$119–C$139 (US$95–US$111) double. Kitchen C$20 (US$16) extra. AE, DISC, MC, V. **Amenities:** Restaurant; indoor and outdoor pools w/water slide; Jacuzzi; playground; barbecue. *In room:* A/C, TV, dataport, fridge, coffeemaker.

Hostelling International–Penticton   Right in the heart of downtown, this hostel is in a historic home once owned by a pioneer banker. Private rooms are available.

464 Ellis St., Penticton, BC V2A 4M2. © **250/492-3992.** Fax 250/492-8755. www.hihostels.ca. 50 beds. High season C$17–C$21 (US$14–US$17) dorm bed; C$38–C$42 (US$30–US$34) private unit. MC, V. **Amenities:** Bike rentals; tour desk; coin-op laundry; Internet access; kitchen.

Naramata Heritage Inn & Spa 🕿🕿   Built in 1908, the Naramata Inn served as a hotel, private residence, and girls' school before undergoing extensive and loving renovation as a classic wine country inn. If you're coming to the Okanagan for a romantic getaway, or simply have an aversion to the mom-and-pop motels and corporate hotels that dominate wine-country lodging, then look no further. This inn, which is a half-hour northwest of Penticton on the quiet side of Lake Okanagan, overlooks vineyards and the lake itself. It offers very charming rooms (note that some are authentically small), restored to glow with period finery, but modern luxury—the linens are top-notch and the bathroom's heated tile floors are a nice touch on a cool morning. In addition to en suite bathrooms with showers, rooms also have a claw-foot tub in the bedroom for soaking and relaxing. The inn also offers a spa for upscale pampering, plus the best dining in the area. There are few places in the otherwise utilitarian Okanagan as nice as this.

3625 First St., Naramata, BC V0H 1N0 (19km/12 miles north of Penticton on the east side of Okanagan Lake). © **866/617-1188** or 250/496-5001. www.naramatainn.com. 12 units. High season C$182–C$510 (US$147–US$408) double. Continental breakfast included in rates. Lower off-season rates. AE, MC, V. **Amenities:** Restaurant (see "Where to Dine," below); wine bar; spa; limited room service; wireless Internet access. *In room:* A/C, hair dryer, iron, balcony (in some rooms), no phone.

Penticton Lakeside Resort Convention Centre & Casino 🕿   Set on the water's edge, the Penticton Lakeside Resort has its own stretch of sandy Lake Okanagan beachfront, where guests can sunbathe or stroll along the adjacent pier. The deluxe suites feature Jacuzzis, and the lakeside rooms are highly recommended for their view. All rooms and suites are smartly furnished with quality furniture; all rooms have balconies (some suites have two-person Jacuzzi tubs). The menus at the Okanagan Surf N' Turf Company Restaurant and the Barking Parrot Bar & Patio feature locally grown ingredients. Other facilities include an extensive pool and health club facility, and a casino.

21 W. Lakeshore Dr., Penticton, BC V2A 7M5. © **800/663-9400** or 250/493-8221. Fax 250/493-0607. www.rpb hotels.com. 204 units. C$197–C$222 (US$156–US$178) double; from C$255 (US$204) suite. Lower off-season rates. AE, DC, DISC, MC, V. Free parking. When you arrive in town, follow the signs to Main St. Lakeshore Dr. is at the north end of Main St. Pets accepted with C$20 (US$16) fee. **Amenities:** Restaurant; lounge; indoor pool; tennis courts; health club; Jacuzzi; sauna; watersports equipment rental; children's center; concierge; tour desk; business center; 24-hr. room service; babysitting; same-day dry cleaning; volleyball court. *In room:* A/C, TV/VCR w/pay movies, dataport, coffeemaker, hair dryer, iron.

Spanish Villa Resort   Of the many motels that line Lakeshore Drive, the Spanish Villa, directly across the street from the Okanagan Lake beaches, is the most attractive and best maintained. Rooms are furnished with a Mediterranean flair; the most expensive units boast great views. The Villa is close to dozens of restaurants and shops, right in the thick of things.

890 Lakeshore Dr., Penticton, BC V2A 1C1. © **800/552-9199** or 250/492-2922. Fax 250/492-2922. www.spanish villa.penticton.com. 60 units. High season C$98–C$150 (US$78–US$120) double. Kitchen C$20 (US$16) extra. AE, DISC, MC, V. **Amenities:** Indoor pool; coin-op laundry. *In room:* A/C, TV, dataport, kitchenette, fridge, coffeemaker, hair dryer.

Travelodge Penticton *Value*   A moderately priced motel within walking distance of Okanagan Lake and next door to the convention center, the Travelodge offers clean, unfussy rooms with lots of extras (most have an enclosed balcony). All in all, one of the best values in Penticton.

950 Westminster Ave., Penticton, BC V2A 1L2. © **800/578-7878** or 250/492-0225. Fax 250/493-8340. www. travelodge.penticton.com. 34 units. C$119–C$124 (US$95–US$99) double. Lower off-season rates. Kitchen C$10 (US$8) extra. AE, MC, V. **Amenities:** Restaurant; outdoor and indoor pools with water slide; Jacuzzi; sauna; coin-op laundry. *In room:* A/C, TV, fridge, coffeemaker.

Waterfront Inn   This older, standard-issue motel is right across from a park with beach access to Lake Skaha. The rooms are clean and basic, but if you're here for the lakefront action, you'll enjoy the relative quiet of this location and the fact that you won't have to cross four lanes of traffic to get to the water.

3688 Parkview St., Penticton, BC V2A 6H1. © **800/563-6006** or 250/492-8228. Fax 250/492-8228. www.waterfront inn.net. 21 units. High season C$80–C$125 (US$64–US$100) double. Kitchen C$10 (US$8) extra. AE, MC, V. Closed mid-Oct to Apr. **Amenities:** Sauna; splash pool; coin-op laundry; playground. *In room:* A/C, TV, fridge.

WHERE TO DINE

Cellar Door Bistro ✿ CONTINENTAL   This attractive choice is hidden inside the Sumac Ridge Estate Winery in Summerland, just north of Penticton. The menu, which changes monthly, has a hearty country French finesse, as in the savory mushroom tart, roast duck breast with chanterelle-studded potatoes, and chardonnay-poached salmon. The dishes are paired with wines from Sumac Ridge.

17403 Hwy. 97, Summerland, 17km (11 miles) north of Penticton. © **250/494-3316.** www.cellardoorbistro.com. Reservations recommended. Main courses C$16–C$31 (US$13–US$25). AE, MC, V. Tues–Sat 11:30am–2:30pm and 5–9pm.

Granny Bogners CONTINENTAL   Granny Bogners, in a shake-sided heritage home in a quiet residential area, tops the list when it comes to locals' favorite special-occasion restaurant. The menu is slightly old-fashioned but reassuringly so and admirably prepared: Choices include chicken cordon bleu, filet mignon with béarnaise sauce, grilled salmon, veal medallions in port-and-mushroom sauce, and a number of

German specialties. Despite the white linen and crystal, the dining room retains a kind of rustic nonchalance. In summer, dine out on the lovely garden patio.

302 W. Eckhardt Ave. ✆ 250/493-2711. Reservations required. Main courses C$16–C$32 (US$13–US$26). AE, MC, V. Tues–Sun 5:30–9:30pm.

Naramata Inn ✿ NORTHWEST CUISINE Resplendent in early-20th-century character, the Naramata Inn's Rock Oven Dining Room overlooks gardens and vineyards, and serves some of the most sophisticated food in the Okanagan Valley. Using only the freshest ingredients—many from its own garden—the Rock Oven offers a selection of six- to nine-course specialty menus that focus on regional ingredients; the inn offers a very impressive wine list and wine pairings are available for each of the menus. Expect such refined dishes as barbecued rabbit leg with lavender jelly glaze and English green pea risotto, and sockeye salmon filet baked with pumpkin seed crust. While the Rock Oven has limited hours and is only open seasonally, excellent a la carte meals are available at the inn's Cobblestone Wine Bar and Restaurant throughout the year.

3625 First St., Naramata (19km/12 miles north of Penticton on the east side of Okanagan Lake). ✆ 250/496-5001. www.naramatainn.com. 6-course menu C$50–C$60 (US$40–US$48); 9-course menu C$90 (US$72); wine pairings C$50 (US$40). MC, V. Rock Oven Dining Room: May–Oct Thurs–Sun 6–9pm. Cobblestone Wine Bar and Restaurant: Apr–Oct Thurs–Sun 11:30am–10pm.

Theo's Greek Restaurant *Value* GREEK Don't be surprised when previous visitors to Penticton immediately offer testimonials about Theo's, a popular place with excellent, flavorful cooking. The taverna-style dining room has whitewashed walls, a stone floor, and lush greenery. The menu features delectable calamari, succulent marinated lamb, and specialties like seared chicken livers and a standout moussaka. Even the requisite local salmon is wrapped in phyllo pastry with feta cheese and baked until flaky and golden.

687 Main St. ✆ 250/492-4019. www.eatsquid.com. Reservations recommended. Main courses C$10–C$18 (US$8–US$15). AE, DC, MC, V. Mon–Thurs 11am–10pm; Fri–Sat 11am–11pm; Sun 4–10pm.

Villa Rossa Ristorante ITALIAN Villa Rossa is one of the top Penticton options for more traditional Italian cuisine. It has an especially attractive patio shaded by grapevines, just the spot on a warm evening. The menu is varied, with classic dishes such as *osso buco,* chicken Marsala, and pasta joining Canadian specialties such as steaks and salmon. Good wine list, too.

795 W. Westminster Ave. ✆ 250/490-9595. www.thevillarosa.com. Reservations suggested. Main courses C$13–C$27 (US$10–US$22). AE, MC, V. Mon–Fri 11:30am–2:30pm; daily 5–10pm.

Zia's Stonehouse Restaurant ✿ CONTINENTAL Located north of Penticton in Summerland, this restaurant is set inside a historic stone home that was built a century ago by an Italian immigrant. An appealing international menu is served inside the landmark building. Although the menu focuses on Mediterranean preparations of local meats and produce, there are also gestures toward Asian and American cuisine as well. Zia's, with its dedication to the memory of Italian aunts and their home-style cooking, is often selected by Okanagan locals as the area's most romantic restaurant.

14015 Rosedale Ave., Summerland. ✆ 250/494-1105. www.ziasstonehouse.com. Reservations required. Main courses C$11–C$24 (US$8.80–US$19). AE, DC, MC, V. Daily 11:30am–2:30pm and 5:30–10pm.

5 Kelowna

395km (245 miles) E of Vancouver

Kelowna (pop. 148,000) is the largest city in the Okanagan, and one of the fastest-growing areas in Canada. You won't have to spend much time here to understand why: The city sits astride 128km-long (79-mile) Okanagan Lake at the center of a vast fruit-, wine-, and vegetable-growing area, with lots of sun and a resort lifestyle. This is about as close to California as it gets in Canada. Kelowna is especially popular with retirees, who stream here to escape the Pacific pall of Vancouver and the winter cold of Alberta. Predictably, watersports and golf are the main leisure activities, and it's hard to imagine a better outdoor-oriented family-vacation spot.

With plenty of marinas and a beautiful beachfront park that flanks downtown, you'll have no problem finding a place to get wet. In fact, Kelowna's only problem is its popularity. The greater area now has a population of 180,000. Traffic is very heavy, especially on the Okanagan Lake Floating Bridge, which simply can't handle its present traffic load.

ESSENTIALS

GETTING THERE   The Kelowna airport is north of the city on Highway 97. **Air Canada Jazz** (© 888/247-8747) offers regular flights from Calgary and Vancouver. **Horizon Air** (© 800/547-9308; www.alaskaair.com) offers service from Seattle. **WestJet** (© 888/937-8538; www.westjet.com) operates flights from Vancouver, Victoria, Calgary, and Edmonton.

Greyhound Canada (© 800/661-8747) travels between Vancouver and Kelowna daily. The adult fare is C$62 (US$50). Three buses per day continue on to Calgary. The Coquihalla Highway (Hwy. 5) links Kelowna and the Okanagan to the Vancouver area. The 395km (245-mile) drive from Vancouver takes 4 hours. From Kelowna to Calgary, it's 623km (386 miles) over slower roads.

VISITOR INFORMATION   The **Kelowna Visitor Info Centre** is at 544 Harvey Ave. (© 800/663-4345 or 250/861-1515; www.kelownachamber.org).

GETTING AROUND   The local bus service is operated by **Kelowna Transit System** (© 250/860-8121). A one-zone fare is C$1.75 (US$1.40). For a taxi, call **Checkmate Cabs** (© 250/861-1111).

EXPLORING THE CITY

Greater Kelowna is a big, sprawling place that has engulfed both sides of Okanagan Lake, but the sights of most interest are contained in a relatively small area. And that's good, because traffic in Kelowna can be vexing. Beware of the heavily traveled **Harvey Street** and the **Okanagan Lake Floating Bridge;** on the latter, delays of an hour are not uncommon.

Downtown is a pleasant retail area that retains a number of older buildings that now house shops, galleries, and cafes. The main commercial strip is **Bernard Street.** The showpiece of Kelowna is lovely **City Park,** which flanks downtown and the bridge's east side and has over half a mile of wide sandy beach. At the north edge is a marina where you can rent boats and recreational equipment, or sign up to learn to water-ski and parasail. Here, too, is where you board the **MV *Fintry Queen,*** which offers boat tours of the lake (see below).

Kelowna

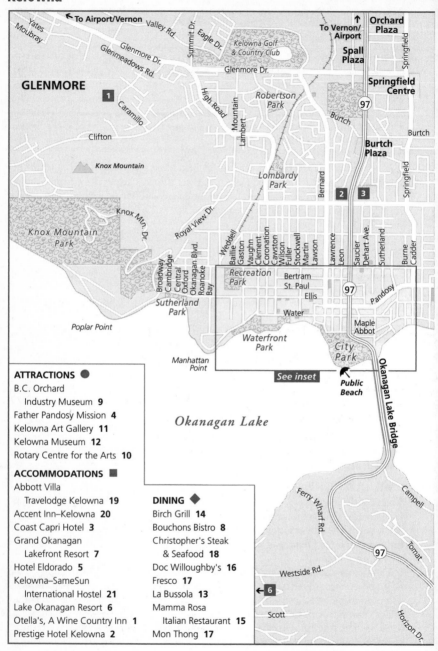

ATTRACTIONS ●

B.C. Orchard
  Industry Museum **9**
Father Pandosy Mission **4**
Kelowna Art Gallery **11**
Kelowna Museum **12**
Rotary Centre for the Arts **10**

ACCOMMODATIONS ■

Abbott Villa
  Travelodge Kelowna **19**
Accent Inn–Kelowna **20**
Coast Capri Hotel **3**
Grand Okanagan
  Lakefront Resort **7**
Hotel Eldorado **5**
Kelowna–SameSun
  International Hostel **21**
Lake Okanagan Resort **6**
Otella's, A Wine Country Inn **1**
Prestige Hotel Kelowna **2**

DINING ◆

Birch Grill **14**
Bouchons Bistro **8**
Christopher's Steak
  & Seafood **18**
Doc Willoughby's **16**
Fresco **17**
La Bussola **13**
Mamma Rosa
  Italian Restaurant **15**
Mon Thong **17**

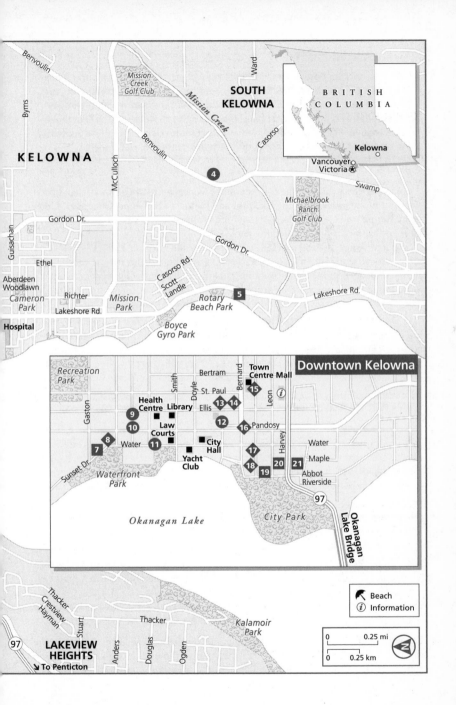

Tips **Special Events**

Kelowna gets its busy summer festival season off to a bang with the **Knox Mountain Hill Climb** (© 250/861-1990), held for nearly half a century on the second-to-last weekend in May. This motor-sport race involves both cars and motorcycles, and is the longest hill-climb race in North America. The **Okanagan Wine Festival** (© 250/861-6654; www.owfs.com) is celebrated in late September and early October in wineries and restaurants throughout the area.

Continue north through the busy marina to **Waterfront Park,** with an island band shell and promenades along the lakefront and lagoons. The **Grand Okanagan Lakefront Resort** towers above the park, and it's worth a stop to step inside the opulent lobby, or to enjoy a drink beside the pool.

The new **Rotary Center for the Arts,** 421 Cawston Ave. (© 250/717-5304), is a multipurpose venue with a 330-seat performing arts theater, plus two art galleries and a number of open studios for artists and craftspeople. It's a fun place to wander, watching artists at work, and you may find a gift to buy or a piece to add to your collection. The center also contains a lunchtime cafe with soup and sandwiches.

B.C. Orchard Industry Museum   This museum, housed in an old apple-packing plant, tells the story of the region's apple-and-soft-fruit industry, with archival photos, equipment, and a hands-on discovery corner. Sharing space with the Orchard Museum is the **Wine Museum** (© 250/868-0441), with a few exhibits on the history of Okanagan wine production. The shop sells a good selection of regional vintages.

1304 Ellis St. © 250/763-0433. www.kelownamuseum.ca. Admission by donation. Mon–Sat 10am–5pm.

Father Pandosy Mission   The first non-Native person to settle in the Kelowna area was the oblate Father Pandosy, who established a mission here to convert the Native Okanagans. On the original site now stands a life-size replica of the log mission buildings, which are filled with period household items. Also on the grounds are a collection of horse-drawn wagons and carriages. A free brochure leads you on a self-guided tour.

3685 Benvoulin Rd. (at Casorso Rd.). © 250/860-8369. Admission C$3 (US$2.40). Easter to mid-Oct daily 9am–dusk. From downtown, take Richter St. south. Take a left on Cedar, then right on Casorso.

Kelowna Art Gallery   Kelowna's 1,394-sq.-m (15,000-sq.-ft.) regional gallery hosts nearly 20 shows per year of work by regional, national, and international artists. The permanent collection is a good body of works by primarily British Columbian artists. The shop is a great place for unique handcrafted gifts.

1315 Water St. © 250/762-2226. www.galleries.bc.ca/kelowna. C$4 (US$3.20) adult, C$3 (US$2.40) senior and student, C$8 (US$6.40) family. Tues–Sat 10am–5pm (Thurs to 9pm); Sun 1–4pm.

Kelowna Museum   This ambitious museum touches on the history of life in the Okanagan Valley. Starting out with local fossils, exhibits move through the prehistoric culture of the Native Okanagans and on to the lives of the farmers and ranchers.

Eclectic only begins to describe the collection—radios, dolls, books—but everything is well curated, and you're sure to find something of interest.

470 Queensway Ave. (℃ 250/763-2417. www.kelownamuseum.ca. Admission by donation. Mon–Sat 10am–5pm.

TOURING THE WINERIES

Calona Wines, 1125 Richter St., Kelowna (℃ **250/762-3332;** www.calonavineyards. ca), conducts daily tours through western Canada's oldest and largest (since 1932) winery. Many antique winemaking machines are on display, alongside the state-of-the-art equipment the winery now uses.

An experience worth savoring even if you're not an oenophile is the **Quail's Gate Estate,** 3303 Boucherie Rd., Kelowna (℃ **250/769-4451;** www.quailsgate.com), famous for its ice wines. Tours are conducted daily from mid-May to mid-October. The tasting room is in the restored log home of pioneers who arrived in the valley during the 1870s. The **Old Vines Patio Restaurant** is open for lunch and dinner.

The neighboring town of Westbank is home to **Mission Hill Wines,** 1730 Mission Hill Rd. (℃ **250/768-7611;** www.missionhillwinery.com), one of the most architecturally eye-catching wineries in the Okanagan. The tasting room is open daily, except for major winter holidays; check the website for tours.

North of Kelowna is **Gray Monk Estate Winery,** 1055 Camp Rd., Okanagan Centre (℃ **800/663-4205** or 250/766-3168; www.graymonk.com). Noted for its pinot noirs, Gray Monk boasts a patio lounge and gives winery tours daily. The tasting room is open daily year-round.

ORGANIZED TOURS & EXCURSIONS

Built in 1948, the paddle-wheeler **MV _Fintry Queen,_** on the dock off Bernard Avenue (℃ **250/763-2780;** www.fintryqueen.com), was once a working ferry but is now a tour boat and restaurant. Call for details on sailings and special lunch and dinner cruises.

If you want to visit the wineries and leave the driving to someone else, contact **Okanagan Wine Country Tours** (℃ **866/689-9463** or 250/868-9463; www.okwine tours.com), which offers packages ranging from a 3-hour Afternoon Delight for C$55 (US$44) to the Daytripper for C$130 (US$104).

OUTDOOR PURSUITS

BIKING The Kettle Valley Railway's **Myra Canyon** route near Kelowna lost over half of its 18 trestle bridges during the Okanagan wild fires in 2003. The central part of the route remains closed though work proceeds on rebuilding the trestles. Inquire at **Sports Rent,** 3000 Pandosy St. (℃ **250/861-5699**), for other mountain biking routes in the area, including detours that link the intact beginning and ending stretches of the Kettle Valley Railroad route.

GOLF There are more than a dozen courses in the area, and golf is second only to watersports as the region's recreational drawing card. The greens fees throughout the Okanagan Valley range from C$50 to C$135 (US$40–US$108)—a good value not only for the beautiful locations but also for the quality of service you'll find at each club.

Gallagher's Canyon Golf and Country Club, 4320 McCulloch Rd. (℃ **250/861-4240**), has a Les Furber–designed 18-hole course that features one hole overlooking the precipice of a gaping canyon and another that's perched on the brink of a ravine. It also has a 9-hole course, midlength course, and double-ended learning center. **Harvest Golf Club,** 2725 Klo Rd. (© 250/862-3103), is one of the finest courses in the Okanagan, a championship course in an orchard setting. The **Okanagan Golf Club** ✪, off Highway 97 near the airport (© 800/898-2449 or 250/765-5955), has two 18-hole courses, the Jack Nicklaus–designed Bear Course and the Les Furber–designed Quail Course.

HIKING　The closest trails to Kelowna are in **Knox Mountain Park,** immediately north of the city. From downtown, follow Ellis Street to its terminus, where there's a parking area and trail head. The most popular trail climbs up the cactus-clad mountainside to the summit, from which you'll enjoy magnificent views of the lake and orchards.

SKIING & SNOWBOARDING　One of British Columbia's largest ski areas and one of North America's snowboarding capitals, **Big White Ski Resort** ✪, Parkinson Way, Kelowna (© 250/765-3101, 250/765-SNOW for snow report, or 250/765-8888 for lodge reservations; www.bigwhite.com), is famed for its hip-deep champagne powder snow. The resort spreads over a broad mountain, featuring long, wide runs. Skiers here cruise open bowls and tree-lined glades. There's an annual average of 5m (18 ft.) of fluffy powder, so it's no wonder the resort's 102 named runs are so popular. There are three high-speed quad chairs, a fixed-grip quad, a triple quad, a double chair, a T-bar, a beginner tow, and a platter lift. The resort also offers more than 25km (16 miles) of groomed cross-country ski trails, a recreational racing program, and night skiing. Adult lift tickets are C$64 (US$51). Big White is 55km (34 miles) southeast of Kelowna off Highway 33.

Only a 15-minute drive from Westbank, **Crystal Mountain Resorts Ltd.** (© 250/768-5189, or 250/768-3753 for snow report; www.crystalresort.com) has a range of programs for all types of skiers, specializing in clinics for children, women, and seniors. This friendly, family-oriented resort has 20 runs, 80% of which are intermediate-to-novice grade. They're serviced by a double chair and two T-bars, and are equipped for day and night skiing. There's also a half pipe for snowboarders. Lift tickets start at C$39 (US$31) for adults.

Farther afield is the **Silver Star Mountain Resort** ✪, 20km (12 miles) northeast of Vernon (© 800/663-4431 or 250/542-0224; www.silverstarmtn.com). It boasts two ski hills with 84 runs and a vertical drop of 762m (2,500 ft.). The Vance Creek side offers long, rolling cruisers, and the Putnam Creek side is a little wilder with groomed and ungroomed double-blacks, glades, and bumps. For snowboarders, there's a half pipe and a terrain park. Silver Star has nine lifts, including two high-speed detachable quads. For cross-country skiers, there are 85km (53 miles) of groomed and track-set trails. Day lift tickets are C$64 (US$51) for adults.

WATERSPORTS　The marina just north of City Park has a great many outfitters that can rent you a boat, jet ski, windsurfing board, or paddle boat. If you want to call ahead, try **Dockside Marine Centre** (© 250/765-3995), which offers a wide range of boats and watercraft. To try parasailing, call **Kelowna Parasail Adventures** (© 250/868-4838), which offers flights for C$50 (US$40).

WHERE TO STAY

Abbott Villa Travelodge Kelowna *(Value)*   For the money, this is one of the best places to stay in Kelowna, as it has one of the best locations downtown—right across from the City Park beaches. You'll be able to walk to the lakefront and to your favorite restaurants. The standard-issue motel units are clean and well maintained.

1627 Abbott St., Kelowna, BC V1Y 1A9. *(C)* **800/578-7878** or 250/763-7771. Fax 250/762-2402. www.travelodge.com. 52 units. High season C$119–C$144 (US$95–US$115) double. Kitchen C$10 (US$8) extra. AE, MC, V. **Amenities:** Restaurant; heated outdoor pool; Jacuzzi; sauna. *In room:* A/C, TV, coffeemaker.

Accent Inn–Kelowna   So you're heading into Kelowna on a summer weekend, and even though you're dreaming of a beachfront hotel, you didn't call 6 months ago to secure a room. Every place is absolutely booked and you're going to have to stay in a decent, basic motel, and you just hope it's clean, new, and functional. This is it.

1140 Harvey Ave., Kelowna, BC V1Y 6E7. *(C)* **800/663-0298** or 250/862-8888. Fax 250/862-8884. www.accentinns.com. 101 units. High season C$129–C$159 (US$103–US$127) double. Kitchen C$10 (US$8) extra. MC, V. **Amenities:** Restaurant; outdoor pool; exercise room; Jacuzzi; sauna. *In room:* A/C, TV, coffeemaker.

Coast Capri Hotel   Somewhat apart from the downtown area, the Coast Capri offers large, newly furbished rooms, most with balconies. You'll need to drive to the beaches from here, and the surrounding blocks are filled with strip malls, but if you can't get into one of the beachfront hotels yet still want high-quality lodgings, then this is your next-best choice. The **Vintage Dining Room** is a great old-fashioned steakhouse—probably the best place in town for an elegant dinner of prime rib or steak.

1171 Harvey Ave., Kelowna, BC V1Y 6E8. *(C)* **800/663-1144** or 250/860-6060. Fax 250/762-3430. www.coasthotels.com. 185 units. High season C$160–C$220 (US$128–US$176) double. AE, MC, V. **Amenities:** 2 restaurants; 2 bars; heated outdoor pool; fitness center; Jacuzzi. *In room:* A/C, TV, dataport.

Grand Okanagan Lakefront Resort & Conference Centre *(Kids)*   This elegant lakeshore resort sits on 10 hectares (25 acres) of beach and parkland; its atmosphere is reminiscent of Miami Beach in the 1920s. The atrium lobby of the modern hotel has a fountain with a sculpted dolphin as its centerpiece. The rooms are spacious and regally outfitted with opulent furniture and upholstery, with views from every window. Suites offer Jacuzzi tubs and separate showers, and deluxe condos offer full kitchens—good for families. This is an ideal location for visitors who want to feel pampered in sophisticated surroundings while maintaining easy access to the waterfront. The restaurant and lounge overlook the resort's private marina, where guests can moor their small boats. Motorized swans and boats sized for kids offer fun for children in a protected waterway.

1310 Water St., Kelowna, BC V1Y 9P3. *(C)* **800/465-4651** or 250/763-4500. Fax 250/763-4565. www.grandokanagan.com. 320 units. C$262–C$349 (US$209–US$279) double; C$369–C$549 (US$295–US$439) suite or condo. Extra person C$15 (US$12). Off-season discounts available. AE, DC, MC, V. From Vancouver, on Hwy. 97, cross the Lake Okanagan Bridge. At the 1st set of lights, turn left onto Abbott St. At the 2nd set of lights, turn onto Water St. **Amenities:** 3 restaurants; pub; lounge; indoor/outdoor pool; health club with spa; watersports equipment rentals; concierge; business center; shopping arcade; salon; 24-hr. room service; laundry service; same-day dry cleaning. *In room:* A/C, TV, dataport, minibar (on request), coffeemaker, hair dryer, iron.

Hotel Eldorado *(★★)*   One of Kelowna's oldest hotels (from 1926), this charming historic inn was floated down the lake from its original location to its present site on the water's edge south of downtown. It has been fully restored and is now decorated with a unique mix of antiques; a wing with 30 new guest rooms and six luxury suites was added in 2005. All rooms are individually decorated, and there's a wide mix of floor plans and layouts. The third-floor guest rooms with views of the lake are the largest and quietest. Some rooms also feature lakeside balconies. On the premises are a boardwalk cafe, lounge, spa, and dining room. The staff can arrange boat moorage, boat rentals, and water-skiing lessons.

500 Cook Rd. (at Lakeshore Rd.), Kelowna, BC V1W 3G9. ℂ 250/763-7500. Fax 250/861-4779. www.sunnyokanagan. com/el. 55 units. C$169–C$279 (US$135–US$223) double; C$349–C$379 (US$279–US$303) suite. Lower off-season rates. AE, DC, MC, V. Free parking. From downtown follow Pandosy Rd. south 1.5km (1 mile). Turn right on Cook Rd. **Amenities:** Fine-dining restaurant; boardwalk cafe; bar; indoor pool; fitness center; Jacuzzi; steam room; marina. *In room:* A/C, TV, coffeemaker, hair dryer, iron.

Kelowna-SameSun International Hostel   If you're on a budget, this brand-new, centrally located backpackers' lodge is just the ticket. You'll be close to the beach as well as downtown eats and nightlife. Extras include private rooms, a huge kitchen, and a common room with TV.

245 Harvey Ave., Kelowna, BC V1Y 6C2. ℂ 877/562-2783 or 250/763-9814. Fax 250/763-9814. www.samesun.com. 67 beds. C$25 (US$20) single. MC, V. **Amenities:** Coin-op laundry; kitchen. *In room:* No phone.

Lake Okanagan Resort ⭐   The long, winding road that leads to this secluded hideaway is a sports-car driver's dream come true. And there are many more activities to keep guests occupied once they arrive at this woodsy resort with its country-club atmosphere. Located on 122 hectares (301 acres) of Okanagan Lake's hilly western shore, it offers one-, two-, three-, and five-bedroom units, plus all the facilities you'd expect. Because the resort is built on a hillside, every room has a terrific view.

2751 Westside Rd., Kelowna, BC V1Z 3T1. ℂ 800/663-3273 or 250/769-3511. Fax 250/769-6665. www.lakeokanagan. com. 135 units. C$239–C$269 (US$191–US$215) studio suite; C$299–C$329 (US$239–C$261) 1-bedroom suite. Off-season discounts and packages available. AE, MC, V. Free parking. Drive 18km (11 miles) up Westside Rd. **Amenities:** 2 restaurants; 2 bars; 3 outdoor pools; par-3 golf course; tennis courts; health club and spa; Jacuzzis; watersports-equipment rentals; summer children's camp; concierge; business center; salon; laundry service. *In room:* A/C, TV, data-port, kitchen, fridge, coffeemaker, hair dryer, iron.

Otella's, A Wine Country Inn ⭐   Otella's is located in the hills behind Kelowna, in a quiet, upscale neighborhood. The owners knew they didn't want a frilly B&B: Instead, they transformed this modern A-frame into a coolly elegant, sophisticated guesthouse filled with quality furniture, local art, and restrained good taste. The two nicest rooms, which share a small balcony, are on the third floor. There's also a two-bedroom suite that sleeps four. All the rooms sport extras such as fine linens and bathrobes. The intriguing setting is at the end of a steep cul-de-sac against the desert hillside; the backyard incorporates ledges of rock that form a two-tiered lawn. It's favored by local quail, which stroll down for a peck at the manicured grasses. One of the owners is a professionally trained chef, so expect the three-course breakfast to be exemplary.

42 Altura Rd., Kelowna, BC V1V 1B6. ℂ 888/858-8596 or 250/763-4922. Fax 250/763-4982. www.otellas.com. 3 units. High season from C$150 (US$120) double. MC, V. Free parking. **Amenities:** Laundry service. *In room:* A/C, TV, fridge, hair dryer, iron.

Prestige Hotel Kelowna   One of the closest hotels to the City Park beaches, the Prestige Hotel is a cornerstone of downtown Kelowna. Rooms are nicely furnished,

large, and comfortable, with glass-fronted balconies; suites come with canopy beds, robes, VCRs, double Jacuzzis; several have themes, such as the medieval or South Pacific suites. The Blue Gator Bar and Grill is one of Kelowna's premier clubs for live blues and jazz.

1675 Abbott St., Kelowna, BC V1Y 8S3. ℭ 87/PRESTIGE or 250/860-7900. Fax 250/860-7997. www.prestigeinn. com. 66 units. High season C$149–C$219 (US$119–US$175) double. Suites from C$399 (US$319). AE, DISC, MC, V. **Amenities:** Restaurant; bar; indoor pool; exercise room; Jacuzzi; concierge; room service; massage; laundry service; same-day dry cleaning. In room: A/C, TV w/pay movies, dataport, fridge, coffeemaker, hair dryer, iron.

CAMPING

Okanagan Lake Provincial Park (ℭ **250/494-6500**), 11km (7 miles) north of Summerland and 44km (27 miles) south of Kelowna on Highway 97, has 168 campsites nestled amid 10,000 imported trees. Sites go for C$22 (US$18). Facilities include free hot showers, flush toilets, a sani-station, and a boat launch.

Closer to Kelowna is **Bear Creek Provincial Park** (ℭ **250/494-6500**), 9km (5½ miles) north of Highway 97 on Westside Road, about 3km (1¾ miles) west of the Okanagan Lake Floating Bridge. The park has 80 sites for C$22 (US$18) each.

WHERE TO DINE

For the kind of hearty cooking that fulfills gastronomic stereotypes, try **Mamma Rosa Italian Restaurant,** 561 Lawrence Ave. (ℭ **250/763-4114**), a third-generation Italian family restaurant which serves up affordable house-made pastas and very good pizzas.

Birch Grill CONTINENTAL   This sophisticated little bistro has a daily changing menu that features lots of appetizers and small plates, plus pasta dishes—such as portobello ravioli with tomato-cream sauce—and grilled fish and chicken. The staff is friendly and professional.

526 Bernard Ave. ℭ 250/860-3103. Reservations recommended. Main courses C$12–C$21 (US$9.60–US$17). AE, MC, V. Mon–Fri 11:30am–2:30pm and 5–10pm; Sat 5–11pm.

Bouchons Bistro ℱ FRENCH   This Gallic transplant offers classic French bistro fare just a few blocks from the Okanagan lakefront. The dining room, with ochre walls, stained glass panels, and hand-written menus, actually feels Parisian. The menu doesn't stray far from classic French cuisine, though dishes are prepared with the freshest and best of local products—the level of cooking at Bouchons will make you appreciate French cuisine once again. Cassoulet is a house specialty, and you can't go wrong with duck confit glazed with honey and spices. A recent game-meat-focused menu offered wonderful wild fowl consommé with foie gras wontons. The wine list is half French, half Okanagan vintages. In summer, there's alfresco dining in the gardenlike patio.

1180 Sunset Dr. ℭ 250/763-6595. Reservations suggested. Main courses C$17–C$29 (US$14–US$23). MC, V. Daily 5:30–10pm.

Christopher's Steak & Seafood STEAKHOUSE   Christopher's is a local favorite for drinks and steaks in a dark, fern bar–like dining room. The decor and menu haven't changed much since the early years of the Reagan administration, but that's a plus if you're looking for Alberta beef served up in simple abundance. Pasta, chicken, and seafood are also offered.

242 Lawrence Ave. © **250/861-3464.** Reservations recommended. Main courses C$10–C$33 (US$8–US$26). AE, DC, MC, V. Sun–Thurs 4:30–10pm; Fri–Sat 4:30–11pm.

Doc Willoughby's Pub CANADIAN   For a scene that's casual but on the edge of trendy, with a publike atmosphere but with better food, try Doc Willoughby's, in the heart of downtown. The building was once a pioneer drugstore (note the hammered-tin ceiling), but the interior has been done up in a strikingly contemporary design. This is a good spot for lunch, as the entire front of the restaurant opens to the street; you can watch the to-ing and fro-ing of tourists as you choose from salads, burgers, and sandwiches. At dinner, the eclectic menu offers lots of fish, chicken, and pasta dishes.

353 Bernard Ave. © **250/868-8288.** Reservations not needed. Main courses C$8–C$15 (US$6.40–US$12). AE, MC, V. Mon–Thurs 11:30am–11pm; Fri–Sat 11:30am–midnight; Sun 4:30–10pm.

Fresco ⭐⭐ NEW CANADIAN   This is the hottest of dining spots in Kelowna, and the first solo venture of chef/owner Rod Butters, who has worked at some of western Canada's top restaurants. The cooking focuses on fresh, relatively unfussy regional cuisine. Start with a ginger-cured salmon with tea-poached scallops, and move on to a main dish of roast pheasant breast with foie gras spring roll, or prosciutto wrapped rockfish and shellfish sausage. Service is top-notch; the wine list celebrates the vintages of the Okanagan Valley.

1560 Water St. © **250/868-8805.** www.frescorestaurant.net. Reservations recommended. Main courses C$19–C$32 (US$15–$26). Tues–Sat 5:30–10pm.

La Bussola ITALIAN   La Bussola is a solid and dependable traditional Italian restaurant with a big local reputation. All of your favorites are here—pasta al pesto, lasagna, chicken piccata—along with an especially large selection of veal specialties. The house signature dish is grilled chicken breast with a creamy white-vermouth sauce.

1451 Ellis St. © **250/763-3110.** www.labussolarestaurant.com. Reservations recommended. AE, MC, V. Main courses C$14–C$36 (US$11–US$29). Mon–Sat 5–10pm.

Mon Thong Thai Restaurant ⭐ THAI   Mon Thong has an encyclopedic menu of house specialties, making this the best Thai restaurant in the Okanagan. Almost all dishes can be made vegetarian. Choose from red, green, or yellow curries, or from signature dishes like *goong pad num prick pao,* stir-fried shrimp with fresh vegetables in fiery Thai sauce.

1530 Water St. © **250/763-8600.** Reservations not needed. Main courses C$9–C$15 (US$7.20–US$12). MC, V. Daily 11am–2:30pm and 5–11pm.

13

Southeastern British Columbia & the Kootenay Valley

With the high-flying Rockies to the east and the rugged Purcell and Selkirk mountain ranges to the west, southeastern British Columbia has as much beauty and recreation to offer as anywhere else in the province. If you're looking to avoid the crowds at Banff and Jasper national parks on the Alberta side of the Rockies, try one of the smaller parks covered in this chapter.

Trenched by the mighty Kootenay and Columbia rivers, this region has a long history of mining, river transport, and ranching. More recently, the ranches have given way to golf courses, but development out in this rural area of British Columbia is still low-key. And while that means that you may not have the ultimate dining experience here, it also means that prices are lower across the board—and you won't have to compete with tour-bus hordes while you hike the trails.

In pre-Contact Native America and the early years of western exploration, the Kootenay Valley was a major transportation corridor. Due to a curious accident of geology, the headwaters of the vast Columbia River—which flows north from Columbia Lake for 275km (171 miles) before bending south and flowing to the Pacific at Astoria, Oregon—are separated from the south-flowing Kootenay

River by a low, 2km-wide (1¼-mile) berm of land called Canal Flats. The Kootenay River then zigzags down into the United States before flowing back north into Canada to join the Columbia at Castlegar, British Columbia.

Because a short portage was all that separated these two powerful rivers, Canal Flats was an important crossroads when canoes and riverboats were the primary means of transport. The fact that an easily breached ridge was all that separated two major rivers caught the imagination of an early entrepreneur, William Adolph Baillie-Grohman. In the 1880s, he conceived a plan to breach Canal Flats and divert much of the Kootenay's flow into the Columbia. Unsurprisingly, he ran into opposition from people living and working on the Columbia, and had to settle for building a canal and lock system between the two rivers. Only two ships ever passed through the canal, and today this curiosity is preserved as Canal Flats Provincial Park, 44km (27 miles) north of Cranbrook, with picnic tables and a boat launch on Columbia Lake.

For advance information on southeastern British Columbia, contact **Kootenay Rockies Tourism,** P.O. Box 10, Kimberley, BC V1A 2Y5 (© **250/427-4838;** www.bcrockies.com).

1 Revelstoke

410km (254 miles) W of Calgary; 565km (350 miles) NE of Vancouver

Located on the Columbia River at the foot of Mount Revelstoke National Park, Revelstoke sits in a narrow fir-cloaked valley between the Selkirk and the Monashee mountains. It's a spectacular, big-as-all-outdoors setting, and unsurprisingly, Revelstoke makes the most of the outdoor-recreation opportunities on its doorstep. Winter is high season here, as the city is a major center for heli-skiing and snowmobiling. Summer activities include rafting, hiking, and horseback riding.

The town was established in the 1880s, when the Canadian Pacific Railway pushed through. Much of the handsome downtown core was built then; most restaurants and hotels are housed in century-old buildings. For all its beauty and charm, Revelstoke is surprisingly unheralded. With a setting that rivals Banff and Jasper, Revelstoke's congenial and sleepy isolation can't last. Plan a visit before the throngs arrive.

ESSENTIALS

GETTING THERE   Revelstoke is 192km (119 miles) from Kelowna on Highway 1. It's 565km (350 miles) northwest of Vancouver and 410km (254 miles) west of Calgary. **Greyhound Canada** (© **800/661-8747** or 403/260-0877; www.greyhound.ca) operates four buses daily from Vancouver, costing C$83 (US$66) one-way. From Revelstoke to Calgary costs C$54 (US$43) one-way.

VISITOR INFORMATION   Contact the **Revelstoke Visitor Information Centre,** 204 Campbell St. (© **800/487-1493** or 250/837-5345; www.revelstokecc.bc.ca).

EXPLORING THE TOWN

Downtown Revelstoke (pop. 8,500) sits on a shelf of land above the confluence of the Columbia and Illecillewaet rivers. Founded in the 1880s, the town center retains a number of original storefronts and is pleasant to explore. You'll see plenty of coffeehouses, galleries, and some standout architectural jewels, like the domed **Revelstoke Courthouse,** 1123 Second St. W. **Grizzly Plaza,** near Victoria Road and Campbell Avenue, is lined with redbrick storefronts. It's the site of the Saturday farmers' market, as well as free live music from July to Labour Day, Monday through Saturday from 7 to 10pm.

Revelstoke Museum   Located in the town's original post office, this small museum contains memorabilia from Revelstoke's pioneer mining and railroading days. Upstairs is the community art gallery, with works by local and regional artists.

315 W. First St. © 250/837-3067. Admission by donation. Mid-May to Labour Day Mon–Fri 1–5pm; Labour Day to mid-May Mon, Wed, and Fri 1–4:30pm.

Revelstoke Railway Museum   It's the railroad that really put Revelstoke on the map, and this noteworthy museum—built to resemble an original Canadian Pacific Railway shop—tells the story of western Canadian rail history. Its collection of antique rolling stock includes a beautifully restored CPR steam engine from the 1940s. Other exhibits focus on the building of the first transcontinental line across Canada and the communications systems that kept the trains running safely.

719 Track St. W., across from downtown on Victoria Rd. © 250/837-6060. www.railwaymuseum.com. Admission C$6 (US$4.80) adults, C$5 (US$4) seniors, C$3 (US$2.40) students, free for children 5 and under. July–Labour Day daily 9am–8pm; Mar–June and Labour Day–Nov daily 9am–5pm; rest of year Mon–Fri 1–5pm.

TOURING THE DAMS

The Columbia River has the steepest descent of any large river in North America, and in terms of volume, is the continent's third-largest river, making it irresistible to hydroelectric dam builders. Two of the many electricity-generating dams on the river are near Revelstoke, and both are open for tours. **Revelstoke Dam,** 4km (2½ miles) north of Revelstoke on Highway 23, is 470m (1,541 ft.) across and 175m (574 ft.) high. Self-guided tours of the visitor center explain how hydroelectricity is produced and how the dams impact the local ecosystem. An elevator shoots to the top of the dam, where you'll get a feeling for the immensity of this structure. The visitor center is open May to mid-June and mid-September to mid-October daily from 9am to 5pm, and mid-June to mid-September daily from 8am to 8pm. Admission is free.

A 140km (87-mile) drive up Highway 23 along the shores of Revelstoke Lake takes you to **Mica Dam,** the first large dam on the Columbia—and large it is, much larger than Revelstoke Dam. More than 792m (2,597 ft.) across and 200m (656 ft.) high, Mica Dam forms Kinbasket Lake, which stretches for more than 160km (99 miles) and contains 14.8 trillion cubic meters of water. The visitor center is open mid-June to Labour Day daily from 10:30am to 4:30pm. Tours are offered at 11am and 1:30pm.

OUTDOOR PURSUITS

Revelstoke is surrounded by rugged mountains with extremely heavy snowfalls (almost 18m/59 ft. annually). The town is particularly known as a center for heli-skiing, a sport that employs helicopters to deposit expert skiers high on mountain ridges, far from lifts and ski areas.

BIKING The mountains around Revelstoke are etched with old logging roads that have been converted into mountain-bike trails; ask at the visitor center for a map.

GOLF **Revelstoke Golf Club** (② 800/991-4455 or 250/837-4276) is an 18-hole, par-72 championship course established in 1924, with narrow fairways lined with mammoth conifers and small lakes. The club—one of the oldest in British Columbia—has a driving range, clubhouse with lounge and restaurant, and pro shop. Greens fees are C$53 (US$42) for 18 holes.

SKIING **Powder Springs Ski Area,** 6km (3¾ miles) south of Revelstoke on Camozzi Road (② 877/422-8754 or 250/837-5151), has 305m (1,000 ft.) of vertical drop, with 1,067m (3,500 ft.) of total runs. There are two lifts, a T-bar, and a rope tow; lift tickets are C$28 (US$22) weekdays to C$32 (US$27) on weekends.

CMH Heli-Skiing (② 800/661-0252; www.cmhski.com) offers helicopter skiing to remote slopes and glaciers in the Monashee and Selkirk mountains. CMH offers 7- or 10-day trips to 12 different locations; prices begin at C$5,155 (US$4,124) including lodging, food, and transport from Calgary.

The long-established **Selkirk Tangiers Heli-Skiing** (② 800/663-7080; www.selkirk-tangiers.com) offers helicopter-assisted skiing and snowboarding trips to more than 200 approved areas in the Monashee and Selkirk mountains, with some runs up to 2,195m (7,200 ft.) in length. In addition, the company's Albert Canyon base, 35km (22 miles) east of Revelstoke on Highway 1, offers heli-skiing in the Selkirks. A week of midwinter skiing goes for C$6,963 (US$5,570).

Cat Powder Skiing (© 800/991-4455; www.catpowder.com) uses Snowcats to transport skiers and snowboarders to backcountry slopes. The Snowcat takes you to the 2,286m (7,498-ft.) elevation of Mount Mackenzie, where you can choose from a number of runs up to 1,067m (3,500 ft.) long, including a half pipe and a terrain park. Packages include guide service, lodging, and meals; a 3-day option costs C$1,620 (US$1,296).

SNOWMOBILING   A detailed brochure of snowmobiling trails is available from the visitor center; contact **Great Canadian Snowmobile Tours** (© 800/667-8865 or 250/837-6500; www.snowmobilerevelstoke.com) for guided trips.

WHITE-WATER RAFTING   **Apex Rafting Company** (© 888/232-6666 or 250/837-6376; www.apexrafting.com) offers excursions down the Illecillewaet River's Albert Canyon. The trip provides thrills, but nothing too extreme. In summer, daily 4-hour trips cost C$74 (US$59) for adults and C$62 (US$50) for kids 16 and under.

WHERE TO STAY

Martha Creek Provincial Park, just north of Revelstoke on Highway 23 (© 250/825-3500), sits on Lake Revelstoke and has 28 campsites that go for C$14 (US$11) each.

Glacier House Resort   Just 5 minutes north from Revelstoke, across the Columbia River in a meadow overlooking the Monashee and Selkirk mountains, is this quiet alpine resort with outstanding amenities and a recreational focus. There are cozy, simply decorated rooms in the spacious lodge building, plus 10 free-standing log chalets which range from one to three bedrooms. Each chalet has a fireplace and deck, and some have TVs, hot tubs, and kitchenettes. In addition to a spa, indoor pool, and sauna, Glacier House also has a restaurant and bar, plus it operates an outfitting company to provide guided hiking, biking, and snowmobiling trips. This is a great destination for a family that wants a backcountry-style vacation without roughing it.

679 Westsyde Rd. (Box 250), Revelstoke, BC V0E 2S0. © 877/837-9594 or 250/837-9594. Fax 250/837-9592. www.glacierhouse.com. 25 units. High season C$115–C$150 (US$92–US$120) lodge room; C$165–C$245 (US$132–US$196) chalet. MC, V. **Amenities:** Restaurant; pub with pool tables; indoor pool; fitness center; spa; sauna; sports equipment rentals. *In room:* TVs (in all lodge rooms and larger chalets), coffeemaker, hair dryer, fireplace.

The Hillcrest Hotel, A Coast Resort 𝒜   On the eastern edge of Revelstoke, this new hotel does its best to look like a grand mountain lodge, complete with turrets, balconies, log beams, stone walls, and a vast lobby dominated by a river-rock fireplace. The Hillcrest has the most complete facilities in Revelstoke, and its rooms are large and comfortable—many offer mountain views, and suites come with Jacuzzis. The only downside is that you'll need to drive to get to downtown Revelstoke.

3km (2 miles) east of Revelstoke on Hwy. 1 (Box 1979), Revelstoke, BC V0E 2S0. © 250/837-3322. Fax 250/837-3340. 75 units. C$145–C$205 (US$116–US$164) double; C$205–C$285 (US$164–US$228) suite. AE, MC, V. **Amenities:** Restaurant; lounge; exercise room; Jacuzzis; sauna; game room. *In room:* A/C, TV, coffeemaker, hair dryer, iron, safe.

Mulvehill Creek Wilderness Inn and Bed & Breakfast 𝒜𝒜 *Finds*   One of the best small lodgings in all of British Columbia, this inn sits in a clearing in the forest, just steps from Arrow Lake and a magnificent 90m (295-ft.) waterfall. The cedar shake–sided lodge has three queen rooms, one king room, and two units with twin beds, plus two suites (one with Jacuzzi and private deck). All rooms are beautifully decorated with locally made pine furniture and original folk art. The lounge is lined with bookcases; grab a novel and curl up by the fireplace. From the deck, look onto the organic garden, which supplies much of the produce served here; the inn's hens provide the eggs. Your hosts will happily arrange cross-country-skiing, snowshoeing, horseback-riding, biking, and fishing excursions. A couple of days at Mulvehill may well be the highlight of your trip to British Columbia. Children are welcome.

4200 Hwy. 23 S. (19km/12 miles south of Revelstoke), P.O. Box 1220, Revelstoke, BC V0E 2S0. © **877/837-8649** or 250/837-8649. www.mulvehillcreek.com. 8 units. C$125–C$165 (US$100–US$132) double; C$225 (US$180) suite. Rates include breakfast. AE, MC, V. **Amenities:** Heated outdoor pool; Jacuzzi; playground; free canoes. *In room:* Hair dryer, no phone.

Regent Inn ☞ The finest lodging in downtown Revelstoke, the Regent is a refurbished heritage hotel facing historic Grizzly Plaza. The large bedrooms are individually decorated with restrained good taste; some have private Jacuzzis. The One Twelve Restaurant offers fine dining (see "Where to Dine," below).

112 First St. E., Revelstoke, BC V0E 2S0. © **888/245-5523** or 250/837-2107. Fax 250/837-9669. www.regent inn.com. 50 units. C$109–C$169 (US$87–US$135) double. Rates include continental breakfast. AE, DC, MC, V. Pets accepted in limited rooms for C$10 (US$8). **Amenities:** Restaurant; lounge; pub; outdoor heated pool; golf course nearby; access to adjacent health club; Jacuzzi; sauna. *In room:* A/C, TV, hair dryer, iron, safe.

SameSun Budget Lodge Located on the edge of downtown, the hostel is in a spacious older home with oak floors and French doors. There are tent sites in the large backyard.

400 Second St. W., Revelstoke, BC V0E 2S0. © **877/562-2783** or 250/837-4050. Fax 250/837-6410. www. samesun.com. 90 beds. C$21 (US$17) per person bunk; C$43 (US$34) per person private room. MC, V. **Amenities:** Bike rentals; kitchen; TV lounge; computer and Internet access. *In room:* No phone.

Three Valley Lake Chateau (*Value*) With its bright-red, steeply pitched, four-story tin roof cleaved by dozens of sharply peaked gables, this huge hotel and entertainment complex stands out, to put it mildly. The hotel sits amid formal gardens at the head of Three Valley Lake, a small body of water with sandy swimming beaches. Guest rooms are quite large, most with balconies; if you're interested, ask about the theme suites (the interior of the Cave Suite is lined completely in native stone). The hotel's Walter Moberly Theatre hosts a nightly revue with cowboy songs and skits. Also part of the development is Historic Town, a collection of historic buildings that have been moved to the property to form an ad hoc ghost town.

19km (12 miles) west of Revelstoke on Hwy. 1 (P.O. Box 860), Revelstoke, BC V0E 2S0. © **888/667-2109** or 250/ 837-2109. Fax 250/837-5220. www.3valley.com. 200 units. High season C$115–C$150 (US$95–US$120) double. Closed mid-Oct to mid-Apr. AE, DC, DISC, MC, V. **Amenities:** 2 dining rooms; cafeteria; lounge; indoor pool; whirlpool; coin-op laundry. *In room:* A/C, TV.

WHERE TO DINE

One Twelve Restaurant WESTERN CANADIAN This handsome restaurant is Revelstoke's fine-dining option, with a good selection of steaks, seafood (about half the menu options), and Continental cuisine. Veal is served with a wild-mushroom sauce, and fresh New Brunswick lobster tails come with drawn butter. Good service, an intriguing wine list, the woodsy but elegant decor, and a fireplace all enhance the experience.

In the Regent Inn, 112 First St. E. © **250/837-2107.** www.regentinn.com. Reservations suggested. Main courses C$12–C$31 (US$9.60–US$25). AE, MC, V. Mon–Sat 11:30am–2pm and 5:30–9pm.

Three Bears Bistro CASUAL DINING   The Three Bears is a convivial spot in Grizzly Plaza with sidewalk patio seating as well as deck seating in the garden. At lunch, the menu includes homemade soup, salads, wraps, and fajitas; the evening offerings shift to pasta, potpies, and paella. The bistro also has good desserts, espresso drinks, and specialty teas.

144 Mackenzie Ave. © **250/837-9575.** Reservations not accepted. Main courses C$5–C$12 (US$4–US$9.60). MC, V. July–Labour Day Mon–Sat 8:30am–10pm, Sun 11am–10pm; Labour Day–June Mon–Sat 8:30am–5pm.

2 Mount Revelstoke National Park

Just west of Glacier National Park is Mount Revelstoke National Park, a glacier-clad collection of craggy peaks in the **Selkirk Range.** Comprising only 417 sq. km (163 sq. miles), Mount Revelstoke can't produce the kind of awe that its larger neighbor, Glacier National Park, can in good weather; it does, however, offer easier access to the high country and alpine meadows.

The park is flanked on the south by Highway 1, the Trans-Canada Highway. It has no services or campgrounds, but all tourist services are available in the neighboring town of Revelstoke (see above).

For information, contact **Mount Revelstoke National Park** (© **250/837-7500;** www.pc.gc.ca/pn-np/bc/revelstoke). Entry to the park costs C$6 (US$4.80) for adults, C$5 (US$4) for seniors, C$3 (US$2.40) for children 6 to 16, and C$15 (US$12) per family.

EXPLORING THE PARK

The most popular activity in the park is the drive up to the top of 1,829m (5,999-ft.) **Mount Revelstoke,** with great views of the Columbia River and the peaks of Glacier Park. To reach Mount Revelstoke, take the paved Meadows in the Sky Parkway north from the town of Revelstoke and follow it 23km (14 miles) to Balsam Lake. The parkway is closed to trailers and motor coaches, as it is a very narrow mountain road with 16 steep switchbacks.

At **Balsam Lake,** at the Meadows in the Sky area, free shuttles operated by the parks department make the final ascent up to the top of Mount Revelstoke, but only after the road is clear of snow, usually from early July to late September. If the shuttle isn't running, you have a choice of several easy hiking trails around Balsam Lake that lead past rushing brooks through wildflower meadows. The **Eagle Knoll Trail** and the **Parapets** are two options that take under an hour. At the summit are longer trails, including the 6km (3¾-mile) **Eva Lake Trail.**

If you don't make the trip up to the Meadows in the Sky area, you can enjoy a short hike in the park from along Highway 1. The **Skunk Cabbage Trail** winds through a marsh that explodes with bright yellow and odoriferous flowers in early summer. Another popular hike is the **Giant Cedars Trail,** a short boardwalk out into a grove of old-growth cedars that are more than 1,000 years old.

3 Glacier National Park

72km (45 miles) E of Revelstoke; 80km (50 miles) W of Golden

Located amid the highest peaks of the Selkirk Mountains, Canada's Glacier National Park amply lives up to its name. More than 400 glaciers repose here, with 14% of the park's 2,168 sq. km (846 sq. miles) lying under permanent snowpack. The reason that this high country is so covered with ice is the same reason that this is one of the more unpopulated places to visit in the mountain West: It snows and rains a lot here.

For information, contact **Glacier National Park** (© 250/837-7500; www.pc.gc.ca/pn-np/bc/glacier). The visitor center is at Rogers Pass. There's no charge if you pass through the park on Highway 1 without stopping, but if you do stop to hike or picnic, the entry fee is C$6 (US$4.80) for adults, C$5 (US$4) for seniors, C$3 (US$2.40) for children, or C$15 (US$12) per family.

EXPLORING THE PARK

The primary attractions in the park are viewpoints onto craggy peaks and hiking trails leading to wildflower meadows and old-growth groves; heavy snow and rainfall lend a near-rainforest feel to the hikes. Spring hikers and cross-country skiers should beware of avalanche conditions, a serious problem in areas with high snowfall and steep slopes. Call the park information number (© **250/837-7500**) for weather updates.

Glacier Park is crossed by the Trans-Canada Highway and the Canadian Pacific Railway tracks. Each has had to build snowsheds to protect its transportation system from the effects of heavy snows and avalanches. **Park headquarters** are just east of 1,250m (4,100-ft.) Rogers Pass; stop here to watch videos and see the displays on natural and human history in the park. New exhibits focus on the role of the railroads in opening up this rugged area of Canada. You can sign up for ranger-led interpretive hikes here as well. On a typically gray and wet day, the visitor center may be the driest place to enjoy the park.

HIKING

Several easy trails leave from the park's Rogers Pass visitor center. **Abandoned Rails Trail** follows a rails-to-trails section of the old CPR track for a 1-hour round-trip journey along a gentle grade through a wildflower-studded basin. The **Balu Pass Trail** is a more strenuous 5km (3-mile) hike up to the base of the glaciers on 2,728m (8,950-ft.) Ursus Major.

The other important trail head is at **Illecillewaet Campground,** west of Rogers Pass along Highway 1. Seven major trails head up into the peaks from here, including the **Asulkan Valley Trail,** which follows a stream up a narrow valley to a hikers' hut. These trails require more exertion than the trails at Rogers Pass, and will take most of a day to complete.

Further down the Illecillewaet Valley are two other popular routes. **Loop Brook Trail** is a 1-hour saunter through a riparian wetland. The .5km (⅓-mile) **Rockgarden Trail** climbs up a valley wall of moss-and-lichen-covered boulders to a vista point onto 2,880m (9,446-ft.) Smart Peak. Stop at the **Hemlock Grove Picnic Area** and follow the boardwalk through the old-growth hemlock forest.

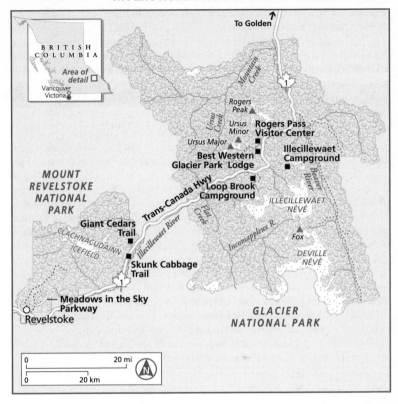

Mount Revelstoke & Glacier National Parks

To Golden

BRITISH
COLUMBIA

*Area of
detail* □

Vancouver
Victoria

Mountain Creek

Rogers
Peak ▲

Ursus Creek

Ursus
Minor ▲   **Rogers Pass
Visitor Center** ■

Ursus Major ▲

**Best Western
Glacier Park Lodge** ■

**Illecillewaet
Campground** ▲

Beaver River

**MOUNT
REVELSTOKE
NATIONAL
PARK**

Trans-Canada Hwy

**Loop Brook
Campground** ■

*ILLECILLEWAET
NÉVÉ*

Flat Creek

Inconappleux R.

**Giant Cedars
Trail** ■

CLACHNACUDAINN
ICEFIELD

Illecillewaet River

Fox ▲

*DEVILLE
NÉVÉ*

**Skunk Cabbage
Trail** ■

1

**Meadows in the Sky
Parkway**

○
Revelstoke

**GLACIER
NATIONAL PARK**

0   20 mi
0   20 km

N

The longest hike in the park is the 42km (26-mile) **Beaver Valley Trail,** which follows the Beaver River on the eastern edge of the park. This trail takes 3 days, one-way,
to complete. If you plan on backcountry camping, you'll need to register at the visitor center and purchase a C$9 (US$7.20) wilderness pass.

WHERE TO STAY

Illecillewaet and **Loop Brook** campgrounds are just west of Rogers Pass off Highway
1 and along the Illecillewaet River. Both operate on a first-come, first-served basis.
Facilities include flush toilets, kitchen shelters, firewood, and drinking water. Illecillewaet offers guided hikes and fireside programs as well. Rates at both campgrounds are
C$19 (US$15) per night.

Best Western Glacier Park Lodge   This large complex is just below Rogers Pass,
where Highway 1 edges over the Selkirk Range in Glacier National Park. The setting
is spectacular: The glaciered faces of towering peaks crowd around a broad cirque
blanketed with wildflowers and boulders, at the center of which sits this handsome
lodge. One hundred thirty-nine kilometers (86 miles) of hiking and cross-country ski
trails lead out into the wilderness (the hotel will prepare a picnic lunch for you on

request). Guest rooms are comfortable and nicely furnished with extra-long beds; three of the suites are large enough to accommodate families.

Rogers Pass, BC V0E 2S0. (✆) **800/528-1234** or 250/837-2126. Fax 250/837-2130. www.glacierparklodge.ca. 50 units. C$115–C$155 (US$920–US$124) double; C$185 (US$148) suite. AE, DISC, MC, V. **Amenities:** 2 restaurants; bar; heated outdoor pool; Jacuzzi; sauna; limited room service; laundry service. *In room:* TV, coffeemaker, iron.

4 Golden

134km (83 miles) W of Banff; 713km (442 miles) E of Vancouver

For more than a century, Golden (pop. 4,107) has been known primarily as a transport hub, first as a division point on the transcontinental Canadian Pacific Railway, next as the upstream steamboat terminus on the Columbia River, and then as a junction of two of Canada's busiest highway systems.

Nowadays, Golden is known for its outdoor recreation. The town sits in a breathtaking location in the trenchlike Columbia River valley, between the massive Rocky Mountains and the soaring Purcell Range, within a 90-minute drive of five major national parks. The fact that Golden is near—and not in—the parks is largely the reason for the area's recent phenomenal growth. Outfitters that offer heli-skiing, heli-hiking, and other recreation that isn't allowed in the national parks (for conservation reasons) choose to make Golden their base. And with park towns such as nearby Banff trying to limit further development, businesses and outfitters that want a Rocky Mountain hub find Golden a convenient and congenial center.

Golden won't win any awards for quaint charm, however. It's basically a functional little town with lots of motel rooms in a magnificent location.

Note that Golden and the other communities in this part of the Columbia Valley are in the Mountain Time zone, an hour earlier than the rest of British Columbia.

ESSENTIALS

GETTING THERE Golden is at the junction of Highway 1 (the Trans-Canada Hwy.) and Highway 95. The closest airport is in Calgary. **Greyhound Canada** (✆) **800/661-8747** or 403/260-0877; www.greyhound.ca) links Golden to Vancouver, Banff, and Calgary, and to Cranbrook to the south. The one-way fare from Golden to Vancouver is C$104 (US$83); to Calgary, it's C$45 (US$36).

VISITOR INFORMATION Contact the **Golden Visitor Info Centre,** 500 10th Ave. N. (✆) **800/622-4653** or 250/344-7125; www.goldenchamber.bc.ca).

GETTING AROUND If you need a rental car while in Golden, contact **National,** 915 11th Ave. (✆) **250/344-9899;** www.nationalcar.com).

EXPLORING THE AREA

You could spend several days in the Golden area without realizing that the town has an older downtown core. It's a block west of busy 10th Avenue, on **Main Street.** There's not much here—just a handful of shops and cafes—but it's a pleasant break from the commercial sprawl along highways 1 and 95.

The **Golden and District Museum,** 1302 11th Ave. (✆) **250/344-5169**), tells the story of Golden's rail history. It also has an old log schoolhouse and blacksmith's shop. It's open Monday through Friday from 10am to 6pm in May, June, and September, and daily in July and August. Admission is by donation.

> ⌒ *Tips* **Special Events**
>
> The **Golden Festival of Birds and Bears** (🕿 **800/622-4653**) is held during the second week of May. Events include field trips, kids' programs, musical entertainment, and wildlife and conservation seminars. The **Golden Rodeo** brings a bit of the Wild West to the Canadian Rockies during the first weekend of August, with a pancake breakfast, street dance, barbecues, and, of course, bucking bulls and broncos, roping, and races. The rodeo grounds are a mile south of Golden off Highway 95. For information, contact the visitor center.

OUTDOOR PURSUITS

FISHING   The Columbia River runs through town and offers fair fishing for rainbow trout and kokanee salmon. There's better fishing in the **Kinbasket Lake** section of the river, which begins just north of Golden. For guided trips in more remote lakes and streams, contact **Kinbasket Adventures** (🕿 **250/344-6012;** www.rockies.net/~kbasket).

GOLF   **Golden Golf & Country Club** (🕿 **866/727-7222** or 250/344-2700; www.golfgolden.com) is an 18-hole championship course along the Columbia River. Bill Newis designed the front 9 holes; Les Furber took care of the back 9. The clubhouse includes a pro shop with equipment rentals. Greens fees are C$55 to C$59 (US$44–C$47).

HELI-HIKING   Although based in Banff, **CMH Heli-Hiking** (🕿 **800/661-0252** or 403/762-7100; www.cmhhike.com) offers a variety of helicopter-assisted hiking packages in the mountains west of Golden. Three-, four-, or six-day heli-hiking trips involve staying at remote high-country lodges accessible only by long hikes or by helicopter. Prices vary depending on time of year and individual lodge, but 3-day trips begin at C$2,164 (US$1,731); rates include lodging, food, and helicopter transport.

Mid-June through September, **Purcell Helicopter Skiing** (🕿 **877/435-4754** or 250/344-5410; www.purcellhelicopterskiing.com) offers heli-hiking day trips in the Purcell Mountains west of Golden. Guided day hikes go for C$288 to C$485 (US$230–US$388), including lunch. Sightseeing tours start at C$150 (US$120).

HELI-SKIING 🌟   Banff-based **CMH Heli-Skiing** (see "Heli-Hiking," above) has eight high-country lodges in the mountain ranges near Golden. Prices vary greatly depending on the lodge and time of year, but start at C$5,155 all inclusive for a week. Rates include lodging, food, helicopter transport, use of specialized powder skis, and ground transport from the nearest large airport (usually Calgary).

If you prefer more of a DIY approach to heli-skiing, **Purcell Helicopter Skiing** (see "Heli-Hiking," above) offers day trips to peaks in the Selkirk and Purcell ranges. Three-run (C$630/US$504) and seven-run (C$750/US$600) packages are available, and include the helicopter ride, lunch, a guide, and instruction; you'll provide your own skis and lodging.

HORSEBACK RIDING   Located in the lovely Blaeberry River valley, **Triple C Backcountry Riding,** Goat Mountain Lodge, 236 Blaeberry Rd. (🕿 **877/240-RIDE**

or 250/344-6579; www.rockies.net/~goatmtn/TripleC.html), offers a variety of rides. The trails follow the river along the same routes traversed by Native Canadians and early frontier explorers. Full-day trips are C$75 (US$60) for adults and C$65 (US$52) for kids 12 and under; 1- and 2-hour guided rides are also available. The Sundowner trip that includes an evening cookout goes for C$55 (US$44) per adult and C$50 (US$40) per child.

SKIING ✯ **Kicking Horse Mountain Resort** (℃ **866/754-5425;** www.kicking horseresort.com), opened in 2001, is the newest ski resort in the Canadian Rockies. Located 14km (8¾ miles) west of Golden, it features a 1,240m-long (4,067-ft.) vertical drop (Canada's second longest), a gondola lift that takes skiers up above elevations of 2,310m (7,577 ft.), and the Eagle's Eye, the highest-elevation restaurant in Canada. It has six lifts and over 1,620 hectares (4,001 acres) of skiable terrain. Lift tickets are C$59 (US$47) a day. Several lodging options are now available at the resort, including five lodges, three-bedroom town houses, and resort homes. You can also spend a night at the Eagle's Eye restaurant complex and wake up at the crest of the Selkirk Mountains (at C$1,750/US$1,400 per couple, the views won't provide the only unforgettable memory of this overnight stay).

WHITE-WATER RAFTING   The **Kicking Horse River,** which enters the Columbia at Golden, is one of the most exciting white-water runs in Canada, with constant Class III and Class IV rapids as it tumbles down from the Continental Divide through Yoho. A trip down the Kicking Horse will be a highlight of your vacation in the Rockies. Rafting trips are usually offered from mid-May to mid-September.

Alpine Rafting (℃ **888/599-5299** or 250/344-6778; www.alpinerafting.com) offers a daylong trip for C$95 (US$76), including a barbecue steak lunch. A gentler introduction to white water goes for C$60 (US$48) for adults and C$30 (US$24) for children 12 and under.

Canadian Whitewater Adventures (℃ **888/577-8118** or 403/720-8745; www. canadianwhitewater.com) offers rafting trips and combination rafting/hiking or rafting/rappelling trips. Rafting packages include Upper Canyon for C$95 (US$76) and the Upper & Lower Combo for C$150 (US$120). A shuttle from Banff and Lake Louise costs C$15 (US$12) per person.

Glacier Raft Company (℃ **250/344-6521;** www.glacierraft.com) offers a variety of options. The easygoing scenic float day trip goes to the gentle upper valley of the Kicking Horse; it's for those who want an introduction to rafting or who don't want

---

Moments A Bird's-Eye View

Alpenglow Aviation (℃ **888/244-7117** or 250/344-7117; www.rockiesairtours. com) offers a variety of flightseeing trips into the magnificent mountain ranges that ring Golden. The 1¼-hour Columbia Icefields Tour (C$195/US$156) flies along the Continental Divide between Yoho and Banff national parks and also takes in the Columbia Icefield, the largest nonpolar ice cap in the world. The Golden Airport is just west of Golden, off Fisher Road. Alpenglow also offers pickup van service anywhere in Canmore, Banff, or Lake Louise. Simply awe-inspiring!

Exploring the Columbia River Wetlands

South (upstream) from Golden is the Columbia River Wetlands, a 144km-long (89-mile) Wildlife Management Area that supports an incredible diversity of wildlife. More than 270 bird species have been seen in this stretch of river, marsh, and lake. The largest wetlands west of Manitoba, the Columbia River Wetlands is also a major breeding ground for the bald eagle, osprey, and great blue heron. Moose, elk, mink, and beaver make their home here as well.

Kinbasket Adventures (© 250/334-6012; www.rockies.net/~kbasket) has two different wildlife-viewing trips through the wetlands. A leisurely 2½-hour pontoon trip is C$46 (US$37) for adults and C$20 (US$16) for children 12 and under. This is suitable for all ages as well as for those with disabilities. Longer guided canoe excursions have a stronger bird-watching focus. Half-day trips are C$50 (US$40); full-day trips are C$80 (US$64), including lunch. Canoe rentals are available as well.

the thrills of white water. Cost is C$65 (US$52) for adults and C$40 (US$32) for kids 14 and under. Two separate day trips explore the white-water sections of the Kicking Horse and cost C$105 to C$130 (US$84–US$104). Deduct C$10 (US$8) from the white-water trip rates if you take your trip on a weekday. All day trips include a steak barbecue lunch.

Wet 'n' Wild Adventures (© 800/668-9119 or 250/344-6546; www.wetnwild. bc.ca) offers Kicking Horse trips from Banff, Lake Louise, and Golden (the shuttle from Banff and Lake Louise costs C$15/US$11). The standard day trip is C$92 (US$74), including lunch. If you just want to shoot the rapids of the lower canyon, a half-day trip is available for C$63 (US$50). For beginners, a morning introduction to white water is C$58 (US$46) for adults and C$38 (US$30) for children 12 and under, including lunch. These outfitters also offer guided, 2½-hour flat-water kayak trips on the Columbia River for C$59 (US$47).

WHERE TO STAY

Alpine Meadows Lodge 🐾   This family-owned lodge enjoys a great location—high above Golden, looking across onto the face of the Rockies, yet only 10 minutes to skiing, golf, and tourist services. The lodge, which was constructed from timber felled on the property, has a central three-story great room, flanked by wraparound balconies and open staircases. A huge stone fireplace dominates the living area. The guest rooms are light-filled and airy, with simple, unfussy decor; all of them have Jacuzzi tubs in the bathrooms. In addition, a four-bedroom, two-bathroom chalet with full kitchen is also available for rent. Outdoor recreation is literally right out the door, with paths from the lodge leading to hiking trails in neighboring federal forestland. The staff is very helpful and will make it easy for you to get out into the wilderness or onto the fairways.

717 Elk Rd., Golden, BC V0A 1H0. © **888/700-4477** or 250/344-5863. Fax 250/344-5853. www.alpinemeadows lodge.com. 10 units, 1 chalet. C$99–C$119 (US$79–US$95) double; C$300–C$425 (US$240–US$340) chalet, with 3–5 night minimum stay in peak seasons. Rates include breakfast. Golf, skiing, rafting, and flightseeing packages available. MC, V. **Amenities:** Restaurant; lounge (offers TV and Internet access). *In room:* A/C, no phone.

Columbia Valley Lodge This homey lodge sits on a wetlands lake beside the Columbia River, offering a relaxing place to stay for those who want to be close to nature but don't want to backpack to get to it. The flower-bedecked, Tyrolean-style inn overlooks a grassy meadow with picnic tables and play structures for the kids; a 2-minute walk leads to the lake (this is a great place for birders). The rooms are clean and basic; half have balconies.

23km (14 miles) south of Golden on Hwy. 95 (Box 2669), Golden, BC V0A 1H0. © **800/311-5008** or 250/348-2508. Fax 250/348-2505. www.columbiavalleylodge.com. 12 units. C$90–C$105 (US$72–US$84) double. Extra person C$15 (US$12). Rates include full breakfast. Senior, off-season, and weekly discounts available. Children under 6 stay free in parent's room. MC, V. **Amenities:** Restaurant; canoe rentals. *In room:* TV.

Golden Rim Motor Inn Of the dozens of older motels in Golden, this is the pick of the litter. Standing above the precipitous Kicking Horse River valley, just half a mile east of Golden, the Golden Rim boasts sweeping views of the Rockies and the Columbia Valley. It offers standard queen-bed motel rooms, with some kitchen and Jacuzzi units available.

1416 Golden View Rd., Golden, BC V0A 1H0. © **877/311-2216** or 250/344-2216. Fax 250/344-6673. 81 units. C$104 (US$83) double. AE, MC, V. **Amenities:** Restaurant; bar; indoor pool with water slide; Jacuzzi; sauna; coin-op laundry. *In room:* A/C, TV, dataport, hair dryer.

Hillside Lodge & Chalets This stylish, European-style lodge with five stand-alone chalets sits on 24 forested hectares (59 acres) above the quiet Blaeberry River, 16km (10 miles) north of Golden. Guests stay in comfortable lodge rooms or delightful one-bedroom or two-bedroom chalets, the latter with woodstoves, kitchenettes, decks, and handcrafted furniture. All accommodations are newly built, so you'll find everything completely shipshape.

1740 Seward Frontage Rd., Golden, BC V0A 1H0. © **250/344-7281**. Fax 250/344-7281. www.hillsidechalets.com. 14 units. C$98–C$135 (US$78–US$108) lodge double; C$115–C$140 (US$92–US$112) 1-bedroom chalet. Rates include full German-style breakfast. MC, V. **Amenities:** Dining room (guests only); lounge (w/TV); exercise room; sauna. *In room:* Fridge, coffeemaker, hair dryer, no phone.

Kapristo Lodge Homey, lodge-style Kapristo is an excellent choice for the recreation-oriented vacationer. It sits high above the Columbia Valley, with sweeping views of the Purcell Mountains from the large flagstone-and-planking patio. Guest rooms are comfortably furnished with down quilts and handsome furniture; one unit has its own kitchen, fireplace, and Jacuzzi. What sets this apart from other lodges around Golden is its friendly informality and its owner's efforts to ensure that guests have a good time, whether rafting a river, riding horseback, or sunning on the deck.

1297 Campbell Rd., Golden, BC V0A 1H0. © **250/344-6048**. Fax 250/344-6755. www.kapristolodge.com. 6 units. C$180–C$206 (US$144–US$164) double. Rates include breakfast. MC, V. **Amenities:** Dining room (guests only); Jacuzzi; sauna. *In room:* No phone.

Prestige Inn Golden ⚱ Easily the swankest place to stay in Golden, the Prestige Inn is recently built and luxurious, with excellent facilities, a variety of room types, and a good restaurant. Guest rooms are spacious and richly appointed, each with two phones and lots of extras.

1049 Trans-Canada Hwy., Golden, BC V0A 1H0. © 877/737-8443 or 250/344-7990. Fax 250/344-7902. www. prestigeinn.com. 82 units. C$149–C$179 (US$119–US$143) double. AE, DISC, MC, V. **Amenities:** Restaurant; bar; indoor pool; exercise room; Jacuzzi; concierge; shopping arcade; limited room service; laundry service. In room: A/C, TV w/pay movies, dataport, kitchenette, fridge, coffeemaker, hair dryer, iron.

WHERE TO DINE

Cedar House ✿ PACIFIC NORTHWEST   Perched high above the Columbia Valley south of Golden, Cedar House has one of the best views in the region. The log lodge is divided into cozy dining areas and is flanked by decks, all the better to take in the vista. The exciting menu features seasonal specials and local meats and vegetables, all cooked in an open kitchen. Seared wild salmon with lemon balm and chile butter, and grilled pork tenderloin with fig, thyme, and sherry *jus* are standouts.

735 Hefti Rd., 10 min. south of Golden on Hwy 95. © 250/344-4679. http://cedarhousecafe.com. Reservations recommended. Main courses C$17–C$34 (US$14–US$27). MC, V. Sun 10:30am–3:30pm; daily 5–10:30pm.

Eagle's Eye Restaurant ✿✿ NEW CANADIAN   Canada's highest-elevation restaurant, the Eagle's Eye towers above the new Kicking Horse Resort. Diners take the ski gondola 1,200m (3,936 ft.) up to 2,410m (7,905 ft.) above sea level to reach this dining room with a 360-degree view of the nearby Rocky, Selkirk, and Purcell mountain ranges. With a panorama like this, the food needn't be good; it's excellent, however, with an emphasis on Alberta lamb and beef, British Columbia salmon and oysters, and seasonal specials like pistachio-crusted halibut with truffled potatoes.

Kicking Horse Resort, west of Golden on Dyke Rd. © 250/344-8626. Reservations required. Main courses C$21–C$39 (US$17–US$31). AE, MC, V. Off-season Mon–Thurs 10am–3:30pm, Fri–Sun 10am–9pm; summer daily 10am–10pm. Closed mid-Oct to mid-Dec and mid-Apr to mid-May. Call to confirm opening dates.

Kicking Horse Grill INTERNATIONAL   Housed in a historic log cabin near downtown, this bustling restaurant is a culinary League of Nations: The menu changes every season to reflect not only fresh ingredients but also the international travels of the Dutch owners. Start with French onion soup or a Japanese *goma* salad, then move on to an Indonesian *bami goreng* stir-fry or a grilled ahi tuna steak with lime noodles. If you're happy to remain gastronomically in Golden, there's a selection of steaks and chops (including an excellent pork tenderloin in a maple and mint sauce). The dining room is a puzzling mix of white linen, crystal, and the Wild West.

1105 Ninth St. © 250/344-2330. www.thekickinghorsegrill.ca. Reservations recommended. Main courses C$18–C$30 (US$14–US$24). AE, MC, V. Daily 5–10pm.

The Timber Inn *Finds* GERMAN/CONTINENTAL   This country inn in the little community of Parsons contains an excellent dining room (along with handsome guest rooms). The menu offers a number of starter salads, such as the Turino with tuna and onion, plus excellent bruschetta. Moving on to the main courses, choose from schnitzel, steaks, roast lamb, and chicken. The cozy room overlooks the Columbia Valley and the Purcell Mountains. It's a lovely drive from Golden to Parsons on a long summer evening.

3483 Hwy. 95 S., 32km (20 miles) south of Golden. © 250/348-2228. Reservations recommended. Main courses C$13–C$23 (US$10–US$18). MC, V. Daily 5–9pm.

5 The Kootenay Valley: Cranbrook & Nelson

Cranbrook: 80km (50 miles) N of the U.S.–Canada border

CRANBROOK

The largest city in southeastern British Columbia, Cranbrook (pop. 18,780) exists mostly as a trade center for loggers and agriculturists. The town itself has few tourist sights, but Cranbrook is central to a number of historic and recreational areas and offers ample numbers of hotel rooms. Its setting is spectacularly dramatic: a broad forested valley that looks onto the sky-piercing Canadian Rockies and backside of the U.S. Glacier National Park.

ESSENTIALS

GETTING THERE Cranbrook is near the junction of the north-south Highway 93/95 corridor and the east-west Highway 3. **Greyhound Canada** (© 800/661-8747; www.greyhound.ca) operates buses that travel on both of these road systems. One-way service from Cranbrook to Golden costs C$37 (US$30). There's also daily service to Spokane, Washington. **Air Canada Jazz** (© 888/247-2262; www.air canada.ca) operates flights from Vancouver to the Cranbrook Airport, north of town.

VISITOR INFORMATION The **Cranbrook Visitor Info Centre** is at 2279 Cranbrook St. N. (© 800/222-6174 or 250/426-5914; www.cranbrookchamber.com). It's open daily 9am to 6pm.

EXPLORING THE AREA

It's worth getting off the grim Highway 95 strip to visit the pleasant downtown area around Baker Street. As you stroll the broad, tree-lined streets, you'll see a number of heritage brick storefronts and commercial buildings. Especially impressive is the grand, turreted 1909 **Imperial Bank** building at Baker and Eighth streets.

Canadian Museum of Rail Travel ❧ Cranbrook was established as a rail division point, so it's fitting that the town is home to this fascinating museum that preserves a number of historic rail cars, including several "cars of state" designed for royalty. The Royal Alexandra Hall is a 279-sq.-m (3,000-sq.-ft.) oak-paneled dining room salvaged from Winnipeg's Royal Alexandra Hotel, a CPR hotel torn down in 1971. The ornate moldings, panels, and furniture were carefully numbered and stored for nearly 30 years before being reconstructed here. Other highlights include a complete set of 12 cars built in 1929 for the Canadian Pacific Railway's Trans-Canada Limited run. Rather like a traveling luxury hotel, the restored cars gleam with brass and inlaid walnut and mahogany. In summer, the dining car offers tea service.

Tips **Special Events**

Sam Steele Days (© 250/426-4161) celebrate the Wild West heritage of the Cranbrook area. This annual festival, held the third weekend of June, features an indoor rodeo, parade, barbecue, pancake breakfast, street dances, sports tournaments, and more.

---

57 Van Horne St. S. (*C*) **250/489-3918**. www.crowsnest.bc.ca/cmrt. Admission (may vary according to which tours are taken) C$13 (US$10) adults, C$11 (US$8.80) seniors, C$6.55 (US$5.25) students, C$3 children 12 and under, C$32 (US$26) families. July–Aug daily 10am–6pm, dining car daily 10am–6pm; Sept to mid-Oct and Easter–June daily 10am–6pm; mid-Oct to Easter Tues–Sat noon–5pm. Tours given on the half-hour.

Fort Steele Heritage Town *Kids*   During the 1864 gold rush, a cable ferry stretched across a narrow section of the Kootenay River, enabling prospectors to safely cross the turbulent waters. A small settlement sprang up, and after another mining boom—this time for silver, lead, and zinc—Fort Steele had more than 4,000 inhabitants. But when the railroad pushed through, it bypassed Fort Steele in favor of Cranbrook. Within 5 years, all but 150 of the citizens had left. In the 1960s, the crumbling ghost town was declared a heritage site. Today, more than 60 restored and reconstructed buildings grace the town-site, including a hotel, churches, saloons, and a courthouse and jail. In summer, living-history actors give demonstrations of period skills and occupations. There are also a steam train, wagon rides, and a variety show at the Wild Horse Theatre. The International Hotel Restaurant serves Victorian fare.

16km (10 miles) northeast of Cranbrook on Hwy. 93/95. (*C*) **250/426-7352**, or 250/426-7352 for recorded information. www.fortsteele.bc.ca. Daily May–June and Labour Day to mid-Oct 9:30am–5pm; July–Labour Day 9:30am–7pm. Evening entertainment and restaurant July–Labour Day Tues–Sun. Admission to grounds July–Labour Day C$12 (US$9.60) adults, C$11 (US$8.80) seniors, C$4.50 (US$3.60) youths 13–18, C$2.50 (US$2) children 6–12. Reduced admission in shoulder seasons. Tickets good for 2 consecutive days. Free evening admission for theater and restaurant patrons. The grounds remain open in winter, though without services.

OUTDOOR PURSUITS

FISHING   Eighteen area rivers, including the Elk River, St. Mary River, and Kootenay, are often rated among the country's top 10 fly-fishing destinations. Trophy fish are taken all season long. For lake fishing, Moyie Lake, 30km (19 miles) south of Cranbrook, has a good stock of kokanee, rainbow, and bull trout. **Rocky Mountain Angler** (*C* **250/489-4053**; www.geocities.com/rockymountainangler) offers hourly, half-day, and full-day instruction. Women-only trips are available as well.

GOLF   Opened in 2000, the **St. Eugene Mission Golf Resort** (*C* **877/417-3133** or 250/417-3417) is an 18-hole, Les Furber–designed course with a links section. *Golf Digest* has rated the St. Eugene Mission course as one of the top three new courses in Canada. Greens fees are C$82 to C$95 (US$59–US$68). The **Cranbrook Golf Club,** 2700 Second St. S. (*C* **888/211-8855** or 250/426-6462), is a long-established 18-hole course with greens fees starting at C$49 (US$35). The **Mission Hills Golf Course** (*C* **250/489-3009**) has 18 holes and a par-3 rating, plus a clubhouse and restaurant. Greens fees are C$20 (US$16).

SKIING   Ninety-three kilometers (57 miles) east of Cranbrook, on the western face of the Rockies, is one of the best skiing and snowboarding areas in British Columbia. **Fernie Alpine Resort,** Ski Area Road, Fernie (*C* **250/423-4655**; www.skifernie. com), is a relatively unheralded resort that's popular with in-the-know snowboarders. Average snowfall is about 9m (30 ft.), with a vertical drop of 843m (2,765 ft.). There are 97 trails in five alpine bowls, with a total of more than 1,013 hectares (2,500 acres) of skiable terrain served by three quads, two triples, two T-bars, a Poma, and a handle tow with the capacity to handle 12,300 skiers per hour (but it's never *that* busy). Adult lift tickets are C$64 to C$69 (US$51–US$55). Amenities include lodging (© **800/ 258-SNOW** for reservations), restaurants, rentals, and instruction. The resort, lodges, and lifts remain open in summer, with hiking, mountain biking, and horseback riding the main activities.

WHERE TO STAY

Fort Steele Resort & RV Park, 16km (10 miles) north of Cranbrook on Highway 95 (© **250/426-5117**), has 300 sites costing from C$19 to C$25 (US$15–US$20). It offers pull-throughs, a tenting area, hot showers, and a swimming pool.

Cedar Heights B&B This stylish, contemporary home is situated in a residential area just minutes from downtown Cranbrook. The rooms are beautifully furnished and have private entrances. Two lounges contain a fireplace, wet bar, fridge, coffee and tea service, and games. From the spacious deck, take in the view of the magnificent Rockies.

1200 13th St., Cranbrook, BC V1C 5V8. © **800/497-6014** or 250/426-0505. Fax 250/426-0045. www.bb canada.com/cedarheights. 3 units. C$100–C$135 (US$80–US$92) double. Extra person C$30–C$35 (US$24–US$28). Rates include full breakfast. MC, V. Children must be 12 or older. **Amenities:** Jacuzzi; laundry service. *In room:* A/C, TV/VCR, hair dryer.

Nomad Motel *Value* Of the many moderately priced motels along the Highway 95 strip north of Cranbrook, the well-maintained Nomad offers the most facilities for the money. Some rooms offer full kitchens, and the apartment-style family suites have full kitchens and sleeping space for up to six people. And it's right next door to a 24-hour Smitty's and the Apollo steakhouse (see "Where to Dine," below).

910 Cranbrook St. N., Cranbrook, BC V1C 3S3. © **800/863-6999** or 250/426-6266. Fax 250/426-1871. www.nomad motel.bc.ca. 34 units. High seasonC$69–C$99 (US$55–US$79) double; C$109 (US$87) suite. Extra person C$10 (US$8). Kitchen C$10 (US$) extra. Rates include continental breakfast. Lower off-season rates available. AE, MC, V. **Amenities:** Outdoor heated pool; access to nearby health club; business center; coin-op laundry; playground. *In room:* A/C, TV/VCR, dataport, kitchen (some rooms and suites only), fridge, coffeemaker, microwave.

Prestige Rocky Mountain Resort & Convention Centre ✿✿ By far the poshest place to stay in Cranbrook itself, the first-class Prestige resort features very large and stylish rooms with lots of extras; some rooms have kitchenettes. There's fine dining at Delmonico's, drinks and lighter meals at Chattanooga's Bar and Grill, and an espresso bar for your caffeine fix. Other perks include a spa offering aromatherapy and massage.

209 Van Horne St. S., Cranbrook, BC V1C 6R9. © **887/737-8443** or 250/417-0444. Fax 250/417-0400. www. prestigeinn.com. 109 units. C$140–C$179 (US$112–US$143) double; from C$359 (US$287) suite. Extra person C$20 (US$16). Off-season rates and golf/ski packages available. AE, DISC, MC, V. **Amenities:** Restaurant; bar; indoor pool; full health club (fee); spa; Jacuzzi; room service; massage; same-day dry cleaning. *In room:* A/C, TV w/pay movies, kitchenette (in some), fridge, coffeemaker, hair dryer, iron.

St. Eugene Mission Resort ✿ This extraordinary resort is both the newest and one of the oldest places to stay in the Cranbrook area. The resort hotel, along with a noted golf course, spa, casino, and First Nation cultural center, are on the grounds of a former residential school built for the education and acculturation of the local Kootenay Indian band in the late 19th century. The original mission school structure was renovated and now houses a number of unique guest accommodations; a brandnew adjacent lodge also features rooms and suites. The mission's historic barn is now the golf club house and, in 2004, a health club was added. With financial backing from the Ktunaxa Kinbasket Tribal Council and the federal government, the transformation of the old mission has been accomplished with great attention to historic detail, and its affiliation with the respected Delta Hotel chain assures a certain quality of service and comfort. Rooms are simply but elegantly appointed, and the views are magnificent, with miles of open links and pine forest and the Rockies rising to fill the sky.

7731 Mission Rd., Cranbrook, BC VIC 7E5. (Ⓒ) **888/778-5050** or 250/420-2000. Fax 250/420-2001. www.delta hotels.com. 125 units. C$119–C$199 (US$95–US$159) double. Extra person C$20 (US$16). Golf and ski packages available. AE, DC, DISC, MC, V. Off-season rates available. **Amenities:** Restaurant; lounge; indoor and outdoor pool; golf course; tennis; health club; spa; sauna; steam room; business center; casino. *In room:* A/C, TV w/movie channels, coffeemaker, hair dryer, iron, robes.

WHERE TO DINE

Apollo Ristorante & Steak House GREEK/STEAKHOUSE   Ask a local to recommend a restaurant, and Apollo is sure to be among the first choices. The menu covers not only traditional Greek dishes, but also a broad selection of pasta, steaks and prime rib, sandwiches, seafood, even pizza. With such a large dining room and ambitious menu, you might suspect that quality would suffer. But you'll be pleased with the hearty, slightly old-fashioned tastiness of the results.

1012 Cranbrook St. N. (Ⓒ) **250/426-3721.** Main courses C$9–C$24 (US$7.20–US$19). AE, MC, V. Daily 11am–10pm.

Heidi's Restaurant 𝒜 CONTINENTAL   The menu at this pleasantly refined restaurant, with red-brick walls and potted plants, is dominated by the cuisines of Germany and Italy. Appetizers range from empanadas with cumin beef to classic escargots. Entrees include steaks from local beef, schnitzels, pastas, fresh fish, and specialties like seared duck breast with black-currant sauce and spaetzle.

821C Baker St. (Ⓒ) **250/426-7922.** Reservations recommended. Main courses C$11–C$23 (US$8.80–US$18). AE, MC, V. Mon–Thurs 11am–2:30pm and 5–9pm; Fri–Sat 11:30am–2:30pm and 5–10pm; Sun 5–9pm.

NELSON 𝒜𝒜
102km (63 miles) N of the U.S.–Canada border

Nelson (pop. 10,000) is quite possibly the most pleasant and attractive town in the British Columbian interior. The late-19th-century commercial district is still intact, with an eclectic mix of old-fashioned businesses, coffeehouses, and fancy boutiques and galleries. Nelson also offers high-quality B&Bs, hotels, and restaurants, and the setting—along a shelf of land above the West Arm of Kootenay Lake—is splendid.

Nelson was born as a silver-mining town in the 1880s, and its veins proved productive and profitable. By 1900, Nelson was the third-largest city in the province, with an architecturally impressive core of Victorian and Queen Anne–style homes. Today, the gracious town center, coupled with convenient access to recreation in nearby lakes, mountains, and streams, has added to Nelson's newfound luster as an arts capital. Nelson claims to have more artists and craftspeople per capita than any other city in Canada. It certainly has an appealingly youthful, comfortably countercultural feel, and makes a great place to spend a day or two.

ESSENTIALS
GETTING THERE   Nelson is 102km (63 miles) north of the U.S.–Canada border; 242km (150 miles) north of Spokane, Washington; and 657km (407 miles) east of

Vancouver. **Greyhound Canada** (© **800/661-8747;** www.greyhound.ca) operates daily service from Vancouver for C$106 (US$85) one-way.

VISITOR INFORMATION   Contact the **Nelson Visitor Info Centre,** 225 Hall St. (© **250/352-3433;** www.discovernelson.com).

EXPLORING THE AREA

Nelson's main attractions are, in order, the city itself and what's just beyond. As an introduction to the town's wonderful Victorian architecture, stop by the visitor center for brochures on the driving and walking tours of Nelson's significant heritage buildings.

Not to be missed are the château-style **City Hall,** 502 Vernon St., and **Nelson Court House,** designed by F. M. Rattenbury, famed for his designs for the B.C. Parliament Buildings and the Empress Hotel, both of which continue to dominate Victoria. Note the three-story, turreted storefront at the corner of Baker and Ward streets, and the **Mara-Barnard building,** 421–431 Baker St., once the Royal Bank of Canada building, with elaborate brickwork and bay windows.

The story of Nelson's human history is told at the **Nelson Museum,** 402 Anderson St. (© **250/352-9813**), which has a number of artifacts from the Native Ktunaxa and from the silver-mining days when Nelson was one of the richest towns in Canada. There's a fascinating exhibit on the Dukhobors, a Russian Christian sect that settled along Kootenay Lake in the 1890s. Hours are Monday through Saturday from 1 to 6pm. Admission is C$2 (US$1.60) for adults, C$1 (US80¢) for seniors and students.

Nelson has a number of beautiful parks. **Gyro Park,** at Vernon and Park streets, features formal gardens, an outdoor pool, and panoramic views of Kootenay Lake and the Selkirk Mountains. **Lakeside Park,** which flanks Kootenay Lake near the base of the Nelson Bridge, offers swimming beaches, tennis courts, and a playground.

You can explore Nelson's lakefront on foot on the **Waterfront Pathway,** which winds along the shore from near the Prestige Resort to Lakeside Park. Or, in summer, hop on the restored **streetcar no. 23,** which runs from Lakeside Park to Hall Street, along the waterfront. At the turn of the 20th century, Nelson had a streetcar system and was the smallest city in Canada to boast such public transport. The system fell out of use in the 1940s, but a stretch of the track remains intact. From mid-May to Labour Day, the streetcar runs daily from noon to 6pm. Tickets are C$2 (US$1.60) for adults and C$1 (US80¢) for seniors and students.

OUTDOOR PURSUITS

FISHING   Fishing is legendary in 200m-deep (656-ft.) Kootenay Lake, which has 500km (310 miles) of lakefront. For guided trips and advice, contact **Split Shot Charters** (© **877/368-FISH;** www.split-shot.com).

GOLF   **Granite Pointe Golf Club,** 1123 Richards St. W. (© **250/352-5913**), is a hilly 18-hole, par-72 course with fantastic views of Kootenay Lake. Greens fees are C$48 (US$38); rentals, a clubhouse with dining, and a driving range are available.

HIKING   Accessible right in town is a 9km (5½-mile) rails-to-trails system on the old Burlington Northern line that follows the southern edge of the town along the flanks of Toad Mountain. You can join the path at a number of places; from downtown, follow Cedar Street south to find one entry point. The closest wilderness hiking is at

Kokanee Glacier Provincial Park, 21km (13 miles) northeast of Nelson on Highway 3A, then 16km (10 miles) north on a gravel road.

KAYAKING   For rentals or a guided half-day tour (C$65/US$52), contact **Kootenay Kayak Co.,** 579 Baker St. (© **877/229-4959** or 250/229-4959).

MOUNTAIN BIKING   The visitor center has a free map of old logging roads and rail lines that are available for biking. The Burlington Northern rails-to-trails system (see "Hiking," above) is also open to mountain bikers. For rentals and trail conditions, contact **Gerick Cycle & Sports,** 702 Baker St. (© **800/665-4441**).

SKIING   Sixteen kilometers (10 miles) south of Nelson off Highway 6 is the **Whitewater Ski Resort** (© **800/666-9420** or 250/354-4944; www.skiwhitewater.com), with some of British Columbia's best snow conditions. The ski area is in a natural snow-catching bowl below an escarpment of 2,490m (8,167-ft.) peaks. The average snowfall is 12m (39 ft.), and that snow falls as pure powder. The mountain consists of groomed runs, open bowls, glades, chutes, and tree skiing; 80% of the runs are rated either intermediate or advanced. There are two double chairs and a handle tow; the vertical drop is 390m (1,279 ft.). Lift tickets cost C$44 (US$35). Facilities include a day lodge with rentals, dining, and drinks. A new Nordic Centre has 18km (11 miles) of groomed cross-country ski trails.

If you're looking for backcountry skiing, the **Baldface Lodge** (© **250/352-0006;** www.baldface.net) is your ticket. A short helicopter ride takes you from Nelson to the backcountry lodge, where there's exquisite dining and accommodation, plus snowcat access to 14,568 hectares (36,000 acres) of power snow terrain. Rates are C$550 (US$440) per day in peak season, including guided snowcat skiing, all meals, and lodging.

WHERE TO STAY

Best Western Baker Street Inn   The Baker Street Inn stands at the end of the historic downtown area, within easy walking distance of both shopping and dining. Guest rooms are rather basic, but very clean and comfortable.

153 Baker St., Nelson, BC V1L 4H1. © **888/255-3525** or 250/352-3525. Fax 250/352-2995. www.bwbakerstreetinn. com. 70 units. C$129–C$259 (US$103–US$207) double. Extra person C$20 (US$16). AE, DISC, MC, V. **Amenities:** Restaurant; lounge; exercise room; Jacuzzi; business center; coin-op laundry. *In room:* A/C, TV, dataport, fridge, coffeemaker, hair dryer, microwave.

Casa Blanca Bed & Breakfast ☞   This exotic 1938 Art Deco minimansion offers spacious rooms in a great location across from Kootenay Lake. The detailing in the house is amazing: The living room boasts tropical-wood paneling, beveled-glass doors, a quartz fireplace, and inlaid hardwood floors, as well as such modern comforts as a TV, VCR, and CD player. It's an easy walk to downtown Nelson or to Kootenay Lake beaches. If you want more privacy or independence, or just want to make your own breakfast, consider the two-bedroom Blue Parrot cottage now offered by the folks at Casa Blanca. Located just next door to the B&B, it's a charming little house with everything, including a kitchen, that you'll need for a pleasant stay.

724 Second St., Nelson, BC V1L 2L9. © **888/354-4431** or 250/354-4431. Fax 250/354-4431. www.casablancanelson. com. 3 units, 1 with private bathroom; 1 cottage. C$8–C$125 (US$64–US$100) double. Extra person C$15 (US$12). MC, V. *In room:* A/C, no phone.

Dancing Bear Inn *Value*   The Dancing Bear is a first-rate hostel right in the thick of things downtown. The atmosphere and furnishings are more like what you'd expect to find in a B&B—a grimy backpackers' flophouse this is definitely not. The furniture is locally made from pine, beds are made up with down duvets, and paintings by area artists grace the walls. This is not your everyday hostel, and even if you're not into the hostelling scene, you'll find it a great place to meet people.

171 Baker St., Nelson, BC V1L 4H1. (C) **250/352-7573.** Fax 250/352-9818. www.dancingbearinn.com. 35 beds. C$22 (US$18) dorm bed; C$46 (US$39) private unit. Family and group rates, seasonal packages, and discounts for Hostelling International members available. MC, V. **Amenities:** Kitchen; common room with TV/VCR; computer with Internet access; laundry. *In room:* No phone.

Hume Hotel   This beautifully preserved 1898 hotel has been renovated to accommodate modern ideas of comfort while maintaining its vintage charm. For an antique hotel, the rooms are good-size, environmentally friendly, and smartly furnished. You'll want to visit the Hume Hotel even if you're not staying here, just to check out the wonderful bars, nightclub, and lobby area.

422 Vernon St., Nelson, BC V1L 4E5. (C) **877/568-0888** or 250/352-5331. Fax 250/352-5214. www.heritageinn.org. 43 units. C$89–C$105 (US$71–US$84) double. Extra person C$15 (US$12). Rates include breakfast. Golf and ski packages available. AE, MC, V. **Amenities:** 2 restaurants; 2 bars; access to nearby health club; salon; beer-and-wine store. *In room:* TV, high-speed Internet access.

Inn the Garden Bed & Breakfast   This spacious B&B is perched on a hill just a block off Baker Street, with views of the lake and Kootenay Peak. The handsome painted lady–style Victorian has six rooms with a mix of private and shared bathrooms, plus a garden, patio, and deck. A separate three-bedroom cottage, with kitchen and TV/VCR, is perfect for families or groups. Rates for guests staying in the main house include full breakfast; cottage guests get the makings for breakfast plus fresh baked goods delivered to their door.

408 Victoria St., Nelson, BC V1L 4K5. (C) **800/596-2337** or 250/352-3226. Fax 250/352-3284. www.innthegarden. com. 7 units. From C$90 (US$72) double in main house; from C$190 (US$152) cottage. Extra person C$15–C$25 (US$12–US$20). Rates for main house include full breakfast. Golf and ski packages available. AE, MC, V. Children accepted in cottage only. **Amenities:** Lounge with TV. *In room:* No phone.

New Grand Hotel ☆   Originally built in 1914, the Art Deco New Grand Hotel has been lovingly restored and updated as a hip and happening hotel and nightspot for the young at heart. The renovated rooms wear their age gracefully, without attempting to match a period style. The decor is comfortably eclectic, with hardwood floors, oriental rugs, contemporary art, and mid-century reproduction furniture. The result is simple, charming, and clutter free. If you're looking for inexpensive rooms, a number of double and triple rooms are available hostel style, with shared bathrooms and a kitchen area. The hotel's Uptown Tavern is a popular bar and grill, while Louie's Steakhouse offers prime beef and martinis.

616 Vernon St., Nelson, BC V1L 4G1. (C) **888/722-2258** or 250/352-7211. Fax 250/352-2445. www.newgrandhotel.ca. 34 units. C$70–C$109 (US$56–US$87) double; hostel rooms from C$19 (US$15) per person. **Amenities:** Restaurant; bar. *In room:* A/C, TV.

Prestige Lakeside Resort & Convention Centre   Down on the lakeshore, the Prestige is Nelson's full-service resort, offering spacious, beautiful rooms with all the services you'd expect at a luxury hotel. All units have balconies, and a number of theme rooms (including African and prehistoric ones) will spice up a special occasion. Some rooms have kitchenettes. The Prestige chain has opened another lakeshore lodging, in many ways an adjunct to this large hotel. The **Prestige Lakeview Inn,** 1301 Front St., is a smaller boutique hotel with upscale, European-style rooms. Facilities, such as the restaurant and pool, are shared with the sister property; rates are parallel. To contact the Prestige Lakeview Inn directly, call ✆ **250/352-3595.**

701 Lakeside Dr., Nelson, BC V1L 6G3. ✆ **877/737-8443** or 250/352-7222. Fax 250/352-3966. www.prestige inn.com. 101 units. C$149–C$219 (US$119–US$175) double. Extra person C$20 (US$16). Off-season rates available. AE, DC, DISC, MC, V. **Amenities:** Restaurant; coffee bar; bar; indoor pool; exercise room; spa; Jacuzzi; concierge; car-rental desk; limited room service; massage; laundry service; same-day dry cleaning. *In room:* A/C, TV w/pay movies, dataport, kitchenette (in some rooms), fridge, coffeemaker, hair dryer, iron.

WHERE TO DINE

The restaurants at the **Prestige Lakeside Resort** and the **Hume Hotel** (see "Where to Stay," above) are good, and a wander down **Baker Street** will reveal dozens of cafes, coffeehouses, and inexpensive ethnic restaurants. Don't miss the **Dominion Café,** 334 Baker St. (✆ **250/352-1904**), an old diner offering sandwiches, light entrees, baked goods, and a friendly, relaxed atmosphere. A popular hangout, morning to night, is **Jigsaws Coffee Co.,** 503 Baker St. (✆ **250/352-5961**).

All Seasons Café ★★★ NORTHWEST   The All Seasons is reason enough to visit Nelson. Located in a handsome heritage home a block off busy Baker Street, it isn't easy to find, but if you want to eat at British Columbia's best restaurant east of Vancouver, then persevere. Menus, which change seasonally, feature local produce and meats. To start, try the outstanding brie-and-asparagus flan with Italian figs and warm honey, or go for the Dungeness crab and potato latkes with fresh salsa. Main courses include a number of vegetarian and fish options. Spinach fettuccine is tossed with rosemary-infused roasted-tomato sauce and topped with either hempnut balls (a surprisingly flavorful tofu creation rolled in hemp seeds) or lamb meatballs. Skillet-seared halibut cheeks with wasabi whipped potatoes and Pernod-flambéed sea scallops are also outstanding. The wine list has many Okanagan Valley selections, and the service is friendly and professional.

620 Herridge Lane. ✆ **250/352-0101.** www.allseasonscafe.com. Reservations required. Main courses C$17–C$39 (US$14–US$31). AE, MC, V. Daily 5–10pm; Sun brunch 10am–2:30pm.

Max and Irma's Kitchen NEW ITALIAN   The focus at bright, lively Max and Irma's is the wood-fired oven. Located half a block off Baker Street, this restaurant serves very tasty, California-influenced Italian cuisine. The large menu encompasses a selection of individual pizzas, calzones, toasted panini sandwiches, and pastas.

515A Kootenay St. ✆ **250/352-2332.** www.maxandirmaskitchen.com. Reservations not needed. Main courses C$8–C$12 (US$6.40–US$9.60). MC, V. Sun–Thurs 11am–8pm; Fri–Sat 11am–9pm.

14

Gateways to the Canadian Rockies: Calgary & Edmonton

Stretching from the Northwest Territories to the U.S. border of Montana in the south, flanked by the Rocky Mountains in the west and the province of Saskatchewan in the east, Alberta is a big, beautiful, empty chunk of North America. It has 3.2 million inhabitants, roughly half of whom live in and around Edmonton, the provincial capital, and Calgary, a former cow town grown large and wealthy with oil money.

Both Calgary and Edmonton serve as gateways to the famed Canadian Rockies that rise on their western horizons. Since both cities function as air hubs for the major national parks—there are no scheduled flights to destinations within the Canadian Rockies—and since both Calgary and Edmonton are on major east-west road systems, chances are good you'll spend some time here. (See chapter 15 for complete coverage of the Rockies.)

Culturally, Calgary and Edmonton are a beguiling mix of rural Canadian sincerity and big-city swagger and affluence. Both cities are models of modern civic pride and hospitality; in fact, an anonymous behavioral survey recently named Edmonton Canada's friendliest city.

Early settlers first came to Alberta for its wealth of furs; the Hudson's Bay Company established Edmonton House on the North Saskatchewan River in 1795. The Blackfoot, one of the West's most formidable Indian nations, maintained control of the prairies until the 1870s, when the Royal Canadian Mounted Police arrived to enforce the white man's version of law and order. The Mounties' Fort Calgary was established on the Bow River in 1875. Open-range cattle ranching prospered on the rich grasslands, and agriculture is still the basis of the rural economy. Vast oil reserves were discovered beneath the prairies in the 1960s, introducing a tremendous boom across the province.

Plan to take a day or two to explore these lively cities—more, if your itineray will accommodate it. Calgary has excellent museums and one of the most exciting restaurant scenes in Canada. Edmonton, dominated by its university and its capital status, has a vital arts scene and—not to be dismissed lightly—one of the largest shopping malls–cum–entertainment palaces in the world. And with the recent blockbuster success of the award-winning *Brokeback Mountain,* which was fictionally set in Wyoming but actually filmed entirely on location in Alberta, film buffs are making pilgrimages to the area in droves for the not-to-be-missed rugged scenery.

1 Calgary: Home of the Annual Stampede ⟨★⟨★

128km (79 miles) E of Banff; 296km (184 miles) N of the U.S. border

Calgary dates back to 1875, when a detachment of the Northwest Mounted Police reached the confluence of the Bow and Elbow rivers. Gradually, the lush prairie lands drew tremendous beef herds, and Calgary grew into a cattle metropolis and meat-packing center. When World War II ended, the placid city numbered barely 100,000.

The oil boom erupted in the late 1960s, and in a single decade utterly changed the complexion of the city. The population shot up at a pace that made statisticians dizzy. Office high-rises, hotels, and shopping centers went up so fast that even locals weren't sure what was around the next corner.

The 1980s recession caused by the world's oil glut cooled Calgary's overheated growth considerably. But—at least from the visitor's angle—this enhanced the city's attractiveness. The once-ubiquitous rooftop cranes that marred its skyline have largely disappeared; however, Calgary continues to prosper. Since the mid-1990s and on through today, the oil market has continued to boom, and Alberta's pro-business political climate tempted national companies to build their headquarters here. And in 1988, Calgary was the site of the Winter Olympics, giving it the opportunity to roll out the welcome mat on a truly international scale. The city outdid itself in hospitality, erecting a whole network of facilities, including the Canada Olympic Park west of downtown.

Calgary now has an imposing skyline with dozens of business towers topping 40 stories. Despite this, the city doesn't seem urban. With its many parks and convivial populace, Calgary retains the atmosphere of a much smaller, friendlier town.

ESSENTIALS

GETTING THERE   By Plane   Calgary International Airport (www.calgaryairport. com) lies 16km (10 miles) northeast of the city. You can go through U.S. Customs right here if you're flying home via Calgary. The airport is served by **Air Canada** (© 888/247-2262), **Delta** (© 800/221-1212), **American Airlines** (© 800/433-7300), **United** (© 800/241-6522), **Continental** (© 800/525-0280), and **Northwest** (© 800/447-4747), as well as several commuter lines.

Air Canada operates an air shuttle service to and from Edmonton almost hourly. Cab fare to downtown hotels comes to around C$25 (US$18). The **Airporter bus** (© **403/531-3909**) takes you downtown for C$9 (US$6.50).

By Car   From the U.S. border in the south, Highway 2 runs to Calgary and continues north to Edmonton (via Red Deer). From Vancouver in the west to Regina in the east, take the Trans-Canada Highway.

By Train   The nearest **VIA Rail** station is in Edmonton (see "Edmonton: Capital of Alberta," later in this chapter). You can, however, take a scenic train ride to/from Vancouver/Calgary on the *Rocky Mountaineer,* operated by **Rocky Mountaineer Vacations** (© **800/665-7245** or 604/606-7245; www.rockymountaineer.com). The lowest-priced tickets begin at C$889 (US$699) for 2 days of daylight travel, which includes four meals and overnight accommodation in Kamloops; many other packages are available.

By Bus   Greyhound buses (© **800/661-8747** or 403/260-0877; www.greyhound.ca) link Calgary with most other points in Canada, including Banff and Edmonton, as well as towns in the United States. The depot is at 877 Greyhound Way SW, west of downtown near the corner of Ninth Avenue SW and 16th Street SW.

VISITOR INFORMATION   The downtown **Visitor Service Centre,** now in the Riley & McCormick store at 220 8th Ave. SW, and at the airport, provide free literature, maps, and information. These are run by **Tourism Calgary,** 200, 238 11th Ave. SE, Calgary, AB T2G 0X8 (© **800/661-1678** or 403/263-8510; www.tourism calgary.com).

CITY LAYOUT   Central Calgary lies between the Bow River in the north and the Elbow River to the south. The two rivers meet at the eastern end of the city, forming **St. George's Island,** which houses a park and the zoo. South of the island stands Fort Calgary, birthplace of the city. The Bow River makes a bend north of downtown, and in this bend nestles **Prince's Island Park** and **Eau Claire Market.** The Canadian Pacific Railway tracks run between 9th and 10th avenues, and **Central Park** and **Stampede Park,** scene of Calgary's greatest annual festival, stretch south of the tracks. Northwest, across the Bow River, is the **University of Calgary**'s lovely campus. The airport is northwest of the city.

Moments **The Calgary Stampede**

Each July, Calgary puts on the biggest, wildest, woolliest western fling on earth: the **Calgary Stampede** ✸✸✸. The whole city goes mildly crazy, donning western gear, whooping, hollering, dancing, and generally behaving uproariously.

The top attractions are the **rodeo events,** the largest and most prestigious of their kind in North America, in which cowboys from all over the world compete for prize money totaling C$1.1 million (US$880,000).

Parts of Stampede Park become amusement areas, whirling, spinning, and rotating with rides. Other areas are just for the kids, who romp through Kids' World and the Petting Zoo. Still other sections host livestock shows, a food fair, handicraft exhibitions, an art show, lectures, a bazaar, a casino, lotteries, and entertainment on several stages.

Reserving accommodations well ahead is essential—as many months ahead of your arrival as you can possibly foresee. Some downtown watering holes even take reservations for space at the bar; that should give you an idea of how busy Calgary gets.

The same advice applies to reserving tickets for Stampede events. Tickets begin at C$27 (US$22) but go up from there, depending on the event, the seats, and whether the event takes place in the afternoon or evening. For mail order bookings, contact the Calgary Exhibition and Stampede, P.O. Box 1060, Station M, Calgary, AB T2P 2K8 (© **800/661-1767;** fax 403/223-9736; www.calgarystampede.com).

Alberta

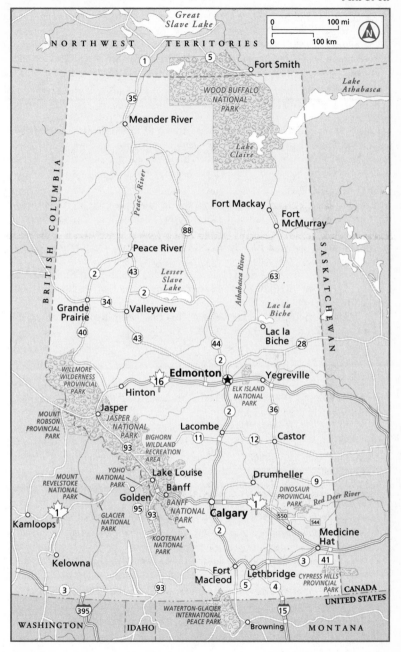

Tips **A Word about Walking**

The "Plus-15" system is a series of enclosed walkways, connecting downtown buildings, 4.5m (15 ft.) above street level. These walkways enable you to shop in living-room comfort, regardless of the weather. Watch for the little "+15" signs on the streets for access points.

Calgary is divided into four segments: **northeast** (NE), **southeast** (SE), **northwest** (NW), and **southwest** (SW), with avenues running east–west and streets north–south. The north and south numbers begin at Centre Avenue, the east and west numbers at Centre Street—a recipe for confusion if ever there was one.

GETTING AROUND   Calgary Transit System ☎ 403/276-1000; www.calgary transit.com) operates buses and a light-rail system called the C-Train. You can transfer from the light rail to buses on the same ticket. The ride costs C$2 (US$1.60) for adults and C$1.25 (US$1) for children; the C-Train is free (buses are not) in the downtown stretch between 10th Street and City Hall. Tickets are only good for travel in one direction.

Car-rental firms include **Avis,** 211 6th Ave. SW (☎ **403/269-6166**); **Budget,** 140 6th Ave. SE (☎ **403/226-0000**); and **Hertz,** 227 6th Ave. SW (☎ **403/221-1681**). Each of these has a bureau at the airport.

To summon a taxi, call **Checker Cabs** ☎ **403/299-9999**), **Red Top Cabs** ☎ **403/974-4444**), or **Yellow Cabs** ☎ **403/974-1111**).

FAST FACTS: **Calgary**

American Express The office at 421 Seventh Ave. SW (☎ **403/261-5982**) is open Monday to Friday 9am to 5pm.

Doctors & Hospitals If you need non-emergency medical attention, check the phone number for the closest branch of **Medicentre,** a group of walk-in clinics open daily 7am to midnight. If you need immediate attention, try **Foothills Hospital,** 1403 29th St. NW (☎ **403/670-1110**).

Drugstores Check the phone book for **Shoppers Drug Mart,** which has more than a dozen stores in Calgary, most open till midnight. The branch at the Chinook Centre, 6455 Macleod Trail S. (☎ **403/253-2424**), is open 24 hours.

Newspapers Calgary's two dailies, the *Calgary Herald* (www.calgaryherald. com) and the *Calgary Sun* (www.calgarysun.com), are both morning papers. *Ffwd* (www.ffwdweekly.com) is a youth-oriented newsweekly and a good place to look for information on the local music and arts scene.

Police & Emergencies The 24-hour number is ☎ **403/266-1234**. Dial ☎ **911** in emergencies.

Post Office The main post office is at 207 9th Ave. (☎ **403/974-2078**). Call ☎ 403/292-5434 to find other branches.

Calgary

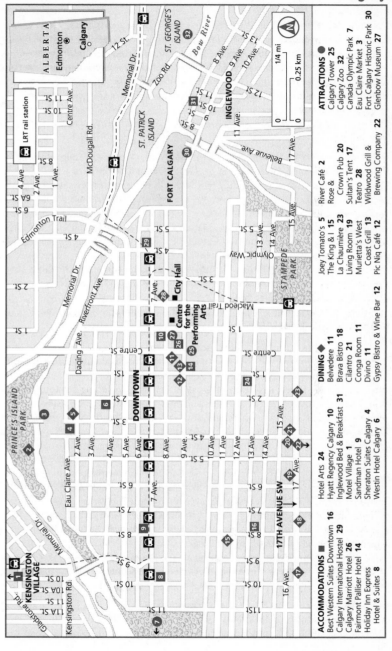

ACCOMMODATIONS ■
Best Western Suites Downtown **16**
Calgary International Hostel **29**
Calgary Marriott Hotel **26**
Fairmont Palliser Hotel **14**
Holiday Inn Express
Hotel & Suites **8**
Hotel Arts **24**
Hyatt Regency Calgary **10**
Inglewood Bed & Breakfast **31**
Motel Village **1**
Sandman Hotel **9**
Sheraton Suites Calgary **4**
Westin Hotel Calgary **6**

DINING ◆
Belvedere **11**
Brava Bistro **18**
Cilantro **21**
Conga Room **11**
Divino **11**
Gypsy Bistro & Wine Bar **12**
Joey Tomato's **5**
The King & I **15**
La Chaumière **23**
Living Room **19**
Murietta's West
Coast Grill **13**
Pic Niq Café **12**
River Café **2**
Rose &
Crown Pub **20**
Sultan's Tent **17**
Teatro **28**
Wildwood Grill &
Brewing Company **22**

ATTRACTIONS ●
Calgary Tower **25**
Calgary Zoo **32**
Canada Olympic Park **7**
Eau Claire Market **3**
Fort Calgary Historic Park **30**
Glenbow Museum **27**

321

EXPLORING THE CITY

Calgary Tower   Reaching 762 steps or 191m (626 ft.) into the sky, this Calgary landmark is topped by an observation terrace offering unparalleled views of the city and the mountains and prairies beyond. The elevator whisks you to the top in just 63 seconds. A stairway from the terrace leads to the cocktail lounge, where you can enjoy drinks and a panoramic vista. Photography from up here is fantastic. The **Panorama Restaurant** (✆ **403/508-5822**) is the near-mandatory revolving restaurant.

9th Ave. and Centre St. SW. ✆ **403/266-7171**. www.calgarytower.com. Elevator ride C$12 (US$9.55) adults, C$9.95 (US$7.95) seniors, C$8.95 (US$7.15) youths 13–17, C$6.95 (US$5.55) children 3–12. June 15–Sept 15 daily 7am–11pm (last lift 10:30pm); Sept 16–June 14 daily 9am–11pm (last lift 9pm). LRT: 1st St. E.

Calgary Zoo, Botanical Garden & Prehistoric Park 🐾 *Kids*   Calgary's large and thoughtfully designed zoo resides on St. George's Island in the Bow River. The Calgary Zoo comes as close to providing natural habitats for its denizens as is technically possible. You'll particularly want to see the troop of majestic lowland gorillas and the African warthogs. The flora and fauna of western and northern Canada are on display in the Botanical Garden, and there's an amazing year-round tropical butterfly enclosure as well. Adjoining the zoo is the Prehistoric Park, a three-dimensional textbook of ancient dinosaur habitats populated by 22 amazingly realistic replicas—these imposing reproductions will give Barney-loving children something to think about. Call to inquire about special summer events, such as Thursday Jazz Nights and free interpretive talks called "Nature Tales."

1300 Zoo Rd. NE. ✆ **403/232-9300**. www.calgaryzoo.ab.ca. Admission C$16 (US$13) adults, C$14 (US$11) seniors, C$10 (US$8) youths 13–17, C$8 (US$6.40) children 3–12. Daily 9am–5pm. LRT: Zoo station.

Canada Olympic Park *Kids*   This lasting memento of Calgary's role as host of the 1988 Winter Olympics stands in Olympic Park, which was the site for ski jumping, luge, and bobsledding during the games. The Olympic Hall of Fame and Museum features the world's largest collection of Olympic artifacts, including the torch used to bring the flame from Greece; costumes and equipment used by the athletes; superb photographs; and a gallery of all medal winners. The reason that the park is still an exciting destination is the availability of activities and lessons. In winter, both adults and children can take downhill and cross-country ski lessons, learn to ski jump or snowboard, or get an introduction to snow skating. More exciting are the opportunities to ride a luge or bobsled. In winter, for C$120 (US$96) per person, you can experience the twists and turns of the Olympic Track in a bobsled. Luge rides are available July and August in the Ice House, an athletes' indoor training facility, and will get the adrenaline pumping for road-trip weary teenagers. Other summer activities include a mountain-bike course and chairlift rides up to the ski-jump tower, which is the highest vantage point in Calgary.

88 Canada Olympic Park Rd. SW. ✆ **403/247-5452**. www.coda.ab.ca. Admission and audio tour C$15 (US$12) per person, C$48 (US$38) per family; separate fees for activities and lessons. Museum only C$6 (US$4.80). Daily 10am–6pm. Ski hill Mon–Sat 9am–9pm, Sun 9am–5pm, weather permitting.

Eau Claire Market & Prince's Island Park   Eau Claire Market is part of a car-free pedestrian zone north of downtown on the banks of the Bow River; it links to lovely Prince's Island Park, a bucolic island lined with paths, shaded by cottonwood trees, and populated by hordes of Canada geese. This is where much of downtown Calgary comes to eat, drink, shop, sunbathe, jog, and hang out in good weather. The market itself no longer offers much for the traveler except a few eateries (better options are the pubs in the plaza outside the market) though it remains busy with a four-screen cinema and an **IMAX Theatre** (© **403/974-4629**) with a five-story domed screen.

Near 2nd Ave. SW and 3rd St. SW. © 403/264-6450. Free admission. Market building 9am–9pm, shops and restaurants have varying hours. LRT: 3rd St. W.

Fort Calgary Historic Park *Kids*   On the occasion of the city's centennial in 1975, Fort Calgary became a public park of 16 hectares (40 acres), spread around the ruins of the original Mounted Police stronghold. In 2001, volunteers completed a replica of the 1888 barracks using traditional methods and building materials. The Interpretive Centre captures the history of Calgary, from its genesis as a military fort to the beginnings of 20th-century hegemony as an agricultural and oil boomtown. Kids can do time in the 1875-era jail, or dress up as a Mountie. There are a number of interesting videos and docent-led displays; always in focus are the adventures and hardships of the Mounties a century ago. The rigors of their westward march and the almost unbelievable isolation these pioneer troopers endured now seems incredible. If all this history whets your appetite, cross the Elbow River on 9th Avenue and head to the Deane House. This historic home was built by a Fort Calgary superintendent nearly 100 years ago and is now the **Deane House Restaurant** operated by Fort Calgary (© **403/269-7747**), open Monday to Friday from 11am to 3pm, Saturday and Sunday from 10am to 3pm.

750 9th Ave. SE. © 403/290-1875. www.fortcalgary.ab.ca. Admission C$10 (US$8) adults, C$8 (US$6.40) seniors and students, C$5 (US$4) youths 7–17; free for children under 6. Daily 9am–5pm. LRT: Bridgeland.

Glenbow Museum   One of the country's finest museums, the Glenbow is a must for anyone with an interest in the history and culture of western Canada. What sets it apart from other museums chronicling the continent's Native cultures and pioneer settlement is the excellence of its interpretation. Especially notable is the third floor, with its vivid evocation of Native cultures—particularly of the local Blackfoot—and compelling descriptions of western Canada's exploration and settlement. You'll enjoy the brief asides into whimsy, such as the display of early washing machines. Other floors contain displays of West African carvings, gems and minerals, and a cross-cultural look at arms and warfare.

130 9th Ave. SE (at 1st St.). © 403/268-4100. www.glenbow.org. Admission C$12 (US$9.60) adults (weekend C$14/US$11), C$9 (US$7.20) seniors (weekend C$11/US$8.80), C$8 (US$6.40) students and children (C$9/US$7.20 weekend), C$38 (US$30) families (C$44/US$35 weekend); free for children under 3. Daily 9am–5pm, Thurs to 9pm. LRT: 1st St. E.

WHERE TO STAY

Finding inexpensive lodging in Calgary can be difficult. The city's booming economy means that many of the older hotels that once offered perfectly pleasant but moderately priced accommodations have gentrified. If you enjoy B&Bs, try the **Bed and Breakfast Association of Calgary** (www.bbcalgary.com), which has several dozen listings for Calgary. The many hotels in **Motel Village** (see below), which link to city center via the C-Train, are another option; you can often find these rooms at discount hotel websites.

DOWNTOWN
Very Expensive & Expensive
Calgary Marriott Hotel ⚜ The Marriott is about as central as things get in Calgary: Linked to the convention center and convenient to the goings-on at the Centre for the Performing Arts and the Glenbow Museum, the hotel is also linked via skywalk with Palliser Square, Calgary Tower, and loads of downtown shopping. Yes, it's a convention hotel—But its large guest rooms received a total makeover in 2005 and are subtly decorated and outfitted with niceties such as windows that open, lots of mirrors, and desks set up for business travelers. The even larger, tasteful suites are worth the extra money—especially the French Parlour suites, with lots of room to decompress.

110 9th Ave. SE (at Centre St.), Calgary, AB T2G 5A6. ℂ **800/228-9290** or 403/266-7331. Fax 403/269-1961. www.calgarymarriott.com. 384 units. C$109–C$279 (US$87–US$223) double; C$259–C$329 (US$207–US$263) suite. Extra person C$20 (US$16). Weekend packages available. AE, DC, DISC, MC, V. Valet parking C$24 (US$19) per day; self-parking C$18 (US$14). **Amenities:** 2 restaurants; lounge; indoor pool; exercise room; Jacuzzi; sauna; concierge; business center; limited room service; same-day dry cleaning. *In room:* A/C, TV, dataport, fridge, coffeemaker, hair dryer, iron, microwave, high-speed Internet.

The Fairmont Palliser ⚜⚜⚜ This is the classiest address in all of Calgary. Opened in 1914 as one of the Canadian Pacific Railroad hotels, the Palliser is Calgary's landmark historic hotel. The vast marble-floored lobby, surrounded by columns and lit by gleaming chandeliers, is the very picture of Edwardian sumptuousness. You'll feel like an Alberta Cattle King in the Rimrock Dining Room, with vaulted ceilings, period murals, a massive stone fireplace, and hand-tooled leather panels on teak beams. The lounge bar looks like a gentlemen's West End club. Guest rooms are large for a hotel of this vintage—the Pacific Premier rooms would be suites at most other properties—and they preserve the period charm while incorporating modern luxuries. Fairmont Gold rooms come with their own concierge and a private lounge with breakfast, drinks, and hors d'oeuvres included. A C$30-million (US$24-million) renovation delivered new carpets, upholstery, and furniture throughout.

133 9th Ave. SW, Calgary, AB T2P 2M3. ℂ **800/441-1414** or 403/262-1234. Fax 403/260-1260. www.fairmont.com. 405 units. C$149–C$399 (US$119–US$319) double; from C$209–C$489 (US$146–US$391) suite. AE, DC, DISC, MC, V. Valet parking C$29 (US$23) per day; self-parking C$22 (US$18). **Amenities:** Restaurant; bar; indoor pool; health club and spa; concierge; business services; salon; 24-hr. room service; babysitting; laundry service; same-day dry cleaning; concierge-level rooms. *In room:* A/C, TV, dataport w/high-speed Internet, minibar, hair dryer, iron.

Hyatt Regency Calgary ⚜⚜ Downtown's most upscale hotel, the Hyatt is linked to the TELUS Convention Centre and is convenient to shopping and arts venues. Guest rooms are large, measuring roughly 37 sq. m (400 sq. ft.), with comfy furniture and great views. Suites are truly spacious, with most of the comforts of home. All rooms come with high-speed Internet access and two-line speaker phones, just the thing for the busy traveler. The hotel's Stillwater Spa is a full-service day spa, with a combination of massage and hydro therapies, body wraps, and beauty treatments. The fitness center and saline pool offer majestic views across the city skyline to the Rockies. The Hyatt flanks historic Stephen Avenue; and rather than leveling the 1890s stone storefronts, the Hyatt cleverly incorporates them into the hotel's facade. Original art worth C$2 million (US$1.4 million) is on display in the hotel lobby and corridors.

700 Center St. S., Calgary, AB T2G 5P6. ✆ **800/233-1234** or 403/717-1234. Fax 403/537-4444. www.hyatt.com. 355 units. From C$159 (US$127) double; from C$234 (US$187) suite. AE, DC, DISC, MC, V. Valet parking C$21 (US$17); self-parking C$15 (US$12). **Amenities:** Restaurant; lounge; indoor pool, Jacuzzi, sauna; health club; spa; concierge; business center; babysitting; laundry service; same-day dry cleaning; 24-hr. room service. *In room:* A/C, TV, dataport w/high-speed Internet, minibar, coffeemaker, hair dryer, iron, laptop safe, voice mail.

Sheraton Suites Calgary 😊😊   The Sheraton Suites overlooks the Eau Claire Market area, just steps away from both the Bow River Greenway and downtown business towers. As an all-suite hotel, the Sheraton offers large and thoughtfully designed rooms that put luxury and business ease foremost. The decor is strikingly modern, with quality and notably-comfortable furniture, plus easy access to high-tech tools to help a business traveler multitask. The built-in cabinetry makes it feel very homelike, as do the Prairie-influenced art, plants, and two TVs in every room. Corner king suites are especially nice, with huge bathrooms, tiled showers, and Jacuzzi tubs.

255 Barclay Parade SW, Calgary AB T2P 5C2. ✆ **888/784-8370** or 403/266-7200. Fax 403/266-1300. www. sheratonsuites.com. 323 suites. C$149–C$574 (US$119–US$459) double. Extra person C$30 (US$24). AE, DC, DISC, MC, V. Valet parking C$27 (US$22). **Amenities:** 2 restaurants; lounge; indoor pool; water slide; exercise room; Jacuzzi; sauna; in-suite spa services; concierge; business center; 24-hr. room service; salon; babysitting; laundry service; wireless Internet access in public spaces. *In room:* A/C, TV w/games and movie channels, dataport w/high-speed Internet access, fridge, coffeemaker, hair dryer, iron, safe, microwave.

Westin Hotel Calgary 😊😊 *Kids*   The Westin completes a C$6-million (US$4.8-million) renovation in 2006, with newly upgraded rooms and new lobby. Despite its anonymous business-hotel exterior, the interior has a subtle western feel that's reflected in the mission-style furniture, sunny colors, and period photos. Beautiful barn-wood breakfronts and lowboys dispel the feeling that you're in one of the city's most modern properties. While standard rooms are very comfortable, corner suites come with balconies. For extra quiet, request one of the Tower rooms, which are normally reserved for business travelers. The Westin also offers high-speed Internet throughout, large working desks, and two-line phones. Upgraded "Heavenly" beds ensure a good night's sleep while dual shower heads enhance your morning ablution. The hotel rolls out the welcome mat for kids, with a "kids club" offering children's furniture, babysitting, and a children's menu—and even games and special treats from room service. Special needs are anticipated, from strollers to room-service delivery of fresh diapers. Even dogs, which are welcome, have specialty beds!

320 4th Ave. SW, Calgary, AB T2P 2S6. ✆ **800/937-8461** or 403/266-1611. Fax 403/233-7471. www.westin.com/calgary. 525 units. C$99–C$299 (US$79–US$239) double; from C$349 (US$279) suite. Extra person C$20 (US$16). Family and senior rates available. AE, DC, DISC, MC, V. Parking C$14 (US$11) per day. **Amenities:** 7 restaurants; lounge; panoramic roof-top indoor pool; health club and spa; sauna and whirlpool; concierge; business center; 24-hr. room service; laundry service; same-day dry cleaning. *In room:* A/C, TV, dataport, minibar, coffeemaker, hair dryer, iron.

Moderate & Inexpensive

Travelers on a budget have excellent though limited choices in downtown Calgary. Luckily, the light-rail system makes it easy to stay outside the city center—particularly in Motel Village in Northwest Calgary—yet have access to the restaurants and sights of downtown.

Best Western Suites Downtown   This well-maintained older hotel is an excellent value. The rooms are quite large, some almost apartment-size, and are fitted with quality furniture; some come with efficiency kitchens. It's located between downtown and trendy 17th Avenue.

1330 8th St. SW, Calgary, AB T2R 1B3. ⓒ 800/981-2555 or 403/228-6900. Fax 403/228-5535. www.bestwestern suitescalgary.com. 123 units. C$99–C$149 (US$79–US$119) junior suite; C$109–C$169 (US$87–US$135) 1-bedroom suite; C$119–C$189 (US$95–151) 2-bedroom suite. Extra person C$10 (US$8). Senior, weekly, and monthly rates available. AE, DISC, MC, V. Free parking. **Amenities:** Restaurant; Jacuzzi; guest laundry. *In room:* A/C, TV, dataport, kitchenette, coffeemaker, hair dryer.

Calgary International Hostel   The 120 beds at the Calgary hostel are the city's most affordable lodgings—but there are reasons beyond economy to stay here. The hostel is on the edge of downtown, convenient to bars and restaurants along Stephen Avenue and theaters near the performing-arts center. Facilities include two family rooms, a common area, and a small convenience store.

520 7th Ave. SE, Calgary, AB T2G 0J6. ⓒ 403/269-8239. Fax 403/283-6503. www.hihostels.ca. Members C$23 (US$18); nonmembers C$27 (US$22). MC, V. Free parking. **Amenities:** Coin-op laundry.

Holiday Inn Express Hotel & Suites Calgary Downtown *Value*   This conveniently located older hotel has just undergone a major makeover, emerging as part of the Holiday Inn Express chain. The rooms are large and nicely furnished; all have balconies and large workstations with high-speed Internet. It's just a block from the C-Train, which will put you in the heart of things in 5 minutes. With free parking, this is one of the best deals in the downtown area.

1020 8th Ave. SW, Calgary AB T2P 1J2, ⓒ 800/661-6017 or 403/269-8262. Fax 403/269-4868. www.hiexpress.c om/calgarydt. 56 units. C$129–C$199 (US$103–C$159) double. Rates include continental breakfast. AE, MC, V. Free parking. **Amenities:** Restaurant; pub; fitness center; business center; guest laundry; free local calls. *In room:* A/C, dataport, fridge, coffeemaker, hair dryer, iron, microwave, free high-speed Internet access.

Hotel Arts   At press time, the long-time Holiday Inn just south of downtown Calgary, in what is now labeled the "Arts District," is undergoing transformation into a Euro-chic, one-of-a-kind boutique hotel focusing on the arts scene in Calgary. The entire hotel will be filled with contemporary visual art; guest rooms feature briskly modern decor and upscale amenities. The poolside bar and cafe is destined to set the scene for the hotel. Hotel Arts is scheduled for completion in 2006. Call or check the website for current information.

119 12th Ave. SW, Calgary, AB T2R 0G8. ⓒ 800/661-9378 or 403/266/4611. Fax 403/237-0978. www.hotelarts.ca. 188 units. From C$129 (US$103) double. AE, DC, DISC, MC, V. Free parking. **Amenities:** Restaurant; lounge; outdoor pool; exercise room; concierge. *In room:* A/C, TV, dataport, coffeemaker, hair dryer, iron.

Sandman Hotel Downtown Calgary *&* *Value*   This hotel on the west end of downtown is one of Calgary's best deals. The Sandman is conveniently located on the free rapid-transit mall, just west of the main downtown core. The standard rooms are a good size, but the real winners are the very large corner units, which feature small kitchens and great views. The Sandman is a popular place with corporate clients, due to its central location and good value. It also boasts a complete fitness facility. Its private health club, available free to guests, has a lap pool, three squash courts, aerobics, and weight-training facilities.

888 7th Ave. SW, Calgary, AB T2P 3J3. ⓒ 800/726-3626 or 403/237-8626. Fax 403/290-1238. www.sandman hotels.com. 301 units. C$119–C$159 (US$95–US$127) double. Children under 16 stay free in parent's room. AE, DC,

DISC, MC, V. Parking C$12 (US$9.60). **Amenities:** Restaurant; bar; indoor pool; health club; concierge; business center; limited room service; laundry service; same-day dry cleaning. *In room:* A/C, TV, dataport, fridge, coffeemaker, hair dryer, iron, microwave, high-speed Internet.

IN INGLEWOOD

Inglewood Bed & Breakfast ✶ *Finds*   It's a great location: minutes from downtown, on a quiet residential street backed up to a park and the swift waters of the Bow River. The Inglewood is a rambling modern structure in Queen Anne style built as a B&B. The three guest rooms are simply but stylishly furnished with handmade pine furniture and antiques; all have private bathrooms. Two of the turret rooms have great views over the river. If in Calgary with a family or on an extended stay, ask about the suite, with full kitchen facilities, a fireplace, and TV. Both owners are professional chefs, so expect an excellent breakfast.

1006 8th Ave. SE, Calgary, AB T2G 0M4. ℭ **403/262-6570.** www.inglewoodbedandbreakfast.com. 3 units. C$80–C$130 (US$64–US$104) double. Rates include breakfast. MC, V. Free parking. *In room:* TV/VCR.

MOTEL VILLAGE

Northwest of downtown, this triangle of more than 20 large motels, plus restaurants, stores, and gas stations forms a self-contained hamlet near the University of Calgary. Enclosed by Crowchild Trail, the Trans-Canada Highway, and Highway 1A, the village's costlier establishments flank the highway and the cheaper ones lie off Crowchild Trail. If you're driving and don't want to deal with downtown traffic, just head here to find a room; for C-Train service, use Lions Park or Banff Park stops.

Except during the Stampede, you'll be able to find a vacancy without reservations. Use discount hotel Web sites such as Travelocity to find deals here. Popular chain hotels are located here, including **Comfort Inn Calgary Motel Village,** 2369 Banff Trail NW (ℭ **800/228-5150** or 403/289-2581), **Best Western Village Park Inn,** 1804 Crowchild Trail NW (ℭ **888/774-7716** or 403/289-4645), **Travelodge North,** 2304 16th Ave. NW (ℭ **800/578-7878** or 403/289-0211), and the **Quality Inn University,** 2359 Banff Trail NW (ℭ **800/661-4667** or 403/289-1973).

CAMPING

The **Calgary West Campground,** on the Trans-Canada Highway West (Box 10, Site 12, SS no. 1), Calgary, AB T2M 4N3 ℭ **403/288-0411**), allows tents and pets. Facilities include washrooms, toilets, laundry, a dumping station, hot showers, groceries, and a pool. The price for full hook-up with two people is C$39 (US$31) per night; tent sites are C$27 (US$21) per night.

WHERE TO DINE

Calgary has very stylish and exciting restaurants. The city is going through an unparalleled period of prosperity, and the citizenry's average age is just over 30. Put these two factors together and you've got the ingredients for a vibrant bar-and-restaurant scene. The focus for downtown dining has moved to the pedestrian-friendly **Stephen Avenue** area (that is, Eighth Ave. near First St. SW), with more casual bistros and restaurants found along 17th Avenue.

DOWNTOWN
Expensive
Belvedere ✶✶✶ NEW CANADIAN   The very stylish Belvedere is one of the most impressive of Calgary's restaurants. The dining room exudes a darkly elegant, 1930s

atmosphere. The menu blends traditional favorites with stand-up-and-take-notice preparations. Foie gras frequently appears as an appetizer, perhaps seared with a tart Macintosh apple tart tatin, all robed with Sauterne wine reduction. Main courses feature local meats and seasonal produce; favorite main courses include pork chops with apple and rutabaga risotto, Meursault wine-poached lobster, and roast duck with blood orange sauce. The bar is a quiet and sophisticated spot for a drink.

107 8th Ave. SW. © 403/265-9595. www.thebelvedere.ca. Reservations recommended. Main courses C$31–C$42 (US$25–US$33). AE, DC, MC, V. Mon–Fri 11:30am–10pm; Sat 5:30–10pm.

Murietta's West Coast Grill REGIONAL CANADIAN   Just around the corner from the vibrant Stephen Avenue restaurant scene, Murietta's is a popular and stylish bar and dining room that combines the best of historic and contemporary Calgary. Located on the second story of the 1890s Alberta Hotel, Murietta's huge bar is a favorite watering hole for urban professionals, and the art-filled, two-story stone-walled dining room is the place for Alberta steaks and local lamb, pork, and game. For appetizers, choose fresh oysters or tuna tartare, and if red meat's not your thing, Murietta's offers a daily changing selection of fresh fish with a choice of sauces—perhaps saffron vanilla butter on wild Pacific salmon.

808 1st St. SW. © 403/269-7707. Reservations suggested. Main courses C$16–C$42 (US$13–US$33). AE, DC, MC, V. Mon–Wed 11am–midnight; Thurs 11am–1am; Fri–Sat 11am–2am; Sun 4pm–10pm.

River Café ✦✦ NEW CANADIAN   If you have one meal in Calgary, it should be here. To reach the aptly named River Café, it takes a short walk through the Eau Claire Market area, then over the footbridge to lovely Prince's Island Park. On a lovely summer evening, the walk is a plus, as are the restaurant's lovely park-side decks (no vehicles hurtling by). Wood-fired, free-range, and wild-gathered foods teamed with organic whole breads and fresh-baked desserts form the backbone of the excellent menu. There's a wide range of appetizers and light dishes—many vegetarian—as well as pizzalike flat breads topped with zippy cheese, vegetables, and fruit. Specialties from the grill include braised pheasant breast with mustard spaetzle, black-cherry oil, and roasted apple. Menus change seasonally and read like a very tasty adventure novel.

Prince's Island Park. © 403/261-7670. www.river-cafe.com. Reservations recommended. Main courses C$12–C$40 (US$9.60–US$32). AE, MC, V. Mon–Fri 11am–11pm; Sat–Sun 10am–11pm. Closed Jan.

Téatro ✦✦ ITALIAN   Located in the historic Dominion Bank building just across from the Centre for the Performing Arts, Téatro delivers the best New Italian cooking in Calgary. The high-ceilinged dining room is dominated by columns and huge panel windows, bespeaking class and elegance. The extensive menu is based on "Italian market cuisine," featuring what's seasonally best and freshest; some of the best dishes come from the wood-fired oven that dominates one wall. For lighter appetites, there's a large selection of antipasti, boutique pizzas, and salads; the entrees, featuring Alberta beef, veal, pasta, and seafood, are prepared with flair and innovation. Lobster and scallop ravioli is a favorite. Service is excellent.

200 8th Ave. SE. © 403/290-1012. www.teatro-rest.com. Reservations recommended. Main courses C$12–C$40 (US$9.60–US$32). AE, DC, MC, V. Mon–Fri 11:30am–11pm; Sat 5pm–midnight; Sun 5–10pm.

Moderate & Inexpensive

Conga Room CUBAN   A little bit of Old Havana off Stephens Avenue, Conga offers flavors (and sounds) of Latin America. A large tapas menu provides finger food for two or lunch if you're dining solo; try the ceviche, empanadas, or camarones (shrimp) with mango chipotle aioli. The main menu is very broad, from Argentine-style steaks to paella to sweet chile salmon with fruit salsa. The long, narrow restaurant opens up in back to a dance floor, with live salsa bands on Thursday through Saturday evenings.

109 8th Ave. SE. © **403/262-7248.** Main courses C$18–C$32 (US$14–US$26). MC, V. Daily 11:30am–10pm; limited menu until 1pm.

Divino 🐾🐾 BISTRO   This estimable bar and restaurant calls itself a "wine and cheese bistro," and while a casual spot for a drink and cheese platter is welcome on busy Stephen Avenue, Divino offers a lot more. This bustling, stylish gathering spot offers intriguing light entrees from sandwiches—lamb confit melt with fig jam—to pasta (cannelloni filled with lobster and chanterelles) in addition to full-flavored and satisfying main courses such as roast chicken with herb mustard gnocchi. A class act.

113 8th Ave. SW. © **403/234-0403.** Reservations recommended. Main courses C$12–C$30 (US$9.60–US$24). AE, DC, MC, V. Daily 11am–11pm.

Gypsy Bistro & Wine Bar BISTRO   A small jewel box of a restaurant, the Gypsy Bistro is in the historic Grain Exchange building, and features deep red walls, odd nooks and crannies, and a soft-focus bordello ambience. The menu is extensive and Mediterranean-focused. For light appetites, there's a broad selection of pizzas, entree salads, and specialty sandwiches, such as a lamb and dried cranberry burger. The Gypsy is also the spot for a chic, low-key dinner with main courses such as roast lamb with lavender honey mustard and pancetta-wrapped salmon. The wine list is beguiling and the service friendly—this is the perfect spot for leisurely dinner and conversation.

817 1st St. SW. © **403/263-5869.** Reservations recommended. Main courses C$11–C$24 (US$8.80–US$19). AE, MC, V. Daily 11am–10pm.

Joey Tomato's 🐾 ITALIAN   In the popular Eau Claire Market complex, the lively Joey Tomato's serves Italian/Asian fusion cooking to throngs of appreciative Calgarians. And no wonder it's often packed with the city's young and tanned: The food is really good, the prices moderate (by the city's standards), and there's a lively bar scene. Thin-crust pizzas come with zippy, cosmopolitan choices such as tandoori chicken. Pasta dishes are just as unorthodox, with dishes such as linguini and smoked chicken, jalapeño, cilantro, and lime-cream sauce. The broad menu includes steaks, fresh fish, and stir-fried veggies. It's always a fun, high-energy place to eat.

208 Barclay Parade SW. © **403/263-6336.** Reservations not accepted. Pizza and pasta C$9–C$15 (US$7.20–US$12). AE, MC, V. Sun–Thurs 11am–midnight; Fri–Sat 11am–1am.

The King & I THAI   This restaurant was the first to introduce Thai cuisine to Calgary, and it still ranks high. Chicken, seafood, and vegetables predominate—one of the outstanding dishes is chicken filet sautéed with eggplant and peanuts in chile-bean sauce. For more seasoned palates, there are eight regional curry courses, ranging from mild to downright devilish.

820 11th Ave. SW. © **403/264-7241.** Main courses C$7–C$20 (US$5.60–US$16). AE, DC, MC, V. Mon–Thurs 11:30am–10:30pm; Fri 11:30am–11:30pm; Sat 4:30–11:30pm; Sun 4:30–9:30pm.

Pic Niq Café ⚄ BISTRO   The Pic Niq is as casual and enjoyable as it sounds—an intimate little wine bar and bistro that's perfect for both a quick pre-event meal or a full dinner. You can assemble a meal from the selection of small plates—such as the trio of Canadian smoked salmon—or indulge in made-to-share dishes such as one of the specialty pizzas or pork tenderloin with Calvados. Or if time and appetite allow, make a night of it and order main courses such as seared chipotle prawns or wild mushroom profiteroles. Pic Niq is upstairs from Beat Niq, a popular jazz bar.

811 1st St. SW. © **403/263-1650.** Reservations required. Main courses C$14–C$21 (US$11–US$17). AE, MC, V. Mon–Tues 11am–2pm; Wed–Fri 11am–2pm and 5–10pm; Sat 5–10pm.

ON 17TH AVENUE
Roughly between 4th Street SW and 10th Street SW, 17th Avenue is home to many casual restaurants and bistros (and the scene has recently edged south along 4th St. SW). Take a cab or drive over and walk the busy cafe-lined streets, perusing the menus; the restaurants listed below are just the beginning.

Expensive
La Chaumière ⚄ FRENCH   Winner of multiple awards, La Chaumière is a discreetly luxurious temple of fine dining. A meal here is an occasion to dress up, and this is one of the few spots in town that enforces a dress code. In addition to the coolly elegant dining room, La Chaumière offers plenty of patio seating in summer. The impressively broad menu is based on classic French preparations, but features local Alberta meats, game, and produce.

139 17th Ave. SW. © **403/228-5690.** www.lachaumiere.ca. Reservations required. Jacket and tie required for men. Main courses C$25–C$35 (US$20–US$28). AE, DC, MC, V. Mon–Fri noon–2pm; Mon–Sat 6pm–midnight.

Moderate
Brava Bistro ⚄⚄ NEW CANADIAN   Brava began as an offshoot of a successful catering company, and has now evolved to a Mediterranean-style bistro. In the relaxed, beautifully lit dining room, you can try anything from elegant appetizers and boutique pizzas to contemporary main courses. For an appetizer, try seared scallops with buttered spinach and truffled vichyssoise. Among the entrees, the sautéed salmon with beets and horseradish is deliciously complex and colorful, while the homey rotisserie chicken or beef ribs with creamy polenta are tempting when comfort food feels more appropriate. The wine list is large and well-priced.

723 17th Ave. SW. © **403/228-1854.** www.bravabistro.com. Reservations recommended. Main courses C$15–C$21 (US$12–US$17). AE, DC, MC, V. Mon–Wed 11:30am–3pm and 5–10pm; Thurs–Sat 11:30am–3pm and 5pm–midnight; Sunday 5–10pm.

Cilantro INTERNATIONAL   Cilantro has a forlorn stucco storefront that would look New Mexican if it weren't on a urban strip of 17th Avenue. The walls hide a tucked-away garden courtyard with a veranda bar. The food here is eclectic with feints toward California and Santa Fe. You can snack on sandwiches, pasta, or burgers (in this case, an elk burger), or have a full meal of grilled buffalo rib-eye or grilled sea bass. The wood-fired pizzas—with mostly Mediterranean ingredients—are great for lunch. The food is always excellent, and the setting casual and friendly.

338 17th Ave. SW. *©* **403/229-1177.** Reservations recommended on weekends. Main courses C$9–C$30 (US$7.20–US$24). AE, DC, MC, V. Mon–Thurs 11am–11pm; Fri 11am–midnight; Sat–Sun 5pm–11pm.

Living Room   This popular new restaurant is the antithesis of a small-plates tapas bar. Located in a heritage home fronting onto 17th Avenue, with tables inside and on the lovely shaded patio (heated by outdoor fireplaces in chilly weather), the Living Room specializes in "contemporary interactive cuisine," which translates as French, Italian, and Canadian classics that are meant to be shared: double-size portions of fondues, bouillabaisse, double-cut prime rib, and lobster Newburg. Individual portions are also served, though in the same spirit of interactive sharing. Local produce and meats are featured: the rack of local lamb with almond and cranberry mustard crust is a standout.

514 17th Ave. SW. *©* **403/228-9830.** www.thelivingroomrestaurant.com. Reservations suggested. Main courses C$19–C$39 (US$15–US$31). MC, V. Tues–Fri 11:30am–2:30pm and 5pm–midnight; Sat–Mon 5pm–midnight.

Rose and Crown Pub PUB FARE   This traditional English pub has lots of quiet outdoor seating, good ales, and a menu featuring sandwiches, fish and chips, and other light entrees. This is a good place to gather if you find the scene on 17th Avenue a little too precious.

1503 4th St. SW. (just off 17th Ave. SW). *©* **403/244-7757.** Reservations not accepted. Main courses C$7–C$13 (US$5.60–US$10). MC, V. Mon–Sat 11am–2am; Sun 10am–2pm.

Sultan's Tent *⚜* MOROCCAN   The Sultan's Tent's interior has been transformed by carpets and tapestries into a pretty good imitation of a Saharan tent. If you like great couscous, you should definitely make this a stop. Go all out and order the C$42/US$37 Sultan's Feast (the vegetarian version is C$36/US$29), which includes all the trimmings and provides an evening's worth of entertainment.

909 17th Ave. SW. *©* **403/244-2333.** Reservations recommended on weekends. Main courses C$14–C$23 (US$11–US$18). AE, DC, MC, V. Mon–Sat 5:30–11pm.

Wildwood Grill & Brewing Company *⚜*BREWPUB   A few blocks south of 17th Avenue's scene is this nouveau hunting lodge–style brew pub. Don't think pub grub (though you can get a good burger here) because Wildwood Grill offers high-end cuisine to match their house-made ales. In addition to pasta, wood-fired pizza (lemon thyme chicken with goat cheese is a delicious choice), and upscale standards like chicken breast sautéed with thyme and truffles, the pub specializes in game dishes. Caribou scaloppini with sour cherry–ginger sauce is a standout for adventurous meat-eaters. In good weather, the patio is a great spot to sample the excellent draughts.

2417 SE 4th St. SW. *©* **403/228-0100.** www.wildwoodgrill.ca. Reservations suggested. Main courses C$13–C$36 (US$10–US$29). AE, MC, V. Mon–Thurs 11am–midnight; Fri 11am–2am; Sat 5pm–11pm; Sun 5pm–10pm.

DAY TRIPS FROM CALGARY: THE OLD WEST

The Old West isn't very old in Alberta. If you're interested in the life and culture of the cowboy and rancher, drive through the ranch country along the foothills of the Rockies and stop at the historic Bar U Ranch. This short side trip into the Old West is just a short detour on the way from Calgary to the Rocky Mountains.

Bar U Ranch National Historic Site ❧❧   An hour southwest of Calgary is this a well-preserved and still-operating cattle ranch that celebrates both past and present traditions of the Old West. Tours of the ranch's 35 original buildings (some date from the 1880s) are available; a video of the area's ranching history is shown in the interpretive center. Special events include displays of ranching activities and techniques; since this is a real ranch, you might get to watch a branding or roundup.

Follow Hwy. 22 South from Calgary to the little community of Longview. © **403/395-2212**. www.pc.gc.ca. Admission C$6.50 (US$5.20) adults, C$5.50 (US$4.40) seniors, C$3 (US$2.40) for children. Late May to early Oct 10am–6pm.

2 Edmonton: Capital of Alberta

283km (175 miles) N of Calgary, 361km (224 miles) E of Jasper

Edmonton, Alberta's capital, is located on the banks of the North Saskatchewan River. It's a sophisticated city of around 1 million citizens that's noted for its summer festivals and easygoing friendliness.

Edmonton grew in spurts, following a boom-and-bust pattern as exciting as it was unreliable. During World War II, the boom came in the form of the Alaska Highway, with Edmonton as the material base and temporary home of 50,000 American troops and construction workers. The ultimate boom, however, gushed from the ground in 1947, when a drill at Leduc, 40km (25 miles) southwest of the city, sent a fountain of crude oil soaring skyward. Some 10,000 other wells followed, and in their wake came the petrochemical industry and the refining and supply conglomerates. In 20 years, the population quadrupled, the skyline mushroomed with glass-and-concrete office towers, a rapid-transit system was created, and a C$150-million (US$120-million) civic center rose. Edmonton had become what it is today—the oil capital of Canada.

ESSENTIALS

GETTING THERE   By Plane   Edmonton International Airport (© **800/268-7134;** www.edmontonairports.com) is served by **Air Canada** (© 800/372-9500) and **Northwest** (© 800/447-4747), among other airlines. The airport lies 29km (18 miles) south of the city on Highway 2, about 45 minutes away. By cab, the trip costs about C$35 (US$25); by Airporter bus, C$10 (US$8).

By Car   Edmonton straddles the Yellowhead Highway, western Canada's east–west interprovincial highway. Just west of Edmonton, the Yellowhead is linked to the Alaska Highway. The city is 515km (319 miles) north of the U.S. border, 283km (175 miles) north of Calgary.

By Train   The **VIA Rail** (© **800/561-8630** or 780/422-6032; www.viarail.ca) station is at 104th Avenue and 100th Street.

By Bus   Greyhound (© **780/413-8747;** www.greyhound.ca) buses link Edmonton to points in Canada and the United States from the depot at 10324 103rd St.

VISITOR INFORMATION   Contact **Edmonton Tourism,** 9990 Jasper Ave. NW, Edmonton, AB T5J 1N9 (© **800/463-4667** or 780/496-8400; www.edmonton. com). There are also visitor centers located at City Hall and at Gateway Park, both open from 9am to 6pm, and on the Calgary Trail at the southern edge of the city, open from 9am to 9pm.

Edmonton

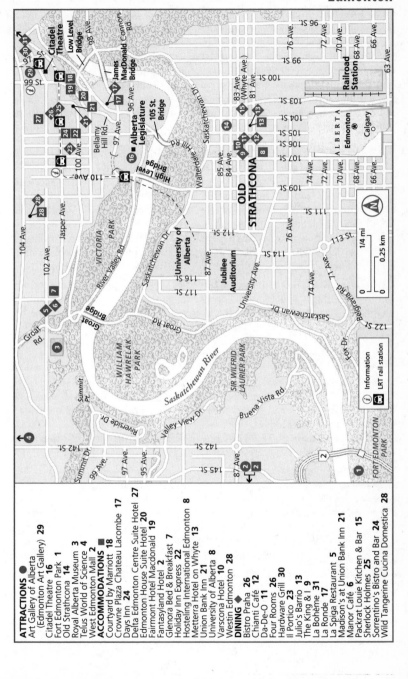

ATTRACTIONS ●
Art Gallery of Alberta
  (Edmonton Art Gallery) **29**
Citadel Theatre **16**
Fort Edmonton Park **1**
Old Strathcona **14**
Royal Alberta Museum **3**
Telus World of Science **4**
West Edmonton Mall **2**

ACCOMMODATIONS ■
Courtyard by Marriott **18**
Crowne Plaza Chateau Lacombe **17**
Days Inn **24**
Delta Edmonton Centre Suite Hotel **27**
Edmonton House Suite Hotel **20**
Fairmont Hotel Macdonald **19**
Fantasyland Hotel **2**
Glenora Bed & Breakfast **7**
Holiday Inn Express **22**
Hostelling International Edmonton **8**
Metterra Hotel on Whyte **13**
Union Bank Inn **21**
University of Alberta **8**
Varscona Hotel **10**
Westin Edmonton **28**

DINING ◆
Bistro Praha **26**
Chianti Café **12**
Da-De-O **11**
Four Rooms **26**
Hardware Grill **30**
Il Portico **23**
Julio's Barrio **9**
The King & I **9**
La Bohème **31**
La Ronde **17**
La Spiga Restaurant **5**
Madison's at Union Bank Inn **21**
Manor Café **6**
Packrat Louie Kitchen & Bar **15**
Sherlock Holmes **25**
Sorrentino's Bistro and Bar **24**
Wild Tangerine Cucina Domestica **28**

CITY LAYOUT The winding **North Saskatchewan River** flows right through the heart of the city, dividing it into roughly equal halves. Most of this steep-banked valley has been turned into public parklands.

Edmonton's main street is **Jasper Avenue** (actually 101st Ave.), running north of the river. At 97th Street, on Jasper Avenue, rises the massive pink **Canada Place,** the only planned government complex of its kind in Canada. Across the street is the **Edmonton Convention Centre,** which stair-steps down the hillside to the river.

Beneath the downtown core stretches a network of climate-controlled pedestrian walkways—called **Pedways**—connecting hotels, restaurants, and malls with the library, City Hall, and Citadel Theatre.

At the northern approach to the High Level Bridge stand the buildings of the **Alberta Legislature.** Across the bridge, to the west, stretches the vast campus of the **University of Alberta.** East of the U of A is **Old Strathcona,** a bustling neighborhood of cafes, galleries, and hip shops that is a haven for the alternative crowd. The main arterial through Old Strathcona is **Whyte Avenue,** or 82nd Avenue. Running south from here is 104th Street, which becomes the **Calgary Trail** and leads to the airport.

West of downtown, Jasper Avenue eventually becomes Stony Plain Road, which passes near **West Edmonton Mall,** the world's largest shopping and entertainment center, before merging with Highway 16 on its way to Jasper National Park.

GETTING AROUND **Edmonton Transit** (© 780/496-1611) operates the buses and the LRT (Light Rail Transit). This electric rail service connects downtown with Northlands Park to the north and the University of Alberta to the south. The LRT and buses have the same fares: C$2 (US$1.60) for adults and C$1.35 (US$1.10) for seniors and children; a day pass goes for C$7 (US$5.60). Monday through Friday from 9am to 3pm, downtown LRT travel is free between Churchill, Central, Bay, Corona, and Grandin stations.

In addition to the following downtown locations, **National,** 10133 100A St. NW. (© 800/CAR-RENT); **Budget,** 10016 106th St. (© 800/268-8900 in Canada, 800/527-0700 in the U.S.); and **Hertz,** 10815 Jasper Ave. (© 780/423-3431) each has a car-rental bureau at the airport.

Call **CO-OP Taxi** (© 780/425-2525 or 780/425-8310) for a ride in a driver/owner-operated cab.

FAST FACTS: Edmonton

American Express The office at 10180 101st St., at 102nd Avenue (© **780/421-0608;** LRT: Corona), is open Monday to Friday from 9am to 5pm.

Doctors & Hospitals **Medicentre** offers walk-in medical services daily. The closest hospital with emergency service to downtown Edmonton is the **Royal Alexandra Hospital,** 10240 Kingsway Ave. (© **780/477-4111;** bus: 9).

Emergency For fire, medical, or crime emergencies, dial © **911.**

Newspapers The *Edmonton Journal* (www.edmontonjournal.com) and *Edmonton Sun* (www.edmontonsun.com) are the local daily papers. Arts, entertainment, and nightlife listings can be found in the weekly *See* (www.seemagazine.com).

Pharmacies **Shoppers Drug Mart** has over a dozen locations, most open till midnight. One central location is 8210 109th St. (© **780/433-2424;** bus 6).

Post Office The main post office is at 103A Avenue and 99th Street (LRT: Churchill).

EXPLORING THE CITY

Edmonton Art Gallery   The Edmonton Art Gallery (EAG) occupies a stately building in the heart of downtown, east of City Hall. The interior, however, is state-of-the-art modern, subtly lit, and expertly arranged. Exhibits consist of contemporary Canadian and international art, and touring works from every corner of the globe. The Gallery shop sells an array of items, from books to locally made crafts. The EAG recently unveiled plans for a total redesign of the gallery—and announced a new name, **Art Gallery of Alberta.** Construction is scheduled to commence in 2007.

2 Sir Winston Churchill Sq. © **780/422-6223.** www.edmontonartgallery.com. Admission C$10 (US$8) adults, C$7 (US$5.60) seniors and students, C$5 (US$4) children 6–12; free for children under 6. Mon–Wed 10:30am–5pm; Thurs–Fri 10:30am–8pm; Sat–Sun and holidays 11am–5pm. LRT: Churchill.

Fort Edmonton Park 🐾 *Kids*   Fort Edmonton Park literally reconstructs four distinct eras of Edmonton's history. Perhaps most interesting is the complete reconstruction of the old Fort Edmonton fur trading post from the turn of the 18th century. This vast wooden structure is a warren of rooms and activities: Blacksmiths, bakers, and other docents ply their trades. On 1885 Street, you'll see Frontier Edmonton, complete with saloons, general store, and Jasper House Hotel, which serves hearty pioneer meals. 1905 Street celebrates the agricultural boom years of the early 19th century, when

---

Moments **Edmonton's Klondike Days**

Since 1962, Edmonton has commemorated its gold-rush past with one of the greatest and most colorful extravaganzas in Canada. The Klondike Days are held annually in late July, with street festivities and the great Klondike Days Exposition at Northlands Park lasting 10 days.

The 16,000-seat Coliseum holds nightly spectacles of rock, pop, variety, or western entertainment. Northlands Park turns into Klondike Village, complete with the Chilkoot Gold Mine, Silver Slipper Saloon, and gambling casino—legal for this occasion only. The Walterdale Playhouse drops serious stage endeavors for a moment and puts on hilarious melodramas with mustachioed villains to hiss and dashing heroes to cheer.

Immense "Klondike breakfasts" are served in the open air, marching bands compete in the streets, and 100 of the weirdest-looking home-built rafts ever seen compete in the "World Championship Sourdough River Raft Race."

For more information, contact **Klondike Days** (© **888/800-PARK** or 780/471-7210; www.klondikedays.com).

Edmonton thronged with new immigrants and was named provincial capital. On 1920 Street, sip an old-fashioned ice-cream soda at Bill's confectionery and see the changes wrought in the rural West by World War I. If the variety of activities at Fort Edmonton appeals to your family, consider spending a night at the park's **Hotel Selkirk,** a very handsome replica of a 1910s hotel, but with all modern comforts (© **888/962-2522** or 780/496-7227; www.hotelselkirk.com)

On Whitemud Dr. at Fox Dr. © **780/496-8787.** www.edmonton.ca/fort. Admission C$9.25 (US$7.40) adults, C$7 (US$5.60) seniors and youths, C$4.75 (US$3.80) children, C$30 (US$24) families. Mid-May to late June Mon–Fri 10am–4pm, Sat–Sun 10am–6pm; late June to early Sept daily 10am–6pm. LRT to University Station, then bus no. 32.

Old Strathcona ⚑⚑   This historic district used to be a separate township, but was amalgamated with Edmonton in 1912 and still contains some of the best-preserved landmarks in the city. It's best seen on foot, guided by the brochures given out at the **Old Strathcona Foundation,** 10324 82nd Ave., fourth floor (© **780/433-5866**). It's easy to spend an afternoon here, just wandering the shops, sitting at street-side cafes, and people-watching. This is hipster-central for Edmonton, where students, artists, and the city's alternative community come to hang out. In addition, if you're looking for good value in restaurants or the center of pubs and nightlife, Old Strathcona is ground zero: Come take in the sometimes rowdy evening scene. Be sure to stop by the **Old Strathcona Farmers Market** (© **780/439-1844**), at 83rd Avenue and 103rd Street. It's open Saturday year-round, plus Tuesday and Thursday afternoons in summer.

Around 82nd Ave., between 103rd and 105th sts. Bus: 46 from downtown.

Royal Alberta Museum ⚑ (Kids)   Expertly laid out, this 18,500-sq.-m (200,000-sq.-ft.) modern museum displays Alberta's natural and human history in three permanent galleries. Wild Alberta, the museum's new permanent exhibit, represents Alberta's diverse natural history with astonishingly lifelike dioramas and interactive displays utilizing computers, microscopes and other hands-on tools. The Gallery of Aboriginal Culture tells the 11,000-year story of Alberta's First Nations inhabitants, incorporating artifacts, film, interactive media, and Native interpreters. The Natural History Gallery has fossils, minerals, and a live-bug room.

12845 102nd Ave. © **780/453-9100.** Fax 780/454-6629. www.royalalbertamuseum.ca. Admission confirm C$10 (US$8) adults, C$8 (US$6.40) seniors, C$7 (US$5.60) students, C$5 (US$4) youths 7–17, C$28 (US$22) families; free for children under 7; Sat–Sun half-price admission 9–11am. Sat–Thurs 9am–5pm, Fri 9am–9pm. Bus: 1

TELUS World of Science ⚑ (Kids)   This is one of the most advanced science centers in the world. Its wonders include an **IMAX theater** (& 780/493-4250), the largest planetarium theater in Canada, high-tech exhibits (including a virtual-reality showcase and a display on robotics), and an observatory open on clear afternoons and evenings. Exhibits include a journey through the human body (including the Gallery of the Gross!) and Mystery Avenue, where young sleuths can try their hands.

11211 142nd St., Coronation Park. © **780/451-3344.** www.odyssium.com. Admission C$9.95 (US$8) adults, C$7.95 (US$6.40) seniors and youths, C$6.95 (US$5.60) children 3–12, C$39 (US$31) families. Summer daily 10am–9pm; winter Sun–Thurs and holidays 10am–5pm, Fri–Sat 10am–9pm. Bus: 17 or 22. Free parking.

West Edmonton Mall (Kids)   You won't find many shopping malls mentioned in this book, but the West Edmonton Mall is something else. In fact, locals even call it the

"Eighth Wonder of the World." Although it contains 800 stores and services, including 100 eateries, it looks and sounds more like a theme park than a mall. In a space equal to 48 city blocks, it houses the world's largest indoor amusement park, including a titanic roller coaster, bungee-jumping platform, and enclosed wave-lake, complete with a beach and enough artificial waves to surf on. It has walk-through aviaries, a huge ice-skating palace, 19 movie theaters, a lagoon with performing dolphins, and a submarine adventure ride to the "ocean floor." Roll your eyes all you want, but do go. You have to see the West Edmonton Mall to believe it.

8882 170th St. © **800/661-8890** or 780/444-5200. www.westedmontonmall.com. Bus: 10.

WHERE TO STAY

For B&Bs, try **Alberta and Pacific Bed and Breakfast** (© **604/944-1793;** fax 604/ 552-1659) or the **Alberta Bed and Breakfast Association** (www.bbalberta.com).

EXPENSIVE

Crowne Plaza Chateau Lacombe   Centrally located downtown, the Crowne Plaza, a round 24-story tower sitting on the edge of a cliff overlooking the North Saskatchewan River, possesses some of the city's best views (best seen from **La Ronde,** the hotel's revolving restaurant; see below). The nicely furnished standard rooms aren't huge, though the wedge-shaped design means that they are broadest toward the windows, where you'll spend time looking over the city. The Crown Plaza's Sleep Advantage program focuses on high-quality linens, pillows, plus interesting extras like relaxation CDs and aromatherapeutic lavender atomizers for the sheets. For just a C$30 (US$24) upgrade, Executive Suites offer twice the square footage of standard rooms, and a full living room with foldout bed—a sweet deal.

10111 Bellamy Hill, Edmonton, AB T5J 1N7. © **800/661-8801** or 780/428-6611. Fax 780/425-6564. www.chateau lacombe.com. 307 units. From C$139 (US$111) double. Extra person C$10 (US$8). Weekend packages available. AE, DC, DISC, MC, V. Parking C$8 (US$6.40) per day. **Amenities:** Revolving restaurant; lounge; cafe; coffee bar; exercise room; business center; room service; babysitting; laundry service; nonsmoking rooms. *In room:* A/C, TV, dataport, coffeemaker, hair dryer, iron, wireless Internet, CD player.

Delta Edmonton Centre Suite Hotel   This all-suite establishment forms part of the upscale City Centre shopping mall in the heart of downtown. Without having to stir out of doors, you can access 170 shops, plus movie theaters and an indoor putting green. Three-quarters of the windows look into the mall, so you can stand behind the tinted one-way glass (in your pajamas, if you like) and watch the shopping action outside. Most units are deluxe executive suites, each with a large sitting area (with TV and wet bar) and separate bedroom (with another glass wall). If you need lots of room, or have work to do in Edmonton, these very spacious rooms are just the ticket.

Eaton Centre, 10222 102nd St., Edmonton, AB T5J 4C5. © **800/661-6655** or 780/429-3900. Fax 780/428-1566. www.deltahotels.com. 169 units. C$164–C$209 (US$131–US$167) standard business suite; C$269 (US$215) deluxe executive suite. Ask about summer family discounts, weekend packages, and special rates for business travelers. AE, DC, MC, V. Parking C$12 (US$9.60) per day; valet parking C$15 (US$12) per day. **Amenities:** Restaurant; bar; exercise room; Jacuzzi; sauna; children's center; concierge; business center; limited room service; babysitting; coin-op laundry and laundry service; same-day dry cleaning. *In room:* A/C, TV w/pay movies, dataport, minibar, coffeemaker, hair dryer, iron.

Fairmont Hotel Macdonald   From the outside, with its limestone facade and gargoyles, the Mac looks like a feudal château—It's no wonder that this is where

Queen Elizabeth II stays when she's in town. Originally opened in 1915, the restored Hotel Macdonald has retained signature elements such as its deep tubs, brass door plates, and paneled doors. Everything, including the service, is absolutely top-notch— including the views over the North Saskatchewan River. Rooms are large and beautifully furnished with luxurious upholstery, feather duvets, and original art. Even pets get special treatment: a gift bag of treats and a map of pet-friendly parks. Needless to say, there aren't many hotels like this in Edmonton, or in Canada for that matter.

10065 100th St., Edmonton, AB T5J 0N6. ✆ **800/441-1414** or 780/424-5181. Fax 780/429-6481. www.fairmont. com. 198 units. High season C$299–C$329 (US$239–US$263) deluxe standard room; C$289–C$799 (US$231– US$639) premier suite. Weekend and off-season discounts available. AE, DC, DISC, MC, V. Parking C$22 (US$18) per day. **Amenities:** Restaurant; lounge; indoor pool; health club and spa; concierge; business center; 24-hr. room service; babysitting; laundry service; same-day dry cleaning; concierge-level rooms; squash court. *In room:* A/C, TV/VCR w/pay movies, dataport w/high-speed Internet access, minibar, coffeemaker, hair dryer, iron.

Fantasyland Hotel *(Kids* With 116 theme rooms decorated in 12 different styles, Fantasyland is a cross between a hotel and Las Vegas. Theme rooms aren't just a matter of subtle touches; these units are exceedingly clever, very comfortable, and way over the top. Take the Truck Room: Your bed is located in the back end of a real pickup; the bench seats fold down into a child's bed; and the lights on the vanity are real stoplights. In the Igloo Room, a round bed is encased in a shell of faux ice blocks; statues of sled dogs keep you company; and the walls are painted with amazingly lifelike arctic murals. The themes continue, through the Canadian Rail Room (train berths for beds), the African Room, and more. All theme rooms come with immense four-person Jacuzzis and plenty of amenities. The hotel offers tours of the different theme types on Saturdays at 2pm.

It's not all fantasy, though. 238 large, well-furnished, non-theme rooms are divided into superior rooms, with either a king-size or two queen-size beds, and executive rooms, with a king-size bed and Jacuzzi. The hotel's restaurant is quite good; of course, you have all-weather access to the world's largest mall and its many eateries as well.

17700 87th Ave. (at the end of the West Edmonton Mall), Edmonton, AB T5T 4V4. ✆ **800/737-3783** or 780/444-3000. Fax 780/444-3294. www.fantasylandhotel.com. 355 units. C$219–C$269 (US$175–US$215) double. Extra person C$10 (US$8). Weekend and off-season packages available. AE, MC, V. Free parking. **Amenities:** Restaurant; bar; exercise room; concierge; 24-hr. room service; babysitting; laundry service; same-day dry cleaning. *In room:* A/C, TV w/pay movies, fax, dataport, fridge, coffeemaker, hair dryer, iron, wireless Internet.

Metterra Hotel on Whyte *★★* The lively Old Strathcona neighborhood, filled with students and artists, great nightlife, and dining, now also boasts the Metterra: a swank boutique hotel that's contemporary and sleek, but with homey warmth. The lobby sets the tone with striking art, two-story rundlestone wall and waterfall, while the guest rooms are large, with contemporary and Indonesian art adding some funk. Some rooms offer fireplaces, others feature recliners. Rates include a continental breakfast and afternoon wine and cheese. Though not a typical business hotel, Metterra offers all the features and services sophisticated business and leisure travelers require.

10454 82nd Ave., Edmonton, AB T6E 4Z7. ✆ **866/465-8150** or 780/465-8150. Fax 780/465-8174. www. metterra.com. 98 units. From C$165 (US$132) double. Rates include breakfast. AE, MC, V. Free valet parking. **Amenities:** Fitness center; business center; room service. *In room:* A/C, TV, fridge, coffeemaker, hair dryer, iron and board, high-speed Internet, wireless Internet.

Union Bank Inn 🌟🌟 If you're tired of unmemorable business hotels, this is a wonderful choice. The stylish Union Bank, built in 1910, now houses an elegant restaurant and intimate boutique hotel. The owner asked Edmonton's top interior designers to each design a room; and the results are charming, with each unique guest room displaying its own style, colors, furniture, and fabrics. All units, however, have the same amenities, including fireplaces, voice mail, feather duvets, and upscale toiletries. Joining the original inn are 20 business-class rooms in a new addition—each equally idiosyncratic and uniquely designed. The older rooms aren't incredibly big; so if you're in town with work to do, ask for one of the newer and larger units. The restaurant/bar Madison's is a great place to meet friends (see "Where to Dine," below).

10053 Jasper Ave., Edmonton, AB T5J 1S5. © 780/423-3600. Fax 780/423-4623. www.unionbankinn.com. 34 units. C$159–C$299 (US$127–US$239) double. Rates include full breakfast. AE, DC, MC, V. Free parking. **Amenities:** Restaurant; bar; exercise room; access to nearby health club; business center; limited room service; same-day dry cleaning. *In room:* A/C, TV, dataport, fridge, hair dryer, iron, fireplace.

Westin Edmonton 🌟🌟 Located in the heart of downtown shopping and entertainment, this modern hotel offers some of the city's largest and most comfortable rooms—the beds feature custom mattresses designed for near-perfect support; showers have dual shower heads; and the decor is a clean, contemporary look right out of *Architectural Digest*. Standard rooms come with one king-size bed or two doubles, while deluxe rooms are designed for business travelers, and come with two phone lines, wireless Internet, and other telecom and amenities upgrades. Suites are gracious and large, with separate bedrooms, large dressing room and bathroom, and a swank sitting room with black, leather furniture. These stylish and comfortable rooms will quickly take the pain out of both business and leisure travel.

10135 100th St., Edmonton, AB T5J 0N7. © 800/228-3000 or 780/426-3636. Fax 780/428-1454. www.thewestin edmonton.com. 413 units. From C$179 (US$143) double. AE, DC, DISC, MC, V. Parking C$14 (US$11) per day; valet parking C$17 (US$14) per day. **Amenities:** 2 restaurants; lounge; indoor pool; exercise room; Jacuzzi; sauna; concierge; business center; 24-hr. room service; babysitting; laundry service. *In room:* A/C, TV, dataport, minibar, fridge, coffeemaker, hair dryer, iron.

MODERATE

Courtyard by Marriott 🌟 Don't let the name fool you; This is anything but a could-be-anywhere business hotel. Rooms are comfortable and well furnished, but it's the setting and facilities that really stand out. Edmontonians have voted the downtown bar and restaurant patio—cantilevered hundreds of feet above the North Saskatchewan River—as the city's top spot for outdoor drinks and dining. Located on the cliff-edge with vistas over city center and the breadth of the valley, this Courtyard (formerly the Warwick) must have the best views in the entire chain.

One Thornton Court (99 St. and Jasper Ave.), Edmonton, AB T5J 2E7. © 866/441-7591 or 780/423-9999. Fax 780/ 423-9998. 177 units. C$99–C$149 (US$79–US$119) double. Parking C$15 (US$12) per day. **Amenities:** Restaurant; lounge; business center. *In room:* A/C, TV, coffeemaker, iron, hair dryer.

Edmonton House Suite Hotel This is a great alternative to pricier downtown hotels: The rooms are big and well decorated, and you don't have to pay stiff parking fees. With a great location right above the North Saskatchewan River, the all-suite hotel has one of the best views in the city. Each suite comes with a full kitchen and dining area, bedroom, separate sitting area with foldout couch, balcony, and two phones. Edmonton House is within easy walking distance of most downtown office areas and public transport.

10205 100th Ave., Edmonton, AB T5J 4B5. © **800/661-6562** or 780/420-4000. Fax 780/420-4008. www.edmonton house.com. 305 units. C$139–C$179 (US$111–US$143) 1-bedroom suite. Extra person C$15 (US$12). Weekend packages and weekly/monthly rates available. AE, DC, MC, V. Free parking. **Amenities:** Restaurant; lounge; indoor pool; exercise room; business center; limited room service. *In room:* TV, dataport, high-speed Internet, kitchens, fridge, microwave, coffeemaker, hair dryer, iron.

Glenora Bed & Breakfast ★   Located in the heart of the artsy High Street district, just west of downtown, the Glenora occupies the upper floors of a converted 1912 heritage apartment building. While lots of care has been taken to retain the period character and charm of the rooms, the rooms have been thoroughly updated—all but three have private bathrooms, and some have full kitchen facilities. Most appealing is the happy mix of unique period furnishings and snappy interior design—absolutely every room is unique. There are five styles of rooms, from simple bedroom units with shared bathrooms to one-bedroom apartment suites with kitchens. Free parking and access to a handsome Edwardian common room and a second-story deck is included. Complimentary breakfast is offered in an adjacent restaurant, and two top restaurants are a block away. The Glenora is an excellent value—and fun to boot.

12327 102nd Ave. NW, Edmonton, AB T5N 0I8. © **877/453-6672** or 780/488-6766. Fax 780/488-5168. www.glenora bnb.com. 18 units. C$90–C$160 (US$72–US$128) double; specialty room packages available. Rates include continental breakfast. AE, MC, V. **Amenities:** Restaurant and bar downstairs; access to nearby health club; coin-op laundry. *In room:* TV/VCR, dataport, minibar, coffeemaker, hair dryer, iron.

Holiday Inn Express *Value*   This convenient hotel in a wooded neighborhood setting is tucked between downtown and the Legislature building—a five-minute walk will get you to shopping or lobbying. Although rooms aren't huge, they are newly remodeled and a good alternative to expensive hotels nearby. All rooms have balconies, parking is free, and lots of cafes and pubs are within walking distance.

10010 104 Street, Edmonton, Alberta T5J 0Z1, Canada. © **877/423-4656** or 780/423-2450 Fax 780/425-1783. www.hiexdowntown.com. 140 units. From C$120 (US$96) double. AE, DISC, MC, V. Free parking, complimentary breakfast. **Amenities:** Indoor pool; whirlpool; guest laundry; fitness center. *In room:* A/C, TV, high-speed Internet, iron, coffeemaker, hair dryer, CD player, voice mail.

Varscona Hotel *Value*   A sister hotel to the boldly contemporary Metterra just down the street, the Varscona offers the same excellent quality of lodging and service but with a choice of either more traditional hotel rooms in dark cherry and floral upholstery or more zippy rooms with features like glass-brick showers. Rates include continental breakfast and evening wine and cheese tasting. Old Strachcona's shopping, dining, and nightlife is just outside your door.

8208 106 St., Edmonton, AB, T6E 6R9. © **888/515-3355** or 780/434-6111. Fax 780/439-1195. www.varscona.com. 89 rooms. C$115–C$130 (US$92–US$104) double. AE, MC, V. Free valet parking. **Amenities:** Complimentary breakfast. *In room:* A/C, TV, bathrobe, coffeemaker, dataport, high-speed Internet, iron, hair dryer.

INEXPENSIVE

Days Inn *Value*   For the price, this is one of downtown Edmonton's best deals. Located just a 5 minute's walk from the city center, the motor inn has everything you need for a pleasant stay, including comfortably furnished rooms and easy access to public transport. If all you need for a night or two is a clean and basic room in a convenient location, this is a top choice.

10041 106th St., Edmonton, AB T5J 1G3. ⓒ 800/267-2191 or 780/423-1925. Fax 780/424-5302. www.daysinn.ca. 76 units. C$69–C$99 (US$55–US$79) double. Senior, AAA, and corporate discounts available. AE, DC, DISC, MC, V. Free parking. **Amenities:** Restaurant; bar; limited room service; coin-op laundry; same-day dry cleaning. *In room:* A/C, TV, dataport, wireless Internet, coffeemaker, hair dryer, iron.

Hosteling International Edmonton   Well-located near the university in the lively Old Strathcona neighborhood, this pleasant hostel has shared kitchen facilities and spacious common rooms. Some family rooms are available, and check-in is at 3pm.

10647 81st Ave. ⓒ 780/988-6836. Fax 780/988-8698. www.hihostels.ca. 88 beds. Members C$21–C$24 (US$17–US$19); nonmembers C$26–C$29 (US$21–US$23). MC, V. **Amenities:** Self-catering kitchen; coin-op laundry; bike rental.

University of Alberta   In May through August, two dorms are thrown open to visitors. Some are standard shared-bathroom rooms, single (C$35/US$28) or twin (C$45/US$36), while others are single (C$45/US$36) or twins (C$50/US$40) with private washroom. Also, the university has a number of hotel-style guest rooms with private bathrooms (C$72/US$58). UA is on the LRT line, not far from Old Strathcona.

87th Ave. and 116th St. ⓒ 780/492-4281. Fax 780/492-0064. www.hfs.ualberta.ca. MC, V. Parking C$3 (US$2.15) per day. **Amenities:** Food service nearby; coin-op laundry.

WHERE TO DINE

Edmonton has a vigorous dining scene, with hip new eateries joining traditional steak and seafood restaurants. In general, fine dining is found downtown and on High Street, close to the centers of politics and business. Over in Old Strathcona, south of the river, are trendy—and less expensive—cafes and bistros.

DOWNTOWN
Expensive

Hardware Grill 𝄢𝄢𝄢 NEW CANADIAN   This is easily one of western Canada's most exciting restaurants. The building may be historic (and within walking distance of most downtown hotels), but there's nothing antique about the dining room. Postmodern without being stark, the room is edged with glass partitions, and exposed pipes and ducts painted a smoky rose. There are as many appetizers as entrees, making it tempting to graze through a series of smaller dishes. Bison carpaccio is served with Québec Migneron cheese, and hand-cut potato gnocchi are dressed in morel cream and shaved black truffle. But it's hard to resist entrees such as plank-roasted salmon with fresh corn relish, grilled lamb tenderloin with chokecherry sauce, or Alberta beef tenderloin with chorizo-gratin potatoes.

9698 Jasper Ave. ⓒ 780/423-0969. www.hardwaregrill.com. Reservations suggested. Main courses C$24–C$42 (US$19–US$33). AE, DC, MC, V. Mon–Fri 11:30am–2pm; Mon–Thurs 5–9:30pm; Fri–Sat 5–10pm. Closed 1st week of July.

La Bohème FRENCH   La Bohème consists of two small, lace-curtained dining rooms in a historic building northeast of downtown (at the turn of the 20th century, this structure was a luxury apartment building—the upper floors are now available as B&B accommodations). The cuisine is French, and so is the wine, with the accent on Rhône Valley vintages. There's a wide selection of appetizers and light dishes, including a number of good salads. The entrees are hearty, classically French preparations of lamb, chicken, and seafood; there's also a five-course table d'hôte menu for C$50 (US$40). The restaurant also features daily vegetarian entrees. Desserts are outstanding.

6427 112th Ave. ℂ 780/474-5693. www.laboheme.ca. Reservations required. Main courses C$17–C$32 (US$14–US$26). AE, MC, V. Daily 5–11pm.

La Ronde ⊛ REGIONAL CANADIAN   On the 24th floor of the Crowne Plaza, the revolving La Ronde offers the best views of any restaurant in Edmonton. The Alberta-focused menu also puts on quite a show—chef Jasmin Kobajica is passionate about local organic meats and produce, and his menu is rich in Alberta-raised beef, lamb, and game prepared with a focus on indigenous flavors. Local bison rib-eye is served with prairie mushrooms and wheat berry potato cake, while pork medallions are served with native blackberry *jus*. A number of Albertan cheeses appear as starters. The intensely regional menu makes a brilliant companion to the ever-changing, revolving vista of city towers and river valley.

10111 Bellamy Hill. ℂ 780/428-6611. Reservations required. Main courses C$26–C$35 (US$21–US$28). AE, MC, V. Daily 5:30–10pm

Madison's at Union Bank Inn ⊛ NEW CANADIAN   Madison's is one of the loveliest dining rooms and casual cocktail bars in Edmonton. Once an early-20th-century bank, the building's formal architectural details remain, but they now share the light-and-airy space with modern art and excellent food. The menu is contemporary, bridging Continental European cuisine with regional Canadian ingredients. The menu features grilled and roast fish and meat, plus pasta dishes and interesting salads (one special featured rose petals, baby lettuce, and shaved white chocolate). Other standouts include smoked-tomato ravioli, and a pork chop stuffed with wild mushrooms and goat cheese in a pear reduction sauce.

10053 Jasper Ave. ℂ 780/423-3600. Reservations suggested. Main courses C$14–C$32 (US$11–US$27). AE, MC, V. Mon–Thurs 7–10am, 11am–2pm, and 5–10pm; Fri 7–10am, 11am–2pm, and 5–11pm; Sat 5–11pm; Sun 5–8pm.

Sorrentino's Bistro and Bar ITALIAN   This upscale branch of a local chain is a good addition to the downtown scene. The sophisticated dining room—flanked by the Havana Room, where Cuban cigars are available with port and single-malt Scotch—is a popular meeting place for the city's business and social elite. At lunch, order from the menu or choose sauces and noodles from a pasta buffet. The daily appetizer table features grilled vegetables, salads, and marinated anchovies. Entrees range from risotto to wood-fired pizza to the more imaginative tournedos of salmon and scallops.

10162 100th St. ℂ 780/424-7500. www.sorrentinos.com. Reservations suggested. Main courses C$23–C$35 (US$18–US$28). AE, DC, MC, V. Mon–Fri 11:30am–2:30pm and 5–11pm; Sat 5–11pm.

MODERATE & INEXPENSIVE

Bistro Praha CENTRAL EUROPEAN   Bistro Praha is one of several side-by-side casual restaurants—all with summer street-side seating—that take up 100A Street. It's also the best of these restaurants, and features a charming, wood-paneled interior, a mural-covered wall, and very good Eastern European cooking. The menu offers a wide selection of light dishes, convenient for a quick meal or mid-afternoon snack. The entrees center on schnitzels, as well as a wonderful roast goose with sauerkraut. Desserts tend toward fancy, imposing confections such as Sacher torte. The clientele here is mainly young, stylish, and cosmopolitan. Service is friendly and relaxed.

10168 100A St. 📞 **780/424-4218.** Reservations recommended on weekends. Main courses C$13–C$18 (US$10–US$14). AE, DC, MC, V. Daily 11:30am–2am.

Four Rooms ✱   This comfortable, easy-on-the-pocket restaurant and watering hole is a nice alternative to the meat fest at most upscale downtown restaurants. The menu is a hybrid of Asian and North American cooking with lots of appetizers, salads, and tapas coming in under C$10 (US$8). Confit duck pot stickers, chicken enchiladas, beef bulgogi, and seared tuna salad with daikon are all delicious. The same high quality and diversity extends through the main courses. Come Thursday through Saturday to catch live jazz in the lounge. Service is both friendly and professional.

137 Edmonton City Centre East (102 Ave. and 100 A St.). 📞 **780/426-4767.** Reservations recommended on weekends. Main courses C$18–C$29 (US$15–23). MC, V. Mon–Thurs 11 am–midnight; Fri 11 am–2 am; Sat noon–2 am; Sun 5 pm–midnight.

Il Portico ✱✱ ITALIAN   Popular among locals, Il Portico has a wide menu of well-prepared traditional but updated dishes. With excellent selections of grilled meats, pastas, and pizza, it's one of those rare restaurants where you want to try everything. The Caesar salad will remind you how wonderful these salads can be. Service is impeccable, and the wine list one of the best in the city. The dining room is nicely informal, but classy; in summer, a lovely Tuscan-style courtyard offers alfresco dining.

10012 107th St. 📞 **780/424-0707.** Reservations recommended on weekends. Main courses C$13–C$27 (US$10–US$21). AE, DC, DISC, MC, V. Mon–Fri 11:30am–2pm; Mon–Sat 5:30–11pm.

Sherlock Holmes ENGLISH   The Sherlock Holmes is a tremendously popular English-style pub with local and regional beers on tap (as well as Guinness) and a very well-executed bar menu. The Holmes offers up a few traditional English dishes—fish and chips, steak-and-kidney pie—but there's a strong emphasis on new pub grub; the tandoori chicken and goat cheese quesadilla is excellent. The pub—in a charming Tudor-style building with a picket fence around the outdoor patio—is completely surrounded by high-rise towers.

10012 101A Ave. 📞 **780/426-7784.** www.thesherlockholmes.com. Main courses C$7–C$13 (US$5.60–US$10). AE, MC, V. Mon–Sat 11:30am–2am; Sun noon–8pm.

Wild Tangerine Cucina Domestica ✱   Wild Tangerine is one of many new restaurants (and condos) springing up in the former rail yards west of downtown. This very hip and colorful restaurant offers updated, addictive versions of traditional Asian cuisine, with flavors and textures as bright and crisp as the decor. Shrimp lollipops with wasabi yogurt start the meal off with a bang. Five-spice octopus salad with peppers, taro, lotus root, and a citrus dressing is an explosion of color and flavor, and the jocular owner wanders from table to table. Besides this friendly welcome and the wonderful and affordable food, the green tea–based cocktails are ample reason to return.

10393 112 St. (entrance on 104th Ave.). 📞 **780/429-3131.** Reservations not accepted. Main courses C$11–C$20 (US$9–US$16). AE, MC, V. Mon–Fri 11:30am–10:30pm, Sat 5–11pm.

HIGH STREET

La Spiga Restaurant ✱ ITALIAN   La Spiga, located along High Street's gallery row in a 1913 heritage home, offers nouveau Italian cooking with an emphasis on fresh, stylish ingredients and unusual tastes and textures. There's a large selection of appetizers for starters or light dining. The rack of lamb is marinated in fresh herbs and

---

Tips **Summertime Festivals**

Edmonton Folk Music Festival (© 780/429-1899; www.efmf.ab.ca) is the largest folk festival in North America. Held outdoors in early August, it draws musicians from around the world, plus major rock stars playing unplugged.

For 11 days in mid-August, Old Strathcona is transformed into a series of stages for the renowned **Edmonton International Fringe Theatre Festival** (© 780/448-9000; www.fringetheatreadventures.ca). Only Edinburgh's fringe festival is larger than Edmonton's—more than 150 troupes attend from around the world as does an audience of over 600,000. The festival has 12 indoor theater stages and two outdoor stages, offering more than 1,000 individual performances.

---

grappa, while the prawns and scallops are paired with a white-wine lemon sauce and served over angel-hair pasta. The dining room is casual and comfortable, and in summer there is alfresco dining. Service is laid-back but astute.

10133 125th St. © 780/482-3100. Reservations recommended on weekends. Main courses C$18–C$39 (US$14–US$31). AE, DC, MC, V. Mon–Thurs 5–10pm, Fri–Sat 5–11pm.

Manor Cafe ☞ INTERNATIONAL   The Manor Cafe offers one of the most fashionable outdoor dining patios in Edmonton. This longtime Edmonton favorite offers fusion and international cuisine, from Italian pastas—Manor Pasta with chicken, spinach, goat cheese, and tomato gin cream sauce is the signature dish—to a delicious Moroccan curry or traditional Wiener schnitzel. Food is eclectic, but always delicious.

10109 125th St. © 780/482-7577. www.manorcafe.com. Reservations recommended on weekends. Main courses C$15–C$29 (US$12–US$23). AE, MC, V. Sun–Thurs 11am–10pm; Fri–Sat 11am–midnight.

OLD STRATHCONA

Chianti Cafe ITALIAN   Chianti is a rarity among Italian restaurants: very good and very inexpensive. Pasta dishes include fettuccine with scallops, smoked salmon, curry, and garlic; or try one of the veal dishes (more than a dozen are offered) or seafood specials. Chianti is located in a handsomely remodeled post-office building; the restaurant isn't a secret, so it can be a busy and fairly crowded experience.

10501 82nd Ave. © 780/439-9829. Reservations required. Main courses C$7–C$18 (US$5.60–US$14). AE, DC, DISC, MC, V. Sun–Thurs 11am–11pm; Fri–Sat 11am–midnight.

Da-De-O CAJUN/SOUTHERN   This New Orleans–style diner is authentic right down to the low-tech, jukebox at your table. The food is top-notch, with good and goopy po' boys, fresh oysters, and five kinds of jambalaya. Especially tasty is the Louisiana Linguine, with crawfish and clams in basil cream. Relax in a vinyl booth, listen to Billie Holiday, and graze through some crab fritters.

10548A 82nd Ave. © 780/433-0930. Main courses C$6–C$15 (US$4.80–US$12). AE, MC, V. Mon–Wed 11:30am–11pm; Thurs–Sat 11:30am–midnight; Sun 10am–10pm.

Julio's Barrio MEXICAN   If you like Mexican food, it's (surprisingly for Canada) worth a detour to Julio's. The food ranges from enchiladas and nachos to sizzling shrimp fajitas. This Mexican watering hole is a great place to snack on several light dishes while quaffing drinks with friends. The atmosphere is youthful, high energy, and minimalist hip: no kitschy piñatas or scratchy recordings of marimba bands here.

10450 82nd Ave. ℂ 780/431-0774. Main courses C$9–C$19 (US$7.20–US$15). AE, MC, V. Mon–Wed 11:45am–11pm; Thurs 11:45am–midnight; Fri–Sat noon–1am; Sun noon–11pm.

The King & I ✿ THAI   This member of a well-respected Alberta chain (see p. 329 for a review of the Calgary branch) is the place for excellent, zesty Thai food, which can be a real treat after the beef-rich cooking of western Canada. Many dishes are vegetarian, almost a novelty in Alberta. Various curries, ranging from mild to sizzling, and rice and noodle dishes are the house specialties. For a real treat, try the lobster in curry sauce with asparagus.

8208 107th St. ℂ 780/433-2222. Main courses C$12–C$25 (US$9.60–US$20). AE, MC, V. Mon–Thurs 11:30am–10:30pm; Fri 11:30am–11:30pm; Sat 4:30–11:30pm.

Packrat Louie Kitchen & Bar ✿✿ ITALIAN   Bright and lively, this very popular bistro has a somewhat unlikely name, given that it's one of the best casual Italian trattorie in Edmonton. Menu choices range from specialty pizzas to fine entree salads—I loved the seared goat cheese salad with mushrooms, pumpkin seeds, and smoked pear dressing—to grilled meats, chicken, and pasta. Most dishes tend toward light or healthy preparations without sacrificing complexity. A rack of lamb comes with lemon lentils, and pork rib-eye comes with blueberry pepper sauce.

10335 83rd Ave. ℂ 780/433-0123. Reservations recommended on weekends. Main courses C$12–C$32 (US$9.60–US$26). MC, V. Tues–Sat 11:30am–11:30pm.

15

The Canadian Rockies: Banff & Jasper National Parks & More

The Canadian Rockies rise to the west of the Alberta prairies and contain some of the finest mountain scenery on earth. Between them, Banff and Jasper national parks preserve much of this mountain beauty, but vast and equally spectacular regions of the Rockies (as well as portions of nearby British Columbia's Selkirk and Purcell mountain ranges; see chapter 13) are protected by other national and provincial parks. Because Banff and Jasper are so popular and expensive, these smaller, less thronged, but equally dramatic parks—which include Waterton Lakes, Yoho, and Kootenay national parks, as well as a host of provincial parks—are excellent destinations for those travelers who are looking for wilderness adventure, and not just luxury shopping and dining in a mountain setting.

Hiking, biking, and pack trips on horseback have long pedigrees in the parks, as does superlative skiing—the Winter Olympics were held in Calgary and on the eastern face of the Rockies in 1988. Outfitters throughout the region offer whitewater and float trips on mighty rivers; calmer pursuits such as fishing and canoeing are also popular.

In addition, some of the country's finest and most famous hotels are in the Canadian Rockies. The incredible mountain lodges and châteaux built by early rail entrepreneurs are still in operation, offering unforgettable experiences in luxury and stunning scenery. If you're looking for a more rural holiday, head to one of the Rockies' many guest ranches, where you can saddle up, poke some doggies, and end the evening at a steak barbecue.

The Canadian Rockies boast an excellent network of paved roads, which makes exploring by car safe and easy—if slow, during the busy summer season. From Calgary, it's a stunning 1-hour drive up the Bow River to Banff on Highway 1, and driving from Edmonton to Jasper on the Yellowhead Highway (Hwy. 16) takes from 3 to 4 hours. Both these roads (which continue over the Rockies into British Columbia), along with the Icefields Parkway between Lake Louise and Jasper, remain open year-round.

1 Exploring the Canadian Rockies

Few places in the world are more dramatically beautiful than the Canadian Rockies. Banff and Jasper national parks are famous for their mountain lakes, flower-spangled meadows, spirelike peaks choked by glaciers, and abundant wildlife. Nearly the entire spine of the Rockies—from the U.S. border north for 1,127km (700 miles)—is preserved as parkland or wilderness.

That's the good news. The bad news is that lovers of solitude who come here will find themselves surrounded by increasingly larger numbers of visitors. Advance planning is absolutely necessary if you're going to stay or eat where you want, or if you hope to evade the swarms of visitors that throng the parks during the high season, from mid-June to the end of August.

ORIENTATION

Canada's Rocky Mountain parks include Jasper and Banff, which together comprise 17,519 sq. km (6,764 sq. miles); the provincial parklands of the Kananaskis Country and Mount Robson; and Yoho and Kootenay national parks, to the west in British Columbia.

The parks are traversed by one of the most scenic highway systems in Canada, plus innumerable nature trails leading to more remote valleys and peaks. The two "capitals," Banff and Jasper, lie 287km (178 miles) apart, connected by Highway 93, one of the most scenic routes you'll ever drive. Banff is 128km (79 miles) from Calgary via Highway 1; Jasper, 375km (232 miles) from Edmonton on Route 16, the famous Yellowhead Highway.

Entry to the Banff, Jasper, Yoho, and Kootenay network of parks costs C$8 (US$6.40) per person per day, or C$16 (US$13) per group or family per day.

VISITOR INFORMATION

For information on the entire province of Alberta, contact **Travel Alberta** (© **800/ 661-8888;** www.travelalberta.com). Ask for copies of the accommodations and visitors guides, as well as the excellent *Traveler's Guide* and a road map. There's a separate guide for campers as well.

Alberta has no provincial sales tax. There's only the 7% national goods and services tax (GST), plus a 5% accommodations tax. On the other side of the Rockies, the province of British Columbia levies another 7% tax on purchases and services.

TOURS & EXCURSIONS

You'll get used to the name Brewster, associated with many things in these parts. In particular, these folks operate the park system's principal tour-bus operation. **Brewster Transportation and Tours,** 100 Gopher St., Banff, AB T0L 0C0 (© **403/762- 6767;** www.brewster.ca), covers most of the outstanding scenic spots in both parks. Call for a full brochure, or ask the concierge at your hotel to arrange a trip. A few sample packages:

- **Banff to Jasper** (or vice versa): Some 9½ hours through unrivaled scenery, this tour takes in Lake Louise and a view of the ice field along the parkway. (The return trip requires an overnight stay, not included in the price.) In summer, the one-way fare is C$106 (US$85) for adults, C$53 (US$42) for children. If you don't want the tour, there's also a daily express bus between Banff and Jasper for C$69 (US$55) one-way; children pay half price.
- **Columbia Icefields:** On this 9½-hour tour from Banff, you stop at the Icefields Centre and get time off for lunch and a Snocoach ride up the glacier. Adults pay C$106 (US$85) in summer; children pay C$53 (US$42). The Snocoach Tour costs an extra C$30 (US$24) for adults and C$15 (US$12) for children; tickets must be purchased in advance.

The Canadian Rockies

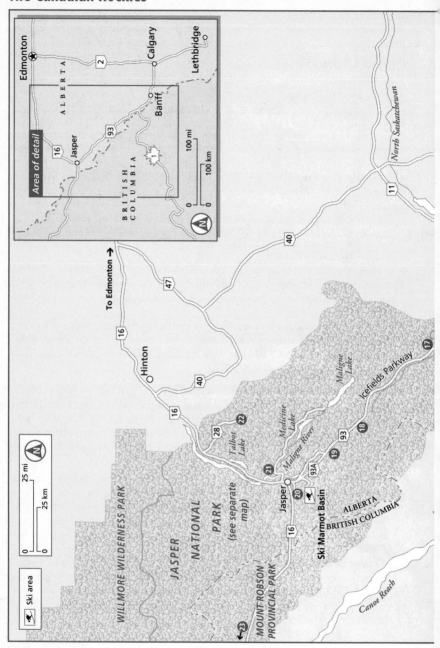

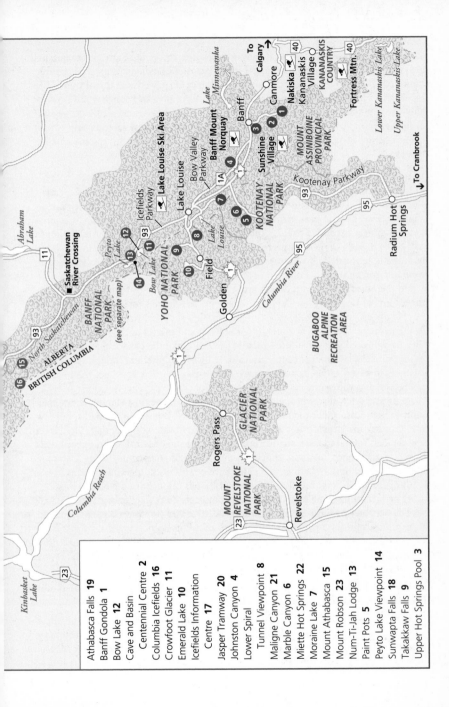

Athabasca Falls **19**
Banff Gondola **1**
Bow Lake **12**
Cave and Basin
  Centennial Centre **2**
Columbia Icefields **16**
Crowfoot Glacier **11**
Emerald Lake **10**
Icefields Information
  Centre **17**
Jasper Tramway **20**
Johnston Canyon **4**
Lower Spiral
  Tunnel Viewpoint **8**
Maligne Canyon **21**
Marble Canyon **6**
Miette Hot Springs **22**
Moraine Lake **7**
Mount Athabasca **15**
Mount Robson **23**
Num-Ti-Jah Lodge **13**
Paint Pots **5**
Peyto Lake Viewpoint **14**
Sunwapta Falls **18**
Takakkaw Falls **9**
Upper Hot Springs Pool **3**

SEASONS

The parks have two peak seasons during which hotels charge top rates and restaurants are jammed. The first is summer, mid-June to late August, when it doesn't get terribly hot, rarely above 77°F (25°C), though the sun's rays are powerful at this altitude. The other peak time is winter, the skiing season from December to February; this is probably the finest skiing terrain in all Canada. March to May is decidedly off season: Hotels offer bargain room rates, and you can choose the best table in any eatery. There's plenty of rain in the warmer months, so don't forget to bring some suitable rainwear.

LODGING IN THE ROCKIES

On any given day in high season, up to 50,000 people wind through the Canadian Rocky national parks. Because growth in the parks is strictly regulated, there's not an abundance of hotel rooms waiting. The result is strong competition for a limited number of very expensive rooms. Adding to the squeeze is the fact that many hotels have 80% to 90% of their rooms reserved for coach tours in summer. To avoid disappointment, particularly if you want to stay in one of the landmark hotels, *reserve your room as far in advance as possible.*

On the other hand, if you don't mind uncertainty and are traveling with a laptop, the advent of discount hotel websites opens up possibilities for those who want to gamble on last-minute room availability. Using sites such as Travelocity—or just type in the name of your favorite hotel into a browser and marvel at the number of websites ready to sell you discounted rooms—you can take the chance that top-ranked hotels will have last-minute cancellations to sell over the Internet. In high season, the savings can be up to 50%, though there is no guarantee that you'll get the hotel or room type that you want.

Regarding price, it seems that lodgings can ask for and get just about any rate they want in high season. For the most part, hotels are well kept up in the parks, but few would justify these high prices anywhere else in the world. Knowing that, there are a few choices. You can decide whether or not to splurge on one of the world-class hotels here, actually only a bit more expensive than the midrange competition. Camping is another good option, because the parks have dozens of campgrounds with varying levels of facilities. There are also a number of hostels throughout the parks.

If you are having trouble locating a room, or simply don't want to deal with the hassle, contact **Rocky Mountain Reservations** (© 877/902-9455; www.rockymountain reservations.com) for a free hotel and activities booking service.

In the off season, prices drop dramatically, often as much as 50%. Most hotels offer ski packages in winter, as well as other attractive getaway incentives. Ask about any special rates, especially at the larger hotels.

BED-AND-BREAKFASTS   If you're looking for a B&B, try the **Alberta Bed and Breakfast Association** (www.bbalberta.com).

HOSTELS   Hostels in the Rocky Mountain national parks are often the most affordable lodging option. Hostels aren't just for youths anymore; all **Hostelling International** properties welcome guests of any age. To find out more about Alberta hostels, check out **www.hihostels.ca.**

GUEST RANCHES   Alberta has been ranch country for well over a century, and the Old West lifestyle is deeply ingrained in Albertan culture. Indulge in a cowboy fantasy and spend a few days at one of the area's many historic guest ranches.

At Seebe, in the Kananaskis Country near the entrance to Banff National Park, are a couple of the oldest and most famous ranches. **Rafter Six Ranch** (© **888/267-2624** or 403/673-3691; www.raftersix.com) has a beautiful old log lodge. The original Brewster homestead was transformed in 1923 into the **Brewster's Kananaskis Guest Ranch** ☞ (© **800/691-5085** or 403/673-3737; www.kananaskisguestranch.com). The **Black Cat Guest Ranch** (© **800/859-6840** or 403/865-3084; www.blackcat guestranch.ca), near Hinton, was once a winter horse camp. At all of these, horseback riding and trail rides are the main focus, but other Western activities, such as rodeos, barbecues, and country dancing, are usually on the docket. Gentler pursuits like fishing, hiking, and lolling by the hot tub are equally possible. Meals are usually served in the lodge; accommodations are either in cabins or the main lodge. A night at a guest ranch usually ranges from C$90 to C$200 (US$72–US$160), depending on what style of room you choose, and includes breakfast. Full bed-and-board packages are available for longer stays. There's usually an additional fee for horseback riding.

Home stays at smaller working ranches are also possible. Here you can pitch in and help your ranch-family hosts with their work, or simply relax. For a stay on a real mom-and-pop farm, obtain a list of member ranches from **Alberta Country Vacations Association** (© **403/722-3053;** www.albertacountryvacation.com).

THE GREAT OUTDOORS

Banff and Jasper national parks have long been the center of mountain recreation for Alberta. If you're staying in Banff, Jasper, or Lake Louise, you'll find that outfitters and rental operations in these centers are pretty sophisticated and professional: They make it easy and convenient to get outdoors. Most hotels will offer a concierge service that can arrange activities for you; for many, you need little or no advance registration. Shuttle buses to more distant activities are usually available as well.

You don't even have to break a sweat to enjoy the magnificent scenery—hire a horse and ride to the backcountry, or take an afternoon trail ride. Jasper, Banff, and Lake Louise have gondolas to lift travelers from valley floor to mountaintop. Bring a picnic, or plan a ridge-top hike. If you're not ready for white water, the scenic cruises on Lake Minnewanka and Maligne Lake offer a more relaxed waterborne adventure.

BACKPACKING   Backcountry trips through high mountain meadows and remote lakes provide an unforgettable experience; Banff Park alone has 3,059km (1,897 miles) of hiking trails.

BIKING   Both parks provide free maps of local mountain-bike trails; the Bow Valley Parkway between Banff and Lake Louise and Parkway 93A in Jasper Park are both good, less trafficked roads for road biking. Bike rentals are easily available nearly everywhere in the parks.

ROCK CLIMBING, ICE CLIMBING & MOUNTAINEERING   The sheer rock faces on Mount Rundle near Banff and the Palisades near Jasper are popular with rock climbers, and the area's many waterfalls become frozen ascents for ice climbers in winter. Instruction in mountaineering skills is offered by **Yamnuska Inc. Mountain School,** based in Canmore (© **403/678-4164;** www.yamnuska.com).

SKIING   There are downhill areas at Banff, Lake Louise, Jasper, and the former Olympic site at Nakiska in the Kananaskis Country. Skiing can be superb here: The snowpack is copious, the scenery beautiful, après-ski festivities indulgent, and accommodations world-class. There's a lot of value in an Alberta ski holiday—lift tickets here are generally cheaper than at comparable ski areas in the United States.

Heli-skiing isn't allowed in the national parks but is popular in the adjacent mountain ranges near Golden in British Columbia. **CMH Heli-Skiing,** 217 Bear St., Banff (© **800/661-0252** or 402/762-7100; fax 403/762-5879; www.cmhski.com), is the leader in this increasingly popular sport, which uses helicopters to deposit skiers on virgin slopes far from the lift lines and runs of ski resorts. CMH offers 7- and 10-day trips to 12 locations; prices begin at C$5,155 (US$4,124) including lodging, food, and transport from Calgary.

Cross-country skiers will find a lot to like in the Canadian Rockies. The 1988 Winter Olympic cross-country runs are now open as **Canmore Nordic Centre** ☞, © **403/ 678-2400**), and are administered as an all-season provincial park. A number of snowbound mountain lodges remain open throughout the winter and serve as bases for adventurous Nordic skiers. The historic **Emerald Lake Lodge,** in Yoho National Park (© **800/663-6336** or 250/343-6321), is one of the finest.

WHITE-WATER RAFTING & CANOEING   The Rockies' many glaciers and snowfields are the source of mighty rivers. Outfitters throughout the region offer white-water rafting and canoe trips of varying lengths and difficulty—you can spend a single morning on the river, or plan a 5-day expedition. Jasper is central to a number of good white-water rivers. **Maligne Rafting Adventures Ltd.** (© **780/852- 3370;** www.mra.ab.ca) offers packages for rafters of all experience levels.

WILDLIFE-VIEWING   If you're thrilled by seeing animals in the wild, you've turned to the right chapter. No matter which one you choose, the Rocky Mountain national parks are all teeming with wildlife—bighorn sheep, grizzly and black bears, deer, mountain goats, moose, coyotes, lynxes, wolves, and more. See "Park Wildlife & You," below, for important warnings on how to handle wildlife encounters in the parks responsibly and safely.

PARK WILDLIFE & YOU

The parklands are swarming with wildlife, with some animals meandering along and across highways and hiking trails, within easy camera range. However tempting, *don't feed the animals and don't touch them!* For starters, you can be fined up to C$500 (US$400) for feeding any wildlife. There's also the distinct possibility you may end up paying more than cash for disregarding this warning.

It isn't easy to resist the blithely fearless bighorn sheep, mountain goats, elk, soft-eyed deer, and lumbering moose you meet. (You'll have very little chance of meeting the coyotes, lynxes, and occasional wolves, since they give humans a wide berth.) But the stuff you feed them can kill them. Bighorns get accustomed to summer handouts of bread, candy, potato chips, and marshmallows when they should be grazing on the high-protein vegetation that'll help them survive through the winter.

Moose involve additional dangers. They've been known to take over entire picnics after being given an initial snack, chase off the picnickers, and eat up everything in sight—including cutlery, dishes, and the tablecloth.

Portions of the parks may sometimes be closed to hikers and bikers during elk calving season. A mother elk can mistake your recreation for an imminent attack on her newborn; or an unsuspecting hiker could frighten a mother from her calf, separating the two for good. Pay attention to—and obey—postings at trail heads.

Bears pose the worst problems. The parks contain two breeds: the big grizzly, standing up to 2m (6½ ft.) on its hind legs, and the smaller black bear, about 1.5m (5 ft.) long. The grizzly spends most of the summer in high alpine ranges, well away from tourist haunts. As one of North America's largest carnivores, its appearance and reputation are awesome enough to make you beat a retreat on sight. But the cuddly looks and circus antics of the black bear tend to obscure the fact that these too are wild animals: powerful, faster than a horse, and completely unpredictable.

Hiking in bear country (and virtually all parkland is bear country) necessitates certain precautions—ignore them at your peril. Never hike alone and never take a dog along. Dogs often yap at bears, then when the animal charges, they run toward their owners for protection, bringing the pursuer with them. Above all, never go near a cub. The mother is usually close by, and a female defending her young is the most ferocious creature you'll ever face—and possibly the last.

2 Kananaskis Country & Canmore

31km (19 miles) E of Banff; 97km (60 miles) W of Calgary

Kananaskis Country is the name given to three Alberta provincial parks on the Rocky Mountains' eastern slope, southeast of Banff National Park. Once considered only a gateway region to more glamorous Banff, the Kananaskis has developed into a recreation destination on a par with more famous brand-name resorts in the Rockies.

Located just west of the Kananaskis and just outside the eastern boundary of Banff National Park, **Canmore** is a sprawl of condominium and resort developments in a dramatic location beneath the soaring peaks of **Three Sisters Mountain.** Only 20 minutes from Banff, Canmore hasn't yet topped the list of Canadian resort destinations, but the scenery is magnificent and the accommodations generally much less expensive and considerably less overbooked than those in Banff.

Weather is generally warmer and sunnier here, which is conducive to great golf: The championship course at **Kananaskis** is considered one of the best in North America.

When the 1988 Olympics were held in Calgary, the national park service wouldn't allow the alpine ski events to be held inside the parks. **Nakiska,** in the Kananaskis, became the venue instead, vaulting this ski area to international prominence.

The Kananaskis offers stunning scenery without Banff's crowds and high prices. Also, because Kananaskis Country isn't governed by national-park restrictions, there's better road access to out-of-the-way lakeside campgrounds and trail heads, which makes this a more convenient destination for family getaways (there are more than 3,000 campsites in the area!). This provincial parkland also allows "mixed use," including some traditional (though heavily regulated) ranching. Some of the best guest ranches in Alberta operate here.

The main road through Kananaskis Country is Highway 40, which cuts south from Highway 1 at the gateway to the Rockies and follows the Kananaskis River. **Kananaskis Village,** a collection of resort hotels and shops, is the center of activities in the Kananaskis and is convenient to most recreation areas. Highway 40 eventually climbs up to 2,206m (7,237-ft.) Highwood Pass, the highest pass in Alberta, before looping around to meet Highway 22 south of Calgary.

ESSENTIALS

GETTING THERE Canmore is served by **Greyhound Canada** (© **800/661-8747** or 403/260-0877; www.greyhound.ca) and **Brewster** (© **403/762-6767;** www.brewster. ca) buses and by private shuttle services that run between Banff and Calgary; see "Getting There" under "Banff Townsite," later in this chapter.

VISITOR INFORMATION For information on Kananaskis and Canmore, contact Kananaskis Country (© **866/432-4322;** www.kananaskisvalley.com) or the Barrier Lake Visitor Information Centre (© **403/673-3985**). The province-wide Travel Alberta Visitor Information Centre, at the Bow Valley Trail exit off Highway 1 at Canmore (© **403/678-5277**), also has lots of information on Canmore.

EXPLORING CANMORE

You could drive past Canmore many times—indeed, you could pull off the freeway and drive down the hotel- and mall-laden Bow Valley Trail—and think you've seen all the town has to offer. In fact, the booming modern development that you'll glimpse from the freeway started before the 1988 Olympics, when Canmore was the center for cross-country ski competition. The pace of development has greatly quickened in the last decade, as Canmore has become a retirement mecca, and vast subdivisions now rise from the slopes of the Bow Valley just outside the gates to Banff National Park. However, the old town center has been largely bypassed by this kind of "progress" and is pleasant to explore.

Canmore has actually been around since the 1880s, when it was the headquarters for the coal mines that fueled the Canadian Pacific Railroad's transcontinental trains as they climbed up over the Rockies. The old downtown area is on an island in the Bow River, and is reached by turning onto Main Street off Railway Avenue. Downtown is undeveloped by Banff standards, but three pleasant, pedestrian-friendly blocks are lined with shops, brewpubs, restaurants, and boutiques. The **Canmore Museum,** at Seventh Avenue and Ninth Street (© **403/678-2462**), tells the story of the community from its days as a coal-mining camp to its pinnacle as Olympic host.

OUTDOOR PURSUITS

It's the excellent access to outdoor activities that makes Canmore and the Kananaskis such a prime destination. From its offices in Kananaskis Village and in Canmore at 999 Bow Valley Trail, **Canmore Rafting Centre/Mirage Adventure Tours** (© **888/ 312-7238** in western Canada or 403/678-4919; www.canmoreraftingcentre.com) represents most local outfitters. You'll find bike trips, trail rides, rafting, hiking, and sightseeing tours on offer. Mirage also rents cross-country skis and equipment.

CROSS-COUNTRY SKIING & MORE The **Canmore Nordic Centre** ⚘, south of town off Spray Lakes Road, at 1988 Olympic Way, Canmore, AB T1W 2T6 (© **403/678-2400**), was developed for the Olympics' cross-country skiing competition, though the facility is now open year-round. Today, it's administered as an all-season provincial park (www.cd.gov.ab.ca/parks/kananaskis). In winter, the center offers 70km of scenic cross-country trails, plus the on-site **Trail Sports** shop (© **403/678-6764**) for rentals, repairs, and sales. In summer, hikers and mountain bikers take over the trails, and Trail Sports offers bike rentals, skill-building courses, and guided rides.

DOWNHILL SKIING   Kananaskis gained worldwide attention when it hosted the alpine ski events for the Winter Olympics in 1988, and skiing remains a primary attraction in the area. At **Nakiska** (𝄐 **800/258-7669** or 403/591-7777; www.ski nakiska.com), skiers can follow in the tracks of past Winter Olympians. A second ski area, **Fortress Mountain** (𝄐 **800/258-7669** or 403/591-7108; www.skifortress.com), is 19km (12 miles) south of Kananaskis Village. Although overshadowed by Nakiska's Olympic reputation, Fortress Mountain offers an escape from the resort crowd and features overnight accommodations in an on-site dormitory. Both areas offer terrain for every age and ability, and are open from early December to mid-April. Adult lift tickets cost C$49 (US$39) at Nakiska, C$40 (US$32) at Fortress; tickets are completely transferable between the two areas.

GOLF   Kananaskis features four championship golf courses and one of Canada's premier golf resorts. **Kananaskis Country Golf Course** 𝄐 boasts two 18-hole, par-72 courses set among alpine forests and streams, and featuring water hazards on 20 holes, 140 sand traps, and four tee positions. Kananaskis is rated among the top courses in Canada. For information, contact **Golf Kananaskis,** Kananaskis Country Golf Course, P.O. Box 1710, Kananaskis Village, AB T0L 2H0 (𝄐 **877/591-2525** or 403/591-7272; www.kananaskisgolf.com). Greens fees are C$80 (US$64).

    Near Canmore, the 18-hole **Canmore Golf Course** is right along the Bow River at 2000 Eighth Ave. (𝄐 **403/678-4785;** www.canmoregolf.net). Greens fees are C$65 (US$52).

    The Les Furber–designed **SilverTip Golf Course** 𝄐 (𝄐 **403/678-1600;** www.silver tipresort.com) is an 18-hole, par-72 course high above Canmore, off SilverTip Drive. You'll look eye-to-eye with the Canadian Rockies here. Boasting a length of 7,300 yards, the course has sand bunkers on all holes, and water on eight. Greens fees range from C$119 to C$145 (US$95–US$116). Also at Canmore is the new **Stewart Creek Golf Club** (𝄐 **877/993-4653;** www.stewartcreekgolf.com), with 18 holes, 32 bunkers, and a beautiful location below the Three Sisters peaks. The course measures 7,150 yards and incorporates natural lakes, streams, and even historic mine entrances. Greens fees range from C$145 to C$165 (US$116–US$132), and include use of a golf cart.

HORSEBACK TRIPS   The Kananaskis is noted for its dude ranches (see "Riding Herd at a Guest Ranch," below), which offer a variety of horseback adventures from short trail rides to multiday pack trips. A 2-hour guided ride will generally cost C$50 to C$60 (US$40–US$48). In addition, **Boundary Ranch,** just south of Kananaskis Village on Highway 40 (𝄐 **877/591-7177** or 403/591-7171; www.boundaryranch. com), offers a variety of trail rides including a horseback lunch excursion.

RAFTING   The Kananaskis and Bow rivers are the main draw here. In addition to a range of half-day (C$45–C$79/US$36–US$63), full-day (C$115/US$92), and 2-day (C$259/US$207) white-water trips, there are excursions that combine a half-day of horseback riding with an afternoon of rafting (C$139/US$111). Contact **Canmore Rafting Centre,** above, for information.

WHERE TO STAY
KANANASKIS VILLAGE
The lodgings in Kananaskis Village were built for the Olympics, so all are fairly new and well maintained. In fact, Kananaskis was the site of the G8 Summit in 2002, so

you may well stay in a room once graced by a world leader. There's no more than a stone's throw between the hotels, and to a high degree, public facilities are shared among all the hotels.

Delta Lodge at Kananaskis 🍂 This resort hotel consists of two separate buildings that face each other across a pond at the center of Kananaskis Village. The Lodge is the larger building, with a more rustic facade, a shopping arcade, and a number of drinking and dining choices. Its guest rooms are large and well furnished; many have balconies and some have fireplaces. The Signature Club service rooms are in the smaller—and quieter—of the two lodge buildings. Rooms here are generally more spacious than those in the Lodge, and even more sumptuously furnished. Additionally, the Signature Club rooms include deluxe continental breakfast, afternoon hors d'oeuvres, honor bar, and full concierge service. The new Summit Spa and Fitness Centre provides health and beauty treatments for both men and women.

Kananaskis Village, AB T0L 2H0. ⓒ **800/268-1133** or 403/591-7711. Fax 403/591-7770. www.deltalodgeatkananaskis. ca. 321 units. High season C$249–C$349 (US$199–US$279) double. Ski/golf package rates and discounts available. AE, DC, MC, V. Parking C$12 (US$9.60); valet parking C$16 (US$13). **Amenities:** 4 restaurants; bar; indoor pool; golf courses nearby; tennis courts; health club; complete spa with salt water pool, whirlpool, and beauty treatments; bike rental; concierge; tour desk; car-rental desk; business center; shopping arcade; room service (7am–1am); babysitting; laundry service; dry cleaning; concierge-level rooms. *In room:* A/C (Signature Club), TV/VCR w/pay movies, dataport (Signature Club), minibar, fridge, coffeemaker, hair dryer, iron.

Executive Resort at Kananaskis This handsome, wood-fronted hotel offers newly renovated rooms with lush new linens and upscale furnishings. All rooms have balconies or patios, and most suites have a gas fireplace. The hotel offers a wide variety of room types including many loft units that can sleep up to six. There are mountain views from practically every room.

P.O. Box 10, Kananaskis Village, AB T0L 2H0. ⓒ **888/591-7501** or 403/591-7500. Fax 403/591-7633. www. kananaskisresort.com. 90 units. C$229–C$259 (US$183–US$207) double; C$179–C$270 (US$143–US$216) suite. AE, DC, DISC, MC, V. Free parking. **Amenities:** Restaurant; pub; golf courses nearby; tennis courts; health club and spa; exercise room; concierge; tour desk; business center; room service (7am–1am); babysitting; laundry service; dry cleaning. *In room:* TV w/pay movies, dataport, fridge, coffeemaker, hair dryer, iron.

Kananaskis Wilderness Hostel This is a great place for a recreation-loving traveler on a budget. The hostel is located at the Nakiska ski area, within walking distance of Kananaskis Village, and is close to 60 mountain-biking, hiking, and cross-country trails. Area outfitters offer special discounts to hostel guests. The hostel has a common room with a fireplace and four private family rooms.

At Nakiska Ski Area. ⓒ **866/762-4122** or 403/670-7580 for reservations, or 403/591-7333 for the hostel itself. www.hihostels.ca. 47 beds. C$23 (US$18) members; C$27 (US$21) nonmembers. MC, V. Free parking. **Amenities:** Laundry. *In room:* No phone.

CANMORE

About half of the hotel development in Canmore dates from the 1988 Olympics, and the rest dates from—oh, the last 15 minutes. Canmore is presently going through an intense period of growth, with new lodgelike hotels (the pine timbered facades typically disguise standard hotel rooms inside) springing out of the forest like mushrooms. To a large degree, this is due to the restrictions on development within the national parks to the west: Hoteliers, outfitters, and other businesses designed to serve the needs of park visitors find Canmore, right on the park boundary, a much easier place to locate than Banff. As a result, Canmore is booming, and is now a destination in its own right.

The main reason to stay in Canmore is the price of hotel rooms. Rates here are between a half and a third lower than in Banff, and the small downtown area is blossoming with interesting shops and good restaurants. The hotels listed below are, in relative terms, the older properties in Canmore. Built for the Olympics, they generally have more facilities than today's batch of hotels. Canmore hotels can represent especially good deals on discount hotel websites.

For a complete list of B&Bs, contact the **Canmore–Bow Valley B&B Association,** P.O. Box 8005, Canmore, AB T1W 2T8 (www.bbcanmore.com).

Best Western Green Gables Inn   Located along Canmore's hotel strip, this pleasant Best Western has queen-size beds throughout, with many units boasting whirlpool baths and fireplaces. Most rooms have private patios or balconies. The restaurant, Chez François, offers Canmore's best French dining.

1602 Second Ave., Canmore, AB T1W 1M8. ⓒ **800/661-2133** or 403/678-5488. Fax 403/678-2670. www.bestwestern. com. 61 units. C$169–C$209 (US$135–US$167) double. Children under 18 stay free in parent's room. AE, DISC, MC, V. Free parking. **Amenities:** Restaurant; bar; exercise room; Jacuzzi. *In room:* A/C, TV, dataport, fridge, hair dryer.

Best Western Pocaterra Inn 🐾   One of the nicest of the hotels along the Bow Valley Trail strip is the Pocaterra Inn. All rooms are spacious and come with gas fireplaces,

---

⌒Moments Riding Herd at a Guest Ranch

Brewster's Kananaskis Guest Ranch 🐾, 30 minutes east of Banff on Highway 1, P.O. Box 340, Exhaw, AB T0L 2C0 (ⓒ **800/691-5085** or 403/673-3737; www. brewsteradventures.com), the original family homestead from the 1880s, was transformed into a guest ranch in 1923. The 33 fully modern guest rooms, in chalets and cabins, have full bathrooms. Doubles are C$98 to C$114 per person (US$78–US$91), breakfast and dinner included. Activities include horseback riding, rafting, canoeing, hiking, golfing, and more. Long-distance backcountry horseback rides are a specialty—a 2-day trip costs around C$320 (US$256)—and backcountry campsites have newly constructed sleeping cabins.

Another old-time guest ranch with a long pedigree, **Rafter Six Ranch Resort,** P.O. Box 6, Seebe, AB T0L 1X0 (ⓒ **888/26-RANCH** or 403/673-3622; www.raftersix.com), is located in a meadow right on the banks of the Kananaskis River. This full-service resort is open year-round and accommodates guests in an especially inviting old log lodge (with restaurant, barbecue deck, and lounge), in various sizes of log cabins, and in large chalets that sleep up to six and have full kitchens. All units have private bathrooms. Doubles go for C$110 to C$250 (US$79–US$180) in the lodge, C$125 to C$250 (US$100–US$200) in cabins and chalets. Casual horseback and longer pack rides are offered, as well as raft and canoe trips. Seasonal special events might include rodeos, country dances, and hay or sleigh rides.

and lots of thoughtful niceties. The King suites on the top floor are especially spacious and have grand views of the Rockies. Free high-speed wireless Internet service is available throughout the hotel, and there's a complimentary Internet kiosk in the lobby.

1725 Mountain Ave., Canmore, AB T1W 2W1. © **888/678-6786** or 403/678-4334. Fax 403/678-3999. www.pocaterra inn.com. 83 units. C$179–C$269 (US$143–US$215) double. Children under 18 stay free in parent's room. Rates include continental breakfast. AE, DISC, MC, V. Free parking. **Amenities:** Indoor pool with water slide; exercise room; Jacuzzi; sauna; coin-op laundry. *In room:* A/C, TV, dataport, fridge, coffeemaker, hair dryer, microwave.

Chateau Canmore ✮

You can't miss this enormous complex along the hotel strip. Like a series of 10 four-story conjoined chalets, the all-suite Chateau Canmore offers some of the largest rooms in the area. The accommodations are very nicely decorated in a comfortable rustic style, while the lobby and common rooms look like they belong in a log lodge. Each standard suite has a fireplace and separate bedroom, while the deluxe one- or two-bedroom suites add a living room and dining area. Just like home, but with a better view.

1720 Bow Valley Trail, Canmore, AB T1W 2X3. © **800/261-8551** or 403/678-6699. Fax 403/678-6954. www.chateau canmore.com. 120 units. From C$184 (US$147) standard suite; from C$204 (US$163) deluxe suite. AE, DC, DISC, MC, V. Free parking. **Amenities:** Dining room; lounge; indoor pool; health club; spa; limited room service. *In room:* AC, TV, dataport, fridge, hair dryer, microwave.

Paintbox Lodge ✮

One of the few lodgings in Canmore's charming town center, the Paintbox Lodge is a small and luxurious boutique inn that mingles rustic mountain charm and refined sophistication. The lodge offers seven guest rooms in the main building and a two-bedroom suite with a full kitchen in a separate lodge, all just steps from the Bow River and the lively cafes and shops of Canmore.

701 Mallard Alley, Canmore, AB T1W 2A2. © **888/678-3100** or 403/609-0482. Fax 403/609-0481 www.paintbox lodge.com. 8 units. C$259–C$379 (US$207–US$303) double. Rates include full breakfast. MC, V. Free parking. *In room:* TV w/movie channels, dataport, minibar, fridge, high-speed Internet access, CD player.

Radisson Hotel and Conference Centre Canmore

This vast complex is Canmore's largest hotel and also serves as the town's convention center. With all of the functions and services offered here, it's almost a self-contained community. There are two styles of accommodations: standard guest rooms in the main building, all with balconies and quality furnishings, or luxury lodge rooms, most with kitchenettes and fireplaces. A few two-bedroom lodge units with full kitchens are available as well (call for rates).

511 Bow Valley Trail, Canmore, AB T1W 1N7. © **800/333-3333** or 403/678-3625. Fax 403/678-3765. www.radisson. com/canmoreca. 224 units. C$169–C$199 (US$135–US$159) double. AE, DC, DISC, MC, V. Free parking. **Amenities:** Restaurant; bar; indoor pool; exercise room; Jacuzzi; sauna; car-rental desk; limited room service; babysitting; laundry service; same-day dry cleaning. *In room:* A/C, TV w/pay movies, dataport, coffeemaker, hair dryer, iron.

CAMPING

Kananaskis is a major camping destination for families, and the choice of **campgrounds** in Calgary is wide. There's a concentration of campgrounds at Upper and Lower Kananaskis Lakes, some 32km (20 miles) south of Kananaskis Village. A few campgrounds are scattered nearer to Kananaskis Village, around Barrier Lake and Ribbon Creek. For a full-service campground with RV hookups, go to **Mount Kidd RV Park** (© **403/591-7700**) just south of the Kananaskis golf course.

WHERE TO DINE

The dining rooms at both **Rafter Six Ranch Resort** and **Brewster's Kananaskis Guest Ranch** (see "Riding Herd at a Guest Ranch," above) are open to nonguests with reservations. Pub dining in Canmore is also noteworthy; most pubs have pleasant garden patios. **Grizzly Paw Pub,** 622 Main St. (© **403/678-9983**), makes its own excellent ales and serves good food. The **Rose and Crown,** 749 Railway Ave. (© **403/ 678-5168**), overlooking the river, wins for the best deck.

Copper Door NEW CANADIAN   Tucked away on quiet Ninth Street, this cozy dining room offers up-to-date dining in a stylish but informal setting. Appetizers include "salmonkapita," smoked salmon, horseradish, and feta cheese in phyllo pastry, while main dishes include sherried-raisin-and-wild-mushroom-stuffed wild Pacific salmon wrapped with grape leaves; grilled pork tenderloin with caramelized pears and pear brandy cream; and vegetable strudel. The dining room is small, so come early or phone for reservations.

726 Ninth St. © 403/678-5233. Reservations recommended. Main courses C$17–C$34 (US$14–US$27). AE, MC, V. Daily 5–10pm in summer. Closed Sun and Mon Oct–June.

Murrieta's Bar & Grill ☙☙ STEAKHOUSE/FISH   A story above Canmore's busy main street, Murrieta's is a stylish and lively steakhouse and bar with attractive lodge decor, and a soaring 24-foot cathedral ceiling. The food is lofty as well—in addition to steak and chops, Murrieta's offers a broad selection of fresh fish and seafood. The grilled shrimp with vanilla saffron sauce is outstanding, and for a break from beef, try the chile-roasted pork rib-eye with red onion marmalade. On Friday and Saturday nights, the bar features live jazz.

200-737 Main St. © 403/609-9500. www.murrietas.ca. Reservations recommended. Main courses C$10–C$32 (US$8–US$26). AE, MC, V. Mon–Thurs 11am–11pm; Fri–Sat 11am–1pm; Sun 11am–10pm.

Quarry Bistro ☙ CONTINENTAL   A friendly, informal spot for intriguing cooking based on French and Italian classics but translated into New Canadian vernacular by chef David Wyse. Using local and organic ingredients, Wyse creates a seasonal cuisine that's sophisticated but low-key. Wild mushroom and lemon thyme raviolis make an excellent appetizer, and one evening's special, a grilled organic pork chop with fresh crab-apple tarragon relish, was full of fall flavors. It sounds unlikely, but the housemade blueberry basil sorbet is delightful. This bright and lively spot is right on Main Street, with a few street-side tables.

718 Main St. © 403/678-6088. Reservations suggested. Main courses C$14–C$28 (US$11–US$22). MC, V. Mon–Fri 11:30am–2:30pm and 5–10pm; Sat–Sun 9:30am–2:30pm and 5–10pm.

Sherwood House CANADIAN   This handsome log restaurant on the busiest corner of downtown Canmore (which isn't that busy) is a longtime favorite. The wideranging and well-executed menu, which offers everything from pizza and pasta to prime Angus steaks, has something for everyone, but what makes this one of Canmore's favorite gathering spots is the wonderful landscaped deck. In summer, there's no better place to spend the afternoon. In winter, you'll enjoy the traditional lodge building with its cozy fireplace.

At Main St. and Eighth Ave. © 403/678-5211. Reservations recommended. Main courses C$13–C$29 (US$10–US$23). AE, MC, V. Daily 7am–10pm.

Tapas Restaurant SPANISH/PORTUGUESE   Many restaurants use the term tapas to refer to finger food and appetizers from just about any cuisine, forgetting that tapas are supposed to be Spanish. There's no such mistake here: Tapas Restaurant serves up a very broad selection of authentically Spanish and Portuguese favorites including chile-and-cilantro mussels *escabeche,* seafood skewers, roasted peppers, anchovies, and olives. The restaurant also focuses on dishes to be shared by two, including *cataplana,* a Portuguese seafood stew served in a copper pot, and three kinds of paella. The intimate dining room is painted with Iberian murals, and with the scent of garlic and sausage in the air, you might just believe you're in Seville.

633 10th St. © **403/609-0583.** Reservations suggested. Tapas C$4–C$12 (US$3.20–US$9.60); main courses (for 2) C$30–C$40 (US$24–US$36). AE, MC, V. Summer daily 8am–11pm; winter daily 5:30–11pm.

Zona's Late Night Bistro INTERNATIONAL   Come to this friendly hangout, popular with Canmore's young outdoorsy crowd, if you don't want to spend a fortune, but still seek sophisticated food with zip. The menu trots the globe: assemble tapas such as Mediterranean vegetable tart or Thai turkey meat balls into a meal, or consider a main course such as Mexican three-bean pie or Moroccan molasses lamb curry. Zona's offers ample vegetarian options plus outdoor seating in summer.

710 Ninth St. © **403/609-2000.** Reservations recommended. Main courses C$15–C$21 (US$12–US$17); tapas C$7–C$9 (US$5.60–US$7.20). MC, V. Daily 5pm–midnight.

3 Banff National Park

Banff Townsite: 129km (80 miles) W of Calgary

Banff, Canada's oldest national park, encompasses 6,641 sq. km (2,590 sq. miles) of incredibly dramatic mountain landscape, glaciers, high morainal lakes, and rushing rivers. Its two towns, Lake Louise and Banff, are both splendid counterpoints to the wilderness, with beautiful historic hotels, fine restaurants, and lively nightlife.

If there's a downside to all this sophisticated beauty, it's that Banff is generally considered Canada's number-one tourist destination. About five million people visit Banff yearly, with the vast majority squeezing in during June, July, and August.

Happily, the wilderness invites visitors to get away from the crowds and congestion. Banff Park is blessed with many great outfitters who make it easy to get on a raft, bike, or horse and find a little solitude. Alternatively, consider visiting the park off season, when prices are lower, the locals are friendlier, and the scenery is just as stunning.

For more information on the park, contact **Banff National Park,** P.O. Box 900, Banff, AB T1L 1K2 (© **403/762-1550;** www.pc.gc.ca).

OUTDOOR PURSUITS IN THE PARK

Lots of great recreational activities are available in Banff National Park, so don't just spend your vacation shopping the boutiques on Banff Avenue. There are many more outfitters in Banff than the ones I list, but the offerings and prices below are typical of what's available.

BIKING   The most popular cycling adventure in the Canadian Rockies is the 287km (178-mile) trip between Banff and Jasper along the Icefields Parkway, one of the world's most magnificent mountain roads.

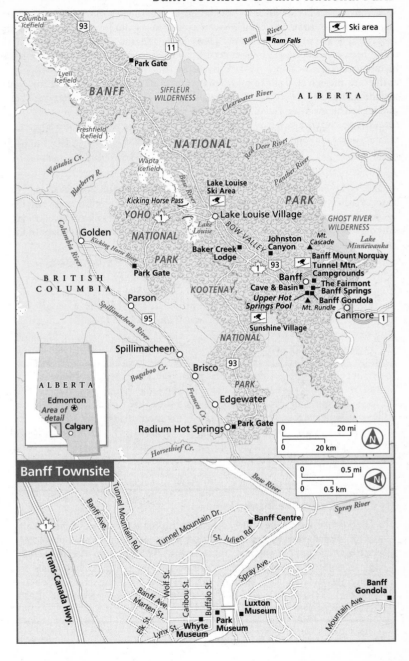

Banff Townsite & Banff National Park

Ski area

Columbia Icefield

93

11

Ram River

Ram Falls

Park Gate

Lyell Icefield

BANFF

SIFFLEUR WILDERNESS

Clearwater River

ALBERTA

Freshfield Icefield

NATIONAL

Red Deer River

Waitabit Cr.

Wapta Icefield

Panther River

Blaeberry R.

Bow River

Lake Louise Ski Area

PARK

Kicking Horse Pass

YOHO

1

Lake Louise Village

GHOST RIVER WILDERNESS

Columbia River

Golden

NATIONAL

Lake Louise

BOW VALLEY

Johnston Canyon

Mt. Cascade

Lake Minnewanka

Kicking Horse River

Baker Creek Lodge

1

93

Banff Mount Norquay

PARK

Park Gate

BRITISH COLUMBIA

KOOTENAY

Banff

Tunnel Mtn. Campgrounds

Parson

Cave & Basin

The Fairmont Banff Springs

Spillimacheen River

Upper Hot Springs Pool

Mt. Rundle

Banff Gondola

Canmore

1

95

NATIONAL

Sunshine Village

Spillimacheen

Bugaboo Cr.

Brisco

93

ALBERTA

PARK

Frances Cr.

Edmonton

Area of detail

Edgewater

Calgary

Radium Hot Springs

Park Gate

Horsethief Cr.

0   20 mi

0   20 km

N

Banff Townsite

0   0.5 mi

0   0.5 km

N

Bow River

Tunnel Mountain Rd.

Banff Ave.

Tunnel Mountain Dr.

Banff Centre

Spray River

1

St. Julien Rd.

Spray Ave.

Trans-Canada Hwy.

Wolf St.

Banff Ave.

Caribou St.

Marten St.

Buffalo St.

Luxton Museum

Banff Gondola

Elk St.

Lynx St.

Whyte Museum

Park Museum

Mountain Ave.

If you're fit and ready for a high elevation ride, but don't want to bother with the logistics yourself, consider signing on with a bike-touring outfitter. An Internet search will reveal dozens of tour operators; **Canusa Cycle Tours** (© 800/938-7986 or 403/703-5566; www.canusacycletours.com) offers 6-day supported trips starting at C$975 (US$780).

If you'd prefer a self-guided tour, simply rent a bike in Banff or Lake Louise and peddle along the Bow Valley Parkway—Highway 1A—between Banff and Lake Louise, which makes an easy day trip for the average cyclist.

FISHING   **Banff Fishing Unlimited** (© 403/762-4936; www.banff-fishing.com) offers a number of fly-fishing expeditions on the Bow River as well as lake fishing at Lake Minnewanka. All levels of anglers are accommodated, and packages include part- or whole-day trips.

GOLF   The **Fairmont Banff Springs Golf Course** ☝ (© 403/762-6801) rolls out along the Bow River beneath towering mountain peaks. One of the most venerable courses in Canada, and one of the most expensive, it offers 27 holes of excellent golf. Although associated with the resort hotel, the course is open to the public. In high summer season, greens fees for 18 holes are C$180 (US$144).

HIKING   One of the great virtues of Banff is that many of its most scenic areas are easily accessible by day hikes. The park has more than 80 maintained trails, ranging from interpretive nature strolls to long-distance expeditions (you'll need a permit if you're planning on camping in the backcountry). For a good listing of popular hikes, pick up the free *Banff/Lake Louise Drives and Walks* brochure from the national park information center at 224 Banff Avenue.

One of the best day hikes is up **Johnston Canyon** ☝, 24km (15 miles) north of Banff on Highway 1A. This relatively easy hike up a limestone canyon passes seven waterfalls before reaching a series of jade-green springs known as the **Inkpots.** Part of the fun of this trail is the narrowness of the canyon—the walls are more than 30m (99 ft.) high, but only 5m (16 ft.) across; the path skirts the cliff face, tunnels through walls, and winds across wooden footbridges for more than a mile. The waterfalls plunge down through the canyon, soaking hikers with spray; watch for black swifts diving in the mist. The hike through the canyon to Upper Falls takes 1½ hours; all the way to the Inkpots will take at least 4 hours.

Tips A Bird's-Eye View

If you'd like to see the beautiful scenery of the Canadian Rockies from the air, contact **Alpine Helicopters** (© 403/678-4802; www.alpinehelicopter.com), which operates out of Canmore. This company's flights over the Rockies start at C$80 (US$64) with a minimum of three passengers. See p. 11 for details on **Alpenglow Aviation** (© 888/244-7117 or 250/344-7117; www.rockiesair tours.com), which offers a variety of flight-seeing trips starting at C$110 (US$88) per person.

It's easy to strike out from **Banff Townsite** and find any number of satisfying short hikes. Setting off on foot can be as simple as following the paths along both sides of the Bow River. From the west end of the Bow River Bridge, trails lead east to Bow Falls, past the Fairmount Banff Springs to the Upper Hot Springs. Another popular hike just beyond town is the **Fenlands Trail,** which begins past the train station and makes a loop through marshland wildlife habitat near the Vermillion Lakes.

Two longer trails leave from the Cave and Basin Centennial Centre. The **Sundance Trail** follows the Bow River for nearly 5km (3 miles) past beaver dams and wetlands, ending at the entrance to Sundance Canyon. Keen hikers can continue up the canyon another 2.5km (1½ miles) to make a loop past Sundance Falls. The Marsh Loop winds 2.5km (1½ miles) past the Bow River and marshy lakes.

If you'd prefer a guided hike, Parks Canada offers several hikes daily. Ask at the Banff Information Centre or check the chalkboard outside to find out what hiking options are available. Some walks are free, while others (like the popular evening Wildlife Research Walks) charge a small fee; both require preregistration. For information and preregistration, call © **403/762-9818.**

HORSEBACK RIDING See Banff on horseback with **Warner Guiding and Outfitting** (© **800/661-8352** or 403/762-4551; fax 403/762-8130; www.horseback. com). Multiday trail rides, which start at C$615 (US$492) for a 3-day lodge-to-lodge trip and peak at C$1,236 (US$988) for a 6-day backcountry tenting trip, explore some of the most remote areas of the park. Some rides climb up to backcountry lodges, which serve as base camps for further exploration; other trips involve a backcountry circuit, with lodging in tents. Shorter day rides are also offered from two stables near the townsite. A morning ride with brunch goes for C$88 (US$70).

Operating out of Lake Louise, **Timberline Tours** (© **888/858-3388** or 403/ 522-3743; www.timberlinetours.ca) offers day trips to some of the area's more prominent beauty sites, starting at C$50 (US$40) for 90 minutes of riding. Three- to 10-day pack trips are also offered.

RAFTING & CANOEING Family float trips on the Bow River just below Banff are popular 2-hour diversions, available from **Canadian Rockies Rafting Company** (© **877/226-7625** or 403/678-6535; www.rafting.ca). Trips are C$42 (US$34) for adults and C$30 (US$24) for children 6 to 16, with free pickup at Banff and Canmore hotels. Longer, more challenging trips on area rivers are also available.

For serious white water, the closest option is the **Kicking Horse River** ⊛, past Lake Louise just over the Continental Divide near Field, British Columbia. **Hydra River Guides** (© **800/644-8888** or 403/762-4554; www.raftbanff.com) offers transport from Banff and Lake Louise (an extra C$15/US$12), then a 2½-hour run down the Kicking Horse through Class IV rapids. Trips go for C$90 (US$72), which includes gear and barbecue lunch.

SKIING Banff Park has three ski areas, which together have formed a partnership for booking and promotional purposes. For information on all of the following, contact **Ski Banff/Lake Louise,** Box 1085, Banff, AB T0l 0C0 (© **403/762-4561;** fax 403/762-8185; www.skibig3.com).

Banff Mount Norquay (© **403/762-4421;** www.banffnorquay.com) has twin runs just above the town of Banff. They cater to family skiing and offer day care, instruction, and night skiing. Rates start at C$52 (US$41) for adults.

Skiers must ski or take a gondola to the main lifts at **Sunshine Village** (© 403/762-6500; www.skibanff.com) and the Sunshine Inn, a ski-in/ski-out hotel. Sunshine, located 15 minutes west of Banff off Highway 1, receives more snow than any ski area in the Canadian Rockies (more than 9m/30 ft. per year!). Lift tickets here start at C$65 (US$52) for adults.

Lake Louise Ski Area (© 800/258-SNOW in North America, or 403/552-3555) has been named the most scenic ski resort in North America by *Ski* magazine. It's also one of the largest in Canada, with 1,680 skiable hectares (4,200 acres) and 113 named runs. Rates are C$64 (US$51) for adults. Snowmaking machines keep the lifts running from November to early May.

A special lift pass for Banff Mount Norquay, Sunshine Village, and Lake Louise Ski Area allows skiers unlimited access to all three resorts (and free rides on shuttle buses between the ski areas). Passes for 3 days (minimum) start at C$195 (US$156) for adults and C$61 (US$49) for children.

BANFF TOWNSITE

Few towns in the world boast as beautiful a setting as Banff. The mighty Bow River courses right through town, while massive mountain blocks rear up on Banff's outskirts. Mount Rundle, a finlike mountain that somehow got tipped over on its side, parades off to the south. Mount Cascade rises up immediately north of downtown.

This is a stunning, totally unlikely place for a town, and Banff has been trading on its beauty for more than a century. The Fairmount Banff Springs was built in 1888 as a destination resort by the Canadian Pacific Railroad. As outdoor-recreation enthusiasts began to frequent the area, the little town of Banff grew up to service their needs.

While the setting hasn't changed since the early days of the park, the town certainly has. Today, the streets of Banff are lined with exclusive boutiques; trendy cafes spill out onto the sidewalks; and bus after bus filled with tourists choke the streets. There's a vital and cosmopolitan feel to the town; just don't come here expecting a bucolic alpine village—Banff in summer is a very busy place.

ESSENTIALS

GETTING THERE   If you're flying into Calgary and heading straight to Banff, call and reserve a seat on the **Banff Airporter** (© 403/762-3330; www.banffairporter.com). Vans depart from Calgary Airport roughly every 2 hours; a one-way ticket costs C$47 (US$38).

The closest VIA Rail **train** service is at Jasper, 287 kilometers (178 miles) north. **Brewster Transport** (© 403/762-6767) offers an express bus between the two park centers five times weekly for C$69 (US$55) one-way.

Greyhound (© 800/661-8747 or 403/260-0877; www.greyhound.ca) operates **buses** that pass through Banff on the way from Calgary to Vancouver. One-way fare between Banff and Calgary is C$23 (US$18). The depot is at 100 Gopher St. (© 403/762-6767).

If you're **driving,** the Trans-Canada Highway takes you right to Banff's main street; the town is 129km (80 miles) west of Calgary.

VISITOR INFORMATION   The **Banff Information Centre,** at 224 Banff Ave., houses both the Banff Tourism Bureau and a national-park information center. Contact the office at P.O. Box 1298, Banff, AB T0L 0C0 (© 403/762-0270; fax

---

(*Tips* **Special Events**

The **Banff Centre**, St. Julien Road ((C) **800/413-8368** or 403/762-6300; www.banff
centre.ca), is devoted to the arts in the widest sense. From June to August, it
hosts the **Banff Arts Festival** ❀, offering a stimulating mixture of drama, opera,
jazz, ballet, classical and pop music, and the visual arts. Tickets for some of the
events cost from pay-what-you-can to C$25 (US$20); a great many are
absolutely free. In November, the center is home to the **Festival of Mountain
Films**. Find out what's currently on by checking out the website.

403/762-8545; www.bannfflakelouise.com). The center is open daily June 15 to October 15 from 9am to 9pm and the rest of the year from 9am to 5pm. Be sure to ask for
the *Official Visitors Guide,* which is packed with information about local businesses
and recreation. For information on the park, go to **www.pc.gc.ca**.

ORIENTATION   Getting your bearings is easy. The **Greyhound and Brewster Bus
Depot** is located at the corner of Gopher and Lynx streets ((C) **403/762-2286**). The
main street—Banff Avenue—starts at the southern end of town at the Bow River and
runs north until it's swallowed by the Trans-Canada Highway.

Just beyond the river stands the park administration building amid a beautifully
landscaped garden. Here the road splits: **Fairmount Banff Springs** and the **Banff
Gondola** are to the left; to the right are the **Cave and Basin Hot Springs,** Banff
National Park's original site. At the northwestern edge of town is the old railroad
station, and a little farther northwest the road branches off to Lake Louise and Jasper.
In the opposite direction, northeast, is the highway going to Calgary.

GETTING AROUND   Banff offers local bus service along two routes designed to
pass through downtown and by most hotels. Service on the **Banff Bus** ((C) **403/
760-8294**) is pretty informal, but there's generally a bus every half-hour. One route
runs from the Fairmount Banff Springs down Banff Avenue to the northern end of
town; the other runs between the train station and the Banff Hostel on Tunnel Mountain; the fare is C$1 (US80¢). The bus operates in summer only.

For a taxi, call **Banff Taxi and Limousine** at (C) **403/762-4444.**

For a rental car, contact **National,** at Caribou and Lynx streets ((C) **403/762-2688**),
or **Banff Rent A Car,** 204 Lynx St. ((C) **403/762-3352**), for a less expensive but reliable vehicle. Avis, Budget, and Hertz also have offices in Banff. Reserve well in
advance as cars are frequently sold out.

EXPLORING THE AREA

Banff Gondola ❀   Apart from helicopter excursions (see above), the best way to get
an overall view of Banff's landscape is this high-wire act (formerly the Sulphur Mountain Gondola). In 8 minutes, the enclosed gondolas lift you 698m (2,292 ft.) from the
valley floor up to the top of Sulphur Mountain, at 2,281m (7,486 ft.). Up here, at the
crest of the mountains behind Banff, the panoramas are stunning. Trails lead out along
the mountain ridges; hike back to the bottom of the mountain, or spend the day
exploring the subarctic zone along the mountaintop. Also, the upper terminal has two

restaurants, a snack bar, and gift shop. Lines to get on the gondola can be very long in summer; if you are set on riding up to the high country, try to go as early as possible.

The lower terminal is 6km (4 miles) southeast of town on Mountain Ave. ℭ **403/762-5438**. www.banffgondola. com. Admission C$23 (US$18) adults, C$11 (US$9) children 6–15. May 1 to Labour Day 7:30am–9pm; check website for off-season schedule.

Banff Park Museum   Housed in a lovely building dating from 1903, this museum beside the Bow River Bridge is largely a paean to taxidermy, but there's a lot to learn here about the wildlife of the park and how the various ecosystems interrelate. The real pleasure, though, is the rustic, lodge-style building, now preserved as a National Historic Site.

Banff Ave. and Buffalo St. ℭ **403/762-1558**. Admission C$4 (US$3.20) adults, C$3.50 (US$2.80) seniors, C$3 (US$2.40) youths 6–16. Summer daily 10am–6pm; off season daily 1–5pm.

Buffalo Nations Luxton Museum   Housed in a log fort south of the Bow River, just across the bridge from downtown Banff, this museum is devoted to the history of the First Nations peoples of the Canadian Rockies and Northern Plains. It offers realistic dioramas, tepees, a sun-dance exhibit, artifacts, and ornaments.

1 Birch Ave. ℭ **403/762-2388**. Admission C$8 (US$6.40) adults, C$6 (US$4.80) seniors and students, C$2.50 (US$2) children 6–12. Daily 9am–5pm.

Cave and Basin National Historic Site ⚐   Although most people now associate Banff with skiing or hiking, in the early days of the park, travelers streamed in to visit the curative hot springs. In fact, it was the discovery of the hot springs now preserved at this historic site that spurred the creation of the national park in 1888. During the 1910s, these hot mineral waters, which rise in a limestone cave, were piped into a rather grand natatorium. Although the Cave and Basin springs are no longer open for swimming or soaking, the old pool area and the original cave have been preserved; interpretive displays and films round out the experience.

1.5km (1 mile) west of Banff; turn right at the west end of the Bow River Bridge. ℭ **403/762-1566**. Admission C$4 (US$3.20) adults, C$3 (US$2.40) seniors and youths 6–18. May 15–Sept 30 daily 9am–6pm; Oct 1–May 14 Mon–Fri 11am–4pm, Sat–Sun 9:30am–5pm.

Lake Minnewanka Boat Tours   These very popular scenic and wildlife-viewing trips in glassed-in motor cruisers take place on Lake Minnewanka, a glacial lake wedged between two mountain ranges. These trips—usually 2 hours long—are among those excursions that nearly every visitor to Banff ends up taking, so unless you want to be part of a huge shuffling throng, try to go early in the day. Reservations are suggested. In high season, there are five sailings a day and buses depart daily from Banff to meet these departures, both from the bus station and from most hotels.

24km (15 miles) north of Banff. ℭ **403/762-3473**. Fax 403/762-2800. www.minnewankaboattours.com. Tickets C$32 (US$26) adults, C$15 (US$12) children 5–11. Mid-May to early Oct.

Upper Hot Springs Pool   If visiting the Cave and Basin makes you long for a soak in mountain hot springs, then drive up Mountain Avenue to this spa. In addition to the redesigned swimming pool filled with hot, sulfurous waters, you'll find a restaurant, snack bar, and home spa boutique. If you're looking more for a cure than a splash, try the adjacent **Upper Hot Springs Spa** (ℭ **403/760-2500**) with a steam room, massage, plunge pools, and aromatherapy treatments.

At the top of Mountain Ave., 5km (3 miles) west of Banff. ☏ **403/762-1515.** Pool admission C$7.50 (US$6) adults, C$6.50 (US$5.20) seniors and children, C$22 (US$18) per family. Spa treatments begin at C$32 (US$26) and are open to adults only. Daily 9am–11pm with reduced hours in winter.

Whyte Museum of the Canadian Rockies Part art gallery, part local-history museum, this is the only museum in North America that collects, exhibits, and interprets the history and culture of the Canadian Rockies. Two furnished heritage homes on the grounds are open in summer and stand as a memorial to the pioneers of the Rockies. Interpretive programs and tours are offered year-round. The Elizabeth Rummel Tea Room is open from mid-May to mid-October and serves light lunches, desserts, and coffee.

111 Bear St. ☏ **403/762-2291.** www.whyte.org. Admission C$6 (US$4.30) adults, C$3.50 (US$2.80) seniors and students, C$15 (US$12) family; free for children under 5. Daily 10am–5pm.

SHOPPING

The degree to which you like the town of Banff will depend largely upon your taste for shopping. **Banff Avenue** is increasingly an open-air boutique mall, with throngs of shoppers milling around. Of course, you would expect to find excellent outdoor-gear and sporting-goods stores here, as well as the usual T-shirt and gift emporiums. What's more surprising are the boutiques devoted to Paris and New York designers, the upscale jewelry stores, and the high-end galleries. What's most surprising of all is that many visitors seem to actually prefer to while away their time in this masterpiece of nature called Banff by shopping for English soaps or Italian shoes. There are no secrets to shopping here: Arcade after arcade opens onto Banff Avenue, where you'll find everything you need. Quality and prices are both quite high.

WHERE TO STAY

All accommodation prices listed are for high season, normally mid-May to mid-October; nearly all hotels have discounts for late fall, holidays, winter, late winter, and spring lodging. If you're having trouble finding affordable lodgings in Banff, try properties in Canmore, located 20 minutes away (see "Kananaskis Country & Canmore," earlier in this chapter).

If you want to camp, Banff National Park offers hundreds of campsites within easy distance of Banff. The closest are the three **Tunnel Mountain campgrounds** ⚸, just past the youth hostel west of town. Two of the campgrounds are for RVs only and have both partial and full hookups (C$33/US$26); the third has showers and is usually reserved for tenters (C$24/US$19). For more information, call the park's visitor center (☏ **403/762-1500**). Campsites within the park cannot be reserved in advance.

Very Expensive

Banff Park Lodge Resort Hotel and Conference Centre ⚸ A handsome cedar-and-oak structure with a cosmopolitan air, the Banff Park Lodge is a quiet block-and-a-half off the town's main street, near the Bow River. Calm and sophisticated are the key words here: All rooms are soundproof, and wild, après-ski cavorting isn't the norm, or even much encouraged. The lodge will feel like a tranquil retreat after a day in frantic Banff. The standard rooms are spacious and exceptionally well furnished, all with balconies. Most suites have a whirlpool, jetted tub, and fireplace. With its abundant ground-floor rooms and wide hallways, this lodging is popular with travelers with accessibility or mobility concerns.

222 Lynx St., Banff, AB T1L 1K5. Ⓒ **800/661-9266** or 403/762-4433. Fax 403/762-3553. www.banffparklodge.com. 211 units. C$279 (US$223) double; from C$399 (US$319) suite. Extra person C$12–C$18 (US$9.60–US$14). Children 16 and under stay free in parent's room. Off-season and ski packages available. AE, DC, MC, V. Free parking. **Amenities:** Formal and family restaurants; bar; indoor pool; access to nearby health club; spa; Jacuzzi; steam room; concierge; tour and activities desk; business center; shopping arcade; salon; room service (7am–midnight); babysitting; laundry service; same-day dry cleaning. *In room:* A/C, TV w/movie channels, dataport, coffeemaker, hair dryer, iron, voice mail.

Buffalo Mountain Lodge 👓👓 The most handsome of the properties on Tunnel Mountain, 1.6km (1 mile) northeast of Banff, this is the perfect choice if you'd rather avoid the frenetic pace of downtown and yet remain central to restaurants and activities. Its quiet location and beautiful lodge make this a good alternative to equally priced hotels in the heart of town (the Banff Bus stops right out the front door). The lodge building itself is an enormous log cabin, with a lobby supported by massive rafters. A fieldstone fireplace dominates the lounge, while the restaurant overlooks the grounds. An enormous, 25-person hot tub sits between the lodge and the guest rooms. Accommodations are scattered around the forested 3-hectare (8-acre) property. They range from one-bedroom suites with kitchens to the exceptionally handsome Premier rooms, which feature slate-tiled bathrooms with both claw-foot tubs and slate-walled showers. The pine-and-twig furniture lends a rustic look to the otherwise sophisticated decor. All units have fireplaces (wood is stacked near your door), DVD players, high-speed Internet access, balconies or patios, and beds made up with feather duvets. These are some of the most attractive rooms in Banff.

1.6km (1 mile) northeast of Banff on Tunnel Mountain Rd., P.O. Box 1326, Banff, AB T1L 1B3. Ⓒ **800/661-1367** or 403/762-2400. Fax 403/760-4492. www.buffalomountainlodge.com. 108 units. C$239 (US$191) double; C$325 (US$260) 1-bedroom apt. AE, MC, V. Free parking. Follow Otter St. from downtown. **Amenities:** 2 restaurants (see "Where to Dine," later in this chapter); lounge; exercise room; Jacuzzi; steam room; laundry service; same-day dry cleaning. *In room:* TV, dataport, coffeemaker, hair dryer, iron.

The Fairmont Banff Springs Standing north of Bow River Falls like an amazing Scottish baronial fortress, the Banff Springs is one of the most beautiful and famous hotels in North America. Founded in 1888 as an opulent destination resort by the Canadian Pacific Railroad, this stone castle of a hotel is still the best address in Banff. Expect sumptuous linens, fancy soaps and lotions, real art, and quality furniture. This venerable hotel doesn't offer the largest rooms in Banff, but the amenities are superlative. With the views, the spa, the history, and the near pageantry of service (the Springs maintains a staff of 1,200), this is an amazing testament to luxury. Is it worth the money? Perhaps, if you're looking for a totally unique experience in historic lodging—but there is far better value, even at the top end, at other Banff lodgings.

405 Spray Ave. (P.O. Box 960), Banff, AB T1L 1J4. Ⓒ **800/441-1414** or 403/762-2211. Fax 403/762-5755. www. fairmont.com. 770 units. C$476–C$656 (US$381–US$524) double; C$657–C$1,007 (US$525–US$806) suite. Rates include full breakfast and service charges. AE, DC, DISC, MC, V. Valet parking C$26 (US$22); self-parking C$19 (US$16). **Amenities:** 15 restaurants; 3 lounges; Olympic-size pool; the famed Banff Springs golf course (considered one of the most scenic in the world); 4 tennis courts; the European-style Solace Spa, with mineral baths, a full range of beauty and health treatments, plus fitness training, nutritional consultation, and lifestyle programs; Jacuzzi; bike rental; concierge; tour and activities desk; business center; shopping arcade; 24-hr. room service; babysitting; laundry service; same-day dry cleaning. *In room:* A/C, TV/VCR w/pay movies and video games, dataport, coffeemaker, hair dryer, iron.

Rimrock Resort Hotel If you seek modern luxury and great views, this is your hotel. From its roadside lobby entrance, the enormous, stunningly beautiful Rimrock drops nine floors down a steep mountain slope, affording tremendous views from nearly all of its rooms. Aiming for the same quality of architecture and majesty of scale as venerable older lodges, the Rimrock offers a massive glass-fronted lobby that's lined with cherry wood, tiled with unpolished marble floors, and filled with inviting chairs and Oriental rugs. The limestone fireplace, open on two sides, is so large that staff members step inside it to ready the kindling. Guest rooms are large and well appointed with handsome furnishings; some have balconies. Standard rooms are all the same size; their prices vary only depending on the view. The suites are truly large, with balconies, wet bars, and loads of cozy couches.

Mountain Ave. (5km/3 miles south of Banff), P.O. Box 1110, Banff, AB T1L 1J2. (C) **800/661-1587** or 403/762-3356. Fax 403/762-1842. www.rimrockresort.com. 346 units. C$400–C$550 (US$320–US$440) double; C$550–C$1,300 (US$440–US$1,040) suite. AE, DC, DISC, MC, V. Valet parking C$10 (US$8); free self-parking in heated garage. **Amenities:** 2 restaurants; 2 bars; health club with pool, squash court, hot tub, aerobics, beauty treatments. massage, wraps, and more weight training and fitness devices than many professional gyms; concierge; tour and activities desk; business center; shopping arcade; 24-hr. room service; babysitting; laundry service; same-day dry cleaning. *In room:* A/C, TV w/pay movies and video games, dataport, minibar, coffeemaker, hair dryer, iron.

Thea's House

Thea's House The most upscale and elegant bed-and-breakfast in Banff, Thea's is the perfect spot for a romantic getaway. Just a couple minutes walk from downtown, this striking log-and-stone structure boasts 8m (25-ft.) ceilings, antiques, exquisite artwork, and discreet and friendly service. Guest rooms are large and beautifully outfitted, with vaulted pine ceilings, fir floors, rustic pine and antique furniture, fireplaces, sitting areas, cassette and CD players, and private balconies. Guests have access to a lounge area with a stocked minibar and refrigerator and a coffee and tea service; a full breakfast is included, and ski packages are also available. "Elegant Alpine" is how Thea's describes itself, and you'll have no trouble imagining yourself in a fairy-tale mountain lodge.

138 Otter St. (Box 1237), Banff, AB T1L 1B2. (C) **403/762-2499.** Fax 403/762-2496. www.theashouse.com. 3 units. C$250–C$275 (US$200–US$220) double. MC, V. Free parking. **Amenities:** Complimentary health club pass available; bike rental. *In room:* TV/DVD, hair dryer, iron, stereo, gas fireplace.

Expensive

Banff Aspen Lodge ☆ *Value* Located a 5-minute walk from downtown, the Banff Aspen is a very well-maintained motel that offers reasonably good value for the dollar—remember, this is Banff. Rooms are quite large and pleasantly decorated, all with twin vanities and king- or queen-size beds. Some are divided into two sleeping areas by the bathroom, a great configuration for families or groups. All units have balconies or patio access.

401 Banff Ave., Banff, AB T1L 1A9. (C) **877/886-6660** or 403/762-4401. Fax 403/762-5905. www.banffaspen lodge.com. 89 units. C$205 (US$164) double. Continental breakfast included in all rates. AE, MC, V. Free parking. **Amenities:** Hot tub; sauna; steam room; coin-op laundry; Internet access terminal; gift shop. *In room:* TV, coffeemaker.

Banff Caribou Lodge The Caribou, with its gabled green roof, outdoor patio, bay windows, and wooden balconies, has a Western-lodge look that blends well with the alpine landscape. The interior is equally impressive, especially the vast lobby with slate-tile floor, peeled-log woodwork, and huge stone fireplace. The finely furnished bedrooms continue the Western theme with rustic pine chairs and beds decked out with snug down comforters. The bathrooms are spacious; some of the rooms have balconies. The lodge is long on service and friendliness. The Keg is a local favorite for steaks. A free shuttle bus ferries guests to destinations throughout Banff.

521 Banff Ave., Banff, AB T1L 1A4. ⓒ **800/563-8764** or 403/762-5887. Fax 403/762-5918. www.bestofbanff.com. 207 units. C$220–C$235 (US$176–US$188) double; C$300–C$350 (US$240–US$280) suite. Up to 2 children under 16 stay free in parent's room. AE, DC, DISC, MC, V. Free heated parking. **Amenities:** Restaurant; bar; exercise room; Jacuzzi; sauna; concierge; room service (7:30am–10pm). *In room:* TV w/pay movies, dataport, coffeemaker, hair dryer, iron.

Brewster's Mountain Lodge ⟨Value⟩

All in all, for the comfort, convenience, and moderately (by Banff standards) priced rooms, this is one of the top picks in central Banff. This handsome lodgelike hotel, right in the heart of Banff, is operated by the Brewster family, who dominate much of the local recreation, guest ranching, and transportation. The modern hotel does its best to look rustic: Peeled log posts and beams fill the lobby and foyer, while quality pine furniture and paneling grace the spacious guest rooms. Wheelchair-accessible rooms are available. Although there's no fine dining in the hotel, you'll find plenty adjacent in central Banff. The Brewster affiliation makes it simple to take advantage of lodging and adventure packages involving horseback riding and hiking.

208 Caribou St., Banff, AB T1L 1C1. ⓒ **888/762-2900** or 403/762-2900. Fax 403/762-2970. www.brewstermountain lodge.com. 73 units. From C$229 (US$183) double. AE, MC, V. Self parking C$6 (US$4.80). **Amenities:** Restaurant; Jacuzzi; sauna; car-rental desk; same-day dry cleaning. *In room:* TV/VCR, dataport, hair dryer, iron.

Hidden Ridge Resort

Located up on Tunnel Mountain, a 5-minute drive from downtown Banff, is a collection of well-traveled condo developments. There's a good reason that these properties are popular—they are out of the busy center of town, and they offer large units that can accommodate families and groups. One of these, Hidden Ridge Resort, is undergoing a major renovation and general spiffing up and offers some excellent deals for travelers who want self-catering accommodations. Condos range from king one-bedroom units to two-bedroom condos with lofts that comfortably sleep eight—even before opening out the sofa bed. All units have full maplewood kitchens with granite counters, stone fireplace, dining area, living room, and balcony or patio. Added features include a giant outdoor hot tub, a covered barbecue area, and incredible views onto Mount Rundle.

901 Hidden Ridge Way, Banff, AB T1L 1H8. ⓒ **800/661-1372** or 403/762-3544. www.bestofbanff.com/hrr. 94 units. C$219–C$229 (US$175–US$183) double. AE, MC, V. Free parking. **Amenities:** Hot tub; barbecue. *In room:* TV, kitchen, coffeemaker, hair dryer.

Moderate

Banff Inn

One of the newer accommodations in Banff, the Banff Inn is a very handsome, mountain-lodgelike structure. Like most of the other hotels along the Banff Avenue strip, the illusion of the lodge ends at the lobby—rooms are comfortable, nicely furnished, and identical to corporate hotel rooms across North America, except that some units have private balconies and fireplaces. Facilities include a breakfast-only coffee shop and heated underground parking. The Banff Inn is located about a mile from downtown. The inexpensive Banff Bus has a stop right outside the hotel, with frequent transport to the city center.

501 Banff Ave. (P.O. Box 1018), Banff, AB T1L 1A9. ⓒ **800/667-1464** or 403/762-8844. Fax 403/762-4418. www. banffinn.com. 99 units. C$159–C$209 (US$127–US$167) double. Extra person C$15 (US$12). Children under 13 stay free in parent's room. Early-bird specials available. AE, MC, V. Free parking. **Amenities:** Breakfast room; Jacuzzi; sauna. *In room:* A/C, TV, hair dryer.

Blue Mountain Lodge   This rambling place east of downtown began its life in 1908 as a boardinghouse. As you may expect in an older building constructed at the edge of the wilderness, the bedrooms were never exactly palatial to begin with—and when the rooms were redesigned to include private bathrooms, they got even smaller. That's the bad news. The good news is that the lodge is full of charm and funny nooks and crannies. Those small rooms just mean that you'll be spending time with new friends in the lounge and common kitchen. Breakfast is served buffet-style, or you can cook up some eggs on your own. Many guests here are avid outdoorsy types, making this a great place to stay if you're on your own and would appreciate meeting other people to hike with. Sound familiar? The owner admits that guests refer to the Blue Mountain Lodge as an upscale hostel, and it's an accurate characterization. Whatever you call it, it's one of the least expensive and friendliest places to stay in central Banff. The staff is young, friendly, and eager to help you get out on the trails.

137 Muskrat St. (Box 2763), Banff, AB T1L 1C4. © **403/762-5134.** Fax 403/762-8081. www.bluemtnlodge.com. 10 units. From C$99–C$149 (US$79–C$119) double. Extra person C$10 (US$8). Rates include continental breakfast and afternoon hot beverages and homemade cookies. Extended-stay discounts available. MC, V. Free off-street parking. *In room:* TV.

Homestead Inn *(Value)*   One of the best lodging deals in Banff is the Homestead Inn, only a block from all the action on Banff Avenue. Though the amenities are modest compared to upscale alternatives, the rooms are tastefully furnished and equipped with armchairs and stylish bathrooms. Factor in the free downtown parking and this well-maintained older motel seems all the more enticing.

217 Lynx St., Banff, AB T1L 1A7. © **800/661-1021** or 403/762-4471. Fax 403/762-8877. www.homesteadinn banff.com. 27 units. C$139 (US$111) double. Extra person C$10 (US$8). Children under 12 stay free in parent's room. AE, MC, V. Free parking. **Amenities:** Family restaurant. *In room:* TV, hair dryer.

King Edward Hotel *(Value)*   Youthful travelers—and others who don't mind the bustle (read, *noise*)—will like the newly remodeled King Edward, one of Banff's originals, dating from 1904. The accommodations are basic but clean and comfortable; all rooms have private bathrooms. Best of all is the location, in the heart of town.

137 Banff Ave., Banff, AB T1L 1A5. © **800/344-4232** or 403/762-2202. Fax 403/762-0876. 21 units. C$129 (US$103) double. AE, MC, V. Limited free parking. **Amenities:** Restaurant; bar. *In room:* TV, coffeemaker, hair dryer.

Mountain Home Bed & Breakfast ☆   If you're looking for a bit of historic charm coupled with modern comforts, this excellent B&B may be it. It was originally built as a tourist lodge in the 1940s, and then served as a private home for years before being restored and turned back into a guesthouse. The present decor manages to be evocative without being too fussy. The bedrooms are airy and nicely furnished with quality furniture and antiques; all have an en-suite bathroom and telephone. Especially nice is the cozy Rundle Room, with its own slate fireplace. Breakfast is a full cooked meal with homemade baked goods. Downtown Banff is just a 2-minute walk away.

129 Muskrat St. (P.O. Box 272), Banff, AB T1L 01A4. © **403/762-3889.** Fax 403/762-3254. www.mountainhome bb.com. 3 units. C$135–C$165 (US$108–US$132) double. Extra person C$20 (US$16). Rates include full breakfast. MC, V. Free parking. *In room:* TV/VCR w/pay movies, dataport, hair dryer, iron, wireless Internet access.

Pension Tannenhof *(Value)*   This rambling historic home in a quiet neighborhood and just an 8-minute stroll from downtown has a curious story. Built during World

War II, when no new construction was allowed, the owner "remodeled" by building around the two preexisting cabins, eventually tearing them down from the inside. Most rooms are quite large and simply furnished. In a separate chalet at the back of the inn are two king suites, each with a fireplace and jetted tub. Pension Tannenhof is an excellent value and a good place to stay if you want clean, unfussy accommodations.

121 Cave Ave. (P.O. Box 1914), Banff, AB T1L 1B7. © **877/999-5011** or 403/762-4636. Fax 403/762-5660. www. pensiontannenhof.com. 10 units. C$95–C$165 (US$76–US$132) double. Extra person C$20 (US$16). Rates include full breakfast. AE, MC, V. Free parking. **Amenities:** Jacuzzi; sauna; coin-op laundry; use of "the world's oldest barbecue"—made of dinosaur bones. *In room:* TV.

Red Carpet Inn *Value*   A handsome brick building with a balcony along the top floors, the Red Carpet Inn is located on the long, main street leading to downtown. Well maintained and more than adequately furnished, this is one of the best deals in Banff. Guest rooms are furnished with easy chairs and desks. There's an excellent restaurant just right next door. The entire facility is shipshape and very clean—just the thing if you don't want to spend a fortune.

425 Banff Ave., Banff, AB T1L 1B6. © **800/563-4609** or 403/762-4184. Fax 403/762-4894. 52 units. C$99–C$150 (US$79–US$120) double. AE, MC, V. Free parking. **Amenities:** Jacuzzi in winter only. *In room:* A/C, TV, dataport, fridge, coffeemaker, hair dryer, iron.

Rocky Mountain B&B *Kids*   A former boardinghouse converted into a B&B, this pleasant and rambling inn offers comfortable, clean, and cozy rooms and a location just a few minutes from downtown. Accommodations have a mix of private and shared bathrooms. Four units have kitchenettes. Families are welcome.

223 Otter St. (Box 2528), Banff, AB T1L 1C3. ©/fax **403/762-4811**. www.rockymtnbb.com. 10 units. From C$95 (US$76) double. Extra person C$15 (US$12). Rates include breakfast. MC, V. Free parking. Closed Dec 1–Apr 30. *In room:* TV.

Inexpensive

Banff Y Mountain Lodge (YWCA) *Value*   The YWCA is a bright, modern building with good amenities, just across the Bow River bridge from downtown. The Y welcomes both genders—singles, couples, and family groups—with accommodations in private or dorm rooms. Some units have private bathrooms.

102 Spray Ave. (P.O. Box 520), Banff, AB T1L 1A6. © **800/813-4138** or 403/760-3207. Fax 403/760-3202. www.ymountainlodge.com. 80 beds, 43 private rooms. C$32–C$37 (US$27–US$30) bunk in dorm room (sleeping bag required); C$63–C$125 (US$50–US$100) double. MC, V. Free parking. **Amenities:** Restaurant; coin-op laundry; Internet terminal; common room w/TV; lockers.

HI-Banff Alpine Centre   With a mix of two-, four-, and six-bed rooms, this hostel is the most pleasant budget lodging in Banff. Couple and family rooms are available. Facilities include a recreation room, kitchen, laundry, and lounge with fireplace. Meals are available at the Cougar Pete's Kitchen and Lookout; there's also an on-site pub. Reserve at least a month in advance for summer stays.

On Tunnel Mountain Rd., 1.6km (1 mile) west of Banff (P.O. Box 1358), Banff, AB T1L 1B3. © **866/762-4122** or 403/760-7580. Fax 403/762-3441. www.hihostels.ca. 216 beds. C$29 (US$23) members; C$33 (US$26) nonmembers. Private rooms available. MC, V. Free parking. **Amenities:** Restaurant; access to health club across the street; bike rental; activities desk; coin-op laundry. *In room:* No phone.

WHERE TO DINE

Food is generally good in Banff, although you pay handsomely for what you get. The difference in price between a simply okay meal in an Alpine-theme restaurant and a nice meal in a classy dining room can be quite small. Service is often indifferent, as many restaurant staff members have become used to waiting on the in-and-out-in-a-hurry tour-bus crowds. An abundance of eateries line **Banff Avenue,** and most hotels have at least one dining room. The following recommendations are just the beginning of what's available in a very concentrated area.

Expensive

Buffalo Mountain Lodge ★★ NEW CANADIAN   One of the most pleasing restaurants in Banff, the dining room at the Buffalo Mountain Lodge occupies half of the lodge's soaring, three-story lobby, set in a quiet wooded location just outside town. As satisfying as all this is to the eye and the spirit, the food here is even more notable. The chef brings together the best of regional ingredients—Alberta beef, lamb, pheasant, venison, trout, and B.C. salmon—and prepares each in a seasonally changing, contemporary style. Fresh herbs come from the lodge's gardens. The fireplace-dominated bar is a lovely place for an intimate cocktail.

1.5km (1 mile) west of Banff on Tunnel Mountain Rd. ☎ **403/762-2400.** www.buffalomountainlodge.com. Reservations recommended on weekends. Main courses C$19–C$39 (US$15–US$31). AE, DC, MC, V. Daily 6–10pm.

Fuze Finer Dining ★ INTERNATIONAL   This new and welcome addition to the Banff dining scene brings together bold flavors and sophisticated preparations. While "fuze" suggestions fusion cuisine, in fact, most preparations are updates on French cooking, though there are a number of tempting dishes that reflect Indian and Indonesian influences. Start your meal with Masala prawns with mango in a pappadum basket, or a fricassee of escargot and oyster mushrooms. Butter-poached lobster comes with pesto risotto and tomato marmalade, and Alberta beef tenderloin is served with foie gras, oxtails, and truffled Madeira sauce. The dining room is chic and modern; a lighter menu is available in the lounge.

110 Banff Ave. (2nd floor). ☎ **403/760-0853.** www.fuzedining.com. Reservations suggested. Main courses C$24–C$39 (US$19–US$31). AE, MC, V. Daily 11:30am–10pm.

Grizzly House FONDUE   Grizzly House has nothing to do with bears except a rustic log-cabin atmosphere. The specialty here is fondue—from cheese to hot chocolate, and everything in between, including seafood, rattlesnake, frogs' legs, alligator, and buffalo. Steaks and game dishes are the Grizzly's other specialties. The setting is frontier Banff, not the Swiss shtick you may expect from a fondue palace, and the fare excellent.

207 Banff Ave. ☎ **403/762-4055.** Fax 403/762-4359. Reservations appreciated. A la carte fondue for 2 C$30–C$48 (US$24–US$38). AE, MC, V. Daily 11:30am–midnight.

Maple Leaf Grille & Spirits ★★ NEW CANADIAN   This excellent restaurant serves innovative pan-Canadian cuisine. The dining rooms and bar, all wood-paneled with river-rock columns, occupy two stories in the very center of Banff, and are linked by a long open staircase. The menu features regional meats, produce, and fish prepared with a sure and sophisticated hand. Bison stroganoff is exceptionally rich and satisfying, while pan-seared halibut is crusted with lavender and mint. Alberta steaks, elk, and lamb round out the menu.

137 Banff Ave. ☎ **403/760-7680.** Reservations suggested. C$14–C$40 (US$11–US$32). AE, MC, V. Daily 11am–11pm, limited menu until 2am.

Moderate

Balkan Restaurant GREEK   You'll find this airy blue-and-white dining room up a flight of stairs, with windows overlooking the street below. The fare consists of reliable Hellenic favorites, well prepared and served with a flourish; pasta and steaks are available as well. The Greek platter for two consists of a small mountain of beef souvlaki, ribs, moussaka, lamb chops, tomatoes, and salad. If you're dining alone, you can't do better than the *lagos stifado* (rabbit stew) with onions and red wine.

120 Banff Ave. ℂ **403/762-3454.** Reservations recommended. Main courses C$12–C$25 (US$9.60–US$20). AE, MC, V. Daily 11am–11pm.

Coyotes Deli & Grill ✦ SOUTHWEST/MEDITERRANEAN   One of the few places in Banff where you can find lighter, healthier food, Coyote's is an attractive bistrolike restaurant with excellent contemporary southwestern cuisine. There's a broad selection of vegetarian dishes, as well as fresh fish, grilled meats, and multiethnic dishes prepared with an eye to spices and full flavors. There's also a deli, where you can get the makings for a picnic and head to the park. This is a very popular place, so go early or make reservations if you don't want to stand in line.

206 Caribou St. ℂ **403/762-3963.** Reservations recommended. Main courses C$14–C$22 (US$11–US$18). AE, DC, MC, V. Daily 7:30am–11pm.

Giorgio's Trattoria ITALIAN   Giorgio's is a cozy eatery with an Italian country-inn theme. Giorgio's serves authentic old-country specialties at eminently reasonable prices. Entrees range from pizza with smoked salmon, to *osso buco* and Genoa fish stew. Don't miss the *gnocchi alla piemontese* (potato dumplings in meat sauce).

219 Banff Ave. ℂ **403/762-5114.** Reservations accepted for groups of 8 or more. Main courses C$12–C$26 (US$9.60–US$20). MC, V. Daily 5–10pm.

Magpie & Stump Restaurant & Cantina ✦ MEXICAN   The false-fronted Magpie & Stump doesn't really match up architecturally with the rest of smart downtown Banff—and neither does the food and atmosphere, thank goodness. The food here is traditional Mexican and Tex-Mex, done up with style and heft: Someone in the kitchen sure knows how to handle a tortilla. This isn't high cuisine, just well-prepared favorites such as enchiladas, tamales, tacos, and the like. Barbecued ribs and chicken are also delicious. Meals are well-priced for Banff, and you won't leave hungry. The interior looks like a dark and cozy English pub, except for the buffalo heads and cactus plants everywhere—plus a lot of Southwest kitsch. The Cantina is a good place for a lively late-night drink, as the town's young summer waitstaff likes to pack in here to unwind with an after-shift beverage—usually a beer served in a jam jar.

203 Caribou St. ℂ **403/762-4067.** Reservations accepted for groups of 10 or more. Main courses C$8–C$18 (US$6.40–US$14). AE, MC, V. Daily noon–2am.

St. James Gate Irish Pub IRISH   The St. James Gate is owned by Guinness, a company that knows a thing or two about Irish pubs. Newly created to resemble a traditional draft house, this lively pub also offers an extensive menu of bar meals to accompany its selection of beers and ales. Halibut fish and chips are a specialty, as are traditional meat pies and sandwiches. Full meals are available as well. This is a lively place, and, in the Irish tradition, you never know when a table full of dislocated Finnians will break into a heartfelt ballad or two.

207 Wolf St. ℂ **403/762-9355.** Reservations not accepted. Main courses C$10–C$17 (US$8–US$14). MC, V. Food service available Mon–Fri 11am–2pm; Sat–Sun 10am–2pm.

Inexpensive

If you're really on a budget, you'll probably get used to the deli case at **Safeway,** at Martin and Elk streets, as even inexpensive food is costly here. There's also a food court in the basement of **Cascade Plaza Mall,** at Banff and Wolf streets. Another favorite for cheap and quick food is **Evelyn's Coffee Bar,** 201 Banff Ave. (© **403/762-0352**), for great home-baked muffins and rolls. The **Jump Start Coffee and Sandwich Place,** 206 Buffalo St. (© **403/762-0332**), offers sandwiches, soup, salads, pastries, and picnics to go. For all-day and all-night pizza, head to **Aardvark Pizza,** 304a Caribou St. (© **403/762-5500**), open daily to 4am.

Bruno's Cafe and Grill CANADIAN   Named for Bruno Engler, a famed outdoor guide and photographer, Bruno's serves burgers, pizza, wraps, and hearty Canadian-style entrees—all best washed down with locally brewed draft beer. This cozy and casual little joint is open late, a rarity in Banff.

304 Caribou St. © **403/762-8115.** Reservations not accepted. Main courses C$8–C$15 (US$6.40–US$12). MC, V. Daily 7am–1am.

Melissa's Restaurant and Bar CANADIAN   Banff's original hostelries weren't all as grand as the Fairmount Banff Springs. There was also the Homestead Inn, established in the 1910s, with its much-loved restaurant, Melissa's. The original hotel has been replaced with a more modern structure, but the half-timbered cabin that houses Melissa's remains. The food has been updated in the last century, but old-fashioned, traditionally Canadian foods still dominate the menu. Breakfasts are famed, especially the apple hot cakes. Lunch and dinner brings burgers, sandwiches, local trout, and steaks.

218 Lynx St. © **403/762-5511.** Reservations recommended. Main courses C$8–C$25 (US$6.40–US$20). AE, MC, V. Restaurant 7am–9pm daily; bar 11am–2am daily.

BANFF AFTER DARK

Most of Banff's larger hotels and restaurants offer some form of nightly entertainment. However, for a more lively selection, head to downtown's Banff Avenue.

One of the best spots is the legendary **Wild Bill's Saloon,** 203 Banff Ave. (© **403/762-0333**), where you can watch tourists in cowboy hats learning to line dance. Alt-rock bands dominate on Monday and Tuesday evenings; Wednesday to Saturday, it's all country rock, all the time. The venerable **Rose and Crown Pub,** 202 Banff Ave. (© **403/762-2121**), used to be the only place to hear live music in Banff. It's still one of the best. Bands range from Celtic to folk to rock. In summer, sit on the rooftop bar and watch the stars. Popular with foreign tourists, **The Barbary Coast,** 119 Banff Ave. (© **403/762-4616**), is a California-style bar and restaurant that features live music among the potted plants. Bands range from '80s cover bands to light jazz.

It took the ultra-cool cocktail lounge format a while to reach Banff, but here it is: **Aurora,** 110 Banff Ave. (© **403/760-5300**). Dance nightly to DJ-spun rock while sipping something delicious in a martini glass. Banff's most popular dance club, **Outabounds,** 137 Banff Ave. (© **403/762-8434**), is in the basement of the old King Eddy Hotel. DJs spin the tunes while young white-water guides chat and dance with impressionable young tourists. Thursday night is ladies night.

LAKE LOUISE ✷✷✷

Deep-green Lake Louise, 56km (35 miles) northwest of Banff and surrounded by snowcapped mountains, is one of the most famed beauty spots in a park renowned for its scenery. Lake Louise, in the valley below, boasts the largest ski area in Canada and easy hiking access to the remote high country along the Continental Divide.

The lake and the skiing may be spectacular, but probably as many people wind up the road to Lake Louise to see its most famous resort, the Chateau Lake Louise (p. 377). Built by the Canadian Pacific Railroad, the Chateau is, along with the Fairmount Banff Springs (p. 377), one of the most celebrated hotels in Canada.

The reason Lake Louise looks so green is that sunlight refracts off minerals in the glacial runoff, creating vivid colors. You'll want to at least stroll around the shore and gawk at the glaciers and the massive Chateau. The gentle **Lakeshore Trail** follows the northern shore to the end of Lake Louise. For more exercise and even better views, continue on the trail as it begins to climb. Now called the **Plain of Six Glaciers Trail** ✷, it passes a teahouse 5km (3 miles) from the Chateau, and is open in summer only, on its way to a tremendous viewpoint over Victoria Glacier and Lake Louise.

SEEING THE SIGHTS

The **Lake Louise Summer Sightseeing Lift** (© **403/522-3555**) offers a 14-minute ride up to 2,088 m (6,850 ft.) on Mt. Whitehorn, midway up the Lake Louise Ski Area. From here, the views of Lake Louise and the mountains along the Continental Divide are magnificent. Hikers can follow one of many trails into alpine meadows, visit the Wildlife Interpretation Centre, or join a free naturalist-led walk to explore the delicate ecosystem. The round-trip costs C$22 (US$18) for adults, C$20 (US$16) for seniors and students, and C$12 (US$9.20) for children ages 6 to 15. The lift operates from mid-May to mid-September. At the base, the Lodge of Ten Peaks offers buffet dining; ride-and-dine packages are available.

To many visitors, **Moraine Lake** ✷✷ is even more beautiful than Lake Louise, its more famous twin. Ten spirelike peaks, each over 3,000m (10,000 ft.) high, rise precipitously from the shores of this tiny gem-blue lake. It's an unforgettable sight, and definitely worth the short 13km (8-mile) drive from Lake Louise. A trail follows the lake's north shore to the mountain cliffs. There's a lodge offering meals. If the panorama looks familiar, you may recognize it from the back of a Canadian $20 bill.

WHERE TO STAY

Lake Louise is an expensive place to spend the night—let's face it: It's costly to run a hotel within view of the Continental Divide. A lesser-priced option is the **Lake Louise Hostel,** on Village Road, Box 115, Lake Louise, Alberta T0L 1E0 (© **866/762-4122** or 403/522-2202; www.hihostels.ca). Jointly owned by Hostelling International and the Alpine Club of Canada, the hostel offers guide-led hikes daily. Linens are included in the rates: C$34/C$38 (US$27/US$30) member/nonmember for dorm rooms, C$99/C$112 (US$79/US$90) for private rooms.

Baker Creek Lodge ✷ Secluded and rustic, Baker Creek Lodge offers log-built lodge, cabin, and chalet accommodations just off the quiet Bow Valley Parkway (Hwy. 1A). This very charming, family-owned resort sits right on the banks of Baker Creek amid firs and pines, and is the perfect destination for families who want their memories of Banff park to be of mountains and woods, not the shops of Banff townsite.

Accommodations range from top-of-the-line one-bedroom Trapper's Cabins with wood-burning fireplace, double Jacuzzi, and a gas barbecue on the porch, to a selection of large chalets and suites that can comfortably sleep six. Call ahead and discuss your needs with the staff, as there are a number of room configurations; all have fireplaces, full or efficiency kitchens, decks, and locally built pine furniture. The Baker Creek Bistro is one of the top places to dine in this part of Alberta.

15km (9 miles) east of Lake Louise on Hwy. 1A, P.O. Box 66, Lake Louise, AB T0L 1E0. ℂ 403/522-3761. Fax 403/522-2270. www.bakercreek.com. 33 units. C$205–C$355 (US$164–US$284) double. Lower off-season rates. AE, MC, V. Free parking. **Amenities:** Restaurant; lounge; gym; steam room; sauna. *In room:* Kitchen, coffeemaker, fireplace, no phone.

Deer Lodge   The Chateau Lake Louise isn't the only historic lodge at the lake. Built in the 1920s, the original Deer Lodge was a teahouse for the early mountaineers who came to the area to hike (the original tearoom is now the Mount Fairview Dining Room and bar, offering Northwest cuisine). Although Lake Louise itself is a 3-minute stroll away, the charming Deer Lodge features a sense of privacy and solitude that the busy Chateau can't offer. Choose from three eras of rooms: small, basic rooms in the original lodge; larger rooms in the newer Tower Wing; and Heritage Rooms, the largest rooms in the newest wing. All are unfussy and comfortable, though it's the handsome common rooms, particularly the bar and the log-and-stone sitting room, that will create memories.

109 Lake Louise Dr., Lake Louise (P.O. Box 1598), Banff, AB T0L 0C0. ℂ 800/661-1595 or 403/522-3747. Fax 403/522-4222. www.deerlodgelakelouise.com. 73 units. C$150–C$220 (US$120–US$176) double. AE, MC, V. Free parking. **Amenities:** Restaurant; lounge; rooftop Jacuzzi; sauna; coin-op laundry; dry cleaning. *In room:* TV.

The Fairmont Chateau Lake Louise 🎔🎔🎔   The Chateau Lake Louise is one of the best-loved hotels in North America—and one of the most expensive. If you want to splurge on only one place in the Canadian Rockies, make it this one—you won't be sorry. This massive, formal structure is blue-roofed and turreted, furnished with Edwardian sumptuousness and alpine charm. Built in stages over the course of a century by the Canadian Pacific Railroad, the entire hotel was remodeled and upgraded in 1990, and now stays open year-round. The cavernous grand lobby, with its curious figurative chandeliers, gives way to a sitting room filled with overstuffed chairs and couches; these and other common areas overlook the Chateau's gardens and the deep blue-green lake in its glacier-hung cirque. The guest rooms' marble-tiled bathrooms, crystal barware, and comfy down duvets are indicative of the attention to detail and luxury you can expect here. The Chateau can sometimes feel like Grand Central Station—so many guests and so many visitors crowding into the hotel. But the guest rooms are truly sumptuous and the service highly professional. New construction in 2003 added a conference center and additional guest rooms to the Chateau.

Lake Louise, AB T0L 1E0. ℂ 800/441-1414 or 403/522-3511. Fax 403/522-3834. www.fairmont.com. 513 units. High season C$569–C$670 (US$455–US$536) double. Rates vary depending on whether you want a view of the lake or mountains. Off-season rates and packages available. Children under 17 stay free in parent's room. AE, DC, DISC, MC, V. Parking C$18 (US$14) per day. **Amenities:** 9 restaurants in high season, including the exquisite Edelweiss Room and the jolly Walliser Stube Wine Bar (see "Where to Dine," below); 2 bars; indoor pool; health club; exercise room; Jacuzzi; sauna; bike and canoe rental; concierge; tour desk; business center; shopping arcade; salon; 24-hr. room service; massage; babysitting; laundry service; same-day dry cleaning; concierge-level rooms. *In room:* A/C, TV, dataport, minibar, coffeemaker, hair dryer, iron.

Lake Louise Inn   The Lake Louise Inn stands in a wooded 3-hectare (8-acre) estate at the base of the moraine, 7 driving minutes from the fabled lake. You'll stay in a room with forest all around and snowcapped mountains peering over the trees outside your window. The inn consists of five different buildings—a central lodge with pool, whirlpool, steam room, restaurant, bar, and lounge, and four additional lodging units. There are five different room types, starting with standard units with double beds. The superior queen and executive rooms in Building Five are the newest and nicest, with pine-railed balconies and sitting areas. For families, the superior lofts are capable of sleeping up to eight, with two separate bedrooms, two bathrooms, full kitchen, living room, fireplace, and a fold-out couch—just the ticket for a big group.

210 Village Rd. (P.O. Box 209), Lake Louise, AB T0L 1E0. ✆ **800/661-9237** or 403/522-3791. Fax 403/522-2018. www.lakelouiseinn.com. 232 units. High season C$159–C$261 (US$127–US$208) double. AE, DC, MC, V. Free parking. **Amenities:** Restaurant; bar; pool; Jacuzzi; sauna; business center; coin-op laundry. *In room:* TV, dataport, fridge, coffeemaker, hair dryer, microwave.

Moraine Lake Lodge   The only lodging at beautiful Moraine Lake is this handsome lakeside lodge. The original building houses eight basic rooms, each with two double beds. In the newer Wenkchemna Wing are six rooms with queen-size beds and fireplaces. The cabins contain either one king-size or two twin beds, plus a sunken seating area with fireplace. One suite is available as well, with a fireplace, Jacuzzi, king-size bed, and views over the lake. All accommodations are simply but nicely furnished with pine furniture. The dining room is open for three meals daily and serves excellent Northwest cuisine. Room rates include continental breakfast, afternoon tea, use of canoes, and naturalist presentations and hikes.

13km (8 miles) south of Lake Louise at Moraine Lake (Box 70), Banff, AB T0L 0C0. ✆ **403/522-3733.** Fax 403/522-3719. www.morainelake.com. 33 units. C$415–C$460 (US$332–US$368) double; C$540 (US$432) suite; C$535 (US$428) cabin. AE, MC, V. Free parking. **Amenities:** 2 restaurants; bar; canoe rental; concierge. *In room:* Hair dryer, no phone.

Post Hotel 🥇🥇🥇   Discreetly elegant and beautifully furnished, this wonderful log hotel with a distinctive red roof began its life in 1942 as a humble ski lodge. Between 1988 and 1993, new owners completely rebuilt the old lodge, transforming it into one of the most luxurious getaways in the Canadian Rockies; in fact, the Post Hotel is one of only a few properties in western Canada that has been admitted into the French network, Relais & Châteaux. The entire lodge is built of traditional log-and-beam construction, preserving the rustic flavor of the old structure and its mountain setting. The public rooms are lovely, from the renowned dining room (preserved intact from the original hotel) to the arched, two-story, wood-paneled library (complete with rolling track ladders and river-stone fireplace). New in 2005 is the full service "Temple Mountain Spa" with eight treatment rooms, his and hers steam rooms and plunge pools, a beautiful lounging area with fireplace, a rundle-stone "water wall," and a new state-of-the-art fitness area.

Accommodations throughout are beautifully furnished with rustic pine pieces and rich upholstery. Most units have stone fireplaces, balconies, and whirlpool tubs. Due to the rambling nature of the property, there are a bewildering 14 different layouts available. Families will like the "N" rooms, as each has a separate bedroom with queen-size bed, a loft with queen-size and twin beds, a fireplace, and balconies. The "F" units are fantastic, featuring a huge tiled bathroom with both shower and Jacuzzi, a separate bedroom, a large balcony, and a sitting area with couch, river-stone fireplace, and daybed. Amenities include a notably attractive glass-encased pool facility. Hospitality and service here are top-notch.

P.O. Box 69, Lake Louise, AB T0L 1E0. ℂ 800/661-1586 or 403/522-3989. Fax 403/522-3966. www.posthotel.com. 98 units. High season C$305–C$630 (US$244–US$504) double; C$520 (US$416) suite; C$360–C$650 (US$288–US$520) cabin. AE, MC, V. Free parking. Closed Nov. **Amenities:** Restaurant (see "Where to Dine," below); 2 bars; indoor pool; Jacuzzi; sauna; massage; babysitting; laundry service; dry cleaning. *In room:* TV/VCR, dataport, hair dryer, iron, safe.

WHERE TO DINE

Baker Creek Bistro 🐾🐾 NEW CANADIAN   Just 9 miles east of Lake Louise on Highway 1A (the Bow Valley Pkwy.), and thankfully far from its crowds, the charming log-lodge Baker Creek Bistro is a real find—excellent regional cuisine in a quiet sylvan setting. Although the atmosphere is rustic, the food is uptown: Salmon and sesame cannoli come with cucumber salsa, and turducken breast is stuffed with pine nuts. An ale-brined pork loin is served with tangy pear jus. Desserts are noteworthy.

15km (9 miles) east of Lake Louise on Hwy. 1A (P.O. Box 66). ℂ 403/522-2182. Reservations suggested. Main courses C$25–C$31 (US$20–US$25). MC, V. Daily 8–2pm and 5–10pm.

Lake Louise Station STEAKS/SEAFOOD   This handsome and historic log building served as the Lake Louise train station for nearly a century, before rail service ceased in the 1980s. Guests now dine in the old waiting room, or enjoy a quiet drink in the old ticketing lobby. Two dining cars sit on the sidings beside the station and are open for fine dining in the evening. The most popular dish is rib-eye steak with whiskey and green peppercorn sauce, though fresh tuna loin with warm pineapple and coconut sauce provides a delicious change of pace.

200 Sentinel Rd. ℂ 403/522-2600. Reservations recommended on weekends. Main courses C$15–C$36 (US$12–US$29). AE, MC, V. Daily 11:30am–4:40pm and 5–9:30pm.

Post Hotel Dining Room 🐾🐾🐾 INTERNATIONAL   Let's face it: Your trip through the Canadian Rockies is costing you a lot more than you planned. But don't start economizing on food just yet because the Post Hotel offers some of the finest dining in western Canada. The food was famous long before the rebuilding and renovation of the old hotel, but in recent years, the restaurant has maintained such a degree of excellence that it has won the highly prized endorsement of the French Relais & Châteaux organization; the 1,800-bottle wine list received the "Grand Award" from *Wine Spectator,* one of only four Canadian restaurants to win such an honor. Guests dine in a long, rustic room with wood beams and windows looking out onto glaciered peaks. The menu focuses on full-flavored meat and fish preparations. For an appetizer, you might try Pacific marlin carpaccio with heirloom tomato tartar and three mustard sauces, or buffalo strip loin with blackberry maple-syrup butter and corn fritters. Desserts are equally imaginative, and service is excellent. With 30,000 bottles in the wine cellar, some good values are even discreetly hidden in the (mostly French) selection.

In the Post Hotel, Lake Louise. ℂ 403/522-3989. www.posthotel.com. Reservations required. Main courses C$30–C$42 (US$24–US$34). AE, MC, V. Daily 7–11am, 11:30am–2pm, and 5–10pm.

Walliser Stube Wine Bar 🐾 SWISS   While the Chateau Lake Louise operates four major restaurants, including the formal Edelweiss Room, the most fun and relaxing place to eat is the Walliser Stube, a small dining room that serves excellent Swiss-style food and some of the best fondue ever. The back dining room is called the Library, and is indeed lined with tall and imposing wood cases and rolling library ladders. Happily, the cases are filled with wine, not books. A meal in the Walliser Stube is an evening's worth of eating and drinking, as the best foods—a variety of fondues and raclettes—make for convivial and communal dining experiences. The cheese fondue, C$35 (US$17) for two, is fabulous; forget the stringy glutinous experience you had in the 1970s and give it another chance. Raclettes are another communal operation, involving heat lamps that melt chunks of cheese until bubbly; the aromatic, molten result is spread on bread. It's all great fun in a great atmosphere—go with friends and have a blast.

In Chateau Lake Louise. ☎ 403/522-1817. Reservations required. Main courses C$18–C$36 (US$14–US$29); fondues for 2 C$35–C$48 (US$28–US$38). AE, DISC, MC, V. Daily 5–11:30pm.

THE ICEFIELDS PARKWAY ✶✶✶

Between Lake Louise and Jasper winds one of the most spectacular mountain roads in the world. Called the Icefields Parkway, the road climbs through three deep river valleys, beneath soaring, glacier-notched mountains, and past dozens of hornlike peaks shrouded with permanent snowfields. Capping this 287km (178-mile) route is the **Columbia Icefields,** a massive dome of glacial ice and snow straddling the top of the continent. From this mighty cache of ice—the largest nonpolar ice cap in the world—flow the Columbia, the Athabasca, and the North Saskatchewan rivers.

Although you can drive the Icefields Parkway in 3 hours, plan to take enough time to stop at eerily green lakes, hike to a waterfall, and take an excursion up onto the Columbia Icefields. There's also a good chance that you'll see wildlife: ambling bighorn sheep, mountain goats, elks with huge shovel antlers, and mama bears with cubs—all guaranteed to halt traffic and set cameras clicking.

After Lake Louise, the highway divides: Highway 1 continues west toward Golden, British Columbia, while Highway 93 (the Icefields Pkwy.) continues north along the Bow River. **Bow Lake,** the river's source, glimmers below enormous **Crowfoot Glacier;** when the glacier was named, a third "toe" was more in evidence, lending a resemblance to a bird's claw. **Num-Ti-Jah Lodge,** on the shores of Bow Lake, is a good place to stop for lunch and to take some photographs; this venerable lodge also offers accommodations in traditional guest rooms.

The road mounts Bow Summit and drops into the North Saskatchewan River drainage. Stop at the **Peyto Lake Viewpoint** and hike up a short but steep trail to glimpse this startling blue-green body of water.

The parkway then begins to climb up in earnest toward the Sunwapta Pass. Here, in the shadows of 3,490m (11,450-ft.) **Mount Athabasca,** the icy tendrils of the **Columbia Icefields** come into view. However impressive these glaciers may seem from the road, they're nothing compared to the massive amounts of centuries-old ice and snow hidden by mountain peaks; the Columbia Icefields cover nearly 518 sq. km (200 sq. miles) and are more than 760m (2,500 ft.) thick. From the parkway, the closest fingers of the ice field are **Athabasca Glacier,** which fills the horizon to the west of the **Columbia Icefields Centre** (☎ 780/852-7032), a recently rebuilt lodge with a restaurant open from 8am to 10pm and double rooms starting at C$215 (US$172). The **Icefields Information Centre** (☎ 780/852-7030), a park service office that answers questions about the area, stands beside the lodge. It's open May 1 to June 14, daily from 9am to 5pm; June 15 to September 7, daily from 9am to 6pm; and September 8 to October 15, daily from 9am to 5pm. It is closed October 15 to May 1.

From the **Brewster Snocoach Tours** ticket office (© **403/762-6735**), specially designed buses take visitors out onto the glacier. The 90-minute excursion includes a chance to hike the surface of Athabasca Glacier. The Snocoach Tour is C$32 (US$26) for adults and C$16 (US$13) for children. If you don't have the time for the tour, you can drive to the toe of the glacier and walk up onto its surface. Use extreme caution when on the glacier; accidents can result in broken limbs or even death.

From the Columbia Icefields, the parkway descends steeply into the Athabasca River drainage. From the parking area for **Sunwapta Falls,** travelers can choose to crowd around the chain-link fence and peer at this turbulent falls, or take the half-hour hike to equally impressive but less crowded Lower Sunwapta Falls. **Athabasca Falls,** farther north along the parkway, is another must-see. Here, the wide and powerful Athabasca River constricts into a roaring torrent before dropping 25m (82 ft.) into a narrow canyon. The parkway continues along the Athabasca River, through a landscape of meadows and lakes, before entering the Jasper Townsite.

WHERE TO STAY

Facilities are few along the parkway. Hikers and bikers will be pleased to know that there are **rustic hostels** at Mosquito Creek, Rampart Creek, Hilda Creek, Beauty Creek, Athabasca Falls, and Mount Edith Cavell. Reservations for all Icefields Parkway hostels can be made by calling © **866/762-4122.** A shuttle runs between the Calgary International Hostel and hostels in Banff, Lake Louise, and along the Icefields Parkway to Jasper. You must have reservations at the destination hostel to use the service. Call © **403/283-5551** for more information.

Num-Ti-Jah Lodge   Many Rocky Mountain hotels are newly constructed to look vintage—however, Num-Ti-Jah Lodge is the real thing. Sitting on the edge of Bow Lake, with a view of glaciers and soaring peaks to rival that at Lake Louise, this beloved lodge with the bright red roof had its beginnings when pioneering outfitter Jimmy Simpson stood on this site in 1898 and vowed one day to "build a shack here." Over the next 50 years, Simpson and his family did just that, though the handsome log and stone lodge now presiding over this astonishing vista is quite a bit more than a shack. Num-Ti-Jah Lodge (from the First Nation word for pine marten) breathes frontier tradition, with its huge stone fireplaces, stuffed moose heads and antlers on the log walls, and cozy library and lounge areas amply supplied with comfy chairs and couches. Num-Ti-Jah is best for those who appreciate the heritage of a traditional lodge: some will be charmed, others will consider this roughing it. Don't expect upscale guest rooms; though they are clean and nicely furnished, they are authentic to the period in which they were built. All but five rooms have private bathrooms. The dining room is a wonderful spot for lunch, and three-course dinners are available for C$50 (US$40) in addition to a la carte dining.

40km (25 miles) north of Lake Louise on Hwy. 93, P.O. Box 39, Lake Louise, AB T0L 1E0. © **403/522-2167.** Fax 403/522-2425. www.num-ti-jah.com. 25 units. C$195–C$300 (US$156–US$240) double. Extra person C$15 (US$12). Free parking. Closed mid-Oct to early Dec. **Amenities:** Restaurant; lounge with pool table; gift shop. *In room:* No phone.

4 Jasper National Park

Jasper Townsite: 287km (178 miles) NW of Banff

Jasper, now Canada's largest mountain park, was established in 1907, although it already boasted a "guesthouse" of sorts in the 1840s. A visiting painter described it as "composed of two rooms of about 14 and 15 feet square. One of them is used by all comers and goers, Indians, voyageurs and traders, men, women, and children being huddled together indiscriminately, the other room being devoted to the exclusive occupation of Colin Fraser (postmaster) and his family."

Things have changed. Slightly less busy than Banff to the south, Jasper National Park attracts a much more outdoors-oriented crowd, with hiking, biking, climbing, horseback riding, and rafting the main activities. Sure, there's shopping and fine dining in Jasper, but it's not the focus of activity as it is in Banff. Travelers seem a bit more determined and rugged-looking, as if they've just stumbled in from a long-distance hiking trail or off the face of a rock.

For more information on the park, contact **Jasper National Park,** P.O. Box 10, Jasper, AB T0E 1E0 (© **780/852-6176;** www.pc.gc.ca).

OUTDOOR PURSUITS IN THE PARK

The **Jasper Adventure Centre,** 604 Connaught Dr. (© **800/565-7547** in western Canada, or 780/852-5595; www.jasperadventurecentre.com), is a clearinghouse of local outfitters and guides. White-water rafting and canoeing trips, horseback rides, guided hikes, and other activities can be arranged out of this office, which is open June 1 to October 1 daily from 9am to 9pm.

A number of shops rent most of the equipment you'll need. Mountain bikes, canoes and rafts, tents, fishing gear, and skis are available for rent from **On-Line Sport and Tackle,** 600 Patricia St. (© **780/852-3630**), which can also set you up on guided rafting and fishing trips. Snowboards, cross-country ski equipment, and more bikes are available from **Freewheel Cycle,** 618 Patricia St. (© **780/852-3898**).

FISHING   Currie's Guiding (© **780/852-5650;** www.curriesguidingjasper.com) conducts fishing trips to beautiful Maligne Lake; the cost is C$149 (US$119) per person (minimum of two persons) for an 8-hour day. Tackle, bait, boat, and lunch are included. Ask about special single and group rates. Patricia and Pyramid lakes, north of Jasper, are more convenient to Jasper-based anglers who fancy trying their luck at trout fishing.

GOLF   The 18-hole course at Jasper Park Lodge ☆ (© **780/852-6090**), east of Jasper Townsite, is one of the most popular and challenging courses in the Rockies, with 73 sand traps and other, more natural hazards—such as visiting wildlife. *Score Magazine* ranked this the best golf course in Alberta.

**HIKING   Overnight and long-distance hikers will find an abundance of backcountry trails around Jasper, reaching into some of the most spectacular scenery in the Canadian Rockies. Day hikers have fewer, but still good, choices.

The complex of trails around **Maligne Canyon** ☆ makes a good choice for a group, as there are a number of access points (across six different footbridges). The less keen can make the loop back and meet fellow hikers (after getting the car) farther down the canyon. Trails ring parklike Beauvert and Annette lakes (the latter is

Jasper Townsite & Jasper National Park

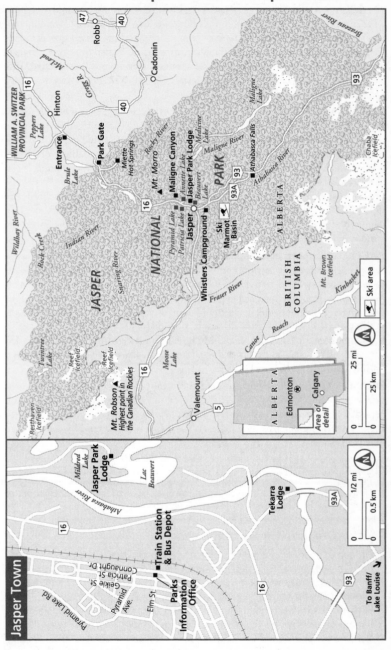

Jasper Town

Mildred Lake

Jasper Park Lodge

Lac Beauvert

Athabasca River

16

1/2 mi

0.5 km

93A

Tekarra Lodge

Train Station & Bus Depot

Parks Information Office

Connaught Dr.

Patricia St.

Geikie St.

Pyramid Ave.

Elm St.

Pyramid Lake Rd.

16

93

To Banff/ Lake Louise

Robb

47

40

McLeod

Cadomin

Brazeau River

16

WILLIAM A. SWITZER PROVINCIAL PARK

Peppers Lake

Hinton

40

Greg R.

93

Entrance

Park Gate

Miette Hot Springs

Brule Lake

Rocky River

Mt. Morro

Maligne Canyon

Annette Lake

Jasper Park Lodge

Beauvert Lake

Medicine Lake

Maligne Lake

Maligne River

Athabasca Falls

Athabasca River

Chaba Icefield

JASPER

NATIONAL

PARK

93A

93

ALBERTA

16

Pyramid Lake

Patricia Lake

Jasper

Whistlers Campground

Ski Marmot Basin

Wildhay River

Rock Creek

Indian River

Snaring River

BRITISH COLUMBIA

Mt. Brown Icefield

Kinbasket

Twintree Lake

Reef Icefield

Reef Icefield

Moose Lake

Fraser River

Canoe Reach

16

Valemount

5

Resthaven Icefield

Mt. Robson ▲ Highest point in the Canadian Rockies

Ski area

25 mi

25 km

ALBERTA

Edmonton

Calgary

Area of detail

383

wheelchair accessible), both near Jasper Park Lodge. Likewise, Pyramid and Patricia lakes just north of town have loop trails but more of a backcountry atmosphere.

The brochure *Day Hikers' Guide to Jasper National Park* details dozens of hikes throughout the park. It costs C$1 (US80¢) at the visitor center. Several outfitters lead guided hikes; contact **Jasper Park Lodge Mountaineering and Interpretive Hiking** (© 780/852-3301) or **Walk and Talks Jasper** (© 780/852-4945; www.walksntalks. com) for a selection of half- and full-day hikes.

HORSEBACK RIDING   One of the most exhilarating experiences the park can offer is trail riding. Guides take your riding prowess (or lack of it) into account and select trails slow enough to keep you mounted. The horses used are steady, reliable animals not given to sudden antics. For a short ride, call **Pyramid Stables** (© 780/852-7433), which offers 1- to 3-hour trips (C$30–C$75/US$24–US$60) around Pyramid and Patricia lakes.

Long-distance trail rides take you into the backcountry. **Skyline Trail Rides** (© 888/582-7787 or 780/852-4215; www.skylinetrail.com) offers a number of short day trips costing roughly C$35 (US$28) per hour, as well as 3- to 4-day trips to a remote, albeit modernized, lodge. Sleigh rides are offered in winter.

RAFTING   Jasper is the jumping-off point for float and white-water trips down several rivers. A raft trip is a good option for that inevitable drizzly day, as you're going to get wet anyway. The mild rapids (Class II–III) of the Athabasca River make a good introductory trip, with rates starting at C$47 (US$38) adult and C$24 (US$19) children under 13; wilder runs down the Maligne River (Class III) will appeal to those needing something to brag about. Jasper is loaded with rafting outfitters; ask your hotel concierge for assistance, or call **Maligne River Adventures** (© 780/852-3370; www.mra.ab.ca), which offers trips down both rivers, as well as a 3-day wilderness trip on the Kakwa River (Class IV-plus).

SKIING   Jasper's downhill ski area is **Ski Marmot Basin** (© 780/852-3816; www. skimarmot.com), located 19km (12 miles) west of Jasper on Highway 93. Marmot is generally underrated as a ski resort; it doesn't get the crowds of Banff, nor does it get the infamous Chinook winds. The resort has 52 runs and seven lifts, and rarely any lines. Lift tickets start at C$56 (US$45).

JASPER TOWNSITE

Jasper isn't Banff, and to listen to most residents of Jasper, that's just fine with them. Born as a railroad division point, Jasper Townsite lacks its southern neighbor's glitz

---

Tips Organized Tours of the Park

Organized tours of the park's major sites—notably the Athabasca snowfields (C$76/US$61) and a Maligne Lake cruise (C$86/US$69)—are offered by **Brewster** (© 780/852-3332; www.brewster.ca) and **Maligne Tours** (© 780/852-3370; www.malignelake.com). **Beyond the Beaten Path** (© 780/852-5650; www. jasperbeyondthebeatenpath.com) also offers excursions to these popular destinations, as well as trips to Miette Hot Springs (C$50/US$40) and more intimate sightseeing, photography, wildlife-viewing, and picnic options. The company offers a shuttle for hikers and rafting parties.

and slightly precious air of an internationalized alpine fantasyland. Instead, it gives off a lived-in, community-oriented feel that's largely lacking in Banff. The streets are thronged with avid young hikers and mountain bikers rather than the shopping hordes.

However, development is rapidly approaching: New nightclubs, restaurants, and shops geared toward tourists are springing up along Patricia Street, and that sound you hear in the distance is the thunder of tour buses.

ESSENTIALS

GETTING THERE   Jasper is on the Yellowhead Highway System, linking it with Vancouver, Prince George, and Edmonton—and is therefore an important transportation hub. The town is 287km (178 miles) northwest of Banff.

VIA Rail connects Jasper to Vancouver and Edmonton with three trains weekly; the *Skeena* line connects with Prince George and Prince Rupert on the Pacific coast. The train station ((C) **780/852-4102**) is at the town center, along Connaught Street. The train tracks run due north before they start the long easterly sweep that leads to Edmonton. Also headquartered at the train station is the **Greyhound** bus station ((C) **780/852-3926**) and **Brewster Transportation** ((C) **780/852-3332**), which offers express service to Banff, as well as a large number of sightseeing excursions.

VISITOR INFORMATION   For information on the townsite, contact **Jasper Tourism and Commerce,** P.O. Box 98, Jasper, AB T0E 1E0 ((C) **780/852-3858;** www.jaspercanadianrockies.com).

ORIENTATION   Jasper Townsite is much smaller than Banff. The main street, **Connaught Drive,** runs alongside the Canadian National Railway tracks, and is the address of the majority of Jasper's hotels. **Patricia Street,** a block west, is quickly becoming the boutique street, with new shops and cafes springing up. Right in the center of town, surrounded by delightful shady gardens, is the **Parks Information Offices** ((C) **780/852-6146**). The post office is at the corner of Patricia and Elm streets. At the northern end of Connaught and Geike streets, a half kilometer (¼ mile) from downtown, is another complex of hotels.

GETTING AROUND   For a rental car, contact **National,** 607 Connaught Dr. ((C) **780/852-1117**). Call a taxi at (C) **780/852-5558** or 780/852-3600.

EXPLORING THE AREA

Just northeast of Jasper, off the Jasper Park Lodge access road, the Maligne River drops from its high mountain valley to cut an astounding canyon into a steep limestone face on its way to meet the Athabasca River. The chasm of **Maligne Canyon** is up to 46m (151 ft.) deep at points, yet only 3m (10 ft.) across. A sometimes-steep trail follows the canyon down the mountainside, bridging the gorge six times. In summer, a teahouse operates at the top of the canyon.

An incredibly blue mountain lake buttressed by a ring of high-flying peaks, **Maligne Lake** is 45 minutes east of Jasper and is one of the park's great beauty spots. Maligne is the largest glacier-fed lake in the Rockies, and the second largest in the world. Droves of tour buses go to the "hidden lake," and the area is a popular destination for hikers, anglers, trail riders, and rafters. No matter what else they do, most visitors take a boat cruise to **Spirit Island,** at the head of the lake. The 90-minute cruise leaves from below the **Maligne Lake Lodge,** an attractive summer-only facility with a restaurant and bar (but no lodging). Cruise tickets cost C$35 (US$28) for adults, C$29 (US$23) for seniors, and C$18 (US$15) for kids.

Maligne Lake waters are alive with rainbow and eastern brook trout, and the Maligne Lake Boathouse is stocked with licenses, tackle, bait, and boats. Guided **fishing** trips include equipment, lunch, and hotel transportation, with half-day excursions starting at C$195 (US$156). You can rent a boat, canoe, or sea kayak to ply the waters. All facilities at Maligne Lake, including lake cruises, fishing, trail rides, and a white-water raft outfitter that offers trips down three Jasper Park rivers, are operated by **Maligne Tours** (www.malignelake.com). Offices are located at the lake, next to the lodge in Jasper at 626 Connaught Dr. (© **780/852-3370**) and at the Jasper Park Lodge (© **780/852-4779**). Maligne Tours also operates a shuttle bus between Jasper and the lake.

Downstream from Maligne Lake, the Maligne River flows into **Medicine Lake.** This large body of water appears regularly every spring, grows 8km (5 miles) long and 18m (59 ft.) deep, and then vanishes in fall through a system of underground drainage caves, leaving only a dry gravel bed through the winter. According to First Nations belief, spirits were responsible for the lake's annual disappearance, hence the name.

Jasper Tramway   Canada's longest and highest aerial tramway tour starts at the foot of Whistler's Mountain, 6km (3¾ miles) south of Jasper off Highway 93. Each car takes 30 passengers and hoists them 2km (1¼ miles) up to the summit (2,220m/ 7,283 ft.) in a breathtaking sky ride. At the upper terminal, you'll step out into alpine tundra and a wonderful picnic area carpeted with mountain grass. Combo tickets that include meals at the upper terminal's Treeline Restaurant are also available.

Off Hwy. 93, south of Jasper. © 780/852-3093. www.jaspertramway.com. Tickets C$22 (US$18) adults, C$11 (US$8.80) children, C$52 (US$42) family. Lifts operate June 1 to Labour Day daily 8:30am–10pm. Cars depart every 10–15 min. Call for off-season rates. Closed mid-Oct to Apr.

Miette Hot Springs   The hot mineral water pools are only one reason to make the side trip to Miette Hot Springs. The drive is also one of the best wildlife-viewing routes in the park. Watch for elk, deer, coyotes, and moose en route. The springs can be enjoyed in a beautiful swimming pool or in two soaker pools, surrounded by forest and an imposing mountain backdrop. Campgrounds and an attractive lodge with refreshments are nearby.

60k (37 miles) northeast of Jasper off Hwy. 16. © 780/866-3939. Admission C$6.25 (US$5) adults, C$5.25 (US$4.20) children and seniors, C$18 (US$14) family. June 22–Sept 9 daily 8:30am–10:30pm; May 11–June 21 and Sept 10–Oct 8 daily 10:30am–9pm.

SHOPPING

Weather can be unpredictable in Jasper. If it's raining, you can while away an afternoon in the town's shops and boutiques—the town is especially rich in shops for outdoor gear and recreation clothing. In Jasper itself, Patricia Street and Connaught Drive contain most of the high-quality choices. A number of galleries feature Inuit and Native arts and crafts: Check out **Our Native Land,** 601 Patricia St. (© **780/852-5592**). The arcade at the Jasper Park Lodge, called the **Beauvert Promenade,** has a number of excellent clothing and gift shops.

WHERE TO STAY

As in Banff, there's a marked difference in rates between high season and the rest of the year, so if you can avoid the June-to-September crush, you may save up to 50%. All prices listed below are for high season. Call for off-season rates, as they usually follow a complex price structure. Reserve well in advance if possible. If you can't find a room, contact **Rocky Mountain Reservations** (© **877/902-9455** or 780/852-9455; www.rockymountainreservations.com), which offers a free booking service for Jasper accommodations and activities.

If you find the prices too astronomical in Jasper, or just can't find a room, consider staying east of the park near Hinton (see below).

Very Expensive

Chateau Jasper   Chateau Jasper is a refined three-story lodging with some of the best staff and service in town, and the large guest rooms come with all the amenities you'd expect at a four-star property, with prices to match. If anything, the rooms are a tad overdecorated—considering the dramatic views from every window, you don't need the slightly boudoir-y upholstery and wall coverings.

96 Geikie St., Jasper, AB T0E 1E0. © **800/661-9323** or 780/852-5644. Fax 780/852-4860. www.decorehotels.com. 119 units. C$286 (US$228) double; C$418–C$462 (US$334–US$369) suite. AE, DC, DISC, MC, V. Parking C$8 (US$6.40) per day. **Amenities:** Restaurant; bar; indoor pool; Jacuzzi; concierge; limited room service; babysitting; laundry service; same-day dry cleaning. *In room:* A/C, TV, dataport, coffeemaker, hair dryer, safe.

Fairmont Jasper Park Lodge ⟨ℛℛ⟩   Jasper's most exclusive lodging, the Jasper Park Lodge was built by the Canadian Pacific Railroad and has an air of luxury and gentility, but with a more woodsy feel—sort of like an upscale summer camp. The hotel's wooded, elk-inhabited grounds—over 900 acres!—are located along Lac Beauvert, about 8km (5 miles) east of Jasper proper. The central lodge's lofty great room offers huge fireplaces to snuggle by. Accommodations are extremely comfortable, though a bit hard to characterize, as there are a wide variety of cabins, lodge rooms, chalets, and cottages available—all from different eras, all set amid the forest. It's a good idea to call and find out what suits your budget and needs. Groups can opt for one of the wonderful housekeeping cabins, some of which have up to eight bedrooms.

P.O. Box 40, Jasper, AB T0E 1E0. © **800/441-1414** or 780/852-3301. Fax 780/852-5107. www.fairmont.com. 446 units. C$299–C$499 (US$239–US$399) double; from C$469–C$789 (US$375–US$631) lakefront suite; from C$1,756 (US$1,404) cabin. AE, DC, DISC, MC, V. Free parking. **Amenities:** 9 restaurants, including the 4-star Edith Cavell Dining Room and the Moose's Nook Northern Grill (see "Where to Dine," below, for more on the latter); 3 lounges; heated outdoor pool; one of Canada's finest golf courses—Jasper Park Lodge Golf Course; tennis courts; health club; canoe, paddle-boat, and bike rentals; children's center; concierge; tour desk; business center; shopping arcade; 24-hr. room service; babysitting; laundry service; same-day dry cleaning; horseback riding. *In room:* TV w/pay movies, dataport, coffeemaker, hair dryer, iron, complimentary Internet access.

Expensive

Jasper Inn Alpine Resort ⟨ℛ⟩   The Jasper Inn, on the northern end of town but set back off the main road, is one of the nicest lodgings in town. Rooms are available in three different buildings and in many configurations. If you're looking for good value, look past the standard units (which are perfectly nice, mind you); instead, fork over C$13 (US$10) more and reserve a spacious suite with fireplace and kitchen. Even nicer are the rooms in the separate Maligne Suites building, which come with marble-and-granite bathrooms, fireplaces, Jacuzzis, and balconies. Two-bedroom chalet-style rooms can sleep up to seven.

98 Geikie St. (P.O. Box 879), Jasper, AB T0E 1E0. © **800/661-1933** or 780/852-4461. Fax 780/852-5916. www.jasper inn.com. 143 units. C$212–C$218 (US$169–US$174) double; C$225–C$413 (US$180–US$330) suite. Extra person C$15 (US$12). Children 17 and under stay free in parent's room. AE, DC, MC, V. Free parking. **Amenities:** Restaurant; small indoor pool; Jacuzzi; sauna; babysitting; coin-op laundry; laundry service. *In room:* TV, dataport, fridge, hair dryer, microwave.

Lobstick Lodge *Kids*

The Lobstick Lodge—featuring some of the largest standard units in Jasper—is a longtime favorite for the discerning traveler with an eye to value. Even more impressive are the huge kitchen units, which come with a full kitchen, a sitting room with sofa bed and easy chairs, plus a separate bedroom with either two doubles or a king-size bed. As large as most apartments, these kitchen units are perfect for families and go fast—reserve early. King suites are also large and very comfortably furnished. A complete remodel of the hotel was completed in 2003.

96 Geikie St. (P.O. Box 1200), Jasper, AB T0E 1E0. © **888/852-7737** or 780/852-4431. Fax 780/852-4142. www. lobsticklodge.com. 139 units. C$215 (US$172) double; C$229 (US$183) kitchen unit. Children under 15 stay free in parent's room. AE, DC, MC, V. Free parking. **Amenities:** Restaurant; lounge; indoor pool; 3 Jacuzzis; 2 saunas. *In room:* TV, dataport, coffeemaker, hair dryer, iron.

Marmot Lodge *ℱ*

At the northern end of Jasper's main street, the Marmot Lodge offers pleasant rooms in three different buildings. One building contains large kitchen units with fireplaces, living area, and separate bedrooms with two queen-size beds or a king-size bed. These units are deservedly popular with families—ask for units with balconies off the back and you may see elk grazing on the back lawn. The building facing the street offers smaller, less expensive rooms; the third building features very large deluxe units. All are comfortable according to a relaxing, unfussy aesthetic that's restful after a day of sightseeing.

86 Connaught Dr., Jasper, AB T0E 1E0. © **800/661-6521** or 780/852-4471. Fax 780/852-3280. www.marmot lodge.com. 107 units. C$219 (US$175) double; C$235–C$245 (US$188–US$196) kitchen unit. Children under 15 stay free in parent's room. AE, DC, MC, V. Free parking. **Amenities:** Restaurant; lounge; indoor pool; Jacuzzi; sauna. *In room:* TV w/pay movies, coffeemaker, hair dryer.

Sawridge Inn and Conference Centre *ℱℱ*

The three-story lobby of this hotel is large and airy, opening onto a central atrium lit with skylights and filled with tropical plants. The Sawridge is the classiest of all the Jasper Townsite hotels—the entire hotel was renovated in 2003, and offers large and beautifully furnished rooms. Half the rooms (most with one queen-size bed) overlook the junglelike atrium, which also contains the restaurant, lounge, and pool. The other rooms (most with two queen-size beds) overlook the town and offer large private balconies as well. The king-size bed corner suites are truly large, with two balconies and a jetted tub. New at the Sawridge is the European Beauty and Wellness Centre, a day spa with a selection of beauty, aromatherapy, and massage treatments. The Sawridge, on the northern edge of Jasper, is unique in that it's owned by the Sawridge Cree Indian Band.

82 Connaught Dr. (PO Box 2080), Jasper, AB T0E 1E0. © **800/661-6427** or 780/852-5111. Fax 780/852-5942. www.sawridgejasper.com. 153 units. C$235–C$260 (US$188–US$208) double; C$310–C$360 (US$248–US$288) suite. AE, DC, DISC, MC, V. Free parking. **Amenities:** Restaurant; lounge; indoor pool; Jacuzzi; spa; sauna; business center; room service (7am–10pm); massage; coin-op laundry; laundry service. *In room:* A/C, TV w/movie channels, dataport, fridge, coffeemaker, hair dryer, robes.

Moderate

In high season, it seems that nearly half the dwellings in Jasper let rooms, B&B-style; contact **Jasper Home Accommodation Association,** P.O. Box 758, Jasper, AB T0E

1E0 (www.stayinjasper.com), for a full list. B&Bs listed with the local visitor association have little signs in front; if you arrive early enough in the day, you can comb the streets looking for a likely suspect. Note that B&Bs here are much less grand than those in Banff, and less expensive as well. Double-occupancy accommodations are in the C$60 to C$85 (US$48–US$68) range at most homes. You'll need to pay cash for most. There's no central booking agency in Jasper, so contact your host directly.

If you are really just looking for a motel room, Jasper has a few standard motor lodges to accommodate your needs. The **Maligne Lodge,** on the western edge of Jasper at 900 Connaught Dr. (© **800/661-1315** or 780/852-3143), offers an indoor pool, restaurant, lounge, and clean unfussy rooms starting at C$182 (US$146) double.

Athabasca Hotel _Value_   This hotel's lobby is like a hunting lodge, with a stone fireplace and trophy heads of deer and elk. A gray-stone corner building with a homey, old-fashioned air, the Athabasca was built in 1929, and has long served as one of Jasper's principal gathering spots. Each guest room offers a mountain view, although only half have private bathrooms; while rooms are small, the furnishings are simple and tasteful. The place is really quite pleasant—it's the very image of venerable Canadian charm—and one of the few good values in Jasper.

510 Patricia St., Jasper, AB T0E 1E0. © **877/542-8422** or 780/852-3386. Fax 780/852-4955. www.athabascahotel. com. 61 units, 39 with private bathroom. C$129–C$149 (US$103–US$119) double with private bathroom; C$89 (US$71) double with shared bathroom. AE, DC, MC, V. Free parking. **Amenities:** Restaurant; 2 bars; concierge; room service (7am–11pm). _In room:_ TV, dataport, hair dryer.

Austrian Haven   This large home in a quiet residential section of Jasper offers two very comfortable and spacious suites that are essentially full apartments. The large Family suite offers two queen beds, living room, kitchen, and dining area. The Honeymoon Suite is opulently decorated and has a king bed, cozy down duvet, and private sun-room with outstanding views. Both suites have private bathrooms, fridges, microwaves, TVs and VCRs, and private entrances. Continental breakfast is provided to both suites, and they also share a mountain-view deck with barbecue.

812 Patricia St. (Box 1856), Jasper, AB T0E 1E0. © **780/852-4259.** Fax 780/852-4259. www.austrianhaven.ca. 2 units. C$120–C$140 (US$96–US$112) double. Cash and traveler's checks only. Free parking. **Amenities:** Barbecue deck. _In room:_ TV/VCR, fridge, coffeemaker, microwave, toaster.

Becker's Chalets ￼   This attractive log-cabin resort offers a variety of lodging options in freestanding chalets, set in a glade of trees along the Athabasca River. While the resort dates from the 1940s and retains the feel of an old-fashioned mountain retreat, most of the chalets have been built in the last 10 years, and thus are thoroughly modernized. Cabins come in a wide variety of sizes and styles, ranging from one-room cottages to four-bedroom chalets, with everything in between. Most cabins come with river-stone fireplaces and kitchens. My favorite? Ask for a deluxe one-bedroom log chalet (C$225/US$162) and live your log-cabin fantasies. The dining room at Becker's is also one of Jasper's best.

Hwy. 95, 5km (3 miles) south of Jasper (P.O. Box 579), Jasper, AB T0E 1E0. © **780/852-3779.** Fax 780/852-7202. www.beckerschalets.com. 118 chalets. C$145–C$175 (US$116–US$140) 1-bedroom cabin; C$170–C$240 (US$136–US$192) 2-bedroom cabin; C$210–C$380 (US$168–US$304) 3-bedroom cabin. AE, MC, V. Free parking. **Amenities:** Restaurant; babysitting; coin-op laundry; playground. _In room:_ TV, fridge, coffeemaker, hair dryer, no phone.

Tekarra Lodge ☆ Just east of Jasper, this venerable log-cabin resort is situated above the confluence of the Miette and Athabasca rivers. Accommodations are in the lodge or in vintage cabins that can sleep from two to seven people. The log cabins are nicely furnished, but it's the location that really sets Tekarra apart. Just far enough from the bustle of Jasper, off a quiet road in the forest, it offers the kind of charm that you dream of in a classic mountain-cabin resort. One of Jasper's best restaurants is located in the lodge, making this a great place for a family seeking solitude yet access to good food.

1.5km (1 mile) east of Jasper off Hwy. 93A (P.O. Box 669), Jasper, AB T0E 1E0. ℂ **888/962-2522** or 780/852-3058. Fax 780/852-4636. www.maclabhotels.com. 52 units. C$164 (US$132) lodge room; C$174–C$224 (US$139–US$179) cabin double. 2-night minimum for cabins in summer. Extra person C$10 (US$8). Rates for lodge rooms include continental breakfast. AE, DC, MC, V. Free parking. **Amenities:** Restaurant; bar; bike rental; coin-op laundry. *In room:* Kitchen, coffeemaker, hair dryer, no phone.

Inexpensive

Two Hostelling International **hostels,** both reachable at P.O. Box 387, Jasper, AB T0E 1E0 (ℂ **780/852-3215;** www.hihostels.ca), are the best alternatives for the budget traveler. Advance reservations are strongly advised in summer. The 80-bed **Jasper International Hostel,** on Skytram Road, 6km (4 miles) west of Jasper, charges C$22 (US$18) for members and C$27 (US$22) for nonmembers. The closest hostel to Jasper, it's open year-round. Two family rooms, a barbecue area, indoor plumbing, hot showers, and bike rentals are available. In winter, ask about ski packages. The **Maligne Canyon Hostel,** off Maligne Lake Road, 18km (11 miles) east of Jasper, sleeps 24; rates are C$15 (US$12) for members and C$20 (US$16) for nonmembers. This convenient hostel is just above the astonishing Maligne Canyon. Facilities include a self-catering kitchen and dining area.

In & Around Hinton

Just east of the park gate in and near Hinton are a number of options that offer high-quality accommodations at significantly lower prices than you'll find in Jasper. Downtown Jasper is a 30- to 45-minute drive away from the choices listed below.

Hinton has a number of motel complexes with standard, no-nonsense rooms. The **Best Western White Wolf Inn,** 828 Carmichael Lane (ℂ **800/220-7870** in Canada, or 780/865-7777), has 42 air-conditioned rooms, most with kitchenettes. The **Black Bear Inn,** 571 Gregg Ave. (ℂ **888/817-2888** or 780/817-2000), features an exercise room, hot tub, and restaurant. The **Crestwood Hotel,** 678 Carmichael Lane (ℂ **800/ 661-7288** or 780/865-4001), has a pool and restaurant. Doubles at these motels cost between C$95 and C$120 (US$76–US$96).

Mountain Splendour Bed & Breakfast The spacious rooms at this large, modern home are outfitted with private bathrooms, tables and chairs, and English-theme decor. The largest of the three rooms is the English Garden Suite, a comfortable space with a private deck, fireplace, and large bathroom with Jacuzzi, separate shower, and cathedral ceilings. Guests can lounge by the fireplace or watch TV in the light, airy living room, which has picture windows framing a view of Jasper Park.

17 Folding Mountain Village (P.O. Box 6544), Jasper East, AB T7V 1X8. ℂ **780/866-2116.** Fax 780/866-2117. www.mountainsplendour.com. 3 units. C$149–C$174 (US$119–US$139) double. Rates include breakfast. MC, V. Free parking. **Amenities:** Jacuzzi. *In room:* TV, hair dryer, iron.

Moments   A Local Guest Ranch

The venerable **Black Cat Guest Ranch,** 56km (35 miles) northeast of Jasper, P.O. Box 6267, Hinton, AB T7V 1X6 (© **800/859-6840** or 780/865-3084; www.black catguestranch.ca), boasts a superb mountain setting just outside the park boundaries. The rustic lodge, built in 1978, offers 16 unfussy units, each with private bathroom and an unspoiled view of Jasper Park. Rates of C$192 (US$154) double include three family-style meals. Activities include hiking, horseback riding (C$35/US$28 per hour for guided trips), canoe rentals, murder-mystery weekends, and fishing. The ranch staff will meet your train or bus at Hinton.

Overlander Mountain Lodge ⊛   The Overlander is a historic lodge on the edge of Jasper National Park. The original lodge building houses the Stone Peak Restaurant, a handsome dining room, and a bar with tremendous views of the Rockies, plus cozy guest rooms with queen- or twin-size beds. A newer wing features rooms with gas fireplaces and jetted tubs. The four-plex cabins have two double beds and a gas fireplace. Most of the chalets, which are scattered in the forest behind the lodge, contain a fireplace or wood-burning stove, full kitchen, washer/dryer, and patio. Accommodations throughout have private bathrooms and are decorated handsomely and furnished with country flair. The dining room serves notable tasty international and regional cuisine, with specialties of rack of lamb, venison, and fish. The Overlander's staff is friendly and helpful. This property offers excellent value and makes a charming base for exploring the park.

1km (½ mile) from Jasper Park East Gate (Box 6118), Hinton, AB T7V 1X5. © **877/866-2330** or 780/866-2330. Fax 780/866-2332. www.overlandermountainlodge.com. 29 units. C$175–C$195 (US$140–US$156) lodge room; C$155 (US$124) cabin room; C$295 (US$236) 2-bedroom chalet; C$350 (US$280) 3-bedroom chalet. AE, MC, V. Free parking. **Amenities:** Restaurant; lounge; horseback riding; hiking trails. *In room:* Coffeemaker, hair dryer, no phone.

Suite Dreams B&B   A modern, wheelchair-accessible home built as a B&B, Suite Dreams offers large, comfortable rooms with lots of natural light in a quiet, forested setting. Each room is decorated according to a horticultural theme and features art from several generations of the owner's talented family. All units have private bathrooms, and one can sleep up to four. The spacious living room has a fireplace. The backyard features 100 yards of golf greens. The hostess is happy to make specialty breakfasts for guests with dietary restrictions.

Box 6145 (Lot 3134 Maskuta Estates), Hinton, AB T7V 1X5. © **780/865-8855.** Fax 780/865-2199. www.suite dream.com. 3 units. From C$85 (US$68) double. Extra person C$20 (US$16). Rates include full breakfast. MC, V. Free parking. **Amenities:** Golf greens. *In room:* TV/VCR, fridge.

Wyndswept Bed & Breakfast ⊛   This excellent B&B has a hostess who will make you feel like family. The main-floor guest rooms have private bathrooms, robes, hair dryers, handmade soaps, kettles, and other extras. The suite, which gives out onto a deck, measures 110 sq. m (1,200 sq. ft.) and has a full kitchen, large bathroom, and sitting area; it can sleep up to five. Guests have access to a computer and fax machine. Breakfast is delicious and substantial—there's even a dessert course. Chances are good you'll see wildlife while here: Bears, coyotes, wolves, and deer have all been spotted from the deck. The owner will outfit you with a Wyndswept backpack upon arrival that contains books about hiking, wildlife, mosquito spray, band aids, and other incidentals that make your stay more comfortable and interesting.

4km (2½ miles) east of Jasper Park gates (Box 2683), Hinton, AB T7V 1Y2. © **780/866-3950**. Fax 780/866-3951. www.wyndswept.com. 3 units. C$150–C$185 (US$120–US$148) double. Extra person C$35 (US$28). MC, V. Free parking. *In room:* A/C, TV w/movie channels, dataport, coffeemaker, hair dryer, iron.

CAMPING
There are 10 campgrounds in Jasper National Park; prices range from C$14 (US$11) for primitive tenting sites to C$33 (US$26) for full-service RV sites. You need a special permit to camp anywhere in the parks outside the regular campgrounds—a regulation necessary due to fire hazards. Contact the parks information office (© **780/852-6176**) for permits. The campgrounds range from completely unserviced sites to those providing water, power, sewer connections, laundry facilities, gas, and groceries. The closest to Jasper Townsite is the **Whistlers,** up the road toward the gondola, providing a total of some 700 campsites.

WHERE TO DINE
Expensive
Andy's Bistro ⍟ CONTINENTAL/CANADIAN   This resourceful little restaurant's dining room looks like a wine cellar, and indeed the wine list is noteworthy. The food is classic Continental with a sprinkling of New World specialties thrown in for spice. Starters feature baked brie jubilee—with sour cherry sauce—and black olive toast. Main courses range from pork tenderloin Calvados (with sautéed apples) to lamb *osso buco* with pear compote and cornmeal. Though the menu may seem highbrow, the atmosphere is casual and friendly—one communal table for six is saved for first-come, first-served diners.

606 Patricia St. © **780/852-4559**. Reservations recommended. Main courses C$17–C$33 (US$14–US$26). MC, V. Mid-May to mid-Oct daily 5–11pm; mid-Oct to mid-May Tues–Sat 5–11pm.

Becker's Gourmet Restaurant FRENCH/CANADIAN   Although the name's not very elegant, it's highly descriptive. This inventive restaurant serves what could only be termed gourmet food, observing the mandate to serve what's fresh and local without turning the menu into a list of endangered game animals. Samples include lamb chops with a cider-cream sauce, rainbow trout with pumpkin-maple butter, and pork loin with rhubarb chutney. The dining room is an intimate log-and-glass affair that overlooks the Athabasca River.

At Becker's Chalets, Hwy. 93, 5km (3 miles) south of Jasper. © **780/852-3779**. Reservations required. Main courses C$16–C$35 (US$13–US$28). MC, V. Daily 8am–11am and 5:30–10pm.

Fiddle River Seafood ⍟ SEAFOOD   This rustic-looking retreat has panoramic windows facing the Jasper railroad station and the mountains beyond. The specialty here is fresh fish, though a number of pasta dishes and red-meat entrees will complicate your decision-making process. While there are plenty of good selections on the menu, Fiddle River offers as many daily specials (presented at the table on an easel-propped blackboard). At least 8 or 10 fresh fish and seafood specials are featured, including oysters and several preparations of Pacific salmon, such as pan-seared steelhead salmon filet with a honey, lime, and tarragon butter sauce. For "landlubbers," as the menu denotes the non-fish eaters, there are also excellent steaks: A peppered rib-eye is served with blue-cheese demi glace. The wine list is short but interesting.

620 Connaught Dr. (*) 780/852-3032. Reservations required. Main courses C$15–C$32 (US$12–US$26). AE, MC, V. Daily 5pm–midnight.

Moose's Nook Northern Grill *⊕* CANADIAN   This atmospheric restaurant off the great room of the Jasper Park Lodge features "Canadiana" specialties. With equal parts tradition and innovation, the Moose's Nook offers hearty presentations of native meats, fish, and game. Grilled duck breast is served with figs and celery root, and venison loin comes with a sauce of wild mushrooms and leeks. Lighter appetites will enjoy the vegetarian cabbage rolls.

In the Fairmont Jasper Park Lodge, 8km (5 miles) east of Jasper. (*) 780/852-6052. Reservations recommended. Main courses C$24–$40 (US$19–US$32). AE, DISC, MC, V. Daily 6–10pm.

Sorrentino's Bistro Bar ITALIAN   The Canadian Rockies are filled with restaurants that feature steaks and game—chances are that top-quality Italian cuisine will be a real treat after a couple days in Banff and Jasper. Sorrentino's is an outpost of a highly popular Edmonton Italian restaurant chain, and brings excellent pasta, risotto, and grilled meats to the handsome dining room at Chateau Jasper. Angel hair pasta with wild mushrooms and herbs, veal cannelloni, and pork tenderloin with black currants and macadamia nuts are featured entrees.

In the Chateau Jasper, 96 Geike St. (*) 780/852-5644. www.sorrentinos.com. Reservations recommended. Main courses C$14–C$30 (US$11–US$24); Sun brunch C$20 (US$16) adults, C$15 (US$12) seniors and youths. AE, DC, MC, V. Daily 5:30–10:30pm; Sun 10am–2pm.

Tekarra Lodge Restaurant STEAK/INTERNATIONAL   This local favorite offers excellent international cuisine, as well as steaks and other intriguing dishes such as pan-seared chicken with roast grapes and Pacific bouillabaisse. Lighter dishes such as salads and pastas are also available. The charming lodge dining room is one of Jasper's hidden gems; the service is friendly, and the fireplace-dominated room intimate.

Hwy. 93A, 1.6km (1 mile) east of Jasper (call for directions). (*) 780/852-3058. Reservations advised on weekends. Main courses C$18–C$42 (US$14–US$34). AE, DC, MC, V. Daily 5:30–10pm.

Moderate

Denjiro Japanese Restaurant JAPANESE   Denjiro's is a slice of Japan, complete with sushi bar, karaoke lounge, intimate ozashiki booths, shoeless patrons, soft Asian mood music, and service that's both fast and impeccable. The place has a studied simplicity that goes well with the traditional Japanese fare served: sukiyaki, sashimi, tempura, and teriyaki.

410 Connaught Dr. (*) 780/852-3780. Reservations recommended. Most items C$8–C$22 (US$6.40–US$18). AE, MC, V. Mid-May to mid-Oct daily noon–10pm; mid-Oct to mid-May daily 5–10pm.

Jasper Brewing Company BREWPUB   A welcome addition to Jasper's youthful eating and nightlife scene, this new brewpub made its debut on Food Network's *Opening Soon* series. All the attention has made this a very popular place, though the excellent ales and food—upscale pub grub with a Creole twist—are reason enough to make this your home-away-from-home in Jasper.

624 Connaught Dr. (*) 780/852-4111. Reservations accepted. Main courses C$7–C$18 (US$5.60–US$14). MC, V. Daily 11am–11pm.

Something Else INTERNATIONAL/PIZZA Something Else is accurately named: Fold together a good Greek restaurant and a pizza parlor; add a high-quality Canadian-style restaurant; and stir in a Creole bistro. In short, if you're with a group that can't decide where to eat, this is the place to go. Prime Alberta steaks, fiery Louisiana jambalaya and mesquite chicken, Greek saganaki and moussaka, an array of 21 pizzas—no matter what you choose, it's all well prepared and fresh, and the welcome is friendly.

621 Patricia St. ⓒ 780/852-3850. Reservations not needed. Main courses C$12–C$23 (US$9.60–US$18). AE, DC, MC, V. Daily 11am–11pm.

Inexpensive

For muffins, sandwiches, coffee, desserts, soups, and salads, go to **Soft Rock Cafe,** 632 Connaught Dr. (ⓒ 780/852-5850), in the Connaught Square Mall. You can log onto the Internet from one of its computers. Another casual spot is **Spooner's Coffee Bar,** upstairs at 610 Patricia St. (ⓒ 780/852-4046), with a juice bar, coffee drinks, burritos, soups, sandwiches, and other deli items.

Jasper Pizza Place PIZZA One of Jasper's most popular eateries, the redesigned Pizza Place agreeably combines the features of an upscale boutique pizzeria with a traditional Canadian bar. The pizzas are baked in a wood-fired oven, and come in some very unusual—some would say unlikely—combinations. If you're not quite ready for the escargot pizza, then maybe the smoked salmon, caper, and black-olive version will please. Standard-issue pizzas are also available, as are sandwiches and a mammoth helping of lasagna for C$10 (US$8). The bar side of things is lively, with pool tables and a crowd of summer resort workers on display.

402 Connaught Dr. ⓒ 780/852-3225. Reservations not accepted. Pizza C$7–C$13 (US$5.60–US$10). MC, V. Daily 11am–11pm.

JASPER AFTER DARK

Nearly all of Jasper's nightlife can be found in the bars and lounges of the hotels, motels, and inns. Good news to many: There's no smoking in Jasper clubs as of 2005.

O'Shea's, Athabasca Hotel, 510 Patricia St. (ⓒ 780/852-3386), is a longtime favorite party den, usually just called the Atha'B, or simply The B. It caters to a young clientele with its changing lineup of Top 40 bands, dance floor, and movies shown on the large-screen TV. O'Shea's is in action Monday to Saturday until 2am. If it's a straightforward and straight-head party scene that you're looking for, consider the **D'ed Dog Bar and Grill,** 404 Connaught Dr. (ⓒ 780/852-3351). This is where the young river and hiking guides who work in Jasper every summer gather to compare exploits by shouting above the din of country rock. Jasper's hottest club for music, **Pete's On Patricia,** upstairs at 614 Patricia St. (ⓒ 780/852-6262), presents live alternative and blues bands.

It's a little bit anomalous—Jasper's most exclusive and expensive hotel providing shelter for one of Jasper's most popular twenty-something hangouts. **Tent City** is a youthful gathering place in the bowels of the Jasper Park Lodge, where you'll find billiards, loud music, and a preponderance of the JPL's 650 employees.

You may think of most basement bars as dank and airless, but pleasant **Downstream Bar,** 620 Connaught Dr. (ⓒ 780/852-9449), is a friendly place for a late evening drink, and you won't feel out of place if you're not 25 and totally tan.

5 British Columbia's Rockies: Mount Robson Provincial Park & Yoho & Kootenay National Parks

MOUNT ROBSON PROVINCIAL PARK

24km (15 miles) W of Jasper

The highlight of this beautiful park, just west of Jasper National Park along the Yellowhead Highway, is 3,954m (12,969-ft.) Mount Robson, the highest peak in the Canadian Rockies. This massive sentinel fills the sky from most vantage points, making it a certainty that you'll easily run through a roll of film if the weather's good.

The mighty Fraser River rises in the park, offering a challenging white-water adventure for experienced rafters. A number of Jasper-area outfitters offer trips down the Fraser; see "Outdoor Pursuits in the Park" under "Jasper National Park," earlier.

Two- to 4-hour park tours are offered by **Mount Robson Adventure Holidays** (© **250/566-4386;** fax 250/556-4351). For C$55 (US$44), visitors can choose a guided nature tour by raft, canoe, or van. Longer hiking or backpacking excursions are also available.

For additional information on the park, call © **250/566-4325** or follow the links from **http://wlapwww.gov.bc.ca/bcparks**.

YOHO NATIONAL PARK

East gate is 60km (37 miles) W of Banff, west gate is 20km (12 miles) E of Golden

Located just east of Golden on the western slopes of the Rockies in British Columbia, Yoho National Park preserves some of the most famous rocks in Canada, as well as a historic rail line and the nation's second-highest waterfall. The park is essentially the drainage of the Kicking Horse River—famed for its white-water rafting—and is traversed by the Trans-Canada Highway.

The first white exploration of this area was by scouts looking for a pass over the Rockies that would be suitable for the Canadian Pacific's transcontinental run. Kicking Horse Pass, at 1,626m (5,333 ft.), was surveyed, and the railroad began its service in 1884. However, the first train to attempt the 4½%-grade descent lost control and crashed, killing three men. In 1909, after decades of accidents, the Canadian Pacific solved its problem by curling two spiral rail tunnels into the mountains facing Big Hill. Together, the two tunnels are more than 1,859m (6,098 ft.) long. At the Lower Spiral Tunnel Viewpoint, interpretive displays explain this engineering feat, and you can still watch trains enter and emerge from the tunnels.

ESSENTIALS

The service center for Yoho National Park is the little town of **Field,** with a half-dozen modest accommodations and a few casual restaurants. The park's **visitor center** is just off Highway 1 near the entrance to town. For advance information, contact **Yoho National Park** (© **250/343-6324;** www.parkscanada.pch.gc.ca/yoho).

The daily entrance fee is C$8 (US$6.40) per person per day, or C$16 (US$13) per group or family per day. The pass is good for entry at all of the four contiguous Rocky Mountain national parks.

EXPLORING THE PARK

Thirteen kilometers (8 miles) from the Kicking Horse Pass, turn north onto Yoho Valley Road to find some of the park's most scenic areas. Past another viewpoint of the

Spiral Tunnels, continue 13km (8 miles) to **Takakkaw Falls** ✦, Canada's second highest, which cascades 380m (1,246 ft.) in two drops. A short trail leads from the road's end to a picnic area, where views of this waterfall are even more eye-popping.

Another impressive waterfall is **Wapta Falls,** on the rushing Kicking Horse River. The falls is reached by an easy 2.4km (1.5-mile) hike near the park's western entrance.

The Kicking Horse River descends between Mount Field and Mount Stephen, famous in paleontological circles for the **Burgess Shale,** fossil-rich deposits from the Cambrian era. Interpretive displays on these fossil digs, which have produced organisms that seem to challenge some established evolutionary tenets, are found at the visitor center in Field.

Emerald Lake, a jewel-toned lake in a glacial cirque, is one of the park's most popular stops. Hiking trails ring the lake; the destination is popular for cross-country skiing as well. The **Emerald Lake Lodge** ✦ (© 250/343-6321) is open for meals and lodging year-round (see "Where to Stay," below). In summer, this is a very busy place, but it's worth the drive.

Lake O'Hara is another beautiful mountain lake nestled below the soaring peaks of the Continental Divide. To protect the fragile alpine ecosystem, access to the lake is restricted. Although you can hike into the lake basin—13km (8 miles) one-way—most people reserve a seat on the bus that travels the gravel road leading to the lake, four times per day. Reservations are essential, and in high season difficult to obtain. The buses run mid-June through September; tickets are C$15 (US$12), and the reservation fee is another C$12 (US$9.60). For reservations, call © **250/343-6433.** Check out the Parks Canada website listed above for the most recent information on this area; the restrictions and options are fairly complex. Lake O'Hara is very popular with backcountry hikers, as the wilderness **campground** (C$9/US$7.20 per adult) here serves as a hub for a great many trails. Sitting on the shores is **Lake O'Hara Lodge** (© **250/343-6418;** www.lakeohara.com), a rustic resort with lodge rooms and cabins starting at C$465 (US$372) double, including all meals and bus transport.

HIKING

The trails that lead out from Emerald Lake are among the most popular in the park. The **Emerald Lake Trail** is a 5.2km (3.2-mile), all-abilities nature loop that leads from the parking area to the bridge at the back of the lake. At the end of the lake, it connects to the **Emerald Basin Trail,** an 8.6km (5.3-mile) round-trip hike ending dramatically in a natural amphitheater of hanging glaciers and avalanche paths. The Emerald Lake circuit alone will take 1 to 2 hours; the Emerald Basin Trail is a half-day hike taking from 3 to 4 hours.

The **Yoho Glacier Moraine Trail** is a half-day hike, 8.2km (5 miles) in length, that passes by Laughing Falls en route to Twin Falls, the most popular destination in the valley. Energetic folks can continue to the top of **Twin Falls,** then over the **Whaleback Trail** for some of the most incredible views of glaciers in the park. Before you take this route, ask the staff at the visitor center in Field if the bridge is in. Returning to Takakkaw Falls via the Whaleback and Laughing falls is a 20km (12.4-mile) circuit.

Heading up to the **Burgess Shale** formations is limited to guided hikes. The exquisitely preserved fossils discovered here were like none seen before, and even today are still reshaping our understanding of early evolution of modern animal life. The **Yoho–Burgess Shale Foundation** (© **800/343-3006;** www.burgess-shale.bc.ca) offers educational earth-science hikes from July to mid-September. The Burgess Shale Hike is 20km (12.4 miles) round-trip, a moderately difficult 10-hour trek. The cost is C$65 (US$52) adults and C$35 (US$28) for students. The Mount Stephen Fossil Beds hike is a moderately difficult 6km (3.7 miles), lasting about 6 hours. The cost is C$45 (US$36) adults and C$35 (US$28) for students. Other options include a special hike for seniors and the Mary Vaux Interpretive Hike. Call ahead for reservations.

WHERE TO STAY & DINE
The Emerald Lake Lodge ⚑ The Emerald Lake Lodge sits at the base of a placid aquamarine lake beneath towering cliff-faced mountains. The lake was discovered in 1882, when the Canadian Pacific Railway pushed over Kicking Horse Pass; by 1902, the railway had built a lodge on the lakeshore. The original lodge has expanded since then, but retains a marvelous sense of woodsy venerability and rustic charm. The main lodge houses a formal dining room, a bar, and conference facilities. Guest accommodations are in 24 newly built, cabin-style buildings, designed to harmonize with the historic lodge. Each unit features a fieldstone fireplace, bent-willow chairs, down comforters, and a balcony (most overlook the lake). There's fine dining in the elegant restaurant and lighter cuisine at Cilantro. The lounge features an oak bar salvaged from an 1890s Yukon saloon.

Box 10, Field, BC V0A 1G0. ℂ **800/663-6336** or 250/343-6321. www.crmr.com. 85 units. C$355–C$490 (US$284–US$392) double. Extra person C$25 (US$20). Children 12 and under stay free in parent's room. Off-season rates available. AE, DC, MC, V. Free parking. **Amenities:** 2 restaurants; lounge; Jacuzzi; sauna; canoe and cross-country ski rentals; horseback riding. *In room:* TV, dataport, fridge (in some), hair dryer.

CAMPING
There are five campgrounds in Yoho National Park. East of Field, sites go for C$16 (US$13) at **Monarch** and C$24 (US$19) at **Kicking Horse.** Near the park's western gate, **Hoodoo Creek** charges C$19 (US$115) per site. There's also a walk-in campground near **Takakkaw Falls,** where sites are C$16 (US$13). For information, contact the visitor center at ℂ **250/343-6783.**

KOOTENAY NATIONAL PARK & RADIUM HOT SPRINGS
Radium Hot Springs is 105km (65 miles) SE of Golden; Vermillion Pass is 38km (24 miles) SW of Banff

Kootenay National Park ⚑, just west of Banff on the western slopes of the Canadian Rockies, preserves the valleys of the Kootenay and Vermillion rivers. The park contains prime wildlife habitats and a number of hiking trails. Although Kootenay's scenery is as grand as anywhere else in the Rockies, its trails are considerably less crowded than those in the neighboring parks.

ESSENTIALS
Kootenay National Park is linked to the other Canadian Rockies parks by Highway 93, which departs from Highway 1 at Castle Junction to climb over the Vermillion Pass and descend to **Radium Hot Springs,** the park's western entrance. The town of Radium Hot Springs sits at the junction of Highways 93 and 95. Not an especially attractive place, it nonetheless offers ample motel rooms along the stretch of Highway 93 just before the park gates.

For information on the town, contact **Radium Hot Springs Visitor Information Centre,** Unit #4, Radium Plaza, 7685 Main St. W. (© **800/347-9704** or 250/347-9331; www.radiumhotsprings.com). For information on the park, contact **Kootenay National Park** (© **250/347-9505;** www.pc.gc.ca/pn-np/bc/kootenay).

The entry fee is C$8 (US$6.40) per person per day, or C$16 (US$13) per group or family per day. The pass is good at all of the four contiguous Rocky Mountain national parks.

EXPLORING THE PARK & RADIUM HOT SPRINGS

Kootenay National Park is on the west side of the Continental Divide, just west of Banff. Kootenay has the fewest facilities of the four major Rocky Mountain national parks, and day-hiking options are limited. The drive through the park on Highway 93 does offer spectacular scenery.

Much of the area around **Vermillion Pass,** the eastern entrance to the park, was burned in a massive forest fire in 1968; from the parking area at the pass, the interpretive 15-minute Fireweed Trail leads into the still-devastated forest, describing the process of revegetation.

Seven kilometers (4¼ miles) into the park is another dramatic stop. **Marble Canyon** is a narrow 61m-deep (200-ft.) chasm cut through a formation of limestone. A short trail winds over and through the canyon, bridging the canyon in several places. Just 5 minutes down the road are the **Paint Pots.** Here, cold spring water surfaces in an iron-rich deposit of red and yellow clay, forming intense colored pools.

The highway leaves the Vermillion River valley and climbs up to a viewpoint above the **Hector Gorge,** into which the river flows before meeting the Kootenay River. From here, look out for mountain goats, which can often be seen on the rocky cliffs of Mount Wardle to the north.

The highway passes through one of these narrow limestone canyons after it mounts Sinclair Pass and descends toward Radium Hot Springs. Called **Sinclair Canyon,** the chasm is about 10km (6¼ miles) long, and in places is scarcely wide enough to accommodate the roadbed.

Radium Hot Springs Pool (© **250/347-9485**), a long-established hot springs spa and resort, sits at the mouth of Sinclair Canyon. It's open from mid-May to mid-October daily from 9am to 11pm, and mid-October to mid-May daily from noon to 9pm. Day passes are C$6.50 (US$5.20) for adults, C$5.50 (US$4.40) for seniors and children, and C$20 (US$16) per family. Also here is the **Radium Hot Springs Massage Clinic** (© **250/347-9714**) and other spa services.

There's not much to delay you in the town of Radium Hot Springs unless you need an inexpensive motel room. The town does boast two new championship 18-hole golf courses, the **Springs Course,** along the Columbia just west of town has summer season greens fees of C$68 to C$80 (US$54–US$64), and the **Resort Course,** south of Radium, with summer fees of C$52 (US$42). Both are operated by **Radium Golf Resort** (© **250/347-9311;** www.radiumresort.com), which offers restaurants, clubhouses, pro shops, and luxury accommodations.

WHERE TO STAY

The Chalet Europe ✮ One of the few places to stay in Radium that doesn't have busy Highway 93 as its front yard, the Chalet is perched high above the Columbia Valley, just above the entrance to Kootenay Park. Each of the property's suites has a galley kitchen and private balcony with superlative views of the Rockies and Columbia Valley. *Note:* Smoking isn't permitted inside the rooms.

5063 Madsen Rd., Radium Hot Springs, BC V0A 1M0. © **888/428-9998** or 250/347-9305. Fax 250/347-9316. www. chaleteurope.com. 17 units. C$109–C$179 (US$87–US$143) double. Extra person C$10 (US$8). AE, DISC, MC, V. Free parking. **Amenities:** Exercise room; Jacuzzi; sauna; game room; coin-op laundry; barbecue. *In room:* A/C, TV, dataport, kitchenette, fridge, coffeemaker, hair dryer, microwave, DVD.

Gables Motel   One of the many motels that line the entry road to Kootenay National Park, the Gables is an attractive place with Bavarian-style balconies, lots of flower boxes, and good-size rooms.

5028 Hwy. 93, Radium Hot Springs, BC V0A 1M0. © **250/347-9866.** Fax 250/347-0042. www.radiumhotsprings. com/gables. 17 units. C$89 (US$71) double. AE, MC, V. Free parking. **Amenities:** Jacuzzi; sun deck; barbecue. *In room:* A/C, TV, fridge, coffeemaker.

Motel Tyrol *Value*   Like most other businesses in Radium Hot Springs, Motel Tyrol does its best to look like it belongs in the Alps. Well maintained, with colorful flowers and landscaping, it offers great value for the money. Several rooms have kitchens, and a few have balconies. Consider what a motel like this would cost if it were in Banff!

East on Hwy. 93 (P.O. Box 312), Radium Hot Springs, BC V0A 1M0. © **888/881-1188** or 250/347-9402. www.motel tyrol.com. 22 units. C$69–C$119 (US$55–US$95) double. Kitchen C$10 (US$8) extra. AE, MC, V. Free parking. **Amenities:** Outdoor pool; Jacuzzi. *In room:* TV, kitchen (in some), fridge (in some).

WHERE TO DINE

In addition to the following, consider stopping in for a beer and a light meal at **Horsethief Creek Pub & Eatery,** 7538 Main St. (© **250/347-6400**).

Old Salzburg Restaurant AUSTRIAN   This is one of the most authentic-looking of Radium's ersatz Alpine structures, flanked by filigreed balconies, gables, and flowerpots. The menu features six varieties of schnitzel, but thankfully also contains a broad selection of other Austrian and Continental dishes. *Jagerrostbraten* is grilled beef loin in red wine, bacon, mushroom, and cranberry sauce. Homemade sausages, fish, and steaks round out the menu.

4943 Hwy. 93. © **250/347-6553.** Reservations recommended. Main courses C$13–C$25 (US$10–US$20). AE, MC, V. Daily 11am–10pm.

6 Waterton Lakes National Park 🖈

264km (164 miles) S of Calgary

In the southwestern corner of the province, Waterton Lakes National Park is linked with Glacier National Park in neighboring Montana; together these two beautiful tracts of wilderness compose Waterton-Glacier International Peace Park. Once the hunting ground of the Blackfoot, Waterton Park contains superb mountain, prairie, and lake scenery and is home to abundant wildlife.

The transition from plains to mountains in Waterton and Glacier parks is abrupt: The formations that now rise above the prairie were once under the primal Pacific Ocean, but wedges of the ocean's basement rock broke along deep horizontal faults, cutting these rock layers free. The continued impact of the plate tectonics gouged these rocks out and pushed them 56km (35 miles) east over the prairies. Thus, almost 5km (3 miles) high, the rock block of Waterton Park—an overthrust in geological terms—is a late arrival, now sitting on top of the plains.

During the last ice age, the park was filled with glaciers, which deepened and straightened river valleys; those peaks that remained above the ice were carved into distinctive thin, finlike ridges. The park's famous lakes also date from the Ice Age; all three of the Waterton Lakes nestle in glacial basins.

ESSENTIALS

Waterton Park is 264km (164 miles) south of Calgary and 130km (81 miles) west of Lethbridge. From Waterton, it's 100km (62 miles) south across the U.S.–Canada border to St. Mary, at the entrance to Montana's Glacier National Park. **Greyhound Canada** (© **800/661-8747;** www.greyhound.ca) runs buses to Waterton Townsite from late June to Labour Day. Once in Waterton, you can make use of Glacier Park's minivan service, linking Waterton to Glacier National Park to the south. For information, call © **406/226-9311.**

PARK INFORMATION   For information, contact Waterton Park Chamber of Commerce and Visitors Association (© 403/859-5133 in summer, or 403/859-2224 in winter). Check out www.parkscanada.pch.gc.ca/waterton and **www.discoverwaterton. com** as well. Park entry is C$6 (US$4.80) for adults, C$5 (US$4) for seniors, and C$3 (US$2.40) for children.

EXPLORING THE PARK

The park's main entrance road leads to **Waterton Townsite,** the only commercial center, with a number of hotels, restaurants, and tourist facilities. Other roads lead to more remote lakes and trail heads. Akamina Parkway leads from the townsite to Cameron Lake, glimmering beneath the crags of the Continental Divide. Red Rock Parkway follows Blackiston Creek past the park's highest peaks to Red Rock Canyon. From here, three trails lead up deep canyons to waterfalls.

The most popular activity in the park is the **Inter-Nation Shoreline Cruise** (© **403/859-2362;** www.watertoninfo.com/m/cruise.html), which leaves from the townsite and sails Upper Waterton Lake past looming peaks to the ranger station at Goat Haunt, Montana, in Glacier Park. The tour boat operates from June 1 through early October. In the high season, from the last weekend of June through August, there are five tour boat departures daily, with two or three daily in the shoulder seasons (check the website for exact schedules). Only during the high season does the boat land in Montana. The cruise usually takes just over 2 hours, including the stop in Montana. The price is C$27 (US$21) for adults, C$14 (US$11) for youths 13 to 17, and C$10 (US$8) for children 4 to 12.

OUTDOOR PURSUITS

BIKING   Unusual in a national park, mountain biking is allowed on a number of trails. Cameron Lake is a good trail head, offering three different options. Two short but steep trails climb up to Wall and Forum lakes; the Akimina Creek Trail follows an old forestry road 14km (8¾ miles) up Akimina Creek. For rentals, contact **Pat's Cycle Rental** (© 403/859-2266).

GOLF   The **Waterton Park Golf Course** ⚑ (© 403/859-2114) is one of the oldest courses in Alberta. An original Stanley Thompson design (he designed the famed courses at Banff and Jasper), hazards include incredible Rocky Mountain vistas and meandering elk, bear, and moose. Greens fees are C$27 (US$22) for 18 holes.

HIKING   A 3km (1.9-mile) loop trail rings the peninsula that holds Waterton Townsite and links to long-distance trails. **Cameron Falls,** just above the Evergreen Avenue Bridge, is a good place to pick up the trail. From the Red Rock Canyon Trail Head, follow the main trail a mile up the canyon to see rust-red cliffs. From the same trail head, turn south and follow Blackiston Creek to Blackiston Falls, a 1km (.6-mile) leg-stretcher.

The most famous day hike is to **Crypt Lake.** This 17km (11-mile) round-trip is strenuous, but worth the effort for those in shape. The International Shoreline Cruise to Goat Haunt (see above) makes eight stops daily at the trail head.

Long-distance hiking trails skirt the edge of Upper Waterton Lake and link to the trail system in Glacier National Park.

HORSEBACK RIDING   **Alpine Stables,** across from the golf course on Entrance Road (© **403/859-2462**), offers a variety of guided rides on more than 250km (155 miles) of trails.

WHERE TO STAY

All lodgings in the park are in Waterton Townsite, a tiny settlement beside Waterton Lake. No matter where you stay, you won't be more than a 5-minute stroll from the lake.

Aspen Village Inn ✸   Aspen Village offers motel rooms in the Wildflower building, suites in the Aspen building, and duplex cottages. The suites are the newest, and can accommodate up to eight persons each. The entire complex, located 2 blocks from the lake, is hung with flower boxes and is well maintained.

P.O. Box 100, Waterton Lake, AB T0K 2M0. © **888/859-8669** or 403/859-2255. Fax 403/859-2033. www.aspen villageinn.com. 51 units. C$146–C$230 (US$116–US$184) double. Extra person $20 (US$14). Children under 16 stay free in parent's room. AE, DISC, MC, V. Free parking. Closed Oct–May. **Amenities:** Jacuzzi; playground; barbecue and picnic area. *In room:* TV, dataport, coffeemaker, hair dryer, iron.

Crandell Mountain Lodge   A Bavarian guesthouse look-alike, the Crandell is one of the park's original lodges. It has the feel of a charming country inn, with individually decorated rooms ranging from small units under the eaves to suites with kitchens and fireplaces. Two wheelchair-accessible units are available as well. The inn is noted for its friendly staff.

P.O. Box 114, Waterton Lake, AB T0K 2M0. © **866/859-2288.** ©/fax 403/859-2288. www.crandellmountain lodge.com. 17 units. C$129–C$199 (US$103–US$159) double. Extra person C$10 (US$8). DC, MC, V. Free parking. *In room:* TV, fridge, coffeemaker, hair dryer.

Kilmorey Lodge   Beloved by oft-returning guests, the Kilmorey is a rambling old lodge from the park's heyday. One of the few lodgings that has direct lake views, it offers small but elegantly appointed rooms. Expect down comforters, antiques, squeaky floors, and loads of character and charm. The Lamp Post is one of Waterton's most acclaimed restaurants. Also on-site are the Gazebo Café and the Ram's Head Lounge.

P.O. Box 100, Waterton Park, AB T0K 2M0. © **888/859-8669** or 403/859-2334. Fax 403/859-2342. www.kilmorey lodge.com. 23 units. C$123–C$240 (US$98–US$192) double. Extra person C$20 (US$16). Children under 16 stay free in parent's room. AE, DC, DISC, MC, V. Free parking. **Amenities:** Fine-dining restaurant; outdoor cafe; bar. *In room:* Hair dryer, no phone.

Waterton Glacier Suites   These attractive suites are some of the nicest accommodations in Waterton, particularly if you're able to step up and pay for a top-end loft unit. Most expensive are town house–style suites with two bathrooms and a two-person Jacuzzi; one has vaulted ceilings. All units are attractively furnished, with both fireplaces and balconies.

P.O. Box 51, Waterton Park, AB T0K 2M0. ℂ **403/859-2004.** Fax 403/859-2118. www.watertonsuites.com. 26 units. C$169–C$259 (US$135–US$207) double. Extra person C$15 (US$12). AE, MC, V. Free parking. **Amenities:** Jacuzzi. *In room:* A/C, TV, dataport, fridge, coffeemaker, hair dryer, microwave.

Waterton Lakes Lodge ⚇   This new and classy complex sits on 1.5 hectares (4 acres) in the heart of Waterton Townsite. The 80 rooms are in nine separate lodgelike buildings that flank a central courtyard. All are decorated with an environmental theme and appointed with handsome pine furniture. The Wildflower Dining Room, the Good Earth Deli, and the Wolf's Den Lounge are part of the resort complex. Also on the property are a guest and community sports facility, with a large pool, fitness center, and spa. Winter sports and cross-country ski rentals are available.

P.O. Box 4, Waterton Park, AB T0K 2M0. ℂ **888/985-6343** or 403/859-2150. Fax 403/859-2229. www.waterton lakeslodge.com. 80 units. C$174–C$219 (US$139–US$175) double. Extra person C$20 (US$16). Off-season rates available. AE, MC, V. Free parking. Closed Nov–Apr. **Amenities:** 2 restaurants; bar; health club with pool; fitness center and spa; coin-op laundry; nonsmoking rooms.

WHERE TO DINE

Garden Court ⚇ PACIFIC NORTHWEST   This elegant dining room overlooks stunning Waterton Lake, with the towering peaks of Glacier National Park incising the southern horizon. By and large, the food is up to the challenge of competing with the vista. Appetizers include baked brie with sliced apples, crostini, and cranberry coulis; and scallops in chives, mushrooms, and cream in a puff-pastry shell. Entrees range from prime rib to the house specialty Princess chicken, a spinach-and-feta-stuffed breast with a pine-nut crust, served with Saskatoonberry-and-onion chutney.

In Prince of Wales Hotel. ℂ **403/859-2231.** Reservations required. Main courses C$18–C$35 (US$14–US$28). MC, V. May 14–Sept 26 daily 6:30–9:30am, 11:30am–2pm, and 5–9pm.

Kootenai Brown Dining Room CANADIAN   The only restaurant in Waterton that's directly on the lake, the food at Kootenai Brown doesn't try to interfere with the view. The dining room has seen some hard use, but the steaks here are good. The menu is centered on classic Western-style cooking, though a few international and fancy dishes appear, such as chicken tandoori or stuffed trout with mushroom duxelles. The Bayshore complex also contains the Koffee Shop (serving up soup, salads, and sandwiches) and a lounge offering a late-night menu of pizza and burgers.

In the Bayshore Inn, Waterton Ave. ℂ **403/859-2211.** Reservations suggested. Main courses C$19–C$33 (US$15–US$26); breakfast buffet C$12 (US$9.60). AE, DISC, MC, V. Apr 1–Oct 15 daily 7–10am, 11am–2:30pm, and 5–9pm.

Lamp Post Dining Room ⚇ NORTHWEST   This dining room has a big regional reputation, and while the food is good and the ambience pleasant, some of the preparations are better than others. The menu stresses its "mix of cultures," but the most successful dishes are those featuring local beef, regional game and fish, and wild mushrooms and berries. As an appetizer, try the vanilla citrus prawns. Local beef cuts come with a choice of five preparations and sauces—the most unusual is McNally's, a traditional Irish-style brew mixed with a rich beef demi glace and just a hint of dark chocolate. The wine list is extensive, and the service prompt despite the busyness of the room.

In the Kilmorey Lodge. ℂ **403/859-2334.** Reservations required. Main courses C$15–C$41 (US$12–US$33). AE, DISC, MC, V. Daily 7:30am–10pm.

Little Italian Café ITALIAN

This cafe on Waterton's main street is a pleasant place for relatively inexpensive Italian food. Breakfasts feature dishes like eggs Florentine; lunch brings grilled focaccia sandwiches. At night, the menu tilts toward pasta—with more than 20 choices—plus classic preparations of chicken, veal, and beef. The patio is a marvelous spot to people-watch.

110 Waterton Ave. ℂ **403/859-0003.** Reservations not accepted. Main courses C$7–C$23 (US$5.60–US$18). MC, V. Daily 8am–10pm.

Appendix:
British Columbia & the Canadian Rockies in Depth

The more you know about British Columbia and the Canadian Rockies, the more you're likely to enjoy and appreciate everything the region has to offer. The pages that follow include a brief history, a range of highly recommended books, a primer on the unique cuisine of the area, and more.

1 British Columbia: History 101

NATIVE WESTERN CANADA
According to generally accepted theories, the Native peoples of North America arrived on this continent about 15,000 to 20,000 years ago from Asia, crossing a land bridge that spanned the Bering Strait. At the time, much of western Canada was covered with vast glaciers. Successive waves of these peoples moved south down either the coast or a glacier-free corridor that ran along the east face of the Rockies. As the climate warmed and the glaciers receded, the Native peoples moved north, following ice-age game animals like the woolly mammoth.

The ancestors of the tribes and bands that now live on the prairies of Alberta didn't make their year-round homes here in the pre-Contact era. The early plains Indians wintered in the lake and forest country around present-day Manitoba, where they practiced forms of basic agriculture. In summer and fall, hunting parties headed to the prairies of Alberta and Saskatchewan in search of buffalo. The move to a year-round homeland on the Great Plains was a comparatively recent event, caused by Native displacement as the eastern half of North America became increasingly dominated by European colonists. Thus, a number of linguistically and culturally unrelated tribes were forced onto the prairies at the same time, competing for food and shelter.

The Natives of the prairies relied on the buffalo for almost all their needs. The hide provided tepee coverings and leather for moccasins; the flesh was eaten fresh in season and preserved for later consumption; and the bones were used to create a number of tools.

The Native Indians along the Northwest coast had a very different culture and lifestyle, and in all likelihood migrated to the continent much later than the Plains Indians. Living at the verge of the Pacific or along the region's mighty rivers, these early people settled in wooden longhouses in year-round villages, fished for salmon and shellfish, and used the canoe as the primary means of transport. The Pacific Northwest coast was one of the most heavily populated areas in Native America, and an extensive trading network developed. Because the temperate coastal climate and abundant wildlife made this a relatively hospitable place to live, the tribes were reasonably well off, and the arts—carving and weaving in particular—flourished. Villages were organized according to clans, and elaborately carved totem poles portrayed ritual clan myths.

EUROPEAN EXPLORATION The first known contact between Europeans and the Natives of western Canada came in the last half of the 18th century, as the Pacific Northwest coast became a prize in the colonial dreams of distant nations. Russia, Britain, Spain, and the United States each would assert a claim over parts of what would become British Columbia and Alberta.

In 1774, the Spanish explorer Juan Perez landed on the Queen Charlotte Islands and then on the western shores of Vancouver Island, at Nootka Sound. England's James Cook made a pass along the Pacific Northwest coast, spending a couple weeks at Nootka Sound in 1778, where the crew traded trinkets for sea otter pelts. Later in the same journey, when Cook visited China, he discovered that the Chinese were willing to pay a high price for otter furs.

Thus was born the Chinese trade triangle that would dominate British economic interests in the northern Pacific for 30 years. Ships entered the waters of the Pacific Northwest, their crews traded cloth and trinkets with Natives for pelts of sea otters, and then the ships set sail for China, where the skins were traded for tea and luxury items. After the ships returned to London, the Asian goods were sold.

Since the Spanish and the English had competing claims over the Pacific Northwest coast, these nations sent envoys to the region—the Spaniard Don Juan Francisco de la Bodega y Quadra and the British Captain George Vancouver—to further explore the territory and resolve who controlled it. The expeditions led by these explorers resulted in a complete mapping of the region, though the ownership of the territory wasn't resolved until 1793, when Spain renounced its claims.

Fur traders also first explored the interior of British Columbia and the Alberta prairies. Two British fur-trading companies, the Hudson's Bay Company (HBC) and the North West Company, began to expand from their bases along the Great Lakes and Hudson's Bay, following mighty prairie rivers to the Rockies. Seeking to gain advantage over the Hudson's Bay Company, the upstart North West Company sent traders and explorers farther inland to open new trading posts and to find routes to the Pacific. Alexander Mackenzie became the first white man to cross the continent when he followed the Peace River across northern Alberta and British Columbia, crossing the Rockies and the Fraser River Plateau to reach Bella Coola, on the Pacific, in 1793.

Simon Fraser followed much of Mackenzie's route in 1808, though he floated down the Fraser River to its mouth near present-day Vancouver. Another fur trader and explorer was David Thompson, who crossed the Rockies and established Kootenay House trading post on the upper Columbia River. In 1811, Thompson journeyed to the mouth of the Columbia, where he found Fort Astoria, an American fur-trading post, already in place. Competing American and British interests would dominate events in the Pacific Northwest for the next 2 decades.

By the 1820s, seasonal fur-trading forts were established along the major rivers of the region. Cities like Edmonton, Kamloops, Prince George, and Hope all had their beginnings as trading posts. Each of the forts was given an assortment of trade goods to induce the local Indians to trap beaver, otter, fox, and wolf. Although the fur companies generally treated the Native populations with respect and fairness, there were tragic and unintentional consequences to the relationships that developed. While blankets, beads, and cloth were popular with the Natives, nothing was as effective as whiskey: Thousands of gallons of alcohol passed from the trading posts to the

Natives, corrupting traditional culture and creating a cycle of dependence that enriched the traders while poisoning the Indians. The white traders also unwittingly introduced European diseases to the Natives, who had little or no resistance to such deadly scourges as smallpox and measles.

The Louisiana Purchase, which gave the U.S. control of all the territory along the Missouri River up to the 49th parallel and to the Continental Divide, and the Lewis and Clark Expedition from 1804 to 1806 gave the Americans a toe-hold in the Pacific Northwest. As part of the settlement of the War of 1812, the Pacific Northwest—which included all of today's Oregon, Washington, and much of British Columbia—was open to both British and American exploitation, though neither country was allowed to set up governmental institutions. In fact, Britain had effective control of this entire area through its proxies in the Hudson's Bay Company, which had quasi governmental powers over its traders and over relations with the Native peoples, which included pretty much everyone who lived in the region.

B.C. CONSOLIDATES & JOINS CANADA
From its headquarters at Fort Vancouver, on the north banks of the Columbia River near Portland, Oregon, the Hudson's Bay Company held sway over the river's huge drainage, which extended far into present-day Canada. However, with the advent of the Oregon Trail and settlement in what would become the state of Oregon, the HBC's control over this vast territory began to slip. In 1843, the Oregon settlers voted by a slim majority to form a government based on the American model. The HBC and Britain withdrew to the north of the Columbia River, which included most of Washington and British Columbia.

The U.S.–Canada boundary dispute became increasingly antagonistic. The popular slogan of the U.S. 1844 presidential campaign was "54/40 or fight," which urged the United States to occupy all of the Northwest up to the present Alaskan border. Finally, in 1846, the British and the Americans agreed to the present border along the 49th parallel. The HBC headquarters withdrew to Fort Victoria on Vancouver Island; many British citizens moved north as well. In order to better protect its interests and citizens, Vancouver Island became a crown colony in 1849—just in case the Americans grew more expansionist-minded. However, population in the Victoria area—then the only settled area of what would become British Columbia—was still small: In 1854, the population counted only 250 white people.

Then, in 1858, gold-rush fever struck this remote area of the British Empire. The discovery of gold along the Fraser River and in 1862 in the Cariboo Mountains brought in a flood of people. By far the vast majority of the estimated 100,000 who streamed into the area were Americans who came north from the by-now-spent California gold fields. Fearing domination of mainland Canada by the United States, Britain named the mainland a new colony, New Caledonia, in 1858. In 1866, the two colonies—Vancouver Island and the mainland—merged as the British colony of British Columbia.

As population and trade increased, the need for greater political organization grew. As a colony, British Columbia had little local control, and was largely governed by edict from London. In order for British Columbia to have greater freedom and self-determination, the growing colony had two choices: join the prosperous United States to the south, with which it shared many historic and commercial ties, or join the new Dominion of Canada far to the east. After Ottawa promised to build a railroad to link eastern and western Canada, B.C. delegates voted in 1871 to join Canada as the province of British Columbia.

THE RAILROADS LINK CANADA

Meanwhile, the rule of the HBC over the inland territory known as Ruperts Land relaxed as profits from trapping decreased, and in 1869, the Crown bought back the rights to the entire area. The border between the United States and Canada in the prairie regions was hazy at best, lawless at worst. Although selling whiskey to Native people was illegal, in the no-man's-land between Montana and Canada, trade in alcohol was rife.

In response to uprisings and border incursions, the Canadian government created a new national police force, the Royal Canadian Mounted Police. In 1873, a contingent of Mounties began their journey across the Great Plains, establishing Fort Macleod (1874) in southern Alberta along with three other frontier forts, including Fort Calgary at the confluence of the Bow and Elbow rivers. The Mounties succeeded in stopping the illegal whiskey trade and creating conditions favorable for settlement. By 1875, there were 600 residents at Fort Calgary, lured by reports of vast and fertile grasslands.

However, for the prairies and the interior of Canada to support an agrarian economy, these remote areas needed to be linked to the rest of Canada. In 1879, the Canadian Pacific Railroad reached Winnipeg, and in 1883 arrived at Banff. Finding a route over the Rockies proved a major challenge: The grades were very steep, the construction season short, and much of the rail bed had to be hacked out of rock.

Canada's transcontinental railway needed a mainland coastal terminus in British Columbia, as the new province's population center and capital, Victoria, was on an island. Railroad engineers set their sites on the sheltered Burrard Inlet, then a sparse settlement of saloons, lumber mills, and farms. The first train arrived from Montreal in 1886, stopping at a thrown-together, brand-new town called Vancouver. A year later, the first ship docked from China, and Vancouver began its boom as a trading center and transportation hub.

All along the railroad's transcontinental reach, towns, farms, and other industries sprang up for the first time. In Alberta, huge ranches sprawled along the face of the Rockies, and Calgary boomed as a cow town. The railroads also brought foreign immigration. Entire communities of central and eastern European farmers appeared on the prairies overnight, the result of the railroads' extensive promotional campaign in places like the Ukraine. Other settlers came to western Canada seeking religious tolerance; many small towns on the prairies began as utopian colonies for Hutterites, Mennonites, and Dukhobors. Alberta became a province in 1905, and in 1914 the Grand Trunk Railroad, Canada's second transcontinental railroad, opened up the more northerly prairies, linking Saskatoon and Edmonton to Prince George and Prince Rupert. By 1920, Alberta was Canada's leading agricultural exporter.

All this development demanded lumber for construction, and in Canada, lumber—then as now—meant British Columbia. In return for building the transcontinental railroad, the CPR was granted vast tracts of land along its route. As the demand for lumber skyrocketed, these ancient forests met the saw.

As the population, industry, logging, farming, and shipping all increased in western Canada, it was not just the local ecosystem that took a hit. The Natives had at first reasonably cooperative relations with the HBC trappers and traders. Although European diseases wiped out enormous numbers of Indians, these early whites did little to overtly disturb the traditional life and culture of the Natives.

That awaited the arrival of agriculture, town settlements, and Christian missionaries. After the HBC lost its long-standing role in Indian relations, authority was wielded by a federal agency in Ottawa. The Natives received no compensation for the land deeded over to the CPR, and increased contact with the whites who were flooding the region simply increased contact with alcohol, trade goods, and disease. The key social and religious ritual of the coastal Indians—the potlatch, a feast and gift-giving ceremony—was banned in 1884 by the provincial government under the influence of Episcopal missionaries. The massive buffalo herds of the open prairies were slaughtered to near-extinction in the 1870s and 1880s, leaving the once proud Plains Indians little choice but to accept confinement on reservations.

THE 20TH CENTURY The building of the Panama Canal, which was completed in 1914, meant easier access to markets in Europe and along North America's East Coast, bringing about a boom for the western Canadian economy. As big business grew, so did big unions. In Vancouver in the 1910s, workers organized into labor unions to protest working conditions and pay rates. A number of strikes hit key industries, and in several instances resulted in armed confrontations between union members and soldiers. However, one area where the unions, the government, and business could all agree was racism: The growing Chinese and Japanese populations were a problem they felt only punitive legislation and violence could solve. Large numbers of Chinese had moved to the province and were instrumental in building the CPR; they were also important members of hard-rock mining communities and ran small businesses such as laundries. Japanese settlers came slightly later, establishing truck farms and becoming

the area's principal commercial fishermen. On several occasions, Vancouver's Chinatown and Little Tokyo were the scene of white mob violence, and in the 1920s, British Columbia passed legislation that effectively closed its borders to nonwhite immigration.

The period of the World Wars was turbulent on many fronts. Settlers with British roots returned to Europe to fight the Germans in World War I, dying in great numbers and destabilizing the communities they left behind. Following the war, Canada experienced an economic downturn, which led to further industrial unrest and unemployment. After a brief recovery, the Wall Street crash of 1929 brought severe economic depression and hardship. Vancouver, with its comparatively mild climate, became a kind of magnet for young Canadian men—hungry, desperate, and out of work. The city, however, held no easy answers for these problems, and soon the streets were filled with demonstrations and riots. Vancouver was in the grip of widespread poverty.

With the beginning of World War II, anti-German riots took hold of the city streets; and German-owned businesses were burned. In 1941, Japanese-Canadians were removed from their land and their fishing boats and interned by the government on farms and work camps in inland British Columbia, Alberta, and Saskatchewan.

Perversely, for other Canadians, social calm and prosperity returned as World War II progressed: the unemployed enlisting as foot soldiers against the Axis nations, and the shipbuilding and armaments-manufacturing industries bolstering the region's traditional farming, ranching, and lumbering.

Alberta's wild oil boom began in 1947, when drillers struck black gold near Leduc and a period of tremendous economic growth ensued. By the 1960s, Alberta was supplying most of Canada's crude oil and natural gas. In the 1970s, as oil-producing nations joined together to form the Organization of Petroleum Exporting Countries (OPEC) and oil shortages hit North America, Alberta was left holding the hose. The value of the province's petroleum resources tripled almost overnight; by the end of the 1970s, its value had quadrupled again, allowing for a period of nearly unlimited building and infrastructure development. Calgary morphed from a sleepy ranchers' town into a brand-new city of soaring office towers, the financial and business center of Canada's oil industry. Edmonton, the capital of Alberta, boomed as the center of oil technology and refining.

Since the war years, British Columbia generally boomed economically as well, especially under the leadership of the Social Credit Party, supposedly the party of small business. Father and son premiers, W. A. C. and Bill Bennett, effectively ruled the Social Credit Party and the province from 1952 until 1986. With close ties between government ministers and the resources they oversaw, business—especially manufacturing, mining, and logging—certainly boomed, but along with prosperity came significant governmental scandals, opportunistic financial shenanigans, and major resource mismanagement. Social Credit Premier Bill Vander Zalm was forced to resign in 1991. Reform-minded governments have been in place in Victoria since, although Chicago-style corruption still seems rampant in both government and business.

The 1990s saw a vast influx of Hong Kong Chinese to the Vancouver area, the result of fears accompanying the British hand over of Hong Kong to the mainland Chinese in 1997. Unlike earlier migrations of Chinese to North America, these Hong Kong Chinese were middle- and upper-class merchants and business leaders. Real-estate prices shot through the roof, and entire neighborhoods became Chinese enclaves. Currently, Vancouver has the world's largest Chinese population outside of Asia.

Asians are not the only people bolstering western Canada's fast-growing population. Canada has relatively open immigration laws, resulting in a steady flow of newcomers from the Middle East, the Indian subcontinent, and Europe. Additionally, many young Canadians from the economically depressed eastern provinces see a brighter future in the west. With their strong economies and big-as-all-outdoors setting, Vancouver, Edmonton, and Calgary serve as magnets for many seeking new lives and opportunities.

Dateline

- **1670** Hudson's Bay Company is established by English King Charles II.
- **1741** Danish sailor Vitus Bering explores northern Pacific Coast for Russia.
- **1759** English defeat French at Montreal's Plains of Abraham, ending the French and Indian War; British take control of Upper and Lower Canada.
- **1774** Spaniard Juan Perez sails up British Columbian coast from Mexico, landing in the Queen Charlottes and on Vancouver Island; the first European to explore the coast, he claims all of the Pacific Coast for Spain.
- **1776** American colonies declare their independence from Britain; Canada remains royalist.
- **1778** Capt. James Cook of England lands at Nootka Sound, on Vancouver Island, and trades for otter furs on his way to China, establishing the beginning of the Northwest/China trade triangle. Establishes British claim to Northwest.
- **1778** North West Company establishes Fort Chipewyan on Lake Athabasca, the first European settlement in Alberta.

continues

2 British Columbia & the Canadian Rockies Today

Canada's westernmost region has a lot to offer travelers, including dramatic landscapes, a vibrant arts culture, and unparalleled access to outdoor recreation. British Columbia and the Canadian Rockies, which stretch across the provincial border into Alberta, are obviously part of Canada, and have a thoroughly Canadian infrastructure and political system. However, these two giant provinces—British Columbia covers 948,600 sq. km (366,255 sq. miles), Alberta 661,188 sq. km (255,285 sq. miles)—are separated from the nation's capital, Ottawa, and the political and cultural centers of eastern Canada by thousands of miles of farmland.

Much closer is the northwestern tier of the United States. Although British Columbia and Alberta are definitely part of Canada, they are much closer in spirit to the Pacific Northwest states than to, say, Quebec or Nova Scotia. The states of Washington, Oregon, Idaho, and Montana share their northern neighbors' climate, economies, and cultural histories. These regions of Canada and the United States have more in common with each other than with the rest of their respective countries—a reality that seems to please everyone in both the Canadian and the American Pacific Northwest.

There's another cultural overlay at work here, not quite at odds with the above observation, but simultaneously true: In the United States, the westering urge—that uniquely North American drive to keep moving west toward unspecified freedom and opportunity—was diffused across a dozen or so states, each of which developed its own culture and institutions. In Canada, there were just British Columbia and Alberta to absorb all the hopes, idealism, and pragmatism of 150 years' worth of western migration.

British Columbia is often called the California of Canada, with Canada's most temperate climate, a vibrant film industry, a visible and powerful gay and lesbian community, and a soft-focus New Age patina. However, British Columbia is also the Idaho of Canada, the Washington state of Canada, and, incidentally, the Asia of Canada. In terms of cultural diversity and competing interests, there's a lot going on here.

Likewise, the Alberta of prosperous Edmonton and Calgary may seem like an oil- and agriculture-fueled monoculture, but dozens of its rural communities began as colonies of religious refugees whose stories have a lot in common with the Mormons of Utah. And with its

- **1792** Nootka Accord settles British/Spanish dispute over the Northwest coast; Spain renounces claims to the northern coast.
- **1793** British fur trader Alexander Mackenzie arrives in Bella Coola, becoming the first European to traverse North America.
- **1794** Rocky Mountain House, a North West Company trading post, opens at the juncture of the Peace and

Moberly rivers, becoming the first permanent European settlement in British Columbia.
- **1795** Hudson's Bay Company establishes Edmonton House on the banks of the North Saskatchewan River.
- **1804–06** Americans Lewis and Clark journey up the Missouri River and down the Columbia River to the Pacific, then Spanish territory. The journey reveals a great wealth of furs in the

Northwest, piquing American settlement interest.
- **1808** Fur trader Simon Fraser floats the Fraser River from the Rocky Mountains to the site of present-day Vancouver.
- **1811** David Thompson floats the entire length of the Columbia River, arriving at the Pacific to find an already-established American trading post, Fort Astoria.

nouveau-riche wealth and well-rehearsed swagger, Alberta is more like Texas than anywhere else on earth.

As if these factors weren't enough to explain the schizoid nature of the two westernmost provinces, the populace is further divided by highly politicized environmental issues. Although Canadians in general seem more environmentally conscious than Americans, that doesn't mean that individual Canadians want to lose their salmon-fishing jobs to some vague international treaty, or that they want to close down the mine that's employed their families for generations just because

of a little mud in the river. Environmental issues—especially those surrounding logging, agriculture, mining, and fishing—are especially contentious, often pitting urban and rural residents against each other.

It's easy to think of Canada as North America's Scandinavia—well ordered, stable, and culturally just a little sleepy. In fact, during your own travels across British Columbia and the Rocky Mountains, you'll likely find this corner of Canada a fascinating amalgam of cultures, histories, and conflicting interests.

3 A Taste of British Columbia & the Canadian Rockies

Western Canada is home to an excellent and evolving regional cuisine that relies on local produce, farm-raised game, grass-fed beef and lamb, and fresh-caught fish and shellfish. These high-quality ingredients are matched with inventive sauces and accompaniments, often based on native berries and wild mushrooms. In attempting to capture what the French call the *terroir*, or the native taste of the Northwest, chefs from Edmonton and Calgary to Victoria and Vancouver are producing a delicious school of cooking with distinctive regional characteristics.

One of the hallmarks of Northwest cuisine is freshness. In places like Vancouver

Island, chefs meet fishing boats to select the finest of the day's catch. The lower Fraser Valley and the interior of British Columbia are filled with small specialty farms and orchards. Visit Vancouver's Granville Island Market or stop at a roadside farmer's stand to have a look at the incredible bounty of the land.

Cooks in western Canada are also very particular about where the food comes from. Menus often tell you exactly what farm grew your asparagus, what ranch your beef was raised on, which orchard harvested your peaches, and what bay your oysters came from. To capture the distinct flavor of the Northwest—its *terroir*—means using

- **1812** Outbreak of War of 1812; British take control of Fort Astoria.
- **1818** Treaty of Ghent ends War of 1812; Spain renounces claim in Pacific Northwest; United States and Britain agree to "joint occupancy" of Pacific Northwest.
- **1821** Hudson's Bay Company and North West Company merge.
- **1825** Hudson's Bay Company's Fort Vancouver is

established near present-day Portland, becoming the administrative center over nearly all of the Pacific Northwest.

- **1841** Act of Union creates the United Provinces of Canada.
- **1843** Settlers in Oregon decide to set up American-style government, and British withdraw to north of the Columbia River; Fort Victoria

is established on Vancouver Island.

- **1846** U.S.–Canada boundary is established at 49th Parallel.
- **1849** Vancouver Island becomes British colony.
- **1858** Fraser River gold rush begins; the B.C. mainland becomes colony of New Caledonia.
- **1859** First wine grapes are planted along Lake Okanagan

continues

only those products that swam in the waters or grew in or on the soil of the Northwest.

Once you've assembled your extra-fresh, locally produced foodstuffs, you need to cook it according to some kind of esthetic. This is where Northwest cooks get inventive. While many chefs marry the region's superior meat, fish, and produce to traditional French or Italian techniques, other cooks turn elsewhere for inspiration. One popular school of Northwest cooking looks west across the Pacific to Asia. Pacific Rim or Pan Pacific cuisine, as this style of cooking is often called, matches the North American Pacific Coast's excellent fish and seafood with the flavors of Pacific Asia. The results can be subtle—the delicate taste of lemon grass or nori—or intense, with lashings of red curry or wasabi. However, don't expect Pacific Rim cuisine to follow the rules of Asian cooking: One memorable meal at Calgary's Belvedere restaurant (p. 327) matched grilled Pacific salmon with a sauce of Japanese seaweed and reduced red wine, served with heirloom potato cakes.

Other attempts to find the authentic roots of Northwest cooking look back to frontier times or to Native American techniques. There's no better way to experience salmon than at a traditional salmon bake at a Native village—most First Nations communities have an annual festival open to the general public—and many restaurants replicate this method by baking salmon on a cedar plank. Several restaurants in Vancouver and on Vancouver Island specialize in full Northwest Native feasts.

FRUITS OF THE FIELD & FOREST

Although there's nothing exotic about the varieties of vegetables available in western Canada, what will seem remarkable to visitors from distant urban areas is the freshness and quality of the produce here. Many fine restaurants contract directly with small, often organic, farms to make daily deliveries. Heirloom varieties—old-fashioned strains that are often full of flavor but don't ship or keep well—are frequently highlighted.

Fruit trees do particularly well in the hot central valleys of British Columbia, and apples, peaches, apricots, plums, and pears do more than grace the fruit basket. One of the hallmarks of Northwest cuisine is its mixing of fruit with savory meat and chicken dishes. And as long as the chef is slicing apricots to go with sautéed chicken and thyme, he might as well chop up a few hazelnuts (filberts) to toss in: These nuts thrive in the Pacific Northwest.

Berries of all kinds do well in the milder coastal regions. Cranberries grow in low-lying coastal plains. The blueberry and its wild cousin, the huckleberry, are

by Catholic missionary Father Pandosy.

- **1862** Gold is discovered at Barkerville, beginning the Cariboo gold rush.
- **1866** Colonies of Vancouver Island and New Caledonia combine to form colony of British Columbia.
- **1867** Britain grants further independence to the new Dominion of Canada.
- **1871** British Columbia agrees to join the Dominion

of Canada and not the United States, as long as Canada builds the transcontinental railroad.

- **1872** The Dominion Lands Acts, Canada's Homestead Act, opens the prairies to farmers and ranchers.
- **1874** Royal Canadian Mounted Police (RCMP) ride west to establish order on prairies of Ruperts Land (Alberta and Saskatchewan).

- **1875** RCMP establish Fort Calgary at the confluence of the Bow and Elbow rivers.
- **1877** Blackfoot chief Crowfoot signs treaty relegating the tribe, the largest and most powerful of the Canadian Plains tribes, to reservations.
- **1883** Canadian Pacific Railroad reaches Calgary.
- **1885** Canadian Pacific Railroad is completed, and the first train steams from

both used in all manner of cooking, from breads to savory chutneys. In Alberta, another wild cousin, the Saskatoonberry, appears on menus to validate regional cooking aspirations. The astringent wild chokecherry, once used to make pemmican (a sort of Native American energy bar), is also finding its way into fine-dining restaurants.

Wild mushrooms grow throughout western Canada, and harvesting the chanterelles, morels, porcinis, and myriad other varieties is big business. Expect to find forest mushrooms in pasta, alongside a steak, in savory bread puddings, or braised with fish.

MEATS & SEAFOOD   Easily the most iconic of the Northwest's staples is the Pacific salmon. For thousands of years, the Native people have followed the cycles of the salmon, netting or spearing the fish, then smoking and preserving it for later use. The delicious and abundant salmon became the mainstay of settlers and early European residents as well. Although salmon fishing is now highly restricted and some salmon species are endangered, salmon is still very available and easily the most popular fish in the region. Expect to find a salmon dish on practically every fine-dining menu in the Northwest.

However, there are other fish in the sea. The fisheries along Vancouver Island and the Pacific Coast are rich in bottom fish like sole, flounder, and halibut, which grow to enormous size here. Fresh-caught rock and black cod are also delectable, and the Pacific has plentiful tuna, especially ahi and albacore.

Although shellfish and seafood are abundant in the Pacific, it is only recently that many of the varieties have appeared on the dinner table. Oysters grow in a number of bays on Vancouver Island, and while wild mussels blanket rocks the length of the coast, only a few sea farms grow mussels commercially. Fanny Bay, north of Qualicum Beach on Vancouver Island, is noted for both its oysters and its mussels. Another Northwest shellfish delicacy is the razor clam, a long, thin bivalve with a nutty and rich flavor. Shrimp of all sizes thrive off the coast of British Columbia, and one of the clichés of Northwest cooking is the unstinting use of local shrimp on nearly everything, from pizza to polenta. Local squid and octopus are beginning to appear on menus, while sea urchin—abundant along the coast—is harvested mostly for export to Japan.

Both British Columbia and Alberta have excellent ranch-raised beef and lamb. Steaks are a staple throughout the region, as is prime rib. You'll see lamb on menus more often in western Canada than in many areas of the United States.

Montreal to Burrard Inlet, on the Pacific near Vancouver; Banff National Park, Canada's first, is proclaimed by Prime Minister John Macdonald.

- **1886** Vancouver, a rail siding near a popular tavern named Gassy's, is established.
- **1896** Gold is discovered in the Yukon; Edmonton becomes a major outfitting center for overland journey to the Klondike.
- **1904** Butchart Gardens opens to the public.
- **1905** Alberta becomes a province.
- **1914** Grand Trunk Railroad reaches from Winnipeg to Prince Rupert, becoming Canada's second transcontinental railroad.
- **1914** First ski resort opens at Whistler.
- **1914–18** In World War I, 60,000 Canadian troops die

and another 173,000 are wounded.

- **1923** British Columbia restricts immigration by Japanese and Chinese.
- **1930s** The depression and mass unemployment hit Canada. Prairie farms and ranches are especially hard hit; social unrest rocks Vancouver.

continues

Fun Fact **British Columbia in Television & Film**

British Columbia is one of the centers of film in Canada, and many Canadian features are set in Vancouver. Numerous Hollywood films have also been shot in the province: *Legends of the Fall, Little Women, Jumanji,* and *Rambo: First Blood* give an idea of the range of films done here. Television's groundbreaking series, *The X-Files,* was shot in and around the city for its first 4 years of production (Vancouver doubles as many American cities, notably Washington, D.C.).

Game meats are increasingly popular, especially in restaurants dedicated to Northwest cuisine. Buffalo and venison are offered frequently enough to no longer seem unusual, and farm-raised pheasant is easily available. You'll look harder to find meats like caribou or elk, however. Savor it when you can.

FRUITS OF THE VINEYARDS British Columbia wines remain one of western Canada's greatest secrets. Scarcely anyone outside of the region has ever heard of these wines, yet many are delicious and, while not exactly cheap, still less expensive than comparable wines from California. There are wineries on Vancouver and Saturna islands and in the Fraser Valley, but the real center of British Columbia's winemaking is the Okanagan Valley. In this hot and arid climate, noble grapes like cabernet sauvignon, merlot, and chardonnay thrive when irrigated. You'll also find more unusual varietals,

like Ehrenfelser and sangiovese. More than 70 wineries are currently producing wine in the Okanagan Valley; when combined with excellent restaurants in Kelowna and Penticton, this region becomes a great vacation choice for the serious gastronome.

DINING IN RESTAURANTS Canadians enjoy eating out, and you'll find excellent restaurants throughout British Columbia and Alberta. Many of the establishments recommended in this guide serve Northwest regional cuisine, the qualities of which are outlined above.

However, there is also a wealth of other kinds of restaurants available. If you're a meat eater, it's worth visiting a traditional steakhouse in Calgary or Edmonton. In many smaller centers, Greek restaurants double as the local steakhouse. Don't be surprised when you see a sign for, say, Zorba's Steakhouse; both the steaks and the souvlakia will probably be excellent.

- **1935** Social Credit Party forms in response to the Great Depression; becomes leading political party in much of western Canada until 1980s.
- **1939** Canada declares war on Germany.
- **1945** World War II ends; 42,000 Canadians die in the war, another 54,000 are wounded.
- **1947** Native Canadians are granted right to vote in

provincial elections; first major oil reserves are discovered in Alberta.
- **1960** Native Canadians are granted right to vote in federal elections.
- **1967** "Vive le Quebec Libre": de Gaulle visits Quebec, spurring Quebec secessionism.
- **1968** The Official Languages Bill declares French and English the two official languages of Canada.

- **1972** Canada bans whaling off the Pacific Coast.
- **1988** Calgary hosts Winter Olympic Games.
- **1989** Canada–U.S. Free Trade Agreement eliminates all tariffs on goods of national origin moving between the two countries.
- **1993** Environmentalists, loggers, and law enforcement clash near Clayoquot Sound; 800 logging protesters are arrested.

Vancouver is one of the most ethnically diverse places on earth, and the selection of restaurants is mind-boggling. You'll find some of the best Chinese food this side of Hong Kong, as well as the cooking of Russia, Mongolia, Ghana, and Sri Lanka, along with every other country and ethnic group in between.

Several Canadian chain restaurants are handy to know about. White Spot restaurants serve basic but good-quality North American cooking. Often open 24 hours, these are good places for an eggs-and-hash-browns breakfast. Tim Horton's is the place to go for coffee and donuts, plus light snacks. Earl's serves a wide menu and frequently has a lively bar scene. Expect grilled ribs and chicken, steaks, and gourmet burgers. The Keg is another western Canadian favorite, and is a bit more sedate than Earl's, with more of a steakhouse atmosphere.

4 Recommended Reading

In addition to the specialized volumes listed below, we recommend two excellent books as adjuncts to this guide, especially if you're on a road trip. The *Big New B.C. Travel Guide,* published by *Beautiful British Columbia Magazine*—an arm of the provincial tourism office—is out of print, but still available at www.british columbia.com/bookstore. Its wealth of information—an amazing kilometer-by-kilometer guide to the natural and human history of the province, along with all sorts of curious facts and insights—doesn't go out of date. The *Canadian Rockies Super-guide,* by Graeme Pole (Altitude Publishing), has a similarly encyclopedic approach to western Alberta and eastern British Columbia, with lots of history and nature writing, accompanied by attractive photos.

It's also a good source of information on hikes and other outdoor adventures.

CANADIAN HISTORY A basic primer on the country's complex history is *The Penguin History of Canada,* by Kenneth McNaught. *The Canadians,* by Andrew H. Malcolm (St. Martin's Press), is an insightful and highly readable rumination on what it is to be Canadian, written by the former *New York Times* Canada bureau chief.

Peter C. Newman has produced an intriguing history of the Hudson's Bay Company, *Caesars of the Wilderness* (Publications of the Minnesota Historial Society), beginning with the early fur-trading days. *The Great Adventure,* by David Cruise and Alison Griffiths (St. Martin's Press), tells the story of the Mounties and their role in the subduing of the Canadian west.

- **1995** Quebec votes narrowly to remain in Canada.
- **1997** Britain hands over Hong Kong to mainland Chinese. Major emigration of Hong Kong Chinese to Vancouver area precedes the repatriation; Port Hardy fishermen and -women blockade Alaska Marine Highway ferry in protest of Alaskan fishing practices.
- **1999** Nunavut becomes a stand-alone territory, splitting off from the Northwest Territories—the first new territory in over a century.
- **2000** Jean Chrétien is re-elected for a third consecutive term, defeating Stockwell Day of the right-wing Canadian Alliance Party.
- **2003** In the worst Canadian forest fire year in recent history, wildfires burn vast tracts of forest near Kamloops, Kelowna, and Cranbrook; hundreds of homes burn in Kelowna.
- **2003** Vancouver awarded 2010 Olympic Winter Games as tourism starts to rebound following major drop due to SARS outbreak and discovery of mad cow disease in some Alberta cattle.
- **2003** Former Finance Minister Paul Martin is sworn in as Prime Minister after Jean

continues

Pierre Berton, who died in 2004, was the preeminent popular historian of Canada. He wrote over 50 books on Canada's rich past, all well researched and well written. His books range on most Canadian subjects, from the days of the Hudson's Bay Company and the fur trade to ruminations on what it means to be Canadian in the 21st century.

For a specific history of British Columbia, try *British Columbia: An Illustrated History*, by Geoffrey Molyneux (Polestar Books), or *The West Beyond the West: A History of British Columbia*, by Jean Borman (University of Toronto Press). Review Vancouver's past with *Vancouver: A History in Photographs*, by Aynsley Wyse and Dana Wyse (Altitude Publishing).

Alberta: A History in Photographs, by Faye Reinebert Holt (Altitude Publishing), is a good introduction to the history of that province, though the engaging *Alberta History Along the Highway: A Traveler's Guide to the Fascinating Facts, Intriguing Incidents and Lively Legends in Alberta's Remarkable Past*, by Ted Stone (Orca Books), is the book you'll want to take along in the car (the same author has a companion volume on British Columbia).

To learn about Canada's Native peoples, read *Native Peoples and Cultures of Canada*, by Alan D. McMillan (Douglas & McIntyre), which includes both history and current issues. The classic book on Canada's indigenous peoples, *The Indians of Canada* (University of Toronto Press), was written in 1932 by Diamond Jenness. The author's life is an amazing story in its own right, as he spent years living with various indigenous peoples across the country.

NATURAL HISTORY Two good general guides to the natural world in western Canada are the Audubon Society's *Pacific Coast*, by Evelyn McConnaghey, and *Western Forests*, by Stephen Whitney (both published by Knopf).

British Columbia: A Natural History, by Richard Cannings (Douglas & McIntyre), is an in-depth guide to the province's plants, animals, and geography. *Plants and Animals of the Pacific Northwest: An Illustrated Guide to the Natural History of Western Oregon, Washington, and British Columbia*, by Eugene N. Kozloff (University of Washington Press), is another good general resource.

For information on the natural history of Alberta's southern prairies, pick up *From Grasslands to Rockland: An Explorers Guide to the Ecosystems of Southernmost Alberta*, by Peter Douglas Elias (Rocky Mountain Books).

Bird-watchers might want to dig up a copy of *Familiar Birds of the Northwest*, by Harry B. Nehls (Audubon Society of Portland).

Chrétien retires after 10 years in office.

- **2005** Canada's Civil Marriage Act, legalizing same-sex marriage, passes parliament and receives royal assent. Same-sex marriage has been legal in B.C. since 2003; Alberta never permitted it until mandated by federal law.

- **2005** Michaëlle Jean, born in Haiti, becomes the 27th Governor General of Canada, the first black person to hold that position.

Read about the natural history of extinct wildlife in *A Wonderful Life: The Burgess Shale and the Nature of History,* by Stephen Jay Gould (Norton), which details the discovery and scientific ramifications of the fossil beds found in Yoho National Park.

OUTDOOR PURSUITS Edward Weber's *Diving and Snorkeling Guide to the Pacific Northwest* (Lonely Planet) is a good place to start if you're planning a diving holiday in the Northwest.

Mountain Bike Adventures in Southwest British Columbia, by Greg Maurer and Tomas Vrba (Mountaineers), is just one of a cascade of books on off-road biking in western Canada.

A good hiking guide to western British Columbia is *Don't Waste Your Time in the B.C. Coast Mountains: An Opinionated Hiking Guide to Help You Get the Most from This Magnificent Wilderness,* by Kathy Copeland. *A Guide to Climbing and Hiking in Southwestern British Columbia,* by Bruce Fairley, also includes Vancouver Island.

The *Canadian Rockies Access Guide* (Lone Pine), by John Dodd and Gail Helgason, is an excellent resource for hikers and cross-country skiers in the national parks of Alberta. *Hikers Guide to Alberta,* by Will Harmon (Falcon), covers 75 hikes along the eastern face of the Rockies.

FICTION & MEMOIR Alice Munro's short fiction captures the soul of what it is to be Canadian in brief, though often wrenching, prose. Some of the stories in *The Love of a Good Woman* take place in Vancouver. Another good selection of short stories as well as poetry is *Fresh Tracks: Writing the Western Landscape* (Pamela Banting, editor), a collection of writings by western Canadian authors.

The frontier-era conflicts in southern Alberta form the backdrop for the award-winning *The Englishman's Boy,* by Guy Vanderhaeghe, an atmospheric western with a story that travels from Fort Macleod to Hollywood.

Richard P. Hobson, Jr., writes of his experiences as a modern-day cowboy on the grasslands of central British Columbia in an acclaimed series of memoirs titled *Grass Beyond the Mountains: Discovering the Last Great Cattle Frontier on the North American Continent, The Rancher Takes a Wife,* and *Nothing Too Good for a Cowboy.*

Vancouver and southwestern British Columbia are home to a number of noted international authors. *Generation X* chronicler Douglas Coupland lives here, as does Jane Rule, author of *Desert of the Heart.* Science-fiction writer William Gibson's dark vision of the cyber-future attracts a large young audience. W. P. Kinsella *(Shoeless Joe)* and mystery writer Laurali R. Wright also make their homes here. Wright's Karl Alberg mystery series usually takes place in and around Vancouver.

Index

FROMMER'S® COMPLETE TRAVEL GUIDES

FROMMER'S® DOLLAR-A-DAY GUIDES

FROMMER'S® PORTABLE GUIDES

FROMMER'S® CRUISE GUIDES

FROMMER'S® DAY BY DAY GUIDES

Amsterdam	London	Rome
Chicago	New York City	San Francisco
Florence & Tuscany	Paris	Venice

FROMMER'S® NATIONAL PARK GUIDES

Algonquin Provincial Park	National Parks of the American West	Yosemite and Sequoia & Kings
Banff & Jasper	Rocky Mountain	Canyon
Grand Canyon	Yellowstone & Grand Teton	Zion & Bryce Canyon

FROMMER'S® MEMORABLE WALKS

Chicago	New York	Rome
London	Paris	San Francisco

FROMMER'S® WITH KIDS GUIDES

Chicago	National Parks	Toronto
Hawaii	New York City	Walt Disney World® & Orlando
Las Vegas	San Francisco	Washington, D.C.
London		

SUZY GERSHMAN'S BORN TO SHOP GUIDES

Born to Shop: France	Born to Shop: Italy	Born to Shop: New York
Born to Shop: Hong Kong, Shanghai & Beijing	Born to Shop: London	Born to Shop: Paris

FROMMER'S® IRREVERENT GUIDES

Amsterdam	Los Angeles	Rome
Boston	Manhattan	San Francisco
Chicago	New Orleans	Walt Disney World®
Las Vegas	Paris	Washington, D.C.
London		

FROMMER'S® BEST-LOVED DRIVING TOURS

Austria	Germany	Northern Italy
Britain	Ireland	Scotland
California	Italy	Spain
France	New England	Tuscany & Umbria

THE UNOFFICIAL GUIDES®

Adventure Travel in Alaska	Hawaii	Paris
Beyond Disney	Ireland	San Francisco
California with Kids	Las Vegas	South Florida including Miami &
Central Italy	London	the Keys
Chicago	Maui	Walt Disney World®
Cruises	Mexico's Best Beach Resorts	Walt Disney World® for
Disneyland®	Mini Las Vegas	Grown-ups
England	Mini Mickey	Walt Disney World® with Kids
Florida	New Orleans	Washington, D.C.
Florida with Kids	New York City	

SPECIAL-INTEREST TITLES

Athens Past & Present	Frommer's Exploring America by RV
Cities Ranked & Rated	Frommer's NYC Free & Dirt Cheap
Frommer's Best Day Trips from London	Frommer's Road Atlas Europe
Frommer's Best RV & Tent Campgrounds in the U.S.A.	Frommer's Road Atlas Ireland
	Retirement Places Rated

FROMMER'S® PHRASEFINDER DICTIONARY GUIDES

French	Italian	Spanish

THE NEW TRAVELOCITY GUARANTEE

**EVERYTHING YOU BOOK WILL BE RIGHT, OR WE'LL WORK
WITH OUR TRAVEL PARTNERS TO MAKE IT RIGHT, RIGHT AWAY.**

*To drive home the point,
we're going to use the word "right" in every single sentence.*

Let's get right to it. Right to the meat! Only Travelocity guarantees everything about your booking will be right, or we'll work with our travel partners to make it right, right away. Right on!

Here's a picture taken smack dab right in the middle of Antigua, where the guarantee also covers you.

The guarantee covers all but one of the items pictured to the right.

Now, you may be thinking, "Yeah, right, I'm so sure." That's OK; you have the right to remain skeptical. That is until we mention help is always right around the corner. Call us right off the bat, knowing that our customer service reps are there for you 24/7. Righting wrongs. Left and right.

For example, what if the ocean view you booked actually looks out at a downright ugly parking lot? You'd be right to call – we're there for you. And no one in their right mind would be pleased to learn the rental car place has closed and left them stranded. Call Travelocity and we'll help get you back on the right track.

Now if you're guessing there are some things we can't control, like the weather, well you're right. But we can help you with most things – to get all the details in righting,* visit **travelocity.com/guarantee**.

*Sorry, spelling things right is one of the few things not covered under the guarantee.

I'd give my right arm for a guarantee like this, although I'm glad I don't have to.

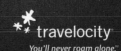

IF YOU BOOK IT, IT SHOULD BE THERE.

Only Travelocity guarantees it will be, or we'll work
with our travel partners to make it right, right away.
So if you're missing a balcony or anything else you
booked, just call us 24/7. 1-888-TRAVELOCITY.

travelocity

You'll never roam alone